# 2022
# Collier Portable Pamphlet

Full Text of the BANKRUPTCY CODE and RULES

Including Rule Amendments Effective December 1, 2021

Selected Provisions of the JUDICIAL CODE
and RELATED STATUTES

Full Text of the FEDERAL RULES OF EVIDENCE


**RICHARD LEVIN**

*Jenner & Block LLP*
*Collier Editor-in-Chief*

**HENRY J. SOMMER**

*President, National Consumer Bankruptcy Rights Center*
*Collier Editor-in-Chief*


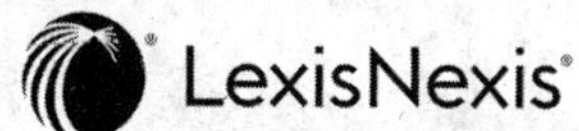

## QUESTIONS ABOUT THIS PUBLICATION?

For questions about the **Editorial Content** appearing in these volumes or reprint permission, please call:

Ryan Kearns, J.D., at .................... (513) 257-9021
Email: .................... ryan.kearns@lexisnexis.com
Outside the United States and Canada, please call .................... (973) 820-2000

For assistance with replacement pages, shipments, billing or other customer service matters, please call:

Customer Services Department at .................... (800) 833-9844
Outside the United States and Canada, please call .................... (518) 487-3385
Fax Number .................... (800) 828-8341
Customer Service Website .................... http://www.lexisnexis.com/custserv/

For information on other Matthew Bender publications, please call
Your account manager or .................... (800) 223-1940
Outside the United States and Canada, please call .................... (937) 247-0293

---

Library of Congress Card Number: 89-640217

Portable Pamphlet ISBN: 978–1–6633–2202–9
Collier Pamphlet Edition ISBN (full set): 978–1–6633–2199–2

---

**Cite this publication as:**

COLLIER PORTABLE PAMPHLET 2022 (Richard Levin & Henry J. Sommer eds., Matthew Bender).

---



Editorial Office
230 Park Ave., 7th Floor, New York, NY 10169 (800) 543-6862
www.lexisnexis.com

MATTHEW BENDER

(12/2021–Pub.221)

# About the Collier Editors-in-Chief

RICHARD LEVIN is a Co-head of Jenner & Block LLP's Restructuring and Bankruptcy Practice, practicing in the New York City office. Mr. Levin's practice concentrates on corporate restructuring, insolvency and bankruptcy issues.

He spent 16 years as a member of the Los Angeles insolvency and corporate reorganization firm of Stutman, Treister & Glatt, where he successfully led the reorganization of Public Service Company of New Hampshire. Mr. Levin also served for three years as General Counsel, Chief Financial Officer and Chief Administrative Officer of Whittaker Corporation, a technology company with aerospace, defense and network communications operations, for 10 years as a partner in Skadden, Arps, Slate, Meagher & Flom LLP in the Corporate Restructuring department and, more recently, 8 years as a partner and head of the restructuring practice at Cravath, Swaine & Moore LLP.

Mr. Levin was named one of the world's leading practitioners in corporate restructuring in the *International Who's Who of Insolvency & Restructuring Lawyers* (3d ed.) and has repeatedly been selected for inclusion in *The Best Lawyers in America* and in *Chambers USA: America's Leading Lawyers for Business*.

From 1975 to 1978, Mr. Levin served as counsel to a subcommittee of the House Judiciary Committee, where he was one of the principal authors of the Bankruptcy Reform Act of 1978. Mr. Levin has remained involved in bankruptcy legislative matters as a member and former Chair of the National Bankruptcy Conference, a select organization of bankruptcy professionals that has acted as an informal advisor to Congress on bankruptcy law since the mid-1930s. He is also a Fellow of the American College of Bankruptcy and a former member of its Board of Trustees (2007–2009). Mr. Levin also served as a consultant to the World Bank and to the Central Bank of Brazil regarding new Brazilian bankruptcy legislation (2001–2004), as Faculty at the Federal Judicial Center (2001–present) and as a Lecturer in Law at Harvard Law School (2004, 2006).

Mr. Levin received an S.B. from the Massachusetts Institute of Technology in 1972, and a J.D. from Yale Law School in 1975, where he was an editor of the *Yale Law Journal*.

HENRY J. SOMMER is a leading authority on consumer bankruptcy law and has litigated many major cases involving bankruptcy, consumer law, civil rights and other issues. He is the President of the National Consumer Bankruptcy Rights Center. He has served in the past as head of the Consumer Law Project at Community Legal Services in Philadelphia and as the Supervising Attorney at the *pro bono* Consumer Bankruptcy Assistance Project in Philadelphia. Mr. Sommer has also taught as a Lecturer-in-Law at the University of Pennsylvania Law School and as an Adjunct Professor at Temple University School of Law. Together with Richard Levin, Mr. Sommer serves as Editor-in-Chief of *Collier on Bankruptcy* (Matthew Bender 16th ed.).

Mr. Sommer is the author of *Collier Consumer Bankruptcy Practice Guide* (Matthew Bender), *Consumer Bankruptcy Law and Practice* (Nat'l Consumer Law Center), *Consumer Bankruptcy* (Wiley) and numerous articles on bankruptcy law. He is co-author of *Collier Family Law and the Bankruptcy Code* (Matthew Bender) and a contributing author to *Collier on Bankruptcy* (Matthew Bender 16th Edition).

## *About the Collier Editors-in-Chief*

From 1991 to 1998, Mr. Sommer was a member of the Advisory Committee on Bankruptcy Rules of the Judicial Conference of the United States. He has testified on many occasions before the House and Senate Judiciary Committees, as well as the National Bankruptcy Review Commission, on bankruptcy and consumer law issues and has appeared as a bankruptcy expert on national and local television and radio shows. He has served on the faculty of numerous continuing legal education programs, including those presented by the Federal Judicial Center, NYU Law School, the National Conference of Bankruptcy Judges, the Southeastern Bankruptcy Law Institute, the Executive Office of U.S. Trustees, ALI-ABA, the National Association of Chapter 13 Trustees, the National Association of Consumer Bankruptcy Attorneys and the ABA Family Law Section.

Mr. Sommer is an elected member of the American Law Institute and the National Bankruptcy Conference, and he is an elected Fellow of the American College of Bankruptcy. He has served as the President of the National Association of Consumer Bankruptcy Attorneys, and is the former Chair of the Eastern District of Pennsylvania Bankruptcy Conference and a former member of the Federal Reserve Board Consumer Advisory Council.

Mr. Sommer was the first recipient of the National Consumer Law Center's Vern Countryman Consumer Law Award and is a recipient of the National Conference of Bankruptcy Judges' Excellence in Education Award and the American College of Bankruptcy Distinguished Service Award. He received his legal education from Harvard Law School (J.D., *cum laude*).

# *Publisher's Editorial Staff*

MICHAEL A. BRUNO
*Practice Area Director*

RYAN KEARNS
*Practice Area Editor*

PATRICK G. HEALY
*Index Editor*

SHARON L. BURNS
*Publishing Operations Manager*

JOHN PRICE
*Publishing Operations Coordinator*

JOHN F. CAPACCIONE
*Publishing Operations Senior Analyst*

# *Collier Portable Pamphlet Table of Contents*

## BANKRUPTCY CODE

## JUDICIAL CODE—SELECTED PROVISIONS



## ADDITIONAL STATUTORY PROVISIONS

## *Collier Portable Pamphlet Table of Contents*

## PART VI Collection and Liquidation of the Estate



## PART VII Adversary Proceedings

**PART IX** **General Provisions**

**TIME PERIODS PRESCRIBED BY THE BANKRUPTCY RULES**



**FEDERAL RULES OF EVIDENCE**

**Article I General Provisions**



**Article II Judicial Notice**



**Article III Presumptions in Civil Cases**



**Article IV Relevance and Its Limits**

**INDEX TO PORTABLE PAMPHLET**

# Bankruptcy Code

## CHAPTER 1
## GENERAL PROVISIONS

### § 101 Definitions

In this title the following definitions shall apply:

(1) The term "accountant" means accountant authorized under applicable law to practice public accounting, and includes professional accounting association, corporation, or partnership, if so authorized.

(2) The term "affiliate" means—

(A) entity that directly or indirectly owns, controls, or holds with power to vote, 20 percent or more of the outstanding voting securities of the debtor, other than an entity that holds such securities—

(i) in a fiduciary or agency capacity without sole discretionary power to vote such securities; or

(ii) solely to secure a debt, if such entity has not in fact exercised such power to vote;

(B) corporation 20 percent or more of whose outstanding voting securities are directly or indirectly owned, controlled, or held with power to vote, by the debtor, or by an entity that directly or indirectly owns, controls, or holds with power to vote, 20 percent or more of the outstanding voting securities of the debtor, other than an entity that holds such securities—

(i) in a fiduciary or agency capacity without sole discretionary power to vote such securities; or

(ii) solely to secure a debt, if such entity has not in fact exercised such power to vote;

(C) person whose business is operated under a lease or operating agreement by a debtor, or person substantially all of whose property is operated under an operating agreement with the debtor; or

(D) entity that operates the business or substantially all of the property of the debtor under a lease or operating agreement.

(3) The term "assisted person" means any person whose debts consist primarily of consumer debts and the value of whose nonexempt property is less than $204,425.[1]

(4) The term "attorney" means attorney, professional law association, corporation, or partnership, authorized under applicable law to practice law.

(4A) The term "bankruptcy assistance" means any goods or services sold or

[1] Ed. Note: For cases commenced in the three-year period before April 1, 2019, the dollar amount is $192,450.

otherwise provided to an assisted person with the express or implied purpose of providing information, advice, counsel, document preparation, or filing, or attendance at a creditors' meeting or appearing in a case or proceeding on behalf of another or providing legal representation with respect to a case or proceeding under this title.

(5) The term "claim" means—

(A) right to payment, whether or not such right is reduced to judgment, liquidated, unliquidated, fixed, contingent, matured, unmatured, disputed, undisputed, legal, equitable, secured, or unsecured; or

(B) right to an equitable remedy for breach of performance if such breach gives rise to a right to payment, whether or not such right to an equitable remedy is reduced to judgment, fixed, contingent, matured, unmatured, disputed, undisputed, secured, or unsecured.

(6) The term "commodity broker" means futures commission merchant, foreign futures commission merchant, clearing organization, leverage transaction merchant, or commodity options dealer, as defined in section 761 of this title, with respect to which there is a customer, as defined in section 761 of this title.

(7) The term "community claim" means claim that arose before the commencement of the case concerning the debtor for which property of the kind specified in section 541(a)(2) of this title is liable, whether or not there is any such property at the time of the commencement of the case.

(7A) The term "commercial fishing operation" means—

(A) the catching or harvesting of fish, shrimp, lobsters, urchins, seaweed, shellfish, or other aquatic species or products of such species; or

(B) for purposes of section 109 and chapter 12, aquaculture activities consisting of raising for market any species or product described in subparagraph (A).

(7B) The term "commercial fishing vessel" means a vessel used by a family fisherman to carry out a commercial fishing operation.

(8) The term "consumer debt" means debt incurred by an individual primarily for a personal, family, or household purpose.

(9) The term "corporation"—

(A) includes—

(i) association having a power or privilege that a private corporation, but not an individual or a partnership, possesses.

(ii) partnership association organized under a law that makes only the capital subscribed responsible for the debts of such association;

(iii) joint-stock company;

(iv) unincorporated company or association; or

(v) business trust; but

(B) does not include limited partnership.

(10) The term "creditor" means—

(A) entity that has a claim against the debtor that arose at the time of or before the order for relief concerning the debtor;

(B) entity that has a claim against the estate of a kind specified in section 348(d), 502(f), 502(g), 502(h) or 502(i) of this title; or

(C) entity that has a community claim.

(10A) The term "current monthly income"—

(A) means the average monthly income from all sources that the debtor receives (or in a joint case the debtor and the debtor's spouse receive) without regard to whether such income is taxable income, derived during the 6-month period ending on—

(i) the last day of the calendar month immediately preceding the date of the commencement of the case if the debtor files the schedule of current income required by section 521(a)(1)(B)(ii); or

(ii) the date on which current income is determined by the court for purposes of this title if the debtor does not file the schedule of current income required by section 521(a)(1)(B)(ii); and

(B) (i) includes any amount paid by any entity other than the debtor (or in a joint case the debtor and the debtor's spouse), on a regular basis for the household expenses of the debtor or the debtor's dependents (and in a joint case the debtor's spouse if not otherwise a dependent); and

(ii) excludes—

(I) benefits received under the Social Security Act (42 U.S.C. 301 et seq.);

(II) payments to victims of war crimes or crimes against humanity on account of their status as victims of such crimes;

(III) payments to victims of international terrorism or domestic terrorism, as those terms are defined in section 2331 of title 18, on account of their status as victims of such terrorism;

(IV) any monthly compensation, pension, pay, annuity, or allowance paid under title 10, 37, or 38 in connection with a disability, combat-related injury or disability, or death of a member of the uniformed services, except that any retired pay excluded under this subclause shall include retired pay paid under chapter 61 of title 10 only to the extent that such retired pay exceeds the amount of retired pay to which the debtor would otherwise be entitled if retired under any provision of title 10 other than chapter 61 of that title; and

(V) Payments made under Federal law relating to the national emergency declared by the President under the National Emergencies Act (50 U.S.C. 1601 et seq.) with respect to the coronavirus disease 2019 (COVID-19).[2]

(11) The term "custodian" means—

(A) receiver or trustee of any of the property of the debtor, appointed in a case or proceeding not under this title;

(B) assignee under a general assignment for the benefit of the debtor's creditors; or

(C) trustee, receiver, or agent under applicable law, or under a contract, that is appointed or authorized to take charge of property of the debtor for the purpose of enforcing a lien against such property, or for the purpose of general administration of such property for the benefit of the debtor's creditors.

(12) The term "debt" means liability on a claim.

(12A) The term "debt relief agency" means any person who provides any bankruptcy assistance to an assisted person in return for the payment of money or other valuable consideration, or who is a bankruptcy petition preparer under section 110, but does not include—

(A) any person who is an officer, director, employee, or agent of a person who provides such assistance or of the bankruptcy petition preparer;

(B) a nonprofit organization that is exempt from taxation under section 501(c)(3) of the Internal Revenue Code of 1986;

(C) a creditor of such assisted person, to the extent that the creditor is assisting such assisted person to restructure any debt owed by such assisted person to the creditor;

(D) a depository institution (as defined in section 3 of the Federal Deposit Insurance Act) or any Federal credit union or State credit union (as those terms are defined in section 101 of the Federal Credit Union Act), or any affiliate or subsidiary of such depository institution or credit union; or

(E) an author, publisher, distributor, or seller of works subject to copyright protection under title 17, when acting in such capacity.

(13) The term "debtor" means person or municipality concerning which a case under this title has been commenced.

(13A) The term "debtor's principal residence"—

---

[2] Ed. Note: Underscored material applies to cases commenced before, on or after March 27, 2020. *See* Coronavirus, Aid, Relief, and Economic Security Act, Pub. L. No. 116-136, § 1113(b)(D)(i) (2020). It will expire two years after March 27, 2020. *See* COVID-19 Bankruptcy Relief Extension Act of 2021, Pub. L. No. 117-5 (2021).

(A) means a residential structure if used as the principal residence by the debtor, including incidental property, without regard to whether that structure is attached to real property; and

(B) includes an individual condominium or cooperative unit, a mobile or manufactured home, or trailer if used as the principal residence by the debtor.

(14) The term "disinterested person" means a person that—

(A) is not a creditor, an equity security holder, or an insider;

(B) is not and was not, within 2 years before the date of the filing of the petition, a director, officer, or employee of the debtor; and

(C) does not have an interest materially adverse to the interest of the estate or of any class of creditors or equity security holders, by reason of any direct or indirect relationship to, connection with, or interest in, the debtor, or for any other reason.

(14A) The term "domestic support obligation" means a debt that accrues before, on, or after the date of the order for relief in a case under this title, including interest that accrues on that debt as provided under applicable nonbankruptcy law notwithstanding any other provision of this title, that is—

(A) owed to or recoverable by—

(i) a spouse, former spouse, or child of the debtor or such child's parent, legal guardian, or responsible relative; or

(ii) a governmental unit;

(B) in the nature of alimony, maintenance, or support (including assistance provided by a governmental unit) of such spouse, former spouse, or child of the debtor or such child's parent, without regard to whether such debt is expressly so designated;

(C) established or subject to establishment before, on, or after the date of the order for relief in a case under this title, by reason of applicable provisions of—

(i) a separation agreement, divorce decree, or property settlement agreement;

(ii) an order of a court of record; or

(iii) a determination made in accordance with applicable nonbankruptcy law by a governmental unit; and

(D) not assigned to a nongovernmental entity, unless that obligation is assigned voluntarily by the spouse, former spouse, child of the debtor, or such child's parent, legal guardian, or responsible relative for the purpose of collecting the debt.

(15) The term "entity" includes person, estate, trust, governmental unit, and

United States trustee.

(16) The term "equity security" means—

(A) share in a corporation, whether or not transferable or denominated "stock", or similar security;

(B) interest of a limited partner in a limited partnership; or

(C) warrant or right, other than a right to convert, to purchase, sell, or subscribe to a share, security, or interest of a kind specified in subparagraph (A) or (B) of this paragraph.

(17) The term "equity security holder" means holder of an equity security of the debtor.

(18) The term "family farmer" means—

(A) individual or individual and spouse engaged in a farming operation whose aggregate debts do not exceed $10,000,000[3] and not less than 50 percent of whose aggregate noncontingent, liquidated debts (excluding a debt for the principal residence of such individual or such individual and spouse unless such debt arises out of a farming operation), on the date the case is filed, arise out of a farming operation owned or operated by such individual or such individual and spouse, and such individual or such individual and spouse receive from such farming operation more than 50 percent of such individual's or such individual and spouse's gross income for—

(i) the taxable year preceding; or

(ii) each of the 2d and 3d taxable years preceding;

the taxable year in which the case concerning such individual or such individual and spouse was filed; or

(B) corporation or partnership in which more than 50 percent of the outstanding stock or equity is held by one family, or by one family and the relatives of the members of such family, and such family or such relatives conduct the farming operation, and

(i) more than 80 percent of the value of its assets consists of assets related to the farming operation;

(ii) its aggregate debts do not exceed $10,000,000[4] and not less than 50 percent of its aggregate noncontingent, liquidated debts (excluding a debt for one dwelling which is owned by such corporation or partnership and which a shareholder or partner maintains as a principal residence, unless such debt arises out of a farming operation), on the date the case is filed,

---

[3] Ed. Note: Effective April 1, 2019, the amount was increased to $4,411,400. Subsequently, the Family Farmer Relief Act of 2019, Pub. L. No. 116-51 (2019), increased the amount to $10,000,000, and this amount applies to all cases pending on or after August 23, 2019.

[4] Ed. Note: *See* note 3 *supra*.

arise out of the farming operation owned or operated by such corporation or such partnership; and

(iii) if such corporation issues stock, such stock is not publicly traded.

(19) The term "family farmer with regular annual income" means family farmer whose annual income is sufficiently stable and regular to enable such family farmer to make payments under a plan under chapter 12 of this title.

(19A) The term "family fisherman" means—

(A) an individual or individual and spouse engaged in a commercial fishing operation—

(i) whose aggregate debts do not exceed $2,044,225[5] and not less than 80 percent of whose aggregate noncontingent, liquidated debts (excluding a debt for the principal residence of such individual or such individual and spouse, unless such debt arises out of a commercial fishing operation), on the date the case is filed, arise out of a commercial fishing operation owned or operated by such individual or such individual and spouse; and

(ii) who receive from such commercial fishing operation more than 50 percent of such individual's or such individual's and spouse's gross income for the taxable year preceding the taxable year in which the case concerning such individual or such individual and spouse was filed; or

(B) a corporation or partnership—

(i) in which more than 50 percent of the outstanding stock or equity is held by—

(I) 1 family that conducts the commercial fishing operation; or

(II) 1 family and the relatives of the members of such family, and such family or such relatives conduct the commercial fishing operation; and

(ii) (I) more than 80 percent of the value of its assets consists of assets related to the commercial fishing operation;

(II) its aggregate debts do not exceed $2,044,225[6] and not less than 80 percent of its aggregate noncontingent, liquidated debts (excluding a debt for 1 dwelling which is owned by such corporation or partnership and which a shareholder or partner maintains as a principal residence, unless such debt arises out of a commercial fishing operation), on the date the case is filed, arise out of a commercial fishing operation owned or operated by such corporation or such partnership; and

(III) if such corporation issues stock, such stock is not publicly traded.

---

[5] Ed. Note: For cases commenced in the three-year period before April 1, 2019, the dollar amount is $1,924,550.

[6] Ed. Note: For cases commenced in the three-year period before April 1, 2019, the dollar amount is $1,924,550.

(19B) The term "family fisherman with regular annual income" means a family fisherman whose annual income is sufficiently stable and regular to enable such family fisherman to make payments under a plan under chapter 12 of this title.

(20) The term "farmer" means (except when such term appears in the term "family farmer") person that received more than 80 percent of such person's gross income during the taxable year of such person immediately preceding the taxable year of such person during which the case under this title concerning such person was commenced from a farming operation owned or operated by such person.

(21) The term "farming operation" includes farming, tillage of the soil, dairy farming, ranching, production or raising of crops, poultry, or livestock, and production of poultry or livestock products in an unmanufactured state.

(21A) The term "farmout agreement" means a written agreement in which—

(A) the owner of a right to drill, produce, or operate liquid or gaseous hydrocarbons on property agrees or has agreed to transfer or assign all or a part of such right to another entity; and

(B) such other entity (either directly or through its agents or its assigns), as consideration, agrees to perform drilling, reworking, recompleting, testing, or similar or related operations, to develop or produce liquid or gaseous hydrocarbons on the property.

(21B) The term "Federal depository institutions regulatory agency" means—

(A) with respect to an insured depository institution (as defined in section 3(c)(2) of the Federal Deposit Insurance Act) for which no conservator or receiver has been appointed, the appropriate Federal banking agency (as defined in section 3(q) of such Act);

(B) with respect to an insured credit union (including an insured credit union for which the National Credit Union Administration has been appointed conservator or liquidating agent), the National Credit Union Administration;

(C) with respect to any insured depository institution for which the Resolution Trust Corporation has been appointed conservator or receiver, the Resolution Trust Corporation; and

(D) with respect to any insured depository institution for which the Federal Deposit Insurance Corporation has been appointed conservator or receiver, the Federal Deposit Insurance Corporation.

(22) The term "financial institution" means—

(A) a Federal reserve bank, or an entity that is a commercial or savings bank, industrial savings bank, savings and loan association, trust company, federally-insured credit union, or receiver, liquidating agent, or conservator for such entity and, when any such Federal reserve bank, receiver, liquidating agent, conservator or entity is acting as agent or custodian for a customer (whether or not a "customer", as defined in section 741) in connection with a securities contract (as defined in section 741) such customer; or

(B) in connection with a securities contract (as defined in section 741) an investment company registered under the Investment Company Act of 1940.

(22A) The term "financial participant" means—

(A) an entity that, at the time it enters into a securities contract, commodity contract, swap agreement, repurchase agreement, or forward contract, or at the time of the date of the filing of the petition, has one or more agreements or transactions described in paragraph (1), (2), (3), (4), (5), or (6) of section 561(a) with the debtor or any other entity (other than an affiliate) of a total gross dollar value of not less than $1,000,000,000 in notional or actual principal amount outstanding (aggregated across counterparties) at such time or on any day during the 15-month period preceding the date of the filing of the petition, or has gross mark-to-market positions of not less than $100,000,000 (aggregated across counterparties) in one or more such agreements or transactions with the debtor or any other entity (other than an affiliate) at such time or on any day during the 15-month period preceding the date of the filing of the petition; or

(B) a clearing organization (as defined in section 402 of the Federal Deposit Insurance Corporation Improvement Act of 1991).

(23) The term "foreign proceeding" means a collective judicial or administrative proceeding in a foreign country, including an interim proceeding, under a law relating to insolvency or adjustment of debt in which proceeding the assets and affairs of the debtor are subject to control or supervision by a foreign court, for the purpose of reorganization or liquidation.

(24) The term "foreign representative" means a person or body, including a person or body appointed on an interim basis, authorized in a foreign proceeding to administer the reorganization or the liquidation of the debtor's assets or affairs or to act as a representative of such foreign proceeding.

(25) The term "forward contract" means—

(A) a contract (other than a commodity contract as defined in section 761) for the purchase, sale, or transfer of a commodity, as defined in section 761(8) of this title, or any similar good, article, service, right, or interest which is presently or in the future becomes the subject of dealing in the forward contract trade, or product or byproduct thereof, with a maturity date more than two days after the date the contract is entered into, including, but not limited to, a repurchase or reverse repurchase transaction (whether or not such repurchase or reverse repurchase transaction is a "repurchase agreement", as defined in this section)[,] consignment, lease, swap, hedge transaction, deposit, loan, option, allocated transaction, unallocated transaction, or any other similar agreement;

(B) any combination of agreements or transactions referred to in subparagraphs (A) and (C);

(C) any option to enter into an agreement or transaction referred to in subparagraph (A) or (B);

(D) a master agreement that provides for an agreement or transaction referred to in subparagraph (A), (B), or (C), together with all supplements to any such master agreement, without regard to whether such master agreement provides for an agreement or transaction that is not a forward contract under this paragraph, except that such master agreement shall be considered to be a forward contract under this paragraph only with respect to each agreement or transaction under such master agreement that is referred to in subparagraph (A), (B), or (C); or

(E) any security agreement or arrangement, or other credit enhancement related to any agreement or transaction referred to in subparagraph (A), (B), (C), or (D), including any guarantee or reimbursement obligation by or to a forward contract merchant or financial participant in connection with any agreement or transaction referred to in any such subparagraph, but not to exceed the damages in connection with any such agreement or transaction, measured in accordance with section 562.

(26) The term "forward contract merchant" means a Federal reserve bank, or an entity the business of which consists in whole or in part of entering into forward contracts as or with merchants in a commodity (as defined in section 761) or any similar good, article, service, right, or interest which is presently or in the future becomes the subject of dealing in the forward contract trade.

(27) The term "governmental unit" means United States; State; Commonwealth; District; Territory; municipality; foreign state; department, agency, or instrumentality of the United States (but not a United States trustee while serving as a trustee in a case under this title), a State, a Commonwealth, a District, a Territory, a municipality, or a foreign state; or other foreign or domestic government.

(27A) The term "health care business"—

(A) means any public or private entity (without regard to whether that entity is organized for profit or not for profit) that is primarily engaged in offering to the general public facilities and services for—

(i) the diagnosis or treatment of injury, deformity, or disease; and

(ii) surgical, drug treatment, psychiatric, or obstetric care; and

(B) includes—

(i) any—

(I) general or specialized hospital;

(II) ancillary ambulatory, emergency, or surgical treatment facility;

(III) hospice;

(IV) home health agency; and

(V) other health care institution that is similar to an entity referred to in subclause (I), (II), (III), or (IV); and

(ii) any long-term care facility, including any—

(I) skilled nursing facility;

(II) intermediate care facility;

(III) assisted living facility;

(IV) home for the aged;

(V) domiciliary care facility; and

(VI) health care institution that is related to a facility referred to in subclause (I), (II), (III), (IV), or (V), if that institution is primarily engaged in offering room, board, laundry, or personal assistance with activities of daily living and incidentals to activities of daily living.

(27B) The term "incidental property" means, with respect to a debtor's principal residence—

(A) property commonly conveyed with a principal residence in the area where the real property is located;

(B) all easements, rights, appurtenances, fixtures, rents, royalties, mineral rights, oil or gas rights or profits, water rights, escrow funds, or insurance proceeds; and

(C) all replacements or additions.

(28) The term "indenture" means mortgage, deed of trust, or indenture, under which there is outstanding a security, other than a voting-trust certificate, constituting a claim against the debtor, a claim secured by a lien on any of the debtor's property, or an equity security of the debtor.

(29) The term "indenture trustee" means trustee under an indenture.

(30) The term "individual with regular income" means individual whose income is sufficiently stable and regular to enable such individual to make payments under a plan under chapter 13 of this title, other than a stockbroker or a commodity broker.

(31) The term "insider" includes—

(A) if the debtor is an individual—

(i) relative of the debtor or of a general partner of the debtor;

(ii) partnership in which the debtor is a general partner;

(iii) general partner of the debtor; or

(iv) corporation of which the debtor is a director, officer, or person in control;

(B) if the debtor is a corporation—

(i) director of the debtor;

(ii) officer of the debtor;

(iii) person in control of the debtor;

(iv) partnership in which the debtor is a general partner;

(v) general partner of the debtor; or

(vi) relative of a general partner, director, officer, or person in control of the debtor;

(C) if the debtor is a partnership—

(i) general partner in the debtor;

(ii) relative of a general partner in, general partner of, or person in control of the debtor;

(iii) partnership in which the debtor is a general partner;

(iv) general partner of the debtor; or

(v) person in control of the debtor;

(D) if the debtor is a municipality, elected official of the debtor or relative of an elected official of the debtor;

(E) affiliate, or insider of an affiliate as if such affiliate were the debtor; and

(F) managing agent of the debtor.

(32) The term "insolvent" means—

(A) with reference to an entity other than a partnership and a municipality, financial condition such that the sum of such entity's debts is greater than all of such entity's property, at a fair valuation, exclusive of—

(i) property transferred, concealed, or removed with intent to hinder, delay, or defraud such entity's creditors; and

(ii) property that may be exempted from property of the estate under section 522 of this title;

(B) with reference to a partnership, financial condition such that the sum of such partnership's debts is greater than the aggregate of, at a fair valuation—

(i) all of such partnership's property, exclusive of property of the kind specified in subparagraph (A)(i) of this paragraph; and

(ii) the sum of the excess of the value of each general partner's nonpartnership property, exclusive of property of the kind specified in subparagraph (A) of this paragraph, over such partner's nonpartnership debts; and

(C) with reference to a municipality, financial condition such that the municipality is—

(i) generally not paying its debts as they become due unless such debts are the subject of a bona fide dispute; or

(ii) unable to pay its debts as they become due.

(33) The term "institution-affiliated party"—

(A) with respect to an insured depository institution (as defined in section 3(c)(2) of the Federal Deposit Insurance Act), has the meaning given it in section 3(u) of the Federal Deposit Insurance Act; and

(B) with respect to an insured credit union, has the meaning given it in section 206(r) of the Federal Credit Union Act.

(34) The term "insured credit union" has the meaning given it in section 101(7) of the Federal Credit Union Act.

(35) The term "insured depository institution"—

(A) has the meaning given it in section 3(c)(2) of the Federal Deposit Insurance Act; and

(B) includes an insured credit union (except in the case of paragraphs (21B) and (33)(A) of this subsection).

(35A) The term "intellectual property" means—

(A) trade secret;

(B) invention, process, design, or plant protected under title 35;

(C) patent application;

(D) plant variety;

(E) work of authorship protected under title 17; or

(F) mask work protected under chapter 9 of title 17;

to the extent protected by applicable nonbankruptcy law.

(36) The term "judicial lien" means lien obtained by judgment, levy, sequestration, or other legal or equitable process or proceeding.

(37) The term "lien" means charge against or interest in property to secure payment of a debt or performance of an obligation.

(38) The term "margin payment" means, for purposes of the forward contract provisions of this title, payment or deposit of cash, a security or other property, that is commonly known in the forward contract trade as original margin, initial margin, maintenance margin, or variation margin, including mark-to-market payments, or variation payments.

(38A) The term "master netting agreement"—

(A) means an agreement providing for the exercise of rights, including rights of netting, setoff, liquidation, termination, acceleration, or close out, under or in connection with one or more contracts that are described in any one or more of paragraphs (1) through (5) of section 561(a), or any security agreement or arrangement or other credit enhancement related to one or more of the foregoing, including any guarantee or reimbursement obligation related to 1 or more of the foregoing; and

(B) if the agreement contains provisions relating to agreements or transactions that are not contracts described in paragraphs (1) through (5) of section 561(a), shall be deemed to be a master netting agreement only with respect to those agreements or transactions that are described in any one or more of paragraphs (1) through (5) of section 561(a).

(38B) The term "master netting agreement participant" means an entity that, at any time before the date of the filing of the petition, is a party to an outstanding master netting agreement with the debtor.

(39) The term "mask work" has the meaning given it in section 901(a)(2) of title 17.

(39A) The term "median family income" means for any year—

(A) the median family income both calculated and reported by the Bureau of the Census in the then most recent year; and

(B) if not so calculated and reported in the then current year, adjusted annually after such most recent year until the next year in which median family income is both calculated and reported by the Bureau of the Census, to reflect the percentage change in the Consumer Price Index for All Urban Consumers during the period of years occurring after such most recent year and before such current year.

(40) The term "municipality" means political subdivision or public agency or instrumentality of a State.

(40A) The term "patient" means any individual who obtains or receives services from a health care business.

(40B) The term "patient records" means any record relating to a patient, including a written document or a record recorded in a magnetic, optical, or other form of electronic medium.

(41) The term "person" includes individual, partnership, and corporation, but does not include governmental unit, except that a governmental unit that—

(A) acquires an asset from a person—

(i) as a result of the operation of a loan guarantee agreement; or

(ii) as receiver or liquidating agent of a person;

(B) is a guarantor of a pension benefit payable by or on behalf of the debtor or an affiliate of the debtor; or

(C) is the legal or beneficial owner of an asset of—

(i) an employee pension benefit plan that is a governmental plan, as defined in section 414(d) of the Internal Revenue Code of 1986; or

(ii) an eligible deferred compensation plan, as defined in section 457(b) of the Internal Revenue Code of 1986;

shall be considered, for purposes of section 1102 of this title, to be a person with respect to such asset or such benefit.

(41A) The term "personally identifiable information" means—

(A) if provided by an individual to the debtor in connection with obtaining a product or a service from the debtor primarily for personal, family, or household purposes—

(i) the first name (or initial) and last name of such individual, whether given at birth or time of adoption, or resulting from a lawful change of name;

(ii) the geographical address of a physical place of residence of such individual;

(iii) an electronic address (including an e-mail address) of such individual;

(iv) a telephone number dedicated to contacting such individual at such physical place of residence;

(v) a social security account number issued to such individual; or

(vi) the account number of a credit card issued to such individual; or

(B) if identified in connection with 1 or more of the items of information specified in subparagraph (A)—

(i) a birth date, the number of a certificate of birth or adoption, or a place of birth; or

(ii) any other information concerning an identified individual that, if disclosed, will result in contacting or identifying such individual physically or electronically.

(42) The term "petition" means petition filed under section 301, 302, 303 and 1504 of this title, as the case may be, commencing a case under this title.

(42A) The term "production payment" means a term overriding royalty satisfiable in cash or in kind—

(A) contingent on the production of a liquid or gaseous hydrocarbon from particular real property; and

(B) from a specified volume, or a specified value, from the liquid or gaseous hydrocarbon produced from such property, and determined without regard to production costs.

(43) The term "purchaser" means transferee of a voluntary transfer, and includes immediate or mediate transferee of such a transferee.

(44) The term "railroad" means common carrier by railroad engaged in the transportation of individuals or property or owner of trackage facilities leased by such a common carrier.

(45) The term "relative" means individual related by affinity or consanguinity within the third degree as determined by the common law, or individual in a step or adoptive relationship within such third degree.

(46) The term "repo participant" means an entity that, at any time before the filing of the petition, has an outstanding repurchase agreement with the debtor.

(47) The term "repurchase agreement" (which definition also applies to a reverse repurchase agreement)—

(A) means—

(i) an agreement, including related terms, which provides for the transfer of one or more certificates of deposit, mortgage related securities (as defined in section 3 of the Securities Exchange Act of 1934), mortgage loans, interests in mortgage related securities or mortgage loans, eligible bankers' acceptances, qualified foreign government securities (defined as a security that is a direct obligation of, or that is fully guaranteed by, the central government of a member of the Organization for Economic Cooperation and Development), or securities that are direct obligations of, or that are fully guaranteed by, the United States or any agency of the United States against the transfer of funds by the transferee of such certificates of deposit, eligible bankers' acceptances, securities, mortgage loans, or interests, with a simultaneous agreement by such transferee to transfer to the transferor thereof certificates of deposit, eligible bankers' acceptance, securities, mortgage loans, or interests of the kind described in this clause, at a date certain not later than 1 year after such transfer or on demand, against the transfer of funds;

(ii) any combination of agreements or transactions referred to in clauses (i) and (iii);

(iii) an option to enter into an agreement or transaction referred to in clause (i) or (ii);

(iv) a master agreement that provides for an agreement or transaction referred to in clause (i), (ii), or (iii), together with all supplements to any such master agreement, without regard to whether such master agreement provides for an agreement or transaction that is not a repurchase agreement under this paragraph, except that such master agreement shall be considered to be a repurchase agreement under this paragraph only with respect to each agreement or transaction under the master agreement that is referred to in clause (i), (ii), or (iii); or

(v) any security agreement or arrangement or other credit enhancement related to any agreement or transaction referred to in clause (i), (ii), (iii), or (iv), including any guarantee or reimbursement obligation by or to a repo participant or financial participant in connection with any agreement or transaction referred to in any such clause, but not to exceed the damages in connection with any such agreement or transaction, measured in accordance with section 562 of this title; and

(B) does not include a repurchase obligation under a participation in a commercial mortgage loan.

(48) The term "securities clearing agency" means person that is registered as a clearing agency under section 17A of the Securities Exchange Act of 1934, or exempt from such registration under such section pursuant to an order of the Securities and Exchange Commission, or whose business is confined to the performance of functions of a clearing agency with respect to exempted securities, as defined in section 3(a)(12) of such Act for the purposes of such section 17A.

(48A) The term "securities self regulatory organization" means either a securities association registered with the Securities and Exchange Commission under section 15A of the Securities Exchange Act of 1934 or a national securities exchange registered with the Securities and Exchange Commission under section 6 of the Securities Exchange Act of 1934.

(49) The term "security"—

(A) includes—

(i) note;

(ii) stock;

(iii) treasury stock;

(iv) bond;

(v) debenture;

(vi) collateral trust certificate;

(vii) pre-organization certificate or subscription;

(viii) transferable share;

(ix) voting-trust certificate;

(x) certificate of deposit;

(xi) certificate of deposit for security;

(xii) investment contract or certificate of interest or participation in a profit-sharing agreement or in an oil, gas, or mineral royalty or lease, if such contract or interest is required to be the subject of a registration statement filed with the Securities and Exchange Commission under the provisions of the Securities Act of 1933, or is exempt under section 3(b) of such Act from the requirement to file such a statement;

(xiii) interest of a limited partner in a limited partnership;

(xiv) other claim or interest commonly known as "security"; and

(xv) certificate of interest or participation in, temporary or interim certificate for, receipt for, or warrant or right to subscribe to or purchase or sell, a security; but

(B) does not include—

(i) currency, check, draft, bill of exchange, or bank letter of credit;

(ii) leverage transaction, as defined in section 761 of this title;

(iii) commodity futures contract or forward contract;

(iv) option, warrant, or right to subscribe to or purchase or sell a commodity futures contract;

(v) option to purchase or sell a commodity;

(vi) contract or certificate of a kind specified in subparagraph (A)(xii) of this paragraph that is not required to be the subject of a registration statement filed with the Securities and Exchange Commission and is not exempt under section 3(b) of the Securities Act of 1933 from the requirement to file such a statement; or

(vii) debt or evidence of indebtedness for goods sold and delivered or services rendered.

(50) The term "security agreement" means agreement that creates or provides for a security interest.

(51) The term "security interest" means lien created by an agreement.

(51A) The term "settlement payment" means, for purposes of the forward contract provisions of this title, a preliminary settlement payment, a partial settlement payment, an interim settlement payment, a settlement payment on account, a final settlement payment, a net settlement payment, or any other similar payment commonly used in the forward contract trade.

(51B) The term "single asset real estate" means real property constituting a single property or project, other than residential real property with fewer than 4 residential units, which generates substantially all of the gross income of a debtor who is not a family farmer and on which no substantial business is being conducted by a debtor other than the business of operating the real property and activities incidental thereto.

(51C) The term "small business case" means a case filed under chapter 11 of this title in which the debtor is a small business debtor and has not elected that subchapter V of chapter 11 of this title shall apply.

(51D) The term "small business debtor"—

(A) subject to subparagraph (B), means a person engaged in commercial or business activities (including any affiliate of such person that is also a debtor under this title and excluding a person whose primary activity is the business of owning single asset real estate that has aggregate noncontingent liquidated secured and unsecured debts as of the date of the filing of the petition or the date of the order for relief in an amount not more than $2,725,625[7] (excluding debts owed to 1 or more affiliates or insiders) not less than 50 percent of which arose from the commercial or business activities of the debtor; and

(B) does not include—

(i) any member of a group of affiliated debtors that has aggregate noncontingent liquidated secured and unsecured debts in an amount greater than $2,725,625[8] (excluding debt owed to 1 or more affiliates or insiders);

(ii) any debtor that is a corporation subject to the reporting requirements under section 13 or 15(d) of the Securities Exchange Act of 1934 (15 U.S.C. 78m, 78o(d)); or

(iii) any debtor that is an affiliate of an issuer (as defined in section 3 of the Securities Exchange Act of 1934 (15 U.S.C. 78c)).

(52) The term "State" includes the District of Columbia and Puerto Rico, except for the purpose of defining who may be a debtor under chapter 9 of this title.

(53) The term "statutory lien" means lien arising solely by force of a statute on specified circumstances or conditions, or lien of distress for rent, whether or not statutory, but does not include security interest or judicial lien, whether or not such interest or lien is provided by or is dependent on a statute and whether or not such interest or lien is made fully effective by statute.

(53A) The term "stockbroker" means person—

(A) with respect to which there is a customer, as defined in section 741 of this title; and

(B) that is engaged in the business of effecting transactions in securities[9]—

(i) for the account of others; or

(ii) with members of the general public, from or for such person's own account.

(53B) The term "swap agreement"—

---

[7] Ed. Note: For cases commenced in the three year period before April 1, 2019, the dollar amount is $2,566,050.

[8] Ed. Note: For cases commenced in the three-year period before April 1, 2019, the dollar amount is $2,566,050.

[9] Ed. Note: 15 U.S.C. 78c-5(g), enacted as part of the Dodd-Frank Wall Street Reform and Consumer Protection Act, Pub. L. 111-203, 124 Stat. 1775 (2010), provides: "A security-based swap, as defined in section 78c(a)(68) of this title shall be considered to be a security as such term is used in section 101(53A)(B) and subchapter III of Title 11."

(A) means—

(i) any agreement, including the terms and conditions incorporated by reference in such agreement, which is—

(I) an interest rate swap, option, future, or forward agreement, including a rate floor, rate cap, rate collar, cross-currency rate swap, and basis swap;

(II) a spot, same day-tomorrow, tomorrow-next, forward, or other foreign exchange, precious metals, or other commodity agreement;

(III) a currency swap, option, future, or forward agreement;

(IV) an equity index or equity swap, option, future, or forward agreement;

(V) a debt index or debt swap, option, future, or forward agreement;

(VI) a total return, credit spread or credit swap, option, future, or forward agreement;

(VII) a commodity index or a commodity swap, option, future, or forward agreement;

(VIII) a weather swap, option, future, or forward agreement;

(IX) an emissions swap, option, future, or forward agreement; or

(X) an inflation swap, option, future, or forward agreement;

(ii) any agreement or transaction that is similar to any other agreement or transaction referred to in this paragraph and that—

(I) is of a type that has been, is presently, or in the future becomes, the subject of recurrent dealings in the swap or other derivatives markets (including terms and conditions incorporated by reference therein); and

(II) is a forward, swap, future, option, or spot transaction on one or more rates, currencies, commodities, equity securities, or other equity instruments, debt securities or other debt instruments, quantitative measures associated with an occurrence, extent of an occurrence, or contingency associated with a financial, commercial, or economic consequence, or economic or financial indices or measures of economic or financial risk or value;

(iii) any combination of agreements or transactions referred to in this subparagraph;

(iv) any option to enter into an agreement or transaction referred to in this subparagraph;

(v) a master agreement that provides for an agreement or transaction referred to in clause (i), (ii), (iii), or (iv), together with all supplements to any such master agreement, and without regard to whether the master agreement contains an agreement or transaction that is not a swap agreement under this paragraph, except that the master agreement shall be considered to be a swap agreement under this paragraph only with respect to each agreement or transaction under the master agreement that is referred to in clause (i), (ii), (iii), or (iv); or

(vi) any security agreement or arrangement or other credit enhancement related to any agreements or transactions referred to in clause (i) through (v), including any guarantee or reimbursement obligation by or to a swap participant or financial participant in connection with any agreement or transaction referred to in any such clause, but not to exceed the damages in connection with any such agreement or transaction, measured in accordance with section 562; and

(B) is applicable for purposes of this title only, and shall not be construed or applied so as to challenge or affect the characterization, definition, or treatment of any swap agreement under any other statute, regulation, or rule, including the Gramm-Leach-Bliley Act, the Legal Certainty for Bank Products Act of 2000, the securities laws (as such term is defined in section 3(a)(47) of the Securities Exchange Act of 1934) and the Commodity Exchange Act;

(53C) The term "swap participant" means an entity that, at any time before the filing of the petition, has an outstanding swap agreement with the debtor.

(56A)[10] The term "term overriding royalty" means an interest in liquid or gaseous hydrocarbons in place or to be produced from particular real property that entitles the owner thereof to a share of production, or the value thereof, for a term limited by time, quantity, or value realized.

(53D) The term "timeshare plan" means and shall include that interest purchased in any arrangement, plan, scheme, or similar device, but not including exchange programs, whether by membership, agreement, tenancy in common, sale, lease, deed, rental agreement, license, right to use agreement, or by any other means, whereby a purchaser, in exchange for consideration, receives a right to use accommodations, facilities, or recreational sites, whether improved or unimproved, for a specific period of time less than a full year during any given year, but not necessarily for consecutive years, and which extends for a period of more than three years. A "timeshare interest" is that interest purchased in a timeshare plan which grants the purchaser the right to use and occupy accommodations, facilities, or recreational sites, whether improved or unimproved, pursuant to a timeshare plan.

(54) The term "transfer" means—

(A) the creation of a lien;

---

[10] ED. NOTE: The Bankruptcy Reform Act of 1994, Pub. L. No. 103-394, to correct a numbering error, redesignated certain definitions as paragraphs (53A) to (53D). However, the 1994 Act added a new definition after the definition of "swap participant" but failed to redesignate it. As a result, the definition of "term overriding royalty" is designated as (56A) and the definition of "timeshare plan" is designated as (53D). These two definitions should be redesignated as (53D) and (53E) respectively.

(B) the retention of title as a security interest;

(C) the foreclosure of a debtor's equity of redemption; or

(D) each mode, direct or indirect, absolute or conditional, voluntary or involuntary, of disposing of or parting with—

(i) property; or

(ii) an interest in property.

(54A) The term "uninsured State member bank" means a State member bank (as defined in section 3 of the Federal Deposit Insurance Act) the deposits of which are not insured by the Federal Deposit Insurance Corporation.

(55) The term "United States", when used in a geographical sense, includes all locations where the judicial jurisdiction of the United States extends, including territories and possessions of the United States.

BANKRUPTCY RULE REFERENCES: 1020, 1021, 9001 and 9002

**§ 102 Rules of construction**

In this title—

(1) "after notice and a hearing", or a similar phrase—

(A) means after such notice as is appropriate in the particular circumstances, and such opportunity for a hearing as is appropriate in the particular circumstances; but

(B) authorizes an act without an actual hearing if such notice is given properly and if—

(i) such a hearing is not requested timely by a party in interest; or

(ii) there is insufficient time for a hearing to be commenced before such act must be done, and the court authorizes such act;

(2) "claim against the debtor" includes claim against property of the debtor;

(3) "includes" and "including" are not limiting;

(4) "may not" is prohibitive, and not permissive;

(5) "or" is not exclusive;

(6) "order for relief" means entry of an order for relief;

(7) the singular includes the plural;

(8) a definition, contained in a section of this title that refers to another section of this title, does not, for the purpose of such reference, affect the meaning of a term used in such other section; and

(9) "United States trustee" includes a designee of the United States trustee.

BANKRUPTCY RULE REFERENCES: 1001, 2002, 9001, 9002, 9007 and 9008

## § 103 Applicability of chapters

(a) Except as provided in section 1161 of this title, chapters 1, 3, and 5 of this title apply in a case under chapter 7, 11, 12, or 13 of this title, and this chapter, sections 307, 362(o), 555 through 557, and 559 through 562 apply in a case under chapter 15.

(b) Subchapters I and II of chapter 7 of this title apply only in a case under such chapter.

(c) Subchapter III of chapter 7 of this title applies only in a case under such chapter concerning a stockbroker.

(d) Subchapter IV of chapter 7 of this title applies only in a case under such chapter concerning a commodity broker.

(e) Scope of Application.—Subchapter V of chapter 7 of this title shall apply only in a case under such chapter concerning the liquidation of an uninsured State member bank, or a corporation organized under section 25A of the Federal Reserve Act, which operates, or operates as, a multilateral clearing organization pursuant to section 409 of the Federal Deposit Insurance Corporation Improvement Act of 1991.

(f) Except as provided in section 901 of this title, only chapters 1 and 9 of this title apply in a case under such chapter 9.

(g) Except as provided in section 901 of this title, subchapters I, II, and III of chapter 11 of this title apply only in a case under such chapter.

(h) Subchapter IV of chapter 11 of this title applies only in a case under such chapter concerning a railroad.

(i) Subchapter V of chapter 11 of this title applies only in a case under chapter 11 in which a debtor (as defined in section 1182) elects that subchapter V of chapter 11 shall apply.

(j) Chapter 13 of this title applies only in a case under such chapter.

(k) Chapter 12 of this title applies only in a case under such chapter.

(*l*) Chapter 15 applies only in a case under such chapter, except that—

(1) sections 1505, 1513, and 1514 apply in all cases under this title; and

(2) section 1509 applies whether or not a case under this title is pending.

## § 104 Adjustment of dollar amounts

(a) On April 1, 1998, and at each 3-year interval ending on April 1 thereafter, each dollar amount in effect under sections 101(3), 101(18), 101(19A), 101(51D), 109(e), 303(b), 507(a), 522(d), 522(f)(3) and 522(f)(4), 522(n), 522(p), 522(q), 523(a)(2)(C), 541(b), 547(c)(9), 707(b), 1322(d), 1325(b), and 1326(b)(3) of this title and section 1409(b) of title 28 immediately before such April 1 shall be adjusted—

(1) to reflect the change in the Consumer Price Index for All Urban

Consumers, published by the Department of Labor, for the most recent 3-year period ending immediately before January 1 preceding such April 1, and

(2) to round to the nearest $25 the dollar amount that represents such change.

(b) Not later than March 1, 1998, and at each 3-year interval ending on March 1 thereafter, the Judicial Conference of the United States shall publish in the Federal Register the dollar amounts that will become effective on such April 1 under sections 101(3), 101(18), 101(19A), 101(51D), 109(e), 303(b), 507(a), 522(d), 522(f)(3) and 522(f)(4), 522(n), 522(p), 522(q), 523(a)(2)(C), 541(b), 547(c)(9), 707(b), 1322(d), 1325(b), and 1326(b)(3) of this title and section 1409(b) of title 28.

(c) Adjustments made in accordance with subsection (a) shall not apply with respect to cases commenced before the date of such adjustments.

BANKRUPTCY RULE REFERENCE: 1006

## § 105 Power of court

(a) The court may issue any order, process, or judgment that is necessary or appropriate to carry out the provisions of this title. No provision of this title providing for the raising of an issue by a party in interest shall be construed to preclude the court from, sua sponte, taking any action or making any determination necessary or appropriate to enforce or implement court orders or rules, or to prevent an abuse of process.

(b) Notwithstanding subsection (a) of this section, a court may not appoint a receiver in a case under this title.

(c) The ability of any district judge or other officer or employee of a district court to exercise any of the authority or responsibilities conferred upon the court under this title shall be determined by reference to the provisions relating to such judge, officer, or employee set forth in title 28. This subsection shall not be interpreted to exclude bankruptcy judges and other officers or employees appointed pursuant to chapter 6 of title 28 from its operation.

(d) The court, on its own motion or on the request of a party in interest—

(1) shall hold such status conferences as are necessary to further the expeditious and economical resolution of the case; and

(2) unless inconsistent with another provision of this title or with applicable Federal Rules of Bankruptcy Procedure, may issue an order at any such conference prescribing such limitations and conditions as the court deems appropriate to ensure that the case is handled expeditiously and economically, including an order that—

(A) sets the date by which the trustee must assume or reject an executory contract or unexpired lease; or

(B) in a case under chapter 11 of this title-

(i) sets a date by which the debtor, or trustee if one has been appointed, shall file a disclosure statement and plan;

(ii) sets a date by which the debtor, or trustee if one has been appointed, shall solicit acceptances of a plan;

(iii) sets the date by which a party in interest other than a debtor may file a plan;

(iv) sets a date by which a proponent of a plan, other than the debtor, shall solicit acceptances of such plan;

(v) fixes the scope and format of the notice to be provided regarding the hearing on approval of the disclosure statement; or

(vi) provides that the hearing on approval of the disclosure statement may be combined with the hearing on confirmation of the plan.

Bankruptcy Rule References: 7001, 7065 and 9020

## § 106 Waiver of sovereign immunity

(a) Notwithstanding an assertion of sovereign immunity, sovereign immunity is abrogated as to a governmental unit to the extent set forth in this section with respect to the following:

(1) Sections 105, 106, 107, 108, 303, 346, 362, 363, 364, 365, 366, 502, 503, 505, 506, 510, 522, 523, 524, 525, 542, 543, 544, 545, 546, 547, 548, 549, 550, 551, 552, 553, 722, 724, 726, 744, 749, 764, 901, 922, 926, 928, 929, 944, 1107, 1141, 1142, 1143, 1146, 1201, 1203, 1205, 1206, 1227, 1231, 1301, 1303, 1305, and 1327 of this title.

(2) The court may hear and determine any issue arising with respect to the application of such sections to governmental units.

(3) The court may issue against a governmental unit an order, process, or judgment under such sections or the Federal Rules of Bankruptcy Procedure, including an order or judgment awarding a money recovery, but not including an award of punitive damages. Such order or judgment for costs or fees under this title or the Federal Rules of Bankruptcy Procedure against any governmental unit shall be consistent with the provisions and limitations of section 2412(d)(2)(A) of title 28.

(4) The enforcement of any such order, process, or judgment against any governmental unit shall be consistent with appropriate nonbankruptcy law applicable to such governmental unit and, in the case of a money judgment against the United States, shall be paid as if it is a judgment rendered by a district court of the United States.

(5) Nothing in this section shall create any substantive claim for relief or cause of action not otherwise existing under this title, the Federal Rules of Bankruptcy Procedure, or nonbankruptcy law.

(b) A governmental unit that has filed a proof of claim in the case is deemed to have waived sovereign immunity with respect to a claim against such governmental unit that is property of the estate and that arose out of the same transaction or occurrence out of which the claim of such governmental unit arose.

(c) Notwithstanding any assertion of sovereign immunity by a governmental unit, there shall be offset against a claim or interest of a governmental unit any claim against such governmental unit that is property of the estate.

## § 107 Public access to papers

(a) Except as provided in subsections (b) and (c) and subject to section 112, a paper filed in a case under this title and the dockets of a bankruptcy court are public records and open to examination by an entity at reasonable times without charge.

(b) On request of a party in interest, the bankruptcy court shall, and on the bankruptcy court's own motion, the bankruptcy court may–

(1) protect an entity with respect to a trade secret or confidential research, development, or commercial information; or

(2) protect a person with respect to scandalous or defamatory matter contained in a paper filed in a case under this title.

(c) (1) The bankruptcy court, for cause, may protect an individual, with respect to the following types of information to the extent the court finds that disclosure of such information would create undue risk of identity theft or other unlawful injury to the individual or the individual's property:

(A) Any means of identification (as defined in section 1028(d) of title 18) contained in a paper filed, or to be filed, in a case under this title.

(B) Other information contained in a paper described in subparagraph (A).

(2) Upon ex parte application demonstrating cause, the court shall provide access to information protected pursuant to paragraph (1) to an entity acting pursuant to the police or regulatory power of a domestic governmental unit.

(3) The United States trustee, bankruptcy administrator, trustee, and any auditor serving under section 586(f) of title 28–

(A) shall have full access to all information contained in any paper filed or submitted in a case under this title; and

(B) shall not disclose information specifically protected by the court under this title.

BANKRUPTCY RULE REFERENCES: 1007, 2013, 5001, 5003, 7027, 9014 and 9018

## § 108 Extension of time

(a) If applicable nonbankruptcy law, an order entered in a nonbankruptcy proceeding, or an agreement fixes a period within which the debtor may commence an action, and such period has not expired before the date of the filing of the petition, the trustee may commence such action only before the later of–

(1) the end of such period, including any suspension of such period occurring on or after the commencement of the case; or

(2) two years after the order for relief.

(b) Except as provided in subsection (a) of this section, if applicable nonbankruptcy law, an order entered in a nonbankruptcy proceeding, or an agreement fixes a period within which the debtor or an individual protected under section 1201 or 1301 of this title may file any pleading, demand, notice, or proof of claim or loss, cure a default, or perform any other similar act, and such period has not expired before the date of the filing of the petition, the trustee may only file, cure, or perform, as the case may be, before the later of—

(1) the end of such period, including any suspension of such period occurring on or after the commencement of the case; or

(2) 60 days after the order for relief.

(c) Except as provided in section 524 of this title, if applicable nonbankruptcy law, an order entered in a nonbankruptcy proceeding, or an agreement fixes a period for commencing or continuing a civil action in a court other than a bankruptcy court on a claim against the debtor, or against an individual with respect to which such individual is protected under section 1201 or 1301 of this title, and such period has not expired before the date of the filing of the petition, then such period does not expire until the later of—

(1) the end of such period, including any suspension of such period occurring on or after the commencement of the case; or

(2) 30 days after notice of the termination or expiration of the stay under section 362, 922, 1201, or 1301 of this title, as the case may be, with respect to such claim.

BANKRUPTCY RULE REFERENCE: 9006

## § 109 Who may be a debtor

(a) Notwithstanding any other provision of this section, only a person that resides or has a domicile, a place of business, or property in the United States, or a municipality, may be a debtor under this title.

(b) A person may be a debtor under chapter 7 of this title only if such person is not—

(1) a railroad;

(2) a domestic insurance company, bank, savings bank, cooperative bank, savings and loan association, building and loan association, homestead association, a New Markets Venture Capital company as defined in section 351 of the Small Business Investment Act of 1958, a small business investment company licensed by the Small Business Administration under section 301 of the Small Business Investment Act of 1958, credit union, or industrial bank or similar institution which is an insured bank as defined in section 3(h) of the Federal Deposit Insurance Act, except that an uninsured State member bank, or a corporation organized under section 25A of the Federal Reserve Act, which operates, or operates as, a multilateral clearing organization pursuant to section 409 of the Federal Deposit Insurance Corporation Improvement Act of

1991 may be a debtor if a petition is filed at the direction of the Board of Governors of the Federal Reserve System; or

(3) (A) a foreign insurance company, engaged in such business in the United States; or

(B) a foreign bank, savings bank, cooperative bank, savings and loan association, building and loan association, or credit union, that has a branch or agency (as defined in section 1(b) of the International Banking Act of 1978) in the United States.

(c) An entity may be a debtor under chapter 9 of this title if and only if such entity—

(1) is a municipality;

(2) is specifically authorized, in its capacity as a municipality or by name, to be a debtor under such chapter by State law, or by a governmental officer or organization empowered by State law to authorize such entity to be a debtor under such chapter;

(3) is insolvent;

(4) desires to effect a plan to adjust such debts; and

(5) (A) has obtained the agreement of creditors holding at least a majority in amount of the claims of each class that such entity intends to impair under a plan in a case under such chapter;

(B) has negotiated in good faith with creditors and has failed to obtain the agreement of creditors holding at least a majority in amount of the claims of each class that such entity intends to impair under a plan in a case under such chapter;

(C) is unable to negotiate with creditors because such negotiation is impracticable; or

(D) reasonably believes that a creditor may attempt to obtain a transfer that is avoidable under section 547 of this title.

(d) Only a railroad, a person that may be a debtor under chapter 7 of this title (except a stockbroker or a commodity broker), and an uninsured State member bank, or a corporation organized under section 25A of the Federal Reserve Act, which operates, or operates as, a multilateral clearing organization pursuant to section 409 of the Federal Deposit Insurance Corporation Improvement Act of 1991 may be a debtor under chapter 11 of this title.

(e) Only an individual with regular income that owes, on the date of the filing of the petition, noncontingent, liquidated, unsecured debts of less than $419,275[11]

---

[11] ED. NOTE: For cases commenced in the three-year period before April 1, 2019, the dollar amount is $394,725.

and noncontingent, liquidated, secured debts of less than $1,257,850,[12] or an individual with regular income and such individual's spouse, except a stockbroker or a commodity broker, that owe, on the date of the filing of the petition, noncontingent, liquidated, unsecured debts that aggregate less than $419,275[13] and noncontingent, liquidated, secured debts of less than $1,257,850[14] may be a debtor under chapter 13 of this title.

(f) Only a family farmer or family fisherman with regular annual income may be a debtor under chapter 12 of this title.

(g) Notwithstanding any other provision of this section, no individual or family farmer may be a debtor under this title who has been a debtor in a case pending under this title at any time in the preceding 180 days if—

(1) the case was dismissed by the court for willful failure of the debtor to abide by orders of the court, or to appear before the court in proper prosecution of the case; or

(2) the debtor requested and obtained the voluntary dismissal of the case following the filing of a request for relief from the automatic stay provided by section 362 of this title.

(h) (1) Subject to paragraphs (2) and (3), and notwithstanding any other provision of this section other than paragraph (4) of this subsection, an individual may not be a debtor under this title unless such individual has, during the 180-day period ending on the date of filing of the petition by such individual, received from an approved nonprofit budget and credit counseling agency described in section 111(a) an individual or group briefing (including a briefing conducted by telephone or on the Internet) that outlined the opportunities for available credit counseling and assisted such individual in performing a related budget analysis.

(2) (A) Paragraph (1) shall not apply with respect to a debtor who resides in a district for which the United States trustee (or the bankruptcy administrator, if any) determines that the approved nonprofit budget and credit counseling agencies for such district are not reasonably able to provide adequate services to the additional individuals who would otherwise seek credit counseling from such agencies by reason of the requirements of paragraph (1).

(B) The United States trustee (or the bankruptcy administrator, if any) who makes a determination described in subparagraph (A) shall review such determination not later than 1 year after the date of such determination, and not less frequently than annually thereafter. Notwithstanding the preceding

[12] Ed. Note: For cases commenced in the three-year period before April 1, 2019, the dollar amount is $1,184,200.

[13] Ed. Note: For cases commenced in the three-year period before April 1, 2019, the dollar amount is $394,725.

[14] Ed. Note: For cases commenced in the three-year period before April 1, 2019, the dollar amount is $1,184,200.

sentence, a nonprofit budget and credit counseling agency may be disapproved by the United States trustee (or the bankruptcy administrator, if any) at any time.

(3) (A) Subject to subparagraph (B), the requirements of paragraph (1) shall not apply with respect to a debtor who submits to the court a certification that—

(i) describes exigent circumstances that merit a waiver of the requirements of paragraph (1);

(ii) states that the debtor requested credit counseling services from an approved nonprofit budget and credit counseling agency, but was unable to obtain the services referred to in paragraph (1) during the 7-day period beginning on the date on which the debtor made that request; and

(iii) is satisfactory to the court.

(B) With respect to a debtor, an exemption under subparagraph (A) shall cease to apply to that debtor on the date on which the debtor meets the requirements of paragraph (1), but in no case may the exemption apply to that debtor after the date that is 30 days after the debtor files a petition, except that the court, for cause, may order an additional 15 days.

(4) The requirements of paragraph (1) shall not apply with respect to a debtor whom the court determines, after notice and hearing, is unable to complete those requirements because of incapacity, disability, or active military duty in a military combat zone. For the purposes of this paragraph, "incapacity" means that the debtor is impaired by reason of mental illness or mental deficiency so that he is incapable of realizing and making rational decisions with respect to his financial responsibilities; and "disability" means that the debtor is so physically impaired as to be unable, after reasonable effort, to participate in an in person, telephone, or Internet briefing required under paragraph (1).

Bankruptcy Rule References: 1007, 1014 and 1016

## § 110 Penalty for persons who negligently or fraudulently prepare bankruptcy petitions

(a) In this section—

(1) "bankruptcy petition preparer" means a person, other than an attorney for the debtor or an employee of such attorney under the direct supervision of such attorney, who prepares for compensation a document for filing; and

(2) "document for filing" means a petition or any other document prepared for filing by a debtor in a United States bankruptcy court or a United States district court in connection with a case under this title.

(b) (1) A bankruptcy petition preparer who prepares a document for filing shall sign the document and print on the document the preparer's name and address. If a bankruptcy petition preparer is not an individual, then an officer, principal, responsible person, or partner of the bankruptcy petition preparer shall be required to—

(A) sign the document for filing; and

(B) print on the document the name and address of that officer, principal, responsible person, or partner.

(2) (A) Before preparing any document for filing or accepting any fees from or on behalf of a debtor, the bankruptcy petition preparer shall provide to the debtor a written notice which shall be on an official form prescribed by the Judicial Conference of the United States in accordance with rule 9009 of the Federal Rules of Bankruptcy Procedure.

(B) The notice under subparagraph (A)—

(i) shall inform the debtor in simple language that a bankruptcy petition preparer is not an attorney and may not practice law or give legal advice;

(ii) may contain a description of examples of legal advice that a bankruptcy petition preparer is not authorized to give, in addition to any advice that the preparer may not give by reason of subsection (e)(2); and

(iii) shall—

(I) be signed by the debtor and, under penalty of perjury, by the bankruptcy petition preparer; and

(II) be filed with any document for filing.

(c) (1) A bankruptcy petition preparer who prepares a document for filing shall place on the document, after the preparer's signature, an identifying number that identifies individuals who prepared the document.

(2) (A) Subject to subparagraph (B), for purposes of this section, the identifying number of a bankruptcy petition preparer shall be the Social Security account number of each individual who prepared the document or assisted in its preparation.

(B) If a bankruptcy petition preparer is not an individual, the identifying number of the bankruptcy petition preparer shall be the Social Security account number of the officer, principal, responsible person, or partner of the bankruptcy petition preparer.

(d) A bankruptcy petition preparer shall, not later than the time at which a document for filing is presented for the debtor's signature, furnish to the debtor a copy of the document.

(e) (1) A bankruptcy petition preparer shall not execute any document on behalf of a debtor.

(2) (A) A bankruptcy petition preparer may not offer a potential bankruptcy debtor any legal advice, including any legal advice described in subparagraph (B).

(B) The legal advice referred to in subparagraph (A) includes advising the debtor—

(i) whether—

(I) to file a petition under this title; or

(II) commencing a case under chapter 7, 11, 12, or 13 is appropriate;

(ii) whether the debtor's debts will be discharged in a case under this title;

(iii) whether the debtor will be able to retain the debtor's home, car, or other property after commencing a case under this title;

(iv) concerning—

(I) the tax consequences of a case brought under this title; or

(II) the dischargeability of tax claims;

(v) whether the debtor may or should promise to repay debts to a creditor or enter into a reaffirmation agreement with a creditor to reaffirm a debt;

(vi) concerning how to characterize the nature of the debtor's interests in property or the debtor's debts; or

(vii) concerning bankruptcy procedures and rights.

(f) A bankruptcy petition preparer shall not use the word "legal" or any similar term in any advertisements, or advertise under any category that includes the word "legal" or any similar term.

(g) A bankruptcy petition preparer shall not collect or receive any payment from the debtor or on behalf of the debtor for the court fees in connection with filing the petition.

(h) (1) The Supreme Court may promulgate rules under section 2075 of title 28, or the Judicial Conference of the United States may prescribe guidelines, for setting a maximum allowable fee chargeable by a bankruptcy petition preparer. A bankruptcy petition preparer shall notify the debtor of any such maximum amount before preparing any document for filing for the debtor or accepting any fee from or on behalf of the debtor.

(2) A declaration under penalty of perjury by the bankruptcy petition preparer shall be filed together with the petition, disclosing any fee received from or on behalf of the debtor within 12 months immediately prior to the filing of the case, and any unpaid fee charged to the debtor. If rules or guidelines setting a maximum fee for services have been promulgated or prescribed under paragraph (1), the declaration under this paragraph shall include a certification that the bankruptcy petition preparer complied with the notification requirement under paragraph (1).

(3) (A) The court shall disallow and order the immediate turnover to the

bankruptcy trustee any fee referred to in paragraph (2)—

(i) found to be in excess of the value of any services rendered by the bankruptcy petition preparer during the 12-month period immediately preceding the date of the filing of the petition; or

(ii) found to be in violation of any rule or guideline promulgated or prescribed under paragraph (1).

(B) All fees charged by a bankruptcy petition preparer may be forfeited in any case in which the bankruptcy petition preparer fails to comply with this subsection or subsection (b), (c), (d), (e), (f), or (g).

(C) An individual may exempt any funds recovered under this paragraph under section 522(b).

(4) The debtor, the trustee, a creditor, the United States trustee (or the bankruptcy administrator, if any) or the court, on the initiative of the court, may file a motion for an order under paragraph (3).

(5) A bankruptcy petition preparer shall be fined not more than $500 for each failure to comply with a court order to turn over funds within 30 days of service of such order.

(i) (1) If a bankruptcy petition preparer violates this section or commits any act that the court finds to be fraudulent, unfair, or deceptive, on the motion of the debtor, trustee, United States trustee (or the bankruptcy administrator, if any), and after notice and a hearing, the court shall order the bankruptcy petition preparer to pay to the debtor—

(A) the debtor's actual damages;

(B) the greater of—

(i) $2,000; or

(ii) twice the amount paid by the debtor to the bankruptcy petition preparer for the preparer's services; and

(C) reasonable attorneys' fees and costs in moving for damages under this subsection.

(2) If the trustee or creditor moves for damages on behalf of the debtor under this subsection, the bankruptcy petition preparer shall be ordered to pay the movant the additional amount of $1,000 plus reasonable attorneys' fees and costs incurred.

(j) (1) A debtor for whom a bankruptcy petition preparer has prepared a document for filing, the trustee, a creditor, or the United States trustee in the district in which the bankruptcy petition preparer resides, has conducted business, or the United States trustee in any other district in which the debtor resides may bring a civil action to enjoin a bankruptcy petition preparer from engaging in any conduct in violation of this section or from further acting as a bankruptcy petition preparer.

(2) (A) In an action under paragraph (1), if the court finds that—

(i) a bankruptcy petition preparer has—

(I) engaged in conduct in violation of this section or of any provision of this title;

(II) misrepresented the preparer's experience or education as a bankruptcy petition preparer; or

(III) engaged in any other fraudulent, unfair, or deceptive conduct; and

(ii) injunctive relief is appropriate to prevent the recurrence of such conduct, the court may enjoin the bankruptcy petition preparer from engaging in such conduct.

(B) If the court finds that a bankruptcy petition preparer has continually engaged in conduct described in subclause (I), (II), or (III) of clause (i) and that an injunction prohibiting such conduct would not be sufficient to prevent such person's interference with the proper administration of this title, has not paid a penalty imposed under this section, or failed to disgorge all fees ordered by the court, the court may enjoin the person from acting as a bankruptcy petition preparer.

(3) The court, as part of its contempt power, may enjoin a bankruptcy petition preparer that has failed to comply with a previous order issued under this section. The injunction under this paragraph may be issued on the motion of the court, the trustee, or the United States trustee (or the bankruptcy administrator, if any).

(4) The court shall award to a debtor, trustee, or creditor that brings a successful action under this subsection reasonable attorneys' fees and costs of the action, to be paid by the bankruptcy petition preparer.

(k) Nothing in this section shall be construed to permit activities that are otherwise prohibited by law, including rules and laws that prohibit the unauthorized practice of law.

(l) (1) A bankruptcy petition preparer who fails to comply with any provision of subsection (b), (c), (d), (e), (f), (g), or (h) may be fined not more than $500 for each such failure.

(2) The court shall triple the amount of a fine assessed under paragraph (1) in any case in which the court finds that a bankruptcy petition preparer—

(A) advised the debtor to exclude assets or income that should have been included on applicable schedules;

(B) advised the debtor to use a false Social Security account number;

(C) failed to inform the debtor that the debtor was filing for relief under this title; or

(D) prepared a document for filing in a manner that failed to disclose the identity of the bankruptcy petition preparer.

(3) A debtor, trustee, creditor, or United States trustee (or the bankruptcy administrator, if any) may file a motion for an order imposing a fine on the bankruptcy petition preparer for any violation of this section.

(4) (A) Fines imposed under this subsection in judicial districts served by United States trustees shall be paid to the United States trustees, who shall deposit an amount equal to such fines in the United States Trustee Fund.

(B) Fines imposed under this subsection in judicial districts served by bankruptcy administrators shall be deposited as offsetting receipts to the fund established under section 1931 of title 28, and shall remain available until expended to reimburse any appropriation for the amount paid out of such appropriation for expenses of the operation and maintenance of the courts of the United States.

Bankruptcy Rule References: 2016 and 9010

## § 111 Nonprofit budget and credit counseling agencies; financial management instructional courses

(a) The clerk shall maintain a publicly available list of—

(1) nonprofit budget and credit counseling agencies that provide 1 or more services described in section 109(h) currently approved by the United States trustee (or the bankruptcy administrator, if any); and

(2) instructional courses concerning personal financial management currently approved by the United States trustee (or the bankruptcy administrator, if any), as applicable.

(b) The United States trustee (or bankruptcy administrator, if any) shall only approve a nonprofit budget and credit counseling agency or an instructional course concerning personal financial management as follows:

(1) The United States trustee (or bankruptcy administrator, if any) shall have thoroughly reviewed the qualifications of the nonprofit budget and credit counseling agency or of the provider of the instructional course under the standards set forth in this section, and the services or instructional courses that will be offered by such agency or such provider, and may require such agency or such provider that has sought approval to provide information with respect to such review.

(2) The United States trustee (or bankruptcy administrator, if any) shall have determined that such agency or such instructional course fully satisfies the applicable standards set forth in this section.

(3) If a nonprofit budget and credit counseling agency or instructional course did not appear on the approved list for the district under subsection (a) immediately before approval under this section, approval under this subsection of such agency or such instructional course shall be for a probationary period not to exceed 6 months.

(4) At the conclusion of the applicable probationary period under paragraph (3), the United States trustee (or bankruptcy administrator, if any) may only approve for an additional 1-year period, and for successive 1-year periods thereafter, an agency or instructional course that has demonstrated during the probationary or applicable subsequent period of approval that such agency or instructional course—

(A) has met the standards set forth under this section during such period; and

(B) can satisfy such standards in the future.

(5) Not later than 30 days after any final decision under paragraph (4), an interested person may seek judicial review of such decision in the appropriate district court of the United States.

(c) (1) The United States trustee (or the bankruptcy administrator, if any) shall only approve a nonprofit budget and credit counseling agency that demonstrates that it will provide qualified counselors, maintain adequate provision for safekeeping and payment of client funds, provide adequate counseling with respect to client credit problems, and deal responsibly and effectively with other matters relating to the quality, effectiveness, and financial security of the services it provides.

(2) To be approved by the United States trustee (or the bankruptcy administrator, if any), a nonprofit budget and credit counseling agency shall, at a minimum—

(A) have a board of directors the majority of which—

(i) are not employed by such agency; and

(ii) will not directly or indirectly benefit financially from the outcome of the counseling services provided by such agency;

(B) if a fee is charged for counseling services, charge a reasonable fee, and provide services without regard to ability to pay the fee;

(C) provide for safekeeping and payment of client funds, including an annual audit of the trust accounts and appropriate employee bonding;

(D) provide full disclosures to a client, including funding sources, counselor qualifications, possible impact on credit reports, and any costs of such program that will be paid by such client and how such costs will be paid;

(E) provide adequate counseling with respect to a client's credit problems that includes an analysis of such client's current financial condition, factors that caused such financial condition, and how such client can develop a plan to respond to the problems without incurring negative amortization of debt;

(F) provide trained counselors who receive no commissions or bonuses based on the outcome of the counseling services provided by such agency, and who have adequate experience, and have been adequately trained to provide counseling services to individuals in financial difficulty, including the matters described in subparagraph (E);

(G) demonstrate adequate experience and background in providing credit counseling; and

(H) have adequate financial resources to provide continuing support services for budgeting plans over the life of any repayment plan.

(d) The United States trustee (or the bankruptcy administrator, if any) shall only approve an instructional course concerning personal financial management—

(1) for an initial probationary period under subsection (b)(3) if the course will provide at a minimum—

(A) trained personnel with adequate experience and training in providing effective instruction and services;

(B) learning materials and teaching methodologies designed to assist debtors in understanding personal financial management and that are consistent with stated objectives directly related to the goals of such instructional course;

(C) adequate facilities situated in reasonably convenient locations at which such instructional course is offered, except that such facilities may include the provision of such instructional course by telephone or through the Internet, if such instructional course is effective;

(D) the preparation and retention of reasonable records (which shall include the debtor's bankruptcy case number) to permit evaluation of the effectiveness of such instructional course, including any evaluation of satisfaction of instructional course requirements for each debtor attending such instructional course, which shall be available for inspection and evaluation by the Executive Office for United States Trustees, the United States trustee (or the bankruptcy administrator, if any), or the chief bankruptcy judge for the district in which such instructional course is offered; and

(E) if a fee is charged for the instructional course, charge a reasonable fee, and provide services without regard to ability to pay the fee; and[15]

(2) for any 1-year period if the provider thereof has demonstrated that the course meets the standards of paragraph (1) and, in addition—

(A) has been effective in assisting a substantial number of debtors to understand personal financial management; and

(B) is otherwise likely to increase substantially the debtor's understanding of personal financial management.

(e) The district court may, at any time, investigate the qualifications of a nonprofit budget and credit counseling agency referred to in subsection (a), and request production of documents to ensure the integrity and effectiveness of such

---

[15] Ed. Note: So in original. This period should probably be a semicolon.

agency. The district court may, at any time, remove from the approved list under subsection (a) a nonprofit budget and credit counseling agency upon finding such agency does not meet the qualifications of subsection (b).

(f) The United States trustee (or the bankruptcy administrator, if any) shall notify the clerk that a nonprofit budget and credit counseling agency or an instructional course is no longer approved, in which case the clerk shall remove it from the list maintained under subsection (a).

(g) (1) No nonprofit budget and credit counseling agency may provide to a credit reporting agency information concerning whether a debtor has received or sought instruction concerning personal financial management from such agency.

(2) A nonprofit budget and credit counseling agency that willfully or negligently fails to comply with any requirement under this title with respect to a debtor shall be liable for damages in an amount equal to the sum of—

(A) any actual damages sustained by the debtor as a result of the violation; and

(B) any court costs or reasonable attorneys' fees (as determined by the court) incurred in an action to recover those damages.

## § 112 Prohibition on disclosure of name of minor children

The debtor may be required to provide information regarding a minor child involved in matters under this title but may not be required to disclose in the public records in the case the name of such minor child. The debtor may be required to disclose the name of such minor child in a nonpublic record that is maintained by the court and made available by the court for examination by the United States trustee, the trustee, and the auditor (if any) serving under section 586(f) of title 28, in the case. The court, the United States trustee, the trustee, and such auditor shall not disclose the name of such minor child maintained in such nonpublic record.

# CHAPTER 3
# CASE ADMINISTRATION

## SUBCHAPTER I
## Commencement of a Case

### § 301 Voluntary cases

(a) A voluntary case under a chapter of this title is commenced by the filing with the bankruptcy court of a petition under such chapter by an entity that may be a debtor under such chapter.

(b) The commencement of a voluntary case under a chapter of this title constitutes an order for relief under such chapter.

BANKRUPTCY RULE REFERENCES: 1002, 1004, 1004.1, 1005, 1006, 1007, 2002, 5001, 5005 and 9009

### § 302 Joint cases

(a) A joint case under a chapter of this title is commenced by the filing with the bankruptcy court of a single petition under such chapter by an individual that may be a debtor under such chapter and such individual's spouse. The commencement of a joint case under a chapter of this title constitutes an order for relief under such chapter.

(b) After the commencement of a joint case, the court shall determine the extent, if any, to which the debtors' estates shall be consolidated.

BANKRUPTCY RULE REFERENCES: 1014, 1015 and 2009

### § 303 Involuntary cases

(a) An involuntary case may be commenced only under chapter 7 or 11 of this title, and only against a person, except a farmer, family farmer, or a corporation that is not a moneyed, business, or commercial corporation, that may be a debtor under the chapter under which such case is commenced.

(b) An involuntary case against a person is commenced by the filing with the bankruptcy court of a petition under chapter 7 or 11 of this title–

(1) by three or more entities, each of which is either a holder of a claim against such person that is not contingent as to liability or the subject of a bona fide dispute as to liability or amount, or an indenture trustee representing such a holder, if such noncontingent, undisputed claims aggregate at least $16,750[16] more than the value of any lien on property of the debtor securing such claims held by the holders of such claims;

(2) if there are fewer than 12 such holders, excluding any employee or insider of such person and any transferee of a transfer that is voidable under section 544, 545, 547, 548, 549, or 724(a) of this title, by one or more of such holders

[16] ED. NOTE: For cases commenced in the three-year period before April 1, 2019, the dollar amount is $15,775.

that hold in the aggregate at least $16,750[17] of such claims;

(3) if such person is a partnership—

(A) by fewer than all of the general partners in such partnership; or

(B) if relief has been ordered under this title with respect to all of the general partners in such partnership, by a general partner in such partnership, the trustee of such a general partner, or a holder of a claim against such partnership; or

(4) by a foreign representative of the estate in a foreign proceeding concerning such person.

(c) After the filing of a petition under this section but before the case is dismissed or relief is ordered, a creditor holding an unsecured claim that is not contingent, other than a creditor filing under subsection (b) of this section, may join in the petition with the same effect as if such joining creditor were a petitioning creditor under subsection (b) of this section.

(d) The debtor, or a general partner in a partnership debtor that did not join in the petition, may file an answer to a petition under this section.

(e) After notice and a hearing, and for cause, the court may require the petitioners under this section to file a bond to indemnify the debtor for such amounts as the court may later allow under subsection (i) of this section.

(f) Notwithstanding section 363 of this title, except to the extent that the court orders otherwise, and until an order for relief in the case, any business of the debtor may continue to operate, and the debtor may continue to use, acquire, or dispose of property as if an involuntary case concerning the debtor had not been commenced.

(g) At any time after the commencement of an involuntary case under chapter 7 of this title but before an order for relief in the case, the court, on request of a party in interest, after notice to the debtor and a hearing, and if necessary to preserve the property of the estate or to prevent loss to the estate, may order the United States trustee to appoint an interim trustee under section 701 of this title to take possession of the property of the estate and to operate any business of the debtor. Before an order for relief, the debtor may regain possession of property in the possession of a trustee ordered appointed under this subsection if the debtor files such bond as the court requires, conditioned on the debtor's accounting for and delivering to the trustee, if there is an order for relief in the case, such property, or the value, as of the date the debtor regains possession, of such property.

(h) If the petition is not timely controverted, the court shall order relief against the debtor in an involuntary case under the chapter under which the petition was filed. Otherwise, after trial, the court shall order relief against the debtor in an

---

[17] ED. NOTE: ED. NOTE: For cases commenced in the three-year period before April 1, 2019, the dollar amount is $15,775.

involuntary case under the chapter under which the petition was filed, only if—

(1) the debtor is generally not paying such debtor's debts as such debts become due unless such debts are the subject of a bona fide dispute as to liability or amount; or

(2) within 120 days before the date of the filing of the petition, a custodian, other than a trustee, receiver, or agent appointed or authorized to take charge of less than substantially all of the property of the debtor for the purpose of enforcing a lien against such property, was appointed or took possession.

(i) If the court dismisses a petition under this section other than on consent of all petitioners and the debtor, and if the debtor does not waive the right to judgment under this subsection, the court may grant judgment—

(1) against the petitioners and in favor of the debtor for—

(A) costs; or

(B) a reasonable attorney's fee; or

(2) against any petitioner that filed the petition in bad faith, for—

(A) any damages proximately caused by such filing; or

(B) punitive damages.

(j) Only after notice to all creditors and a hearing may the court dismiss a petition filed under this section—

(1) on the motion of a petitioner;

(2) on consent of all petitioners and the debtor; or

(3) for want of prosecution.

(k) (1) If—

(A) the petition under this section is false or contains any materially false, fictitious, or fraudulent statement;

(B) the debtor is an individual; and

(C) the court dismisses such petition,

the court, upon the motion of the debtor, shall seal all the records of the court relating to such petition, and all references to such petition.

(2) If the debtor is an individual and the court dismisses a petition under this section, the court may enter an order prohibiting all consumer reporting agencies (as defined in section 603(f) of the Fair Credit Reporting Act (15 U.S.C. 1681a(f)) from making any consumer report (as defined in section 603(d) of that Act) that contains any information relating to such petition or to the case commenced by the filing of such petition.

(3) Upon the expiration of the statute of limitations described in section 3282 of title 18, for a violation of section 152 or 157 of such title, the court,

upon the motion of the debtor and for good cause, may expunge any records relating to a petition filed under this section.

BANKRUPTCY RULE REFERENCES: 1002, 1003, 1004, 1005, 1006, 1007, 1010, 1011, 1013, 1018, 5005, 7004, 7019, 7020, 7021, 7024 and 9009

### § 304 Cases ancillary to foreign proceedings [Repealed in 2005]

### § 305 Abstention

(a) The court, after notice and a hearing, may dismiss a case under this title or may suspend all proceedings in a case under this title, at any time if–

(1) the interests of creditors and the debtor would be better served by such dismissal or suspension; or

(2) (A) a petition under section 1515 for recognition of a foreign proceeding has been granted; and

(B) the purposes of chapter 15 of this title would be best served by such dismissal or suspension.

(b) A foreign representative may seek dismissal or suspension under subsection (a)(2) of this section.

(c) An order under subsection (a) of this section dismissing a case or suspending all proceedings in a case, or a decision not so to dismiss or suspend, is not reviewable by appeal or otherwise by the court of appeals under section 158(d), 1291, or 1292 of title 28 or by the Supreme Court of the United States under section 1254 of title 28.

BANKRUPTCY RULE REFERENCES: 1017, 2002 and 5011

### § 306 Limited appearance

An appearance in a bankruptcy court by a foreign representative in connection with a petition or request under section 303 or 305 of this title does not submit such foreign representative to the jurisdiction of any court in the United States for any other purpose, but the bankruptcy court may condition any order under section 303 or 305 of this title on compliance by such foreign representative with the orders of such bankruptcy court.

### § 307 United States trustee

The United States trustee may raise and may appear and be heard on any issue in any case or proceeding under this title but may not file a plan pursuant to section 1121(c) of this title.

BANKRUPTCY RULE REFERENCES: 2002, 2014, 2015, 2016, 5005, 8004, 8016, 9003, 9019, 9034 and 9035

### § 308 Debtor reporting requirements.

(a) For purposes of this section, the term "profitability" means, with respect to a debtor, the amount of money that the debtor has earned or lost during current and recent fiscal periods.

(b) A debtor in a small business case shall file periodic financial and other reports containing information including—

(1) the debtor's profitability;

(2) reasonable approximations of the debtor's projected cash receipts and cash disbursements over a reasonable period;

(3) comparisons of actual cash receipts and disbursements with projections in prior reports;

(4) whether the debtor is—

(A) in compliance in all material respects with postpetition requirements imposed by this title and the Federal Rules of Bankruptcy Procedure; and

(B) timely filing tax returns and other required government filings and paying taxes and other administrative expenses when due;

(5) if the debtor is not in compliance with the requirements referred to in paragraph (4)(A) or filing tax returns and other required government filings and making the payments referred to in paragraph (4)(B), what the failures are and how, at what cost, and when the debtor intends to remedy such failures; and

(6) such other matters as are in the best interests of the debtor and creditors, and in the public interest in fair and efficient procedures under chapter 11 of this title.

## Subchapter II
## Officers

### § 321 Eligibility to serve as trustee

(a) A person may serve as trustee in a case under this title only if such person is—

(1) an individual that is competent to perform the duties of trustee and, in a case under chapter 7, 12, or 13 of this title, resides or has an office in the judicial district within which the case is pending, or in any judicial district adjacent to such district; or

(2) a corporation authorized by such corporation's charter or bylaws to act as trustee, and, in a case under chapter 7, 12, or 13 of this title, having an office in at least one of such districts.

(b) A person that has served as an examiner in the case may not serve as trustee in the case.

(c) The United States trustee for the judicial district in which the case is pending is eligible to serve as trustee in the case if necessary.

Bankruptcy Rule References: 2008, 2009, 2010, 2011, 2012, 2013, 2014, 2015, 2016, 2017 and 5002

### § 322 Qualification of trustee

(a) Except as provided in subsection (b)(1), a person selected under section 701, 702, 703, 1104, 1163, 1183, 1202, or 1302 of this title to serve as trustee in a case under this title qualifies if before seven days after such selection, and before beginning official duties, such person has filed with the court a bond in favor of the United States conditioned on the faithful performance of such official duties.

(b) (1) The United States trustee qualifies wherever such trustee serves as trustee in a case under this title.

(2) The United States trustee shall determine—

(A) the amount of a bond required to be filed under subsection (a) of this section; and

(B) the sufficiency of the surety on such bond.

(c) A trustee is not liable personally or on such trustee's bond in favor of the United States for any penalty or forfeiture incurred by the debtor.

(d) A proceeding on a trustee's bond may not be commenced after two years after the date on which such trustee was discharged.

Bankruptcy Rule References: 1010, 2008, 2009, 2010, 2011, 2012, 2013, 2014, 2015, 2016, 2017 and 5002

### § 323 Role and capacity of trustee

(a) The trustee in a case under this title is the representative of the estate.

(b) The trustee in a case under this title has capacity to sue and be sued.

BANKRUPTCY RULE REFERENCES: 2008, 2009, 2010, 2011, 2012, 2013, 2015 and 6009

### § 324 Removal of trustee or examiner

(a) The court, after notice and a hearing, may remove a trustee, other than the United States trustee, or an examiner, for cause.

(b) Whenever the court removes a trustee or examiner under subsection (a) in a case under this title, such trustee or examiner shall thereby be removed in all other cases under this title in which such trustee or examiner is then serving unless the court orders otherwise.

BANKRUPTCY RULE REFERENCES: 2012 and 9014

### § 325 Effect of vacancy

A vacancy in the office of trustee during a case does not abate any pending action or proceeding, and the successor trustee shall be substituted as a party in such action or proceeding.

BANKRUPTCY RULE REFERENCE: 2012

### § 326 Limitation on compensation of trustee

(a) In a case under chapter 7 or 11, other than a case under subchapter V of chapter 11, the court may allow reasonable compensation under section 330 of this title of the trustee for the trustee's services, payable after the trustee renders such services, not to exceed 25 percent on the first $5,000 or less, 10 percent on any amount in excess of $5,000 but not in excess of $50,000, 5 percent on any amount in excess of $50,000 but not in excess of $1,000,000, and reasonable compensation not to exceed 3 percent of such moneys in excess of $1,000,000, upon all moneys disbursed or turned over in the case by the trustee to parties in interest, excluding the debtor, but including holders of secured claims.

(b) In a case under subchapter V of chapter 11 or chapter 12 or 13 of this title, the court may not allow compensation for services or reimbursement of expenses of the United States trustee or of a standing trustee appointed under section 586(b) of title 28, but may allow reasonable compensation under section 330 of this title of a trustee appointed under section 1202(a) or 1302(a) of this title for the trustee's services, payable after the trustee renders such services, not to exceed five percent upon all payments under the plan.

(c) If more than one person serves as trustee in the case, the aggregate compensation of such persons for such service may not exceed the maximum compensation prescribed for a single trustee by subsection (a) or (b) of this section, as the case may be.

(d) The court may deny allowance of compensation for services or reimbursement of expenses of the trustee if the trustee failed to make diligent inquiry into facts that would permit denial of allowance under section 328(c) of this title or, with knowledge of such facts, employed a professional person under section 327 of this title.

BANKRUPTCY RULE REFERENCES: 2002, 2013, 2016, 5002 and 5004

## § 327 Employment of professional persons

(a) Except as otherwise provided in this section, the trustee, with the court's approval, may employ one or more attorneys, accountants, appraisers, auctioneers, or other professional persons, that do not hold or represent an interest adverse to the estate, and that are disinterested persons, to represent or assist the trustee in carrying out the trustee's duties under this title.

(b) If the trustee is authorized to operate the business of the debtor under section 721, 1202, or 1108 of this title, and if the debtor has regularly employed attorneys, accountants, or other professional persons on salary, the trustee may retain or replace such professional persons if necessary in the operation of such business.

(c) In a case under chapter 7, 12, or 11 of this title, a person is not disqualified for employment under this section solely because of such person's employment by or representation of a creditor, unless there is objection by another creditor or the United States trustee, in which case the court shall disapprove such employment if there is an actual conflict of interest.

(d) The court may authorize the trustee to act as attorney or accountant for the estate if such authorization is in the best interest of the estate.

(e) The trustee, with the court's approval, may employ, for a specified special purpose, other than to represent the trustee in conducting the case, an attorney that has represented the debtor, if in the best interest of the estate, and if such attorney does not represent or hold any interest adverse to the debtor or to the estate with respect to the matter on which such attorney is to be employed.

(f) The trustee may not employ a person that has served as an examiner in the case.

BANKRUPTCY RULE REFERENCES: 2013, 2014, 2016, 5002, 5004, 6005 and 9001

## § 328 Limitation on compensation of professional persons

(a) The trustee, or a committee appointed under section 1102 of this title, with the court's approval, may employ or authorize the employment of a professional person under section 327 or 1103 of this title, as the case may be, on any reasonable terms and conditions of employment, including on a retainer, on an hourly basis, on a fixed or percentage fee basis, or on a contingent fee basis. Notwithstanding such terms and conditions, the court may allow compensation different from the compensation provided under such terms and conditions after the conclusion of such employment, if such terms and conditions prove to have been improvident in light of developments not capable of being anticipated at the time of the fixing of such terms and conditions.

(b) If the court has authorized a trustee to serve as an attorney or accountant for the estate under section 327(d) of this title, the court may allow compensation for the trustee's services as such attorney or accountant only to the extent that the trustee performed services as attorney or accountant for the estate and not for performance of any of the trustee's duties that are generally performed by a trustee without the assistance of an attorney or accountant for the estate.

(c) Except as provided in section 327(c), 327(e), or 1107(b) of this title, the court may deny allowance of compensation for services and reimbursement of expenses of a professional person employed under section 327 or 1103 of this title if, at any time during such professional person's employment under section 327 or 1103 of this title, such professional person is not a disinterested person, or represents or holds an interest adverse to the interest of the estate with respect to the matter on which such professional person is employed.

Bankruptcy Rule References: 2013, 2014, 2016, 5002, 5004, 6005 and 9001

## § 329 Debtor's transactions with attorneys

(a) Any attorney representing a debtor in a case under this title, or in connection with such a case, whether or not such attorney applies for compensation under this title, shall file with the court a statement of the compensation paid or agreed to be paid, if such payment or agreement was made after one year before the date of the filing of the petition, for services rendered or to be rendered in contemplation of or in connection with the case by such attorney, and the source of such compensation.

(b) If such compensation exceeds the reasonable value of any such services, the court may cancel any such agreement, or order the return of any such payment, to the extent excessive, to—

(1) the estate, if the property transferred—

(A) would have been property of the estate; or

(B) was to be paid by or on behalf of the debtor under a plan under chapter 11, 12, or 13 of this title; or

(2) the entity that made such payment.

Bankruptcy Rule References: 2013, 2014, 2016, 2017, 5002, 5004, 6005 and 9001

## § 330 Compensation of officers

(a) (1) After notice to the parties in interest and the United States Trustee and a hearing, and subject to sections 326, 328, and 329, the court may award to a trustee, a consumer privacy ombudsman appointed under section 332, an examiner, an ombudsman appointed under section 333, or a professional person employed under section 327 or 1103—

(A) reasonable compensation for actual, necessary services rendered by the trustee, examiner, ombudsman, professional person, or attorney and by any paraprofessional person employed by any such person; and

(B) reimbursement for actual, necessary expenses.

(2) The court may, on its own motion or on the motion of the United States Trustee, the United States Trustee for the District or Region, the trustee for the estate, or any other party in interest, award compensation that is less than the

amount of compensation that is requested.

(3) In determining the amount of reasonable compensation to be awarded to an examiner, trustee under chapter 11, or professional person, the court shall consider the nature, the extent, and the value of such services, taking into account all relevant factors, including—

(A) the time spent on such services;

(B) the rates charged for such services;

(C) whether the services were necessary to the administration of, or beneficial at the time at which the service was rendered toward the completion of, a case under this title;

(D) whether the services were performed within a reasonable amount of time commensurate with the complexity, importance, and nature of the problem, issue, or task addressed;

(E) with respect to a professional person, whether the person is board certified or otherwise has demonstrated skill and experience in the bankruptcy field; and

(F) whether the compensation is reasonable based on the customary compensation charged by comparably skilled practitioners in cases other than cases under this title.

(4) (A) Except as provided in subparagraph (B), the court shall not allow compensation for—

(i) unnecessary duplication of services; or

(ii) services that were not—

(I) reasonably likely to benefit the debtor's estate; or

(II) necessary to the administration of the case.

(B) In a chapter 12 or chapter 13 case in which the debtor is an individual, the court may allow reasonable compensation to the debtor's attorney for representing the interests of the debtor in connection with the bankruptcy case based on a consideration of the benefit and necessity of such services to the debtor and the other factors set forth in this section.

(5) The court shall reduce the amount of compensation awarded under this section by the amount of any interim compensation awarded under section 331, and, if the amount of such interim compensation exceeds the amount of compensation awarded under this section, may order the return of the excess to the estate.

(6) Any compensation awarded for the preparation of a fee application shall be based on the level and skill reasonably required to prepare the application.

(7) In determining the amount of reasonable compensation to be awarded to a trustee, the court shall treat such compensation as a commission, based on

section 326.

(b) (1) There shall be paid from the filing fee in a case under chapter 7 of this title $45 to the trustee serving in such case, after such trustee's services are rendered.

(2) The Judicial Conference of the United States—

(A) shall prescribe additional fees of the same kind as prescribed under section 1914(b) of title 28; and

(B) may prescribe notice of appearance fees and fees charged against distributions in cases under this title;

to pay $15 to trustees serving in cases after such trustees' services are rendered. Beginning 1 year after the date of the enactment of the Bankruptcy Reform Act of 1994, such $15 shall be paid in addition to the amount paid under paragraph (1).

(c) Unless the court orders otherwise, in a case under chapter 12 or 13 of this title the compensation paid to the trustee serving in the case shall not be less than $5 per month from any distribution under the plan during the administration of the plan.

(d) In a case in which the United States trustee serves as trustee, the compensation of the trustee under this section shall be paid to the clerk of the bankruptcy court and deposited by the clerk into the United States Trustee System Fund established by section 589a of title 28.

(e) (1) There is established a fund in the Treasury of the United States, to be known as the "Chapter 7 Trustee Fund", which shall be administered by the Director of the Administrative Office of the United States Courts.

(2) Deposits into the Chapter 7 Trustee Fund under section 589a(f)(1)(C) of title 28 shall be available until expended for the purposes described in paragraph (3).

(3) For fiscal years 2021 through 2026, the Chapter 7 Trustee Fund shall be available to pay the trustee serving in a case that is filed under chapter 7 or a case that is converted to a chapter 7 case in the most recent fiscal year (referred to in this subsection as a 'chapter 7 case') the amount described in paragraph (4) for the chapter 7 case in which the trustee has rendered services in that fiscal year.

(4) The amount described in this paragraph shall be the lesser of—

(A) $60; or

(B) a pro rata share, for each chapter 7 case, of the fees collected under section 1930(a)(6) of title 28 and deposited to the United States Trustee System Fund under section 589a(f)(1) of title 28, less the amounts specified in section 589a(f)(1)(A) and (B) of title 28.

(5) The payment received by a trustee under paragraph (3) shall be paid in addition to the amount paid under subsection (b).

(6) Not later than September 30, 2021, the Director of the Administrative Office of the United States Courts shall promulgate regulations for the administration of this subsection.

BANKRUPTCY RULE REFERENCES: 2013, 2014, 2016, 2017, 5002, 5004, 6005 and 9001

## § 331 Interim compensation

A trustee, an examiner, a debtor's attorney, or any professional person employed under section 327 or 1103 of this title may apply to the court not more than once every 120 days after an order for relief in a case under this title, or more often if the court permits, for such compensation for services rendered before the date of such an application or reimbursement for expenses incurred before such date as is provided under section 330 of this title. After notice and a hearing, the court may allow and disburse to such applicant such compensation or reimbursement.

BANKRUPTCY RULE REFERENCES: 2013, 2014, 2016, 2017, 5002, 5004, 6005 and 9001

## § 332 Consumer privacy ombudsman

(a) If a hearing is required under section 363(b)(1)(B), the court shall order the United States trustee to appoint, not later than 7 days before the commencement of the hearing, 1 disinterested person (other than the United States trustee) to serve as the consumer privacy ombudsman in the case and shall require that notice of such hearing be timely given to such ombudsman.

(b) The consumer privacy ombudsman may appear and be heard at such hearing and shall provide to the court information to assist the court in its consideration of the facts, circumstances, and conditions of the proposed sale or lease of personally identifiable information under section 363(b)(1)(B). Such information may include presentation of–

(1) the debtor's privacy policy;

(2) the potential losses or gains of privacy to consumers if such sale or such lease is approved by the court;

(3) the potential costs or benefits to consumers if such sale or such lease is approved by the court; and

(4) the potential alternatives that would mitigate potential privacy losses or potential costs to consumers.

(c) A consumer privacy ombudsman shall not disclose any personally identifiable information obtained by the ombudsman under this title.

BANKRUPTCY RULE REFERENCES: 2002 and 6004

## § 333 Appointment of patient care ombudsman

(a) (1) If the debtor in a case under chapter 7, 9, or 11 is a health care business, the court shall order, not later than 30 days after the commencement of the case, the appointment of an ombudsman to monitor the quality of patient care and to represent the interests of the patients of the health care business unless the court finds that the appointment of such ombudsman is not necessary for the protection of patients under the specific facts of the case.

(2) (A) If the court orders the appointment of an ombudsman under paragraph (1), the United States trustee shall appoint 1 disinterested person (other than the United States trustee) to serve as such ombudsman.

(B) If the debtor is a health care business that provides long-term care, then the United States trustee may appoint the State Long-Term Care Ombudsman appointed under the Older Americans Act of 1965 for the State in which the case is pending to serve as the ombudsman required by paragraph (1).

(C) If the United States trustee does not appoint a State Long-Term Care Ombudsman under subparagraph (B), the court shall notify the State Long-Term Care Ombudsman appointed under the Older Americans Act of 1965 for the State in which the case is pending, of the name and address of the person who is appointed under subparagraph (A).

(b) An ombudsman appointed under subsection (a) shall—

(1) monitor the quality of patient care provided to patients of the debtor, to the extent necessary under the circumstances, including interviewing patients and physicians;

(2) not later than 60 days after the date of appointment, and not less frequently than at 60-day intervals thereafter, report to the court after notice to the parties in interest, at a hearing or in writing, regarding the quality of patient care provided to patients of the debtor; and

(3) if such ombudsman determines that the quality of patient care provided to patients of the debtor is declining significantly or is otherwise being materially compromised, file with the court a motion or a written report, with notice to the parties in interest immediately upon making such determination.

(c) (1) An ombudsman appointed under subsection (a) shall maintain any information obtained by such ombudsman under this section that relates to patients (including information relating to patient records) as confidential information. Such ombudsman may not review confidential patient records unless the court approves such review in advance and imposes restrictions on such ombudsman to protect the confidentiality of such records.

(2) An ombudsman appointed under subsection (a)(2)(B) shall have access to patient records consistent with authority of such ombudsman under the Older Americans Act of 1965 and under non-Federal laws governing the State Long-Term Care Ombudsman program.

Bankruptcy Rule References: 1021, 2007.2, 2015.1 and 2015.2

## Subchapter III
## Administration

### § 341 Meetings of creditors and equity security holders.[18]

(a) Within a reasonable time after the order for relief in a case under this title, the United States trustee shall convene and preside at a meeting of creditors.

(b) The United States trustee may convene a meeting of any equity security holders.

(c) The court may not preside at, and may not attend, any meeting under this section including any final meeting of creditors. Notwithstanding any local court rule, provision of a State constitution, any otherwise applicable nonbankruptcy law, or any other requirement that representation at the meeting of creditors under subsection (a) be by an attorney, a creditor holding a consumer debt or any representative of the creditor (which may include an entity or an employee of an entity and may be a representative for more than 1 creditor) shall be permitted to appear at and participate in the meeting of creditors in a case under chapter 7 or 13, either alone or in conjunction with an attorney for the creditor. Nothing in this subsection shall be construed to require any creditor to be represented by an attorney at any meeting of creditors.

(d) Prior to the conclusion of the meeting of creditors or equity security holders, the trustee shall orally examine the debtor to ensure that the debtor in a case under chapter 7 of this title is aware of—

(1) the potential consequences of seeking a discharge in bankruptcy, including the effects on credit history;

(2) the debtor's ability to file a petition under a different chapter of this title;

(3) the effect of receiving a discharge of debts under this title; and

(4) the effect of reaffirming a debt, including the debtor's knowledge of the provisions of section 524(d) of this title.

(e) Notwithstanding subsections (a) and (b), the court, on the request of a party

---

[18] Ed. Note: The following is a related provision of the Bankruptcy Reform Act of 1994, Pub. L. No. 103-394 (1994), which gives certain powers to bankruptcy administrators:

**Sec. 105. Participation by Bankruptcy Administrator at Meetings of Creditors and Equity Security Holders.**

(a) Presiding Officer.—A bankruptcy administrator appointed under section 302(d)(3)(I) of the Bankruptcy Judges, United States Trustees, and Family Farmer Bankruptcy Act of 1986 (28 U.S.C. 581 note; Public Law 99-554; 100 Stat. 3123), as amended by section 317(a) of the Federal Courts Study Committee Implementation Act of 1990 (Public Law 101-650; 104 Stat. 5115), or the bankruptcy administrator's designee may preside at the meeting of creditors convened under section 341(a) of title 11, United States Code. The bankruptcy administrator or the bankruptcy administrator's designee may preside at any meeting of equity security holders convened under section 341(b) of title 11, United States Code.

(b) Examination of the Debtor.—The bankruptcy administrator or the bankruptcy administrator's designee may examine the debtor at the meeting of creditors and may administer the oath required under section 343 of title 11, United States Code.

in interest and after notice and a hearing, for cause may order that the United States trustee not convene a meeting of creditors or equity security holders if the debtor has filed a plan as to which the debtor solicited acceptances prior to the commencement of the case.

Bankruptcy Rule References: 1007-I, 2002, 2003, 2004, 4002 and 9001.

### § 342 Notice

(a) There shall be given such notice as is appropriate, including notice to any holder of a community claim, of an order for relief in a case under this title.

(b) Before the commencement of a case under this title by an individual whose debts are primarily consumer debts, the clerk shall give to such individual written notice containing—

(1) a brief description of—

(A) chapters 7, 11, 12, and 13 and the general purpose, benefits, and costs of proceeding under each of those chapters; and

(B) the types of services available from credit counseling agencies; and

(2) statements specifying that—

(A) a person who knowingly and fraudulently conceals assets or makes a false oath or statement under penalty of perjury in connection with a case under this title shall be subject to fine, imprisonment, or both; and

(B) all information supplied by a debtor in connection with a case under this title is subject to examination by the Attorney General.

(c) (1) If notice is required to be given by the debtor to a creditor under this title, any rule, any applicable law, or any order of the court, such notice shall contain the name, address, and last 4 digits of the taxpayer identification number of the debtor. If the notice concerns an amendment that adds a creditor to the schedules of assets and liabilities, the debtor shall include the full taxpayer identification number in the notice sent to that creditor, but the debtor shall include only the last 4 digits of the taxpayer identification number in the copy of the notice filed with the court.

(2) (A) If, within the 90 days before the commencement of a voluntary case, a creditor supplies the debtor in at least 2 communications sent to the debtor with the current account number of the debtor and the address at which such creditor requests to receive correspondence, then any notice required by this title to be sent by the debtor to such creditor shall be sent to such address and shall include such account number.

(B) If a creditor would be in violation of applicable nonbankruptcy law by sending any such communication within such 90-day period and if such creditor supplies the debtor in the last 2 communications with the current account number of the debtor and the address at which such creditor requests to receive correspondence, then any notice required by this title to be sent by the debtor to such creditor shall be sent to such address and shall include such account number.

(d) In a case under chapter 7 of this title in which the debtor is an individual and in which the presumption of abuse arises under section 707(b), the clerk shall give written notice to all creditors not later than 10 days after the date of the filing of the petition that the presumption of abuse has arisen.

(e) (1) In a case under chapter 7 or 13 of this title of a debtor who is an individual, a creditor at any time may both file with the court and serve on the debtor a notice of address to be used to provide notice in such case to such creditor.

(2) Any notice in such case required to be provided to such creditor by the debtor or the court later than 7 days after the court and the debtor receive such creditor's notice of address, shall be provided to such address.

(f) (1) An entity may file with any bankruptcy court a notice of address to be used by all the bankruptcy courts or by particular bankruptcy courts, as so specified by such entity at the time such notice is filed, to provide notice to such entity in all cases under chapters 7 and 13 pending in the courts with respect to which such notice is filed, in which such entity is a creditor.

(2) In any case filed under chapter 7 or 13, any notice required to be provided by a court with respect to which a notice is filed under paragraph (1), to such entity later than 30 days after the filing of such notice under paragraph (1) shall be provided to such address unless with respect to a particular case a different address is specified in a notice filed and served in accordance with subsection (e).

(3) A notice filed under paragraph (1) may be withdrawn by such entity.

(g) (1) Notice provided to a creditor by the debtor or the court other than in accordance with this section (excluding this subsection) shall not be effective notice until such notice is brought to the attention of such creditor. If such creditor designates a person or an organizational subdivision of such creditor to be responsible for receiving notices under this title and establishes reasonable procedures so that such notices receivable by such creditor are to be delivered to such person or such subdivision, then a notice provided to such creditor other than in accordance with this section (excluding this subsection) shall not be considered to have been brought to the attention of such creditor until such notice is received by such person or such subdivision.

(2) A monetary penalty may not be imposed on a creditor for a violation of a stay in effect under section 362(a) (including a monetary penalty imposed under section 362(k)) or for failure to comply with section 542 or 543 unless the conduct that is the basis of such violation or of such failure occurs after such creditor receives notice effective under this section of the order for relief.

Bankruptcy Rule References: 1002, 2002, 4002, 5008, 9001 and 9002

## § 343 Examination of the debtor

The debtor shall appear and submit to examination under oath at the meeting of creditors under section 341(a) of this title. Creditors, any indenture trustee, any trustee or examiner in the case, or the United States trustee may examine the debtor. The United States trustee may administer the oath required under this section.

BANKRUPTCY RULE REFERENCES: 2002, 2003, 2004, 2005, 4002, 9001 and 9010.

## § 344 Self-incrimination; immunity

Immunity for persons required to submit to examination, to testify, or to provide information in a case under this title may be granted under part V of title 18.

BANKRUPTCY RULE REFERENCES: 2004, 2005, 4002, 9001 and 9016

## § 345 Money of estates

(a) A trustee in a case under this title may make such deposit or investment of the money of the estate for which such trustee serves as will yield the maximum reasonable net return on such money, taking into account the safety of such deposit or investment.

(b) Except with respect to a deposit or investment that is insured or guaranteed by the United States or by a department, agency, or instrumentality of the United States or backed by the full faith and credit of the United States, the trustee shall require from an entity with which such money is deposited or invested—

(1) a bond—

(A) in favor of the United States;

(B) secured by the undertaking of a corporate surety approved by the United States trustee for the district in which the case is pending, and

(C) conditioned on—

(i) a proper accounting for all money so deposited or invested and for any return on such money;

(ii) prompt repayment of such money and return; and

(iii) faithful performance of duties as a depository; or

(2) the deposit of securities of the kind specified in section 9303 of title 31; unless the court for cause orders otherwise.

(c) An entity with which such moneys are deposited or invested is authorized to deposit or invest such moneys as may be required under this section.

## § 346 Special provisions related to the treatment of State and local taxes

(a) Whenever the Internal Revenue Code of 1986 provides that a separate taxable estate or entity is created in a case concerning a debtor under this title, and the income, gain, loss, deductions, and credits of such estate shall be taxed to or claimed by the estate, a separate taxable estate is also created for purposes of any State and local law imposing a tax on or measured by income and such income, gain, loss, deductions, and credits shall be taxed to or claimed by the estate and may not be taxed to or claimed by the debtor. The preceding sentence shall not apply if the case is dismissed. The trustee shall make tax returns of income required under any such State or local law.

(b) Whenever the Internal Revenue Code of 1986 provides that no separate taxable estate shall be created in a case concerning a debtor under this title, and the income, gain, loss, deductions, and credits of an estate shall be taxed to or claimed by the debtor, such income, gain, loss, deductions, and credits shall be taxed to or claimed by the debtor under a State or local law imposing a tax on or measured by income and may not be taxed to or claimed by the estate. The trustee shall make such tax returns of income of corporations and of partnerships as are required under any State or local law, but with respect to partnerships, shall make such returns only to the extent such returns are also required to be made under such Code. The estate shall be liable for any tax imposed on such corporation or partnership, but not for any tax imposed on partners or members.

(c) With respect to a partnership or any entity treated as a partnership under a State or local law imposing a tax on or measured by income that is a debtor in a case under this title, any gain or loss resulting from a distribution of property from such partnership, or any distributive share of any income, gain, loss, deduction, or credit of a partner or member that is distributed, or considered distributed, from such partnership, after the commencement of the case, is gain, loss, income, deduction, or credit, as the case may be, of the partner or member, and if such partner or member is a debtor in a case under this title, shall be subject to tax in accordance with subsection (a) or (b).

(d) For purposes of any State or local law imposing a tax on or measured by income, the taxable period of a debtor in a case under this title shall terminate only if and to the extent that the taxable period of such debtor terminates under the Internal Revenue Code of 1986.

(e) The estate in any case described in subsection (a) shall use the same accounting method as the debtor used immediately before the commencement of the case, if such method of accounting complies with applicable nonbankruptcy tax law.

(f) For purposes of any State or local law imposing a tax on or measured by income, a transfer of property from the debtor to the estate or from the estate to the debtor shall not be treated as a disposition for purposes of any provision assigning tax consequences to a disposition, except to the extent that such transfer is treated as a disposition under the Internal Revenue Code of 1986.

(g) Whenever a tax is imposed pursuant to a State or local law imposing a tax on or measured by income pursuant to subsection (a) or (b), such tax shall be imposed at rates generally applicable to the same types of entities under such State or local law.

(h) The trustee shall withhold from any payment of claims for wages, salaries, commissions, dividends, interest, or other payments, or collect, any amount required to be withheld or collected under applicable State or local tax law, and shall pay such withheld or collected amount to the appropriate governmental unit at the time and in the manner required by such tax law, and with the same priority as the claim from which such amount was withheld or collected was paid.

(i) (1) To the extent that any State or local law imposing a tax on or measured by income provides for the carryover of any tax attribute from one taxable period to a subsequent taxable period, the estate shall succeed to such tax attribute in any case in which such estate is subject to tax under subsection (a).

(2) After such a case is closed or dismissed, the debtor shall succeed to any tax attribute to which the estate succeeded under paragraph (1) to the extent consistent with the Internal Revenue Code of 1986.

(3) The estate may carry back any loss or tax attribute to a taxable period of the debtor that ended before the date of the order for relief under this title to the extent that—

(A) applicable State or local tax law provides for a carryback in the case of the debtor; and

(B) the same or a similar tax attribute may be carried back by the estate to such a taxable period of the debtor under the Internal Revenue Code of 1986.

(j) (1) For purposes of any State or local law imposing a tax on or measured by income, income is not realized by the estate, the debtor, or a successor to the debtor by reason of discharge of indebtedness in a case under this title, except to the extent, if any, that such income is subject to tax under the Internal Revenue Code of 1986.

(2) Whenever the Internal Revenue Code of 1986 provides that the amount excluded from gross income in respect of the discharge of indebtedness in a case under this title shall be applied to reduce the tax attributes of the debtor or the estate, a similar reduction shall be made under any State or local law imposing a tax on or measured by income to the extent such State or local law recognizes such attributes. Such State or local law may also provide for the reduction of other attributes to the extent that the full amount of income from the discharge of indebtedness has not been applied.

(k) (1) Except as provided in this section and section 505, the time and manner of filing tax returns and the items of income, gain, loss, deduction, and credit of any taxpayer shall be determined under applicable nonbankruptcy law.

(2) For Federal tax purposes, the provisions of this section are subject to the Internal Revenue Code of 1986 and other applicable Federal nonbankruptcy law.

### § 347 Unclaimed property

(a) Ninety days after the final distribution under section 726, 1194, 1226, or 1326 of this title in a case under chapter 7, subchapter V of chapter 11, 12, or 13 of this title, as the case may be, the trustee shall stop payment on any check remaining unpaid, and any remaining property of the estate shall be paid into the court and disposed of under chapter 129 of title 28.

(b) Any security, money, or other property remaining unclaimed at the expiration of the time allowed in a case under chapter 9, 11, or 12 of this title for the presentation of a security or the performance of any other act as a condition to participation in the distribution under any plan confirmed under section 943(b), 1129, 1173, 1191, or 1225 of this title, as the case may be, becomes the property of the debtor or of the entity acquiring the assets of the debtor under the plan, as the case may be.

BANKRUPTCY RULE REFERENCES: 3010, 3011 and 3021

## § 348 Effect of conversion

(a) Conversion of a case from a case under one chapter of this title to a case under another chapter of this title constitutes an order for relief under the chapter to which the case is converted, but, except as provided in subsections (b) and (c) of this section, does not effect a change in the date of the filing of the petition, the commencement of the case, or the order for relief.

(b) Unless the court for cause orders otherwise, in sections 701(a), 727(a)(10), 727(b),[19] 1102(a), 1110(a)(1), 1121(b), 1121(c), 1141(d)(4),[20] 1201(a), 1221, 1228(a), 1301(a), and 1305(a) of this title, "the order for relief under this chapter" in a chapter to which a case has been converted under section 706, 1112, 1208, or 1307 of this title means the conversion of such case to such chapter.

(c) Sections 342 and 365(d) of this title apply in a case that has been converted under section 706, 1112, 1208, or 1307 of this title, as if the conversion order were the order for relief.

(d) A claim against the estate or the debtor that arises after the order for relief but before conversion in a case that is converted under section 1112, 1208, or 1307 of this title, other than a claim specified in section 503(b) of this title, shall be treated for all purposes as if such claim had arisen immediately before the date of the filing of the petition.

(e) Conversion of a case under section 706, 1112, 1208, or 1307 of this title terminates the service of any trustee or examiner that is serving in the case before such conversion.

(f) (1) Except as provided in paragraph (2), when a case under chapter 13 of this title is converted to a case under another chapter under this title—

(A) property of the estate in the converted case shall consist of property of the estate, as of the date of filing of the petition, that remains in the

---

[19] ED. NOTE: Section 719(b)(1) of Pub. L. No. 109-8 (2005) (the "2005 Act") removed section 728 from the Code.

[20] ED. NOTE: Section 719(b)(3) of the 2005 Act removed Code section 1146(a) and (b) and redesignated section 1146(c) and (d) as section 1146(a) and (b), respectively. The cross-references to former section 1146(a) and (b) in section 348(b) should probably have been removed accordingly.

possession of or is under the control of the debtor on the date of conversion;

(B) valuations of property and of allowed secured claims in the chapter 13 case shall apply only in a case converted to a case under chapter 11 or 12, but not in a case converted to a case under chapter 7, with allowed secured claims in cases under chapters 11 and 12 reduced to the extent that they have been paid in accordance with the chapter 13 plan; and

(C) with respect to cases converted from chapter 13—

(i) the claim of any creditor holding security as of the date of the filing of the petition shall continue to be secured by that security unless the full amount of such claim determined under applicable nonbankruptcy law has been paid in full as of the date of conversion, notwithstanding any valuation or determination of the amount of an allowed secured claim made for the purposes of the case under chapter 13; and

(ii) unless a prebankruptcy default has been fully cured under the plan at the time of conversion, in any proceeding under this title or otherwise, the default shall have the effect given under applicable nonbankruptcy law.

(2) If the debtor converts a case under chapter 13 of this title to a case under another chapter under this title in bad faith, the property of the estate in the converted case shall consist of the property of the estate as of the date of conversion.

Bankruptcy Rule References: 1017 and 1019

## § 349 Effect of dismissal

(a) Unless the court, for cause, orders otherwise, the dismissal of a case under this title does not bar the discharge, in a later case under this title, of debts that were dischargeable in the case dismissed; nor does the dismissal of a case under this title prejudice the debtor with regard to the filing of a subsequent petition under this title, except as provided in section 109(g) of this title.

(b) Unless the court, for cause, orders otherwise, a dismissal of a case other than under section 742 of this title—

(1) reinstates—

(A) any proceeding or custodianship superseded under section 543 of this title;

(B) any transfer avoided under section 522, 544, 545, 547, 548, 549, or 724(a) of this title, or preserved under section 510(c)(2), 522(i)(2), or 551 of this title; and

(C) any lien voided under section 506(d) of this title;

(2) vacates any order, judgment, or transfer ordered, under section 522(i)(1), 542, 550, or 553 of this title; and

(3) revests the property of the estate in the entity in which such property was

vested immediately before the commencement of the case under this title.

BANKRUPTCY RULE REFERENCES: 1017 and 2002

**§ 350 Closing and reopening cases**

(a) After an estate is fully administered and the court has discharged the trustee, the court shall close the case.

(b) A case may be reopened in the court in which such case was closed to administer assets, to accord relief to the debtor, or for other cause.

BANKRUPTCY RULE REFERENCES: 3022, 5009, 5010 and 9024

**§ 351 Disposal of patient records**

If a health care business commences a case under chapter 7, 9, or 11, and the trustee does not have a sufficient amount of funds to pay for the storage of patient records in the manner required under applicable Federal or State law, the following requirements shall apply:

(1) The trustee shall—

(A) promptly publish notice, in 1 or more appropriate newspapers, that if patient records are not claimed by the patient or an insurance provider (if applicable law permits the insurance provider to make that claim) by the date that is 365 days after the date of that notification, the trustee will destroy the patient records; and

(B) during the first 180 days of the 365-day period described in subparagraph (A), promptly attempt to notify directly each patient that is the subject of the patient records and appropriate insurance carrier concerning the patient records by mailing to the most recent known address of that patient, or a family member or contact person for that patient, and to the appropriate insurance carrier an appropriate notice regarding the claiming or disposing of patient records.

(2) If, after providing the notification under paragraph (1), patient records are not claimed during the 365-day period described under that paragraph, the trustee shall mail, by certified mail, at the end of such 365-day period a written request to each appropriate Federal agency to request permission from that agency to deposit the patient records with that agency, except that no Federal agency is required to accept patient records under this paragraph.

(3) If, following the 365-day period described in paragraph (2) and after providing the notification under paragraph (1), patient records are not claimed by a patient or insurance provider, or request is not granted by a Federal agency to deposit such records with that agency, the trustee shall destroy those records by—

(A) if the records are written, shredding or burning the records; or

(B) if the records are magnetic, optical, or other electronic records, by otherwise destroying those records so that those records cannot be retrieved.

BANKRUPTCY RULE REFERENCE: 6011

## Subchapter IV
## Administrative Powers

### § 361 Adequate protection

When adequate protection is required under section 362, 363, or 364 of this title of an interest of an entity in property, such adequate protection may be provided by—

(1) requiring the trustee to make a cash payment or periodic cash payments to such entity, to the extent that the stay under section 362 of this title, use, sale, or lease under section 363 of this title, or any grant of a lien under section 364 of this title results in a decrease in the value of such entity's interest in such property;

(2) providing to such entity an additional or replacement lien to the extent that such stay, use, sale, lease, or grant results in a decrease in the value of such entity's interest in such property; or

(3) granting such other relief, other than entitling such entity to compensation allowable under section 503(b)(1) of this title as an administrative expense, as will result in the realization by such entity of the indubitable equivalent of such entity's interest in such property.

Bankruptcy Rule Reference: 4001

### § 362 Automatic stay

(a) Except as provided in subsection (b) of this section, a petition filed under section 301, 302, or 303 of this title, or an application filed under section 5(a)(3) of the Securities Investor Protection Act of 1970, operates as a stay, applicable to all entities, of—

(1) the commencement or continuation, including the issuance or employment of process, of a judicial, administrative, or other action or proceeding against the debtor that was or could have been commenced before the commencement of the case under this title, or to recover a claim against the debtor that arose before the commencement of the case under this title;

(2) the enforcement, against the debtor or against property of the estate, of a judgment obtained before the commencement of the case under this title;

(3) any act to obtain possession of property of the estate or of property from the estate or to exercise control over property of the estate;

(4) any act to create, perfect, or enforce any lien against property of the estate;

(5) any act to create, perfect, or enforce against property of the debtor any lien to the extent that such lien secures a claim that arose before the commencement of the case under this title;

(6) any act to collect, assess, or recover a claim against the debtor that arose before the commencement of the case under this title;

(7) the setoff of any debt owing to the debtor that arose before the

commencement of the case under this title against any claim against the debtor; and

(8) the commencement or continuation of a proceeding before the United States Tax Court concerning a tax liability of a debtor that is a corporation for a taxable period the bankruptcy court may determine or concerning the tax liability of a debtor who is an individual for a taxable period ending before the date of the order for relief under this title.

(b) The filing of a petition under section 301, 302, or 303 of this title, or of an application under section 5(a)(3) of the Securities Investor Protection Act of 1970, does not operate as a stay—

(1) under subsection (a) of this section, of the commencement or continuation of a criminal action or proceeding against the debtor;

(2)[21] under subsection (a)—

(A) of the commencement or continuation of a civil action or proceeding—

(i) for the establishment of paternity;

(ii) for the establishment or modification of an order for domestic support obligations;

(iii) concerning child custody or visitation;

(iv) for the dissolution of a marriage, except to the extent that such proceeding seeks to determine the division of property that is property of the estate; or

(v) regarding domestic violence;

(B) of the collection of a domestic support obligation from property that is not property of the estate;

(C) with respect to the withholding of income that is property of the estate or property of the debtor for payment of a domestic support obligation under a judicial or administrative order or a statute;

(D) of the withholding, suspension, or restriction of a driver's license, a professional or occupational license, or a recreational license, under State law, as specified in section 466(a)(16) of the Social Security Act;

(E) of the reporting of overdue support owed by a parent to any consumer reporting agency as specified in section 466(a)(7) of the Social Security Act;

---

[21] Ed. Note: The following is a related provision of section 304 ("Protection of Child Support and Alimony") of the Bankruptcy Reform Act of 1994, Pub. L. No. 103-394 (1994):

(g) Appearance Before Court.—Child support creditors or their representatives shall be permitted to appear and intervene without charge, and without meeting any special local court rule requirement for attorney appearances, in any bankruptcy case or proceeding in any bankruptcy court or district court of the United States if such creditors or representatives file a form in such court that contains information detailing the child support debt, its status, and other characteristics.

(F) of the interception of a tax refund, as specified in sections 464 and 466(a)(3) of the Social Security Act or under an analogous State law; or

(G) of the enforcement of a medical obligation, as specified under title IV of the Social Security Act;

(3) under subsection (a) of this section, of any act to perfect, or to maintain or continue the perfection of, an interest in property to the extent that the trustee's rights and powers are subject to such perfection under section 546(b) of this title or to the extent that such act is accomplished within the period provided under section 547(e)(2)(A) of this title;

(4) under paragraph (1), (2), (3), or (6) of subsection (a) of this section, of the commencement or continuation of an action or proceeding by a governmental unit or any organization exercising authority under the Convention on the Prohibition of the Development, Production, Stockpiling and Use of Chemical Weapons and on Their Destruction, opened for signature on January 13, 1993, to enforce such governmental unit's or organization's police and regulatory power, including the enforcement of a judgment other than a money judgment, obtained in an action or proceeding by the governmental unit to enforce such governmental unit's or organization's police or regulatory power;

(5) [Repealed.]

(6) under subsection (a) of this section, of the exercise by a commodity broker, forward contract merchant, stockbroker, financial institution, financial participant, or securities clearing agency of any contractual right (as defined in section 555 or 556) under any security agreement or arrangement or other credit enhancement forming a part of or related to any commodity contract, forward contract or securities contract, or of any contractual right (as defined in section 555 or 556) to offset or net out any termination value, payment amount, or other transfer obligation arising under or in connection with 1 or more such contracts, including any master agreement for such contracts;

(7) under subsection (a) of this section, of the exercise by a repo participant or financial participant of any contractual right (as defined in section 559) under any security agreement or arrangement or other credit enhancement forming a part of or related to any repurchase agreement, or of any contractual right (as defined in section 559) to offset or net out any termination value, payment amount, or other transfer obligation arising under or in connection with 1 or more such agreements, including any master agreement for such agreements;

(8) under subsection (a) of this section, of the commencement of any action by the Secretary of Housing and Urban Development to foreclose a mortgage or deed of trust in any case in which the mortgage or deed of trust held by the Secretary is insured or was formerly insured under the National Housing Act and covers property, or combinations of property, consisting of five or more living units;

(9) under subsection (a), of—

(A) an audit by a governmental unit to determine tax liability;

(B) the issuance to the debtor by a governmental unit of a notice of tax deficiency;

(C) a demand for tax returns; or

(D) the making of an assessment for any tax and issuance of a notice and demand for payment of such an assessment (but any tax lien that would otherwise attach to property of the estate by reason of such an assessment shall not take effect unless such tax is a debt of the debtor that will not be discharged in the case and such property or its proceeds are transferred out of the estate to, or otherwise revested in, the debtor).

(10) under subsection (a) of this section, of any act by a lessor to the debtor under a lease of nonresidential real property that has terminated by the expiration of the stated term of the lease before the commencement of or during a case under this title to obtain possession of such property;

(11) under subsection (a) of this section, of the presentment of a negotiable instrument and the giving of notice of and protesting dishonor of such an instrument;

(12) under subsection (a) of this section, after the date which is 90 days after the filing of such petition, of the commencement or continuation, and conclusion to the entry of final judgment, of an action which involves a debtor subject to reorganization pursuant to chapter 11 of this title and which was brought by the Secretary of Transportation under section 31325 of title 46 (including distribution of any proceeds of sale) to foreclose a preferred ship or fleet mortgage, or a security interest in or relating to a vessel or vessel under construction, held by the Secretary of Transportation under chapter 537 of title 46 or section 109(h) of title 49, or under applicable State law;

(13) under subsection (a) of this section, after the date which is 90 days after the filing of such petition, of the commencement or continuation, and conclusion to the entry of final judgment, of an action which involves a debtor subject to reorganization pursuant to chapter 11 of this title and which was brought by the Secretary of Commerce under section 31325 of title 46 (including distribution of any proceeds of sale) to foreclose a preferred ship or fleet mortgage in a vessel or a mortgage, deed of trust, or other security interest in a fishing facility held by the Secretary of Commerce under chapter 537 of title 46;

(14) under subsection (a) of this section, of any action by an accrediting agency regarding the accreditation status of the debtor as an educational institution;

(15) under subsection (a) of this section, of any action by a State licensing body regarding the licensure of the debtor as an educational institution;

(16) under subsection (a) of this section, of any action by a guaranty agency, as defined in section 435(j) of the Higher Education Act of 1965 or the Secretary

of Education regarding the eligibility of the debtor to participate in programs authorized under such Act;

(17) under subsection (a) of this section, of the exercise by a swap participant or financial participant of any contractual right (as defined in section 560) under any security agreement or arrangement or other credit enhancement forming a part of or related to any swap agreement, or of any contractual right (as defined in section 560) to offset or net out any termination value, payment amount, or other transfer obligation arising under or in connection with 1 or more such agreements, including any master agreement for such agreements;

(18) under subsection (a) of the creation or perfection of a statutory lien for an ad valorem property tax, or a special tax or special assessment on real property whether or not ad valorem, imposed by a governmental unit, if such tax or assessment comes due after the date of the filing of the petition;

(19) under subsection (a), of withholding of income from a debtor's wages and collection of amounts withheld, under the debtor's agreement authorizing that withholding and collection for the benefit of a pension, profit-sharing, stock bonus, or other plan established under section 401, 403, 408, 408A, 414, 457, or 501(c) of the Internal Revenue Code of 1986, that is sponsored by the employer of the debtor, or an affiliate, successor, or predecessor of such employer—

(A) to the extent that the amounts withheld and collected are used solely for payments relating to a loan from a plan under section 408(b)(1) of the Employee Retirement Income Security Act of 1974 or is subject to section 72(p) of the Internal Revenue Code of 1986; or

(B) a loan from a thrift savings plan permitted under subchapter III of chapter 84 of title 5, that satisfies the requirements of section 8433(g) of such title;

but nothing in this paragraph may be construed to provide that any loan made under a governmental plan under section 414(d), or a contract or account under section 403(b), of the Internal Revenue Code of 1986 constitutes a claim or a debt under this title;

(20) under subsection (a), of any act to enforce any lien against or security interest in real property following entry of the order under subsection (d)(4) as to such real property in any prior case under this title, for a period of 2 years after the date of the entry of such an order, except that the debtor, in a subsequent case under this title, may move for relief from such order based upon changed circumstances or for other good cause shown, after notice and a hearing;

(21) under subsection (a), of any act to enforce any lien against or security interest in real property—

(A) if the debtor is ineligible under section 109(g) to be a debtor in a case under this title; or

(B) if the case under this title was filed in violation of a bankruptcy court order in a prior case under this title prohibiting the debtor from being a debtor in another case under this title;

(22) subject to subsection (*l*), under subsection (a)(3), of the continuation of any eviction, unlawful detainer action, or similar proceeding by a lessor against a debtor involving residential property in which the debtor resides as a tenant under a lease or rental agreement and with respect to which the lessor has obtained before the date of the filing of the bankruptcy petition, a judgment for possession of such property against the debtor;

(23) subject to subsection (m), under subsection (a)(3), of an eviction action that seeks possession of the residential property in which the debtor resides as a tenant under a lease or rental agreement based on endangerment of such property or the illegal use of controlled substances on such property, but only if the lessor files with the court, and serves upon the debtor, a certification under penalty of perjury that such an eviction action has been filed, or that the debtor, during the 30-day period preceding the date of the filing of the certification, has endangered property or illegally used or allowed to be used a controlled substance on the property;

(24) under subsection (a), of any transfer that is not avoidable under section 544 and that is not avoidable under section 549;

(25) under subsection (a), of–

(A) the commencement or continuation of an investigation or action by a securities self regulatory organization to enforce such organization's regulatory power;

(B) the enforcement of an order or decision, other than for monetary sanctions, obtained in an action by such securities self regulatory organization to enforce such organization's regulatory power; or

(C) any act taken by such securities self regulatory organization to delist, delete, or refuse to permit quotation of any stock that does not meet applicable regulatory requirements;

(26) under subsection (a), of the setoff under applicable nonbankruptcy law of an income tax refund, by a governmental unit, with respect to a taxable period that ended before the date of the order for relief against an income tax liability for a taxable period that also ended before the date of the order for relief, except that in any case in which the setoff of an income tax refund is not permitted under applicable nonbankruptcy law because of a pending action to determine the amount or legality of a tax liability, the governmental unit may hold the refund pending the resolution of the action, unless the court, on the motion of the trustee and after notice and a hearing, grants the taxing authority adequate protection (within the meaning of section 361) for the secured claim of such authority in the setoff under section 506(a);

(27) under subsection (a) of this section, of the exercise by a master netting agreement participant of any contractual right (as defined in section 555, 556, 559, or 560) under any security agreement or arrangement or other credit

enhancement forming a part of or related to any master netting agreement, or of any contractual right (as defined in section 555, 556, 559, or 560) to offset or net out any termination value, payment amount, or other transfer obligation arising under or in connection with 1 or more such master netting agreements to the extent that such participant is eligible to exercise such rights under paragraph (6), (7), or (17) for each individual contract covered by the master netting agreement in issue;

(28) under subsection (a), of the exclusion by the Secretary of Health and Human Services of the debtor from participation in the medicare program or any other Federal health care program (as defined in section 1128B(f) of the Social Security Act pursuant to title XI or XVIII of such Act); and

(29) under subsection (a)(1) of this section, of any action by—

(A) an amateur sports organization, as defined in section 220501(b) of title 36, to replace a national governing body, as defined in that section, under section 220528 of that title; or

(B) the corporation, as defined in section 220501(b) of title 36, to revoke the certification of a national governing body, as defined in that section, under section 220521 of that title.

The provisions of paragraphs (12) and (13) of this subsection shall apply with respect to any such petition filed on or before December 31, 1989.

(c) Except as provided in subsections (d), (e), (f) and (h) of this section—

(1) the stay of an act against property of the estate under subsection (a) of this section continues until such property is no longer property of the estate;

(2) the stay of any other act under subsection (a) of this section continues until the earliest of—

(A) the time the case is closed;

(B) the time the case is dismissed; or

(C) if the case is a case under chapter 7 of this title concerning an individual or a case under chapter 9, 11, 12, or 13 of this title, the time a discharge is granted or denied;

(3) if a single or joint case is filed by or against a debtor who is an individual in a case under chapter 7, 11, or 13, and if a single or joint case of the debtor was pending within the preceding 1-year period but was dismissed, other than a case refiled under a chapter other than chapter 7 after dismissal under section 707(b)—

(A) the stay under subsection (a) with respect to any action taken with respect to a debt or property securing such debt or with respect to any lease shall terminate with respect to the debtor on the 30th day after the filing of the later case;

(B) on the motion of a party in interest for continuation of the automatic stay and upon notice and a hearing, the court may extend the stay in particular cases as to any or all creditors (subject to such conditions or limitations as the court may then impose) after notice and a hearing completed before the expiration of the 30-day period only if the party in interest demonstrates that the filing of the later case is in good faith as to the creditors to be stayed; and

(C) for purposes of subparagraph (B), a case is presumptively filed not in good faith (but such presumption may be rebutted by clear and convincing evidence to the contrary)—

(i) as to all creditors, if—

(I) more than 1 previous case under any of chapters 7, 11, and 13 in which the individual was a debtor was pending within the preceding 1-year period;

(II) a previous case under any of chapters 7, 11, and 13 in which the individual was a debtor was dismissed within such 1-year period, after the debtor failed to—

(aa) file or amend the petition or other documents as required by this title or the court without substantial excuse (but mere inadvertence or negligence shall not be a substantial excuse unless the dismissal was caused by the negligence of the debtor's attorney);

(bb) provide adequate protection as ordered by the court; or

(cc) perform the terms of a plan confirmed by the court; or

(III) there has not been a substantial change in the financial or personal affairs of the debtor since the dismissal of the next most previous case under chapter 7, 11, or 13 or any other reason to conclude that the later case will be concluded—

(aa) if a case under chapter 7, with a discharge; or

(bb) if a case under chapter 11 or 13, with a confirmed plan that will be fully performed; and

(ii) as to any creditor that commenced an action under subsection (d) in a previous case in which the individual was a debtor if, as of the date of dismissal of such case, that action was still pending or had been resolved by terminating, conditioning, or limiting the stay as to actions of such creditor; and

(4) (A) (i) if a single or joint case is filed by or against a debtor who is an individual under this title, and if 2 or more single or joint cases of the debtor were pending within the previous year but were dismissed, other than a case refiled under a chapter other than chapter 7 after dismissal under section 707(b), the stay under subsection (a) shall not go into effect upon the filing of the later case; and

(ii) on request of a party in interest, the court shall promptly enter an order confirming that no stay is in effect;

(B) if, within 30 days after the filing of the later case, a party in interest requests the court may order the stay to take effect in the case as to any or all creditors (subject to such conditions or limitations as the court may impose), after notice and a hearing, only if the party in interest demonstrates that the filing of the later case is in good faith as to the creditors to be stayed;

(C) a stay imposed under subparagraph (B) shall be effective on the date of the entry of the order allowing the stay to go into effect; and

(D) for purposes of subparagraph (B), a case is presumptively filed not in good faith (but such presumption may be rebutted by clear and convincing evidence to the contrary)—

(i) as to all creditors if—

(I) 2 or more previous cases under this title in which the individual was a debtor were pending within the 1-year period;

(II) a previous case under this title in which the individual was a debtor was dismissed within the time period stated in this paragraph after the debtor failed to file or amend the petition or other documents as required by this title or the court without substantial excuse (but mere inadvertence or negligence shall not be substantial excuse unless the dismissal was caused by the negligence of the debtor's attorney), failed to provide adequate protection as ordered by the court, or failed to perform the terms of a plan confirmed by the court; or

(III) there has not been a substantial change in the financial or personal affairs of the debtor since the dismissal of the next most previous case under this title, or any other reason to conclude that the later case will not be concluded, if a case under chapter 7, with a discharge, and if a case under chapter 11 or 13, with a confirmed plan that will be fully performed; or

(ii) as to any creditor that commenced an action under subsection (d) in a previous case in which the individual was a debtor if, as of the date of dismissal of such case, such action was still pending or had been resolved by terminating, conditioning, or limiting the stay as to such action of such creditor.

(d) On request of a party in interest and after notice and a hearing, the court shall grant relief from the stay provided under subsection (a) of this section, such as by terminating, annulling, modifying, or conditioning such stay—

(1) for cause, including the lack of adequate protection of an interest in property of such party in interest;

(2) with respect to a stay of an act against property under subsection (a) of this section, if—

(A) the debtor does not have an equity in such property; and

(B) such property is not necessary to an effective reorganization;

(3) with respect to a stay of an act against single asset real estate under subsection (a), by a creditor whose claim is secured by an interest in such real estate, unless, not later than the date that is 90 days after the entry of the order for relief (or such later date as the court may determine for cause by order entered within that 90-day period) or 30 days after the court determines that the debtor is subject to this paragraph, whichever is later—

(A) the debtor has filed a plan of reorganization that has a reasonable possibility of being confirmed within a reasonable time; or

(B) the debtor has commenced monthly payments that—

(i) may, in the debtor's sole discretion, notwithstanding section 363(c)(2), be made from rents or other income generated before, on, or after the date of the commencement of the case by or from the property to each creditor whose claim is secured by such real estate (other than a claim secured by a judgment lien or by an unmatured statutory lien); and

(ii) are in an amount equal to interest at the then applicable nondefault contract rate of interest on the value of the creditor's interest in the real estate; or

(4) with respect to a stay of an act against real property under subsection (a), by a creditor whose claim is secured by an interest in such real property, if the court finds that the filing of the petition was part of a scheme to delay, hinder, or defraud creditors that involved either—

(A) transfer of all or part ownership of, or other interest in, such real property without the consent of the secured creditor or court approval; or

(B) multiple bankruptcy filings affecting such real property.

If recorded in compliance with applicable State laws governing notices of interests or liens in real property, an order entered under paragraph (4) shall be binding in any other case under this title purporting to affect such real property filed not later than 2 years after the date of the entry of such order by the court, except that a debtor in a subsequent case under this title may move for relief from such order based upon changed circumstances or for good cause shown, after notice and a hearing. Any Federal, State, or local governmental unit that accepts notices of interests or liens in real property shall accept any certified copy of an order described in this subsection for indexing and recording.

(e) (1) Thirty days after a request under subsection (d) of this section for relief from the stay of any act against property of the estate under subsection (a) of this section, such stay is terminated with respect to the party in interest making such request, unless the court, after notice and a hearing, orders such stay continued in effect pending the conclusion of, or as a result of, a final hearing and determination under subsection (d) of this section. A hearing under this subsection may be a preliminary hearing, or may be consolidated with the final hearing under subsection (d) of this section. The court shall order such stay continued in effect pending the conclusion of the final hearing under subsection (d) of this section if there is a reasonable likelihood that the party opposing relief from such stay will prevail at the conclusion of such final hearing. If the hearing under this subsection is a preliminary hearing, then such final hearing shall be concluded not later than thirty days after the conclusion of such preliminary hearing, unless the 30-day period is extended with the consent of the parties in interest or for a specific time which the court finds is required by compelling circumstances.

(2) Notwithstanding paragraph (1), in a case under chapter 7, 11, or 13 in which the debtor is an individual, the stay under subsection (a) shall terminate on the date that is 60 days after a request is made by a party in interest under subsection (d), unless—

(A) a final decision is rendered by the court during the 60-day period beginning on the date of the request; or

(B) such 60-day period is extended—

(i) by agreement of all parties in interest; or

(ii) by the court for such specific period of time as the court finds is required for good cause, as described in findings made by the court.

(f) Upon request of a party in interest, the court, with or without a hearing, shall grant such relief from the stay provided under subsection (a) of this section as is necessary to prevent irreparable damage to the interest of an entity in property, if such interest will suffer such damage before there is an opportunity for notice and a hearing under subsection (d) or (e) of this section.

(g) In any hearing under subsection (d) or (e) of this section concerning relief from the stay of any act under subsection (a) of this section—

(1) the party requesting such relief has the burden of proof on the issue of the debtor's equity in property; and

(2) the party opposing such relief has the burden of proof on all other issues.

(h) (1) In a case in which the debtor is an individual, the stay provided by subsection (a) is terminated with respect to personal property of the estate or of the debtor securing in whole or in part a claim, or subject to an unexpired lease, and such personal property shall no longer be property of the estate if the debtor fails within the applicable time set by section 521(a)(2)—

(A) to file timely any statement of intention required under section 521(a)(2) with respect to such personal property or to indicate in such statement that the debtor will either surrender such personal property or retain it and, if retaining such personal property, either redeem such personal property pursuant to section 722, enter into an agreement of the kind specified in section 524(c) applicable to the debt secured by such personal property, or assume such unexpired lease pursuant to section 365(p) if the trustee does not do so, as applicable; and

(B) to take timely the action specified in such statement, as it may be amended before expiration of the period for taking action, unless such statement specifies the debtor's intention to reaffirm such debt on the original contract terms and the creditor refuses to agree to the reaffirmation on such terms.

(2) Paragraph (1) does not apply if the court determines, on the motion of the trustee filed before the expiration of the applicable time set by section 521(a)(2), after notice and a hearing, that such personal property is of consequential value or benefit to the estate, and orders appropriate adequate protection of the creditor's interest, and orders the debtor to deliver any collateral in the debtor's possession to the trustee. If the court does not so determine, the stay provided by subsection (a) shall terminate upon the conclusion of the hearing on the motion.

(i) If a case commenced under chapter 7, 11, or 13 is dismissed due to the creation of a debt repayment plan, for purposes of subsection (c)(3), any subsequent case commenced by the debtor under any such chapter shall not be presumed to be filed not in good faith.

(j) On request of a party in interest, the court shall issue an order under subsection (c) confirming that the automatic stay has been terminated.

(k) (1) Except as provided in paragraph (2), an individual injured by any willful violation of a stay provided by this section shall recover actual damages, including costs and attorneys' fees, and, in appropriate circumstances, may recover punitive damages.

(2) If such violation is based on an action taken by an entity in the good faith belief that subsection (h) applies to the debtor, the recovery under paragraph (1) of this subsection against such entity shall be limited to actual damages.

(l) (1) Except as otherwise provided in this subsection, subsection (b)(22) shall apply on the date that is 30 days after the date on which the bankruptcy petition is filed, if the debtor files with the petition and serves upon the lessor a certification under penalty of perjury that—

(A) under nonbankruptcy law applicable in the jurisdiction, there are circumstances under which the debtor would be permitted to cure the entire monetary default that gave rise to the judgment for possession, after that judgment for possession was entered; and

(B) the debtor (or an adult dependent of the debtor) has deposited with the clerk of the court, any rent that would become due during the 30-day period after the filing of the bankruptcy petition.

(2) If, within the 30-day period after the filing of the bankruptcy petition, the debtor (or an adult dependent of the debtor) complies with paragraph (1) and files with the court and serves upon the lessor a further certification under penalty of perjury that the debtor (or an adult dependent of the debtor) has cured, under nonbankruptcy law applicable in the jurisdiction, the entire monetary default that gave rise to the judgment under which possession is sought by the lessor, subsection (b)(22) shall not apply, unless ordered to apply by the court under paragraph (3).

(3) (A) If the lessor files an objection to any certification filed by the debtor under paragraph (1) or (2), and serves such objection upon the debtor, the court shall hold a hearing within 10 days after the filing and service of such objection to determine if the certification filed by the debtor under paragraph (1) or (2) is true.

(B) If the court upholds the objection of the lessor filed under subparagraph (A)—

(i) subsection (b)(22) shall apply immediately and relief from the stay provided under subsection (a)(3) shall not be required to enable the lessor to complete the process to recover full possession of the property; and

(ii) the clerk of the court shall immediately serve upon the lessor and the debtor a certified copy of the court's order upholding the lessor's objection.

(4) If a debtor, in accordance with paragraph (5), indicates on the petition that there was a judgment for possession of the residential rental property in which the debtor resides and does not file a certification under paragraph (1) or (2)—

(A) subsection (b)(22) shall apply immediately upon failure to file such certification, and relief from the stay provided under subsection (a)(3) shall not be required to enable the lessor to complete the process to recover full possession of the property; and

(B) the clerk of the court shall immediately serve upon the lessor and the debtor a certified copy of the docket indicating the absence of a filed certification and the applicability of the exception to the stay under subsection (b)(22).

(5) (A) Where a judgment for possession of residential property in which the debtor resides as a tenant under a lease or rental agreement has been obtained by the lessor, the debtor shall so indicate on the bankruptcy petition and shall provide the name and address of the lessor that obtained that pre-petition judgment on the petition and on any certification filed under this subsection.

(B) The form of certification filed with the petition, as specified in this subsection, shall provide for the debtor to certify, and the debtor shall certify—

(i) whether a judgment for possession of residential rental housing in which the debtor resides has been obtained against the debtor before the date of the filing of the petition; and

(ii) whether the debtor is claiming under paragraph (1) that under nonbankruptcy law applicable in the jurisdiction, there are circumstances under which the debtor would be permitted to cure the entire monetary default that gave rise to the judgment for possession, after that judgment of possession was entered, and has made the appropriate deposit with the court.

(C) The standard forms (electronic and otherwise) used in a bankruptcy proceeding shall be amended to reflect the requirements of this subsection.

(D) The clerk of the court shall arrange for the prompt transmittal of the rent deposited in accordance with paragraph (1)(B) to the lessor.

(m) (1) Except as otherwise provided in this subsection, subsection (b)(23) shall apply on the date that is 15 days after the date on which the lessor files and serves a certification described in subsection (b)(23).

(2) (A) If the debtor files with the court an objection to the truth or legal sufficiency of the certification described in subsection (b)(23) and serves such objection upon the lessor, subsection (b)(23) shall not apply, unless ordered to apply by the court under this subsection.

(B) If the debtor files and serves the objection under subparagraph (A), the court shall hold a hearing within 10 days after the filing and service of such objection to determine if the situation giving rise to the lessor's certification under paragraph (1) existed or has been remedied.

(C) If the debtor can demonstrate to the satisfaction of the court that the situation giving rise to the lessor's certification under paragraph (1) did not exist or has been remedied, the stay provided under subsection (a)(3) shall remain in effect until the termination of the stay under this section.

(D) If the debtor cannot demonstrate to the satisfaction of the court that the situation giving rise to the lessor's certification under paragraph (1) did not exist or has been remedied—

(i) relief from the stay provided under subsection (a)(3) shall not be required to enable the lessor to proceed with the eviction; and

(ii) the clerk of the court shall immediately serve upon the lessor and the debtor a certified copy of the court's order upholding the lessor's certification.

(3) If the debtor fails to file, within 15 days, an objection under paragraph (2)(A)—

(A) subsection (b)(23) shall apply immediately upon such failure and relief from the stay provided under subsection (a)(3) shall not be required to enable the lessor to complete the process to recover full possession of the property; and

(B) the clerk of the court shall immediately serve upon the lessor and the debtor a certified copy of the docket indicating such failure.

(n) (1) Except as provided in paragraph (2), subsection (a) does not apply in a case in which the debtor—

(A) is a debtor in a small business case pending at the time the petition is filed;

(B) was a debtor in a small business case that was dismissed for any reason by an order that became final in the 2-year period ending on the date of the order for relief entered with respect to the petition;

(C) was a debtor in a small business case in which a plan was confirmed in the 2-year period ending on the date of the order for relief entered with respect to the petition; or

(D) is an entity that has acquired substantially all of the assets or business of a small business debtor described in subparagraph (A), (B), or (C), unless such entity establishes by a preponderance of the evidence that such entity acquired substantially all of the assets or business of such small business debtor in good faith and not for the purpose of evading this paragraph.

(2) Paragraph (1) does not apply—

(A) to an involuntary case involving no collusion by the debtor with creditors; or

(B) to the filing of a petition if—

(i) the debtor proves by a preponderance of the evidence that the filing of the petition resulted from circumstances beyond the control of the debtor not foreseeable at the time the case then pending was filed; and

(ii) it is more likely than not that the court will confirm a feasible plan, but not a liquidating plan, within a reasonable period of time.

(o) The exercise of rights not subject to the stay arising under subsection (a) pursuant to paragraph (6), (7), (17), or (27) of subsection (b) shall not be stayed by any order of a court or administrative agency in any proceeding under this title.

Bankruptcy Rule Reference: 4001

## § 363 Use, sale, or lease of property

(a) In this section, "cash collateral" means cash, negotiable instruments, documents of title, securities, deposit accounts, or other cash equivalents whenever acquired in which the estate and an entity other than the estate have an interest and includes the proceeds, products, offspring, rents, or profits of property and the fees, charges, accounts or other payments for the use or occupancy of rooms and other public facilities in hotels, motels, or other lodging properties subject to a security interest as provided in section 552(b) of this title, whether existing before or after the commencement of a case under this title.

(b) (1) The trustee, after notice and a hearing, may use, sell, or lease, other than in the ordinary course of business, property of the estate, except that if the debtor in connection with offering a product or a service discloses to an individual a policy prohibiting the transfer of personally identifiable information about individuals to persons that are not affiliated with the debtor and if such policy is in effect on the date of the commencement of the case, then the trustee may not sell or lease personally identifiable information to any person unless—

(A) such sale or such lease is consistent with such policy; or

(B) after appointment of a consumer privacy ombudsman in accordance with section 332, and after notice and a hearing, the court approves such sale or such lease—

(i) giving due consideration to the facts, circumstances, and conditions of such sale or such lease; and

(ii) finding that no showing was made that such sale or such lease would violate applicable nonbankruptcy law.

(2) If notification is required under subsection (a) of section 7A of the Clayton Act in the case of a transaction under this subsection, then—

(A) notwithstanding subsection (a) of such section, the notification required by such subsection to be given by the debtor shall be given by the trustee; and

(B) notwithstanding subsection (b) of such section, the required waiting period shall end on the 15th day after the date of the receipt, by the Federal Trade Commission and the Assistant Attorney General in charge of the Antitrust Division of the Department of Justice, of the notification required under such subsection (a), unless such waiting period is extended—

(i) pursuant to subsection (e)(2) of such section, in the same manner as such subsection (e)(2) applies to a cash tender offer;

(ii) pursuant to subsection (g)(2) of such section; or

(iii) by the court after notice and a hearing.

(c) (1) If the business of the debtor is authorized to be operated under section 721, 1108, 1183, 1184, 1203, 1204, or 1304 of this title and unless the court orders otherwise, the trustee may enter into transactions, including the sale or lease of property of the estate, in the ordinary course of business, without notice or a hearing, and may use property of the estate in the ordinary course of business without notice or a hearing.

(2) The trustee may not use, sell, or lease cash collateral under paragraph (1) of this subsection unless—

(A) each entity that has an interest in such cash collateral consents; or

(B) the court, after notice and a hearing, authorizes such use, sale, or lease in accordance with the provisions of this section.

(3) Any hearing under paragraph (2)(B) of this subsection may be a preliminary hearing or may be consolidated with a hearing under subsection (e) of this section, but shall be scheduled in accordance with the needs of the debtor. If the hearing under paragraph (2)(B) of this subsection is a preliminary hearing, the court may authorize such use, sale, or lease only if there is a reasonable likelihood that the trustee will prevail at the final hearing under subsection (e) of this section. The court shall act promptly on any request for authorization under paragraph (2)(B) of this subsection.

(4) Except as provided in paragraph (2) of this subsection, the trustee shall segregate and account for any cash collateral in the trustee's possession, custody, or control.

(d) The trustee may use, sell, or lease property under subsection (b) or (c) of this section—

(1) in the case of a debtor that is a corporation or trust that is not a moneyed business, commercial corporation, or trust, only in accordance with nonbankruptcy law applicable to the transfer of property by a debtor that is such a corporation or trust; and

(2) only to the extent not inconsistent with any relief granted under subsection (c), (d), (e), or (f) of section 362.

(e) Notwithstanding any other provision of this section, at any time, on request of an entity that has an interest in property used, sold, or leased, or proposed to be used, sold, or leased, by the trustee, the court, with or without a hearing, shall prohibit or condition such use, sale, or lease as is necessary to provide adequate protection of such interest. This subsection also applies to property that is subject to any unexpired lease of personal property (to the exclusion of such property being subject to an order to grant relief from the stay under section 362).

(f) The trustee may sell property under subsection (b) or (c) of this section free and clear of any interest in such property of an entity other than the estate, only if—

(1) applicable nonbankruptcy law permits sale of such property free and clear of such interest;

(2) such entity consents;

(3) such interest is a lien and the price at which such property is to be sold is greater than the aggregate value of all liens on such property;

(4) such interest is in bona fide dispute; or

(5) such entity could be compelled, in a legal or equitable proceeding, to accept a money satisfaction of such interest.

(g) Notwithstanding subsection (f) of this section, the trustee may sell property under subsection (b) or (c) of this section free and clear of any vested or contingent right in the nature of dower or curtesy.

(h) Notwithstanding subsection (f) of this section, the trustee may sell both the estate's interest, under subsection (b) or (c) of this section, and the interest of any co-owner in property in which the debtor had, at the time of the commencement of the case, an undivided interest as a tenant in common, joint tenant, or tenant by the entirety, only if—

(1) partition in kind of such property among the estate and such co-owners is impracticable;

(2) sale of the estate's undivided interest in such property would realize

significantly less for the estate than sale of such property free of the interests of such co-owners;

(3) the benefit to the estate of a sale of such property free of the interests of co-owners outweighs the detriment, if any, to such co-owners; and

(4) such property is not used in the production, transmission, or distribution, for sale, of electric energy or of natural or synthetic gas for heat, light, or power.

(i) Before the consummation of a sale of property to which subsection (g) or (h) of this section applies, or of property of the estate that was community property of the debtor and the debtor's spouse immediately before the commencement of the case, the debtor's spouse, or a co-owner of such property, as the case may be, may purchase such property at the price at which such sale is to be consummated.

(j) After a sale of property to which subsection (g) or (h) of this section applies, the trustee shall distribute to the debtor's spouse or the co-owners of such property, as the case may be, and to the estate, the proceeds of such sale, less the costs and expenses, not including any compensation of the trustee, of such sale, according to the interests of such spouse or co-owners, and of the estate.

(k) At a sale under subsection (b) of this section of property that is subject to a lien that secures an allowed claim, unless the court for cause orders otherwise the holder of such claim may bid at such sale, and, if the holder of such claim purchases such property, such holder may offset such claim against the purchase price of such property.

(l) Subject to the provisions of section 365, the trustee may use, sell, or lease property under subsection (b) or (c) of this section, or a plan under chapter 11, 12, or 13 of this title may provide for the use, sale, or lease of property, notwithstanding any provision in a contract, a lease, or applicable law that is conditioned on the insolvency or financial condition of the debtor, on the commencement of a case under this title concerning the debtor, or on the appointment of or the taking possession by a trustee in a case under this title or a custodian, and that effects, or gives an option to effect, a forfeiture, modification, or termination of the debtor's interest in such property.

(m) The reversal or modification on appeal of an authorization under subsection (b) or (c) of this section of a sale or lease of property does not affect the validity of a sale or lease under such authorization to an entity that purchased or leased such property in good faith, whether or not such entity knew of the pendency of the appeal, unless such authorization and such sale or lease were stayed pending appeal.

(n) The trustee may avoid a sale under this section if the sale price was controlled by an agreement among potential bidders at such sale, or may recover from a party to such agreement any amount by which the value of the property sold exceeds the price at which such sale was consummated, and may recover any costs, attorneys' fees, or expenses incurred in avoiding such sale or recovering such amount. In addition to any recovery under the preceding sentence, the court may grant judgment for punitive damages in favor of the estate and against any such party that entered into such an agreement in willful disregard of this subsection.

(o) Notwithstanding subsection (f), if a person purchases any interest in a consumer credit transaction that is subject to the Truth in Lending Act or any interest in a consumer credit contract (as defined in section 433.1 of title 16 of the Code of Federal Regulations (January 1, 2004), as amended from time to time), and if such interest is purchased through a sale under this section, then such person shall remain subject to all claims and defenses that are related to such consumer credit transaction or such consumer credit contract, to the same extent as such person would be subject to such claims and defenses of the consumer had such interest been purchased at a sale not under this section.

(p) In any hearing under this section—

(1) the trustee has the burden of proof on the issue of adequate protection; and

(2) the entity asserting an interest in property has the burden of proof on the issue of the validity, priority, or extent of such interest.

BANKRUPTCY RULE REFERENCES: 2002, 4001, 6004, 7001 and 9014.

## § 364 Obtaining credit

(a) If the trustee is authorized to operate the business of the debtor under section 721, 1108, 1183, 1184, 1203, 1204, or 1304 of this title, unless the court orders otherwise, the trustee may obtain unsecured credit and incur unsecured debt in the ordinary course of business allowable under section 503(b)(1) of this title as an administrative expense.

(b) The court, after notice and a hearing, may authorize the trustee to obtain unsecured credit or to incur unsecured debt other than under subsection (a) of this section, allowable under section 503(b)(1) of this title as an administrative expense.

(c) If the trustee is unable to obtain unsecured credit allowable under section 503(b)(1) of this title as an administrative expense, the court, after notice and a hearing, may authorize the obtaining of credit or the incurring of debt—

(1) with priority over any or all administrative expenses of the kind specified in section 503(b) or 507(b) of this title;

(2) secured by a lien on property of the estate that is not otherwise subject to a lien; or

(3) secured by a junior lien on property of the estate that is subject to a lien.

(d) (1) The court, after notice and a hearing, may authorize the obtaining of credit or the incurring of debt secured by a senior or equal lien on property of the estate that is subject to a lien only if—

(A) the trustee is unable to obtain such credit otherwise; and

(B) there is adequate protection of the interest of the holder of the lien on the property of the estate on which such senior or equal lien is proposed to be granted.

(2) In any hearing under this subsection, the trustee has the burden of proof on the issue of adequate protection.

(e) The reversal or modification on appeal of an authorization under this section to obtain credit or incur debt, or of a grant under this section of a priority or a lien, does not affect the validity of any debt so incurred, or any priority or lien so granted, to an entity that extended such credit in good faith, whether or not such entity knew of the pendency of the appeal, unless such authorization and the incurring of such debt, or the granting of such priority or lien, were stayed pending appeal.

(f) Except with respect to an entity that is an underwriter as defined in section 1145(b) of this title, section 5 of the Securities Act of 1933, the Trust Indenture Act of 1939, and any State or local law requiring registration for offer or sale of a security or registration or licensing of an issuer of, underwriter of, or broker or dealer in, a security does not apply to the offer or sale under this section of a security that is not an equity security.

(g) (1) The court, after notice and a hearing, may authorize a debtor in possession or a trustee that is authorized to operate the business of the debtor under section 1183, 1184, 1203, 1204, or 1304 of this title to obtain a loan under paragraph (36) or (37) of section 7(a) of the Small Business Act (15 U.S.C. 636(a)), and such loan shall be treated as a debt to the extent the loan is not forgiven in accordance with section 7A of the Small Business Act or subparagraph (J) of such paragraph (37), as applicable, with priority equal to a claim of the kind specified in subsection (c)(1) of this section.

(2) The trustee may incur debt described in paragraph (1) notwithstanding any provision in a contract, prior order authorizing the trustee to incur debt under this section, prior order authorizing the trustee to use cash collateral under section 363, or applicable law that prohibits the debtor from incurring additional debt.

(3) The court shall hold a hearing within 7 days after the filing and service of the motion to obtain a loan described in paragraph (1). Notwithstanding the Federal Rules of Bankruptcy Procedure, at such hearing, the court may grant relief on a final basis.[22]

---

[22] Ed. Note: Underscored language enacted by the Consolidated Appropriations Act, 2021, Pub. L. No. 116-260, div. N, § 320(a). The amendment will:

(A) take effect on the date on which the Administrator submits to the Director of the Executive Office for United States Trustees a written determination that, subject to satisfying any other eligibility requirements, any debtor in possession or trustee that is authorized to operate the business of the debtor under section 1183, 1184, 1203, 1204, or 1304 of title 11, United States Code, would be eligible for a loan under paragraphs (36) and (37) of section 7(a) of the Small Business Act (15 U.S.C. 636(a)); and

(B) apply to any case pending on or commenced on or after the date described in subparagraph (A).

BANKRUPTCY RULE REFERENCES: 4001, 9014 and 9034

## § 365 Executory contracts and unexpired leases

(a) Except as provided in sections 765 and 766 of this title and in subsections (b), (c), and (d) of this section, the trustee, subject to the court's approval, may assume or reject any executory contract or unexpired lease of the debtor.

(b) (1) If there has been a default in an executory contract or unexpired lease of the debtor, the trustee may not assume such contract or lease unless, at the time of assumption of such contract or lease, the trustee—

(A) cures, or provides adequate assurance that the trustee will promptly cure, such default other than a default that is a breach of a provision relating to the satisfaction of any provision (other than a penalty rate or penalty provision) relating to a default arising from any failure to perform nonmonetary obligations under an unexpired lease of real property, if it is impossible for the trustee to cure such default by performing nonmonetary acts at and after the time of assumption, except that if such default arises from a failure to operate in accordance with a nonresidential real property lease, then such default shall be cured by performance at and after the time of assumption in accordance with such lease, and pecuniary losses resulting from such default shall be compensated in accordance with the provisions of this paragraph;

(B) compensates, or provides adequate assurance that the trustee will promptly compensate, a party other than the debtor to such contract or lease, for any actual pecuniary loss to such party resulting from such default; and

(C) provides adequate assurance of future performance under such contract or lease.

(2) Paragraph (1) of this subsection does not apply to a default that is a breach of a provision relating to—

(A) the insolvency or financial condition of the debtor at any time before the closing of the case;

(B) the commencement of a case under this title;

(C) the appointment of or taking possession by a trustee in a case under this title or a custodian before such commencement; or

(D) the satisfaction of any penalty rate or penalty provision relating to a default arising from any failure by the debtor to perform nonmonetary obligations under the executory contract or unexpired lease.

---

The amendment will sunset "effective on the date that is 2 years after the date of enactment" of the Act, which was December 27, 2020. Pub. L. No. 116-260, div. N, § 320(f). On April 8, 2021, the Small Business Administration issued a procedural notice stating that chapter 11, 12 and 13 debtors are eligible to receive Paycheck Protection Program loans after confirmation of a plan. *See* SBA, "Paycheck Protection Program Loans, FAQs," Q. 67 (July 29, 2021), https://www.sba.gov/sites/default/files/2021-07/FINAL%20FAQ%20Update%207.29.21-508.pdf.

(3) For the purposes of paragraph (1) of this subsection and paragraph (2)(B) of subsection (f), adequate assurance of future performance of a lease of real property in a shopping center includes adequate assurance—

(A) of the source of rent and other consideration due under such lease, and in the case of an assignment, that the financial condition and operating performance of the proposed assignee and its guarantors, if any, shall be similar to the financial condition and operating performance of the debtor and its guarantors, if any, as of the time the debtor became the lessee under the lease;

(B) that any percentage rent due under such lease will not decline substantially;

(C) that assumption or assignment of such lease is subject to all the provisions thereof, including (but not limited to) provisions such as a radius, location, use, or exclusivity provision, and will not breach any such provision contained in any other lease, financing agreement, or master agreement relating to such shopping center; and

(D) that assumption or assignment of such lease will not disrupt any tenant mix or balance in such shopping center.

(4) Notwithstanding any other provision of this section, if there has been a default in an unexpired lease of the debtor, other than a default of a kind specified in paragraph (2) of this subsection, the trustee may not require a lessor to provide services or supplies incidental to such lease before assumption of such lease unless the lessor is compensated under the terms of such lease for any services and supplies provided under such lease before assumption of such lease.

(c) The trustee may not assume or assign any executory contract or unexpired lease of the debtor, whether or not such contract or lease prohibits or restricts assignment of rights or delegation of duties, if—

(1) (A) applicable law excuses a party, other than the debtor, to such contract or lease from accepting performance from or rendering performance to an entity other than the debtor or the debtor in possession, whether or not such contract or lease prohibits or restricts assignment of rights or delegation of duties; and

(B) such party does not consent to such assumption or assignment; or

(2) such contract is a contract to make a loan, or extend other debt financing or financial accommodations, to or for the benefit of the debtor, or to issue a security of the debtor; or

(3) such lease is of nonresidential real property and has been terminated under applicable nonbankruptcy law prior to the order for relief.

(d) (1) In a case under chapter 7 of this title, if the trustee does not assume or reject an executory contract or unexpired lease of residential real property or of personal property of the debtor within 60 days after the order for relief, or within such additional time as the court, for cause, within such 60-day period, fixes, then such contract or lease is deemed rejected.

(2) In a case under chapter 9, 11, 12, or 13 of this title, the trustee may assume or reject an executory contract or unexpired lease of residential real property or of personal property of the debtor at any time before the confirmation of a plan but the court, on the request of any party to such contract or lease, may order the trustee to determine within a specified period of time whether to assume or reject such contract or lease.

(3) (A) The trustee shall timely perform all the obligations of the debtor, except those specified in section 365(b)(2), arising from and after the order for relief under any unexpired lease of nonresidential real property, until such lease is assumed or rejected, notwithstanding section 503(b)(1) of this title. The court may extend, for cause, the time for performance of any such obligation that arises within 60 days after the date of the order for relief, but the time for performance shall not be extended beyond such 60-day period, except as provided in subparagraph (B). This subsection shall not be deemed to affect the trustee's obligations under the provisions of subsection (b) or (f) of this section. Acceptance of any such performance does not constitute waiver or relinquishment of the lessor's rights under such lease or under this title.

(B) In a case under subchapter V of chapter 11, the time for performance of an obligation described in subparagraph (A) arising under any unexpired lease of nonresidential real property may be extended by the court if the debtor is experiencing or has experienced a material financial hardship due, directly or indirectly, to the coronavirus disease 2019 (COVID-19) pandemic until the earlier of—

(i) the date that is 60 days after the date of the order for relief, which may be extended by the court for an additional period of 60 days if the court determines that the debtor is continuing to experience a material financial hardship due, directly or indirectly, to the coronavirus disease 2019 (COVID-19) pandemic; or

(ii) the date on which the lease is assumed or rejected under this section.

(C) An obligation described in subparagraph (A) for which an extension is granted under subparagraph (B) shall be treated as an administrative expense described in section 507(a)(2) for the purpose of section 1191(e).[23]

(4) (A) Subject to subparagraph (B), an unexpired lease of nonresidential real property under which the debtor is the lessee shall be deemed rejected, and the trustee shall immediately surrender that nonresidential real property to

---

[23] Ed. Note: Underscored material enacted by the Consolidated Appropriations Act, 2021, Pub. L. No. 116-260, div. FF, tit. X, § 1001(f)(1)(A). The amendment will sunset two years after the date of enactment of the Act, which was December 27, 2020. Pub. L. No. 116-260, div. FF, tit. X, § 1001(f)(2)(A).

the lessor, if the trustee does not assume or reject the unexpired lease by the earlier of–

(i) the date that is ~~120~~ 210[24] days after the date of the order for relief; or

(ii) the date of the entry of an order confirming a plan.

(B) (i) The court may extend the period determined under subparagraph (A), prior to the expiration of the ~~120~~240-day period, for 90 days on the motion of the trustee or lessor for cause.

(ii) If the court grants an extension under clause (i), the court may grant a subsequent extension only upon prior written consent of the lessor in each instance.

(5) The trustee shall timely perform all of the obligations of the debtor, except those specified in section 365(b)(2), first arising from or after 60 days after the order for relief in a case under chapter 11 of this title under an unexpired lease of personal property (other than personal property leased to an individual primarily for personal, family, or household purposes), until such lease is assumed or rejected notwithstanding section 503(b)(1) of this title, unless the court, after notice and a hearing and based on the equities of the case, orders otherwise with respect to the obligations or timely performance thereof. This subsection shall not be deemed to affect the trustee's obligations under the provisions of subsection (b) or (f). Acceptance of any such performance does not constitute waiver or relinquishment of the lessor's rights under such lease or under this title.

(e) (1) Notwithstanding a provision in an executory contract or unexpired lease, or in applicable law, an executory contract or unexpired lease of the debtor may not be terminated or modified, and any right or obligation under such contract or lease may not be terminated or modified, at any time after the commencement of the case solely because of a provision in such contract or lease that is conditioned on–

(A) the insolvency or financial condition of the debtor at any time before the closing of the case;

(B) the commencement of a case under this title; or

(C) the appointment of or taking possession by a trustee in a case under this title or a custodian before such commencement.

(2) Paragraph (1) of this subsection does not apply to an executory contract or unexpired lease of the debtor, whether or not such contract or lease prohibits or restricts assignment of rights or delegation of duties, if–

---

[24] Section 365(d)(4) was amended by the Consolidated Appropriations Act, 2021, Pub. L. No. 116-260, div. FF, tit. X, § 1001(f)(2)(B). New material is underscored; removed material is stricken out. The amendment will sunset two years after the date of enactment of the Act, which was December 27, 2020. Pub. L. No. 116-260, div. FF, tit. X, § 1001(f)(2)(A).

(A) (i) applicable law excuses a party, other than the debtor, to such contract or lease from accepting performance from or rendering performance to the trustee or to an assignee of such contract or lease, whether or not such contract or lease prohibits or restricts assignment of rights or delegation of duties; and

(ii) such party does not consent to such assumption or assignment; or

(B) such contract is a contract to make a loan, or extend other debt financing or financial accommodations, to or for the benefit of the debtor, or to issue a security of the debtor.

(f) (1) Except as provided in subsections (b) and (c) of this section, notwithstanding a provision in an executory contract or unexpired lease of the debtor, or in applicable law, that prohibits, restricts, or conditions the assignment of such contract or lease, the trustee may assign such contract or lease under paragraph (2) of this subsection.

(2) The trustee may assign an executory contract or unexpired lease of the debtor only if—

(A) the trustee assumes such contract or lease in accordance with the provisions of this section; and

(B) adequate assurance of future performance by the assignee of such contract or lease is provided, whether or not there has been a default in such contract or lease.

(3) Notwithstanding a provision in an executory contract or unexpired lease of the debtor, or in applicable law that terminates or modifies, or permits a party other than the debtor to terminate or modify, such contract or lease or a right or obligation under such contract or lease on account of an assignment of such contract or lease, such contract, lease, right, or obligation may not be terminated or modified under such provision because of the assumption or assignment of such contract or lease by the trustee.

(g) Except as provided in subsections (h)(2) and (i)(2) of this section, the rejection of an executory contract or unexpired lease of the debtor constitutes a breach of such contract or lease—

(1) if such contract or lease has not been assumed under this section or under a plan confirmed under chapter 9, 11, 12, or 13 of this title, immediately before the date of the filing of the petition; or

(2) if such contract or lease has been assumed under this section or under a plan confirmed under chapter 9, 11, 12, or 13 of this title—

(A) if before such rejection the case has not been converted under section 1112, 1208, or 1307 of this title, at the time of such rejection; or

(B) if before such rejection the case has been converted under section 1112, 1208, or 1307 of this title—

(i) immediately before the date of such conversion, if such contract or lease was assumed before such conversion; or

(ii) at the time of such rejection, if such contract or lease was assumed after such conversion.

(h) (1) (A) If the trustee rejects an unexpired lease of real property under which the debtor is the lessor and—

(i) if the rejection by the trustee amounts to such a breach as would entitle the lessee to treat such lease as terminated by virtue of its terms, applicable nonbankruptcy law, or any agreement made by the lessee, then the lessee under such lease may treat such lease as terminated by the rejection; or

(ii) if the term of such lease has commenced, the lessee may retain its rights under such lease (including rights such as those relating to the amount and timing of payment of rent and other amounts payable by the lessee and any right of use, possession, quiet enjoyment, subletting, assignment, or hypothecation) that are in or appurtenant to the real property for the balance of the term of such lease and for any renewal or extension of such rights to the extent that such rights are enforceable under applicable nonbankruptcy law.

(B) If the lessee retains its rights under subparagraph (A)(ii), the lessee may offset against the rent reserved under such lease for the balance of the term after the date of the rejection of such lease and for the term of any renewal or extension of such lease, the value of any damage caused by the nonperformance after the date of such rejection, of any obligation of the debtor under such lease, but the lessee shall not have any other right against the estate or the debtor on account of any damage occurring after such date caused by such nonperformance.

(C) The rejection of a lease of real property in a shopping center with respect to which the lessee elects to retain its rights under subparagraph (A)(ii) does not affect the enforceability under applicable nonbankruptcy law of any provision in the lease pertaining to radius, location, use, exclusivity, or tenant mix or balance.

(D) In this paragraph, "lessee" includes any successor, assign, or mortgagee permitted under the terms of such lease.

(2) (A) If the trustee rejects a timeshare interest under a timeshare plan under which the debtor is the timeshare interest seller and—

(i) if the rejection amounts to such a breach as would entitle the timeshare interest purchaser to treat the timeshare plan as terminated under its terms, applicable nonbankruptcy law, or any agreement made by timeshare interest purchaser, the timeshare interest purchaser under the timeshare plan may treat the timeshare plan as terminated by such rejection; or

(ii) if the term of such timeshare interest has commenced, then the timeshare interest purchaser may retain its rights in such timeshare interest for the balance of such term and for any term of renewal or extension of such timeshare interest to the extent that such rights are enforceable under applicable nonbankruptcy law.

(B) If the timeshare interest purchaser retains its rights under subparagraph (A), such timeshare interest purchaser may offset against the moneys due for such timeshare interest for the balance of the term after the date of the rejection of such timeshare interest, and the term of any renewal or extension of such timeshare interest, the value of any damage caused by the nonperformance after the date of such rejection, of any obligation of the debtor under such timeshare plan, but the timeshare interest purchaser shall not have any right against the estate or the debtor on account of any damage occurring after such date caused by such nonperformance.

(i) (1) If the trustee rejects an executory contract of the debtor for the sale of real property or for the sale of a timeshare interest under a timeshare plan, under which the purchaser is in possession, such purchaser may treat such contract as terminated, or, in the alternative, may remain in possession of such real property or timeshare interest.

(2) If such purchaser remains in possession—

(A) such purchaser shall continue to make all payments due under such contract, but may, offset against such payments any damages occurring after the date of the rejection of such contract caused by the nonperformance of any obligation of the debtor after such date, but such purchaser does not have any rights against the estate on account of any damages arising after such date from such rejection, other than such offset; and

(B) the trustee shall deliver title to such purchaser in accordance with the provisions of such contract, but is relieved of all other obligations to perform under such contract.

(j) A purchaser that treats an executory contract as terminated under subsection (i) of this section, or a party whose executory contract to purchase real property from the debtor is rejected and under which such party is not in possession, has a lien on the interest of the debtor in such property for the recovery of any portion of the purchase price that such purchaser or party has paid.

(k) Assignment by the trustee to an entity of a contract or lease assumed under this section relieves the trustee and the estate from any liability for any breach of such contract or lease occurring after such assignment.

(l) If an unexpired lease under which the debtor is the lessee is assigned pursuant to this section, the lessor of the property may require a deposit or other security for the performance of the debtor's obligations under the lease substantially the same as would have been required by the landlord upon the initial leasing to a similar tenant.

(m) For purposes of this section 365 and sections 541(b)(2) and 362(b)(10), leases of real property shall include any rental agreement to use real property.

(n) (1) If the trustee rejects an executory contract under which the debtor is a licensor of a right to intellectual property, the licensee under such contract may elect–

(A) to treat such contract as terminated by such rejection if such rejection by the trustee amounts to such a breach as would entitle the licensee to treat such contract as terminated by virtue of its own terms, applicable nonbankruptcy law, or an agreement made by the licensee with another entity; or

(B) to retain its rights (including a right to enforce any exclusivity provision of such contract, but excluding any other right under applicable nonbankruptcy law to specific performance of such contract) under such contract and under any agreement supplementary to such contract, to such intellectual property (including any embodiment of such intellectual property to the extent protected by applicable nonbankruptcy law), as such rights existed immediately before the case commenced, for–

(i) the duration of such contract; and

(ii) any period for which such contract may be extended by the licensee as of right under applicable nonbankruptcy law.

(2) If the licensee elects to retain its rights, as described in paragraph (1)(B) of this subsection, under such contract–

(A) the trustee shall allow the licensee to exercise such rights;

(B) the licensee shall make all royalty payments due under such contract for the duration of such contract and for any period described in paragraph (1)(B) of this subsection for which the licensee extends such contract; and

(C) the licensee shall be deemed to waive–

(i) any right of setoff it may have with respect to such contract under this title or applicable nonbankruptcy law; and

(ii) any claim allowable under section 503(b) of this title arising from the performance of such contract.

(3) If the licensee elects to retain its rights, as described in paragraph (1)(B) of this subsection, then on the written request of the licensee the trustee shall–

(A) to the extent provided in such contract, or any agreement supplementary to such contract, provide to the licensee any intellectual property (including such embodiment) held by the trustee; and

(B) not interfere with the rights of the licensee as provided in such contract, or any agreement supplementary to such contract, to such intellectual property (including such embodiment) including any right to obtain such intellectual property (or such embodiment) from another entity.

(4) Unless and until the trustee rejects such contract, on the written request of the licensee the trustee shall–

(A) to the extent provided in such contract or any agreement supplementary to such contract—

(i) perform such contract; or

(ii) provide to the licensee such intellectual property (including any embodiment of such intellectual property to the extent protected by applicable nonbankruptcy law) held by the trustee; and

(B) not interfere with the rights of the licensee as provided in such contract, or any agreement supplementary to such contract, to such intellectual property (including such embodiment), including any right to obtain such intellectual property (or such embodiment) from another entity.

(o) In a case under chapter 11 of this title, the trustee shall be deemed to have assumed (consistent with the debtor's other obligations under section 507), and shall immediately cure any deficit under, any commitment by the debtor to a Federal depository institutions regulatory agency (or predecessor to such agency) to maintain the capital of an insured depository institution, and any claim for a subsequent breach of the obligations thereunder shall be entitled to priority under section 507. This subsection shall not extend any commitment that would otherwise be terminated by any act of such an agency.

(p) (1) If a lease of personal property is rejected or not timely assumed by the trustee under subsection (d), the leased property is no longer property of the estate and the stay under section 362(a) is automatically terminated.

(2) (A) If the debtor in a case under chapter 7 is an individual, the debtor may notify the creditor in writing that the debtor desires to assume the lease. Upon being so notified, the creditor may, at its option, notify the debtor that it is willing to have the lease assumed by the debtor and may condition such assumption on cure of any outstanding default on terms set by the contract.

(B) If, not later than 30 days after notice is provided under subparagraph (A), the debtor notifies the lessor in writing that the lease is assumed, the liability under the lease will be assumed by the debtor and not by the estate.

(C) The stay under section 362 and the injunction under section 524(a)(2) shall not be violated by notification of the debtor and negotiation of cure under this subsection.

(3) In a case under chapter 11 in which the debtor is an individual and in a case under chapter 13, if the debtor is the lessee with respect to personal property and the lease is not assumed in the plan confirmed by the court, the lease is deemed rejected as of the conclusion of the hearing on confirmation. If the lease is rejected, the stay under section 362 and any stay under section 1301 is automatically terminated with respect to the property subject to the lease.

BANKRUPTCY RULE REFERENCES: 1007, 6004, 6006, and 9014

## § 366 Utility service

(a) Except as provided in subsections (b) and (c) of this section, a utility may not alter, refuse, or discontinue service to, or discriminate against, the trustee or the debtor solely on the basis of the commencement of a case under this title or that a debt owed by the debtor to such utility for service rendered before the order for relief was not paid when due.

(b) Such utility may alter, refuse, or discontinue service if neither the trustee nor the debtor, within 20 days after the date of the order for relief, furnishes adequate assurance of payment, in the form of a deposit or other security, for service after such date. On request of a party in interest and after notice and a hearing, the court may order reasonable modification of the amount of the deposit or other security necessary to provide adequate assurance of payment.

(c) (1) (A) For purposes of this subsection, the term "assurance of payment" means–

(i) a cash deposit;

(ii) a letter of credit;

(iii) a certificate of deposit;

(iv) a surety bond;

(v) a prepayment of utility consumption; or

(vi) another form of security that is mutually agreed on between the utility and the debtor or the trustee.

(B) For purposes of this subsection an administrative expense priority shall not constitute an assurance of payment.

(2) Subject to paragraphs (3) and (4), with respect to a case filed under chapter 11, a utility referred to in subsection (a) may alter, refuse, or discontinue utility service, if during the 30-day period beginning on the date of the filing of the petition, the utility does not receive from the debtor or the trustee adequate assurance of payment for utility service that is satisfactory to the utility.

(3) (A) On request of a party in interest and after notice and a hearing, the court may order modification of the amount of an assurance of payment under paragraph (2).

(B) In making a determination under this paragraph whether an assurance of payment is adequate, the court may not consider–

(i) the absence of security before the date of the filing of the petition;

(ii) the payment by the debtor of charges for utility service in a timely manner before the date of the filing of the petition; or

(iii) the availability of an administrative expense priority.

(4) Notwithstanding any other provision of law, with respect to a case subject to this subsection, a utility may recover or set off against a security deposit provided to the utility by the debtor before the date of the filing of the petition

without notice or order of the court.

(d) Notwithstanding any other provision of this section, a utility may not alter, refuse, or discontinue service to a debtor who does not furnish adequate assurance of payment under this section if the debtor—

(1) is an individual;

(2) makes a payment to the utility for any debt owed to the utility for service provided during the 20-day period beginning on the date of the order for relief; and

(3) after the date on which the 20-day period beginning on the date of the order for relief ends, makes a payment to the utility for services provided during the pendency of case when such a payment becomes due.[25]

---

[25] Ed. Note: Underscored material enacted by the Consolidated Appropriations Act, 2021, Pub. L. No. 116-260, div. FF, tit. X, § 1001(h)(1). The amendment will sunset one year after the date of enactment of the Act, which was December 27, 2020. Pub. L. No. 116-260, div. FF, tit. X, § 1001(h)(2).

# CHAPTER 5
# CREDITORS, THE DEBTOR, AND THE ESTATE

## SUBCHAPTER I
## Creditors and Claims

### § 501 Filing of proofs of claims or interests

(a) A creditor or an indenture trustee may file a proof of claim. An equity security holder may file a proof of interest.

(b) If a creditor does not timely file a proof of such creditor's claim, an entity that is liable to such creditor with the debtor, or that has secured such creditor, may file a proof of such claim.

(c) If a creditor does not timely file a proof of such creditor's claim, the debtor or the trustee may file a proof of such claim.

(d) A claim of a kind specified in section 502(e)(2), 502(f), 502(g), 502(h) or 502(i) of this title may be filed under subsection (a), (b), or (c) of this section the same as if such claim were a claim against the debtor and had arisen before the date of the filing of the petition.

(e) A claim arising from the liability of a debtor for fuel use tax assessed consistent with the requirements of section 31705 of title 49 may be filed by the base jurisdiction designated pursuant to the International Fuel Tax Agreement (as defined in section 31701 of title 49) and, if so filed, shall be allowed as a single claim.

(f) (1) In this subsection—

(A) the term "CARES forbearance claim" means a supplemental claim for the amount of a Federally backed mortgage loan or a Federally backed multifamily mortgage loan that was not received by an eligible creditor during the forbearance period of a loan granted forbearance under section 4022 or 4023 of the CARES Act (15 U.S.C. 9056, 9057);

(B) the term "eligible creditor" means a servicer (as defined in section 6(i) of the Real Estate Settlement Procedures Act of 1974 (12 U.S.C. 2605(i)) with a claim for a Federally backed mortgage loan or a Federally backed multifamily mortgage loan of the debtor that is provided for by a plan under section 1322(b)(5);

(C) the term "Federally backed mortgage loan" has the meaning given the term in section 4022(a) of the CARES Act (15 U.S.C. 9056(a)); and

(D) the term "Federally backed multifamily mortgage loan" has the meaning given the term in section 4023(f) of the CARES Act (15 U.S.C. 9057(f)).

(2) (A) Only an eligible creditor may file a supplemental proof of claim for a CARES forbearance claim.

(B) If an underlying mortgage loan obligation has been modified or deferred by an agreement of the debtor and an eligible creditor of the mortgage loan in connection with a mortgage forbearance granted under section 4022 or 4023 of the CARES Act (15 U.S.C. 9056, 9057) in order to cure mortgage payments forborne under the forbearance, the proof of claim filed under subparagraph (A) shall include—

(i) the relevant terms of the modification or deferral;

(ii) for a modification or deferral that is in writing, a copy of the modification or deferral; and

(iii) a description of the payments to be deferred until the date on which the mortgage loan matures.[26]

BANKRUPTCY RULE REFERENCES: 1019, 2002, 3001, 3002, 3003, 3004, 3005, 3006 and 5005

## § 502 Allowance of claims or interests

(a) A claim or interest, proof of which is filed under section 501 of this title, is deemed allowed, unless a party in interest, including a creditor of a general partner in a partnership that is a debtor in a case under chapter 7 of this title, objects.

(b) Except as provided in subsections (e)(2), (f), (g), (h) and (i) of this section, if such objection to a claim is made, the court, after notice and a hearing, shall determine the amount of such claim in lawful currency of the United States as of the date of the filing of the petition, and shall allow such claim in such amount, except to the extent that—

(1) such claim is unenforceable against the debtor and property of the debtor, under any agreement or applicable law for a reason other than because such claim is contingent or unmatured;

(2) such claim is for unmatured interest;

(3) if such claim is for a tax assessed against property of the estate, such claim exceeds the value of the interest of the estate in such property;

(4) if such claim is for services of an insider or attorney of the debtor, such claim exceeds the reasonable value of such services;

(5) such claim is for a debt that is unmatured on the date of the filing of the petition and that is excepted from discharge under section 523(a)(5) of this title;

(6) if such claim is the claim of a lessor for damages resulting from the termination of a lease of real property, such claim exceeds—

(A) the rent reserved by such lease, without acceleration, for the greater of one year, or 15 percent, not to exceed three years, of the remaining term of such lease, following the earlier of—

---

[26] ED. NOTE: Underscored material enacted by the Consolidated Appropriations Act, 2021, Pub. L. No. 116-260, div. FF, tit. X, § 1001(d)(1). The amendment will sunset one year after the date of enactment of the Act, which was December 27, 2020. Pub. L. No. 116-260, div. FF, tit. X, § 1001(d)(3)(A).

(i) the date of the filing of the petition; and

(ii) the date on which such lessor repossessed or the lessee surrendered, the leased property; plus

(B) any unpaid rent due under such lease, without acceleration, on the earlier of such dates;

(7) if such claim is the claim of an employee for damages resulting from the termination of an employment contract, such claim exceeds—

(A) the compensation provided by such contract, without acceleration, for one year following the earlier of—

(i) the date of the filing of the petition; or

(ii) the date on which the employer directed the employee to terminate, or such employee terminated, performance under such contract; plus

(B) any unpaid compensation due under such contract, without acceleration, on the earlier of such dates;

(8) such claim results from a reduction, due to late payment, in the amount of an otherwise applicable credit available to the debtor in connection with an employment tax on wages, salaries, or commissions earned from the debtor; or

~~(9) proof of such claim is not timely filed, except to the extent tardily filed as permitted under paragraph (1), (2), or (3) of section 726(a) of this title or under the Federal Rules of Bankruptcy Procedure, except that a claim of a governmental unit shall be timely filed if it is filed before 180 days after the date of the order for relief or such later time as the Federal Rules of Bankruptcy Procedure may provide, and except that in a case under chapter 13, a claim of a governmental unit for a tax with respect to a return filed under section 1308 shall be timely if the claim is filed on or before the date that is 60 days after the date on which such return was filed as required.~~

(9) proof of such claim is not timely filed, except to the extent tardily filed as permitted under paragraph (1), (2), or (3) of section 726(a) or under the Federal Rules of Bankruptcy Procedure, except that—

(A) a claim of a governmental unit shall be timely filed if it is filed before 180 days after the date of the order for relief or such later time as the Federal Rules of Bankruptcy Procedure may provide;

(B) in a case under chapter 13, a claim of a governmental unit for a tax with respect to a return filed under section 1308 shall be timely if the claim is filed on or before the date that is 60 days after the date on which such return was filed as required; and

(C) a CARES forbearance claim (as defined in section 501(f)(1)) shall be timely filed if the claim is filed before the date that is 120 days after the expiration of the forbearance period of a loan granted forbearance under section 4022 or 4023 of the CARES Act (15 U.S.C. 9056, 9057).[27]

(c) There shall be estimated for purpose of allowance under this section—

(1) any contingent or unliquidated claim, the fixing or liquidation of which, as the case may be, would unduly delay the administration of the case; or

(2) any right to payment arising from a right to an equitable remedy for breach of performance.

(d) Notwithstanding subsections (a) and (b) of this section, the court shall disallow any claim of any entity from which property is recoverable under section 542, 543, 550, or 553 of this title or that is a transferee of a transfer avoidable under section 522(f), 522(h), 544, 545, 547, 548, 549, or 724(a) of this title, unless such entity or transferee has paid the amount, or turned over any such property, for which such entity or transferee is liable under section 522(i), 542, 543, 550, or 553 of this title.

(e) (1) Notwithstanding subsections (a), (b), and (c) of this section and paragraph (2) of this subsection, the court shall disallow any claim for reimbursement or contribution of an entity that is liable with the debtor on or has secured the claim of a creditor, to the extent that—

(A) such creditor's claim against the estate is disallowed;

(B) such claim for reimbursement or contribution is contingent as of the time of allowance or disallowance of such claim for reimbursement or contribution; or

(C) such entity asserts a right of subrogation to the rights of such creditor under section 509 of this title.

(2) A claim for reimbursement or contribution of such an entity that becomes fixed after the commencement of the case shall be determined, and shall be allowed under subsection (a), (b), or (c) of this section, or disallowed under subsection (d) of this section, the same as if such claim had become fixed before the date of the filing of the petition.

(f) In an involuntary case, a claim arising in the ordinary course of the debtor's business or financial affairs after the commencement of the case but before the earlier of the appointment of a trustee and the order for relief shall be determined as of the date such claim arises, and shall be allowed under subsection (a), (b), or (c) of this section or disallowed under subsection (d) or (e) of this section, the same as if such claim had arisen before the date of the filing of the petition.

(g) (1) A claim arising from the rejection, under section 365 of this title or under a plan under chapter 9, 11, 12, or 13 of this title, of an executory contract or unexpired lease of the debtor that has not been assumed shall be determined,

---

[27] Ed. Note: Section 502(b)(9) was amended by the Consolidated Appropriations Act, 2021, Pub. L. No. 116-260, div. FF, tit. X, § 1001(d)(2). New material is underscored; removed material is stricken out. One year after the date of enactment, which was December 27, 2020, subparagraph (C) of section 502(b)(9) shall sunset. Pub. L. No. 116-260, div. FF, tit. X, § 1001(d)(3)(B).

and shall be allowed under subsection (a), (b), or (c) of this section or disallowed under subsection (d) or (e) of this section, the same as if such claim had arisen before the date of the filing of the petition.

(2) A claim for damages calculated in accordance with section 562 shall be allowed under subsection (a), (b), or (c), or disallowed under subsection (d) or (e), as if such claim had arisen before the date of the filing of the petition.

(h) A claim arising from the recovery of property under section 522, 550, or 553 of this title shall be determined, and shall be allowed under subsection (a), (b), or (c) of this section, or disallowed under subsection (d) or (e) of this section, the same as if such claim had arisen before the date of the filing of the petition.

(i) A claim that does not arise until after the commencement of the case for a tax entitled to priority under section 507(a)(8) of this title shall be determined, and shall be allowed under subsection (a), (b), or (c) of this section, or disallowed under subsection (d) or (e) of this section, the same as if such claim had arisen before the date of the filing of the petition.

(j) A claim that has been allowed or disallowed may be reconsidered for cause. A reconsidered claim may be allowed or disallowed according to the equities of the case. Reconsideration of a claim under this subsection does not affect the validity of any payment or transfer from the estate made to a holder of an allowed claim on account of such allowed claim that is not reconsidered, but if a reconsidered claim is allowed and is of the same class as such holder's claim, such holder may not receive any additional payment or transfer from the estate on account of such holder's allowed claim until the holder of such reconsidered and allowed claim receives payment on account of such claim proportionate in value to that already received by such other holder. This subsection does not alter or modify the trustee's right to recover from a creditor any excess payment or transfer made to such creditor.

(k) (1) The court, on the motion of the debtor and after a hearing, may reduce a claim filed under this section based in whole on an unsecured consumer debt by not more than 20 percent of the claim, if—

(A) the claim was filed by a creditor who unreasonably refused to negotiate a reasonable alternative repayment schedule proposed on behalf of the debtor by an approved nonprofit budgeting and credit counseling agency described in section 111;

(B) the offer of the debtor under subparagraph (A)—

(i) was made at least 60 days before the date of the filing of the petition; and

(ii) provided for payment of at least 60 percent of the amount of the debt over a period not to exceed the repayment period of the loan, or a reasonable extension thereof; and

(C) no part of the debt under the alternative repayment schedule is nondischargeable.

(2) The debtor shall have the burden of proving, by clear and convincing evidence, that—

(A) the creditor unreasonably refused to consider the debtor's proposal; and

(B) the proposed alternative repayment schedule was made prior to expiration of the 60-day period specified in paragraph (1)(B)(i).

BANKRUPTCY RULE REFERENCES: 3001, 3002, 3007, 3008, 9014, 9023 and 9024

## § 503 Allowance of administrative expenses

(a) An entity may timely file a request for payment of an administrative expense, or may tardily file such request if permitted by the court for cause.

(b) After notice and a hearing, there shall be allowed, administrative expenses, other than claims allowed under section 502(f) of this title, including—

(1) (A) the actual, necessary costs and expenses of preserving the estate, including—

(i) wages, salaries, and commissions for services rendered after the commencement of the case; and

(ii) wages and benefits awarded pursuant to a judicial proceeding or a proceeding of the National Labor Relations Board as back pay attributable to any period of time occurring after commencement of the case under this title, as a result of a violation of Federal or State law by the debtor, without regard to the time of the occurrence of unlawful conduct on which such award is based or to whether any services were rendered, if the court determines that payment of wages and benefits by reason of the operation of this clause will not substantially increase the probability of layoff or termination of current employees, or of nonpayment of domestic support obligations, during the case under this title;

(B) any tax—

(i) incurred by the estate whether secured or unsecured, including property taxes for which liability is in rem, in personam, or both, except a tax of a kind specified in section 507(a)(8) of this title; or

(ii) attributable to an excessive allowance of a tentative carryback adjustment that the estate received, whether the taxable year to which such adjustment relates ended before or after the commencement of the case;

(C) any fine, penalty, or reduction in credit relating to a tax of a kind specified in subparagraph (B) of this paragraph; and

(D) notwithstanding the requirements of subsection (a), a governmental unit shall not be required to file a request for the payment of an expense described in subparagraph (B) or (C), as a condition of its being an allowed administrative expense;

(2) compensation and reimbursement awarded under section 330(a) of this title;

(3) the actual, necessary expenses, other than compensation and reimbursement specified in paragraph (4) of this subsection, incurred by–

(A) a creditor that files a petition under section 303 of this title;

(B) a creditor that recovers, after the court's approval, for the benefit of the estate any property transferred or concealed by the debtor;

(C) a creditor in connection with the prosecution of a criminal offense relating to the case or to the business or property of the debtor;

(D) a creditor, an indenture trustee, an equity security holder, or a committee representing creditors or equity security holders other than a committee appointed under section 1102 of this title, in making a substantial contribution in a case under chapter 9 or 11 of this title;

(E) a custodian superseded under section 543 of this title, and compensation for the services of such custodian; or

(F) a member of a committee appointed under section 1102 of this title, if such expenses are incurred in the performance of the duties of such committee;

(4) reasonable compensation for professional services rendered by an attorney or an accountant of an entity whose expense is allowable under subparagraph (A), (B), (C), (D), or (E) of paragraph (3) of this subsection, based on the time, the nature, the extent, and the value of such services, and the cost of comparable services other than in a case under this title, and reimbursement for actual, necessary expenses incurred by such attorney or accountant;

(5) reasonable compensation for services rendered by an indenture trustee in making a substantial contribution in a case under chapter 9 or 11 of this title, based on the time, the nature, the extent, and the value of such services, and the cost of comparable services other than in a case under this title;

(6) the fees and mileage payable under chapter 119 of title 28;

(7) with respect to a nonresidential real property lease previously assumed under section 365, and subsequently rejected, a sum equal to all monetary obligations due, excluding those arising from or relating to a failure to operate or a penalty provision, for the period of 2 years following the later of the rejection date or the date of actual turnover of the premises, without reduction or setoff for any reason whatsoever except for sums actually received or to be received from an entity other than the debtor, and the claim for remaining sums due for the balance of the term of the lease shall be a claim under section 502(b)(6);

(8) the actual, necessary costs and expenses of closing a health care business incurred by a trustee or by a Federal agency (as defined in section 551(1) of title 5) or a department or agency of a State or political subdivision thereof,

including any cost or expense incurred—

(A) in disposing of patient records in accordance with section 351; or

(B) in connection with transferring patients from the health care business that is in the process of being closed to another health care business; ~~and~~

(9) the value of any goods received by the debtor within 20 days before the date of commencement of a case under this title in which the goods have been sold to the debtor in the ordinary course of such debtor's business ~~.~~; and

(10) any debt incurred under section 364(g)(1) of this title.[28]

(c) Notwithstanding subsection (b), there shall neither be allowed, nor paid—

(1) a transfer made to, or an obligation incurred for the benefit of, an insider of the debtor for the purpose of inducing such person to remain with the debtor's business, absent a finding by the court based on evidence in the record that—

(A) the transfer or obligation is essential to retention of the person because the individual has a bona fide job offer from another business at the same or greater rate of compensation;

(B) the services provided by the person are essential to the survival of the business; and

(C) either—

(i) the amount of the transfer made to, or obligation incurred for the benefit of, the person is not greater than an amount equal to 10 times the amount of the mean transfer or obligation of a similar kind given to nonmanagement employees for any purpose during the calendar year in which the transfer is made or the obligation is incurred; or

(ii) if no such similar transfers were made to, or obligations were incurred for the benefit of, such nonmanagement employees during such

---

[28] Ed. Note: Section 503(b) was amended by the Consolidated Appropriations Act, 2021, Pub. L. No. 116-260, div. N, § 320(b). New material is underscored; removed material is stricken out. The amendment will:

(A) take effect on the date on which the Administrator submits to the Director of the Executive Office for United States Trustees a written determination that, subject to satisfying any other eligibility requirements, any debtor in possession or trustee that is authorized to operate the business of the debtor under section 1183, 1184, 1203, 1204, or 1304 of title 11, United States Code, would be eligible for a loan under paragraphs (36) and (37) of section 7(a) of the Small Business Act (15 U.S.C. 636(a)); and

(B) apply to any case pending on or commenced on or after the date described in subparagraph (A).

The amendment will sunset "effective on the date that is 2 years after the date of enactment" of the Act, which was December 27, 2020. Pub. L. No. 116-260, div. N, § 320(f). On April 8, 2021, the Small Business Administration issued a procedural notice stating that chapter 11, 12 and 13 debtors are eligible to receive Paycheck Protection Program loans after confirmation of a plan. *See* SBA, "Paycheck Protection Program Loans, FAQs," Q. 67 (July 29, 2021), https://www.sba.gov/sites/default/files/2021-07/FINAL%20FAQ%20Update%207.29.21-508.pdf.

calendar year, the amount of the transfer or obligation is not greater than an amount equal to 25 percent of the amount of any similar transfer or obligation made to or incurred for the benefit of such insider for any purpose during the calendar year before the year in which such transfer is made or obligation is incurred;

(2) a severance payment to an insider of the debtor, unless—

(A) the payment is part of a program that is generally applicable to all full-time employees; and

(B) the amount of the payment is not greater than 10 times the amount of the mean severance pay given to nonmanagement employees during the calendar year in which the payment is made; or

(3) other transfers or obligations that are outside the ordinary course of business and not justified by the facts and circumstances of the case, including transfers made to, or obligations incurred for the benefit of, officers, managers, or consultants hired after the date of the filing of the petition.

BANKRUPTCY RULE REFERENCES: 5004, 7052 and 9014

### § 504 Sharing of compensation

(a) Except as provided in subsection (b) of this section, a person receiving compensation or reimbursement under section 503(b)(2) or 503(b)(4) of this title may not share or agree to share—

(1) any such compensation or reimbursement with another person; or

(2) any compensation or reimbursement received by another person under such sections.

(b) (1) A member, partner, or regular associate in a professional association, corporation, or partnership may share compensation or reimbursement received under section 503(b)(2) or 503(b)(4) of this title with another member, partner, or regular associate in such association, corporation, or partnership, and may share in any compensation or reimbursement received under such sections by another member, partner, or regular associate in such association, corporation, or partnership.

(2) An attorney for a creditor that files a petition under section 303 of this title may share compensation and reimbursement received under section 503(b)(4) of this title with any other attorney contributing to the services rendered or expenses incurred by such creditor's attorney.

(c) This section shall not apply with respect to sharing, or agreeing to share, compensation with a bona fide public service attorney referral program that operates in accordance with non-Federal law regulating attorney referral services and with rules of professional responsibility applicable to attorney acceptance of referrals.

BANKRUPTCY RULE REFERENCES: 2014, 2016 and 2017

## § 505 Determination of tax liability

(a) (1) Except as provided in paragraph (2) of this subsection, the court may determine the amount or legality of any tax, any fine or penalty relating to a tax, or any addition to tax, whether or not previously assessed, whether or not paid, and whether or not contested before and adjudicated by a judicial or administrative tribunal of competent jurisdiction.

(2) The court may not so determine—

(A) the amount or legality of a tax, fine, penalty, or addition to tax if such amount or legality was contested before and adjudicated by a judicial or administrative tribunal of competent jurisdiction before the commencement of the case under this title;

(B) any right of the estate to a tax refund, before the earlier of—

(i) 120 days after the trustee properly requests such refund from the governmental unit from which such refund is claimed; or

(ii) a determination by such governmental unit of such request; or

(C) the amount or legality of any amount arising in connection with an ad valorem tax on real or personal property of the estate, if the applicable period for contesting or redetermining that amount under applicable nonbankruptcy law has expired.

(b) (1) (A) The clerk shall maintain a list under which a Federal, State, or local governmental unit responsible for the collection of taxes within the district may—

(i) designate an address for service of requests under this subsection; and

(ii) describe where further information concerning additional requirements for filing such requests may be found.

(B) If such governmental unit does not designate an address and provide such address to the clerk under subparagraph (A), any request made under this subsection may be served at the address for the filing of a tax return or protest with the appropriate taxing authority of such governmental unit.

(2) A trustee may request a determination of any unpaid liability of the estate for any tax incurred during the administration of the case by submitting a tax return for such tax and a request for such a determination to the governmental unit charged with responsibility for collection or determination of such tax at the address and in the manner designated in paragraph (1). Unless such return is fraudulent, or contains a material misrepresentation, the estate, the trustee, the debtor, and any successor to the debtor are discharged from any liability for such tax—

(A) upon payment of the tax shown on such return, if—

(i) such governmental unit does not notify the trustee, within 60 days after such request, that such return has been selected for examination; or

(ii) such governmental unit does not complete such an examination and notify the trustee of any tax due, within 180 days after such request or within such additional time as the court, for cause, permits;

(B) upon payment of the tax determined by the court, after notice and a hearing, after completion by such governmental unit of such examination; or

(C) upon payment of the tax determined by such governmental unit to be due.

(c) Notwithstanding section 362 of this title, after determination by the court of a tax under this section, the governmental unit charged with responsibility for collection of such tax may assess such tax against the estate, the debtor, or a successor to the debtor, as the case may be, subject to any otherwise applicable law.

## § 506 Determination of secured status

(a) (1) An allowed claim of a creditor secured by a lien on property in which the estate has an interest, or that is subject to setoff under section 553 of this title, is a secured claim to the extent of the value of such creditor's interest in the estate's interest in such property, or to the extent of the amount subject to setoff, as the case may be, and is an unsecured claim to the extent that the value of such creditor's interest or the amount so subject to setoff is less than the amount of such allowed claim. Such value shall be determined in light of the purpose of the valuation and of the proposed disposition or use of such property, and in conjunction with any hearing on such disposition or use or on a plan affecting such creditor's interest.

(2) If the debtor is an individual in a case under chapter 7 or 13, such value with respect to personal property securing an allowed claim shall be determined based on the replacement value of such property as of the date of the filing of the petition without deduction for costs of sale or marketing. With respect to property acquired for personal, family, or household purposes, replacement value shall mean the price a retail merchant would charge for property of that kind considering the age and condition of the property at the time value is determined.

(b) To the extent that an allowed secured claim is secured by property the value of which, after any recovery under subsection (c) of this section, is greater than the amount of such claim, there shall be allowed to the holder of such claim, interest on such claim, and any reasonable fees, costs, or charges provided for under the agreement or State statute under which such claim arose.

(c) The trustee may recover from property securing an allowed secured claim the reasonable, necessary costs and expenses of preserving, or disposing of, such property to the extent of any benefit to the holder of such claim, including the payment of all ad valorem property taxes with respect to the property.

(d) To the extent that a lien secures a claim against the debtor that is not an allowed secured claim, such lien is void, unless—

(1) such claim was disallowed only under section 502(b)(5) or 502(e) of this title; or

(2) such claim is not an allowed secured claim due only to the failure of any entity to file a proof of such claim under section 501 of this title.

BANKRUPTCY RULE REFERENCES: 3012, 7001 and 9014

## § 507 Priorities

(a) The following expenses and claims have priority in the following order:

(1) First:

(A) Allowed unsecured claims for domestic support obligations that, as of the date of the filing of the petition in a case under this title, are owed to or recoverable by a spouse, former spouse, or child of the debtor, or such child's parent, legal guardian, or responsible relative, without regard to whether the claim is filed by such person or is filed by a governmental unit on behalf of such person, on the condition that funds received under this paragraph by a governmental unit under this title after the date of the filing of the petition shall be applied and distributed in accordance with applicable nonbankruptcy law.

(B) Subject to claims under subparagraph (A), allowed unsecured claims for domestic support obligations that, as of the date of the filing of the petition, are assigned by a spouse, former spouse, child of the debtor, or such child's parent, legal guardian, or responsible relative to a governmental unit (unless such obligation is assigned voluntarily by the spouse, former spouse, child, parent, legal guardian, or responsible relative of the child for the purpose of collecting the debt) or are owed directly to or recoverable by a governmental unit under applicable nonbankruptcy law, on the condition that funds received under this paragraph by a governmental unit under this title after the date of the filing of the petition be applied and distributed in accordance with applicable nonbankruptcy law.

(C) If a trustee is appointed or elected under section 701, 702, 703, 1104, 1202, or 1302, the administrative expenses of the trustee allowed under paragraphs (1)(A), (2), and (6) of section 503(b) shall be paid before payment of claims under subparagraphs (A) and (B), to the extent that the trustee administers assets that are otherwise available for the payment of such claims.

(2) Second, administrative expenses allowed under section 503(b) of this title, unsecured claims of any Federal reserve bank related to loans made through programs or facilities authorized under section 13(3) of the Federal Reserve Act (12 U.S.C. § 343), and any fees and charges assessed against the estate under chapter 123 of title 28.

(3) Third, unsecured claims allowed under section 502(f) of this title.

(4) Fourth, allowed unsecured claims, but only to the extent of $13,650[29] for each individual or corporation, as the case may be, earned within 180 days before the date of the filing of the petition or the date of the cessation of the debtor's business, whichever occurs first, for—

(A) wages, salaries, or commissions, including vacation, severance, and sick leave pay earned by an individual; or

(B) sales commissions earned by an individual or by a corporation with only 1 employee, acting as an independent contractor in the sale of goods or services for the debtor in the ordinary course of the debtor's business if, and only if, during the 12 months preceding that date, at least 75 percent of the amount that the individual or corporation earned by acting as an independent contractor in the sale of goods or services was earned from the debtor.

(5) Fifth, allowed unsecured claims for contributions to an employee benefit plan—

(A) arising from services rendered within 180 days before the date of the filing of the petition or the date of the cessation of the debtor's business, whichever occurs first; but only

(B) for each such plan, to the extent of—

(i) the number of employees covered by each such plan multiplied by $13,650;[30] less

(ii) the aggregate amount paid to such employees under paragraph (4) of this subsection, plus the aggregate amount paid by the estate on behalf of such employees to any other employee benefit plan.

(6) Sixth, allowed unsecured claims of persons—

(A) engaged in the production or raising of grain, as defined in section 557(b) of this title, against a debtor who owns or operates a grain storage facility, as defined in section 557(b) of this title, for grain or the proceeds of grain, or

(B) engaged as a United States fisherman against a debtor who has acquired fish or fish produce from a fisherman through a sale or conversion, and who is engaged in operating a fish produce storage or processing facility—

but only to the extent of $6,725[31] for each such individual.

(7) Seventh, allowed unsecured claims of individuals, to the extent of

---

[29] Ed. Note: For cases commenced in the three-year period before April 1, 2019, the dollar amount is $12,850.

[30] Ed. Note: For cases commenced in the three-year period before April 1, 2019, the dollar amount is $12,850.

[31] Ed. Note: For cases commenced in the three-year period before April 1, 2019, the dollar amount is $6,325.

$3,025[32] for each such individual, arising from the deposit, before the commencement of the case, of money in connection with the purchase, lease, or rental of property, or the purchase of services, for the personal, family, or household use of such individuals, that were not delivered or provided

(8) Eighth, allowed unsecured claims of governmental units, only to the extent that such claims are for—

(A) a tax on or measured by income or gross receipts for a taxable year ending on or before the date of the filing of the petition—

(i) for which a return, if required, is last due, including extensions, after three years before the date of the filing of the petition;

(ii) assessed within 240 days before the date of the filing of the petition, exclusive of—

(I) any time during which an offer in compromise with respect to that tax was pending or in effect during that 240-day period, plus 30 days; and

(II) any time during which a stay of proceedings against collections was in effect in a prior case under this title during that 240-day period, plus 90 days.; or

(iii) other than a tax of a kind specified in section 523(a)(1)(B) or 523(a)(1)(C) of this title, not assessed before, but assessable, under applicable law or by agreement, after, the commencement of the case;

(B) a property tax incurred before the commencement of the case and last payable without penalty after one year before the date of the filing of the petition;

(C) a tax required to be collected or withheld and for which the debtor is liable in whatever capacity;

(D) an employment tax on a wage, salary, or commission of a kind specified in paragraph (4) of this subsection earned from the debtor before the date of the filing of the petition, whether or not actually paid before such date, for which a return is last due, under applicable law or under any extension, after three years before the date of the filing of the petition;

(E) an excise tax on—

(i) a transaction occurring before the date of the filing of the petition for which a return, if required, is last due, under applicable law or under any extension, after three years before the date of the filing of the petition; or

(ii) if a return is not required, a transaction occurring during the three years immediately preceding the date of the filing of the petition;

---

[32] Ed. Note: For cases commenced in the three-year period before April 1, 2019, the dollar amount is $2,850.

(F) a customs duty arising out of the importation of merchandise—

(i) entered for consumption within one year before the date of the filing of the petition;

(ii) covered by an entry liquidated or reliquidated within one year before the date of the filing of the petition; or

(iii) entered for consumption within four years before the date of the filing of the petition but unliquidated on such date, if the Secretary of the Treasury certifies that failure to liquidate such entry was due to an investigation pending on such date into assessment of antidumping or countervailing duties or fraud, or if information needed for the proper appraisement or classification of such merchandise was not available to the appropriate customs officer before such date; or

(G) a penalty related to a claim of a kind specified in this paragraph and in compensation for actual pecuniary loss.

An otherwise applicable time period specified in this paragraph shall be suspended for any period during which a governmental unit is prohibited under applicable nonbankruptcy law from collecting a tax as a result of a request by the debtor for a hearing and an appeal of any collection action taken or proposed against the debtor, plus 90 days; plus any time during which the stay of proceedings was in effect in a prior case under this title or during which collection was precluded by the existence of 1 or more confirmed plans under this title, plus 90 days.

(9) Ninth, allowed unsecured claims based upon any commitment by the debtor to a Federal depository institutions regulatory agency (or predecessor to such agency) to maintain the capital of an insured depository institution.

(10) Tenth, allowed claims for death or personal injuries resulting from the operation of a motor vehicle or vessel if such operation was unlawful because the debtor was intoxicated from using alcohol, a drug, or another substance.

(b) If the trustee, under section 362, 363, or 364 of this title, provides adequate protection of the interest of a holder of a claim secured by a lien on property of the debtor and if, notwithstanding such protection, such creditor has a claim allowable under subsection (a)(2) of this section arising from the stay of action against such property under section 362 of this title, from the use, sale, or lease of such property under section 363 of this title, or from the granting of a lien under section 364(d) of this title, then such creditor's claim under such subsection shall have priority over every other claim allowable under such subsection.

(c) For the purpose of subsection (a) of this section, a claim of a governmental unit arising from an erroneous refund or credit of a tax has the same priority as a claim for the tax to which such refund or credit relates.

(d) An entity that is subrogated to the rights of a holder of a claim of a kind specified in subsection (a)(1), (a)(4), (a)(5), (a)(6), (a)(7)~~, (a)(8)~~, or (a)(9) or subparagraphs (A) through (E) and (G) of subsection (a)(8) of this section is not subrogated to the right of the holder of such claim to priority under such subsection or subparagraph.[33]

## § 508 Effect of distribution other than under this title

If a creditor of a partnership debtor receives, from a general partner that is not a debtor in a case under chapter 7 of this title, payment of, or a transfer of property on account of, a claim that is allowed under this title and that is not secured by a lien on property of such partner, such creditor may not receive any payment under this title on account of such claim until each of the other holders of claims on account of which such holders are entitled to share equally with such creditor under this title has received payment under this title equal in value to the consideration received by such creditor from such general partner.

## § 509 Claims of codebtors

(a) Except as provided in subsection (b) or (c) of this section, an entity that is liable with the debtor on, or that has secured, a claim of a creditor against the debtor, and that pays such claim, is subrogated to the rights of such creditor to the extent of such payment.

(b) Such entity is not subrogated to the rights of such creditor to the extent that—

(1) a claim of such entity for reimbursement or contribution on account of such payment of such creditor's claim is—

(A) allowed under section 502 of this title;

(B) disallowed other than under section 502(e) of this title; or

(C) subordinated under section 510 of this title; or

(2) as between the debtor and such entity, such entity received the consideration for the claim held by such creditor.

(c) The court shall subordinate to the claim of a creditor and for the benefit of such creditor an allowed claim, by way of subrogation under this section, or for reimbursement or contribution, of an entity that is liable with the debtor on, or that has secured, such creditor's claim, until such creditor's claim is paid in full, either through payments under this title or otherwise.

BANKRUPTCY RULE REFERENCES: 3002, 3003, 3004 and 3005

## § 510 Subordination

(a) A subordination agreement is enforceable in a case under this title to the same extent that such agreement is enforceable under applicable nonbankruptcy law.

(b) For the purpose of distribution under this title, a claim arising from

---

[33] ED. NOTE: Section 507(d) was amended by the Consolidated Appropriations Act, 2021, Pub. L. No. 116-260, div. FF, tit. X, § 1001(i)(1). New material is underscored; removed material is stricken out. The amendment will sunset one year after the date of enactment of the Act, which was December 27, 2020. Pub. L. No. 116-260, div. FF, tit. X, § 1001(i)(2).

rescission of a purchase or sale of a security of the debtor or of an affiliate of the debtor, for damages arising from the purchase or sale of such a security, or for reimbursement or contribution allowed under section 502 on account of such a claim, shall be subordinated to all claims or interests that are senior to or equal the claim or interest represented by such security, except that if such security is common stock, such claim has the same priority as common stock.

(c) Notwithstanding subsections (a) and (b) of this section, after notice and a hearing, the court may—

(1) under principles of equitable subordination, subordinate for purposes of distribution all or part of an allowed claim to all or part of another allowed claim or all or part of an allowed interest to all or part of another allowed interest; or

(2) order that any lien securing such a subordinated claim be transferred to the estate.

BANKRUPTCY RULE REFERENCE: 7001

## § 511 Rate of interest on tax claims

(a) If any provision of this title requires the payment of interest on a tax claim or on an administrative expense tax, or the payment of interest to enable a creditor to receive the present value of the allowed amount of a tax claim, the rate of interest shall be the rate determined under applicable nonbankruptcy law.

(b) In the case of taxes paid under a confirmed plan under this title, the rate of interest shall be determined as of the calendar month in which the plan is confirmed.

## SUBCHAPTER II
## Debtor's Duties and Benefits

### § 521 Debtor's duties

(a) The debtor shall

(1) file—

(A) a list of creditors; and

(B) unless the court orders otherwise—

(i) a schedule of assets and liabilities;

(ii) a schedule of current income and current expenditures;

(iii) a statement of the debtor's financial affairs and, if section 342(b) applies, a certificate—

(I) of an attorney whose name is indicated on the petition as the attorney for the debtor, or a bankruptcy petition preparer signing the petition under section 110(b)(1), indicating that such attorney or the bankruptcy petition preparer delivered to the debtor the notice required by section 342 (b); or

(II) if no attorney is so indicated, and no bankruptcy petition preparer signed the petition, of the debtor that such notice was received and read by the debtor;

(iv) copies of all payment advice or other evidence of payment received within 60 days before the date of the filing of the petition, by the debtor from any employer of the debtor;

(v) a statement of the amount of monthly net income, itemized to show how the amount is calculated; and

(vi) a statement disclosing any reasonably anticipated increase in income or expenditures over the 12-month period following the date of the filing of the petition;

(2) if an individual debtor's schedule of assets and liabilities includes debts which are secured by property of the estate—

(A) within thirty days after the date of the filing of a petition under chapter 7 of this title or on or before the date of the meeting of creditors, whichever is earlier, or within such additional time as the court, for cause, within such period fixes, file with the clerk a statement of his intention with respect to the retention or surrender of such property and, if applicable, specifying that such property is claimed as exempt, that the debtor intends to redeem such property, or that the debtor intends to reaffirm debts secured by such property; and

(B) within 30 days after the first date set for the meeting of creditors under section 341(a) or within such additional time as the court, for cause, within such 30-day period fixes, perform his intention with respect to such property, as specified by subparagraph (A) of this paragraph;

except that nothing in subparagraphs (A) and (B) of this paragraph shall alter the debtor's or the trustee's rights with regard to such property under this title, except as provided in section 362(h);

(3) if a trustee is serving in the case or an auditor is serving under section 586(f) of title 28, cooperate with the trustee as necessary to enable the trustee to perform the trustee's duties under this title;

(4) if a trustee is serving in the case or an auditor is serving under section 586(f) of title 28, surrender to the trustee all property of the estate and any recorded information, including books, documents, records, and papers, relating to property of the estate, whether or not immunity is granted under section 344 of this title;

(5) appear at the hearing required under section 524(d) of this title;

(6) in a case under chapter 7 of this title in which the debtor is an individual, not retain possession of personal property as to which a creditor has an allowed claim for the purchase price secured in whole or in part by an interest in such personal property unless the debtor, not later than 45 days after the first meeting of creditors under section 341(a), either—

(A) enters into an agreement with the creditor pursuant to section 524(c) with respect to the claim secured by such property; or

(B) redeems such property from the security interest pursuant to section 722; and

(7) unless a trustee is serving in the case, continue to perform the obligations required of the administrator (as defined in section 3 of the Employee Retirement Income Security Act of 1974) of an employee benefit plan if at the time of the commencement of the case the debtor (or any entity designated by the debtor) served as such administrator.

If the debtor fails to so act within the 45-day period referred to in paragraph (6), the stay under section 362(a) is terminated with respect to the personal property of the estate or of the debtor which is affected, such property shall no longer be property of the estate, and the creditor may take whatever action as to such property as is permitted by applicable nonbankruptcy law, unless the court determines on the motion of the trustee filed before the expiration of such 45-day period, and after notice and a hearing, that such property is of consequential value or benefit to the estate, orders appropriate adequate protection of the creditor's interest, and orders the debtor to deliver any collateral in the debtor's possession to the trustee.

(b) In addition to the requirements under subsection (a), a debtor who is an individual shall file with the court—

(1) a certificate from the approved nonprofit budget and credit counseling agency that provided the debtor services under section 109(h) describing the services provided to the debtor; and

(2) a copy of the debt repayment plan, if any, developed under section 109(h) through the approved nonprofit budget and credit counseling agency referred to in paragraph (1).

(c) In addition to meeting the requirements under subsection (a), a debtor shall file with the court a record of any interest that a debtor has in an education individual retirement account (as defined in section 530(b)(1) of the Internal Revenue Code of 1986), an interest in an account in a qualified ABLE program (as defined in section 529A(b) of such Code), or under a qualified State tuition program (as defined in section 529(b)(1) of such Code).

(d) If the debtor fails timely to take the action specified in subsection (a)(6) of this section, or in paragraphs (1) and (2) of section 362(h), with respect to property which a lessor or bailor owns and has leased, rented, or bailed to the debtor or as to which a creditor holds a security interest not otherwise voidable under section 522(f), 544, 545, 547, 548, or 549, nothing in this title shall prevent or limit the operation of a provision in the underlying lease or agreement that has the effect of placing the debtor in default under such lease or agreement by reason of the occurrence, pendency, or existence of a proceeding under this title or the insolvency of the debtor. Nothing in this subsection shall be deemed to justify limiting such a provision in any other circumstance.

(e) (1) If the debtor in a case under chapter 7 or 13 is an individual and if a creditor files with the court at any time a request to receive a copy of the petition, schedules, and statement of financial affairs filed by the debtor, then the court shall make such petition, such schedules, and such statement available to such creditor.

(2) (A) The debtor shall provide—

(i) not later than 7 days before the date first set for the first meeting of creditors, to the trustee a copy of the Federal income tax return required under applicable law (or at the election of the debtor, a transcript of such return) for the most recent tax year ending immediately before the commencement of the case and for which a Federal income tax return was filed; and

(ii) at the same time the debtor complies with clause (i), a copy of such return (or if elected under clause (i), such transcript) to any creditor that timely requests such copy.

(B) If the debtor fails to comply with clause (i) or (ii) of subparagraph (A), the court shall dismiss the case unless the debtor demonstrates that the failure to so comply is due to circumstances beyond the control of the debtor.

(C) If a creditor requests a copy of such tax return or such transcript and if the debtor fails to provide a copy of such tax return or such transcript to such creditor at the time the debtor provides such tax return or such transcript to the trustee, then the court shall dismiss the case unless the debtor demonstrates that the failure to provide a copy of such tax return or such transcript is due to circumstances beyond the control of the debtor.

(3) If a creditor in a case under chapter 13 files with the court at any time a request to receive a copy of the plan filed by the debtor, then the court shall make available to such creditor a copy of the plan—

(A) at a reasonable cost; and

(B) not later than 7 days after such request is filed.

(f) At the request of the court, the United States trustee, or any party in interest in a case under chapter 7, 11, or 13, a debtor who is an individual shall file with the court—

(1) at the same time filed with the taxing authority, a copy of each Federal income tax return required under applicable law (or at the election of the debtor, a transcript of such tax return) with respect to each tax year of the debtor ending while the case is pending under such chapter;

(2) at the same time filed with the taxing authority, each Federal income tax return required under applicable law (or at the election of the debtor, a transcript of such tax return) that had not been filed with such authority as of the date of the commencement of the case and that was subsequently filed for any tax year of the debtor ending in the 3-year period ending on the date of the commencement of the case;

(3) a copy of each amendment to any Federal income tax return or transcript filed with the court under paragraph (1) or (2); and

(4) in a case under chapter 13—

(A) on the date that is either 90 days after the end of such tax year or 1 year after the date of the commencement of the case, whichever is later, if a plan is not confirmed before such later date; and

(B) annually after the plan is confirmed and until the case is closed, not later than the date that is 45 days before the anniversary of the confirmation of the plan;

a statement, under penalty of perjury, of the income and expenditures of the debtor during the tax year of the debtor most recently concluded before such statement is filed under this paragraph, and of the monthly income of the debtor, that shows how income, expenditures, and monthly income are calculated.

(g) (1) A statement referred to in subsection (f)(4) shall disclose—

(A) the amount and sources of the income of the debtor;

(B) the identity of any person responsible with the debtor for the support of any dependent of the debtor; and

(C) the identity of any person who contributed, and the amount contributed, to the household in which the debtor resides.

(2) The tax returns, amendments, and statement of income and expenditures described in subsections (e)(2)(A) and (f) shall be available to the United States

trustee (or the bankruptcy administrator, if any), the trustee, and any party in interest for inspection and copying, subject to the requirements of section 315(c) of the Bankruptcy Abuse Prevention and Consumer Protection Act of 2005.

(h) If requested by the United States trustee or by the trustee, the debtor shall provide—

(1) a document that establishes the identity of the debtor, including a driver's license, passport, or other document that contains a photograph of the debtor; or

(2) such other personal identifying information relating to the debtor that establishes the identity of the debtor.

(i) (1) Subject to paragraphs (2) and (4) and notwithstanding section 707(a), if an individual debtor in a voluntary case under chapter 7 or 13 fails to file all of the information required under subsection (a)(1) within 45 days after the date of the filing of the petition, the case shall be automatically dismissed effective on the 46th day after the date of the filing of the petition.

(2) Subject to paragraph (4) and with respect to a case described in paragraph (1), any party in interest may request the court to enter an order dismissing the case. If requested, the court shall enter an order of dismissal not later than 7 days after such request.

(3) Subject to paragraph (4) and upon request of the debtor made within 45 days after the date of the filing of the petition described in paragraph (1), the court may allow the debtor an additional period of not to exceed 45 days to file the information required under subsection (a)(1) if the court finds justification for extending the period for the filing.

(4) Notwithstanding any other provision of this subsection, on the motion of the trustee filed before the expiration of the applicable period of time specified in paragraph (1), (2), or (3), and after notice and a hearing, the court may decline to dismiss the case if the court finds that the debtor attempted in good faith to file all the information required by subsection (a)(1)(B)(iv) and that the best interests of creditors would be served by administration of the case.

(j) (1) Notwithstanding any other provision of this title, if the debtor fails to file a tax return that becomes due after the commencement of the case or to properly obtain an extension of the due date for filing such return, the taxing authority may request that the court enter an order converting or dismissing the case.

(2) If the debtor does not file the required return or obtain the extension referred to in paragraph (1) within 90 days after a request is filed by the taxing authority under that paragraph, the court shall convert or dismiss the case, whichever is in the best interests of creditors and the estate.

Bankruptcy Rule References: 1007, 1008, 1009, 2005, 4002 and 9004

## § 522 Exemptions

(a) In this section–

(1) "dependent" includes spouse, whether or not actually dependent; and

(2) "value" means fair market value as of the date of the filing of the petition or, with respect to property that becomes property of the estate after such date, as of the date such property becomes property of the estate.

(b) (1) Notwithstanding section 541 of this title, an individual debtor may exempt from property of the estate the property listed in either paragraph (2) or, in the alternative, paragraph (3) of this subsection. In joint cases filed under section 302 of this title and individual cases filed under section 301 or 303 of this title by or against debtors who are husband and wife, and whose estates are ordered to be jointly administered under Rule 1015(b) of the Federal Rules of Bankruptcy Procedure, one debtor may not elect to exempt property listed in paragraph (2) and the other debtor elect to exempt property listed in paragraph (3) of this subsection. If the parties cannot agree on the alternative to be elected, they shall be deemed to elect paragraph (2), where such election is permitted under the law of the jurisdiction where the case is filed.

(2) Property listed in this paragraph is property that is specified under subsection (d), unless the State law that is applicable to the debtor under paragraph (3)(A) specifically does not so authorize.

(3) Property listed in this paragraph is–

(A) subject to subsections (o) and (p) any property that is exempt under Federal law, other than subsection (d) of this section, or State or local law that is applicable on the date of the filing of the petition to the place in which the debtor's domicile has been located for the 730 days immediately preceding the date of the filing of the petition or if the debtor's domicile has not been located in a single State for such 730-day period, the place in which the debtor's domicile was located for 180 days immediately preceding the 730-day period or for a longer portion of such 180-day period than in any other place;

(B) any interest in property in which the debtor had, immediately before the commencement of the case, an interest as a tenant by the entirety or joint tenant to the extent that such interest as a tenant by the entirety or joint tenant is exempt from process under applicable nonbankruptcy law; and

(C) retirement funds to the extent that those funds are in a fund or account that is exempt from taxation under section 401, 403, 408, 408A, 414, 457, or 501(a) of the Internal Revenue Code of 1986.

If the effect of the domiciliary requirement under subparagraph (A) is to render the debtor ineligible for any exemption, the debtor may elect to exempt property that is specified under subsection (d).

(4) For purposes of paragraph (3)(C) and subsection (d)(12), the following

shall apply:

(A) If the retirement funds are in a retirement fund that has received a favorable determination under section 7805 of the Internal Revenue Code of 1986, and that determination is in effect as of the date of the filing of the petition in a case under this title, those funds shall be presumed to be exempt from the estate.

(B) If the retirement funds are in a retirement fund that has not received a favorable determination under such section 7805, those funds are exempt from the estate if the debtor demonstrates that—

(i) no prior determination to the contrary has been made by a court or the Internal Revenue Service; and

(ii) (I) the retirement fund is in substantial compliance with the applicable requirements of the Internal Revenue Code of 1986; or

(II) the retirement fund fails to be in substantial compliance with the applicable requirements of the Internal Revenue Code of 1986 and the debtor is not materially responsible for that failure.

(C) A direct transfer of retirement funds from 1 fund or account that is exempt from taxation under section 401, 403, 408, 408A, 414, 457, or 501(a) of the Internal Revenue Code of 1986, under section 401(a)(31) of the Internal Revenue Code of 1986, or otherwise, shall not cease to qualify for exemption under paragraph (3)(C) or subsection (d)(12) by reason of such direct transfer.

(D) (i) Any distribution that qualifies as an eligible rollover distribution within the meaning of section 402(c) of the Internal Revenue Code of 1986 or that is described in clause (ii) shall not cease to qualify for exemption under paragraph (3)(C) or subsection (d)(12) by reason of such distribution.

(ii) A distribution described in this clause is an amount that—

(I) has been distributed from a fund or account that is exempt from taxation under section 401, 403, 408, 408A, 414, 457, or 501(a) of the Internal Revenue Code of 1986; and

(II) to the extent allowed by law, is deposited in such a fund or account not later than 60 days after the distribution of such amount.

(c) Unless the case is dismissed, property exempted under this section is not liable during or after the case for any debt of the debtor that arose, or that is determined under section 502 of this title as if such debt had arisen, before the commencement of the case, except—

(1) a debt of a kind specified in paragraph (1) or (5) of section 523(a) (in which case, notwithstanding any provision of applicable nonbankruptcy law to the contrary, such property shall be liable for a debt of a kind specified in such paragraph);

(2) a debt secured by a lien that is—

(A) (i) not avoided under subsection (f) or (g) of this section or under section 544, 545, 547, 548, 549, or 724(a) of this title; and

(ii) not void under section 506(d) of this title; or

(B) a tax lien, notice of which is properly filed;

(3) a debt of a kind specified in section 523(a)(4) or 523(a)(6) of this title owed by an institution-affiliated party of an insured depository institution to a Federal depository institutions regulatory agency acting in its capacity as conservator, receiver, or liquidating agent for such institution; or

(4) a debt in connection with fraud in the obtaining or providing of any scholarship, grant, loan, tuition, discount, award, or other financial assistance for purposes of financing an education at an institution of higher education (as that term is defined in section 101 of the Higher Education Act of 1965 (20 U.S.C. 1001)).

(d) The following property may be exempted under subsection (b)(2) of this section:

(1) The debtor's aggregate interest, not to exceed $25,150[34] in value, in real property or personal property that the debtor or a dependent of the debtor uses as a residence, in a cooperative that owns property that the debtor or a dependent of the debtor uses as a residence, or in a burial plot for the debtor or a dependent of the debtor.

(2) The debtor's interest, not to exceed $4,000[35] in value, in one motor vehicle.

(3) The debtor's interest, not to exceed $625[36] in value in any particular item or $13,400[37] in aggregate value, in household furnishings, household goods, wearing apparel, appliances, books, animals, crops, or musical instruments, that are held primarily for the personal, family, or household use of the debtor or a dependent of the debtor.

(4) The debtor's aggregate interest, not to exceed $1,700[38] in value, in jewelry held primarily for the personal, family, or household use of the debtor or a dependent of the debtor.

---

[34] Ed. Note: For cases commenced in the three-year period before April 1, 2019, the dollar amount is $23,675.

[35] Ed. Note: For cases commenced in the three-year period before April 1, 2019, the dollar amount is $3,775.

[36] Ed. Note: For cases commenced in the three-year period before April 1, 2019, the dollar amount is $600.

[37] Ed. Note: For cases commenced in the three-year period before April 1, 2019, the dollar amount is $12,625.

[38] Ed. Note: For cases commenced in the three-year period before April 1, 2019, the dollar amount is $1,600.

(5) The debtor's aggregate interest in any property, not to exceed in value $1,325[39] plus up to $12,575[40] of any unused amount of the exemption provided under paragraph (1) of this subsection.

(6) The debtor's aggregate interest, not to exceed $2,525[41] in value, in any implements, professional books, or tools, of the trade of the debtor or the trade of a dependent of the debtor.

(7) Any unmatured life insurance contract owned by the debtor, other than a credit life insurance contract.

(8) The debtor's aggregate interest, not to exceed in value $13,400[42] less any amount of property of the estate transferred in the manner specified in section 542(d) of this title, in any accrued dividend or interest under, or loan value of, any unmatured life insurance contract owned by the debtor under which the insured is the debtor or an individual of whom the debtor is a dependent.

(9) Professionally prescribed health aids for the debtor or a dependent of the debtor.

(10) The debtor's right to receive—

(A) a social security benefit, unemployment compensation, or a local public assistance benefit;

(B) a veterans' benefit;

(C) a disability, illness, or unemployment benefit;

(D) alimony, support, or separate maintenance, to the extent reasonably necessary for the support of the debtor and any dependent of the debtor;

(E) a payment under a stock bonus, pension, profitsharing, annuity, or similar plan or contract on account of illness, disability, death, age, or length of service, to the extent reasonably necessary for the support of the debtor and any dependent of the debtor, unless—

(i) such plan or contract was established by or under the auspices of an insider that employed the debtor at the time the debtor's rights under such plan or contract arose;

(ii) such payment is on account of age or length of service; and

(iii) such plan or contract does not qualify under section 401(a), 403(a), 403(b), or 408 of the Internal Revenue Code of 1986.

---

[39] Ed. Note: For cases commenced in the three-year period before April 1, 2019, the dollar amount is $1,250.

[40] Ed. Note: For cases commenced in the three-year period before April 1, 2019, the dollar amount is $11,850.

[41] Ed. Note: For cases commenced in the three-year period before April 1, 2019, the dollar amount is $2,375.

[42] Ed. Note: For cases commenced in the three-year period before April 1, 2019 the dollar amount is $12,625.

(11) The debtor's right to receive, or property that is traceable to—

(A) an award under a crime victim's reparation law;

(B) a payment on account of the wrongful death of an individual of whom the debtor was a dependent, to the extent reasonably necessary for the support of the debtor and any dependent of the debtor;

(C) a payment under a life insurance contract that insured the life of an individual of whom the debtor was a dependent on the date of such individual's death, to the extent reasonably necessary for the support of the debtor and any dependent of the debtor;

(D) a payment, not to exceed $25,150,[43] on account of personal bodily injury, not including pain and suffering or compensation for actual pecuniary loss, of the debtor or an individual of whom the debtor is a dependent; or

(E) a payment in compensation of loss of future earnings of the debtor or an individual of whom the debtor is or was a dependent, to the extent reasonably necessary for the support of the debtor and any dependent of the debtor.

(12) Retirement funds to the extent that those funds are in a fund or account that is exempt from taxation under section 401, 403, 408, 408A, 414, 457, or 501(a) of the Internal Revenue Code of 1986.

(e) A waiver of an exemption executed in favor of a creditor that holds an unsecured claim against the debtor is unenforceable in a case under this title with respect to such claim against property that the debtor may exempt under subsection (b) of this section. A waiver by the debtor of a power under subsection (f) or (h) of this section to avoid a transfer, under subsection (g) or (i) of this section to exempt property, or under subsection (i) of this section to recover property or to preserve a transfer, is unenforceable in a case under this title.

(f) (1) Notwithstanding any waiver of exemptions but subject to paragraph (3), the debtor may avoid the fixing of a lien on an interest of the debtor in property to the extent that such lien impairs an exemption to which the debtor would have been entitled under subsection (b) of this section, if such lien is—

(A) a judicial lien, other than a judicial lien that secures a debt of a kind that is specified in section 523(a)(5); or

(B) a nonpossessory, nonpurchase-money security interest in any—

(i) household furnishings, household goods, wearing apparel, appliances, books, animals, crops, musical instruments, or jewelry that are held primarily for the personal, family, or household use of the debtor or a dependent of the debtor;

---

[43] Ed. Note: For cases commenced in the three-year period before April 1, 2019, the dollar amount is $23,675.

(ii) implements, professional books, or tools, of the trade of the debtor or the trade of a dependent of the debtor; or

(iii) professionally prescribed health aids for the debtor or a dependent of the debtor.

(2) (A) For the purposes of this subsection, a lien shall be considered to impair an exemption to the extent that the sum of—

(i) the lien;

(ii) all other liens on the property; and

(iii) the amount of the exemption that the debtor could claim if there were no liens on the property;

exceeds the value that the debtor's interest in the property would have in the absence of any liens.

(B) In the case of a property subject to more than 1 lien, a lien that has been avoided shall not be considered in making the calculation under subparagraph (A) with respect to other liens.

(C) This paragraph shall not apply with respect to a judgment arising out of a mortgage foreclosure.

(3) In a case in which State law that is applicable to the debtor—

(A) permits a person to voluntarily waive a right to claim exemptions under subsection (d) or prohibits a debtor from claiming exemptions under subsection (d); and

(B) either permits the debtor to claim exemptions under State law without limitation in amount, except to the extent that the debtor has permitted the fixing of a consensual lien on any property or prohibits avoidance of a consensual lien on property otherwise eligible to be claimed as exempt property;

the debtor may not avoid the fixing of a lien on an interest of the debtor or a dependent of the debtor in property if the lien is a nonpossessory, nonpurchase-money security interest in implements, professional books, or tools of the trade of the debtor or a dependent of the debtor or farm animals or crops of the debtor or a dependent of the debtor to the extent the value of such implements, professional books, tools of the trade, animals, and crops exceeds $6,825.[44]

(4) (A) Subject to subparagraph (B), for purposes of paragraph (1)(B), the term "household goods" means—

(i) clothing;

(ii) furniture;

(iii) appliances;

---

[44] Ed. Note: For cases commenced in the three-year period before April 1, 2019, the dollar amount is $6,425.

(iv) 1 radio;

(v) 1 television;

(vi) 1 VCR;

(vii) linens;

(viii) china;

(ix) crockery;

(x) kitchenware;

(xi) educational materials and educational equipment primarily for the use of minor dependent children of the debtor;

(xii) medical equipment and supplies;

(xiii) furniture exclusively for the use of minor children, or elderly or disabled dependents of the debtor;

(xiv) personal effects (including the toys and hobby equipment of minor dependent children and wedding rings) of the debtor and the dependents of the debtor; and

(xv) 1 personal computer and related equipment.

(B) The term "household goods" does not include—

(i) works of art (unless by or of the debtor, or any relative of the debtor);

(ii) electronic entertainment equipment with a fair market value of more than $725[45] in the aggregate (except 1 television, 1 radio, and 1 VCR);

(iii) items acquired as antiques with a fair market value of more than $725[46] in the aggregate;

(iv) jewelry with a fair market value of more than $725[47] in the aggregate (except wedding rings); and

(v) a computer (except as otherwise provided for in this section), motor vehicle (including a tractor or lawn tractor), boat, or a motorized recreational device, conveyance, vehicle, watercraft, or aircraft.

(g) Notwithstanding sections 550 and 551 of this title, the debtor may exempt under subsection (b) of this section property that the trustee recovers under section 510(c)(2), 542, 543, 550, 551, or 553 of this title, to the extent that the

---

[45] Ed. Note: For cases commenced in the three-year period before April 1, 2019, the dollar amount is $675.

[46] Ed. Note: For cases commenced in the three-year period before April 1, 2019, the dollar amount is $675.

[47] Ed. Note: For cases commenced in the three-year period before April 1, 2019, the dollar amount is $675.

debtor could have exempted such property under subsection (b) of this section if such property had not been transferred, if—

(1) (A) such transfer was not a voluntary transfer of such property by the debtor; and

(B) the debtor did not conceal such property; or

(2) the debtor could have avoided such transfer under subsection (f)(1)(B) of this section.

(h) The debtor may avoid a transfer of property of the debtor or recover a setoff to the extent that the debtor could have exempted such property under subsection (g)(1) of this section if the trustee had avoided such transfer, if—

(1) such transfer is avoidable by the trustee under section 544, 545, 547, 548, 549, or 724(a) of this title or recoverable by the trustee under section 553 of this title; and

(2) the trustee does not attempt to avoid such transfer.

(i) (1) If the debtor avoids a transfer or recovers a setoff under subsection (f) or (h) of this section, the debtor may recover in the manner prescribed by, and subject to the limitations of, section 550 of this title, the same as if the trustee had avoided such transfer, and may exempt any property so recovered under subsection (b) of this section.

(2) Notwithstanding section 551 of this title, a transfer avoided under section 544, 545, 547, 548, 549, or 724(a) of this title, under subsection (f) or (h) of this section, or property recovered under section 553 of this title, may be preserved for the benefit of the debtor to the extent that the debtor may exempt such property under subsection (g) of this section or paragraph (1) of this subsection.

(j) Notwithstanding subsections (g) and (i) of this section, the debtor may exempt a particular kind of property under subsections (g) and (i) of this section only to the extent that the debtor has exempted less property in value of such kind than that to which the debtor is entitled under subsection (b) of this section.

(k) Property that the debtor exempts under this section is not liable for payment of any administrative expense except—

(1) the aliquot share of the costs and expenses of avoiding a transfer of property that the debtor exempts under subsection (g) of this section, or of recovery of such property, that is attributable to the value of the portion of such property exempted in relation to the value of the property recovered; and

(2) any costs and expenses of avoiding a transfer under subsection (f) or (h) of this section, or of recovery of property under subsection (i)(1) of this section, that the debtor has not paid.

(l) The debtor shall file a list of property that the debtor claims as exempt under subsection (b) of this section. If the debtor does not file such a list, a dependent of the debtor may file such a list, or may claim property as exempt from property of the estate on behalf of the debtor. Unless a party in interest objects, the property claimed as exempt on such list is exempt.

(m) Subject to the limitation in subsection (b), this section shall apply separately with respect to each debtor in a joint case.

(n) For assets in individual retirement accounts described in section 408 or 408A of the Internal Revenue Code of 1986, other than a simplified employee pension under section 408(k) of such Code or a simple retirement account under section 408(p) of such Code, the aggregate value of such assets exempted under this section, without regard to amounts attributable to rollover contributions under sections 402(c), 402(e)(6), 403(a)(4), 403(a)(5), and 403(b)(8) of the Internal Revenue Code of 1986, and earnings thereon, shall not exceed $1,362,800[48] in a case filed by a debtor who is an individual, except that such amount may be increased if the interests of justice so require.

(o) For purposes of subsection (b)(3)(A), and notwithstanding subsection (a), the value of an interest in—

(1) real or personal property that the debtor or a dependent of the debtor uses as a residence;

(2) a cooperative that owns property that the debtor or a dependent of the debtor uses as a residence;

(3) a burial plot for the debtor or a dependent of the debtor; or

(4) real or personal property that the debtor or a dependent of the debtor claims as a homestead,

shall be reduced to the extent that such value is attributable to any portion of any property that the debtor disposed of in the 10-year period ending on the date of the filing of the petition with the intent to hinder, delay, or defraud a creditor and that the debtor could not exempt, or that portion that the debtor could not exempt, under subsection (b), if on such date the debtor had held the property so disposed of.

(p) (1) Except as provided in paragraph (2) of this subsection and sections 544 and 548, as a result of electing under subsection (b)(3)(A) to exempt property under State or local law, a debtor may not exempt any amount of interest that was acquired by the debtor during the 1215-day period preceding the date of the filing of the petition that exceeds in the aggregate $170,350[49] in value in—

(A) real or personal property that the debtor or a dependent of the debtor uses as a residence;

(B) a cooperative that owns property that the debtor or a dependent of the debtor uses as a residence;

(C) a burial plot for the debtor or a dependent of the debtor; or

---

[48] Ed. Note: For cases commenced in the three-year period before April 1, 2019, the dollar amount is $1,283,025.

[49] Ed. Note: For cases commenced in the three-year period before April 1, 2019, the dollar amount is $160,375.

(D) real or personal property that the debtor or dependent of the debtor claims as a homestead.

(2) (A) The limitation under paragraph (1) shall not apply to an exemption claimed under subsection (b)(3)(A) by a family farmer for the principal residence of such farmer.

(B) For purposes of paragraph (1), any amount of such interest does not include any interest transferred from a debtor's previous principal residence (which was acquired prior to the beginning of such 1215-day period) into the debtor's current principal residence, if the debtor's previous and current residences are located in the same State.

(q) (1) As a result of electing under subsection (b)(3)(A) to exempt property under State or local law, a debtor may not exempt any amount of an interest in property described in subparagraphs (A), (B), (C), and (D) of subsection (p)(1) which exceeds in the aggregate $170,350[50] if—

(A) the court determines, after notice and a hearing, that the debtor has been convicted of a felony (as defined in section 3156 of title 18), which under the circumstances, demonstrates that the filing of the case was an abuse of the provisions of this title; or

(B) the debtor owes a debt arising from—

(i) any violation of the Federal securities laws (as defined in section 3(a)(47) of the Securities Exchange Act of 1934), any State securities laws, or any regulation or order issued under Federal securities laws or State securities laws;

(ii) fraud, deceit, or manipulation in a fiduciary capacity or in connection with the purchase or sale of any security registered under section 12 or 15(d) of the Securities Exchange Act of 1934 or under section 6 of the Securities Act of 1933;

(iii) any civil remedy under section 1964 of title 18; or

(iv) any criminal act, intentional tort, or willful or reckless misconduct that caused serious physical injury or death to another individual in the preceding 5 years.

(2) Paragraph (1) shall not apply to the extent the amount of an interest in property described in subparagraphs (A), (B), (C), and (D) of subsection (p)(1) is reasonably necessary for the support of the debtor and any dependent of the debtor.

BANKRUPTCY RULE REFERENCES: 1007, 4003 and 4004

---

[50] ED. NOTE: For cases commenced in the three-year period before April 1, 2019, the dollar amount is $160,375.

## § 523 Exceptions to discharge.[51]

(a) A discharge under section 727, 1141, 1192, 1228(a), 1228(b), or 1328(b) of this title does not discharge an individual debtor from any debt—

(1) for a tax or a customs duty—

(A) of the kind and for the periods specified in section 507(a)(3) or 507(a)(8) of this title, whether or not a claim for such tax was filed or allowed;

(B) with respect to which a return, or equivalent report or notice, if required—

(i) was not filed or given; or

(ii) was filed or given after the date on which such return, report, or notice was last due, under applicable law or under any extension, and after two years before the date of the filing of the petition; or

(C) with respect to which the debtor made a fraudulent return or willfully attempted in any manner to evade or defeat such tax;

(2) for money, property, services, or an extension, renewal, or refinancing of credit, to the extent obtained by—

(A) false pretenses, a false representation, or actual fraud, other than a statement respecting the debtor's or an insider's financial condition;

(B) use of a statement in writing—

(i) that is materially false;

(ii) respecting the debtor's or an insider's financial condition;

(iii) on which the creditor to whom the debtor is liable for such money, property, services, or credit reasonably relied; and

(iv) that the debtor caused to be made or published with intent to deceive; or

(C) (i) for purposes of subparagraph (A)

(I) consumer debts owed to a single creditor and aggregating more than $725[52] for luxury goods or services incurred by an individual debtor on or within 90 days before the order for relief under this title

---

[51] Ed. Note: The following is a related provision of section 304 ("Protection of Child Support and Alimony") of the Bankruptcy Reform Act of 1994, Pub. L. No. 103-394 (1994):

> (g) Appearance Before Court.—Child support creditors or their representatives shall be permitted to appear and intervene without charge, and without meeting any special local court rule requirement for attorney appearances, in any bankruptcy case or proceeding in any bankruptcy court or district court of the United States if such creditors or representatives file a form in such court that contains information detailing the child support debt, its status, and other characteristics.

[52] Ed. Note: For cases commenced in the three-year period before April 1, 2019, the dollar amount is $675.

are presumed to be nondischargeable; and

(II) cash advances aggregating more than $1,000[53] that are extensions of consumer credit under an open end credit plan obtained by an individual debtor on or within 70 days before the order for relief under this title, are presumed to be nondischargeable; and

(ii) for purposes of this subparagraph—

(I) the terms "consumer", "credit", and "open end credit plan" have the same meanings as in section 103 of the Truth in Lending Act; and

(II) the term "luxury goods or services" does not include goods or services reasonably necessary for the support or maintenance of the debtor or a dependent of the debtor;

(3) neither listed nor scheduled under section 521(a)(1) of this title, with the name, if known to the debtor, of the creditor to whom such debt is owed, in time to permit—

(A) if such debt is not of a kind specified in paragraph (2), (4), or (6) of this subsection, timely filing of a proof of claim, unless such creditor had notice or actual knowledge of the case in time for such timely filing; or

(B) if such debt is of a kind specified in paragraph (2), (4), or (6) of this subsection, timely filing of a proof of claim and timely request for a determination of dischargeability of such debt under one of such paragraphs, unless such creditor had notice or actual knowledge of the case in time for such timely filing and request;

(4) for fraud or defalcation while acting in a fiduciary capacity, embezzlement, or larceny;

(5) for a domestic support obligation;

(6) for willful and malicious injury by the debtor to another entity or to the property of another entity;

(7) to the extent such debt is for a fine, penalty, or forfeiture payable to and for the benefit of a governmental unit, and is not compensation for actual pecuniary loss, other than a tax penalty—

(A) relating to a tax of a kind not specified in paragraph (1) of this subsection; or

(B) imposed with respect to a transaction or event that occurred before three years before the date of the filing of the petition;

(8) unless excepting such debt from discharge under this paragraph would impose an undue hardship on the debtor and the debtor's dependents, for—

(A) (i) an educational benefit overpayment or loan made, insured, or

---

[53] Ed. Note: For cases commenced in the three-year period before April 1, 2019, the dollar amount is $950.

guaranteed by a governmental unit, or made under any program funded in whole or in part by a governmental unit or nonprofit institution; or

(ii) an obligation to repay funds received as an educational benefit, scholarship, or stipend; or

(B) any other educational loan that is a qualified education loan, as defined in section 221(d)(1) of the Internal Revenue Code of 1986, incurred by a debtor who is an individual;

(9) for death or personal injury caused by the debtor's operation of a motor vehicle, vessel, or aircraft if such operation was unlawful because the debtor was intoxicated from using alcohol, a drug, or another substance;

(10) that was or could have been listed or scheduled by the debtor in a prior case concerning the debtor under this title or under the Bankruptcy Act in which the debtor waived discharge, or was denied a discharge under section 727(a)(2), (3), (4), (5), (6), or (7) of this title, or under section 14c(1), (2), (3), (4), (6), or (7) of such Act;

(11) provided in any final judgment, unreviewable order, or consent order or decree entered in any court of the United States or of any State, issued by a Federal depository institutions regulatory agency, or contained in any settlement agreement entered into by the debtor, arising from any act of fraud or defalcation while acting in a fiduciary capacity committed with respect to any depository institution or insured credit union;

(12) for malicious or reckless failure to fulfill any commitment by the debtor to a Federal depository institutions regulatory agency to maintain the capital of an insured depository institution, except that this paragraph shall not extend any such commitment which would otherwise be terminated due to any act of such agency;

(13) for any payment of an order of restitution issued under title 18, United States Code;

(14) incurred to pay a tax to the United States that would be nondischargeable pursuant to paragraph (1);

(14A) incurred to pay a tax to a governmental unit, other than the United States, that would be nondischargeable under paragraph (1);

(14B) incurred to pay fines or penalties imposed under Federal election law;

(15) to a spouse, former spouse, or child of the debtor and not of the kind described in paragraph (5) that is incurred by the debtor in the course of a divorce or separation or in connection with a separation agreement, divorce decree or other order of a court of record, or a determination made in accordance with State or territorial law by a governmental unit;

(16) for a fee or assessment that becomes due and payable after the order for relief to a membership association with respect to the debtor's interest in a unit that has condominium ownership, in a share of a cooperative corporation,

or a lot in a homeowners association, for as long as the debtor or the trustee has a legal, equitable, or possessory ownership interest in such unit, such corporation, or such lot, but nothing in this paragraph shall except from discharge the debt of a debtor for a membership association fee or assessment for a period arising before entry of the order for relief in a pending or subsequent bankruptcy case;

(17) for a fee imposed on a prisoner by any court for the filing of a case, motion, complaint, or appeal, or for other costs and expenses assessed with respect to such filing, regardless of an assertion of poverty by the debtor under subsection (b) or (f)(2) of section 1915 of title 28 (or a similar non-Federal law), or the debtor's status as a prisoner, as defined in section 1915(h) of title 28 (or a similar non-Federal law);

(18) owed to a pension, profit-sharing, stock bonus, or other plan established under section 401, 403, 408, 408A, 414, 457, or 501(c) of the Internal Revenue Code of 1986, under—

(A) a loan permitted under section 408(b)(1) of the Employee Retirement Income Security Act of 1974, or subject to section 72(p) of the Internal Revenue Code of 1986; or

(B) a loan from a thrift savings plan permitted under subchapter III of chapter 84 of title 5, that satisfies the requirements of section 8433(g) of such title;

but nothing in this paragraph may be construed to provide that any loan made under a governmental plan under section 414(d), or a contract or account under section 403(b), of the Internal Revenue Code of 1986 constitutes a claim or a debt under this title; or

(19) that—

(A) is for—

(i) the violation of any of the Federal securities laws (as that term is defined in section 3(a)(47) of the Securities Exchange Act of 1934), any of the State securities laws, or any regulation or order issued under such Federal or State securities laws; or

(ii) common law fraud, deceit, or manipulation in connection with the purchase or sale of any security; and

(B) results, before, on, or after the date on which the petition was filed, from—

(i) any judgment, order, consent order, or decree entered in any Federal or State judicial or administrative proceeding;

(ii) any settlement agreement entered into by the debtor; or

(iii) any court or administrative order for any damages, fine, penalty, citation, restitutionary payment, disgorgement payment, attorney fee, cost, or other payment owed by the debtor.

For purposes of this subsection, the term "return" means a return that satisfies the requirements of applicable nonbankruptcy law (including applicable filing requirements). Such term includes a return prepared pursuant to section 6020(a) of the Internal Revenue Code of 1986, or similar State or local law, or a written stipulation to a judgment or a final order entered by a nonbankruptcy tribunal, but does not include a return made pursuant to section 6020(b) of the Internal Revenue Code of 1986, or a similar State or local law.

(b) Notwithstanding subsection (a) of this section, a debt that was excepted from discharge under subsection (a)(1), (a)(3), or (a)(8) of this section, under section 17a(1), 17a(3), or 17a(5) of the Bankruptcy Act, under section 439A of the Higher Education Act of 1965, or under section 733(g) of the Public Health Service Act in a prior case concerning the debtor under this title, or under the Bankruptcy Act, is dischargeable in a case under this title unless, by the terms of subsection (a) of this section, such debt is not dischargeable in the case under this title.

(c) (1) Except as provided in subsection (a)(3)(B) of this section, the debtor shall be discharged from a debt of a kind specified in paragraph (2), (4), or (6) of subsection (a) of this section, unless, on request of the creditor to whom such debt is owed, and after notice and a hearing, the court determines such debt to be excepted from discharge under paragraph (2), (4), or (6), as the case may be, of subsection (a) of this section.

(2) Paragraph (1) shall not apply in the case of a Federal depository institutions regulatory agency seeking, in its capacity as conservator, receiver, or liquidating agent for an insured depository institution, to recover a debt described in subsection (a)(2), (a)(4), (a)(6), or (a)(11) owed to such institution by an institution-affiliated party unless the receiver, conservator, or liquidating agent was appointed in time to reasonably comply, or for a Federal depository institutions regulatory agency acting in its corporate capacity as a successor to such receiver, conservator, or liquidating agent to reasonably comply, with subsection (a)(3)(B) as a creditor of such institution-affiliated party with respect to such debt.

(d) If a creditor requests a determination of dischargeability of a consumer debt under subsection (a)(2) of this section, and such debt is discharged, the court shall grant judgment in favor of the debtor for the costs of, and a reasonable attorney's fee for, the proceeding if the court finds that the position of the creditor was not substantially justified, except that the court shall not award such costs and fees if special circumstances would make the award unjust.

(e) Any institution-affiliated party of an insured depository institution shall be considered to be acting in a fiduciary capacity with respect to the purposes of subsection (a)(4) or (11).

BANKRUPTCY RULE REFERENCES: 1007, 1009, 1019, 2002, 4007, 5005 and 7001

## § 524 Effect of discharge

(a) A discharge in a case under this title—

(1) voids any judgment at any time obtained, to the extent that such judgment is a determination of the personal liability of the debtor with respect to any debt discharged under section 727, 944, 1141, 1192, 1228, or 1328 of this title, whether or not discharge of such debt is waived;

(2) operates as an injunction against the commencement or continuation of an action, the employment of process, or an act, to collect, recover or offset any such debt as a personal liability of the debtor, whether or not discharge of such debt is waived; and

(3) operates as an injunction against the commencement or continuation of an action, the employment of process, or an act, to collect or recover from, or offset against, property of the debtor of the kind specified in section 541(a)(2) of this title that is acquired after the commencement of the case, on account of any allowable community claim, except a community claim that is excepted from discharge under section 523, 1192, 1228(a)(1), or 1328(a)(1), or that would be so excepted, determined in accordance with the provisions of sections 523(c) and 523(d) of this title, in a case concerning the debtor's spouse commenced on the date of the filing of the petition in the case concerning the debtor, whether or not discharge of the debt based on such community claim is waived.

(b) Subsection (a)(3) of this section does not apply if—

(1) (A) the debtor's spouse is a debtor in a case under this title, or a bankrupt or a debtor in a case under the Bankruptcy Act, commenced within six years of the date of the filing of the petition in the case concerning the debtor; and

(B) the court does not grant the debtor's spouse a discharge in such case concerning the debtor's spouse; or

(2) (A) the court would not grant the debtor's spouse a discharge in a case under chapter 7 of this title concerning such spouse commenced on the date of the filing of the petition in the case concerning the debtor; and

(B) a determination that the court would not so grant such discharge is made by the bankruptcy court within the time and in the manner provided for a determination under section 727 of this title of whether a debtor is granted a discharge.

(c) An agreement between a holder of a claim and the debtor, the consideration for which, in whole or in part, is based on a debt that is dischargeable in a case under this title is enforceable only to any extent enforceable under applicable nonbankruptcy law, whether or not discharge of such debt is waived, only if—

(1) such agreement was made before the granting of the discharge under section 727, 1141, 1192, 1228, or 1328 of this title;

(2) the debtor received the disclosures described in subsection (k) at or

before the time at which the debtor signed the agreement;

(3) such agreement has been filed with the court and, if applicable, accompanied by a declaration or an affidavit of the attorney that represented the debtor during the course of negotiating an agreement under this subsection, which states that—

(A) such agreement represents a fully informed and voluntary agreement by the debtor;

(B) such agreement does not impose an undue hardship on the debtor or a dependent of the debtor; and

(C) the attorney fully advised the debtor of the legal effect and consequences of—

(i) an agreement of the kind specified in this subsection; and

(ii) any default under such an agreement;

(4) the debtor has not rescinded such agreement at any time prior to discharge or within sixty days after such agreement is filed with the court, whichever occurs later, by giving notice of rescission to the holder of such claim;

(5) the provisions of subsection (d) of this section have been complied with; and

(6) (A) in a case concerning an individual who was not represented by an attorney during the course of negotiating an agreement under this subsection, the court approves such agreement as—

(i) not imposing an undue hardship on the debtor or a dependent of the debtor; and

(ii) in the best interest of the debtor.

(B) Subparagraph (A) shall not apply to the extent that such debt is a consumer debt secured by real property.

(d) In a case concerning an individual, when the court has determined whether to grant or not to grant a discharge under section 727, 1141, 1192, 1228, or 1328 of this title, the court may hold a hearing at which the debtor shall appear in person. At any such hearing, the court shall inform the debtor that a discharge has been granted or the reason why a discharge has not been granted. If a discharge has been granted and if the debtor desires to make an agreement of the kind specified in subsection (c) of this section and was not represented by an attorney during the course of negotiating such agreement, then the court shall hold a hearing at which the debtor shall appear in person and at such hearing the court shall—

(1) inform the debtor—

(A) that such an agreement is not required under this title, under nonbankruptcy law, or under any agreement not made in accordance with the provisions of subsection (c) of this section; and

(B) of the legal effect and consequences of—

(i) an agreement of the kind specified in subsection (c) of this section; and

(ii) a default under such an agreement; and

(2) determine whether the agreement that the debtor desires to make complies with the requirements of subsection (c)(6) of this section, if the consideration for such agreement is based in whole or in part on a consumer debt that is not secured by real property of the debtor.

(e) Except as provided in subsection (a)(3) of this section, discharge of a debt of the debtor does not affect the liability of any other entity on, or the property of any other entity for, such debt.

(f) Nothing contained in subsection (c) or (d) of this section prevents a debtor from voluntarily repaying any debt.

(g) (1) (A) After notice and hearing, a court that enters an order confirming a plan of reorganization under chapter 11 may issue, in connection with such order, an injunction in accordance with this subsection to supplement the injunctive effect of a discharge under this section.

(B) An injunction may be issued under subparagraph (A) to enjoin entities from taking legal action for the purpose of directly or indirectly collecting, recovering, or receiving payment or recovery with respect to any claim or demand that, under a plan of reorganization, is to be paid in whole or in part by a trust described in paragraph (2)(B)(i), except such legal actions as are expressly allowed by the injunction, the confirmation order, or the plan of reorganization.

(2) (A) Subject to subsection (h), if the requirements of subparagraph (B) are met at the time an injunction described in paragraph (1) is entered, then after entry of such injunction, any proceeding that involves the validity, application, construction, or modification of such injunction, or of this subsection with respect to such injunction, may be commenced only in the district court in which such injunction was entered, and such court shall have exclusive jurisdiction over any such proceeding without regard to the amount in controversy.

(B) The requirements of this subparagraph are that—

(i) the injunction is to be implemented in connection with a trust that, pursuant to the plan of reorganization—

(I) is to assume the liabilities of a debtor which at the time of entry of the order for relief has been named as a defendant in personal injury, wrongful death, or property-damage actions seeking recovery for damages allegedly caused by the presence of, or exposure to, asbestos or asbestos-containing products;

(II) is to be funded in whole or in part by the securities of 1 or more debtors involved in such plan and by the obligation of such debtor or debtors to make future payments, including dividends;

(III) is to own, or by the exercise of rights granted under such plan would be entitled to own if specified contingencies occur, a majority of the voting shares of—

(aa) each such debtor;

(bb) the parent corporation of each such debtor; or

(cc) a subsidiary of each such debtor that is also a debtor; and

(IV) is to use its assets or income to pay claims and demands; and

(ii) subject to subsection (h), the court determines that—

(I) the debtor is likely to be subject to substantial future demands for payment arising out of the same or similar conduct or events that gave rise to the claims that are addressed by the injunction;

(II) the actual amounts, numbers, and timing of such future demands cannot be determined;

(III) pursuit of such demands outside the procedures prescribed by such plan is likely to threaten the plan's purpose to deal equitably with claims and future demands;

(IV) as part of the process of seeking confirmation of such plan—

(aa) the terms of the injunction proposed to be issued under paragraph (1)(A), including any provisions barring actions against third parties pursuant to paragraph (4)(A), are set out in such plan and in any disclosure statement supporting the plan; and

(bb) a separate class or classes of the claimants whose claims are to be addressed by a trust described in clause (i) is established and votes, by at least 75 percent of those voting, in favor of the plan; and

(V) subject to subsection (h), pursuant to court orders or otherwise, the trust will operate through mechanisms such as structured, periodic, or supplemental payments, pro rata distributions, matrices, or periodic review of estimates of the numbers and values of present claims and future demands, or other comparable mechanisms, that provide reasonable assurance that the trust will value, and be in a financial position to pay, present claims and future demands that involve similar claims in substantially the same manner.

(3) (A) If the requirements of paragraph (2)(B) are met and the order confirming the plan of reorganization was issued or affirmed by the district court that has jurisdiction over the reorganization case, then after the time for appeal of the order that issues or affirms the plan—

(i) the injunction shall be valid and enforceable and may not be revoked or modified by any court except through appeal in accordance with paragraph (6);

(ii) no entity that pursuant to such plan or thereafter becomes a direct or indirect transferee of, or successor to any assets of, a debtor or trust that is the subject of the injunction shall be liable with respect to any claim or demand made against such entity by reason of its becoming such a transferee or successor; and

(iii) no entity that pursuant to such plan or thereafter makes a loan to such a debtor or trust or to such a successor or transferee shall, by reason of making the loan, be liable with respect to any claim or demand made against such entity, nor shall any pledge of assets made in connection with such a loan be upset or impaired for that reason;

(B) Subparagraph (A) shall not be construed to—

(i) imply that an entity described in subparagraph (A)(ii) or (iii) would, if this paragraph were not applicable, necessarily be liable to any entity by reason of any of the acts described in subparagraph (A);

(ii) relieve any such entity of the duty to comply with, or of liability under, any Federal or State law regarding the making of a fraudulent conveyance in a transaction described in subparagraph (A)(ii) or (iii); or

(iii) relieve a debtor of the debtor's obligation to comply with the terms of the plan of reorganization, or affect the power of the court to exercise its authority under sections 1141 and 1142 to compel the debtor to do so.

(4) (A) (i) Subject to subparagraph (B), an injunction described in paragraph (1) shall be valid and enforceable against all entities that it addresses.

(ii) Notwithstanding the provisions of section 524(e), such an injunction may bar any action directed against a third party who is identifiable from the terms of such injunction (by name or as part of an identifiable group) and is alleged to be directly or indirectly liable for the conduct of, claims against, or demands on the debtor to the extent such alleged liability of such third party arises by reason of—

(I) the third party's ownership of a financial interest in the debtor, a past or present affiliate of the debtor, or a predecessor in interest of the debtor;

(II) the third party's involvement in the management of the debtor or a predecessor in interest of the debtor, or service as an officer, director or employee of the debtor or a related party;

(III) the third party's provision of insurance to the debtor or a related party; or

(IV) the third party's involvement in a transaction changing the corporate structure, or in a loan or other financial transaction affecting the financial condition, of the debtor or a related party, including but not limited to—

(aa) involvement in providing financing (debt or equity), or advice to an entity involved in such a transaction; or

(bb) acquiring or selling a financial interest in an entity as part of such a transaction.

(iii) As used in this subparagraph, the term "related party" means—

(I) a past or present affiliate of the debtor;

(II) a predecessor in interest of the debtor; or

(III) any entity that owned a financial interest in—

(aa) the debtor;

(bb) a past or present affiliate of the debtor; or

(cc) a predecessor in interest of the debtor.

(B) Subject to subsection (h), if, under a plan of reorganization, a kind of demand described in such plan is to be paid in whole or in part by a trust described in paragraph (2)(B)(i) in connection with which an injunction described in paragraph (1) is to be implemented, then such injunction shall be valid and enforceable with respect to a demand of such kind made, after such plan is confirmed, against the debtor or debtors involved, or against a third party described in subparagraph (A)(ii), if—

(i) as part of the proceedings leading to issuance of such injunction, the court appoints a legal representative for the purpose of protecting the rights of persons that might subsequently assert demands of such kind, and

(ii) the court determines, before entering the order confirming such plan, that identifying such debtor or debtors, or such third party (by name or as part of an identifiable group), in such injunction with respect to such demands for purposes of this subparagraph is fair and equitable with respect to the persons that might subsequently assert such demands, in light of the benefits provided, or to be provided, to such trust on behalf of such debtor or debtors or such third party.

(5) In this subsection, the term "demand" means a demand for payment, present or future, that—

(A) was not a claim during the proceedings leading to the confirmation of a plan of reorganization;

(B) arises out of the same or similar conduct or events that gave rise to the claims addressed by the injunction issued under paragraph (1); and

(C) pursuant to the plan, is to be paid by a trust described in paragraph (2)(B)(i).

(6) Paragraph (3)(A)(i) does not bar an action taken by or at the direction of

an appellate court on appeal of an injunction issued under paragraph (1) or of the order of confirmation that relates to the injunction.

(7) This subsection does not affect the operation of section 1144 or the power of the district court to refer a proceeding under section 157 of title 28 or any reference of a proceeding made prior to the date of the enactment of this subsection.

(h) Application to Existing Injunctions. For purposes of subsection (g)—

(1) subject to paragraph (2), if an injunction of the kind described in subsection (g)(1)(B) was issued before the date of the enactment of this Act [enacted Oct. 22, 1994], as part of a plan of reorganization confirmed by an order entered before such date, then the injunction shall be considered to meet the requirements of subsection (g)(2)(B) for purposes of subsection (g)(2)(A), and to satisfy subsection (g)(4)(A)(ii), if—

(A) the court determined at the time the plan was confirmed that the plan was fair and equitable in accordance with the requirements of section 1129(b);

(B) as part of the proceedings leading to issuance of such injunction and confirmation of such plan, the court had appointed a legal representative for the purpose of protecting the rights of persons that might subsequently assert demands described in subsection (g)(4)(B) with respect to such plan; and

(C) such legal representative did not object to confirmation of such plan or issuance of such injunction; and

(2) for purposes of paragraph (1), if a trust described in subsection (g)(2)(B)(i) is subject to a court order on the date of the enactment of this Act [enacted Oct. 22, 1994] staying such trust from settling or paying further claims—

(A) the requirements of subsection (g)(2)(B)(ii)(V) shall not apply with respect to such trust until such stay is lifted or dissolved; and

(B) if such trust meets such requirements on the date such stay is lifted or dissolved, such trust shall be considered to have met such requirements continuously from the date of the enactment of this Act [enacted Oct. 22, 1994].

(i) The willful failure of a creditor to credit payments received under a plan confirmed under this title, unless the order confirming the plan is revoked, the plan is in default, or the creditor has not received payments required to be made under the plan in the manner required by the plan (including crediting the amounts required under the plan), shall constitute a violation of an injunction under subsection (a)(2) if the act of the creditor to collect and failure to credit payments in the manner required by the plan caused material injury to the debtor.

(j) Subsection (a)(2) does not operate as an injunction against an act by a creditor that is the holder of a secured claim, if—

(1) such creditor retains a security interest in real property that is the principal residence of the debtor;

(2) such act is in the ordinary course of business between the creditor and the debtor; and

(3) such act is limited to seeking or obtaining periodic payments associated with a valid security interest in lieu of pursuit of in rem relief to enforce the lien.

(k) (1) The disclosures required under subsection (c)(2) shall consist of the disclosure statement described in paragraph (3), completed as required in that paragraph, together with the agreement specified in subsection (c), statement, declaration, motion and order described, respectively, in paragraphs (4) through (8), and shall be the only disclosures required in connection with entering into such agreement.

(2) Disclosures made under paragraph (1) shall be made clearly and conspicuously and in writing. The terms "Amount Reaffirmed" and "Annual Percentage Rate" shall be disclosed more conspicuously than other terms, data or information provided in connection with this disclosure, except that the phrases "Before agreeing to reaffirm a debt, review these important disclosures" and "Summary of Reaffirmation Agreement" may be equally conspicuous. Disclosures may be made in a different order and may use terminology different from that set forth in paragraphs (2) through (8), except that the terms "Amount Reaffirmed" and "Annual Percentage Rate" must be used where indicated.

(3) The disclosure statement required under this paragraph shall consist of the following:

(A) The statement: "Part A: Before agreeing to reaffirm a debt, review these important disclosures:";

(B) Under the heading "Summary of Reaffirmation Agreement", the statement: "This Summary is made pursuant to the requirements of the Bankruptcy Code";

(C) The "Amount Reaffirmed", using that term, which shall be—

(i) the total amount of debt that the debtor agrees to reaffirm by entering into an agreement of the kind specified in subsection (c), and

(ii) the total of any fees and costs accrued as of the date of the disclosure statement, related to such total amount.

(D) In conjunction with the disclosure of the "Amount Reaffirmed", the statements—

(i) "The amount of debt you have agreed to reaffirm"; and

(ii) "Your credit agreement may obligate you to pay additional amounts which may come due after the date of this disclosure. Consult your credit agreement."

(E) The "Annual Percentage Rate", using that term, which shall be disclosed as—

(i) if, at the time the petition is filed, the debt is an extension of credit under an open end credit plan, as the terms "credit" and "open end credit plan" are defined in section 103 of the Truth in Lending Act, then—

(I) the annual percentage rate determined under paragraphs (5) and (6) of section 127(b) of the Truth in Lending Act, as applicable, as disclosed to the debtor in the most recent periodic statement prior to entering into an agreement of the kind specified in subsection (c) or, if no such periodic statement has been given to the debtor during the prior 6 months, the annual percentage rate as it would have been so disclosed at the time the disclosure statement is given to the debtor, or to the extent this annual percentage rate is not readily available or not applicable, then

(II) the simple interest rate applicable to the amount reaffirmed as of the date the disclosure statement is given to the debtor, or if different simple interest rates apply to different balances, the simple interest rate applicable to each such balance, identifying the amount of each such balance included in the amount reaffirmed, or

(III) if the entity making the disclosure elects, to disclose the annual percentage rate under subclause (I) and the simple interest rate under subclause (II); or

(ii) if, at the time the petition is filed, the debt is an extension of credit other than under an open end credit plan, as the terms "credit" and "open end credit plan" are defined in section 103 of the Truth in Lending Act, then—

(I) the annual percentage rate under section 128(a)(4) of the Truth in Lending Act, as disclosed to the debtor in the most recent disclosure statement given to the debtor prior to the entering into an agreement of the kind specified in subsection (c) with respect to the debt, or, if no such disclosure statement was given to the debtor, the annual percentage rate as it would have been so disclosed at the time the disclosure statement is given to the debtor, or to the extent this annual percentage rate is not readily available or not applicable, then

(II) the simple interest rate applicable to the amount reaffirmed as of the date the disclosure statement is given to the debtor, or if different simple interest rates apply to different balances, the simple interest rate applicable to each such balance, identifying the amount of such balance included in the amount reaffirmed, or

(III) if the entity making the disclosure elects, to disclose the annual percentage rate under (I) and the simple interest rate under (II).

(F) If the underlying debt transaction was disclosed as a variable rate transaction on the most recent disclosure given under the Truth in Lending

Act, by stating "The interest rate on your loan may be a variable interest rate which changes from time to time, so that the annual percentage rate disclosed here may be higher or lower."

(G) If the debt is secured by a security interest which has not been waived in whole or in part or determined to be void by a final order of the court at the time of the disclosure, by disclosing that a security interest or lien in goods or property is asserted over some or all of the debts the debtor is reaffirming and listing the items and their original purchase price that are subject to the asserted security interest, or if not a purchase-money security interest then listing by items or types and the original amount of the loan.

(H) At the election of the creditor, a statement of the repayment schedule using 1 or a combination of the following—

(i) by making the statement: "Your first payment in the amount of $____________ is due on ____________ but the future payment amount may be different. Consult your reaffirmation agreement or credit agreement, as applicable.", and stating the amount of the first payment and the due date of that payment in the places provided;

(ii) by making the statement: "Your payment schedule will be:", and describing the repayment schedule with the number, amount, and due dates or period of payments scheduled to repay the debts reaffirmed to the extent then known by the disclosing party; or

(iii) by describing the debtor's repayment obligations with reasonable specificity to the extent then known by the disclosing party.

(I) The following statement: "Note: When this disclosure refers to what a creditor 'may' do, it does not use the word 'may' to give the creditor specific permission. The word 'may' is used to tell you what might occur if the law permits the creditor to take the action. If you have questions about your reaffirming a debt or what the law requires, consult with the attorney who helped you negotiate this agreement reaffirming a debt. If you don't have an attorney helping you, the judge will explain the effect of your reaffirming a debt when the hearing on the reaffirmation agreement is held."

(J) (i) The following additional statements:

"Reaffirming a debt is a serious financial decision. The law requires you to take certain steps to make sure the decision is in your best interest. If these steps are not completed, the reaffirmation agreement is not effective, even though you have signed it.

"1. Read the disclosures in this Part A carefully. Consider the decision to reaffirm carefully. Then, if you want to reaffirm, sign the reaffirmation agreement in Part B (or you may use a separate agreement you and your creditor agree on).

"2. Complete and sign Part D and be sure you can afford to make the payments you are agreeing to make and have received a copy of the disclosure statement and a completed and signed reaffirmation agreement.

"3. If you were represented by an attorney during the negotiation of your reaffirmation agreement, the attorney must have signed the certification in Part C.

"4. If you were not represented by an attorney during the negotiation of your reaffirmation agreement, you must have completed and signed Part E.

"5. The original of this disclosure must be filed with the court by you or your creditor. If a separate reaffirmation agreement (other than the one in Part B) has been signed, it must be attached.

"6. If you were represented by an attorney during the negotiation of your reaffirmation agreement, your reaffirmation agreement becomes effective upon filing with the court unless the reaffirmation is presumed to be an undue hardship as explained in Part D.

"7. If you were not represented by an attorney during the negotiation of your reaffirmation agreement, it will not be effective unless the court approves it. The court will notify you of the hearing on your reaffirmation agreement. You must attend this hearing in bankruptcy court where the judge will review your reaffirmation agreement. The bankruptcy court must approve your reaffirmation agreement as consistent with your best interests, except that no court approval is required if your reaffirmation agreement is for a consumer debt secured by a mortgage, deed of trust, security deed, or other lien on your real property, like your home.

"Your right to rescind (cancel) your reaffirmation agreement. You may rescind (cancel) your reaffirmation agreement at any time before the bankruptcy court enters a discharge order, or before the expiration of the 60-day period that begins on the date your reaffirmation agreement is filed with the court, whichever occurs later. To rescind (cancel) your reaffirmation agreement, you must notify the creditor that your reaffirmation agreement is rescinded (or canceled).

"What are your obligations if you reaffirm the debt? A reaffirmed debt remains your personal legal obligation. It is not discharged in your bankruptcy case. That means that if you default on your reaffirmed debt after your bankruptcy case is over, your creditor may be able to take your property or your wages. Otherwise, your obligations will be determined by the reaffirmation agreement which may have changed the terms of the original agreement. For example, if you are reaffirming an open end credit agreement, the creditor may be permitted by that agreement or applicable law to change the terms of that agreement in the future under certain conditions.

"Are you required to enter into a reaffirmation agreement by any law? No, you are not required to reaffirm a debt by any law. Only agree to reaffirm a debt if it is in your best interest. Be sure you can afford the payments you agree to make.

"What if your creditor has a security interest or lien? Your bankruptcy discharge does not eliminate any lien on your property. A "lien" is often referred to as a security interest, deed of trust, mortgage or security deed. Even if you do not reaffirm and your personal liability on the debt is discharged, because of the lien your creditor may still have the right to take the property securing the lien if you do not pay the debt or default on it. If the lien is on an item of personal property that is exempt under your State's law or that the trustee has abandoned, you may be able to redeem the item rather than reaffirm the debt. To redeem, you must make a single payment to the creditor equal to the amount of the allowed secured claim, as agreed by the parties or determined by the court."

(ii) In the case of a reaffirmation under subsection (m)(2), numbered paragraph 6 in the disclosures required by clause (i) of this subparagraph shall read as follows:

"6. If you were represented by an attorney during the negotiation of your reaffirmation agreement, your reaffirmation agreement becomes effective upon filing with the court."

(4) The form of such agreement required under this paragraph shall consist of the following:

"Part B: Reaffirmation Agreement. I (we) agree to reaffirm the debts arising under the credit agreement described below.

"Brief description of credit agreement:

"Description of any changes to the credit agreement made as part of this reaffirmation agreement:

"Signature: Date:

"Borrower:

"Co-borrower, if also reaffirming these debts:

"Accepted by creditor:

"Date of creditor acceptance:".

(5) The declaration shall consist of the following:

(A) The following certification:

"Part C: Certification by Debtor's Attorney (If Any).

"I hereby certify that (1) this agreement represents a fully informed and voluntary agreement by the debtor; (2) this agreement does not impose an undue hardship on the debtor or any dependent of the debtor; and (3) I have fully advised the debtor of the legal effect and consequences of this agreement and any default under this agreement.

"Signature of Debtor's Attorney: Date:".

(B) If a presumption of undue hardship has been established with respect to such agreement, such certification shall state that, in the opinion of the attorney, the debtor is able to make the payment.

(C) In the case of a reaffirmation agreement under subsection (m)(2), subparagraph (B) is not applicable.

(6) (A) The statement in support of such agreement, which the debtor shall sign and date prior to filing with the court, shall consist of the following:

"Part D: Debtor's Statement in Support of Reaffirmation Agreement.

"1. I believe this reaffirmation agreement will not impose an undue hardship on my dependents or me. I can afford to make the payments on the reaffirmed debt because my monthly income (take home pay plus any other income received) is $______________, and my actual current monthly expenses including monthly payments on post-bankruptcy debt and other reaffirmation agreements total $______________, leaving $______________ to make the required payments on this reaffirmed debt. I understand that if my income less my monthly expenses does not leave enough to make the payments, this reaffirmation agreement is presumed to be an undue hardship on me and must be reviewed by the court. However, this presumption may be overcome if I explain to the satisfaction of the court how I can afford to make the payments here: ______________.

"2. I received a copy of the Reaffirmation Disclosure Statement in Part A and a completed and signed reaffirmation agreement."

(B) Where the debtor is represented by an attorney and is reaffirming a debt owed to a creditor defined in section 19(b)(1)(A)(iv) of the Federal Reserve Act, the statement of support of the reaffirmation agreement, which the debtor shall sign and date prior to filing with the court, shall consist of the following:

"I believe this reaffirmation agreement is in my financial interest. I can afford to make the payments on the reaffirmed debt. I received a copy of the Reaffirmation Disclosure Statement in Part A and a completed and signed reaffirmation agreement."

(7) The motion that may be used if approval of such agreement by the court is required in order for it to be effective, shall be signed and dated by the movant and shall consist of the following:

"Part E: Motion for Court Approval (To be completed only if the debtor is not represented by an attorney.). I (we), the debtor(s), affirm the following to be true and correct:

"I am not represented by an attorney in connection with this reaffirmation agreement.

"I believe this reaffirmation agreement is in my best interest based on the income and expenses I have disclosed in my Statement in Support of this reaffirmation agreement, and because (provide any additional relevant reasons the court should consider):

"Therefore, I ask the court for an order approving this reaffirmation agreement."

(8) The court order, which may be used to approve such agreement, shall consist of the following:

"Court Order: The court grants the debtor's motion and approves the reaffirmation agreement described above."

(*l*) Notwithstanding any other provision of this title the following shall apply:

(1) A creditor may accept payments from a debtor before and after the filing of an agreement of the kind specified in subsection (c) with the court.

(2) A creditor may accept payments from a debtor under such agreement that the creditor believes in good faith to be effective.

(3) The requirements of subsections (c)(2) and (k) shall be satisfied if disclosures required under those subsections are given in good faith.

(m) (1) Until 60 days after an agreement of the kind specified in subsection (c) is filed with the court (or such additional period as the court, after notice and a hearing and for cause, orders before the expiration of such period), it shall be presumed that such agreement is an undue hardship on the debtor if the debtor's monthly income less the debtor's monthly expenses as shown on the debtor's completed and signed statement in support of such agreement required under subsection (k)(6)(A) is less than the scheduled payments on the reaffirmed debt. This presumption shall be reviewed by the court. The presumption may be rebutted in writing by the debtor if the statement includes an explanation that identifies additional sources of funds to make the payments as agreed upon under the terms of such agreement. If the presumption is not rebutted to the satisfaction of the court, the court may disapprove such agreement. No agreement shall be disapproved without notice and a hearing to the debtor and creditor, and such hearing shall be concluded before the entry of the debtor's discharge.

(2) This subsection does not apply to reaffirmation agreements where the creditor is a credit union, as defined in section 19(b)(1)(A)(iv) of the Federal Reserve Act

Bankruptcy Rule References: 4004 and 4008

## § 525 Protection against discriminatory treatment

(a) Except as provided in the Perishable Agricultural Commodities Act, 1930, the Packers and Stockyards Act, 1921, and section 1 of the Act entitled "An Act making appropriations for the Department of Agriculture for the fiscal year ending June 30, 1944, and for other purposes," approved July 12, 1943, a governmental unit may not deny, revoke, suspend, or refuse to renew a license, permit, charter, franchise, or other similar grant to, condition such a grant to, discriminate with respect to such a grant against, deny employment to, terminate the employment of, or discriminate with respect to employment against, a person that is or has been a debtor under this title or a bankrupt or a debtor under the Bankruptcy Act or another person with whom such bankrupt or debtor has been associated, solely because such bankrupt or debtor is or has been a debtor under this title or a bankrupt or debtor under the Bankruptcy Act, has been insolvent before the commencement of the case under this title, or during the case but before the debtor is granted or denied a discharge, or has not paid a debt that is dischargeable in the case under this title or that was discharged under the Bankruptcy Act.

(b) No private employer may terminate the employment of, or discriminate with respect to employment against, an individual who is or has been a debtor under this title, a debtor or bankrupt under the Bankruptcy Act, or an individual associated with such debtor or bankrupt, solely because such debtor or bankrupt—

(1) is or has been a debtor under this title or a debtor or bankrupt under the Bankruptcy Act;

(2) has been insolvent before the commencement of a case under this title or during the case but before the grant or denial of a discharge; or

(3) has not paid a debt that is dischargeable in a case under this title or that was discharged under the Bankruptcy Act.

(c) (1) A governmental unit that operates a student grant or loan program and a person engaged in a business that includes the making of loans guaranteed or insured under a student loan program may not deny a student grant, loan, loan guarantee, or loan insurance to a person that is or has been a debtor under this title or a bankrupt or debtor under the Bankruptcy Act, or another person with whom the debtor or bankrupt has been associated, because the debtor or bankrupt is or has been a debtor under this title or a bankrupt or debtor under the Bankruptcy Act, has been insolvent before the commencement of a case under this title or during the pendency of the case but before the debtor is granted or denied a discharge, or has not paid a debt that is dischargeable in the case under this title or that was discharged under the Bankruptcy Act.

(2) In this section, "student loan program" means any program operated under title IV of the Higher Education Act of 1965 or a similar program operated under State or local law.

(d) A person may not be denied relief under sections 4022 through 4024 of the CARES Act (15 U.S.C. 9056, 9057, 9058) because the person is or has been a debtor under this title.[54]

## § 526 Restrictions on debt relief agencies

(a) A debt relief agency shall not—

(1) fail to perform any service that such agency informed an assisted person or prospective assisted person it would provide in connection with a case or proceeding under this title;

(2) make any statement, or counsel or advise any assisted person or prospective assisted person to make a statement in a document filed in a case or proceeding under this title, that is untrue or misleading, or that upon the exercise of reasonable care, should have been known by such agency to be untrue or misleading;

---

[54] Ed. Note: Underscored material enacted by the Consolidated Appropriations Act, 2021, Pub. L. No. 116-260, div. FF, tit. X, § 1001(c)(1). The amendment will sunset one year after the date of enactment of the Act, which was December 27, 2020. Pub. L. No. 116-260, div. FF, tit. X, § 1001(c)(2).

(3) misrepresent to any assisted person or prospective assisted person, directly or indirectly, affirmatively or by material omission, with respect to—

(A) the services that such agency will provide to such person; or

(B) the benefits and risks that may result if such person becomes a debtor in a case under this title; or

(4) advise an assisted person or prospective assisted person to incur more debt in contemplation of such person filing a case under this title or to pay an attorney or bankruptcy petition preparer a fee or charge for services performed as part of preparing for or representing a debtor in a case under this title.

(b) Any waiver by any assisted person of any protection or right provided under this section shall not be enforceable against the debtor by any Federal or State court or any other person, but may be enforced against a debt relief agency.

(c) (1) Any contract for bankruptcy assistance between a debt relief agency and an assisted person that does not comply with the material requirements of this section, section 527, or section 528 shall be void and may not be enforced by any Federal or State court or by any other person, other than such assisted person.

(2) Any debt relief agency shall be liable to an assisted person in the amount of any fees or charges in connection with providing bankruptcy assistance to such person that such debt relief agency has received, for actual damages, and for reasonable attorneys' fees and costs if such agency is found, after notice and a hearing, to have—

(A) intentionally or negligently failed to comply with any provision of this section, section 527, or section 528 with respect to a case or proceeding under this title for such assisted person;

(B) provided bankruptcy assistance to an assisted person in a case or proceeding under this title that is dismissed or converted to a case under another chapter of this title because of such agency's intentional or negligent failure to file any required document including those specified in section 521; or

(C) intentionally or negligently disregarded the material requirements of this title or the Federal Rules of Bankruptcy Procedure applicable to such agency.

(3) In addition to such other remedies as are provided under State law, whenever the chief law enforcement officer of a State, or an official or agency designated by a State, has reason to believe that any person has violated or is violating this section, the State—

(A) may bring an action to enjoin such violation;

(B) may bring an action on behalf of its residents to recover the actual damages of assisted persons arising from such violation, including any liability under paragraph (2); and

(C) in the case of any successful action under subparagraph (A) or (B), shall be awarded the costs of the action and reasonable attorneys' fees as determined by the court.

(4) The district courts of the United States for districts located in the State shall have concurrent jurisdiction of any action under subparagraph (A) or (B) of paragraph (3).

(5) Notwithstanding any other provision of Federal law and in addition to any other remedy provided under Federal or State law, if the court, on its own motion or on the motion of the United States trustee or the debtor, finds that a person intentionally violated this section, or engaged in a clear and consistent pattern or practice of violating this section, the court may—

(A) enjoin the violation of such section; or

(B) impose an appropriate civil penalty against such person.

(d) No provision of this section, section 527, or section 528 shall—

(1) annul, alter, affect, or exempt any person subject to such sections from complying with any law of any State except to the extent that such law is inconsistent with those sections, and then only to the extent of the inconsistency; or

(2) be deemed to limit or curtail the authority or ability—

(A) of a State or subdivision or instrumentality thereof, to determine and enforce qualifications for the practice of law under the laws of that State; or

(B) of a Federal court to determine and enforce the qualifications for the practice of law before that court.

## § 527 Disclosures

(a) A debt relief agency providing bankruptcy assistance to an assisted person shall provide—

(1) the written notice required under section 342(b)(1); and

(2) to the extent not covered in the written notice described in paragraph (1), and not later than 3 business days after the first date on which a debt relief agency first offers to provide any bankruptcy assistance services to an assisted person, a clear and conspicuous written notice advising assisted persons that—

(A) all information that the assisted person is required to provide with a petition and thereafter during a case under this title is required to be complete, accurate, and truthful;

(B) all assets and all liabilities are required to be completely and accurately disclosed in the documents filed to commence the case, and the replacement value of each asset as defined in section 506 must be stated in those documents where requested after reasonable inquiry to establish such value;

(C) current monthly income, the amounts specified in section 707(b)(2), and, in a case under chapter 13 of this title, disposable income (determined in accordance with section 707(b)(2)), are required to be stated after reasonable inquiry; and

(D) information that an assisted person provides during their case may be audited pursuant to this title, and that failure to provide such information may result in dismissal of the case under this title or other sanction, including a criminal sanction.

(b) A debt relief agency providing bankruptcy assistance to an assisted person shall provide each assisted person at the same time as the notices required under subsection (a)(1) the following statement, to the extent applicable, or one substantially similar. The statement shall be clear and conspicuous and shall be in a single document separate from other documents or notices provided to the assisted person:

"IMPORTANT INFORMATION ABOUT BANKRUPTCY ASSISTANCE SERVICES FROM AN ATTORNEY OR BANKRUPTCY PETITION PREPARER.

"If you decide to seek bankruptcy relief, you can represent yourself, you can hire an attorney to represent you, or you can get help in some localities from a bankruptcy petition preparer who is not an attorney. THE LAW REQUIRES AN ATTORNEY OR BANKRUPTCY PETITION PREPARER TO GIVE YOU A WRITTEN CONTRACT SPECIFYING WHAT THE ATTORNEY OR BANKRUPTCY PETITION PREPARER WILL DO FOR YOU AND HOW MUCH IT WILL COST. Ask to see the contract before you hire anyone.

"The following information helps you understand what must be done in a routine bankruptcy case to help you evaluate how much service you need. Although bankruptcy can be complex, many cases are routine.

"Before filing a bankruptcy case, either you or your attorney should analyze your eligibility for different forms of debt relief available under the Bankruptcy Code and which form of relief is most likely to be beneficial for you. Be sure you understand the relief you can obtain and its limitations. To file a bankruptcy case, documents called a Petition, Schedules, and Statement of Financial Affairs, and in some cases a Statement of Intention, need to be prepared correctly and filed with the bankruptcy court. You will have to pay a filing fee to the bankruptcy court. Once your case starts, you will have to attend the required first meeting of creditors where you may be questioned by a court official called a "trustee" and by creditors.

"If you choose to file a chapter 7 case, you may be asked by a creditor to reaffirm a debt. You may want help deciding whether to do so. A creditor is not permitted to coerce you into reaffirming your debts.

"If you choose to file a chapter 13 case in which you repay your creditors what you can afford over 3 to 5 years, you may also want help with preparing your chapter 13 plan and with the confirmation hearing on your plan which will be before a bankruptcy judge.

"If you select another type of relief under the Bankruptcy Code other than chapter 7 or chapter 13, you will want to find out what should be done from someone familiar with that type of relief.

"Your bankruptcy case may also involve litigation. You are generally permitted to represent yourself in litigation in bankruptcy court, but only attorneys, not bankruptcy petition preparers, can give you legal advice.".

(c) Except to the extent the debt relief agency provides the required information itself after reasonably diligent inquiry of the assisted person or others so as to obtain such information reasonably accurately for inclusion on the petition, schedules or statement of financial affairs, a debt relief agency providing bankruptcy assistance to an assisted person, to the extent permitted by nonbankruptcy law, shall provide each assisted person at the time required for the notice required under subsection (a)(1) reasonably sufficient information (which shall be provided in a clear and conspicuous writing) to the assisted person on how to provide all the information the assisted person is required to provide under this title pursuant to section 521, including—

(1) how to value assets at replacement value, determine current monthly income, the amounts specified in section 707(b)(2) and, in a chapter 13 case, how to determine disposable income in accordance with section 707(b)(2) and related calculations;

(2) how to complete the list of creditors, including how to determine what amount is owed and what address for the creditor should be shown; and

(3) how to determine what property is exempt and how to value exempt property at replacement value as defined in section 506.

(d) A debt relief agency shall maintain a copy of the notices required under subsection (a) of this section for 2 years after the date on which the notice is given the assisted person.

## § 528 Requirements for debt relief agencies

(a) A debt relief agency shall—

(1) not later than 5 business days after the first date on which such agency provides any bankruptcy assistance services to an assisted person, but prior to such assisted person's petition under this title being filed, execute a written contract with such assisted person that explains clearly and conspicuously—

(A) the services such agency will provide to such assisted person; and

(B) the fees or charges for such services, and the terms of payment;

(2) provide the assisted person with a copy of the fully executed and completed contract;

(3) clearly and conspicuously disclose in any advertisement of bankruptcy assistance services or of the benefits of bankruptcy directed to the general public (whether in general media, seminars or specific mailings, telephonic or electronic messages, or otherwise) that the services or benefits are with respect to bankruptcy relief under this title; and

(4) clearly and conspicuously use the following statement in such advertisement: "We are a debt relief agency. We help people file for bankruptcy relief under the Bankruptcy Code." or a substantially similar statement.

(b) (1) An advertisement of bankruptcy assistance services or of the benefits of bankruptcy directed to the general public includes—

(A) descriptions of bankruptcy assistance in connection with a chapter 13 plan whether or not chapter 13 is specifically mentioned in such advertisement; and

(B) statements such as "federally supervised repayment plan" or "Federal debt restructuring help" or other similar statements that could lead a reasonable consumer to believe that debt counseling was being offered when in fact the services were directed to providing bankruptcy assistance with a chapter 13 plan or other form of bankruptcy relief under this title.

(2) An advertisement, directed to the general public, indicating that the debt relief agency provides assistance with respect to credit defaults, mortgage foreclosures, eviction proceedings, excessive debt, debt collection pressure, or inability to pay any consumer debt shall—

(A) disclose clearly and conspicuously in such advertisement that the assistance may involve bankruptcy relief under this title; and

(B) include the following statement: "We are a debt relief agency. We help people file for bankruptcy relief under the Bankruptcy Code." or a substantially similar statement.

## SUBCHAPTER III
## The Estate

### § 541 Property of the estate

(a) The commencement of a case under section 301, 302, or 303 of this title creates an estate. Such estate is comprised of all the following property, wherever located and by whomever held:

(1) Except as provided in subsections (b) and (c)(2) of this section, all legal or equitable interests of the debtor in property as of the commencement of the case.

(2) All interests of the debtor and the debtor's spouse in community property as of the commencement of the case that is—

(A) under the sole, equal, or joint management and control of the debtor; or

(B) liable for an allowable claim against the debtor, or for both an allowable claim against the debtor and an allowable claim against the debtor's spouse, to the extent that such interest is so liable.

(3) Any interest in property that the trustee recovers under section 329(b), 363(n), 543, 550, 553, or 723 of this title.

(4) Any interest in property preserved for the benefit of or ordered transferred to the estate under section 510(c) or 551 of this title.

(5) Any interest in property that would have been property of the estate if such interest had been an interest of the debtor on the date of the filing of the petition, and that the debtor acquires or becomes entitled to acquire within 180 days after such date—

(A) by bequest, devise, or inheritance;

(B) as a result of a property settlement agreement with the debtor's spouse, or of an interlocutory or final divorce decree; or

(C) as a beneficiary of a life insurance policy or of a death benefit plan.

(6) Proceeds, product, offspring, rents, or profits of or from property of the estate, except such as are earnings from services performed by an individual debtor after the commencement of the case.

(7) Any interest in property that the estate acquires after the commencement of the case.

(b) Property of the estate does not include—

(1) any power that the debtor may exercise solely for the benefit of an entity other than the debtor;

(2) any interest of the debtor as a lessee under a lease of nonresidential real property that has terminated at the expiration of the stated term of such lease before the commencement of the case under this title, and ceases to include

any interest of the debtor as a lessee under a lease of nonresidential real property that has terminated at the expiration of the stated term of such lease during the case;

(3) any eligibility of the debtor to participate in programs authorized under the Higher Education Act of 1965 (20 U.S.C. 1001 et seq.; 42 U.S.C. 2751 et seq.), or any accreditation status or State licensure of the debtor as an educational institution;

(4) any interest of the debtor in liquid or gaseous hydrocarbons to the extent that—

(A) (i) the debtor has transferred or has agreed to transfer such interest pursuant to a farmout agreement or any written agreement directly related to a farmout agreement; and

(ii) but for the operation of this paragraph, the estate could include the interest referred to in clause (i) only by virtue of section 365 or 544(a)(3) of this title; or

(B) (i) the debtor has transferred such interest pursuant to a written conveyance of a production payment to an entity that does not participate in the operation of the property from which such production payment is transferred; and

(ii) but for the operation of this paragraph, the estate could include the interest referred to in clause (i) only by virtue of section 365 or 542 of this title;

(5) funds placed in an education individual retirement account (as defined in section 530(b)(1) of the Internal Revenue Code of 1986) not later than 365 days before the date of the filing of the petition in a case under this title, but—

(A) only if the designated beneficiary of such account was a child, stepchild, grandchild, or stepgrandchild of the debtor for the taxable year for which funds were placed in such account;

(B) only to the extent that such funds—

(i) are not pledged or promised to any entity in connection with any extension of credit; and

(ii) are not excess contributions (as described in section 4973(e) of the Internal Revenue Code of 1986); and

(C) in the case of funds placed in all such accounts having the same designated beneficiary not earlier than 720 days nor later than 365 days before such date, only so much of such funds as does not exceed $6,825;[55]

(6) funds used to purchase a tuition credit or certificate or contributed to an account in accordance with section 529(b)(1)(A) of the Internal Revenue Code

---

[55] Ed. Note: For cases commenced in the three-year period before April 1, 2019, the dollar amount is $6,425.

of 1986 under a qualified State tuition program (as defined in section 529(b)(1) of such Code) not later than 365 days before the date of the filing of the petition in a case under this title, but—

(A) only if the designated beneficiary of the amounts paid or contributed to such tuition program was a child, stepchild, grandchild, or stepgrandchild of the debtor for the taxable year for which funds were paid or contributed;

(B) with respect to the aggregate amount paid or contributed to such program having the same designated beneficiary, only so much of such amount as does not exceed the total contributions permitted under section 529(b)(6) of such Code with respect to such beneficiary, as adjusted beginning on the date of the filing of the petition in a case under this title by the annual increase or decrease (rounded to the nearest tenth of 1 percent) in the education expenditure category of the Consumer Price Index prepared by the Department of Labor; and

(C) in the case of funds paid or contributed to such program having the same designated beneficiary not earlier than 720 days nor later than 365 days before such date, only so much of such funds as does not exceed $6,825;[56]

(7) any amount—

(A) withheld by an employer from the wages of employees for payment as contributions—

(i) to—

(I) an employee benefit plan that is subject to title I of the Employee Retirement Income Security Act of 1974 or under an employee benefit plan which is a governmental plan under section 414(d) of the Internal Revenue Code of 1986;

(II) a deferred compensation plan under section 457 of the Internal Revenue Code of 1986; or

(III) a tax-deferred annuity under section 403(b) of the Internal Revenue Code of 1986;

except that such amount under this subparagraph shall not constitute disposable income as defined in section 1325(b)(2); or

(ii) to a health insurance plan regulated by State law whether or not subject to such title; or

(B) received by an employer from employees for payment as contributions—

(i) to—

(I) an employee benefit plan that is subject to title I of the Employee

---

[56] Ed. Note: For cases commenced in the three-year period before April 1, 2019, the dollar amount is $6,425.

Retirement Income Security Act of 1974 or under an employee benefit plan which is a governmental plan under section 414(d) of the Internal Revenue Code of 1986;

(II) a deferred compensation plan under section 457 of the Internal Revenue Code of 1986; or

(III) a tax-deferred annuity under section 403(b) of the Internal Revenue Code of 1986;

except that such amount under this subparagraph shall not constitute disposable income, as defined in section 1325(b)(2); or

(ii) to a health insurance plan regulated by State law whether or not subject to such title;

(8) subject to subchapter III of chapter 5, any interest of the debtor in property where the debtor pledged or sold tangible personal property (other than securities or written or printed evidences of indebtedness or title) as collateral for a loan or advance of money given by a person licensed under law to make such loans or advances, where—

(A) the tangible personal property is in the possession of the pledgee or transferee;

(B) the debtor has no obligation to repay the money, redeem the collateral, or buy back the property at a stipulated price; and

(C) neither the debtor nor the trustee have exercised any right to redeem provided under the contract or State law, in a timely manner as provided under State law and section 108(b);

(9) any interest in cash or cash equivalents that constitute proceeds of a sale by the debtor of a money order that is made—

(A) on or after the date that is 14 days prior to the date on which the petition is filed; and

(B) under an agreement with a money order issuer that prohibits the commingling of such proceeds with property of the debtor (notwithstanding that, contrary to the agreement, the proceeds may have been commingled with property of the debtor),

unless the money order issuer had not taken action, prior to the filing of the petition, to require compliance with the prohibition; ~~or~~

(10) funds placed in an account of a qualified ABLE program (as defined in section 529A(b) of the Internal Revenue Code of 1986) not later than 365 days before the date of the filing of the petition in a case under this title, but—

(A) only if the designated beneficiary of such account was a child, stepchild, grandchild, or stepgrandchild of the debtor for the taxable year for which funds were placed in such account;

(B) only to the extent that such funds—

(i) are not pledged or promised to any entity in connection with any extension of credit; and

(ii) are not excess contributions (as described in section 4973(h) of the Internal Revenue Code of 1986); and

(C) in the case of funds placed in all such accounts having the same designated beneficiary not earlier than 720 days nor later than 365 days before such date, only so much of such funds as does not exceed $6,825~~.~~;[57] or

(11) recovery rebates made under section 6428 of the Internal Revenue Code of 1986.[58]

Paragraph (4) shall not be construed to exclude from the estate any consideration the debtor retains, receives, or is entitled to receive for transferring an interest in liquid or gaseous hydrocarbons pursuant to a farmout agreement.

(c) (1) Except as provided in paragraph (2) of this subsection, an interest of the debtor in property becomes property of the estate under subsection (a)(1), (a)(2), or (a)(5) of this section notwithstanding any provision in an agreement, transfer instrument, or applicable nonbankruptcy law—

(A) that restricts or conditions transfer of such interest by the debtor; or

(B) that is conditioned on the insolvency or financial condition of the debtor, on the commencement of a case under this title, or on the appointment of or taking possession by a trustee in a case under this title or a custodian before such commencement, and that effects or gives an option to effect a forfeiture, modification, or termination of the debtor's interest in property.

(2) A restriction on the transfer of a beneficial interest of the debtor in a trust that is enforceable under applicable nonbankruptcy law is enforceable in a case under this title.

(d) Property in which the debtor holds, as of the commencement of the case, only legal title and not an equitable interest, such as a mortgage secured by real property, or an interest in such a mortgage, sold by the debtor but as to which the debtor retains legal title to service or supervise the servicing of such mortgage or interest, becomes property of the estate under subsection (a)(1) or (2) of this section only to the extent of the debtor's legal title to such property, but not to the extent of any equitable interest in such property that the debtor does not hold.

(e) In determining whether any of the relationships specified in paragraph (5)(A) or (6)(A) of subsection (b) exists, a legally adopted child of an individual

---

[57] Ed. Note: For cases commenced in the three-year period before April 1, 2019, the dollar amount is $6,425.

[58] Ed. Note: Section 541(b) was amended by the Consolidated Appropriations Act, 2021, Pub. L. No. 116-260, div. FF, tit. X, § 1001(a)(1). New material is underscored; removed material is stricken out. The amendment will sunset one year after the date of enactment of the Act, which was December 27, 2020. Pub. L. No. 116-260, div. FF, tit. X, § 1001(a)(2).

(and a child who is a member of an individual's household, if placed with such individual by an authorized placement agency for legal adoption by such individual), or a foster child of an individual (if such child has as the child's principal place of abode the home of the debtor and is a member of the debtor's household) shall be treated as a child of such individual by blood.

(f)[59] Notwithstanding any other provision of this title, property that is held by a debtor that is a corporation described in section 501(c)(3) of the Internal Revenue Code of 1986 and exempt from tax under section 501(a) of such Code may be transferred to an entity that is not such a corporation, but only under the same conditions as would apply if the debtor had not filed a case under this title.

BANKRUPTCY RULE REFERENCES: 1007, 1009, 6002, 6004 and 6006.

## § 542 Turnover of property to the estate

(a) Except as provided in subsection (c) or (d) of this section, an entity, other than a custodian, in possession, custody, or control, during the case, of property that the trustee may use, sell, or lease under section 363 of this title, or that the debtor may exempt under section 522 of this title, shall deliver to the trustee, and account for, such property or the value of such property, unless such property is of inconsequential value or benefit to the estate.

(b) Except as provided in subsection (c) or (d) of this section, an entity that owes a debt that is property of the estate and that is matured, payable on demand, or payable on order, shall pay such debt to, or on the order of, the trustee, except to the extent that such debt may be offset under section 553 of this title against a claim against the debtor.

(c) Except as provided in section 362(a)(7) of this title, an entity that has neither actual notice nor actual knowledge of the commencement of the case concerning the debtor may transfer property of the estate, or pay a debt owing to the debtor, in good faith and other than in the manner specified in subsection (d) of this section, to an entity other than the trustee, with the same effect as to the entity making such transfer or payment as if the case under this title concerning the debtor had not been commenced.

(d) A life insurance company may transfer property of the estate or property of the debtor to such company in good faith, with the same effect with respect to

---

[59] ED. NOTE: Subsections (d) and (e) of section 1221 of the 2005 Act provide:

(d) APPLICABILITY.—The amendments made by this section [including the addition of subsection (f) to Code section 541] shall apply to a case pending under title 11, United States Code, on the date of enactment of this Act [April 20, 2005], or filed under that title on or after that date of enactment, except that the court shall not confirm a plan under chapter 11 of title 11, United States Code, without considering whether this section would substantially affect the rights of a party in interest who first acquired rights with respect to the debtor after the date of the filing of the petition. The parties who may appear and be heard in a proceeding under this section include the attorney general of the State in which the debtor is incorporated, was formed, or does business.

(e) RULE OF CONSTRUCTION.—Nothing in this section shall be construed to require the court in which a case under chapter 11 of title 11, United States Code, is pending to remand or refer any proceeding, issue, or controversy to any other court or to require the approval of any other court for the transfer of property.

such company as if the case under this title concerning the debtor had not been commenced, if such transfer is to pay a premium or to carry out a nonforfeiture insurance option, and is required to be made automatically, under a life insurance contract with such company that was entered into before the date of the filing of the petition and that is property of the estate.

(e) Subject to any applicable privilege, after notice and a hearing, the court may order an attorney, accountant, or other person that holds recorded information, including books, documents, records, and papers, relating to the debtor's property or financial affairs, to turn over or disclose such recorded information to the trustee.

Bankruptcy Rule Reference: 7001

## § 543 Turnover of property by a custodian

(a) A custodian with knowledge of the commencement of a case under this title concerning the debtor may not make any disbursement from, or take any action in the administration of, property of the debtor, proceeds, product, offspring, rents, or profits of such property, or property of the estate, in the possession, custody, or control of such custodian, except such action as is necessary to preserve such property.

(b) A custodian shall–

(1) deliver to the trustee any property of the debtor held by or transferred to such custodian, or proceeds, product, offspring, rents, or profits of such property, that is in such custodian's possession, custody, or control on the date that such custodian acquires knowledge of the commencement of the case; and

(2) file an accounting of any property of the debtor, or proceeds, product, offspring, rents, or profits of such property, that, at any time, came into the possession, custody, or control of such custodian.

(c) The court, after notice and a hearing, shall–

(1) protect all entities to which a custodian has become obligated with respect to such property or proceeds, product, offspring, rents, or profits of such property;

(2) provide for the payment of reasonable compensation for services rendered and costs and expenses incurred by such custodian; and

(3) surcharge such custodian, other than an assignee for the benefit of the debtor's creditors that was appointed or took possession more than 120 days before the date of the filing of the petition, for any improper or excessive disbursement, other than a disbursement that has been made in accordance with applicable law or that has been approved, after notice and a hearing, by a court of competent jurisdiction before the commencement of the case under this title.

(d) After notice and hearing, the bankruptcy court–

(1) may excuse compliance with subsection (a), (b), or (c) of this section if

the interests of creditors and, if the debtor is not insolvent, of equity security holders would be better served by permitting a custodian to continue in possession, custody, or control of such property, and

(2) shall excuse compliance with subsections (a) and (b)(1) of this section if the custodian is an assignee for the benefit of the debtor's creditors that was appointed or took possession more than 120 days before the date of the filing of the petition, unless compliance with such subsections is necessary to prevent fraud or injustice.

BANKRUPTCY RULE REFERENCES: 6002 and 9014

## § 544 Trustee as lien creditor and as successor to certain creditors and purchasers

(a) The trustee shall have, as of the commencement of the case, and without regard to any knowledge of the trustee or of any creditor, the rights and powers of, or may avoid any transfer of property of the debtor or any obligation incurred by the debtor that is voidable by—

(1) a creditor that extends credit to the debtor at the time of the commencement of the case, and that obtains, at such time and with respect to such credit, a judicial lien on all property on which a creditor on a simple contract could have obtained such a judicial lien, whether or not such a creditor exists;

(2) a creditor that extends credit to the debtor at the time of the commencement of the case, and obtains, at such time and with respect to such credit, an execution against the debtor that is returned unsatisfied at such time, whether or not such a creditor exists; or

(3) a bona fide purchaser of real property, other than fixtures, from the debtor, against whom applicable law permits such transfer to be perfected, that obtains the status of a bona fide purchaser and has perfected such transfer at the time of the commencement of the case, whether or not such a purchaser exists.

(b) (1) Except as provided in paragraph (2), the trustee may avoid any transfer of an interest of the debtor in property or any obligation incurred by the debtor that is voidable under applicable law by a creditor holding an unsecured claim that is allowable under section 502 of this title or that is not allowable only under section 502(e) of this title.

(2) Paragraph (1) shall not apply to a transfer of a charitable contribution (as that term is defined in section 548(d)(3)) that is not covered under section 548(a)(1)(B), by reason of section 548(a)(2). Any claim by any person to recover a transferred contribution described in the preceding sentence under Federal or State law in a Federal or State court shall be preempted by the commencement of the case.

BANKRUPTCY RULE REFERENCE: 7001

## § 545 Statutory liens

The trustee may avoid the fixing of a statutory lien on property of the debtor to the extent that such lien—

(1) first becomes effective against the debtor–

(A) when a case under this title concerning the debtor is commenced;

(B) when an insolvency proceeding other than under this title concerning the debtor is commenced;

(C) when a custodian is appointed or authorized to take or takes possession;

(D) when the debtor becomes insolvent;

(E) when the debtor's financial condition fails to meet a specified standard; or

(F) at the time of an execution against property of the debtor levied at the instance of an entity other than the holder of such statutory lien;

(2) is not perfected or enforceable at the time of the commencement of the case against a bona fide purchaser that purchases such property at the time of the commencement of the case, whether or not such a purchaser exists, except in any case in which a purchaser is a purchaser described in section 6323 of the Internal Revenue Code of 1986, or in any other similar provision of State or local law;

(3) is for rent; or

(4) is a lien of distress for rent.

Bankruptcy Rule Reference: 7001

## § 546 Limitations on avoiding powers

(a) An action or proceeding under section 544, 545, 547, 548, or 553 of this title may not be commenced after the earlier of–

(1) the later of

(A) 2 years after the entry of the order for relief; or

(B) 1 year after the appointment or election of the first trustee under section 702, 1104, 1163, 1202, or 1302 of this title if such appointment or such election occurs before the expiration of the period specified in subparagraph (A); or

(2) the time the case is closed or dismissed.

(b) (1) The rights and powers of a trustee under sections 544, 545, and 549 of this title are subject to any generally applicable law that–

(A) permits perfection of an interest in property to be effective against an entity that acquires rights in such property before the date of perfection; or

(B) provides for the maintenance or continuation of perfection of an interest in property to be effective against an entity that acquires rights in such property before the date on which action is taken to effect such maintenance or continuation.

(2) If–

(A) a law described in paragraph (1) requires seizure of such property or commencement of an action to accomplish such perfection, or maintenance or continuation of perfection of an interest in property; and

(B) such property has not been seized or such an action has not been commenced before the date of the filing of the petition;

such interest in such property shall be perfected, or perfection of such interest shall be maintained or continued, by giving notice within the time fixed by such law for such seizure or such commencement.

(c) (1) Except as provided in subsection (d) of this section and in section 507(c), and subject to the prior rights of a holder of a security interest in such goods or the proceeds thereof, the rights and powers of the trustee under sections 544(a), 545, 547, and 549 are subject to the right of a seller of goods that has sold goods to the debtor, in the ordinary course of such seller's business, to reclaim such goods if the debtor has received such goods while insolvent, within 45 days before the date of the commencement of a case under this title, but such a seller may not reclaim such goods unless such seller demands in writing reclamation of such goods–

(A) not later than 45 days after the date of receipt of such goods by the debtor; or

(B) not later than 20 days after the date of commencement of the case, if the 45-day period expires after the commencement of the case.

(2) If a seller of goods fails to provide notice in the manner described in paragraph (1), the seller still may assert the rights contained in section 503(b)(9).

(d) In the case of a seller who is a producer of grain sold to a grain storage facility, owned or operated by the debtor, in the ordinary course of such seller's business (as such terms are defined in section 557 of this title) or in the case of a United States fisherman who has caught fish sold to a fish processing facility owned or operated by the debtor in the ordinary course of such fisherman's business, the rights and powers of the trustee under sections 544(a), 545, 547, and 549 of this title are subject to any statutory or common law right of such producer or fisherman to reclaim such grain or fish if the debtor has received such grain or fish while insolvent, but–

(1) such producer or fisherman may not reclaim any grain or fish unless such producer or fisherman demands, in writing, reclamation of such grain or fish before ten days after receipt thereof by the debtor; and

(2) the court may deny reclamation to such a producer or fisherman with a right of reclamation that has made such a demand only if the court secures such claim by a lien.

(e) Notwithstanding sections 544, 545, 547, 548(a)(1)(B), and 548(b) of this title, the trustee may not avoid a transfer that is a margin payment, as defined in section 101, 741, or 761 of this title, or settlement payment as defined in section 101 or 741 of this title, made by or to (or for the benefit of) a commodity broker, forward contract merchant, stockbroker, financial institution, financial participant, or securities clearing agency, or that is a transfer made by or to (or for the benefit of) a commodity broker, forward contract merchant, stockbroker, financial institution, financial participant, or securities clearing agency, in connection with a securities contract, as defined in section 741(7), commodity contract, as defined in section 761(4), or forward contract, that is made before the commencement of the case, except under section 548(a)(1)(A) of this title.

(f) Notwithstanding sections 544, 545, 547, 548(a)(1)(B), and 548(b) of this title, the trustee may not avoid a transfer made by or to (or for the benefit of) a repo participant or financial participant, in connection with a repurchase agreement and that is made before the commencement of the case, except under section 548(a)(1)(A) of this title.

(g) Notwithstanding sections 544, 545, 547, 548(a)(1)(B) and 548(b) of this title, the trustee may not avoid a transfer, made by or to (or for the benefit of) a swap participant or financial participant, under or in connection with any swap agreement and that is made before the commencement of the case, except under section 548(a)(1)(A) of this title.

(h) Notwithstanding the rights and powers of a trustee under sections 544(a), 545, 547, 549, and 553, if the court determines on a motion by the trustee made not later than 120 days after the date of the order for relief in a case under chapter 11 of this title and after notice and a hearing, that a return is in the best interests of the estate, the debtor, with the consent of a creditor and subject to the prior rights of holders of security interests in such goods or the proceeds of such goods, may return goods shipped to the debtor by the creditor before the commencement of the case, and the creditor may offset the purchase price of such goods against any claim of the creditor against the debtor that arose before the commencement of the case.

(i) (1) Notwithstanding paragraphs (2) and (3) of section 545, the trustee may not avoid a warehouseman's lien for storage, transportation, or other costs incidental to the storage and handling of goods.

(2) The prohibition under paragraph (1) shall be applied in a manner consistent with any State statute applicable to such lien that is similar to section 7-209 of the Uniform Commercial Code, as in effect on the date of enactment of the Bankruptcy Abuse Prevention and Consumer Protection Act of 2005, or any successor to such section 7-209.

(j) Notwithstanding sections 544, 545, 547, 548(a)(1)(B), and 548(b) the trustee may not avoid a transfer made by or to (or for the benefit of) a master netting agreement participant under or in connection with any master netting agreement or any individual contract covered thereby that is made before the commencement of the case, except under section 548(a)(1)(A) and except to the extent that the trustee could otherwise avoid such a transfer made under an individual contract covered by such master netting agreement.

## § 547 Preferences

(a) In this section—

(1) "inventory" means personal property leased or furnished, held for sale or lease, or to be furnished under a contract for service, raw materials, work in process, or materials used or consumed in a business, including farm products such as crops or livestock, held for sale or lease;

(2) "new value" means money or money's worth in goods, services, or new credit, or release by a transferee of property previously transferred to such transferee in a transaction that is neither void nor voidable by the debtor or the trustee under any applicable law, including proceeds of such property, but does not include an obligation substituted for an existing obligation;

(3) "receivable" means right to payment, whether or not such right has been earned by performance; and

(4) a debt for a tax is incurred on the day when such tax is last payable without penalty, including any extension.

(b) Except as provided in subsections (c) ~~and (i)~~, (i), and (j)[60] of this section, the trustee may, based on reasonable due diligence in the circumstances of the case and taking into account a party's known or reasonably knowable affirmative defenses under subsection (c), avoid any transfer of an interest of the debtor in property—

(1) to or for the benefit of a creditor;

(2) for or on account of an antecedent debt owed by the debtor before such transfer was made;

(3) made while the debtor was insolvent;

(4) made—

(A) on or within 90 days before the date of the filing of the petition; or

(B) between ninety days and one year before the date of the filing of the petition, if such creditor at the time of such transfer was an insider; and

(5) that enables such creditor to receive more than such creditor would receive if—

(A) the case were a case under chapter 7 of this title;

(B) the transfer had not been made; and

(C) such creditor received payment of such debt to the extent provided by the provisions of this title.

---

[60] Section 547(b) was amended by the Consolidated Appropriations Act, 2021, Pub. L. No. 116-260, div. FF, tit. X, § 1001(g)(1)(A). New material is underscored; removed material is stricken out. The amendment will sunset two years after the date of enactment of the Act, which was December 27, 2020. Pub. L. No. 116-260, div. FF, tit. X, § 1001(g)(2).

(c) The trustee may not avoid under this section a transfer—

(1) to the extent that such transfer was—

(A) intended by the debtor and the creditor to or for whose benefit such transfer was made to be a contemporaneous exchange for new value given to the debtor; and

(B) in fact a substantially contemporaneous exchange;

(2) to the extent that such transfer was in payment of a debt incurred by the debtor in the ordinary course of business or financial affairs of the debtor and the transferee, and such transfer was—

(A) made in the ordinary course of business or financial affairs of the debtor and the transferee; or

(B) made according to ordinary business terms;

(3) that creates a security interest in property acquired by the debtor—

(A) to the extent such security interest secures new value that was—

(i) given at or after the signing of a security agreement that contains a description of such property as collateral;

(ii) given by or on behalf of the secured party under such agreement;

(iii) given to enable the debtor to acquire such property; and

(iv) in fact used by the debtor to acquire such property; and

(B) that is perfected on or before 30 days after the debtor receives possession of such property;

(4) to or for the benefit of a creditor, to the extent that, after such transfer, such creditor gave new value to or for the benefit of the debtor—

(A) not secured by an otherwise unavoidable security interest; and

(B) on account of which new value the debtor did not make an otherwise unavoidable transfer to or for the benefit of such creditor;

(5) that creates a perfected security interest in inventory or a receivable or the proceeds of either, except to the extent that the aggregate of all such transfers to the transferee caused a reduction, as of the date of the filing of the petition and to the prejudice of other creditors holding unsecured claims, of any amount by which the debt secured by such security interest exceeded the value of all security interests for such debt on the later of—

(A) (i) with respect to a transfer to which subsection (b)(4)(A) of this section applies, 90 days before the date of the filing of the petition; or

(ii) with respect to a transfer to which subsection (b)(4)(B) of this section applies, one year before the date of the filing of the petition; or

(B) the date on which new value was first given under the security agreement creating such security interest;

(6) that is the fixing of a statutory lien that is not avoidable under section 545 of this title;

(7) to the extent such transfer was a bona fide payment of a debt for a domestic support obligation;

(8) if, in a case filed by an individual debtor whose debts are primarily consumer debts, the aggregate value of all property that constitutes or is affected by such transfer is less than $600; or

(9) if, in a case filed by a debtor whose debts are not primarily consumer debts, the aggregate value of all property that constitutes or is affected by such transfer is less than $6,825.[61]

(d) The trustee may avoid a transfer of an interest in property of the debtor transferred to or for the benefit of a surety to secure reimbursement of such a surety that furnished a bond or other obligation to dissolve a judicial lien that would have been avoidable by the trustee under subsection (b) of this section. The liability of such surety under such bond or obligation shall be discharged to the extent of the value of such property recovered by the trustee or the amount paid to the trustee.

(e) (1) For the purposes of this section—

(A) a transfer of real property other than fixtures, but including the interest of a seller or purchaser under a contract for the sale of real property, is perfected when a bona fide purchaser of such property from the debtor against whom applicable law permits such transfer to be perfected cannot acquire an interest that is superior to the interest of the transferee; and

(B) a transfer of a fixture or property other than real property is perfected when a creditor on a simple contract cannot acquire a judicial lien that is superior to the interest of the transferee.

(2) For the purposes of this section, except as provided in paragraph (3) of this subsection, a transfer is made—

(A) at the time such transfer takes effect between the transferor and the transferee, if such transfer is perfected at, or within 30 days after, such time, except as provided in subsection (c)(3)(B);

(B) at the time such transfer is perfected, if such transfer is perfected after such 30 days; or

(C) immediately before the date of the filing of the petition, if such transfer is not perfected at the later of—

(i) the commencement of the case; or

---

[61] ED. NOTE: For cases commenced in the three-year period before April 1, 2019, the dollar amount is $6,425.

(ii) 30 days after such transfer takes effect between the transferor and the transferee.

(3) For the purposes of this section, a transfer is not made until the debtor has acquired rights in the property transferred.

(f) For the purposes of this section, the debtor is presumed to have been insolvent on and during the 90 days immediately preceding the date of the filing of the petition.

(g) For the purposes of this section, the trustee has the burden of proving the avoidability of a transfer under subsection (b) of this section, and the creditor or party in interest against whom recovery or avoidance is sought has the burden of proving the nonavoidability of a transfer under subsection (c) of this section.

(h) The trustee may not avoid a transfer if such transfer was made as a part of an alternative repayment schedule between the debtor and any creditor of the debtor created by an approved nonprofit budgeting and credit counseling agency.

(i) If the trustee avoids under subsection (b) a transfer made between 90 days and 1 year before the date of the filing of the petition, by the debtor to an entity that is not an insider for the benefit of a creditor that is an insider, such transfer shall be considered to be avoided under this section only with respect to the creditor that is an insider.

(j) (1) In this subsection:

(A) The term "covered payment of rental arrearages" means a payment of arrearages that—

(i) is made in connection with an agreement or arrangement—

(I) between the debtor and a lessor to defer or postpone the payment of rent and other periodic charges under a lease of nonresidential real property; and

(II) made or entered into on or after March 13, 2020;

(ii) does not exceed the amount of rental and other periodic charges agreed to under the lease of nonresidential real property described in clause (i)(I) before March 13, 2020; and

(iii) does not include fees, penalties, or interest in an amount greater than the amount of fees, penalties, or interest—

(I) scheduled to be paid under the lease of nonresidential real property described in clause (i)(I); or

(II) that the debtor would owe if the debtor had made every payment due under the lease of nonresidential real property described in clause (i)(I) on time and in full before March 13, 2020.

(B) The term "covered payment of supplier arrearages" means a payment of arrearages that—

(i) is made in connection with an agreement or arrangement—

(I) between the debtor and a supplier of goods or services to defer or postpone the payment of amounts due under an executory contract for goods or services; and

(II) made or entered into on or after March 13, 2020;

(ii) does not exceed the amount due under the executory contract described in clause (i)(I) before March 13, 2020; and

(iii) does not include fees, penalties, or interest in an amount greater than the amount of fees, penalties, or interest—

(I) scheduled to be paid under the executory contract described in clause (i)(I); or

(II) that the debtor would owe if the debtor had made every payment due under the executory contract described in clause (i)(I) on time and in full before March 13, 2020.

(2) The trustee may not avoid a transfer under this section for—

(A) a covered payment of rental arrearages; or

(B) a covered payment of supplier arrearages.[62]

Bankruptcy Rule References: 6010, 7001 and 9017

## § 548 Fraudulent transfers and obligations

(a) (1) The trustee may avoid any transfer (including any transfer to or for the benefit of an insider under an employment contract) of an interest of the debtor in property, or any obligation (including any obligation to or for the benefit of an insider under an employment contract) incurred by the debtor, that was made or incurred on or within 2 years[63] before the date of the filing of the petition, if the debtor voluntarily or involuntarily—

(A) made such transfer or incurred such obligation with actual intent to hinder, delay, or defraud any entity to which the debtor was or became, on or after the date that such transfer was made or such obligation was incurred, indebted; or

(B) (i) received less than a reasonably equivalent value in exchange for such transfer or obligation; and

(ii) (I) was insolvent on the date that such transfer was made or such

---

[62] Ed. note: Underscored material enacted by the Consolidated Appropriations Act, 2021, Pub. L. No. 116-260, div. FF, tit. X, § 1001(g)(1)(B). The amendment will sunset two years after the date of enactment of the Act, which was December 27, 2020. Pub. L. No. 116-260, div. FF, tit. X, § 1001(g)(2).

[63] Ed. note: Section 1406(b)(2) of the 2005 Act provides: "Avoidance period.—The amendment made by section 1402(1) [of the 2005 Act] [changing 'one year' to '2 years' in paragraphs (a)(1) and (b)(1) of Code section 548] shall apply only with respect to cases commenced under title 11 of the United States Code more than 1 year after the date of the enactment of this Act."

obligation was incurred, or became insolvent as a result of such transfer or obligation;

(II) was engaged in business or a transaction, or was about to engage in business or a transaction, for which any property remaining with the debtor was an unreasonably small capital;

(III) intended to incur, or believed that the debtor would incur, debts that would be beyond the debtor's ability to pay as such debts matured; or

(IV) made such transfer to or for the benefit of an insider, or incurred such obligation to or for the benefit of an insider, under an employment contract and not in the ordinary course of business.

(2) A transfer of a charitable contribution to a qualified religious or charitable entity or organization shall not be considered to be a transfer covered under paragraph (1)(B) in any case in which—

(A) the amount of that contribution does not exceed 15 percent of the gross annual income of the debtor for the year in which the transfer of the contribution is made; or

(B) the contribution made by a debtor exceeded the percentage amount of gross annual income specified in subparagraph (A), if the transfer was consistent with the practices of the debtor in making charitable contributions.

(b) The trustee of a partnership debtor may avoid any transfer of an interest of the debtor in property, or any obligation incurred by the debtor, that was made or incurred on or within 2 years[64] before the date of the filing of the petition, to a general partner in the debtor, if the debtor was insolvent on the date such transfer was made or such obligation was incurred, or became insolvent as a result of such transfer or obligation.

(c) Except to the extent that a transfer or obligation voidable under this section is voidable under section 544, 545, or 547 of this title, a transferee or obligee of such a transfer or obligation that takes for value and in good faith has a lien on or may retain any interest transferred or may enforce any obligation incurred, as the case may be, to the extent that such transferee or obligee gave value to the debtor in exchange for such transfer or obligation.

(d) (1) For the purposes of this section, a transfer is made when such transfer is so perfected that a bona fide purchaser from the debtor against whom applicable law permits such transfer to be perfected cannot acquire an interest in the property transferred that is superior to the interest in such property of the transferee, but if such transfer is not so perfected before the commencement of the case, such transfer is made immediately before the date of the filing of the petition.

(2) In this section—

---

[64] Ed. Note: *See* note 63 *supra.*

(A) "value" means property, or satisfaction or securing of a present or antecedent debt of the debtor, but does not include an unperformed promise to furnish support to the debtor or to a relative of the debtor;

(B) a commodity broker, forward contract merchant, stockbroker, financial institution, financial participant, or securities clearing agency that receives a margin payment, as defined in section 101, 741, or 761 of this title, or settlement payment, as defined in section 101 or 741 of this title, takes for value to the extent of such payment;

(C) a repo participant or financial participant that receives a margin payment, as defined in section 741 or 761 of this title, or settlement payment, as defined in section 741 of this title, in connection with a repurchase agreement, takes for value to the extent of such payment;

(D) a swap participant or financial participant that receives a transfer in connection with a swap agreement takes for value to the extent of such transfer; and

(E) a master netting agreement participant that receives a transfer in connection with a master netting agreement or any individual contract covered thereby takes for value to the extent of such transfer, except that, with respect to a transfer under any individual contract covered thereby, to the extent that such master netting agreement participant otherwise did not take (or is otherwise not deemed to have taken) such transfer for value.

(3) In this section, the term "charitable contribution" means a charitable contribution, as that term is defined in section 170(c)[65] of the Internal Revenue

---

[65] ED. NOTE: Internal Revenue Code section 170(c)(1)–(2) states:

(c) Charitable contribution defined.—For purposes of this section, the term "charitable contribution" means a contribution or gift to or for the use of—

(1) A State, a possession of the United States, or any political subdivision of any of the foregoing, or the United States or the District of Columbia, but only if the contribution or gift is made for exclusively public purposes.

(2) A corporation, trust, or community chest, fund, or foundation—

(A) created or organized in the United States or in any possession thereof, or under the law of the United States, any State, the District of Columbia, or any possession of the United States;

(B) organized and operated exclusively for religious, charitable, scientific, literary, or educational purposes, or to foster national or international amateur sports competition (but only if no part of its activities involve the provision of athletic facilities or equipment), or for the prevention of cruelty to children or animals;

(C) no part of the net earnings of which inures to the benefit of any private shareholder or individual; and

(D) which is not disqualified for tax exemption under section 501(c)(3) by reason of attempting to influence legislation, and which does not participate in, or intervene in (including the publishing or distributing of statements), any political campaign on behalf of (or in opposition to) any candidate for public office.

A contribution or gift by a corporation to a trust, chest, fund, or foundation shall be deductible by reason of this paragraph only if it is to be used within the United States or any of its possessions exclusively for purposes specified in subparagraph (B). Rules similar to the rules of section 501(j) shall apply for purposes of this paragraph.

Code of 1986, if that contribution—

(A) is made by a natural person; and

(B) consists of—

(i) a financial instrument (as that term is defined in section 731(c)(2)(C)[66] of the Internal Revenue Code of 1986); or

(ii) cash.

(4) In this section, the term "qualified religious or charitable entity or organization" means—

(A) an entity described in section 170(c)(1) of the Internal Revenue Code of 1986; or

(B) an entity or organization described in section 170(c)(2) of the Internal Revenue Code of 1986.

(e) (1) In addition to any transfer that the trustee may otherwise avoid, the trustee may avoid any transfer of an interest of the debtor in property that was made on or within 10 years before the date of the filing of the petition if—

(A) such transfer was made to a self-settled trust or similar device;

(B) such transfer was by the debtor;

(C) the debtor is a beneficiary of such trust or similar device; and

(D) the debtor made such transfer with actual intent to hinder, delay, or defraud any entity to which the debtor was or became, on or after the date that such transfer was made, indebted.

(2) For the purposes of this subsection, a transfer includes a transfer made in anticipation of any money judgment, settlement, civil penalty, equitable order, or criminal fine incurred by, or which the debtor believed would be incurred by—

(A) any violation of the securities laws (as defined in section 3(a)(47) of the Securities Exchange Act of 1934 (15 U.S.C. 78c(a)(47))), any State securities laws, or any regulation or order issued under Federal securities laws or State securities laws; or

(B) fraud, deceit, or manipulation in a fiduciary capacity or in connection with the purchase or sale of any security registered under section 12 of 15(d) of the Securities Exchange Act of 1934 (15 U.S.C. 78l and 78o(d)) or under section 6 of the Securities Act of 1933 (15 U.S.C. 77f).

Bankruptcy Rule Reference: 7001

---

[66] Ed. note: Internal Revenue Code section 731(c)(2)(C) states:

(C) Financial instrument.—The term "financial instrument" includes stocks and other equity interests, evidences of indebtedness, options, forward or futures contracts, notional principal contracts, and derivatives.

## § 549 Postpetition transactions

(a) Except as provided in subsection (b) or (c) of this section, the trustee may avoid a transfer of property of the estate—

(1) that occurs after the commencement of the case; and

(2) (A) that is authorized only under section 303(f) or 542(c) of this title; or

(B) that is not authorized under this title or by the court.

(b) In an involuntary case, the trustee may not avoid under subsection (a) of this section a transfer made after the commencement of such case but before the order for relief to the extent any value, including services, but not including satisfaction or securing of a debt that arose before the commencement of the case, is given after the commencement of the case in exchange for such transfer, notwithstanding any notice or knowledge of the case that the transferee has.

(c) The trustee may not avoid under subsection (a) of this section a transfer of an interest in real property to a good faith purchaser without knowledge of the commencement of the case and for present fair equivalent value unless a copy or notice of the petition was filed, where a transfer of an interest in such real property may be recorded to perfect such transfer, before such transfer is so perfected that a bona fide purchaser of such real property, against whom applicable law permits such transfer to be perfected, could not acquire an interest that is superior to such interest of such good faith purchaser. A good faith purchaser without knowledge of the commencement of the case and for less than present fair equivalent value has a lien on the property transferred to the extent of any present value given, unless a copy or notice of the petition was so filed before such transfer was so perfected.

(d) An action or proceeding under this section may not be commenced after the earlier of—

(1) two years after the date of the transfer sought to be avoided; or

(2) the time the case is closed

## § 550 Liability of transferee of avoided transfer

(a) Except as otherwise provided in this section, to the extent that a transfer is avoided under section 544, 545, 547, 548, 549, 553(b), or 724(a) of this title, the trustee may recover, for the benefit of the estate, the property transferred, or, if the court so orders, the value of such property, from—

(1) the initial transferee of such transfer or the entity for whose benefit such transfer was made; or

(2) any immediate or mediate transferee of such initial transferee.

(b) The trustee may not recover under section (a)(2) of this section from—

(1) a transferee that takes for value, including satisfaction or securing of a present or antecedent debt, in good faith, and without knowledge of the voidability of the transfer avoided; or

(2) any immediate or mediate good faith transferee of such transferee.

(c) If a transfer made between 90 days and one year before the filing of the petition—

(1) is avoided under section 547(b) of this title; and

(2) was made for the benefit of a creditor that at the time of such transfer was an insider;

the trustee may not recover under subsection (a) from a transferee that is not an insider.

(d) The trustee is entitled to only a single satisfaction under subsection (a) of this section.

(e) (1) A good faith transferee from whom the trustee may recover under subsection (a) of this section has a lien on the property recovered to secure the lesser of—

(A) the cost, to such transferee, of any improvement made after the transfer, less the amount of any profit realized by or accruing to such transferee from such property; and

(B) any increase in the value of such property as a result of such improvement, of the property transferred.

(2) In this subsection, "improvement" includes—

(A) physical additions or changes to the property transferred;

(B) repairs to such property;

(C) payment of any tax on such property;

(D) payment of any debt secured by a lien on such property that is superior or equal to the rights of the trustee; and

(E) preservation of such property.

(f) An action or proceeding under this section may not be commenced after the earlier of—

(1) one year after the avoidance of the transfer on account of which recovery under this section is sought; or

(2) the time the case is closed

Bankruptcy Rule References: 6010 and 7001

## § 551 Automatic preservation of avoided transfer

Any transfer avoided under section 522, 544, 545, 547, 548, 549, or 724(a) of this title, or any lien void under section 506(d) of this title, is preserved for the benefit of the estate but only with respect to property of the estate.

## § 552 Postpetition effect of security interest

(a) Except as provided in subsection (b) of this section, property acquired by the estate or by the debtor after the commencement of the case is not subject to any lien resulting from any security agreement entered into by the debtor before the commencement of the case.

(b) (1) Except as provided in sections 363, 506(c), 522, 544, 545, 547, and 548 of this title, if the debtor and an entity entered into a security agreement before the commencement of the case and if the security interest created by such security agreement extends to property of the debtor acquired before the commencement of the case and to proceeds, products, offspring, or profits of such property, then such security interest extends to such proceeds, products, offspring, or profits acquired by the estate after the commencement of the case to the extent provided by such security agreement and by applicable nonbankruptcy law, except to any extent that the court, after notice and a hearing and based on the equities of the case, orders otherwise.

(2) Except as provided in sections 363, 506(c), 522, 544, 545, 547, and 548 of this title, and notwithstanding section 546(b) of this title, if the debtor and an entity entered into a security agreement before the commencement of the case and if the security interest created by such security agreement extends to property of the debtor acquired before the commencement of the case and to amounts paid as rents of such property or the fees, charges, accounts, or other payments for the use or occupancy of rooms and other public facilities in hotels, motels, or other lodging properties, then such security interest extends to such rents and such fees, charges, accounts, or other payments acquired by the estate after the commencement of the case to the extent provided in such security agreement, except to any extent that the court, after notice and a hearing and based on the equities of the case, orders otherwise.

**§ 553 Setoff**

(a) Except as otherwise provided in this section and in sections 362 and 363 of this title, this title does not affect any right of a creditor to offset a mutual debt owing by such creditor to the debtor that arose before the commencement of the case under this title against a claim of such creditor against the debtor that arose before the commencement of the case, except to the extent that–

(1) the claim of such creditor against the debtor is disallowed;

(2) such claim was transferred, by an entity other than the debtor, to such creditor–

(A) after the commencement of the case; or

(B) (i) after 90 days before the date of the filing of the petition; and

(ii) while the debtor was insolvent (except for a setoff of a kind described in section 362(b)(6), 362(b)(7), 362(b)(17), 362(b)(27), 555, 556, 559, 560, or 561); or

(3) the debt owed to the debtor by such creditor was incurred by such creditor–

(A) after 90 days before the date of the filing of the petition;

(B) while the debtor was insolvent; and

(C) for the purpose of obtaining a right of setoff against the debtor (except for a setoff of a kind described in section 362(b)(6), 362(b)(7), 362(b)(17), 362(b)(27), 555, 556, 559, 560, or 561).

(b) (1) Except with respect to a setoff of a kind described in section 362(b)(6), 362(b)(7), 362(b)(17), 362(b)(27), 555, 556, 559, 560, 561, 365(h), 546(h), or 365(i)(2) of this title, if a creditor offsets a mutual debt owing to the debtor against a claim against the debtor on or within 90 days before the date of the filing of the petition, then the trustee may recover from such creditor the amount so offset to the extent that any insufficiency on the date of such setoff is less than the insufficiency on the later of—

(A) 90 days before the date of the filing of the petition; and

(B) the first date during the 90 days immediately preceding the date of the filing of the petition on which there is an insufficiency.

(2) In this subsection, "insufficiency" means amount, if any, by which a claim against the debtor exceeds a mutual debt owing to the debtor by the holder of such claim.

(c) For the purposes of this section, the debtor is presumed to have been insolvent on and during the 90 days immediately preceding the date of the filing of the petition.

## § 554 Abandonment of property of the estate

(a) After notice and a hearing, the trustee may abandon any property of the estate that is burdensome to the estate or that is of inconsequential value and benefit to the estate.

(b) On request of a party in interest and after notice and a hearing, the court may order the trustee to abandon any property of the estate that is burdensome to the estate or that is of inconsequential value and benefit to the estate.

(c) Unless the court orders otherwise, any property scheduled under section 521(a)(1) of this title not otherwise administered at the time of the closing of a case is abandoned to the debtor and administered for purposes of section 350 of this title.

(d) Unless the court orders otherwise, property of the estate that is not abandoned under this section and that is not administered in the case remains property of the estate.

BANKRUPTCY RULE REFERENCES: 3022, 5009, 6007, 7001, 9013 and 9014

## § 555 Contractual right to liquidate, terminate, or accelerate a securities contract

The exercise of a contractual right of a stockbroker, financial institution, financial participant, or securities clearing agency to cause the liquidation, termination, or acceleration of a securities contract, as defined in section 741 of this title, because of a condition of the kind specified in section 365(e)(1) of this title shall not be stayed, avoided, or otherwise limited by operation of any provision of this title or by order of a court or administrative agency in any proceeding under this title unless such order is authorized under the provisions of the Securities Investor Protection Act of 1970 or any statute administered by the Securities and Exchange Commission. As used in this section, the term "contractual right" includes a right set forth in a rule or bylaw of a derivatives clearing organization (as defined in the Commodity Exchange Act), a multilateral clearing organization (as defined in the Federal Deposit Insurance Corporation Improvement Act of 1991), a national securities exchange, a national securities association, a securities clearing agency, a contract market designated under the Commodity Exchange Act, a derivatives transaction execution facility registered under the Commodity Exchange Act, or a board of trade (as defined in the Commodity Exchange Act), or in a resolution of the governing board thereof, and a right, whether or not in writing, arising under common law, under law merchant, or by reason of normal business practice.

## § 556 Contractual right to liquidate, terminate, or accelerate a commodities contract or forward contract

The contractual right of a commodity broker, financial participant, or forward contract merchant to cause the liquidation, termination, or acceleration of a commodity contract, as defined in section 761 of this title, or forward contract because of a condition of the kind specified in section 365(e)(1) of this title, and the right to a variation or maintenance margin payment received from a trustee with respect to open commodity contracts or forward contracts, shall not be stayed, avoided, or otherwise limited by operation of any provision of this title or by the order of a court in any proceeding under this title. As used in this section, the term "contractual right" includes a right set forth in a rule or bylaw of a derivatives clearing organization (as defined in the Commodity Exchange Act), a multilateral clearing organization (as defined in the Federal Deposit Insurance Corporation Improvement Act of 1991), a national securities exchange, a national securities association, a securities clearing agency, a contract market designated under the Commodity Exchange Act, a derivatives transaction execution facility registered under the Commodity Exchange Act, or a board of trade (as defined in the Commodity Exchange Act) or in a resolution of the governing board thereof and a right, whether or not evidenced in writing, arising under common law, under law merchant or by reason of normal business practice.

## § 557 Expedited determination of interests in, and abandonment or other disposition of grain assets

(a) This section applies only in a case concerning a debtor that owns or operates a grain storage facility and only with respect to grain and the proceeds of grain. This section does not affect the application of any other section of this title to property other than grain and proceeds of grain.

(b) In this section—

(1) "grain" means wheat, corn, flaxseed, grain sorghum, barley, oats, rye, soybeans, other dry edible beans, or rice;

(2) "grain storage facility" means a site or physical structure regularly used to store grain for producers, or to store grain acquired from producers for resale; and

(3) "producer" means an entity which engages in the growing of grain.

(c) (1) Notwithstanding sections 362, 363, 365, and 554 of this title, on the court's own motion the court may, and on the request of the trustee or an entity that claims an interest in grain or the proceeds of grain the court shall, expedite the procedures for the determination of interests in and the disposition of grain and the proceeds of grain, by shortening to the greatest extent feasible such time periods as are otherwise applicable for such procedures and by establishing, by order, a timetable having a duration of not to exceed 120 days for the completion of the applicable procedure specified in subsection (d) of this section. Such time periods and such timetable may be modified by the court, for cause, in accordance with subsection (f) of this section.

(2) The court shall determine the extent to which such time periods shall be shortened, based upon—

(A) any need of an entity claiming an interest in such grain or the proceeds of grain for a prompt determination of such interest;

(B) any need of such entity for a prompt disposition of such grain;

(C) the market for such grain;

(D) the conditions under which such grain is stored;

(E) the costs of continued storage or disposition of such grain;

(F) the orderly administration of the estate;

(G) the appropriate opportunity for an entity to assert an interest in such grain; and

(H) such other considerations as are relevant to the need to expedite such procedures in the case.

(d) The procedures that may be expedited under subsection (c) of this section include—

(1) the filing of and response to—

(A) a claim of ownership;

(B) a proof of claim;

(C) a request for abandonment;

(D) a request for relief from the stay of action against property under section 362(a) of this title;

(E) a request for determination of secured status;

(F) a request for determination of whether such grain or the proceeds of grain—

(i) is property of the estate;

(ii) must be turned over to the estate; or

(iii) may be used, sold, or leased; and

(G) any other request for determination of an interest in such grain or the proceeds of grain;

(2) the disposition of such grain or the proceeds of grain, before or after determination of interests in such grain or the proceeds of grain, by way of—

(A) sale of such grain;

(B) abandonment;

(C) distribution; or

(D) such other method as is equitable in the case;

(3) subject to sections 701, 702, 703, 1104, 1183, 1202, and 1302 of this title, the appointment of a trustee or examiner and the retention and compensation of any professional person required to assist with respect to matters relevant to the determination of interests in or disposition of such grain or the proceeds of grain; and

(4) the determination of any dispute concerning a matter specified in paragraph (1), (2), or (3) of this subsection.

(e) (1) Any governmental unit that has regulatory jurisdiction over the operation or liquidation of the debtor or the debtor's business shall be given notice of any request made or order entered under subsection (c) of this section.

(2) Any such governmental unit may raise, and may appear and be heard on, any issue relating to grain or the proceeds of grain in a case in which a request is made, or an order is entered, under subsection (c) of this section.

(3) The trustee shall consult with such governmental unit before taking any action relating to the disposition of grain in the possession, custody, or control of the debtor or the estate.

(f) The court may extend the period for final disposition of grain or the proceeds of grain under this section beyond 120 days if the court finds that—

(1) the interests of justice so require in light of the complexity of the case; and

(2) the interests of those claimants entitled to distribution of grain or the proceeds of grain will not be materially injured by such additional delay.

(g) Unless an order establishing an expedited procedure under subsection (c) of this section, or determining any interest in or approving any disposition of grain or the proceeds of grain, is stayed pending appeal—

(1) the reversal or modification of such order on appeal does not affect the validity of any procedure, determination, or disposition that occurs before such

reversal or modification, whether or not any entity knew of the pendency of the appeal; and

(2) neither the court nor the trustee may delay, due to the appeal of such order, any proceeding in the case in which such order is issued.

(h) (1) The trustee may recover from grain and the proceeds of grain the reasonable and necessary costs and expenses allowable under section 503(b) of this title attributable to preserving or disposing of grain or the proceeds of grain, but may not recover from such grain or the proceeds of grain any other costs or expenses.

(2) Notwithstanding section 326(a) of this title, the dollar amounts of money specified in such section include the value, as of the date of disposition, of any grain that the trustee distributes in kind.

(i) In all cases where the quantity of a specific type of grain held by a debtor operating a grain storage facility exceeds ten thousand bushels, such grain shall be sold by the trustee and the assets thereof distributed in accordance with the provisions of this section.

Bankruptcy Rule Reference: 3001

## § 558 Defenses of the estate

The estate shall have the benefit of any defense available to the debtor as against any entity other than the estate, including statutes of limitation, statutes of frauds, usury, and other personal defenses. A waiver of any such defense by the debtor after the commencement of the case does not bind the estate.

Bankruptcy Rule References: 3007, 6009, 9013 and 9014

## § 559 Contractual right to liquidate, terminate, or accelerate a repurchase agreement

The exercise of a contractual right of a repo participant or financial participant to cause the liquidation, termination or acceleration of a repurchase agreement because of a condition of the kind specified in section 365(e)(1) of this title shall not be stayed, avoided, or otherwise limited by operation of any provision of this title or by order of a court or administrative agency in any proceeding under this title, unless, where the debtor is a stockbroker or securities clearing agency, such order is authorized under the provisions of the Securities Investor Protection Act of 1970 or any statute administered by the Securities and Exchange Commission. In the event that a repo participant or financial participant liquidates one or more repurchase agreements with a debtor and under the terms of one or more such agreements has agreed to deliver assets subject to repurchase agreements to the debtor, any excess of the market prices received on liquidation of such assets (or if any such assets are not disposed of on the date of liquidation of such repurchase agreements, at the prices available at the time of liquidation of such repurchase agreements from a generally recognized source or the most recent closing bid quotation from such a source) over the sum of the stated repurchase prices and all expenses in connection with the liquidation of such repurchase agreements shall be deemed property of the estate, subject to the available rights of setoff. As used in this section, the term "contractual right" includes a right set forth in a rule or bylaw of a derivatives clearing organization (as defined in the Commodity Exchange Act), a multilateral clearing organization (as defined in the Federal Deposit Insurance Corporation Improvement Act of 1991), a national securities exchange, a national securities association, a securities clearing agency, a contract market designated under the Commodity Exchange Act, a derivatives transaction execution facility registered under the Commodity Exchange Act, or a board of trade (as defined in the Commodity Exchange Act) or in a resolution of the governing board thereof and a right, whether or not evidenced in writing, arising under common law, under law merchant or by reason of normal business practice.

**§ 560 Contractual right to liquidate terminate, or accelerate a swap agreement**

The exercise of any contractual right of any swap participant or financial participant to cause the liquidation, termination, or acceleration of one or more swap agreements because of a condition of the kind specified in section 365(e)(1) of this title or to offset or net out any termination values or payment amounts arising under or in connection with the termination, liquidation, or acceleration of one or more swap agreements shall not be stayed, avoided, or otherwise limited by operation of any provision of this title or by order of a court or administrative agency in any proceeding under this title. As used in this section, the term "contractual right" includes a right set forth in a rule or bylaw of a derivatives clearing organization (as defined in the Commodity Exchange Act), a multilateral clearing organization (as defined in the Federal Deposit Insurance Corporation Improvement Act of 1991), a national securities exchange, a national securities association, a securities clearing agency, a contract market designated under the Commodity Exchange Act, a derivatives transaction execution facility registered under the Commodity Exchange Act, or a board of trade (as defined in the Commodity Exchange Act) or in a resolution of the governing board thereof and a right, whether or not evidenced in writing, arising under common law, under law merchant, or by reason of normal business practice.

**§ 561 Contractual right to terminate, liquidate, accelerate, or offset under a master netting agreement and across contracts; proceedings under chapter 15**

(a) Subject to subsection (b), the exercise of any contractual right, because of a condition of the kind specified in section 365(e)(1), to cause the termination, liquidation, or acceleration of or to offset or net termination values, payment amounts, or other transfer obligations arising under or in connection with one or more (or the termination, liquidation, or acceleration of one or more)—

(1) securities contracts, as defined in section 741(7);

(2) commodity contracts, as defined in section 761(4);

(3) forward contracts;

(4) repurchase agreements;

(5) swap agreements; or

(6) master netting agreements,

shall not be stayed, avoided, or otherwise limited by operation of any provision of this title or by any order of a court or administrative agency in any proceeding under this title.

(b) (1) A party may exercise a contractual right described in subsection (a) to terminate, liquidate, or accelerate only to the extent that such party could exercise such a right under section 555, 556, 559, or 560 for each individual contract covered by the master netting agreement in issue.

(2) If a debtor is a commodity broker subject to subchapter IV of chapter 7—

(A) a party may not net or offset an obligation to the debtor arising under, or in connection with, a commodity contract traded on or subject to the rules of a contract market designated under the Commodity Exchange Act or a derivatives transaction execution facility registered under the Commodity Exchange Act against any claim arising under, or in connection with, other instruments, contracts, or agreements listed in subsection (a) except to the extent that the party has positive net equity in the commodity accounts at the debtor, as calculated under such subchapter; and

(B) another commodity broker may not net or offset an obligation to the debtor arising under, or in connection with, a commodity contract entered into or held on behalf of a customer of the debtor and traded on or subject to the rules of a contract market designated under the Commodity Exchange Act or a derivatives transaction execution facility registered under the Commodity Exchange Act against any claim arising under, or in connection with, other instruments, contracts, or agreements listed in subsection (a).

(3) No provision of subparagraph (A) or (B) of paragraph (2) shall prohibit the offset of claims and obligations that arise under—

(A) a cross-margining agreement or similar arrangement that has been approved by the Commodity Futures Trading Commission or submitted to the Commodity Futures Trading Commission under paragraph (1) or (2) of section 5c(c) of the Commodity Exchange Act and has not been abrogated or rendered ineffective by the Commodity Futures Trading Commission; or

(B) any other netting agreement between a clearing organization (as defined in section 761) and another entity that has been approved by the Commodity Futures Trading Commission.

(c) As used in this section, the term “contractual right” includes a right set forth in a rule or bylaw of a derivatives clearing organization (as defined in the Commodity Exchange Act), a multilateral clearing organization (as defined in the Federal Deposit Insurance Corporation Improvement Act of 1991), a national securities exchange, a national securities association, a securities clearing agency, a contract market designated under the Commodity Exchange Act, a derivatives transaction execution facility registered under the Commodity Exchange Act, or a board of trade (as defined in the Commodity Exchange Act) or in a resolution of the governing board thereof, and a right, whether or not evidenced in writing, arising under common law, under law merchant, or by reason of normal business practice.

(d) Any provisions of this title relating to securities contracts, commodity contracts, forward contracts, repurchase agreements, swap agreements, or master netting agreements shall apply in a case under chapter 15, so that enforcement of contractual provisions of such contracts and agreements in accordance with their terms will not be stayed or otherwise limited by operation of any provision of this title or by order of a court in any case under this title, and to limit avoidance powers to the same extent as in a proceeding under chapter 7 or 11 of this title (such enforcement not to be limited based on the presence or absence of assets of the debtor in the United States).

### § 562 Timing of damage measurement in connection with swap agreements, securities contracts, forward contracts, commodity contracts, repurchase agreements, and master netting agreements

(a) If the trustee rejects a swap agreement, securities contract (as defined in section 741), forward contract, commodity contract (as defined in section 761), repurchase agreement, or master netting agreement pursuant to section 365(a), or if a forward contract merchant, stockbroker, financial institution, securities clearing agency, repo participant, financial participant, master netting agreement participant, or swap participant liquidates, terminates, or accelerates such contract or agreement, damages shall be measured as of the earlier of—

(1) the date of such rejection; or

(2) the date or dates of such liquidation, termination, or acceleration.

(b) If there are not any commercially reasonable determinants of value as of any date referred to in paragraph (1) or (2) of subsection (a), damages shall be measured as of the earliest subsequent date or dates on which there are commercially reasonable determinants of value.

(c) For the purposes of subsection (b), if damages are not measured as of the date or dates of rejection, liquidation, termination, or acceleration, and the forward contract merchant, stockbroker, financial institution, securities clearing agency, repo participant, financial participant, master netting agreement participant, or swap participant or the trustee objects to the timing of the measurement of damages—

(1) the trustee, in the case of an objection by a forward contract merchant, stockbroker, financial institution, securities clearing agency, repo participant, financial participant, master netting agreement participant, or swap participant; or

(2) the forward contract merchant, stockbroker, financial institution, securities clearing agency, repo participant, financial participant, master netting agreement participant, or swap participant, in the case of an objection by the trustee,

has the burden of proving that there were no commercially reasonable determinants of value as of such date or dates.

# CHAPTER 7
# LIQUIDATION

## SUBCHAPTER I
## Officers and Administration

### § 701 Interim trustee

(a) (1) Promptly after the order for relief under this chapter, the United States trustee shall appoint one disinterested person that is a member of the panel of private trustees established under section 586(a)(1) of title 28 or that is serving as trustee in the case immediately before the order for relief under this chapter to serve as interim trustee in the case.

(2) If none of the members of such panel is willing to serve as interim trustee in the case, then the United States trustee may serve as interim trustee in the case.

(b) The service of an interim trustee under this section terminates when a trustee elected or designated under section 702 of this title to serve as trustee in the case qualifies under section 322 of this title.

(c) An interim trustee serving under this section is a trustee in a case under this title.

BANKRUPTCY RULE REFERENCES: 2001, 2005, 2008, 2009, 2010, 2011, 2012, 2013, 2014, 2015, 2016, 5002 and 6009

### § 702 Election of trustee

(a) A creditor may vote for a candidate for trustee only if such creditor—

(1) holds an allowable, undisputed, fixed, liquidated, unsecured claim of a kind entitled to distribution under section 726(a)(2), 726(a)(3), 726(a)(4), 752(a), 766(h), or 766(i) of this title;

(2) does not have an interest materially adverse, other than an equity interest that is not substantial in relation to such creditor's interest as a creditor, to the interest of creditors entitled to such distribution; and

(3) is not an insider.

(b) At the meeting of creditors held under section 341 of this title, creditors may elect one person to serve as trustee in the case if election of a trustee is requested by creditors that may vote under subsection (a) of this section, and that hold at least 20 percent in amount of the claims specified in subsection (a)(1) of this section that are held by creditors that may vote under subsection (a) of this section.

(c) A candidate for trustee is elected trustee if—

(1) creditors holding at least 20 percent in amount of the claims of a kind specified in subsection (a)(1) of this section that are held by creditors that may vote under subsection (a) of this section vote; and

(2) such candidate receives the votes of creditors holding a majority in

amount of claims specified in subsection (a)(1) of this section that are held by creditors that vote for a trustee.

(d) If a trustee is not elected under this section, then the interim trustee shall serve as trustee in the case.

Bankruptcy Rule References: 2003, 2008, 2009, 2010, 2011, 2015, 5002 and 6009

## § 703 Successor trustee

(a) If a trustee dies or resigns during a case, fails to qualify under section 322 of this title, or is removed under section 324 of this title, creditors may elect, in the manner specified in section 702 of this title, a person to fill the vacancy in the office of trustee.

(b) Pending election of a trustee under subsection (a) of this section, if necessary to preserve or prevent loss to the estate, the United States trustee may appoint an interim trustee in the manner specified in section 701(a).

(c) If creditors do not elect a successor trustee under subsection (a) of this section or if a trustee is needed in a case reopened under section 350 of this title, then the United States trustee—

(1) shall appoint one disinterested person that is a member of the panel of private trustees established under section 586(a)(1) of title 28 to serve as trustee in the case; or

(2) may, if none of the disinterested members of such panel is willing to serve as trustee, serve as trustee in the case.

Bankruptcy Rule References: 2001, 2008, 2009, 2010, 2011, 2012, 2013, 2014, 2015, 2016, 5002 and 6009

## § 704 Duties of trustee

(a) The trustee shall—

(1) collect and reduce to money the property of the estate for which such trustee serves, and close such estate as expeditiously as is compatible with the best interests of parties in interest;

(2) be accountable for all property received;

(3) ensure that the debtor shall perform his intention as specified in section 521(a)(2)(B) of this title;

(4) investigate the financial affairs of the debtor;

(5) if a purpose would be served, examine proofs of claims and object to the allowance of any claim that is improper;

(6) if advisable, oppose the discharge of the debtor;

(7) unless the court orders otherwise, furnish such information concerning the estate and the estate's administration as is requested by a party in interest;

(8) if the business of the debtor is authorized to be operated, file with the

court, with the United States trustee, and with any governmental unit charged with responsibility for collection or determination of any tax arising out of such operation, periodic reports and summaries of the operation of such business, including a statement of receipts and disbursements, and such other information as the United States trustee or the court requires;

(9) make a final report and file a final account of the administration of the estate with the court and with the United States trustee;

(10) if with respect to the debtor there is a claim for a domestic support obligation, provide the applicable notice specified in subsection (c);

(11) if, at the time of the commencement of the case, the debtor (or any entity designated by the debtor) served as the administrator (as defined in section 3 of the Employee Retirement Income Security Act of 1974) of an employee benefit plan, continue to perform the obligations required of the administrator; and

(12) use all reasonable and best efforts to transfer patients from a health care business that is in the process of being closed to an appropriate health care business that—

(A) is in the vicinity of the health care business that is closing;

(B) provides the patient with services that are substantially similar to those provided by the health care business that is in the process of being closed; and

(C) maintains a reasonable quality of care.

(b) (1) With respect to a debtor who is an individual in a case under this chapter—

(A) the United States trustee (or the bankruptcy administrator, if any) shall review all materials filed by the debtor and, not later than 10 days after the date of the first meeting of creditors, file with the court a statement as to whether the debtor's case would be presumed to be an abuse under section 707(b); and

(B) not later than 7 days after receiving a statement under subparagraph (A), the court shall provide a copy of the statement to all creditors.

(2) The United States trustee (or bankruptcy administrator, if any) shall, not later than 30 days after the date of filing a statement under paragraph (1), either file a motion to dismiss or convert under section 707(b) or file a statement setting forth the reasons the United States trustee (or the bankruptcy administrator, if any) does not consider such a motion to be appropriate, if the United States trustee (or the bankruptcy administrator, if any) determines that the debtor's case should be presumed to be an abuse under section 707(b) and the product of the debtor's current monthly income, multiplied by 12 is not less than—

(A) in the case of a debtor in a household of 1 person, the median family-income of the applicable State for 1 earner; or

(B) in the case of a debtor in a household of 2 or more individuals, the highest median family income of the applicable State for a family of the same number or fewer individuals.

(c) (1) In a case described in subsection (a)(10) to which subsection (a)(10) applies, the trustee shall—

(A) (i) provide written notice to the holder of the claim described in subsection (a)(10) of such claim and of the right of such holder to use the services of the State child support enforcement agency established under sections 464 and 466 of the Social Security Act for the State in which such holder resides, for assistance in collecting child support during and after the case under this title;

(ii) include in the notice provided under clause (i) the address and telephone number of such State child support enforcement agency; and

(iii) include in the notice provided under clause (i) an explanation of the rights of such holder to payment of such claim under this chapter;

(B) (i) provide written notice to such State child support enforcement agency of such claim; and

(ii) include in the notice provided under clause (i) the name, address, and telephone number of such holder; and

(C) at such time as the debtor is granted a discharge under section 727, provide written notice to such holder and to such State child support enforcement agency of—

(i) the granting of the discharge;

(ii) the last recent known address of the debtor;

(iii) the last recent known name and address of the debtor's employer; and

(iv) the name of each creditor that holds a claim that—

(I) is not discharged under paragraph (2), (4), or (14A) of section 523(a); or

(II) was reaffirmed by the debtor under section 524(c).

(2) (A) The holder of a claim described in subsection (a)(10) or the State child support enforcement agency of the State in which such holder resides may request from a creditor described in paragraph (1)(C)(iv) the last known address of the debtor.

(B) Notwithstanding any other provision of law, a creditor that makes a disclosure of a last known address of a debtor in connection with a request made under subparagraph (A) shall not be liable by reason of making such disclosure.

BANKRUPTCY RULE REFERENCES: 1017, 1019, 2001, 2002, 2008, 2009, 2010, 2011, 2013, 2014, 2015, 2015.2, 2016, 3011, 4002, 5002 and 6009

## § 705 Creditors' committee

(a) At the meeting under section 341(a) of this title, creditors that may vote for a trustee under section 702(a) of this title may elect a committee of not fewer than three, and not more than eleven, creditors, each of whom holds an allowable unsecured claim of a kind entitled to distribution under section 726(a)(2) of this title.

(b) A committee elected under subsection (a) of this section may consult with the trustee or the United States trustee in connection with the administration of the estate, make recommendations to the trustee or the United States trustee respecting the performance of the trustee's duties, and submit to the court or the United States trustee any question affecting the administration of the estate.

BANKRUPTCY RULE REFERENCES: 2002, 2003, 2006 and 2007

## § 706 Conversion

(a) The debtor may convert a case under this chapter to a case under chapter 11, 12, or 13 of this title at any time, if the case has not been converted under section 1112, 1208, or 1307 of this title. Any waiver of the right to convert a case under this subsection is unenforceable.

(b) On request of a party in interest and after notice and a hearing, the court may convert a case under this chapter to a case under chapter 11 of this title at any time.

(c) The court may not convert a case under this chapter to a case under chapter 12 or 13 of this title unless the debtor requests or consents to such conversion.

(d) Notwithstanding any other provision of this section, a case may not be converted to a case under another chapter of this title unless the debtor may be a debtor under such chapter.

BANKRUPTCY RULE REFERENCES: 1019, 2002, 9013 and 9034

## § 707 Dismissal of a case or conversion to a case under chapter 11 or 13

(a) The court may dismiss a case under this chapter only after notice and a hearing and only for cause, including—

(1) unreasonable delay by the debtor that is prejudicial to creditors;

(2) nonpayment of any fees or charges required under chapter 123 of title 28; and

(3) failure of the debtor in a voluntary case to file, within fifteen days or such additional time as the court may allow after the filing of the petition commencing such case, the information required by paragraph (1) of section 521(a), but only on a motion by the United States trustee.

(b) (1) After notice and a hearing, the court, on its own motion or on a motion by the United States trustee, trustee (or bankruptcy administrator, if any), or any party in interest, may dismiss a case filed by an individual debtor under this chapter whose debts are primarily consumer debts, or, with the debtor's consent, convert such a case to a case under chapter 11 or 13 of this title, if it finds that the granting of relief would be an abuse of the provisions of this chapter. In making a determination whether to dismiss a case under this section, the court may not take into consideration whether a debtor has made, or continues to make, charitable contributions (that meet the definition of "charitable contribution" under section 548(d)(3)) to any qualified religious or charitable entity or organization (as that term is defined in section 548(d)(4)).

(2) (A) (i) In considering under paragraph (1) whether the granting of relief would be an abuse of the provisions of this chapter, the court shall presume abuse exists if the debtor's current monthly income reduced by the amounts determined under clauses (ii), (iii), and (iv), and multiplied by 60 is not less than the lesser of—

(I) 25 percent of the debtor's nonpriority unsecured claims in the case, or $8,175,[67] whichever is greater; or

(II) $13,650.[68]

(ii) (I) The debtor's monthly expenses shall be the debtor's applicable monthly expense amounts specified under the National Standards and Local Standards, and the debtor's actual monthly expenses for the categories specified as Other Necessary Expenses issued by the Internal Revenue Service for the area in which the debtor resides, as in effect on the date of the order for relief, for the debtor, the dependents of the debtor, and the spouse of the debtor in a joint case, if the spouse is not otherwise a dependent. Such expenses shall include reasonably necessary health insurance, disability insurance, and health savings account expenses for the debtor, the spouse of the debtor, or the dependents of the debtor. Notwithstanding any other provision of this clause, the monthly expenses of the debtor shall not include any payments for debts. In addition, the debtor's monthly expenses shall include the debtor's reasonably necessary expenses incurred to maintain the safety of the debtor and the family of the debtor from family violence as identified under section 309 of the Family Violence Prevention and Services Act, or other applicable Federal law. The expenses included in the debtor's monthly expenses described in the preceding sentence shall be kept confidential by the court. In addition, if it is demonstrated that it is reasonable and necessary, the debtor's monthly expenses may also include an additional allowance for food and clothing of up to 5 percent of the food and clothing categories as specified by the National Standards issued by the Internal Revenue Service.

---

67 ED. NOTE: For cases commenced in the three-year period before April 1, 2019, the dollar amount is $7,700.

68 ED. NOTE: For cases commenced in the three-year period before April 1, 2019, the dollar amount is $12,850.

(II) In addition, the debtor's monthly expenses may include, if applicable, the continuation of actual expenses paid by the debtor that are reasonable and necessary for care and support of an elderly, chronically ill, or disabled household member or member of the debtor's immediate family (including parents, grandparents, siblings, children, and grandchildren of the debtor, the dependents of the debtor, and the spouse of the debtor in a joint case who is not a dependent) and who is unable to pay for such reasonable and necessary expenses. Such monthly expenses may include, if applicable, contributions to an account of a qualified ABLE program to the extent such contributions are not excess contributions (as described in section 4973(h) of the Internal Revenue Code of 1986) and if the designated beneficiary of such account is a child, stepchild, grandchild, or stepgrandchild of the debtor.

(III) In addition, for a debtor eligible for chapter 13, the debtor's monthly expenses may include the actual administrative expenses of administering a chapter 13 plan for the district in which the debtor resides, up to an amount of 10 percent of the projected plan payments, as determined under schedules issued by the Executive Office for United States Trustees.

(IV) In addition, the debtor's monthly expenses may include the actual expenses for each dependent child less than 18 years of age, not to exceed $2,050[69] per year per child, to attend a private or public elementary or secondary school if the debtor provides documentation of such expenses and a detailed explanation of why such expenses are reasonable and necessary, and why such expenses are not already accounted for in the National Standards, Local Standards, or Other Necessary Expenses referred to in subclause (I).

(V) In addition, the debtor's monthly expenses may include an allowance for housing and utilities, in excess of the allowance specified by the Local Standards for housing and utilities issued by the Internal Revenue Service, based on the actual expenses for home energy costs if the debtor provides documentation of such actual expenses and demonstrates that such actual expenses are reasonable and necessary.

(iii) The debtor's average monthly payments on account of secured debts shall be calculated as the sum of–

(I) the total of all amounts scheduled as contractually due to secured creditors in each month of the 60 months following the date of the filing of the petition; and

(II) any additional payments to secured creditors necessary for the debtor, in filing a plan under chapter 13 of this title, to maintain possession of the debtor's primary residence, motor vehicle, or other

---

[69] ED. NOTE: For cases commenced in the three-year period before April 1, 2019, the dollar amount is $1,925.

property necessary for the support of the debtor and the debtor's dependents, that serves as collateral for secured debts;

divided by 60.

(iv) The debtor's expenses for payment of all priority claims (including priority child support and alimony claims) shall be calculated as the total amount of debts entitled to priority, divided by 60.

(B) (i) In any proceeding brought under this subsection, the presumption of abuse may only be rebutted by demonstrating special circumstances, such as a serious medical condition or a call or order to active duty in the Armed Forces, to the extent such special circumstances that justify additional expenses or adjustments of current monthly income for which there is no reasonable alternative.

(ii) In order to establish special circumstances, the debtor shall be required to itemize each additional expense or adjustment of income and to provide—

(I) documentation for such expense or adjustment to income; and

(II) a detailed explanation of the special circumstances that make such expenses or adjustment to income necessary and reasonable.

(iii) The debtor shall attest under oath to the accuracy of any information provided to demonstrate that additional expenses or adjustments to income are required.

(iv) The presumption of abuse may only be rebutted if the additional expenses or adjustments to income referred to in clause (i) cause the product of the debtor's current monthly income reduced by the amounts determined under clauses (ii), (iii), and (iv) of subparagraph (A) when multiplied by 60 to be less than the lesser of—

(I) 25 percent of the debtor's nonpriority unsecured claims, or $8,175,[70] whichever is greater; or

(II) $13,650.[71]

(C) As part of the schedule of current income and expenditures required under section 521, the debtor shall include a statement of the debtor's current monthly income, and the calculations that determine whether a presumption arises under subparagraph (A)(i), that show how each such amount is calculated.

(D) Subparagraphs (A) through (C) shall not apply, and the court may not dismiss or convert a case based on any form of means testing—

---

[70] Ed. Note: For cases commenced in the three-year period before April 1, 2019, the dollar amount is $7,700.

[71] Ed. Note: For cases commenced in the three-year period before April 1, 2019, the dollar amount is $12,850.

(i) if the debtor is a disabled veteran (as defined in section 3741(1) of title 38), and the indebtedness occurred primarily during a period during which he or she was—

(I) on active duty (as defined in section 101(d)(1) of title 10); or

(II) performing a homeland defense activity (as defined in section 901(1) of title 32); or

(ii)[72] with respect to the debtor, while the debtor is—

(I) on, and during the 540-day period beginning immediately after the debtor is released from, a period of active duty (as defined in section 101(d)(1) of title 10) or not less than 90 days; or

(II) performing, and during the 540 day period beginning immediately after the debtor is no longer performing, a homeland defense activity (as defined in section 901(1) of title 32) performed for a period of not less than 90 days;

if after September 11, 2001, the debtor while a member of a reserve component of the Armed Forces or a member of the National Guard, was called to such active duty or performed such homeland defense activity.

(3) In considering under paragraph (1) whether the granting of relief would be an abuse of the provisions of this chapter in a case in which the presumption in paragraph (2)(A)(i) does not arise or is rebutted, the court shall consider—

(A) whether the debtor filed the petition in bad faith; or

(B) the totality of the circumstances (including whether the debtor seeks to reject a personal services contract and the financial need for such rejection as sought by the debtor) of the debtor's financial situation demonstrates abuse.

(4) (A) The court, on its own initiative or on the motion of a party in interest, in accordance with the procedures described in rule 9011 of the Federal Rules of Bankruptcy Procedure, may order the attorney for the debtor to reimburse the trustee for all reasonable costs in prosecuting a motion filed under section 707(b), including reasonable attorneys' fees, if—

(i) a trustee files a motion for dismissal or conversion under this subsection; and

(ii) the court—

(I) grants such motion; and

(II) finds that the action of the attorney for the debtor in filing a case under this chapter violated rule 9011 of the Federal Rules of Bankruptcy Procedure.

---

[72] Ed. Note: Subdivision (ii) is scheduled to sunset on December 19, 2023. Pub. L. No. 116-53, amending Pub. L. No. 110-438 (2008).

(B) If the court finds that the attorney for the debtor violated rule 9011 of the Federal Rules of Bankruptcy Procedure, the court, on its own initiative or on the motion of a party in interest, in accordance with such procedures, may order—

(i) the assessment of an appropriate civil penalty against the attorney for the debtor; and

(ii) the payment of such civil penalty to the trustee, the United States trustee (or the bankruptcy administrator, if any).

(C) The signature of an attorney on a petition, pleading, or written motion shall constitute a certification that the attorney has—

(i) performed a reasonable investigation into the circumstances that gave rise to the petition, pleading, or written motion; and

(ii) determined that the petition, pleading, or written motion—

(I) is well grounded in fact; and

(II) is warranted by existing law or a good faith argument for the extension, modification, or reversal of existing law and does not constitute an abuse under paragraph (1).

(D) The signature of an attorney on the petition shall constitute a certification that the attorney has no knowledge after an inquiry that the information in the schedules filed with such petition is incorrect.

(5) (A) Except as provided in subparagraph (B) and subject to paragraph (6), the court, on its own initiative or on the motion of a party in interest, in accordance with the procedures described in rule 9011 of the Federal Rules of Bankruptcy Procedure, may award a debtor all reasonable costs (including reasonable attorneys' fees) in contesting a motion filed by a party in interest (other than a trustee or United States trustee (or bankruptcy administrator, if any)) under this subsection if—

(i) the court does not grant the motion; and

(ii) the court finds that—

(I) the position of the party that filed the motion violated rule 9011 of the Federal Rules of Bankruptcy Procedure; or

(II) the attorney (if any) who filed the motion did not comply with the requirements of clauses (i) and (ii) of paragraph (4)(C), and the motion was made solely for the purpose of coercing a debtor into waiving a right guaranteed to the debtor under this title.

(B) A small business that has a claim of an aggregate amount less than $1,375[73] shall not be subject to subparagraph (A)(ii)(I).

---

[73] Ed. Note: For cases commenced in the three-year period before April 1, 2019, the dollar amount is $1,300.

(C) For purposes of this paragraph—

(i) the term "small business" means an unincorporated business, partnership, corporation, association, or organization that—

(I) has fewer than 25 full-time employees as determined on the date on which the motion is filed; and

(II) is engaged in commercial or business activity; and

(ii) the number of employees of a wholly owned subsidiary of a corporation includes the employees of—

(I) a parent corporation; and

(II) any other subsidiary corporation of the parent corporation.

(6) Only the judge or United States trustee (or bankruptcy administrator, if any) may file a motion under section 707(b), if the current monthly income of the debtor, or in a joint case, the debtor and the debtor's spouse, as of the date of the order for relief, when multiplied by 12, is equal to or less than—

(A) in the case of a debtor in a household of 1 person, the median family income of the applicable State for 1 earner;

(B) in the case of a debtor in a household of 2, 3, or 4 individuals, the highest median family income of the applicable State for a family of the same number or fewer individuals; or

(C) in the case of a debtor in a household exceeding 4 individuals, the highest median family income of the applicable State for a family of 4 or fewer individuals, plus $750[74] per month for each individual in excess of 4.

(7) (A) No judge, United States trustee (or bankruptcy administrator, if any), trustee, or other party in interest may file a motion under paragraph (2) if the current monthly income of the debtor, including a veteran (as that term is defined in section 101 of title 38), and the debtor's spouse combined, as of the date of the order for relief when multiplied by 12, is equal to or less than—

(i) in the case of a debtor in a household of 1 person, the median family income of the applicable State for 1 earner;

(ii) in the case of a debtor in a household of 2, 3, or 4 individuals, the highest median family income of the applicable State for a family of the same number or fewer individuals; or

(iii) in the case of a debtor in a household exceeding 4 individuals, the highest median family income of the applicable State for a family of 4 or

---

[74] Ed. Note: For cases commenced in the three-year period before April 1, 2019, the dollar amount is $700.

fewer individuals, plus $750[75] per month for each individual in excess of 4.

(B) In a case that is not a joint case, current monthly income of the debtor's spouse shall not be considered for purposes of subparagraph (A) if—

(i) (I) the debtor and the debtor's spouse are separated under applicable nonbankruptcy law; or

(II) the debtor and the debtor's spouse are living separate and apart, other than for the purpose of evading subparagraph (A); and

(ii) the debtor files a statement under penalty of perjury—

(I) specifying that the debtor meets the requirement of subclause (I) or (II) of clause (i); and

(II) disclosing the aggregate, or best estimate of the aggregate, amount of any cash or money payments received from the debtor's spouse attributed to the debtor's current monthly income.

(c) (1) In this subsection—

(A) the term "crime of violence" has the meaning given such term in section 16 of title 18; and

(B) the term "drug trafficking crime" has the meaning given such term in section 924(c)(2) of title 18.

(2) Except as provided in paragraph (3), after notice and a hearing, the court, on a motion by the victim of a crime of violence or a drug trafficking crime, may when it is in the best interest of the victim dismiss a voluntary case filed under this chapter by a debtor who is an individual if such individual was convicted of such crime.

(3) The court may not dismiss a case under paragraph (2) if the debtor establishes by a preponderance of the evidence that the filing of a case under this chapter is necessary to satisfy a claim for a domestic support obligation.

Bankruptcy Rule References: 1007-I, 1017, 1019, 2002, 2015.2, 4004, 5008, 9011 and 9013

---

[75] Ed. Note: For cases commenced in the three-year period before April 1, 2019, the dollar amount is $700.

## Subchapter II
## Collection, Liquidation, and Distribution of the Estate

### § 721 Authorization to operate business

The court may authorize the trustee to operate the business of the debtor for a limited period, if such operation is in the best interest of the estate and consistent with the orderly liquidation of the estate.

### § 722 Redemption

An individual debtor may, whether or not the debtor has waived the right to redeem under this section, redeem tangible personal property intended primarily for personal, family, or household use, from a lien securing a dischargeable consumer debt, if such property is exempted under section 522 of this title or has been abandoned under section 554 of this title, by paying the holder of such lien the amount of the allowed secured claim of such holder that is secured by such lien in full at the time of redemption.

Bankruptcy Rule References: 1007 and 6008

### § 723 Rights of partnership trustee against general partners

(a) If there is a deficiency of property of the estate to pay in full all claims which are allowed in a case under this chapter concerning a partnership and with respect to which a general partner of the partnership is personally liable, the trustee shall have a claim against such general partner to the extent that under applicable nonbankruptcy law such general partner is personally liable for such deficiency.

(b) To the extent practicable, the trustee shall first seek recovery of such deficiency from any general partner in such partnership that is not a debtor in a case under this title. Pending determination of such deficiency, the court may order any such partner to provide the estate with indemnity for, or assurance of payment of, any deficiency recoverable from such partner, or not to dispose of property.

(c) The trustee has a claim against the estate of each general partner in such partnership that is a debtor in a case under this title for the full amount of all claims of creditors allowed in the case concerning such partnership. Notwithstanding section 502 of this title, there shall not be allowed in such partner's case a claim against such partner on which both such partner and such partnership are liable, except to any extent that such claim is secured only by property of such partner and not by property of such partnership. The claim of the trustee under this subsection is entitled to distribution in such partner's case under section 726(a) of this title the same as any other claim of a kind specified in such section.

(d) If the aggregate that the trustee recovers from the estates of general partners under subsection (c) of this section is greater than any deficiency not recovered under subsection (b) of this section, the court, after notice and a hearing, shall determine an equitable distribution of the surplus so recovered, and the trustee shall distribute such surplus to the estates of the general partners in such partnership according to such determination.

Bankruptcy Rule References: 1004, 1007, 1015 and 2009

## § 724 Treatment of certain liens

(a) The trustee may avoid a lien that secures a claim of a kind specified in section 726(a)(4) of this title.

(b) Property in which the estate has an interest and that is subject to a lien that is not avoidable under this title (other than to the extent that there is a properly perfected unavoidable tax lien arising in connection with an ad valorem tax on real or personal property of the estate) and that secures an allowed claim for a tax, or proceeds of such property, shall be distributed–

(1) first, to any holder of an allowed claim secured by a lien on such property that is not avoidable under this title and that is senior to such tax lien;

(2) second, to any holder of a claim of a kind specified in section 507(a)(1)(C) or 507(a)(2) (except that such expenses under each such section, other than claims for wages, salaries, or commissions that arise after the date of the filing of the petition, shall be limited to expenses incurred under this chapter and shall not include expenses incurred under chapter 11 of this title), 507(a)(1)(A), 507(a)(1)(B), 507(a)(3), 507(a)(4), 507(a)(5), 507(a)(6), or 507(a)(7) of this title, to the extent of the amount of such allowed tax claim that is secured by such tax lien;

(3) third, to the holder of such tax lien, to any extent that such holder's allowed tax claim that is secured by such tax lien exceeds any amount distributed under paragraph (2) of this subsection;

(4) fourth, to any holder of an allowed claim secured by a lien on such property that is not avoidable under this title and that is junior to such tax lien;

(5) fifth, to the holder of such tax lien, to the extent that such holder's allowed claim secured by such tax lien is not paid under paragraph (3) of this subsection; and

(6) sixth, to the estate.

(c) If more than one holder of a claim is entitled to distribution under a particular paragraph of subsection (b) of this section, distribution to such holders under such paragraph shall be in the same order as distribution to such holders would have been other than under this section.

(d) A statutory lien the priority of which is determined in the same manner as the priority of a tax lien under section 6323 of the Internal Revenue Code of 1986 shall be treated under subsection (b) of this section the same as if such lien were a tax lien.

(e) Before subordinating a tax lien on real or personal property of the estate, the trustee shall–

(1) exhaust the unencumbered assets of the estate; and

(2) in a manner consistent with section 506(c), recover from property

securing an allowed secured claim the reasonable, necessary costs and expenses of preserving or disposing of such property.

(f) Notwithstanding the exclusion of ad valorem tax liens under this section and subject to the requirements of subsection (e), the following may be paid from property of the estate which secures a tax lien, or the proceeds of such property:

(1) Claims for wages, salaries, and commissions that are entitled to priority under section 507(a)(4).

(2) Claims for contributions to an employee benefit plan entitled to priority under section 507(a)(5).

Bankruptcy Rule Reference: 7001

## § 725 Disposition of certain property

After the commencement of a case under this chapter, but before final distribution of property of the estate under section 726 of this title, the trustee, after notice and a hearing, shall dispose of any property in which an entity other than the estate has an interest, such as a lien, and that has not been disposed of under another section of this title.

Bankruptcy Rule References: 6007 and 7001

## § 726 Distribution of property of the estate

(a) Except as provided in section 510 of this title, property of the estate shall be distributed—

(1) first, in payment of claims of the kind specified in, and in the order specified in, section 507 of this title, proof of which is timely filed under section 501 of this title or tardily filed on or before the earlier of—

(A) the date that is 10 days after the mailing to creditors of the summary of the trustee's final report; or

(B) the date on which the trustee commences final distribution under this section;

(2) second, in payment of any allowed unsecured claim, other than a claim of a kind specified in paragraph (1), (3), or (4) of this subsection, proof of which is—

(A) timely filed under section 501(a) of this title;

(B) timely filed under section 501(b) or 501(c) of this title; or

(C) tardily filed under section 501(a) of this title, if—

(i) the creditor that holds such claim did not have notice or actual knowledge of the case in time for timely filing of a proof of such claim under section 501(a) of this title; and

(ii) proof of such claim is filed in time to permit payment of such claim;

(3) third, in payment of any allowed unsecured claim proof of which is

tardily filed under section 501(a) of this title other than a claim of the kind specified in paragraph (2)(C) of this subsection;

(4) fourth, in payment of any allowed claim, whether secured or unsecured, for any fine, penalty, or forfeiture, or for multiple, exemplary, or punitive damages, arising before the earlier of the order for relief or the appointment of a trustee, to the extent that such fine, penalty, forfeiture, or damages are not compensation for actual pecuniary loss suffered by the holder of such claim;

(5) fifth, in payment of interest at the legal rate from the date of the filing of the petition, on any claim paid under paragraph (1), (2), (3), or (4) of this subsection; and

(6) sixth, to the debtor.

(b) Payment on claims of a kind specified in paragraph (1), (2), (3), (4), (5), (6), (7), (8), (9), or (10) of section 507(a) of this title, or in paragraph (2), (3), (4), or (5) of subsection (a) of this section, shall be made pro rata among claims of the kind specified in each such particular paragraph, except that in a case that has been converted to this chapter under section 1112, 1208, or 1307 of this title, a claim allowed under section 503(b) of this title incurred under this chapter after such conversion has priority over a claim allowed under section 503(b) of this title incurred under any other chapter of this title or under this chapter before such conversion and over any expenses of a custodian superseded under section 543 of this title.

(c) Notwithstanding subsections (a) and (b) of this section, if there is property of the kind specified in section 541(a)(2) of this title, or proceeds of such property, in the estate, such property or proceeds shall be segregated from other property of the estate, and such property or proceeds and other property of the estate shall be distributed as follows:

(1) Claims allowed under section 503 of this title shall be paid either from property of the kind specified in section 541(a)(2) of this title, or from other property of the estate, as the interest of justice requires.

(2) Allowed claims, other than claims allowed under section 503 of this title, shall be paid in the order specified in subsection (a) of this section, and, with respect to claims of a kind specified in a particular paragraph of section 507 of this title or subsection (a) of this section, in the following order and manner:

(A) First, community claims against the debtor or the debtor's spouse shall be paid from property of the kind specified in section 541(a)(2) of this title, except to the extent that such property is solely liable for debts of the debtor.

(B) Second, to the extent that community claims against the debtor are not paid under subparagraph (A) of this paragraph, such community claims shall be paid from property of the kind specified in section 541(a)(2) of this title that is solely liable for debts of the debtor.

(C) Third, to the extent that all claims against the debtor including community claims against the debtor are not paid under subparagraph (A) or (B) of this paragraph such claims shall be paid from property of the estate other than property of the kind specified in section 541(a)(2) of this title.

(D) Fourth, to the extent that community claims against the debtor or the debtor's spouse are not paid under subparagraph (A), (B), or (C) of this paragraph, such claims shall be paid from all remaining property of the estate.

Bankruptcy Rule References: 3009, 3010 and 9010

## § 727 Discharge

(a) The court shall grant the debtor a discharge, unless—

(1) the debtor is not an individual;

(2) the debtor, with intent to hinder, delay, or defraud a creditor or an officer of the estate charged with custody of property under this title, has transferred, removed, destroyed, mutilated, or concealed, or has permitted to be transferred, removed, destroyed, mutilated, or concealed—

(A) property of the debtor, within one year before the date of the filing of the petition; or

(B) property of the estate, after the date of the filing of the petition;

(3) the debtor has concealed, destroyed, mutilated, falsified, or failed to keep or preserve any recorded information, including books, documents, records, and papers, from which the debtor's financial condition or business transactions might be ascertained, unless such act or failure to act was justified under all of the circumstances of the case;

(4) the debtor knowingly and fraudulently, in or in connection with the case—

(A) made a false oath or account;

(B) presented or used a false claim;

(C) gave, offered, received, or attempted to obtain money, property, or advantage, or a promise of money, property, or advantage, for acting or forbearing to act; or

(D) withheld from an officer of the estate entitled to possession under this title, any recorded information, including books, documents, records, and papers, relating to the debtor's property or financial affairs;

(5) the debtor has failed to explain satisfactorily, before determination of denial of discharge under this paragraph, any loss of assets or deficiency of assets to meet the debtor's liabilities;

(6) the debtor has refused, in the case—

(A) to obey any lawful order of the court, other than an order to respond to a material question or to testify;

(B) on the ground of privilege against self-incrimination, to respond to a material question approved by the court or to testify, after the debtor has been granted immunity with respect to the matter concerning which such privilege was invoked; or

(C) on a ground other than the properly invoked privilege against self-incrimination, to respond to a material question approved by the court or to testify;

(7) the debtor has committed any act specified in paragraph (2), (3), (4), (5), or (6) of this subsection, on or within one year before the date of the filing of the petition, or during the case, in connection with another case, under this title or under the Bankruptcy Act, concerning an insider;

(8) the debtor has been granted a discharge under this section, under section 1141 of this title, or under section 14, 371, or 476 of the Bankruptcy Act, in a case commenced within 8 years before the date of the filing of the petition;

(9) the debtor has been granted a discharge under section 1228 or 1328 of this title, or under section 660 or 661 of the Bankruptcy Act, in a case commenced within six years before the date of the filing of the petition, unless payments under the plan in such case totaled at least—

(A) 100 percent of the allowed unsecured claims in such case; or

(B) (i) 70 percent of such claims; and

(ii) the plan was proposed by the debtor in good faith, and was the debtor's best effort;

(10) the court approves a written waiver of discharge executed by the debtor after the order for relief under this chapter;

(11) after filing the petition, the debtor failed to complete an instructional course concerning personal financial management described in section 111, except that this paragraph shall not apply with respect to a debtor who is a person described in section 109(h)(4) or who resides in a district for which the United States trustee (or the bankruptcy administrator, if any) determines that the approved instructional courses are not adequate to service the additional individuals who would otherwise be required to complete such instructional courses under this section (The United States trustee (or the bankruptcy administrator, if any) who makes a determination described in this paragraph shall review such determination not later than 1 year after the date of such determination, and not less frequently than annually thereafter.); or

(12) the court after notice and a hearing held not more than 10 days before the date of the entry of the order granting the discharge finds that there is reasonable cause to believe that—

(A) section 522(q)(1) may be applicable to the debtor; and

(B) there is pending any proceeding in which the debtor may be found guilty of a felony of the kind described in section 522(q)(1)(A) or liable for a debt of the kind described in section 522(q)(1)(B).

(b) Except as provided in section 523 of this title, a discharge under subsection (a) of this section discharges the debtor from all debts that arose before the date of the order for relief under this chapter, and any liability on a claim that is determined under section 502 of this title as if such claim had arisen before the commencement of the case, whether or not a proof of claim based on any such debt or liability is filed under section 501 of this title, and whether or not a claim based on any such debt or liability is allowed under section 502 of this title.

(c) (1) The trustee, a creditor, or the United States trustee may object to the granting of a discharge under subsection (a) of this section.

(2) On request of a party in interest, the court may order the trustee to examine the acts and conduct of the debtor to determine whether a ground exists for denial of discharge.

(d) On request of the trustee, a creditor, or the United States trustee, and after notice and a hearing, the court shall revoke a discharge granted under subsection (a) of this section if–

(1) such discharge was obtained through the fraud of the debtor, and the requesting party did not know of such fraud until after the granting of such discharge;

(2) the debtor acquired property that is property of the estate, or became entitled to acquire property that would be property of the estate, and knowingly and fraudulently failed to report the acquisition of or entitlement to such property, or to deliver or surrender such property to the trustee;

(3) the debtor committed an act specified in subsection (a)(6) of this section; or

(4) the debtor has failed to explain satisfactorily–

(A) a material misstatement in an audit referred to in section 586(f) of title 28; or

(B) a failure to make available for inspection all necessary accounts, papers, documents, financial records, files, and all other papers, things, or property belonging to the debtor that are requested for an audit referred to in section 586(f) of title 28.

(e) The trustee, a creditor, or the United States trustee may request a revocation of a discharge–

(1) under subsection (d)(1) of this section within one year after such discharge is granted; or

(2) under subsection (d)(2) or (d)(3) of this section before the later of–

(A) one year after the granting of such discharge; and

(B) the date the case is closed.

BANKRUPTCY RULE REFERENCES: 2002, 4004, 4005, 4006, 4008, 5005, 7001, 7009, 7041, 9006, 9021 and 9024

### § 728 Special tax provisions [Repealed in 2005]

## Subchapter III
## Stockbroker Liquidation

### § 741 Definitions for this subchapter[76]

In this subchapter–

(1) "Commission" means Securities and Exchange Commission;

(2) "customer" includes–

(A) entity with whom a person deals as principal or agent and that has a claim against such person on account of a security received, acquired, or held by such person in the ordinary course of such person's business as a stockbroker, from or for the securities account or accounts of such entity–

(i) for safekeeping;

(ii) with a view to sale;

(iii) to cover a consummated sale;

(iv) pursuant to a purchase;

(v) as collateral under a security agreement; or

(vi) for the purpose of effecting registration of transfer; and

(B) entity that has a claim against a person arising out of–

(i) a sale or conversion of a security received, acquired, or held as specified in subparagraph (A) of this paragraph; or

(ii) a deposit of cash, a security, or other property with such person for the purpose of purchasing or selling a security;

(3) "customer name security" means security–

(A) held for the account of a customer on the date of the filing of the petition by or on behalf of the debtor;

(B) registered in such customer's name on such date or in the process of being so registered under instructions from the debtor; and

---

[76] Ed. note: Section 78c-5(g) of title 15, enacted as part of the Dodd-Frank Wall Street Reform and Consumer Protection Act, Pub. L. 111-203, 124 Stat. 1775 (2010), provides:

A security-based swap, as defined in section 78c(a)(68) of this title shall be considered to be a security as such term is used in section 101(53A)(B) and subchapter III of Title 11. An account that holds a security-based swap, other than a portfolio margining account referred to in section 78o(c)(3)(C) of this title shall be considered to be a securities account, as that term is defined in section 741 of Title 11. The definitions of the terms "purchase and sale" in section 78c(a)(13) and (14) of this title shall be applied to the terms "purchase and sale," as used in section 741 of Title 11. The term "customer", as defined in section 741 of Title 11, excludes any person, to the extent that such person has a claim based on any open repurchase agreement, open reverse repurchase agreement, stock borrowed agreement, non-cleared option, or non-cleared security-based swap except to the extent of any margin delivered to or by the customer with respect to which there is a customer protection requirement under section 78o(c)(3) of this title or a segregation requirement.

(C) not in a form transferable by delivery on such date;

(4) "customer property" means cash, security, or other property, and proceeds of such cash, security, or property, received, acquired, or held by or for the account of the debtor, from or for the securities account of a customer—

(A) including—

(i) property that was unlawfully converted from and that is the lawful property of the estate;

(ii) a security held as property of the debtor to the extent such security is necessary to meet a net equity claim of a customer based on a security of the same class and series of an issuer;

(iii) resources provided through the use or realization of a customer's debit cash balance or a debit item includible in the Formula for Determination of Reserve Requirement for Brokers and Dealers as promulgated by the Commission under the Securities Exchange Act of 1934; and

(iv) other property of the debtor that any applicable law, rule, or regulation requires to be set aside or held for the benefit of a customer, unless including such property as customer property would not significantly increase customer property; but

(B) not including—

(i) a customer name security delivered to or reclaimed by a customer under section 751 of this title; or

(ii) property to the extent that a customer does not have a claim against the debtor based on such property;

(5) "margin payment" means payment or deposit of cash, a security, or other property, that is commonly known to the securities trade as original margin, initial margin, maintenance margin, or variation margin, or as a mark-to-market payment, or that secures an obligation of a participant in a securities clearing agency;

(6) "net equity" means, with respect to all accounts of a customer that such customer has in the same capacity—

(A) (i) aggregate dollar balance that would remain in such accounts after the liquidation, by sale or purchase, at the time of the filing of the petition, of all securities positions in all such accounts, except any customer name securities of such customer; minus

(ii) any claim of the debtor against such customer in such capacity that would have been owing immediately after such liquidation; plus

(B) any payment by such customer to the trustee, within 60 days after notice under section 342 of this title, of any business related claim of the debtor against such customer in such capacity;

(7) "securities contract"—

(A) means—

(i) a contract for the purchase, sale, or loan of a security, a certificate of deposit, a mortgage loan, any interest in a mortgage loan, a group or index of securities, certificates of deposit, or mortgage loans or interests therein (including an interest therein or based on the value thereof), or option on any of the foregoing, including an option to purchase or sell any such security, certificate of deposit, mortgage loan, interest, group or index, or option, and including any repurchase or reverse repurchase transaction on any such security, certificate of deposit, mortgage loan, interest, group or index, or option (whether or not such repurchase or reverse repurchase transaction is a "repurchase agreement", as defined in section 101);

(ii) any option entered into on a national securities exchange relating to foreign currencies;

(iii) the guarantee (including by novation) by or to any securities clearing agency of a settlement of cash, securities, certificates of deposit, mortgage loans or interests therein, group or index of securities, or mortgage loans or interests therein (including any interest therein or based on the value thereof), or option on any of the foregoing, including an option to purchase or sell any such security, certificate of deposit, mortgage loan, interest, group or index, or option (whether or not such settlement is in connection with any agreement or transaction referred to in clauses (i) through (xi));

(iv) any margin loan;

(v) any extension of credit for the clearance or settlement of securities transactions;

(vi) any loan transaction coupled with a securities collar transaction, any prepaid forward securities transaction, or any total return swap transaction coupled with a securities sale transaction;

(vii) any other agreement or transaction that is similar to an agreement or transaction referred to in this subparagraph;

(viii) any combination of the agreements or transactions referred to in this subparagraph;

(ix) any option to enter into any agreement or transaction referred to in this subparagraph;

(x) a master agreement that provides for an agreement or transaction referred to in clause (i), (ii), (iii), (iv), (v), (vi), (vii), (viii), or (ix) together with all supplements to any such master agreement, without regard to whether the master agreement provides for an agreement or transaction that is not a securities contract under this subparagraph, except that such master agreement shall be considered to be a securities contract under this subparagraph only with respect to each agreement or transaction under such master agreement that is referred to in clause (i), (ii), (iii), (iv), (v), (vi), (vii), (viii), or (ix); or

(xi) any security agreement or arrangement or other credit enhancement related to any agreement or transaction referred to in this subparagraph, including any guarantee or reimbursement obligation by or to a stockbroker, securities clearing agency, financial institution, or financial participant in connection with any agreement or transaction referred to in this subparagraph, but not to exceed the damages in connection with any such agreement or transaction, measured in accordance with section 562; and

(B) does not include any purchase, sale, or repurchase obligation under a participation in a commercial mortgage loan;

(8) "settlement payment" means a preliminary settlement payment, a partial settlement payment, an interim settlement payment, a settlement payment on account, a final settlement payment, or any other similar payment commonly used in the securities trade; and

(9) "SIPC" means Securities Investor Protection Corporation.

## § 742 Effect of section 362 of this title in this subchapter

Notwithstanding section 362 of this title, SIPC may file an application for a protective decree under the Securities Investor Protection Act of 1970. The filing of such application stays all proceedings in the case under this title unless and until such application is dismissed. If SIPC completes the liquidation of the debtor, then the court shall dismiss the case.

## § 743 Notice

The clerk shall give the notice required by section 342 of this title to SIPC and to the Commission.

## § 744 Executory contracts

Notwithstanding section 365(d)(1) of this title, the trustee shall assume or reject, under section 365 of this title, any executory contract of the debtor for the purchase or sale of a security in the ordinary course of the debtor's business, within a reasonable time after the date of the order for relief, but not to exceed 30 days. If the trustee does not assume such a contract within such time, such contract is rejected.

## § 745 Treatment of accounts

(a) Accounts held by the debtor for a particular customer in separate capacities shall be treated as accounts of separate customers.

(b) If a stockbroker or a bank holds a customer net equity claim against the debtor that arose out of a transaction for a customer of such stockbroker or bank, each such customer of such stockbroker or bank shall be treated as a separate customer of the debtor.

(c) Each trustee's account specified as such on the debtor's books, and supported by a trust deed filed with, and qualified as such by, the Internal Revenue Service, and under the Internal Revenue Code of 1986, shall be treated as a separate customer account for each beneficiary under such trustee account.

### § 746 Extent of customer claims

(a) If, after the date of the filing of the petition, an entity enters into a transaction with the debtor, in a manner that would have made such entity a customer had such transaction occurred before the date of the filing of the petition, and such transaction was entered into by such entity in good faith and before the qualification under section 322 of this title of a trustee, such entity shall be deemed a customer, and the date of such transaction shall be deemed to be the date of the filing of the petition for the purpose of determining such entity's net equity.

(b) An entity does not have a claim as a customer to the extent that such entity transferred to the debtor cash or a security that, by contract, agreement, understanding, or operation of law, is—

(1) part of the capital of the debtor; or

(2) subordinated to the claims of any or all creditors.

### § 747 Subordination of certain customer claims

Except as provided in section 510 of this title, unless all other customer net equity claims have been paid in full, the trustee may not pay in full or pay in part, directly or indirectly, any net equity claim of a customer that was, on the date the transaction giving rise to such claim occurred—

(1) an insider;

(2) a beneficial owner of at least five percent of any class of equity securities of the debtor, other than—

(A) nonconvertible stock having fixed preferential dividend and liquidation rights; or

(B) interests of limited partners in a limited partnership;

(3) a limited partner with a participation of at least five percent in the net assets or net profits of the debtor; or

(4) an entity that, directly or indirectly, through agreement or otherwise, exercised or had the power to exercise control over the management or policies of the debtor.

### § 748 Reduction of securities to money

As soon as practicable after the date of the order for relief, the trustee shall reduce to money, consistent with good market practice, all securities held as property of the estate, except for customer name securities delivered or reclaimed under section 751 of this title.

### § 749 Voidable transfers

(a) Except as otherwise provided in this section, any transfer of property that, but for such transfer, would have been customer property, may be avoided by the trustee, and such property shall be treated as customer property, if and to the extent that the trustee avoids such transfer under section 544, 545, 547, 548, or 549 of this title. For the purpose of such sections, the property so transferred shall be deemed to have been property of the debtor and, if such transfer was made to a customer or for a customer's benefit, such customer shall be deemed, for the purposes of this section, to have been a creditor.

(b) Notwithstanding sections 544, 545, 547, 548, and 549 of this title, the trustee may not avoid a transfer made before seven days after the order for relief if such transfer is approved by the Commission by rule or order, either before or after such transfer, and if such transfer is—

(1) a transfer of a securities contract entered into or carried by or through the debtor on behalf of a customer, and of any cash, security, or other property margining or securing such securities contract; or

(2) the liquidation of a securities contract entered into or carried by or through the debtor on behalf of a customer.

### § 750 Distribution of securities

The trustee may not distribute a security except under section 751 of this title.

### § 751 Customer name securities

The trustee shall deliver any customer name security to or on behalf of the customer entitled to such security, unless such customer has a negative net equity. With the approval of the trustee, a customer may reclaim a customer name security after payment to the trustee, within such period as the trustee allows, of any claim of the debtor against such customer to the extent that such customer will not have a negative net equity after such payment.

### § 752 Customer property

(a) The trustee shall distribute customer property ratably to customers on the basis and to the extent of such customers' allowed net equity claims and in priority to all other claims, except claims of the kind specified in section 507(a)(2) of this title that are attributable to the administration of such customer property.

(b) (1) The trustee shall distribute customer property in excess of that distributed under subsection (a) of this section in accordance with section 726 of this title.

(2) Except as provided in section 510 of this title, if a customer is not paid the full amount of such customer's allowed net equity claim from customer property, the unpaid portion of such claim is a claim entitled to distribution under section 726 of this title.

(c) Any cash or security remaining after the liquidation of a security interest created under a security agreement made by the debtor, excluding property excluded under section 741(4)(B) of this title, shall be apportioned between the general estate and customer property in the same proportion as the general estate of the debtor and customer property were subject to such security interest.

### § 753 Stockbroker liquidation and forward contract merchants, commodity brokers, stockbrokers, financial institutions, financial participants, securities clearing agencies, swap participants, repo participants, and master netting agreement participants

Notwithstanding any other provision of this title, the exercise of rights by a forward contract merchant, commodity broker, stockbroker, financial institution, financial participant, securities clearing agency, swap participant, repo participant, or master netting agreement participant under this title shall not affect the priority of any unsecured claim it may have after the exercise of such rights.

## Subchapter IV
## Commodity Broker Liquidation

### § 761 Definitions for this subchapter

In this subchapter—

(1) "Act" means Commodity Exchange Act;

(2) "clearing organization" means a derivatives clearing organization registered under the Act;

(3) "Commission" means Commodity Futures Trading Commission;

(4) "commodity contract" means—

(A) with respect to a futures commission merchant, contract for the purchase or sale of a commodity for future delivery on, or subject to the rules of, a contract market or board of trade;

(B) with respect to a foreign futures commission merchant, foreign future;

(C) with respect to a leverage transaction merchant, leverage transaction;

(D) with respect to a clearing organization, contract for the purchase or sale of a commodity for future delivery on, or subject to the rules of, a contract market or board of trade that is cleared by such clearing organization, or commodity option traded on, or subject to the rules of, a contract market or board of trade that is cleared by such clearing organization;

(E) with respect to a commodity options dealer, commodity option;

(F) (i) any other contract, option, agreement, or transaction that is similar to a contract, option, agreement, or transaction referred to in this paragraph; and

(ii) with respect to a futures commission merchant or a clearing organization, any other contract, option, agreement, or transaction, in each case, that is cleared by a clearing organization;

(G) any combination of the agreements or transactions referred to in this paragraph;

(H) any option to enter into an agreement or transaction referred to in this paragraph;

(I) a master agreement that provides for an agreement or transaction referred to in subparagraph (A), (B), (C), (D), (E), (F), (G), or (H), together with all supplements to such master agreement, without regard to whether the master agreement provides for an agreement or transaction that is not a commodity contract under this paragraph, except that the master agreement shall be considered to be a commodity contract under this paragraph only with respect to each agreement or transaction under the master agreement that is referred to in subparagraph (A), (B), (C), (D), (E), (F), (G), or (H); or

(J) any security agreement or arrangement or other credit enhancement related to any agreement or transaction referred to in this paragraph, including any guarantee or reimbursement obligation by or to a commodity broker or financial participant in connection with any agreement or transaction referred to in this paragraph, but not to exceed the damages in connection with any such agreement or transaction, measured in accordance with section 562;

(5) "commodity option" means agreement or transaction subject to regulation under section 4c(b) of the Act;

(6) "commodity options dealer" means person that extends credit to, or that accepts cash, a security, or other property from, a customer of such person for the purchase or sale of an interest in a commodity option;

(7) "contract market" means a registered entity;

(8) "contract of sale", "commodity", "derivatives clearing organization", "future delivery", "board of trade", "registered entity", and "futures commission merchant" have the meanings assigned to those terms in the Act;

(9) "customer" means—

(A) with respect to a futures commission merchant—

(i) entity for or with whom such futures commission merchant deals and that holds a claim against such futures commission merchant on account of a commodity contract made, received, acquired, or held by or through such futures commission merchant in the ordinary course of such futures commission merchant's business as a futures commission merchant from or for a commodity contract account of such entity; or

(ii) entity that holds a claim against such futures commission merchant arising out of—

(I) the making, liquidation, or change in the value of a commodity contract of a kind specified in clause (i) of this subparagraph;

(II) a deposit or payment of cash, a security, or other property with such futures commission merchant for the purpose of making or margining such a commodity contract; or

(III) the making or taking of delivery on such a commodity contract;

(B) with respect to a foreign futures commission merchant—

(i) entity for or with whom such foreign futures commission merchant deals and that holds a claim against such foreign futures commission merchant on account of a commodity contract made, received, acquired, or held by or through such foreign futures commission merchant in the ordinary course of such foreign futures commission merchant's business as a foreign futures commission merchant from or for the foreign futures account of such entity; or

(ii) entity that holds a claim against such foreign futures commission merchant arising out of—

(I) the making, liquidation, or change in value of a commodity contract of a kind specified in clause (i) of this subparagraph;

(II) a deposit or payment of cash, a security, or other property with such foreign futures commission merchant for the purpose of making or margining such a commodity contract; or

(III) the making or taking of delivery on such a commodity contract;

(C) with respect to a leverage transaction merchant—

(i) entity for or with whom such leverage transaction merchant deals and that holds a claim against such leverage transaction merchant on account of a commodity contract engaged in by or with such leverage transaction merchant in the ordinary course of such leverage transaction merchant's business as a leverage transaction merchant from or for the leverage account of such entity; or

(ii) entity that holds a claim against such leverage transaction merchant arising out of—

(I) the making, liquidation, or change in value of a commodity contract of a kind specified in clause (i) of this subparagraph;

(II) a deposit or payment of cash, a security, or other property with such leverage transaction merchant for the purpose of entering into or margining such a commodity contract; or

(III) the making or taking of delivery on such a commodity contract;

(D) with respect to a clearing organization, clearing member of such clearing organization with whom such clearing organization deals and that holds a claim against such clearing organization on account of cash, a security, or other property received by such clearing organization to margin, guarantee, or secure a commodity contract in such clearing member's proprietary account or customers' account; or

(E) with respect to a commodity options dealer—

(i) entity for or with whom such commodity options dealer deals and that holds a claim on account of a commodity contract made, received, acquired, or held by or through such commodity options dealer in the ordinary course of such commodity options dealer's business as a commodity options dealer from or for the commodity options account of such entity; or

(ii) entity that holds a claim against such commodity options dealer arising out of—

(I) the making of, liquidation of, exercise of, or a change in value of, a commodity contract of a kind specified in clause (i) of this subparagraph; or

(II) a deposit or payment of cash, a security, or other property with such commodity options dealer for the purpose of making, exercising, or margining such a commodity contract;

(10) "customer property" means cash, a security, or other property, or proceeds of such cash, security, or property, received, acquired, or held by or for the account of the debtor, from or for the account of a customer—

(A) including—

(i) property received, acquired, or held to margin, guarantee, secure, purchase, or sell a commodity contract;

(ii) profits or contractual or other rights accruing to a customer as a result of a commodity contract;

(iii) an open commodity contract;

(iv) specifically identifiable customer property;

(v) warehouse receipt or other document held by the debtor evidencing ownership of or title to property to be delivered to fulfill a commodity contract from or for the account of a customer;

(vi) cash, a security, or other property received by the debtor as payment for a commodity to be delivered to fulfill a commodity contract from or for the account of a customer;

(vii) a security held as property of the debtor to the extent such security is necessary to meet a net equity claim based on a security of the same class and series of an issuer;

(viii) property that was unlawfully converted from and that is the lawful property of the estate; and

(ix) other property of the debtor that any applicable law, rule, or regulation requires to be set aside or held for the benefit of a customer, unless including such property as customer property would not significantly increase customer property; but

(B) not including property to the extent that a customer does not have a claim against the debtor based on such property;

(11) "foreign future" means contract for the purchase or sale of a commodity for future delivery on, or subject to the rules of, a board of trade outside the United States;

(12) "foreign futures commission merchant" means entity engaged in soliciting or accepting orders for the purchase or sale of a foreign future or that, in connection with such a solicitation or acceptance, accepts cash, a security, or other property, or extends credit to margin, guarantee, or secure any trade or contract that results from such a solicitation or acceptance;

(13) "leverage transaction" means agreement that is subject to regulation under section 19 of the Commodity Exchange Act, and that is commonly known to the commodities trade as a margin account, margin contract, leverage account, or leverage contract;

(14) "leverage transaction merchant" means person in the business of engaging in leverage transactions;

(15) "margin payment" means payment or deposit of cash, a security, or other property, that is commonly known to the commodities trade as original margin, initial margin, maintenance margin, or variation margin, including mark-to-market payments, settlement payments, variation payments, daily settlement payments, and final settlement payments made as adjustments to settlement prices;

(16) "member property" means customer property received, acquired, or held by or for the account of a debtor that is a clearing organization, from or for the proprietary account of a customer that is a clearing member of the debtor; and

(17) "net equity" means, subject to such rules and regulations as the Commission promulgates under the Act, with respect to the aggregate of all of a customer's accounts that such customer has in the same capacity—

(A) the balance remaining in such customer's accounts immediately after—

(i) all commodity contracts of such customer have been transferred, liquidated, or become identified for delivery; and

(ii) all obligations of such customer in such capacity to the debtor have been offset; plus

(B) the value, as of the date of return under section 766 of this title, of any specifically identifiable customer property actually returned to such customer before the date specified in subparagraph (A) of this paragraph; plus

(C) the value, as of the date of transfer, of—

(i) any commodity contract to which such customer is entitled that is transferred to another person under section 766 of this title; and

(ii) any cash, security, or other property of such customer transferred to such other person under section 766 of this title to margin or secure such transferred commodity contract.

## § 762 Notice to the Commission and right to be heard

(a) The clerk shall give the notice required by section 342 of this title to the Commission.

(b) The Commission may raise and may appear and be heard on any issue in a case under this chapter.

Bankruptcy Rule Reference: 2002

## § 763 Treatment of accounts

(a) Accounts held by the debtor for a particular customer in separate capacities shall be treated as accounts of separate customers.

(b) A member of a clearing organization shall be deemed to hold such member's proprietary account in a separate capacity from such member's customers' account.

(c) The net equity in a customer's account may not be offset against the net equity in the account of any other customer.

## § 764 Voidable transfers

(a) Except as otherwise provided in this section, any transfer by the debtor of property that, but for such transfer, would have been customer property, may be avoided by the trustee, and such property shall be treated as customer property, if and to the extent that the trustee avoids such transfer under section 544, 545, 547, 548, 549, or 724(a) of this title. For the purpose of such sections, the property so transferred shall be deemed to have been property of the debtor, and, if such transfer was made to a customer or for a customer's benefit, such customer shall be deemed, for the purposes of this section, to have been a creditor.

(b) Notwithstanding sections 544, 545, 547, 548, 549, and 724(a) of this title, the trustee may not avoid a transfer made before seven days after the order for relief, if such transfer is approved by the Commission by rule or order, either before or after such transfer, and if such transfer is—

(1) a transfer of a commodity contract entered into or carried by or through the debtor on behalf of a customer, and of any cash, securities, or other property margining or securing such commodity contract; or

(2) the liquidation of a commodity contract entered into or carried by or through the debtor on behalf of a customer.

## § 765 Customer instructions

(a) The notice required by section 342 of this title to customers shall instruct each customer—

(1) to file a proof of such customer's claim promptly, and to specify in such claim any specifically identifiable security, property, or commodity contract; and

(2) to instruct the trustee of such customer's desired disposition, including transfer under section 766 of this title or liquidation, of any commodity contract specifically identified to such customer.

(b) The trustee shall comply, to the extent practicable, with any instruction received from a customer regarding such customer's desired disposition of any commodity contract specifically identified to such customer. If the trustee has transferred, under section 766 of this title, such a commodity contract, the trustee shall transmit any such instruction to the commodity broker to whom such commodity contract was so transferred.

BANKRUPTCY RULE REFERENCE: 2002

## § 766 Treatment of customer property

(a) The trustee shall answer all margin calls with respect to a specifically identifiable commodity contract of a customer until such time as the trustee returns or transfers such commodity contract, but the trustee may not make a margin payment that has the effect of a distribution to such customer of more than that to which such customer is entitled under subsection (h) or (i) of this section.

(b) The trustee shall prevent any open commodity contract from remaining open after the last day of trading in such commodity contract, or into the first day on which notice of intent to deliver on such commodity contract may be tendered, whichever occurs first. With respect to any commodity contract that has remained open after the last day of trading in such commodity contract or with respect to which delivery must be made or accepted under the rules of the contract market on which such commodity contract was made, the trustee may operate the business of the debtor for the purpose of—

(1) accepting or making tender of notice of intent to deliver the physical commodity underlying such commodity contract;

(2) facilitating delivery of such commodity; or

(3) disposing of such commodity if a party to such commodity contract defaults.

(c) The trustee shall return promptly to a customer any specifically identifiable security, property, or commodity contract to which such customer is entitled, or shall transfer, on such customer's behalf, such security, property, or commodity contract to a commodity broker that is not a debtor under this title subject to such rules or regulations as the Commission may prescribe, to the extent that the value of such security, property, or commodity contract does not exceed the amount to which such customer would be entitled under subsection (h) or (i) of this section if such security, property, or commodity contract were not returned or transferred under this subsection.

(d) If the value of a specifically identifiable security, property, or commodity contract exceeds the amount to which the customer of the debtor is entitled under subsection (h) or (i) of this section, then such customer to whom such security, property, or commodity contract is specifically identified may deposit cash with the trustee equal to the difference between the value of such security, property, or commodity contract and such amount, and the trustee then shall—

(1) return promptly such security, property, or commodity contract to such customer; or

(2) transfer, on such customer's behalf, such security, property, or commodity contract to a commodity broker that is not a debtor under this title, subject to such rules or regulations as the Commission may prescribe.

(e) Subject to subsection (b) of this section, the trustee shall liquidate any commodity contract that—

(1) is identified to a particular customer and with respect to which such customer has not timely instructed the trustee as to the desired disposition of such commodity contract;

(2) cannot be transferred under subsection (c) of this section; or

(3) cannot be identified to a particular customer.

(f) As soon as practicable after the commencement of the case, the trustee shall reduce to money, consistent with good market practice, all securities and other property, other than commodity contracts, held as property of the estate, except for specifically identifiable securities or property distributable under subsection (h) or (i) of this section.

(g) The trustee may not distribute a security or other property except under subsection (h) or (i) of this section.

(h) Except as provided in subsection (b) of this section, the trustee shall distribute customer property ratably to customers on the basis and to the extent of such customers' allowed net equity claims, and in priority to all other claims, except claims of a kind specified in section 507(a)(2) of this title that are attributable to the administration of customer property. Such distribution shall be in the form of—

(1) cash;

(2) the return or transfer, under subsection (c) or (d) of this section, of specifically identifiable customer securities, property, or commodity contracts; or

(3) payment of margin calls under subsection (a) of this section.

Notwithstanding any other provision of this subsection, a customer net equity claim based on a proprietary account, as defined by Commission rule, regulation, or order, may not be paid either in whole or in part, directly or indirectly, out of customer property unless all other customer net equity claims have been paid in full.

(i) If the debtor is a clearing organization, the trustee shall distribute—

(1) customer property, other than member property, ratably to customers on the basis and to the extent of such customers' allowed net equity claims based on such customers' accounts other than proprietary accounts, and in priority to all other claims, except claims of a kind specified in section 507(a)(2) of this title that are attributable to the administration of such customer property; and

(2) member property ratably to customers on the basis and to the extent of such customers' allowed net equity claims based on such customers' proprietary accounts, and in priority to all other claims, except claims of a kind specified in section 507(a)(2) of this title that are attributable to the administration of member property or customer property.

(j) (1) The trustee shall distribute customer property in excess of that distributed under subsection (h) or (i) of this section in accordance with section 726 of this title.

(2) Except as provided in section 510 of this title if a customer is not paid the full amount of such customer's allowed net equity claim from customer property, the unpaid portion of such claim is a claim entitled to distribution under section 726 of this title.

### § 767 Commodity broker liquidation and forward contract merchants, commodity brokers, stockbrokers, financial institutions, financial participants, securities clearing agencies, swap participants, repo participants, and master netting agreement participants

Notwithstanding any other provision of this title, the exercise of rights by a forward contract merchant, commodity broker, stockbroker, financial institution, financial participant, securities clearing agency, swap participant, repo participant, or master netting agreement participant under this title shall not affect the priority of any unsecured claim it may have after the exercise of such rights.

## Subchapter V
## Clearing Bank Liquidation

### § 781 Definitions

For purposes of this subchapter, the following definitions shall apply:

(1) Board. The term "Board" means the Board of Governors of the Federal Reserve System.

(2) Depository institution. The term "depository institution" has the same meaning as in section 3 of the Federal Deposit Insurance Act.

(3) Clearing bank. The term "clearing bank" means an uninsured State member bank, or a corporation organized under section 25A of the Federal Reserve Act, which operates, or operates as, a multilateral clearing organization pursuant to section 409 of the Federal Deposit Insurance Corporation Improvement Act of 1991.

### § 782 Selection of trustee

(a) In General.

(1) Appointment. Notwithstanding any other provision of this title, the conservator or receiver who files the petition shall be the trustee under this chapter, unless the Board designates an alternative trustee.

(2) Successor. The Board may designate a successor trustee if required.

(b) Authority of Trustee. Whenever the Board appoints or designates a trustee, chapter 3 and sections 704 and 705 of this title shall apply to the Board in the same way and to the same extent that they apply to a United States trustee.

### § 783 Additional powers of trustee

(a) Distribution of Property Not of the Estate. The trustee under this subchapter has power to distribute property not of the estate, including distributions to customers that are mandated by subchapters III and IV of this chapter.

(b) Disposition of Institution. The trustee under this subchapter may, after notice and a hearing—

(1) sell the clearing bank to a depository institution or consortium of depository institutions (which consortium may agree on the allocation of the clearing bank among the consortium);

(2) merge the clearing bank with a depository institution;

(3) transfer contracts to the same extent as could a receiver for a depository institution under paragraphs (9) and (10) of section 11(e) of the Federal Deposit Insurance Act;

(4) transfer assets or liabilities to a depository institution; and

(5) transfer assets and liabilities to a bridge depository institution as provided in paragraphs (1), (3)(A), (5), and (6) of section 11(n) of the Federal Deposit Insurance Act, paragraphs (9) through (13) of such section, and

subparagraphs (A) through (H) and subparagraph (K) of paragraph (4) of such section 11(n), except that—

(A) the bridge depository institution to which such assets or liabilities are transferred shall be treated as a clearing bank for the purpose of this subsection; and

(B) any references in any such provision of law to the Federal Deposit Insurance Corporation shall be construed to be references to the appointing agency and that references to deposit insurance shall be omitted.

(c) CERTAIN TRANSFERS INCLUDED. Any reference in this section to transfers of liabilities includes a ratable transfer of liabilities within a priority class.

## § 784 Right to be heard

The Board or a Federal reserve bank (in the case of a clearing bank that is a member of that bank) may raise and may appear and be heard on any issue in a case under this subchapter.

# CHAPTER 9
# ADJUSTMENT OF DEBTS OF A MUNICIPALITY

## SUBCHAPTER I
## General Provisions

### § 901 Applicability of other sections of this title

(a) Sections 301, 333, 344, 347(b), 349, 350(b), 351, 361, 362, 364(c), 364(d), 364(e), 364(f), 365, 366, 501, 502, 503, 504, 506, 507(a)(2), 509, 510, 524(a)(1), 524(a)(2), 544, 545, 546, 547, 548, 549(a), 549(c), 549(d), 550, 551, 552, 553, 555, 556, 557, 559, 560, 561, 562, 1102, 1103, 1109, 1111(b), 1122, 1123(a)(1), 1123(a)(2), 1123(a)(3), 1123(a)(4), 1123(a)(5), 1123(b), 1123(d), 1124, 1125, 1126(a), 1126(b), 1126(c), 1126(e), 1126(f), 1126(g), 1127(d), 1128, 1129(a)(2), 1129(a)(3), 1129(a)(6), 1129(a)(8), 1129(a)(10), 1129(b)(1), 1129(b)(2)(A), 1129(b)(2)(B), 1142(b), 1143, 1144, and 1145 of this title apply in a case under this chapter.

(b) A term used in a section of this title made applicable in a case under this chapter by subsection (a) of this section or section 103(e) of this title has the meaning defined for such term for the purpose of such applicable section, unless such term is otherwise defined in section 902 of this title.

(c) A section made applicable in a case under this chapter by subsection (a) of this section that is operative if the business of the debtor is authorized to be operated is operative in a case under this chapter.

### § 902 Definitions for this chapter

In this chapter—

(1) "property of the estate", when used in a section that is made applicable in a case under this chapter by section 103(e) or 901 of this title, means property of the debtor;

(2) "special revenues" means—

(A) receipts derived from the ownership, operation, or disposition of projects or systems of the debtor that are primarily used or intended to be used primarily to provide transportation, utility, or other services, including the proceeds of borrowings to finance the projects or systems;

(B) special excise taxes imposed on particular activities or transactions;

(C) incremental tax receipts from the benefited area in the case of tax-increment financing;

(D) other revenues or receipts derived from particular functions of the debtor, whether or not the debtor has other functions; or

(E) taxes specifically levied to finance one or more projects or systems, excluding receipts from general property, sales, or income taxes (other than tax-increment financing) levied to finance the general purposes of the debtor;

(3) "special tax payer" means record owner or holder of legal or equitable title to real property against which a special assessment or special tax has been

levied the proceeds of which are the sole source of payment of an obligation issued by the debtor to defray the cost of an improvement relating to such real property;

(4) "special tax payer affected by the plan" means special tax payer with respect to whose real property the plan proposes to increase the proportion of special assessments or special taxes referred to in paragraph (2) of this section assessed against such real property; and

(5) "trustee", when used in a section that is made applicable in a case under this chapter by section 103(e) or 901 of this title, means debtor, except as provided in section 926 of this title.

### § 903 Reservation of State power to control municipalities

This chapter does not limit or impair the power of a State to control, by legislation or otherwise, a municipality of or in such State in the exercise of the political or governmental powers of such municipality, including expenditures for such exercise, but—

(1) a State law prescribing a method of composition of indebtedness of such municipality may not bind any creditor that does not consent to such composition; and

(2) a judgment entered under such a law may not bind a creditor that does not consent to such composition.

### § 904 Limitation on jurisdiction and powers of court

Notwithstanding any power of the court, unless the debtor consents or the plan so provides, the court may not, by any stay, order, or decree, in the case or otherwise, interfere with—

(1) any of the political or governmental powers of the debtor;

(2) any of the property or revenues of the debtor; or

(3) the debtor's use or enjoyment of any income-producing property.

## SUBCHAPTER II
## Administration

### § 921 Petition and proceedings relating to petition

(a) Notwithstanding sections 109(d) and 301 of this title, a case under this chapter concerning an unincorporated tax or special assessment district that does not have such district's own officials is commenced by the filing under section 301 of this title of a petition under this chapter by such district's governing authority or the board or body having authority to levy taxes or assessments to meet the obligations of such district.

(b) The chief judge of the court of appeals for the circuit embracing the district in which the case is commenced shall designate the bankruptcy judge to conduct the case.

(c) After any objection to the petition, the court, after notice and a hearing, may dismiss the petition if the debtor did not file the petition in good faith or if the petition does not meet the requirements of this title.

(d) If the petition is not dismissed under subsection (c) of this section, the court shall order relief under this chapter notwithstanding section 301(b).

(e) The court may not, on account of an appeal from an order for relief, delay any proceeding under this chapter in the case in which the appeal is being taken; nor shall any court order a stay of such proceeding pending such appeal. The reversal on appeal of a finding of jurisdiction does not affect the validity of any debt incurred that is authorized by the court under section 364(c) or 364(d) of this title.

BANKRUPTCY RULE REFERENCES: 1005, 1006 and 1007

### § 922 Automatic stay of enforcement of claims against the debtor

(a) A petition filed under this chapter operates as a stay, in addition to the stay provided by section 362 of this title, applicable to all entities, of—

(1) the commencement or continuation, including the issuance or employment of process, of a judicial, administrative, or other action or proceeding against an officer or inhabitant of the debtor that seeks to enforce a claim against the debtor; and

(2) the enforcement of a lien on or arising out of taxes or assessments owed to the debtor.

(b) Subsections (c), (d), (e), (f), and (g) of section 362 of this title apply to a stay under subsection (a) of this section the same as such subsections apply to a stay under section 362(a) of this title.

(c) If the debtor provides, under section 362, 364, or 922 of this title, adequate protection of the interest of the holder of a claim secured by a lien on property of the debtor and if, notwithstanding such protection such creditor has a claim arising from the stay of action against such property under section 362 or 922 of this title or from the granting of a lien under section 364(d) of this title, then such claim shall be allowable as an administrative expense under section 503(b) of this title.

(d) Notwithstanding section 362 of this title and subsection (a) of this section, a petition filed under this chapter does not operate as a stay of application of pledged special revenues in a manner consistent with section 927 of this title to payment of indebtedness secured by such revenues.

BANKRUPTCY RULE REFERENCES: 4001, 9013 and 9014

**§ 923 Notice**

There shall be given notice of the commencement of a case under this chapter, notice of an order for relief under this chapter, and notice of the dismissal of a case under this chapter. Such notice shall also be published at least once a week for three successive weeks in at least one newspaper of general circulation published within the district in which the case is commenced, and in such other newspaper having a general circulation among bond dealers and bondholders as the court designates.

BANKRUPTCY RULE REFERENCES: 2002, 9007 and 9008

**§ 924 List of creditors**

The debtor shall file a list of creditors.

BANKRUPTCY RULE REFERENCES: 1007, 1008 and 1009

**§ 925 Effect of list of claims**

A proof of claim is deemed filed under section 501 of this title for any claim that appears in the list filed under section 924 of this title, except a claim that is listed as disputed, contingent, or unliquidated.

BANKRUPTCY RULE REFERENCES: 3001, 3003, 3004, 3006, 3007 and 3008

**§ 926 Avoiding powers**

(a) If the debtor refuses to pursue a cause of action under section 544, 545, 547, 548, 549(a), or 550 of this title, then on request of a creditor, the court may appoint a trustee to pursue such cause of action.

(b) A transfer of property of the debtor to or for the benefit of any holder of a bond or note, on account of such bond or note, may not be avoided under section 547 of this title.

BANKRUPTCY RULE REFERENCES: 9013 and 9014

**§ 927 Limitation on recourse**

The holder of a claim payable solely from special revenues of the debtor under applicable nonbankruptcy law shall not be treated as having recourse against the debtor on account of such claim pursuant to section 1111(b) of this title.

**§ 928 Post petition effect of security interest**

(a) Notwithstanding section 552(a) of this title and subject to subsection (b) of this section, special revenues acquired by the debtor after the commencement of the case shall remain subject to any lien resulting from any security agreement entered into by the debtor before the commencement of the case.

(b) Any such lien on special revenues, other than municipal betterment assessments, derived from a project or system shall be subject to the necessary operating expenses of such project or system, as the case may be.

### § 929 Municipal leases

A lease to a municipality shall not be treated as an executory contract or unexpired lease for the purposes of section 365 or 502(b)(6) of this title solely by reason of its being subject to termination in the event the debtor fails to appropriate rent.

### § 930 Dismissal

(a) After notice and a hearing, the court may dismiss a case under this chapter for cause, including—

(1) want of prosecution;

(2) unreasonable delay by the debtor that is prejudicial to creditors;

(3) failure to propose a plan within the time fixed under section 941 of this title;

(4) if a plan is not accepted within any time fixed by the court;

(5) denial of confirmation of a plan under section 943(b) of this title and denial of additional time for filing another plan or a modification of a plan; or

(6) if the court has retained jurisdiction after confirmation of a plan—

(A) material default by the debtor with respect to a term of such plan; or

(B) termination of such plan by reason of the occurrence of a condition specified in such plan.

(b) The court shall dismiss a case under this chapter if confirmation of a plan under this chapter is refused.

BANKRUPTCY RULE REFERENCES: 1017, 2002, 9013 and 9014

## Subchapter III
## The Plan

### § 941 Filing of plan

The debtor shall file a plan for the adjustment of the debtor's debts. If such a plan is not filed with the petition, the debtor shall file such a plan at such later time as the court fixes.

Bankruptcy Rule References: 2002, 3016, 3017, 3018 and 3020

### § 942 Modification of plan

The debtor may modify the plan at any time before confirmation, but may not modify the plan so that the plan as modified fails to meet the requirements of this chapter. After the debtor files a modification, the plan as modified becomes the plan.

Bankruptcy Rule References: 2002, 3016 and 3019

### § 943 Confirmation

(a) A special tax payer may object to confirmation of a plan.

(b) The court shall confirm the plan if—

(1) the plan complies with the provisions of this title made applicable by sections 103(e) and 901 of this title;

(2) the plan complies with the provisions of this chapter;

(3) all amounts to be paid by the debtor or by any person for services or expenses in the case or incident to the plan have been fully disclosed and are reasonable;

(4) the debtor is not prohibited by law from taking any action necessary to carry out the plan;

(5) except to the extent that the holder of a particular claim has agreed to a different treatment of such claim, the plan provides that on the effective date of the plan each holder of a claim of a kind specified in section 507(a)(2) of this title will receive on account of such claim cash equal to the allowed amount of such claim;

(6) any regulatory or electoral approval necessary under applicable nonbankruptcy law in order to carry out any provision of the plan has been obtained, or such provision is expressly conditioned on such approval; and

(7) the plan is in the best interests of creditors and is feasible.

Bankruptcy Rule References: 2002, 3016, 3017, 3018, 3019 and 3020

### § 944 Effect of confirmation

(a) The provisions of a confirmed plan bind the debtor and any creditor, whether or not—

(1) a proof of such creditor's claim is filed or deemed filed under section 501

of this title;

(2) such claim is allowed under section 502 of this title; or

(3) such creditor has accepted the plan.

(b) Except as provided in subsection (c) of this section, the debtor is discharged from all debts as of the time when—

(1) the plan is confirmed;

(2) the debtor deposits any consideration to be distributed under the plan with a disbursing agent appointed by the court; and

(3) the court has determined—

(A) that any security so deposited will constitute, after distribution, a valid legal obligation of the debtor; and

(B) that any provision made to pay or secure payment of such obligation is valid.

(c) The debtor is not discharged under subsection (b) of this section from any debt—

(1) excepted from discharge by the plan or order confirming the plan; or

(2) owed to an entity that, before confirmation of the plan, had neither notice nor actual knowledge of the case.

Bankruptcy Rule Reference: 3020

## § 945 Continuing jurisdiction and closing of the case

(a) The court may retain jurisdiction over the case for such period of time as is necessary for the successful implementation of the plan.

(b) Except as provided in subsection (a) of this section, the court shall close the case when administration of the case has been completed.

Bankruptcy Rule Reference: 3020

## § 946 Effect of exchange of securities before the date of the filing of the petition

The exchange of a new security under the plan for a claim covered by the plan, whether such exchange occurred before or after the date of the filing of the petition, does not limit or impair the effectiveness of the plan or of any provision of this chapter. The amount and number specified in section 1126(c) of this title include the amount and number of claims formerly held by a creditor that has participated in any such exchange.

# CHAPTER 11
# REORGANIZATION

## SUBCHAPTER I
## Officers and Administration

### § 1101 Definitions for this chapter

In this chapter—

(1) "debtor in possession" means debtor except when a person that has qualified under section 322 of this title is serving as trustee in the case;

(2) "substantial consummation" means—

(A) transfer of all or substantially all of the property proposed by the plan to be transferred;

(B) assumption by the debtor or by the successor to the debtor under the plan of the business or of the management of all or substantially all of the property dealt with by the plan; and

(C) commencement of distribution under the plan.

### § 1102 Creditors' and equity security holders' committees

(a)(1) Except as provided in paragraph (3), as soon as practicable after the order for relief under chapter 11 of this title, the United States trustee shall appoint a committee of creditors holding unsecured claims and may appoint additional committees of creditors or of equity security holders as the United States trustee deems appropriate.

(2) On request of a party in interest, the court may order the appointment of additional committees of creditors or of equity security holders if necessary to assure adequate representation of creditors or of equity security holders. The United States trustee shall appoint any such committee.

(3) Unless the court for cause orders otherwise, a committee of creditors may not be appointed in a small business case or a case under subchapter V of this chapter.

(4) On request of a party in interest and after notice and a hearing, the court may order the United States trustee to change the membership of a committee appointed under this subsection, if the court determines that the change is necessary to ensure adequate representation of creditors or equity security holders. The court may order the United States trustee to increase the number of members of a committee to include a creditor that is a small business concern (as described in section 3(a)(1) of the Small Business Act), if the court determines that the creditor holds claims (of the kind represented by the committee) the aggregate amount of which, in comparison to the annual gross revenue of that creditor, is disproportionately large.

(b)(1) A committee of creditors appointed under subsection (a) of this section shall ordinarily consist of the persons, willing to serve, that hold the seven largest claims against the debtor of the kinds represented on such committee, or of the members of a committee organized by creditors before the commencement of the case under this chapter, if such committee was fairly chosen and is representative of the different kinds of claims to be represented.

(2) A committee of equity security holders appointed under subsection (a)(2) of this section shall ordinarily consist of the persons, willing to serve, that hold the seven largest amounts of equity securities of the debtor of the kinds represented on such committee.

(3) A committee appointed under subsection (a) shall—

(A) provide access to information for creditors who—

(i) hold claims of the kind represented by that committee; and

(ii) are not appointed to the committee;

(B) solicit and receive comments from the creditors described in subparagraph (A); and

(C) be subject to a court order that compels any additional report or disclosure to be made to the creditors described in subparagraph (A).

BANKRUPTCY RULE REFERENCES: 1007, 1007-I, 1020, 2003, 2007 and 2019

## § 1103 Powers and duties of committees

(a) At a scheduled meeting of a committee appointed under section 1102 of this title, at which a majority of the members of such committee are present, and with the court's approval, such committee may select and authorize the employment by such committee of one or more attorneys, accountants, or other agents, to represent or perform services for such committee.

(b) An attorney or accountant employed to represent a committee appointed under section 1102 of this title may not, while employed by such committee, represent any other entity having an adverse interest in connection with the case. Representation of one or more creditors of the same class as represented by the committee shall not per se constitute the representation of an adverse interest.

(c) A committee appointed under section 1102 of this title may—

(1) consult with the trustee or debtor in possession concerning the administration of the case;

(2) investigate the acts, conduct, assets, liabilities, and financial condition of the debtor, the operation of the debtor's business and the desirability of the continuance of such business, and any other matter relevant to the case or to the formulation of a plan;

(3) participate in the formulation of a plan, advise those represented by such committee of such committee's determinations as to any plan formulated, and collect and file with the court acceptances or rejections of a plan;

(4) request the appointment of a trustee or examiner under section 1104 of this title; and

(5) perform such other services as are in the interest of those represented.

(d) As soon as practicable after the appointment of a committee under section 1102 of this title, the trustee shall meet with such committee to transact such business as may be necessary and proper.

BANKRUPTCY RULE REFERENCES: 2002, 2014, 5002 and 5004

## § 1104 Appointment of trustee or examiner

(a) At any time after the commencement of the case but before confirmation of a plan, on request of a party in interest or the United States trustee, and after notice and a hearing, the court shall order the appointment of a trustee—

(1) for cause, including fraud, dishonesty, incompetence, or gross mismanagement of the affairs of the debtor by current management, either before or after the commencement of the case, or similar cause, but not including the number of holders of securities of the debtor or the amount of assets or liabilities of the debtor; or

(2) if such appointment is in the interests of creditors, any equity security holders, and other interests of the estate, without regard to the number of holders of securities of the debtor or the amount of assets or liabilities of the debtor.

(b) (1) Except as provided in section 1163 of this title, on the request of a party in interest made not later than 30 days after the court orders the appointment of a trustee under subsection (a), the United States trustee shall convene a meeting of creditors for the purpose of electing one disinterested person to serve as trustee in the case. The election of a trustee shall be conducted in the manner provided in subsections (a), (b), and (c) of section 702 of this title.

(2) (A) If an eligible, disinterested trustee is elected at a meeting of creditors under paragraph (1), the United States trustee shall file a report certifying that election.

(B) Upon the filing of a report under subparagraph (A)—

(i) the trustee elected under paragraph (1) shall be considered to have been selected and appointed for purposes of this section; and

(ii) the service of any trustee appointed under subsection (a) shall terminate.

(C) The court shall resolve any dispute arising out of an election described in subparagraph (A).

(c) If the court does not order the appointment of a trustee under this section, then at any time before the confirmation of a plan, on request of a party in interest or the United States trustee, and after notice and a hearing, the court shall order the appointment of an examiner to conduct such an investigation of the debtor as is appropriate, including an investigation of any allegations of fraud, dishonesty, incompetence, misconduct, mismanagement, or irregularity in the management of the affairs of the debtor of or by current or former management of the debtor, if–

(1) such appointment is in the interests of creditors, any equity security holders, and other interests of the estate; or

(2) the debtor's fixed, liquidated, unsecured debts, other than debts for goods, services, or taxes, or owing to an insider, exceed $5,000,000.

(d) If the court orders the appointment of a trustee or an examiner, if a trustee or an examiner dies or resigns during the case or is removed under section 324 of this title, or if a trustee fails to qualify under section 322 of this title, then the United States trustee, after consultation with parties in interest, shall appoint, subject to the court's approval, one disinterested person other than the United States trustee to serve as trustee or examiner, as the case may be, in the case.

(e) The United States trustee shall move for the appointment of a trustee under subsection (a) if there are reasonable grounds to suspect that current members of the governing body of the debtor, the debtor's chief executive or chief financial officer, or members of the governing body who selected the debtor's chief executive or chief financial officer, participated in actual fraud, dishonesty, or criminal conduct in the management of the debtor or the debtor's public financial reporting.

Bankruptcy Rule References: 2006, 2007.1, 2008, 2009, 2010, 2011, 2012, 2013, 2015, 5002 and 9014

## § 1105 Termination of trustee's appointment

At any time before confirmation of a plan, on request of a party in interest or the United States trustee, and after notice and a hearing, the court may terminate the trustee's appointment and restore the debtor to possession and management of the property of the estate and of the operation of the debtor's business.

## § 1106 Duties of trustee and examiner

(a) A trustee shall–

(1) perform the duties of a trustee, as specified in paragraphs (2), (5), (7), (8), (9), (10), (11), and (12) of section 704(a);

(2) if the debtor has not done so, file the list, schedule, and statement required under section 521(a)(1) of this title;

(3) except to the extent that the court orders otherwise, investigate the acts, conduct, assets, liabilities, and financial condition of the debtor, the operation of the debtor's business and the desirability of the continuance of such business, and any other matter relevant to the case or to the formulation of a plan;

(4) as soon as practicable–

(A) file a statement of any investigation conducted under paragraph (3) of this subsection, including any fact ascertained pertaining to fraud, dishonesty, incompetence, misconduct, mismanagement, or irregularity in the management of the affairs of the debtor, or to a cause of action available to the estate; and

(B) transmit a copy or a summary of any such statement to any creditors' committee or equity security holders' committee, to any indenture trustee, and to such other entity as the court designates;

(5) as soon as practicable, file a plan under section 1121 of this title, file a report of why the trustee will not file a plan, or recommend conversion of the case to a case under chapter 7, 12, or 13 of this title or dismissal of the case;

(6) for any year for which the debtor has not filed a tax return required by law, furnish, without personal liability, such information as may be required by the governmental unit with which such tax return was to be filed, in light of the condition of the debtor's books and records and the availability of such information;

(7) after confirmation of a plan, file such reports as are necessary or as the court orders; and

(8) if with respect to the debtor there is a claim for a domestic support obligation, provide the applicable notice specified in subsection (c).

(b) An examiner appointed under section 1104(d) of this title shall perform the duties specified in paragraphs (3) and (4) of subsection (a) of this section, and, except to the extent that the court orders otherwise, any other duties of the trustee that the court orders the debtor in possession not to perform.

(c) (1) In a case described in subsection (a)(8) to which subsection (a)(8) applies, the trustee shall–

(A) (i) provide written notice to the holder of the claim described in subsection (a)(8) of such claim and of the right of such holder to use the services of the State child support enforcement agency established under sections 464 and 466 of the Social Security Act for the State in which such holder resides, for assistance in collecting child support during and after the case under this title; and

(ii) include in the notice required by clause (i) the address and telephone number of such State child support enforcement agency;

(B) (i) provide written notice to such State child support enforcement agency of such claim; and

(ii) include in the notice required by clause (i) the name, address, and telephone number of such holder; and

(C) at such time as the debtor is granted a discharge under section 1141, provide written notice to such holder and to such State child support enforcement agency of–

(i) the granting of the discharge;

(ii) the last recent known address of the debtor;

(iii) the last recent known name and address of the debtor's employer; and

(iv) the name of each creditor that holds a claim that—

(I) is not discharged under paragraph (2), (4), or (14A) of section 523(a); or

(II) was reaffirmed by the debtor under section 524(c).

(2) (A) The holder of a claim described in subsection (a)(8) or the State child enforcement support agency of the State in which such holder resides may request from a creditor described in paragraph (1)(C)(iv) the last known address of the debtor.

(B) Notwithstanding any other provision of law, a creditor that makes a disclosure of a last known address of a debtor in connection with a request made under subparagraph (A) shall not be liable by reason of making such disclosure.

Bankruptcy Rule References: 2015, 2015.1, 2015.2, 2015.3, 6009 and 9001

## § 1107 Rights, powers, and duties of debtor in possession

(a) Subject to any limitations on a trustee serving in a case under this chapter, and to such limitations or conditions as the court prescribes, a debtor in possession shall have all the rights, other than the right to compensation under section 330 of this title, and powers, and shall perform all the functions and duties, except the duties specified in sections 1106(a)(2), (3), and (4) of this title, of a trustee serving in a case under this chapter.

(b) Notwithstanding section 327(a) of this title, a person is not disqualified for employment under section 327 of this title by a debtor in possession solely because of such person's employment by or representation of the debtor before the commencement of the case.

Bankruptcy Rule References: 2004, 2011, 2014, 2015, 2015.3, 4002, 6009 and 9001

## § 1108 Authorization to operate business

Unless the court, on request of a party in interest and after notice and a hearing, orders otherwise, the trustee may operate the debtor's business.

Bankruptcy Rule References: 2015, 2015.3

## § 1109 Right to be heard

(a) The Securities and Exchange Commission may raise and may appear and be heard on any issue in a case under this chapter, but the Securities and Exchange Commission may not appeal from any judgment, order, or decree entered in the case.

(b) A party in interest, including the debtor, the trustee, a creditors' committee, an equity security holders' committee, a creditor, an equity security holder, or any indenture trustee, may raise and may appear and be heard on any issue in a case under this chapter.

Bankruptcy Rule References: 2018 and 7024

### § 1110 Aircraft equipment and vessels

(a) (1) Except as provided in paragraph (2) and subject to subsection (b), the right of a secured party with a security interest in equipment described in paragraph (3), or of a lessor or conditional vendor of such equipment, to take possession of such equipment in compliance with a security agreement, lease, or conditional sale contract, and to enforce any of its other rights or remedies, under such security agreement, lease, or conditional sale contract, to sell, lease, or otherwise retain or dispose of such equipment, is not limited or otherwise affected by any other provision of this title or by any power of the court.

(2) The right to take possession and to enforce the other rights and remedies described in paragraph (1) shall be subject to section 362 if—

(A) before the date that is 60 days after the date of the order for relief under this chapter, the trustee, subject to the approval of the court, agrees to perform all obligations of the debtor under such security agreement, lease, or conditional sale contract; and

(B) any default, other than a default of a kind specified in section 365(b)(2), under such security agreement, lease, or conditional sale contract—

(i) that occurs before the date of the order is cured before the expiration of such 60-day period;

(ii) that occurs after the date of the order and before the expiration of such 60-day period is cured before the later of—

(I) the date that is 30 days after the date of the default; or

(II) the expiration of such 60-day period; and

(iii) that occurs on or after the expiration of such 60-day period is cured in compliance with the terms of such security agreement, lease, or conditional sale contract, if a cure is permitted under that agreement, lease, or contract.

(3) The equipment described in this paragraph—

(A) is—

(i) an aircraft, aircraft engine, propeller, appliance, or spare part (as defined in section 40102 of title 49) that is subject to a security interest granted by, leased to, or conditionally sold to a debtor that, at the time such transaction is entered into, holds an air carrier operating certificate issued pursuant to chapter 447 of title 49 for aircraft capable of carrying 10 or more individuals or 6,000 pounds or more of cargo; or

(ii) a vessel documented under chapter 121 of title 46 that is subject to a security interest granted by, leased to, or conditionally sold to a debtor that is a water carrier that, at the time such transaction is entered into, holds a certificate of public convenience and necessity or permit issued by the Department of Transportation; and

(B) includes all records and documents relating to such equipment that are required, under the terms of the security agreement, lease, or conditional sale contract, to be surrendered or returned by the debtor in connection with the surrender or return of such equipment.

(4) Paragraph (1) applies to a secured party, lessor, or conditional vendor acting in its own behalf or acting as trustee or otherwise in behalf of another party.

(b) The trustee and the secured party, lessor, or conditional vendor whose right to take possession is protected under subsection (a) may agree, subject to the approval of the court, to extend the 60-day period specified in subsection (a)(1).

(c) (1) In any case under this chapter, the trustee shall immediately surrender and return to a secured party, lessor, or conditional vendor, described in subsection (a)(1), equipment described in subsection (a)(3), if at any time after the date of the order for relief under this chapter such secured party, lessor, or conditional vendor is entitled pursuant to subsection (a)(1) to take possession of such equipment and makes a written demand for such possession to the trustee.

(2) At such time as the trustee is required under paragraph (1) to surrender and return equipment described in subsection (a)(3), any lease of such equipment, and any security agreement or conditional sale contract relating to such equipment, if such security agreement or conditional sale contract is an executory contract, shall be deemed rejected.

(d) With respect to equipment first placed in service on or before October 22, 1994, for purposes of this section—

(1) the term "lease" includes any written agreement with respect to which the lessor and the debtor, as lessee, have expressed in the agreement or in a substantially contemporaneous writing that the agreement is to be treated as a lease for Federal income tax purposes; and

(2) the term "security interest" means a purchase-money equipment security interest.

## § 1111 Claims and interests

(a) A proof of claim or interest is deemed filed under section 501 of this title for any claim or interest that appears in the schedules filed under section 521(a)(1) or 1106(a)(2) of this title, except a claim or interest that is scheduled as disputed, contingent, or unliquidated.

(b) (1) (A) A claim secured by a lien on property of the estate shall be allowed or disallowed under section 502 of this title the same as if the holder of such claim had recourse against the debtor on account of such claim, whether or not such holder has such recourse, unless

(i) the class of which such claim is a part elects, by at least two-thirds in amount and more than half in number of allowed claims of such class, application of paragraph (2) of this subsection; or

(ii) such holder does not have such recourse and such property is sold under section 363 of this title or is to be sold under the plan.

(B) A class of claims may not elect application of paragraph (2) of this subsection if—

(i) the interest on account of such claims of the holders of such claims in such property is of inconsequential value; or

(ii) the holder of a claim of such class has recourse against the debtor on account of such claim and such property is sold under section 363 of this title or is to be sold under the plan.

(2) If such an election is made, then notwithstanding section 506(a) of this title, such claim is a secured claim to the extent that such claim is allowed.

BANKRUPTCY RULE REFERENCES: 1019, 2019, 3002, 3003, 3004, 3005, 3006, 3007, 3008, 3013, 3014, 5005 and 7015

### § 1112 Conversion or dismissal

(a) The debtor may convert a case under this chapter to a case under chapter 7 of this title unless—

(1) the debtor is not a debtor in possession;

(2) the case originally was commenced as an involuntary case under this chapter; or

(3) the case was converted to a case under this chapter other than on the debtor's request.

(b) (1) Except as provided in paragraph (2) and subsection (c), on request of a party in interest, and after notice and a hearing, the court shall convert a case under this chapter to a case under chapter 7 or dismiss a case under this chapter, whichever is in the best interests of creditors and the estate, for cause unless the court determines that the appointment under section 1104(a) of a trustee or an examiner is in the best interests of creditors and the estate.

(2) The court may not convert a case under this chapter to a case under chapter 7 or dismiss a case under this chapter if the court finds and specifically identifies unusual circumstances establishing that converting or dismissing the case is not in the best interests of creditors and the estate, and the debtor or any other party in interest establishes that—

(A) there is a reasonable likelihood that a plan will be confirmed within the timeframes established in sections 1121(e) and 1129(e) of this title, or if such sections do not apply, within a reasonable period of time; and

(B) the grounds for converting or dismissing the case include an act or omission of the debtor other than under paragraph (4)(A)—

(i) for which there exists a reasonable justification for the act or omission; and

(ii) that will be cured within a reasonable period of time fixed by the court.

(3) The court shall commence the hearing on a motion under this subsection not later than 30 days after filing of the motion, and shall decide the motion not later than 15 days after commencement of such hearing, unless the movant expressly consents to a continuance for a specific period of time or compelling circumstances prevent the court from meeting the time limits established by this paragraph.

(4) For purposes of this subsection, the term "cause" includes—

(A) substantial or continuing loss to or diminution of the estate and the absence of a reasonable likelihood of rehabilitation;

(B) gross mismanagement of the estate;

(C) failure to maintain appropriate insurance that poses a risk to the estate or to the public;

(D) unauthorized use of cash collateral substantially harmful to 1 or more creditors;

(E) failure to comply with an order of the court;

(F) unexcused failure to satisfy timely any filing or reporting requirement established by this title or by any rule applicable to a case under this chapter;

(G) failure to attend the meeting of creditors convened under section 341(a) or an examination ordered under rule 2004 of the Federal Rules of Bankruptcy Procedure without good cause shown by the debtor;

(H) failure timely to provide information or attend meetings reasonably requested by the United States trustee (or the bankruptcy administrator, if any);

(I) failure timely to pay taxes owed after the date of the order for relief or to file tax returns due after the date of the order for relief;

(J) failure to file a disclosure statement, or to file or confirm a plan, within the time fixed by this title or by order of the court;

(K) failure to pay any fees or charges required under chapter 123 of title 28;

(L) revocation of an order of confirmation under section 1144;

(M) inability to effectuate substantial consummation of a confirmed plan;

(N) material default by the debtor with respect to a confirmed plan;

(O) termination of a confirmed plan by reason of the occurrence of a condition specified in the plan; and

(P) failure of the debtor to pay any domestic support obligation that first becomes payable after the date of the filing of the petition.

(c) The court may not convert a case under this chapter to a case under chapter 7 of this title if the debtor is a farmer or a corporation that is not a moneyed, business, or commercial corporation, unless the debtor requests such conversion.

(d) The court may convert a case under this chapter to a case under chapter 12 or 13 of this title only if–

(1) the debtor requests such conversion;

(2) the debtor has not been discharged under section 1141(d) of this title; and

(3) if the debtor requests conversion to chapter 12 of this title, such conversion is equitable.

(e) Except as provided in subsections (c) and (f), the court, on request of the United States trustee, may convert a case under this chapter to a case under chapter 7 of this title or may dismiss a case under this chapter, whichever is in the best interest of creditors and the estate if the debtor in a voluntary case fails to file, within fifteen days after the filing of the petition commencing such case or such additional time as the court may allow, the information required by paragraph (1) of section 521(a), including a list containing the names and addresses of the holders of the twenty largest unsecured claims (or of all unsecured claims if there are fewer than twenty unsecured claims), and the approximate dollar amounts of each of such claims.

(f) Notwithstanding any other provision of this section, a case may not be converted to a case under another chapter of this title unless the debtor may be a debtor under such chapter.

Bankruptcy Rule References: 1007, 1017, 1019 and 2002

**§ 1113 Rejection of collective bargaining agreements**

(a) The debtor in possession, or the trustee if one has been appointed under the provisions of this chapter, other than a trustee in a case covered by subchapter IV of this chapter and by title I of the Railway Labor Act, may assume or reject a collective bargaining agreement only in accordance with the provisions of this section.

(b) (1) Subsequent to filing a petition and prior to filing an application seeking rejection of a collective bargaining agreement, the debtor in possession or trustee (hereinafter in this section "trustee" shall include a debtor in possession), shall–

(A) make a proposal to the authorized representative of the employees covered by such agreement, based on the most complete and reliable information available at the time of such proposal, which provides for those necessary modifications in the employees benefits and protections that are necessary to permit the reorganization of the debtor and assures that all creditors, the debtor and all of the affected parties are treated fairly and equitably; and

(B) provide, subject to subsection (d)(3), the representative of the employees with such relevant information as is necessary to evaluate the proposal.

(2) During the period beginning on the date of the making of a proposal provided for in paragraph (1) and ending on the date of the hearing provided for in subsection (d)(1), the trustee shall meet, at reasonable times, with the authorized representative to confer in good faith in attempting to reach mutually satisfactory modifications of such agreement.

(c) The court shall approve an application for rejection of a collective bargaining agreement only if the court finds that—

(1) the trustee has, prior to the hearing, made a proposal that fulfills the requirements of subsection (b)(1);

(2) the authorized representative of the employees has refused to accept such proposal without good cause; and

(3) the balance of the equities clearly favors rejection of such agreement.

(d) (1) Upon the filing of an application for rejection the court shall schedule a hearing to be held not later than fourteen days after the date of the filing of such application. All interested parties may appear and be heard at such hearing. Adequate notice shall be provided to such parties at least ten days before the date of such hearing. The court may extend the time for the commencement of such hearing for a period not exceeding seven days where the circumstances of the case, and the interests of justice require such extension, or for additional periods of time to which the trustee and representative agree.

(2) The court shall rule on such application for rejection within thirty days after the date of the commencement of the hearing. In the interests of justice, the court may extend such time for ruling for such additional period as the trustee and the employees' representative may agree to. If the court does not rule on such application within thirty days after the date of the commencement of the hearing, or within such additional time as the trustee and the employees' representative may agree to, the trustee may terminate or alter any provisions of the collective bargaining agreement pending the ruling of the court on such application.

(3) The court may enter such protective orders, consistent with the need of the authorized representative of the employee to evaluate the trustee's proposal and the application for rejection, as may be necessary to prevent disclosure of information provided to such representative where such disclosure could compromise the position of the debtor with respect to its competitors in the industry in which it is engaged.

(e) If during a period when the collective bargaining agreement continues in effect, and if essential to the continuation of the debtor's business, or in order to avoid irreparable damage to the estate, the court, after notice and a hearing, may authorize the trustee to implement interim changes in the terms, conditions, wages, benefits, or work rules provided by a collective bargaining agreement. Any hearing under this paragraph shall be scheduled in accordance with the needs of the trustee. The implementation of such interim changes shall not render the application for rejection moot.

(f) No provision of this title shall be construed to permit a trustee to unilaterally terminate or alter any provisions of a collective bargaining agreement prior to compliance with the provisions of this section.

BANKRUPTCY RULE REFERENCE: 6006

## § 1114 Payment of insurance benefits to retired employees

(a) For purposes of this section, the term "retiree benefits" means payments to any entity or person for the purpose of providing or reimbursing payments for retired employees and their spouses and dependents, for medical, surgical, or hospital care benefits, or benefits in the event of sickness, accident, disability, or death under any plan, fund, or program (through the purchase of insurance or otherwise) maintained or established in whole or in part by the debtor prior to filing a petition commencing a case under this title.

(b) (1) For purposes of this section, the term "authorized representative" means the authorized representative designated pursuant to subsection (c) for persons receiving any retiree benefits covered by a collective bargaining agreement or subsection (d) in the case of persons receiving retiree benefits not covered by such an agreement.

(2) Committees of retired employees appointed by the court pursuant to this section shall have the same rights, powers, and duties as committees appointed under sections 1102 and 1103 of this title for the purpose of carrying out the purposes of sections 1114 and 1129(a)(13) and, as permitted by the court, shall have the power to enforce the rights of persons under this title as they relate to retiree benefits.

(c) (1) A labor organization shall be, for purposes of this section, the authorized representative of those persons receiving any retiree benefits covered by any collective bargaining agreement to which that labor organization is signatory, unless (A) such labor organization elects not to serve as the authorized representative of such persons, or (B) the court, upon a motion by any party in interest, after notice and hearing, determines that different representation of such persons is appropriate.

(2) In cases where the labor organization referred to in paragraph (1) elects not to serve as the authorized representative of those persons receiving any retiree benefits covered by any collective bargaining agreement to which that labor organization is signatory, or in cases where the court, pursuant to paragraph (1) finds different representation of such persons appropriate, the court, upon a motion by any party in interest, and after notice and a hearing, shall appoint a committee of retired employees if the debtor seeks to modify or not pay the retiree benefits or if the court otherwise determines that it is appropriate, from among such persons, to serve as the authorized representa-

tive of such persons under this section.

(d) The court, upon a motion by any party in interest, and after notice and a hearing, shall order the appointment of a committee of retired employees if the debtor seeks to modify or not pay the retiree benefits or if the court otherwise determines that it is appropriate, to serve as the authorized representative, under this section, of those persons receiving any retiree benefits not covered by a collective bargaining agreement. The United States trustee shall appoint any such committee.

(e) (1) Notwithstanding any other provision of this title, the debtor in possession, or the trustee if one has been appointed under the provisions of this chapter (hereinafter in this section "trustee" shall include a debtor in possession), shall timely pay and shall not modify any retiree benefits, except that—

(A) the court, on motion of the trustee or authorized representative, and after notice and a hearing, may order modification of such payments, pursuant to the provisions of subsections (g) and (h) of this section, or

(B) the trustee and the authorized representative of the recipients of those benefits may agree to modification of such payments, after which such benefits as modified shall continue to be paid by the trustee.

(2) Any payment for retiree benefits required to be made before a plan confirmed under section 1129 of this title is effective has the status of an allowed administrative expense as provided in section 503 of this title.

(f) (1) Subsequent to filing a petition and prior to filing an application seeking modification of the retiree benefits, the trustee shall—

(A) make a proposal to the authorized representative of the retirees, based on the most complete and reliable information available at the time of such proposal, which provides for those necessary modifications in the retiree benefits that are necessary to permit the reorganization of the debtor and assures that all creditors, the debtor and all of the affected parties are treated fairly and equitably; and

(B) provide, subject to subsection (k)(3), the representative of the retirees with such relevant information as is necessary to evaluate the proposal.

(2) During the period beginning on the date of the making of a proposal provided for in paragraph (1), and ending on the date of the hearing provided for in subsection (k)(1), the trustee shall meet, at reasonable times, with the authorized representative to confer in good faith in attempting to reach mutually satisfactory modifications of such retiree benefits.

(g) The court shall enter an order providing for modification in the payment of retiree benefits if the court finds that—

(1) the trustee has, prior to the hearing, made a proposal that fulfills the requirements of subsection (f);

(2) the authorized representative of the retirees has refused to accept such

proposal without good cause; and

(3) such modification is necessary to permit the reorganization of the debtor and assures that all creditors, the debtor, and all of the affected parties are treated fairly and equitably, and is clearly favored by the balance of the equities;

except that in no case shall the court enter an order providing for such modification which provides for a modification to a level lower than that proposed by the trustee in the proposal found by the court to have complied with the requirements of this subsection and subsection (f): Provided, however, That at any time after an order is entered providing for modification in the payment of retiree benefits, or at any time after an agreement modifying such benefits is made between the trustee and the authorized representative of the recipients of such benefits, the authorized representative may apply to the court for an order increasing those benefits which order shall be granted if the increase in retiree benefits sought is consistent with the standard set forth in paragraph (3): Provided further, That neither the trustee nor the authorized representative is precluded from making more than one motion for a modification order governed by this subsection.

(h) (1) Prior to a court issuing a final order under subsection (g) of this section, if essential to the continuation of the debtor's business, or in order to avoid irreparable damage to the estate, the court, after notice and a hearing, may authorize the trustee to implement interim modifications in retiree benefits.

(2) Any hearing under this subsection shall be scheduled in accordance with the needs of the trustee.

(3) The implementation of such interim changes does not render the motion for modification moot.

(i) No retiree benefits paid between the filing of the petition and the time a plan confirmed under section 1129 of this title becomes effective shall be deducted or offset from the amounts allowed as claims for any benefits which remain unpaid, or from the amounts to be paid under the plan with respect to such claims for unpaid benefits, whether such claims for unpaid benefits are based upon or arise from a right to future unpaid benefits or from any benefits not paid as a result of modifications allowed pursuant to this section.

(j) No claim for retiree benefits shall be limited by section 502(b)(7) of this title.

(k) (1) Upon the filing of an application for modifying retiree benefits, the court shall schedule a hearing to be held not later than fourteen days after the date of the filing of such application. All interested parties may appear and be heard at such hearing. Adequate notice shall be provided to such parties at least ten days before the date of such hearing. The court may extend the time for the commencement of such hearing for a period not exceeding seven days where the circumstances of the case, and the interests of justice require such extension, or for additional periods of time to which the trustee and the authorized representative agree.

(2) The court shall rule on such application for modification within ninety days after the date of the commencement of the hearing. In the interests of justice, the court may extend such time for ruling for such additional period as the trustee and the authorized representative may agree to. If the court does not rule on such application within ninety days after the date of the commencement of the hearing, or within such additional time as the trustee and the authorized representative may agree to, the trustee may implement the proposed modifications pending the ruling of the court on such application.

(3) The court may enter such protective orders, consistent with the need of the authorized representative of the retirees to evaluate the trustee's proposal and the application for modification, as may be necessary to prevent disclosure of information provided to such representative where such disclosure could compromise the position of the debtor with respect to its competitors in the industry in which it is engaged.

(l) If the debtor, during the 180-day period ending on the date of the filing of the petition—

(1) modified retiree benefits; and

(2) was insolvent on the date such benefits were modified;

the court, on motion of a party in interest, and after notice and a hearing, shall issue an order reinstating as of the date the modification was made, such benefits as in effect immediately before such date unless the court finds that the balance of the equities clearly favors such modification.

(m) This section shall not apply to any retiree, or the spouse or dependents of such retiree, if such retiree's gross income for the twelve months preceding the filing of the bankruptcy petition equals or exceeds $250,000, unless such retiree can demonstrate to the satisfaction of the court that he is unable to obtain health, medical, life, and disability coverage for himself, his spouse, and his dependents who would otherwise be covered by the employer's insurance plan, comparable to the coverage provided by the employer on the day before the filing of a petition under this title.

Bankruptcy Rule References: 2002, 2014, 2019, 5002 and 5004

## § 1115 Property of the estate

(a) In a case in which the debtor is an individual, property of the estate includes, in addition to the property specified in section 541—

(1) all property of the kind specified in section 541 that the debtor acquires after the commencement of the case but before the case is closed, dismissed, or converted to a case under chapter 7, 12, or 13, whichever occurs first; and

(2) earnings from services performed by the debtor after the commencement of the case but before the case is closed, dismissed, or converted to a case under chapter 7, 12, or 13, whichever occurs first.

(b) Except as provided in section 1104 or a confirmed plan or order confirming a plan, the debtor shall remain in possession of all property of the estate.

BANKRUPTCY RULE REFERENCES: 1007, 1009 and 6004

## § 1116 Duties of trustee or debtor in possession in small business cases

In a small business case, a trustee or the debtor in possession, in addition to the duties provided in this title and as otherwise required by law, shall—

(1) append to the voluntary petition or, in an involuntary case, file not later than 7 days after the date of the order for relief—

(A) its most recent balance sheet, statement of operations, cash-flow statement, and Federal income tax return; or

(B) a statement made under penalty of perjury that no balance sheet, statement of operations, or cash-flow statement has been prepared and no Federal tax return has been filed;

(2) attend, through its senior management personnel and counsel, meetings scheduled by the court or the United States trustee, including initial debtor interviews, scheduling conferences, and meetings of creditors convened under section 341 unless the court, after notice and a hearing, waives that requirement upon a finding of extraordinary and compelling circumstances;

(3) timely file all schedules and statements of financial affairs, unless the court, after notice and a hearing, grants an extension, which shall not extend such time period to a date later than 30 days after the date of the order for relief, absent extraordinary and compelling circumstances;

(4) file all postpetition financial and other reports required by the Federal Rules of Bankruptcy Procedure or by local rule of the district court;

(5) subject to section 363(c)(2), maintain insurance customary and appropriate to the industry;

(6) (A) timely file tax returns and other required government filings; and

(B) subject to section 363(c)(2), timely pay all taxes entitled to administrative expense priority except those being contested by appropriate proceedings being diligently prosecuted; and

(7) allow the United States trustee, or a designated representative of the United States trustee, to inspect the debtor's business premises, books, and records at reasonable times, after reasonable prior written notice, unless notice is waived by the debtor.

BANKRUPTCY RULE REFERENCES: 1007, 1007-I, 1009, 2015, 2015.2, 2015.3 and 4002

## Subchapter II
## The Plan

### § 1121 Who may file a plan

(a) The debtor may file a plan with a petition commencing a voluntary case, or at any time in a voluntary case or an involuntary case.

(b) Except as otherwise provided in this section, only the debtor may file a plan until after 120 days after the date of the order for relief under this chapter.

(c) Any party in interest, including the debtor, the trustee, a creditors' committee, an equity security holders' committee, a creditor, an equity security holder, or any indenture trustee, may file a plan if and only if—

(1) a trustee has been appointed under this chapter;

(2) the debtor has not filed a plan before 120 days after the date of the order for relief under this chapter; or

(3) the debtor has not filed a plan that has been accepted, before 180 days after the date of the order for relief under this chapter, by each class of claims or interests that is impaired under the plan.

(d) (1) Subject to paragraph (2), on request of a party in interest made within the respective periods specified in subsections (b) and (c) of this section and after notice and a hearing, the court may for cause reduce or increase the 120-day period or the 180-day period referred to in this section.

(2) (A) The 120-day period specified in paragraph (1) may not be extended beyond a date that is 18 months after the date of the order for relief under this chapter.

(B) The 180-day period specified in paragraph (1) may not be extended beyond a date that is 20 months after the date of the order for relief under this chapter.

(e) In a small business case—

(1) only the debtor may file a plan until after 180 days after the date of the order for relief, unless that period is—

(A) extended as provided by this subsection, after notice and a hearing; or

(B) the court, for cause, orders otherwise;

(2) the plan and a disclosure statement (if any) shall be filed not later than 300 days after the date of the order for relief; and

(3) the time periods specified in paragraphs (1) and (2), and the time fixed in section 1129(e) within which the plan shall be confirmed, may be extended only if—

(A) the debtor, after providing notice to parties in interest (including the United States trustee), demonstrates by a preponderance of the evidence that it is more likely than not that the court will confirm a plan within a reasonable period of time;

(B) a new deadline is imposed at the time the extension is granted; and

(C) the order extending time is signed before the existing deadline has expired.

BANKRUPTCY RULE REFERENCES: 1020 and 3016

## § 1122 Classification of claims or interests

(a) Except as provided in subsection (b) of this section, a plan may place a claim or an interest in a particular class only if such claim or interest is substantially similar to the other claims or interests of such class.

(b) A plan may designate a separate class of claims consisting only of every unsecured claim that is less than or reduced to an amount that the court approves as reasonable and necessary for administrative convenience.

BANKRUPTCY RULE REFERENCES: 3013 and 3016

## § 1123 Contents of plan

(a) Notwithstanding any otherwise applicable nonbankruptcy law, a plan shall—

(1) designate, subject to section 1122 of this title, classes of claims, other than claims of a kind specified in section 507(a)(2), 507(a)(3), or 507(a)(8) of this title, and classes of interests;

(2) specify any class of claims or interests that is not impaired under the plan;

(3) specify the treatment of any class of claims or interests that is impaired under the plan;

(4) provide the same treatment for each claim or interest of a particular class, unless the holder of a particular claim or interest agrees to a less favorable treatment of such particular claim or interest;

(5) provide adequate means for the plan's implementation, such as—

(A) retention by the debtor of all or any part of the property of the estate;

(B) transfer of all or any part of the property of the estate to one or more entities, whether organized before or after the confirmation of such plan;

(C) merger or consolidation of the debtor with one or more persons;

(D) sale of all or any part of the property of the estate, either subject to or free of any lien, or the distribution of all or any part of the property of the estate among those having an interest in such property of the estate;

(E) satisfaction or modification of any lien;

(F) cancellation or modification of any indenture or similar instrument;

(G) curing or waiving of any default;

(H) extension of a maturity date or a change in an interest rate or other term of outstanding securities;

(I) amendment of the debtor's charter; or

(J) issuance of securities of the debtor, or of any entity referred to in subparagraph (B) or (C) of this paragraph, for cash, for property, for existing securities, or in exchange for claims or interests, or for any other appropriate purpose;

(6) provide for the inclusion in the charter of the debtor, if the debtor is a corporation, or of any corporation referred to in paragraph (5)(B) or (5)(C) of this subsection, of a provision prohibiting the issuance of nonvoting equity securities, and providing, as to the several classes of securities possessing voting power, an appropriate distribution of such power among such classes, including, in the case of any class of equity securities having a preference over another class of equity securities with respect to dividends, adequate provisions for the election of directors representing such preferred class in the event of default in the payment of such dividends;

(7) contain only provisions that are consistent with the interests of creditors and equity security holders and with public policy with respect to the manner of selection of any officer, director, or trustee under the plan and any successor to such officer, director, or trustee; and

(8) in a case in which the debtor is an individual, provide for the payment to creditors under the plan of all or such portion of earnings from personal services performed by the debtor after the commencement of the case or other future income of the debtor as is necessary for the execution of the plan.

(b) Subject to subsection (a) of this section, a plan may—

(1) impair or leave unimpaired any class of claims, secured or unsecured, or of interests;

(2) subject to section 365 of this title, provide for the assumption, rejection, or assignment of any executory contract or unexpired lease of the debtor not previously rejected under such section;

(3) provide for—

(A) the settlement or adjustment of any claim or interest belonging to the debtor or to the estate; or

(B) the retention and enforcement by the debtor, by the trustee, or by a representative of the estate appointed for such purpose, of any such claim or interest;

(4) provide for the sale of all or substantially all of the property of the estate, and the distribution of the proceeds of such sale among holders of claims or interests;

(5) modify the rights of holders of secured claims, other than a claim secured only by a security interest in real property that is the debtor's principal residence, or of holders of unsecured claims, or leave unaffected the rights of holders of any class of claims; and

(6) include any other appropriate provision not inconsistent with the applicable provisions of this title.

(c) In a case concerning an individual, a plan proposed by an entity other than the debtor may not provide for the use, sale, or lease of property exempted under section 522 of this title, unless the debtor consents to such use, sale, or lease.

(d) Notwithstanding subsection (a) of this section and sections 506(b), 1129(a)(7), and 1129(b) of this title, if it is proposed in a plan to cure a default the amount necessary to cure the default shall be determined in accordance with the underlying agreement and applicable nonbankruptcy law.

BANKRUPTCY RULE REFERENCES: 3013, 3016 and 9009

## § 1124 Impairment of claims or interests

Except as provided in section 1123(a)(4) of this title, a class of claims or interests is impaired under a plan unless, with respect to each claim or interest of such class, the plan—

(1) leaves unaltered the legal, equitable, and contractual rights to which such claim or interest entitles the holder of such claim or interest; or

(2) notwithstanding any contractual provision or applicable law that entitles the holder of such claim or interest to demand or receive accelerated payment of such claim or interest after the occurrence of a default—

(A) cures any such default that occurred before or after the commencement of the case under this title, other than a default of a kind specified in section 365(b)(2) of this title or of a kind that section 365(b)(2) expressly does not require to be cured;

(B) reinstates the maturity of such claim or interest as such maturity existed before such default;

(C) compensates the holder of such claim or interest for any damages incurred as a result of any reasonable reliance by such holder on such contractual provision or such applicable law;

(D) if such claim or such interest arises from any failure to perform a nonmonetary obligation, other than a default arising from failure to operate a nonresidential real property lease subject to section 365(b)(1)(A), compensates the holder of such claim or such interest (other than the debtor or an insider) for any actual pecuniary loss incurred by such holder as a result of such failure; and

(E) does not otherwise alter the legal, equitable, or contractual rights to which such claim or interest entitles the holder of such claim or interest.

## § 1125 Postpetition disclosure and solicitation

(a) In this section—

(1) "adequate information" means information of a kind, and in sufficient detail, as far as is reasonably practicable in light of the nature and history of the debtor and the condition of the debtor's books and records, including a discussion of the potential material Federal tax consequences of the plan to the debtor, any successor to the debtor, and a hypothetical investor typical of the holders of claims or interests in the case, that would enable such a hypothetical investor of the relevant class to make an informed judgment about the plan, but adequate information need not include such information about any other possible or proposed plan and in determining whether a disclosure statement provides adequate information, the court shall consider the complexity of the case, the benefit of additional information to creditors and other parties in interest, and the cost of providing additional information; and

(2) "investor typical of holders of claims or interests of the relevant class" means investor having—

(A) a claim or interest of the relevant class;

(B) such a relationship with the debtor as the holders of other claims or interests of such class generally have; and

(C) such ability to obtain such information from sources other than the disclosure required by this section as holders of claims or interests in such class generally have.

(b) An acceptance or rejection of a plan may not be solicited after the commencement of the case under this title from a holder of a claim or interest with respect to such claim or interest, unless, at the time of or before such solicitation, there is transmitted to such holder the plan or a summary of the plan, and a written disclosure statement approved, after notice and a hearing, by the court as containing adequate information. The court may approve a disclosure statement without a valuation of the debtor or an appraisal of the debtor's assets.

(c) The same disclosure statement shall be transmitted to each holder of a claim or interest of a particular class, but there may be transmitted different disclosure statements, differing in amount, detail, or kind of information, as between classes.

(d) Whether a disclosure statement required under subsection (b) of this section contains adequate information is not governed by any otherwise applicable nonbankruptcy law, rule, or regulation, but an agency or official whose duty is to administer or enforce such a law, rule, or regulation may be heard on the issue of whether a disclosure statement contains adequate information. Such an agency or official may not appeal from, or otherwise seek review of, an order approving a disclosure statement.

(e) A person that solicits acceptance or rejection of a plan, in good faith and in compliance with the applicable provisions of this title, or that participates, in good faith and in compliance with the applicable provisions of this title, in the offer, issuance, sale, or purchase of a security, offered or sold under the plan, of the debtor, of an affiliate participating in a joint plan with the debtor, or of a newly organized successor to the debtor under the plan, is not liable, on account of such solicitation or participation, for violation of any applicable law, rule, or regulation governing solicitation of acceptance or rejection of a plan or the offer, issuance, sale, or purchase of securities.

(f) Notwithstanding subsection (b), in a small business case—

(1) the court may determine that the plan itself provides adequate information and that a separate disclosure statement is not necessary;

(2) the court may approve a disclosure statement submitted on standard forms approved by the court or adopted under section 2075 of title 28; and

(3) (A) the court may conditionally approve a disclosure statement subject to final approval after notice and a hearing;

(B) acceptances and rejections of a plan may be solicited based on a conditionally approved disclosure statement if the debtor provides adequate information to each holder of a claim or interest that is solicited, but a conditionally approved disclosure statement shall be mailed not later than 25 days before the date of the hearing on confirmation of the plan; and

(C) the hearing on the disclosure statement may be combined with the hearing on confirmation of a plan.

(g) Notwithstanding subsection (b), an acceptance or rejection of the plan may be solicited from a holder of a claim or interest if such solicitation complies with applicable nonbankruptcy law and if such holder was solicited before the commencement of the case in a manner complying with applicable nonbankruptcy law.

BANKRUPTCY RULE REFERENCES: 1020, 2002, 3016, 3017, 3017.1 and 9009

## § 1126 Acceptance of plan

(a) The holder of a claim or interest allowed under section 502 of this title may accept or reject a plan. If the United States is a creditor or equity security holder, the Secretary of the Treasury may accept or reject the plan on behalf of the United States.

(b) For the purposes of subsections (c) and (d) of this section, a holder of a claim or interest that has accepted or rejected the plan before the commencement of the case under this title is deemed to have accepted or rejected such plan, as the case may be, if—

(1) the solicitation of such acceptance or rejection was in compliance with any applicable nonbankruptcy law, rule, or regulation governing the adequacy of disclosure in connection with such solicitation; or

(2) if there is not any such law, rule, or regulation, such acceptance or rejection was solicited after disclosure to such holder of adequate information, as defined in section 1125(a) of this title.

(c) A class of claims has accepted a plan if such plan has been accepted by creditors, other than any entity designated under subsection (e) of this section, that hold at least two-thirds in amount and more than one-half in number of the allowed claims of such class held by creditors, other than any entity designated under subsection (e) of this section, that have accepted or rejected such plan.

(d) A class of interests has accepted a plan if such plan has been accepted by holders of such interests, other than any entity designated under subsection (e) of this section, that hold at least two-thirds in amount of the allowed interests of such class held by holders of such interests, other than any entity designated under subsection (e) of this section, that have accepted or rejected such plan.

(e) On request of a party in interest, and after notice and a hearing, the court may designate any entity whose acceptance or rejection of such plan was not in good faith, or was not solicited or procured in good faith or in accordance with the provisions of this title.

(f) Notwithstanding any other provision of this section, a class that is not impaired under a plan, and each holder of a claim or interest of such class, are conclusively presumed to have accepted the plan, and solicitation of acceptances with respect to such class from the holders of claims or interests of such class is not required.

(g) Notwithstanding any other provision of this section, a class is deemed not to have accepted a plan if such plan provides that the claims or interests of such class do not entitle the holders of such claims or interests to receive or retain any property under the plan on account of such claims or interests.

BANKRUPTCY RULE REFERENCES: 3003, 3016, 3017, 3017.1 and 3018

## § 1127 Modification of plan

(a) The proponent of a plan may modify such plan at any time before confirmation, but may not modify such plan so that such plan as modified fails to meet the requirements of sections 1122 and 1123 of this title. After the proponent of a plan files a modification of such plan with the court, the plan as modified becomes the plan.

(b) The proponent of a plan or the reorganized debtor may modify such plan at any time after confirmation of such plan and before substantial consummation of such plan, but may not modify such plan so that such plan as modified fails to meet the requirements of sections 1122 and 1123 of this title. Such plan as modified under this subsection becomes the plan only if circumstances warrant such modification and the court, after notice and a hearing, confirms such plan as modified, under section 1129 of this title.

(c) The proponent of a modification shall comply with section 1125 of this title with respect to the plan as modified.

(d) Any holder of a claim or interest that has accepted or rejected a plan is deemed to have accepted or rejected, as the case may be, such plan as modified, unless, within the time fixed by the court, such holder changes such holder's previous acceptance or rejection.

(e) If the debtor is an individual, the plan may be modified at any time after confirmation of the plan but before the completion of payments under the plan, whether or not the plan has been substantially consummated, upon request of the debtor, the trustee, the United States trustee, or the holder of an allowed unsecured claim, to—

(1) increase or reduce the amount of payments on claims of a particular class provided for by the plan;

(2) extend or reduce the time period for such payments; or

(3) alter the amount of the distribution to a creditor whose claim is provided for by the plan to the extent necessary to take account of any payment of such claim made other than under the plan.

(f) (1) Sections 1121 through 1128 and the requirements of section 1129 apply to any modification under subsection (e).

(2) The plan, as modified, shall become the plan only after there has been disclosure under section 1125 as the court may direct, notice and a hearing, and such modification is approved.

BANKRUPTCY RULE REFERENCES: 3016, 3017, 3017.1, 3018 and 3019

## § 1128 Confirmation hearing

(a) After notice, the court shall hold a hearing on confirmation of a plan.

(b) A party in interest may object to confirmation of a plan.

BANKRUPTCY RULE REFERENCES: 2002, 3016, 3017, 3017.1, 3018, 3019, 3020, 9006 and 9014

## § 1129 Confirmation of plan

(a) The court shall confirm a plan only if all of the following requirements are met:[77]

(1) The plan complies with the applicable provisions of this title.

(2) The proponent of the plan complies with the applicable provisions of this title.

(3) The plan has been proposed in good faith and not by any means forbidden by law.

(4) Any payment made or to be made by the proponent, by the debtor, or by a person issuing securities or acquiring property under the plan, for services or for costs and expenses in or in connection with the case, or in connection with the plan and incident to the case, has been approved by, or is subject to the approval of, the court as reasonable.

(5) (A) (i) The proponent of the plan has disclosed the identity and affiliations

---

[77] ED. NOTE: Section 1228(b) of the 2005 Act provides: "CHAPTER 11 AND CHAPTER 13 CASES.—The court shall not confirm a plan of reorganization in the case of an individual under chapter 11 or 13 of title 11, United States Code, unless requested tax documents have been filed with the court."

of any individual proposed to serve, after confirmation of the plan, as a director, officer, or voting trustee of the debtor, an affiliate of the debtor participating in a joint plan with the debtor, or a successor to the debtor under the plan; and

(ii) the appointment to, or continuance in, such office of such individual, is consistent with the interests of creditors and equity security holders and with public policy; and

(B) the proponent of the plan has disclosed the identity of any insider that will be employed or retained by the reorganized debtor, and the nature of any compensation for such insider.

(6) Any governmental regulatory commission with jurisdiction, after confirmation of the plan, over the rates of the debtor has approved any rate change provided for in the plan, or such rate change is expressly conditioned on such approval.

(7) With respect to each impaired class of claims or interests—

(A) each holder of a claim or interest of such class—

(i) has accepted the plan; or

(ii) will receive or retain under the plan on account of such claim or interest property of a value, as of the effective date of the plan, that is not less than the amount that such holder would so receive or retain if the debtor were liquidated under chapter 7 of this title on such date; or

(B) if section 1111(b)(2) of this title applies to the claims of such class, each holder of a claim of such class will receive or retain under the plan on account of such claim property of a value, as of the effective date of the plan, that is not less than the value of such holder's interest in the estate's interest in the property that secures such claims.

(8) With respect to each class of claims or interests—

(A) such class has accepted the plan; or

(B) such class is not impaired under the plan.

(9) Except to the extent that the holder of a particular claim has agreed to a different treatment of such claim, the plan provides that—

(A) with respect to a claim of a kind specified in section 507(a)(2) or 507(a)(3) of this title, on the effective date of the plan, the holder of such claim will receive on account of such claim cash equal to the allowed amount of such claim;

(B) with respect to a class of claims of a kind specified in section 507(a)(1), 507(a)(4), 507(a)(5), 507(a)(6), or 507(a)(7) of this title, each holder of a claim of such class will receive—

(i) if such class has accepted the plan, deferred cash payments of a value, as of the effective date of the plan, equal to the allowed amount of such claim; or

(ii) if such class has not accepted the plan, cash on the effective date of the plan equal to the allowed amount of such claim;

(C) with respect to a claim of a kind specified in section 507(a)(8) of this title, the holder of such claim will receive on account of such claim regular installment payments in cash—

(i) of a total value, as of the effective date of the plan, equal to the allowed amount of such claim;

(ii) over a period ending not later than 5 years after the date of the order for relief under section 301, 302, or 303; and

(iii) in a manner not less favorable than the most favored nonpriority unsecured claim provided for by the plan (other than cash payments made to a class of creditors under section 1122(b)); and

(D) with respect to a secured claim which would otherwise meet the description of an unsecured claim of a governmental unit under section 507(a)(8), but for the secured status of that claim, the holder of that claim will receive on account of that claim, cash payments, in the same manner and over the same period, as prescribed in subparagraph (C).

(10) If a class of claims is impaired under the plan, at least one class of claims that is impaired under the plan has accepted the plan, determined without including any acceptance of the plan by any insider.

(11) Confirmation of the plan is not likely to be followed by the liquidation, or the need for further financial reorganization, of the debtor or any successor to the debtor under the plan, unless such liquidation or reorganization is proposed in the plan.

(12) All fees payable under section 1930 of title 28, as determined by the court at the hearing on confirmation of the plan, have been paid or the plan provides for the payment of all such fees on the effective date of the plan.

(13) The plan provides for the continuation after its effective date of payment of all retiree benefits, as that term is defined in section 1114 of this title, at the level established pursuant to subsection (e)(1)(B) or (g) of section 1114 of this title, at any time prior to confirmation of the plan, for the duration of the period the debtor has obligated itself to provide such benefits.

(14) If the debtor is required by a judicial or administrative order, or by statute, to pay a domestic support obligation, the debtor has paid all amounts payable under such order or such statute for such obligation that first become payable after the date of the filing of the petition.

(15) In a case in which the debtor is an individual and in which the holder of an allowed unsecured claim objects to the confirmation of the plan—

(A) the value, as of the effective date of the plan, of the property to be distributed under the plan on account of such claim is not less than the amount of such claim; or

(B) the value of the property to be distributed under the plan is not less than the projected disposable income of the debtor (as defined in section 1325(b)(2)) to be received during the 5-year period beginning on the date that the first payment is due under the plan, or during the period for which the plan provides payments, whichever is longer.

(16)[78] All transfers of property under the plan shall be made in accordance with any applicable provisions of nonbankruptcy law that govern the transfer of property by a corporation or trust that is not a moneyed, business, or commercial corporation or trust.

(b) (1) Notwithstanding section 510(a) of this title, if all of the applicable requirements of subsection (a) of this section other than paragraph (8) are met with respect to a plan, the court, on request of the proponent under the plan, shall confirm the plan notwithstanding the requirements of such paragraph if the plan does not discriminate unfairly, and is fair and equitable, with respect to each class of claims or interests that is impaired under, and has not accepted, the plan.

(2) For the purpose of this subsection, the condition that a plan be fair and equitable with respect to a class includes the following requirements:

(A) With respect to a class of secured claims, the plan provides—

(i) (I) that the holders of such claims retain the liens securing such claims, whether the property subject to such liens is retained by the debtor or transferred to another entity, to the extent of the allowed amount of such claims; and

(II) that each holder of a claim of such class receive on account of such claim deferred cash payments totaling at least the allowed amount of such claim, of a value, as of the effective date of the plan, of at least the value of such holder's interest in the estate's interest in such property;

(ii) for the sale, subject to section 363(k) of this title, of any property

---

[78] Ed. Note: Subsections (d) and (e) of section 1221 of the 2005 Act provide:

(d) Applicability.—The amendments made by this section [including the addition of paragraph (16) to Code section 1129(a)] shall apply to a case pending under title 11, United States Code, on the date of enactment of this Act, or filed under that title on or after that date of enactment, except that the court shall not confirm a plan under chapter 11 of title 11, United States Code, without considering whether this section would substantially affect the rights of a party in interest who first acquired rights with respect to the debtor after the date of the filing of the petition. The parties who may appear and be heard in a proceeding under this section include the attorney general of the State in which the debtor is incorporated, was formed, or does business.

(e) Rule of Construction.—Nothing in this section shall be construed to require the court in which a case under chapter 11 of title 11, United States Code, is pending to remand or refer any proceeding, issue, or controversy to any other court or to require the approval of any other court for the transfer of property.

that is subject to the liens securing such claims, free and clear of such liens, with such liens to attach to the proceeds of such sale, and the treatment of such liens on proceeds under clause (i) or (iii) of this subparagraph; or

(iii) for the realization by such holders of the indubitable equivalent of such claims.

(B) With respect to a class of unsecured claims—

(i) the plan provides that each holder of a claim of such class receive or retain on account of such claim property of a value, as of the effective date of the plan, equal to the allowed amount of such claim; or

(ii) the holder of any claim or interest that is junior to the claims of such class will not receive or retain under the plan on account of such junior claim or interest any property, except that in a case in which the debtor is an individual, the debtor may retain property included in the estate under section 1115, subject to the requirements of subsection (a)(14) of this section.

(C) With respect to a class of interests—

(i) the plan provides that each holder of an interest of such class receive or retain on account of such interest property of a value, as of the effective date of the plan, equal to the greatest of the allowed amount of any fixed liquidation preference to which such holder is entitled, any fixed redemption price to which such holder is entitled, or the value of such interest; or

(ii) the holder of any interest that is junior to the interests of such class will not receive or retain under the plan on account of such junior interest any property.

(c) Notwithstanding subsections (a) and (b) of this section and except as provided in section 1127(b) of this title, the court may confirm only one plan, unless the order of confirmation in the case has been revoked under section 1144 of this title. If the requirements of subsections (a) and (b) of this section are met with respect to more than one plan, the court shall consider the preferences of creditors and equity security holders in determining which plan to confirm.

(d) Notwithstanding any other provision of this section, on request of a party in interest that is a governmental unit, the court may not confirm a plan if the principal purpose of the plan is the avoidance of taxes or the avoidance of the application of section 5 of the Securities Act of 1933. In any hearing under this subsection, the governmental unit has the burden of proof on the issue of avoidance.

(e) In a small business case, the court shall confirm a plan that complies with the applicable provisions of this title and that is filed in accordance with section 1121(e) not later than 45 days after the plan is filed unless the time for confirmation is extended in accordance with section 1121(e)(3).

BANKRUPTCY RULE REFERENCES: 1020, 2002, 3016, 3017, 3017.1, 3018, 3019, 3020, 9009 and 9014

## Subchapter III
## Postconfirmation Matters

### § 1141 Effect of confirmation

(a) Except as provided in subsections (d)(2) and (d)(3) of this section, the provisions of a confirmed plan bind the debtor, any entity issuing securities under the plan, any entity acquiring property under the plan, and any creditor, equity security holder, or general partner in the debtor, whether or not the claim or interest of such creditor, equity security holder, or general partner is impaired under the plan and whether or not such creditor, equity security holder, or general partner has accepted the plan.

(b) Except as otherwise provided in the plan or the order confirming the plan, the confirmation of a plan vests all of the property of the estate in the debtor.

(c) Except as provided in subsections (d)(2) and (d)(3) of this section and except as otherwise provided in the plan or in the order confirming the plan, after confirmation of a plan, the property dealt with by the plan is free and clear of all claims and interests of creditors, equity security holders, and of general partners in the debtor.

(d) (1) Except as otherwise provided in this subsection, in the plan, or in the order confirming the plan, the confirmation of a plan—

(A) discharges the debtor from any debt that arose before the date of such confirmation, and any debt of a kind specified in section 502(g), 502(h), or 502(i) of this title, whether or not—

(i) a proof of the claim based on such debt is filed or deemed filed under section 501 of this title;

(ii) such claim is allowed under section 502 of this title; or

(iii) the holder of such claim has accepted the plan; and

(B) terminates all rights and interests of equity security holders and general partners provided for by the plan.

(2) A discharge under this chapter does not discharge a debtor who is an individual from any debt excepted from discharge under section 523 of this title.

(3) The confirmation of a plan does not discharge a debtor if—

(A) the plan provides for the liquidation of all or substantially all of the property of the estate;

(B) the debtor does not engage in business after consummation of the plan; and

(C) the debtor would be denied a discharge under section 727(a) of this title if the case were a case under chapter 7 of this title.

(4) The court may approve a written waiver of discharge executed by the debtor after the order for relief under this chapter.

(5) In a case in which the debtor is an individual—

(A) unless after notice and a hearing the court orders otherwise for cause, confirmation of the plan does not discharge any debt provided for in the plan until the court grants a discharge on completion of all payments under the plan;

(B) at any time after the confirmation of the plan, and after notice and a hearing, the court may grant a discharge to the debtor who has not completed payments under the plan if—

(i) the value, as of the effective date of the plan, of property actually distributed under the plan on account of each allowed unsecured claim is not less than the amount that would have been paid on such claim if the estate of the debtor had been liquidated under chapter 7 on such date;

(ii) modification of the plan under section 1127 is not practicable; and

(iii) subparagraph (C) permits the court to grant a discharge; and

(C) the court may grant a discharge if, after notice and a hearing held not more than 10 days before the date of the entry of the order granting the discharge, the court finds that there is no reasonable cause to believe that—

(i) section 522(q)(1) may be applicable to the debtor; and

(ii) there is pending any proceeding in which the debtor may be found guilty of a felony of the kind described in section 522(q)(1)(A) or liable for a debt of the kind described in section 522(q)(1)(B); and if the requirements of subparagraph (A) or (B) are met.

(6) Notwithstanding paragraph (1), the confirmation of a plan does not discharge a debtor that is a corporation from any debt—

(A) of a kind specified in paragraph (2)(A) or (2)(B) of section 523(a) that is owed to a domestic governmental unit, or owed to a person as the result of an action filed under subchapter III of chapter 37 of title 31 or any similar State statute; or

(B) for a tax or customs duty with respect to which the debtor—

(i) made a fraudulent return; or

(ii) willfully attempted in any manner to evade or to defeat such tax or such customs duty.

Bankruptcy Rule References: 1007-I, 2002, 3020, 3021, 4004, 4005, 4006 and 4007

## § 1142 Implementation of plan

(a) Notwithstanding any otherwise applicable nonbankruptcy law, rule, or regulation relating to financial condition, the debtor and any entity organized or to be organized for the purpose of carrying out the plan shall carry out the plan and shall comply with any orders of the court.

(b) The court may direct the debtor and any other necessary party to execute or deliver or to join in the execution or delivery of any instrument required to effect a transfer of property dealt with by a confirmed plan, and to perform any other act, including the satisfaction of any lien, that is necessary for the consummation of the plan.

BANKRUPTCY RULE REFERENCES: 3020, 3021 and 3022

## § 1143 Distribution

If a plan requires presentment or surrender of a security or the performance of any other act as a condition to participation in distribution under the plan, such action shall be taken not later than five years after the date of the entry of the order of confirmation. Any entity that has not within such time presented or surrendered such entity's security or taken any such other action that the plan requires may not participate in distribution under the plan.

BANKRUPTCY RULE REFERENCES: 3020, 3021 and 3022

## § 1144 Revocation of an order of confirmation

On request of a party in interest at any time before 180 days after the date of the entry of the order of confirmation, and after notice and a hearing, the court may revoke such order if and only if such order was procured by fraud. An order under this section revoking an order of confirmation shall—

(1) contain such provisions as are necessary to protect any entity acquiring rights in good faith reliance on the order of confirmation; and

(2) revoke the discharge of the debtor.

BANKRUPTCY RULE REFERENCES: 7001 and 9024

## § 1145 Exemption from securities laws

(a) Except with respect to an entity that is an underwriter as defined in subsection (b) of this section, section 5 of the Securities Act of 1933 and any State or local law requiring registration for offer or sale of a security or registration or licensing of an issuer of, underwriter of, or broker or dealer in, a security do not apply to—

(1) the offer or sale under a plan of a security of the debtor, of an affiliate participating in a joint plan with the debtor, or of a successor to the debtor under the plan—

(A) in exchange for a claim against, an interest in, or a claim for an administrative expense in the case concerning, the debtor or such affiliate; or

(B) principally in such exchange and partly for cash or property;

(2) the offer of a security through any warrant, option, right to subscribe, or conversion privilege that was sold in the manner specified in paragraph (1) of this subsection, or the sale of a security upon the exercise of such a warrant, option, right, or privilege;

(3) the offer or sale, other than under a plan, of a security of an issuer other

than the debtor or an affiliate, if—

(A) such security was owned by the debtor on the date of the filing of the petition;

(B) the issuer of such security is—

(i) required to file reports under section 13 or 15(d) of the Securities Exchange Act of 1934; and

(ii) in compliance with the disclosure and reporting provision of such applicable section; and

(C) such offer or sale is of securities that do not exceed—

(i) during the two-year period immediately following the date of the filing of the petition, four percent of the securities of such class outstanding on such date; and

(ii) during any 180-day period following such two-year period, one percent of the securities outstanding at the beginning of such 180-day period; or

(4) a transaction by a stockbroker in a security that is executed after a transaction of a kind specified in paragraph (1) or (2) of this subsection in such security and before the expiration of 40 days after the first date on which such security was bona fide offered to the public by the issuer or by or through an underwriter, if such stockbroker provides, at the time of or before such transaction by such stockbroker, a disclosure statement approved under section 1125 of this title, and, if the court orders, information supplementing such disclosure statement.

(b) (1) Except as provided in paragraph (2) of this subsection and except with respect to ordinary trading transactions of an entity that is not an issuer, an entity is an underwriter under section 2(a)(11) of the Securities Act of 1933,[79] if such entity—

(A) purchases a claim against, interest in, or claim for an administrative expense in the case concerning, the debtor, if such purchase is with a view to distribution of any security received or to be received in exchange for such a claim or interest;

(B) offers to sell securities offered or sold under the plan for the holders of such securities;

(C) offers to buy securities offered or sold under the plan from the holders of such securities, if such offer to buy is—

(i) with a view to distribution of such securities; and

(ii) under an agreement made in connection with the plan, with the

[79] Ed. Note: The National Securities Markets Improvement Act of 1996, Pub. L. No. 104-290, 110 Stat. 3416 (1996), amended the Securities Act of 1933, redesignating section 2(11) as section 2(a)(11), 15 U.S.C. § 77b(a)(11).

consummation of the plan, or with the offer or sale of securities under the plan; or

(D) is an issuer, as used in such section 2(a)(11),[80] with respect to such securities.

(2) An entity is not an underwriter under section 2(a)(11) of the Securities Act of 1933[81] or under paragraph (1) of this subsection with respect to an agreement that provides only for—

(A) (i) the matching or combining of fractional interests in securities offered or sold under the plan into whole interests; or

(ii) the purchase or sale of such fractional interests from or to entities receiving such fractional interests under the plan; or

(B) the purchase or sale for such entities of such fractional or whole interests as are necessary to adjust for any remaining fractional interests after such matching.

(3) An entity other than an entity of the kind specified in paragraph (1) of this subsection is not an underwriter under section 2(11) of the Securities Act of 1933[82] with respect to any securities offered or sold to such entity in the manner specified in subsection (a)(1) of this section.

(c) An offer or sale of securities of the kind and in the manner specified under subsection (a)(1) of this section is deemed to be a public offering.

(d) The Trust Indenture Act of 1939 does not apply to a note issued under the plan that matures not later than one year after the effective date of the plan.

BANKRUPTCY RULE REFERENCE: 2018

### § 1146 Special tax provisions

(a) The issuance, transfer, or exchange of a security, or the making or delivery of an instrument of transfer under a plan confirmed under section 1129 or 1191 of this title, may not be taxed under any law imposing a stamp tax or similar tax.

(b) The court may authorize the proponent of a plan to request a determination, limited to questions of law, by a State or local governmental unit charged with responsibility for collection or determination of a tax on or measured by income, of the tax effects, under section 346 of this title and under the law imposing such tax, of the plan. In the event of an actual controversy, the court may declare such effects after the earlier of—

(1) the date on which such governmental unit responds to the request under this subsection; or

(2) 270 days after such request.

---

[80] ED. NOTE: *See* note 79 *supra.*

[81] ED. NOTE: *See* note 79 *supra.*

[82] ED. NOTE: *See* note 79 *supra.*

## Subchapter IV
## Railroad Reorganization

### § 1161 Inapplicability of other sections

Sections 341, 343, 1102(a)(1), 1104, 1105, 1107, 1129(a)(7), and 1129(c) of this title do not apply in a case concerning a railroad.

Bankruptcy Rule References: 1002 and 1007

### § 1162 Definition

In this subchapter, "Board" means the "Surface Transportation Board".

### § 1163 Appointment of trustee

As soon as practicable after the order for relief the Secretary of Transportation shall submit a list of five disinterested persons that are qualified and willing to serve as trustees in the case. The United States trustee shall appoint one of such persons to serve as trustee in the case.

Bankruptcy Rule References: 2008, 2009, 2010, 2011, 2012, 2013, 2014, 2015, 2016 and 2017

### § 1164 Right to be heard

The Board, the Department of Transportation, and any State or local commission having regulatory jurisdiction over the debtor may raise and may appear and be heard on any issue in a case under this chapter, but may not appeal from any judgment, order, or decree entered in the case.

Bankruptcy Rule References: 2018 and 9035

### § 1165 Protection of the public interest

In applying sections 1166, 1167, 1169, 1170, 1171, 1172, 1173, and 1174 of this title, the court and the trustee shall consider the public interest in addition to the interests of the debtor, creditors, and equity security holders.

### § 1166 Effect of subtitle IV of title 49 and of Federal, State, or local regulations

Except with respect to abandonment under section 1170 of this title, or merger, modification of the financial structure of the debtor, or issuance or sale of securities under a plan, the trustee and the debtor are subject to the provisions of subtitle IV of title 49 that are applicable to railroads, and the trustee is subject to orders of any Federal, State, or local regulatory body to the same extent as the debtor would be if a petition commencing the case under this chapter had not been filed, but—

(1) any such order that would require the expenditure, or the incurring of an obligation for the expenditure, of money from the estate is not effective unless approved by the court; and

(2) the provisions of this chapter are subject to section 601(b) of the Regional Rail Reorganization Act of 1973.

## § 1167 Collective bargaining agreements

Notwithstanding section 365 of this title, neither the court nor the trustee may change the wages or working conditions of employees of the debtor established by a collective bargaining agreement that is subject to the Railway Labor Act except in accordance with section 6 of such Act.

## § 1168 Rolling stock equipment

(a) (1) The right of a secured party with a security interest in or of a lessor or conditional vendor of equipment described in paragraph (2) to take possession of such equipment in compliance with an equipment security agreement, lease, or conditional sale contract, and to enforce any of its other rights or remedies under such security agreement, lease, or conditional sale contract, to sell, lease, or otherwise retain or dispose of such equipment, is not limited or otherwise affected by any other provision of this title or by any power of the court, except that right to take possession and enforce those other rights and remedies shall be subject to section 362, if—

(A) before the date that is 60 days after the date of commencement of a case under this chapter, the trustee, subject to the court's approval, agrees to perform all obligations of the debtor under such security agreement, lease, or conditional sale contract; and

(B) any default, other than a default of a kind described in section 365(b)(2), under such security agreement, lease, or conditional sale contract—

(i) that occurs before the date of commencement of the case and is an event of default therewith is cured before the expiration of such 60-day period;

(ii) that occurs or becomes an event of default after the date of commencement of the case and before the expiration of such 60-day period is cured before the later of—

(I) the date that is 30 days after the date of the default or event of the default; or

(II) the expiration of such 60-day period; and

(iii) that occurs on or after the expiration of such 60-day period is cured in accordance with the terms of such security agreement, lease, or conditional sale contract, if cure is permitted under that agreement, lease, or conditional sale contract.

(2) The equipment described in this paragraph—

(A) is rolling stock equipment or accessories used on rolling stock equipment, including superstructures or racks, that is subject to a security interest granted by, leased to, or conditionally sold to a debtor; and

(B) includes all records and documents relating to such equipment that are required, under the terms of the security agreement, lease, or conditional sale contract, that is to be surrendered or returned by the debtor in connection with the surrender or return of such equipment.

(3) Paragraph (1) applies to a secured party, lessor, or conditional vendor acting in its own behalf or acting as trustee or otherwise in behalf of another party.

(b) The trustee and the secured party, lessor, or conditional vendor whose right to take possession is protected under subsection (a) may agree, subject to the court's approval, to extend the 60-day period specified in subsection (a)(1).

(c) (1) In any case under this chapter, the trustee shall immediately surrender and return to a secured party, lessor, or conditional vendor, described in subsection (a)(1), equipment described in subsection (a)(2), if at any time after the date of commencement of the case under this chapter such secured party, lessor, or conditional vendor is entitled pursuant to subsection (a)(1) to take possession of such equipment and makes a written demand for such possession of the trustee.

(2) At such time as the trustee is required under paragraph (1) to surrender and return equipment described in subsection (a)(2), any lease of such equipment, and any security agreement or conditional sale contract relating to such equipment, if such security agreement or conditional sale contract is an executory contract, shall be deemed rejected.

(d) With respect to equipment first placed in service on or prior to October 22, 1994, for purposes of this section—

(1) the term "lease" includes any written agreement with respect to which the lessor and the debtor, as lessee, have expressed in the agreement or in a substantially contemporaneous writing that the agreement is to be treated as a lease for Federal income tax purposes; and

(2) the term "security interest" means a purchase-money equipment security interest.

(e) With respect to equipment first placed in service after October 22, 1994, for purposes of this section, the term "rolling stock equipment" includes rolling stock equipment that is substantially rebuilt and accessories used on such equipment.

### § 1169 Effect of rejection of lease of railroad line

(a) Except as provided in subsection (b) of this section, if a lease of a line of railroad under which the debtor is the lessee is rejected under section 365 of this title, and if the trustee, within such time as the court fixes, and with the court's approval, elects not to operate the leased line, the lessor under such lease, after such approval, shall operate the line.

(b) If operation of such line by such lessor is impracticable or contrary to the public interest, the court, on request of such lessor, and after notice and a hearing, shall order the trustee to continue operation of such line for the account of such lessor until abandonment is ordered under section 1170 of this title, or until such operation is otherwise lawfully terminated, whichever occurs first.

(c) During any such operation, such lessor is deemed a carrier subject to the provisions of subtitle IV of title 49 that are applicable to railroads.

BANKRUPTCY RULE REFERENCES: 6006 and 9014

## § 1170 Abandonment of railroad line

(a) The court, after notice and a hearing, may authorize the abandonment of all or a portion of a railroad line if such abandonment is—

(1) (A) in the best interest of the estate; or

(B) essential to the formulation of a plan; and

(2) consistent with the public interest.

(b) If, except for the pendency of the case under this chapter, such abandonment would require approval by the Board under a law of the United States, the trustee shall initiate an appropriate application for such abandonment with the Board. The court may fix a time within which the Board shall report to the court on such application.

(c) After the court receives the report of the Board, or the expiration of the time fixed under subsection (b) of this section, whichever occurs first, the court may authorize such abandonment, after notice to the Board, the Secretary of Transportation, the trustee, any party in interest that has requested notice, any affected shipper or community, and any other entity prescribed by the court, and a hearing.

(d) (1) Enforcement of an order authorizing such abandonment shall be stayed until the time for taking an appeal has expired, or, if an appeal is timely taken, until such order has become final.

(2) If an order authorizing such abandonment is appealed, the court, on request of a party in interest, may authorize suspension of service on a line or a portion of a line pending the determination of such appeal, after notice to the Board, the Secretary of Transportation, the trustee, any party in interest that has requested notice, any affected shipper or community, and any other entity prescribed by the court, and a hearing. An appellant may not obtain a stay of the enforcement of an order authorizing such suspension by the giving of a supersedeas bond or otherwise, during the pendency of such appeal.

(e) (1) In authorizing any abandonment of a railroad line under this section, the court shall require the rail carrier to provide a fair arrangement at least as protective of the interests of employees as that established under section 11326(a) of title 49.

(2) Nothing in this subsection shall be deemed to affect the priorities or timing of payment of employee protection which might have existed in the absence of this subsection.

BANKRUPTCY RULE REFERENCE: 6007

## § 1171 Priority claims

(a) There shall be paid as an administrative expense any claim of an individual or of the personal representative of a deceased individual against the debtor or the estate, for personal injury to or death of such individual arising out of the operation of the debtor or the estate, whether such claim arose before or after the commencement of the case.

(b) Any unsecured claim against the debtor that would have been entitled to priority if a receiver in equity of the property of the debtor had been appointed by a Federal court on the date of the order for relief under this title shall be entitled to the same priority in the case under this chapter.

## § 1172 Contents of plan

(a) In addition to the provisions required or permitted under section 1123 of this title, a plan—

(1) shall specify the extent to and the means by which the debtor's rail service is proposed to be continued, and the extent to which any of the debtor's rail service is proposed to be terminated; and

(2) may include a provision for—

(A) the transfer of any or all of the operating railroad lines of the debtor to another operating railroad; or

(B) abandonment of any railroad line in accordance with section 1170 of this title.

(b) If, except for the pendency of the case under this chapter, transfer of, or operation of or over, any of the debtor's rail lines by an entity other than the debtor or a successor to the debtor under the plan would require approval by the Board under a law of the United States, then a plan may not propose such a transfer or such operation unless the proponent of the plan initiates an appropriate application for such a transfer or such operation with the Board and, within such time as the court may fix, not exceeding 180 days, the Board, with or without a hearing, as the Board may determine, and with or without modification or condition, approves such application, or does not act on such application. Any action or order of the Board approving, modifying, conditioning, or disapproving such application is subject to review by the court only under sections 706(2)(A), 706(2)(B), 706(2)(C), and 706(2)(D) of title 5.

(c) (1) In approving an application under subsection (b) of this section, the Board shall require the rail carrier to provide a fair arrangement at least as protective of the interests of employees as that established under section 11326(a) of title 49.

(2) Nothing in this subsection shall be deemed to affect the priorities or timing of payment of employee protection which might have existed in the absence of this subsection.

Bankruptcy Rule Reference: 3016

**§ 1173 Confirmation of plan**

(a) The court shall confirm a plan if—

(1) the applicable requirements of section 1129 of this title have been met;

(2) each creditor or equity security holder will receive or retain under the plan property of a value, as of the effective date of the plan, that is not less than the value of property that each such creditor or equity security holder would so receive or retain if all of the operating railroad lines of the debtor were sold, and the proceeds of such sale, and the other property of the estate, were distributed under chapter 7 of this title on such date;

(3) in light of the debtor's past earnings and the probable prospective earnings of the reorganized debtor, there will be adequate coverage by such prospective earnings of any fixed charges, such as interest on debt, amortization of funded debt, and rent for leased railroads, provided for by the plan; and

(4) the plan is consistent with the public interest.

(b) If the requirements of subsection (a) of this section are met with respect to more than one plan, the court shall confirm the plan that is most likely to maintain adequate rail service in the public interest.

BANKRUPTCY RULE REFERENCES: 2002, 3016, 3017, 3018, 3019, 3020, 9005 and 9014

**§ 1174 Liquidation**

On request of a party in interest and after notice and a hearing, the court may, or, if a plan has not been confirmed under section 1173 of this title before five years after the date of the order for relief, the court shall, order the trustee to cease the debtor's operation and to collect and reduce to money all of the property of the estate in the same manner as if the case were a case under chapter 7 of this title.

## SUBCHAPTER V
## Small Business Debtor Reorganization[83]

### § 1181 Inapplicability of other sections

(a) IN GENERAL.—Sections 105(d), 1101(1), 1104, 1105, 1106, 1107, 1108, 1115, 1116, 1121, 1123(a)(8), 1123(c), 1127, 1129(a)(15), 1129(b), 1129(c), 1129(e), and 1141(d)(5) of this title do not apply in a case under this subchapter.

(b) COURT AUTHORITY.—Unless the court for cause orders otherwise, paragraphs (1), (2), and (4) of section 1102(a) and sections 1102(b), 1103, and 1125 of this title do not apply in a case under this subchapter.

(c) SPECIAL RULE FOR DISCHARGE.—If a plan is confirmed under section 1191(b) of this title, section 1141(d) of this title shall not apply, except as provided in section 1192 of this title.

### § 1182 Definitions

In this subchapter:

(1) DEBTOR.—The term "debtor"—

(A) subject to subparagraph (B), means a person engaged in commercial or business activities (including any affiliate of such person that is also a debtor under this title and excluding a person whose primary activity is the business of owning single asset real estate) that has aggregate noncontingent liquidated secured and unsecured debts as of the date of the filing of the petition or the date of the order for relief in an amount not more than $7,500,000 (excluding debts owed to 1 or more affiliates or insiders) not less than 50 percent of which arose from the commercial or business activities of the debtor; and

(B) does not include—

(i) any member of a group of affiliated debtors that has aggregate noncontingent liquidated secured and unsecured debts in an amount greater than $7,500,000 (excluding debt owed to 1 or more affiliates or insiders);

(ii) any debtor that is a corporation subject to the reporting requirements under section 13 or 15(d) of the Securities Exchange Act of 1934 (15 U.S.C. 78m, 78o(d)); or

(iii) any debtor that is an affiliate of an issuer, as defined in section 3 of the Securities Exchange Act of 1934 (15 U.S.C. 78c).[84]

---

[83] ED. NOTE: Subchapter V of chapter 11 was added to the Bankruptcy Code by the Small Business Reorganization Act of 2019, Pub. L. No. 116-54, § 2 (2019). The provisions apply to pending cases effective February 19, 2020. *Id.* § 5.

[84] ED. NOTE: This definition (underscored material) is effective in cases commenced on or after March 27, 2020. *See* Coronavirus, Aid, Relief, and Economic Security Act, Pub. L. No. 116-136, § 1113(a)(5). Two years after the effective date, the definition will revert to the previous definition: "The term 'debtor' means a small business debtor." *See* COVID-19 Bankruptcy Relief Extension Act of 2021, Pub. L. No. 117-5 (2021).

[(1) Debtor.—The term “debtor” means a small business debtor.][85]

(2) Debtor in Possession.—The term “debtor in possession” means the debtor, unless removed as debtor in possession under section 1185(a) of this title.

## § 1183 Trustee

(a) In General.—If the United States trustee has appointed an individual under section 586(b) of title 28 to serve as standing trustee in cases under this subchapter, and if such individual qualifies as a trustee under section 322 of this title, then that individual shall serve as trustee in any case under this subchapter. Otherwise, the United States trustee shall appoint one disinterested person to serve as trustee in the case or the United States trustee may serve as trustee in the case, as necessary.

(b) Duties.—The trustee shall—

(1) perform the duties specified in paragraphs (2), (5), (6), (7), and (9) of section 704(a) of this title;

(2) perform the duties specified in paragraphs (3), (4), and (7) of section 1106(a) of this title, if the court, for cause and on request of a party in interest, the trustee, or the United States trustee, so orders;

(3) appear and be heard at the status conference under section 1188 of this title and any hearing that concerns—

(A) the value of property subject to a lien;

(B) confirmation of a plan filed under this subchapter;

(C) modification of the plan after confirmation; or

(D) the sale of property of the estate;

(4) ensure that the debtor commences making timely payments required by a plan confirmed under this subchapter;

(5) if the debtor ceases to be a debtor in possession, perform the duties specified in section 704(a)(8) and paragraphs (1), (2), and (6) of section 1106(a) of this title, including operating the business of the debtor;

(6) if there is a claim for a domestic support obligation with respect to the debtor, perform the duties specified in section 704(c) of this title; and

(7) facilitate the development of a consensual plan of reorganization.

(c) Termination of Trustee Service.—

(1) In General.—If the plan of the debtor is confirmed under section 1191(a) of this title, the service of the trustee in the case shall terminate when the plan has been substantially consummated, except that the United States trustee may

---

[85] Ed. Note: This definition (bracketed material) is effective in cases commenced on or after March 27, 2022. *See* Coronavirus, Aid, Relief, and Economic Security Act, Pub. L. No. 116-136, § 1113(a)(5); COVID-19 Bankruptcy Relief Extension Act of 2021, Pub. L. No. 117-5 (2021).

reappoint a trustee as needed for performance of duties under subsection (b)(3)(C) of this section and section 1185(a) of this title.

(2) SERVICE OF NOTICE OF SUBSTANTIAL CONSUMMATION.—Not later than 14 days after the plan of the debtor is substantially consummated, the debtor shall file with the court and serve on the trustee, the United States trustee, and all parties in interest notice of such substantial consummation.

### § 1184 Rights and powers of a debtor in possession

Subject to such limitations or conditions as the court may prescribe, a debtor in possession shall have all the rights, other than the right to compensation under section 330 of this title, and powers, and shall perform all functions and duties, except the duties specified in paragraphs (2), (3), and (4) of section 1106(a) of this title, of a trustee serving in a case under this chapter, including operating the business of the debtor.

### § 1185 Removal of debtor in possession

(a) IN GENERAL.—On request of a party in interest, and after notice and a hearing, the court shall order that the debtor shall not be a debtor in possession for cause, including fraud, dishonesty, incompetence, or gross mismanagement of the affairs of the debtor, either before or after the date of commencement of the case, or for failure to perform the obligations of the debtor under a plan confirmed under this subchapter.

(b) REINSTATEMENT.—On request of a party in interest, and after notice and a hearing, the court may reinstate the debtor in possession.

### § 1186 Property of the estate

(a) INCLUSIONS.—If a plan is confirmed under section 1191(b) of this title, property of the estate includes, in addition to the property specified in section 541 of this title—

(1) all property of the kind specified in that section that the debtor acquires after the date of commencement of the case but before the case is closed, dismissed, or converted to a case under chapter 7, 12, or 13 of this title, whichever occurs first; and

(2) earnings from services performed by the debtor after the date of commencement of the case but before the case is closed, dismissed, or converted to a case under chapter 7, 12, or 13 of this title, whichever occurs first.

(b) DEBTOR REMAINING IN POSSESSION.—Except as provided in section 1185 of this title, a plan confirmed under this subchapter, or an order confirming a plan under this subchapter, the debtor shall remain in possession of all property of the estate.

### § 1187 Duties and reporting requirements of debtors

(a) FILING REQUIREMENTS.—Upon electing to be a debtor under this subchapter, the debtor shall file the documents required by subparagraphs (A) and (B) of section 1116(1) of this title.

(b) Other Applicable Provisions.—A debtor, in addition to the duties provided in this title and as otherwise required by law, shall comply with the requirements of section 308 and paragraphs (2), (3), (4), (5), (6), and (7) of section 1116 of this title.

(c) Separate Disclosure Statement Exemption.—If the court orders under section 1181(b) of this title that section 1125 of this title applies, section 1125(f) of this title shall apply.

### § 1188 Status conference

(a) In General.—Except as provided in subsection (b), not later than 60 days after the entry of the order for relief under this chapter, the court shall hold a status conference to further the expeditious and economical resolution of a case under this subchapter.

(b) Exception.—The court may extend the period of time for holding a status conference under subsection (a) if the need for an extension is attributable to circumstances for which the debtor should not justly be held accountable.

(c) Report.—Not later than 14 days before the date of the status conference under subsection (a), the debtor shall file with the court and serve on the trustee and all parties in interest a report that details the efforts the debtor has undertaken and will undertake to attain a consensual plan of reorganization.

### § 1189 Filing of the plan

(a) Who May File a Plan.—Only the debtor may file a plan under this subchapter.

(b) Deadline.—The debtor shall file a plan not later than 90 days after the order for relief under this chapter, except that the court may extend the period if the need for the extension is attributable to circumstances for which the debtor should not justly be held accountable.

### § 1190 Contents of plan

A plan filed under this subchapter—

(1) shall include—

(A) a brief history of the business operations of the debtor;

(B) a liquidation analysis; and

(C) projections with respect to the ability of the debtor to make payments under the proposed plan of reorganization;

(2) shall provide for the submission of all or such portion of the future earnings or other future income of the debtor to the supervision and control of the trustee as is necessary for the execution of the plan; and

(3) notwithstanding section 1123(b)(5) of this title, may modify the rights of the holder of a claim secured only by a security interest in real property that is the principal residence of the debtor if the new value received in connection with the granting of the security interest was—

(A) not used primarily to acquire the real property; and

(B) used primarily in connection with the small business of the debtor.

**§ 1191 Confirmation of plan**

(a) Terms.—The court shall confirm a plan under this subchapter only if all of the requirements of section 1129(a), other than paragraph (15) of that section, of this title are met.

(b) Exception.—Notwithstanding section 510(a) of this title, if all of the applicable requirements of section 1129(a) of this title, other than paragraphs (8), (10), and (15) of that section, are met with respect to a plan, the court, on request of the debtor, shall confirm the plan notwithstanding the requirements of such paragraphs if the plan does not discriminate unfairly, and is fair and equitable, with respect to each class of claims or interests that is impaired under, and has not accepted, the plan.

(c) Rule of Construction.—For purposes of this section, the condition that a plan be fair and equitable with respect to each class of claims or interests includes the following requirements:

(1) With respect to a class of secured claims, the plan meets the requirements of section 1129(b)(2)(A) of this title.

(2) As of the effective date of the plan—

(A) the plan provides that all of the projected disposable income of the debtor to be received in the 3-year period, or such longer period not to exceed 5 years as the court may fix, beginning on the date that the first payment is due under the plan will be applied to make payments under the plan; or

(B) the value of the property to be distributed under the plan in the 3-year period, or such longer period not to exceed 5 years as the court may fix, beginning on the date on which the first distribution is due under the plan is not less than the projected disposable income of the debtor.

(3) (A) (i) The debtor will be able to make all payments under the plan; or

(ii) there is a reasonable likelihood that the debtor will be able to make all payments under the plan; and

(B) the plan provides appropriate remedies, which may include the liquidation of nonexempt assets, to protect the holders of claims or interests in the event that the payments are not made.

(d) Disposable Income.—For purposes of this section, the term 'disposable income' means the income that is received by the debtor and that is not reasonably necessary to be expended—

(1) for—

(A) the maintenance or support of the debtor or a dependent of the debtor; or

(B) a domestic support obligation that first becomes payable after the date of the filing of the petition; or

(2) for the payment of expenditures necessary for the continuation, preservation, or operation of the business of the debtor.

(e) Special Rule.—Notwithstanding section 1129(a)(9)(A) of this title, a plan that provides for the payment through the plan of a claim of a kind specified in paragraph (2) or (3) of section 507(a) of this title may be confirmed under subsection (b) of this section.

(f) Special Provision Related to COVID-19 Pandemic.—Notwithstanding section 1129(a)(9)(A) of this title and subsection (e) of this section, a plan that provides for payment of a claim of a kind specified in section 503(b)(10) of this title may be confirmed under subsection (b) of this section if the plan proposes to make payments on account of such claim when due under the terms of the loan giving rise to such claim.[86]

## § 1192 Discharge

If the plan of the debtor is confirmed under section 1191(b) of this title, as soon as practicable after completion by the debtor of all payments due within the first 3 years of the plan, or such longer period not to exceed 5 years as the court may fix, unless the court approves a written waiver of discharge executed by the debtor after the order for relief under this chapter, the court shall grant the debtor a discharge of all debts provided in section 1141(d)(1)(A) of this title, and all other debts allowed under section 503 of this title and provided for in the plan, except any debt—

(1) on which the last payment is due after the first 3 years of the plan, or such other time not to exceed 5 years fixed by the court; or

(2) of the kind specified in section 523(a) of this title.

## § 1193 Modification of plan

(a) Modification Before Confirmation.—The debtor may modify a plan at any time before confirmation, but may not modify the plan so that the plan as modified

---

[86] Ed. Note: Underscored language enacted by the Consolidated Appropriations Act, 2021, Pub. L. No. 116-260, div. N, § 320(c). The amendment will:

(A) take effect on the date on which the Administrator submits to the Director of the Executive Office for United States Trustees a written determination that, subject to satisfying any other eligibility requirements, any debtor in possession or trustee that is authorized to operate the business of the debtor under section 1183, 1184, 1203, 1204, or 1304 of title 11, United States Code, would be eligible for a loan under paragraphs (36) and (37) of section 7(a) of the Small Business Act (15 U.S.C. 636(a)); and

(B) apply to any case pending on or commenced on or after the date described in subparagraph (A).

The amendment will sunset "effective on the date that is 2 years after the date of enactment" of the Act, which was December 27, 2020. Pub. L. No. 116-260, div. N, § 320(f). On April 8, 2021, the Small Business Administration issued a procedural notice stating that chapter 11, 12 and 13 debtors are eligible to receive Paycheck Protection Program loans after confirmation of a plan. *See* SBA, "Paycheck Protection Program Loans, FAQs," Q. 67 (July 29, 2021), https://www.sba.gov/sites/default/files/2021-07/FINAL%20FAQ%20Update%207.29.21-508.pdf.

fails to meet the requirements of sections 1122 and 1123 of this title, with the exception of subsection (a)(8) of such section 1123. After the modification is filed with the court, the plan as modified becomes the plan.

(b) Modification After Confirmation.—If a plan has been confirmed under section 1191(a) of this title, the debtor may modify the plan at any time after confirmation of the plan and before substantial consummation of the plan, but may not modify the plan so that the plan as modified fails to meet the requirements of sections 1122 and 1123 of this title, with the exception of subsection (a)(8) of such section 1123. The plan, as modified under this subsection, becomes the plan only if circumstances warrant the modification and the court, after notice and a hearing, confirms the plan as modified under section 1191(a) of this title.

(c) Certain Other Modifications.—If a plan has been confirmed under section 1191(b) of this title, the debtor may modify the plan at any time within 3 years, or such longer time not to exceed 5 years, as fixed by the court, but may not modify the plan so that the plan as modified fails to meet the requirements of section 1191(b) of this title. The plan as modified under this subsection becomes the plan only if circumstances warrant such modification and the court, after notice and a hearing, confirms such plan, as modified, under section 1191(b) of this title.

(d) Holders of a Claim or Interest.—If a plan has been confirmed under section 1191(a) of this title, any holder of a claim or interest that has accepted or rejected the plan is deemed to have accepted or rejected, as the case may be, the plan as modified, unless, within the time fixed by the court, such holder changes the previous acceptance or rejection of the holder.

## § 1194 Payments

(a) Retention and Distribution by Trustee.—Payments and funds received by the trustee shall be retained by the trustee until confirmation or denial of confirmation of a plan. If a plan is confirmed, the trustee shall distribute any such payment in accordance with the plan. If a plan is not confirmed, the trustee shall return any such payments to the debtor after deducting—

(1) any unpaid claim allowed under section 503(b) of this title;

(2) any payment made for the purpose of providing adequate protection of an interest in property due to the holder of a secured claim; and

(3) any fee owing to the trustee.

(b) Other Plans.—If a plan is confirmed under section 1191(b) of this title, except as otherwise provided in the plan or in the order confirming the plan, the trustee shall make payments to creditors under the plan.

(c) Payments Prior to Confirmation.—Prior to confirmation of a plan, the court, after notice and a hearing, may authorize the trustee to make payments to the holder of a secured claim for the purpose of providing adequate protection of an interest in property.

## § 1195 Transactions with professionals

Notwithstanding section 327(a) of this title, a person is not disqualified for employment under section 327 of this title, by a debtor solely because that person holds a claim of less than $10,000 that arose prior to commencement of the case.

# CHAPTER 12
# ADJUSTMENT OF DEBTS OF A FAMILY FARMER OR FISHERMAN WITH REGULAR ANNUAL INCOME[87]

## SUBCHAPTER I
## Officers, Administration, and the Estate

### § 1201 Stay of action against codebtor

(a) Except as provided in subsections (b) and (c) of this section, after the order for relief under this chapter, a creditor may not act, or commence or continue any civil action, to collect all or any part of a consumer debt of the debtor from any individual that is liable on such debt with the debtor, or that secured such debt, unless—

(1) such individual became liable on or secured such debt in the ordinary course of such individual's business; or

(2) the case is closed, dismissed, or converted to a case under chapter 7 of this title.

(b) A creditor may present a negotiable instrument, and may give notice of dishonor of such an instrument.

(c) On request of a party in interest and after notice and a hearing, the court shall grant relief from the stay provided by subsection (a) of this section with respect to a creditor, to the extent that—

(1) as between the debtor and the individual protected under subsection (a) of this section, such individual received the consideration for the claim held by such creditor;

(2) the plan filed by the debtor proposes not to pay such claim; or

(3) such creditor's interest would be irreparably harmed by continuation of such stay.

(d) Twenty days after the filing of a request under subsection (c)(2) of this section for relief from the stay provided by subsection (a) of this section, such stay is terminated with respect to the party in interest making such request, unless the debtor or any individual that is liable on such debt with the debtor files and serves upon such party in interest a written objection to the taking of the proposed action.

BANKRUPTCY RULE REFERENCES: 4001, 9013 and 9014

---

[87] ED. NOTE: The Family Farmer Bankruptcy Relief Act of 2004, Pub. L. No. 108-369, 118 Stat. 1749 (Oct. 25, 2004), extended the effective date of chapter 12 through July 1, 2005. Section 1001(a) of the 2005 Act permanently reenacts chapter 12, effective July 1, 2005. Section 1001(a) provides:

(a) IN GENERAL.—

(1) IN GENERAL.—Chapter 12 of title 11, United States Code, as reenacted by section 149 of division C of the Omnibus Consolidated and Emergency Supplemental Appropriations Act, 1999 (Public Law 105-277), and as in effect on June 30, 2005, is hereby reenacted.

(2) EFFECTIVE DATE OF REENACTMENT.—Paragraph (1) shall take effect on July 1, 2005.

## § 1202 Trustee

(a) If the United States trustee has appointed an individual under section 586(b) of title 28 to serve as standing trustee in cases under this chapter and if such individual qualifies as a trustee under section 322 of this title, then such individual shall serve as trustee in any case filed under this chapter. Otherwise, the United States trustee shall appoint one disinterested person to serve as trustee in the case or the United States trustee may serve as trustee in the case if necessary.

(b) The trustee shall—

(1) perform the duties specified in sections 704(a)(2), 704(a)(3), 704(a)(5), 704(a)(6), 704(a)(7), and 704(a)(9) of this title;

(2) perform the duties specified in section 1106(a)(3) and 1106(a)(4) of this title if the court, for cause and on request of a party in interest, the trustee, or the United States trustee, so orders;

(3) appear and be heard at any hearing that concerns—

(A) the value of property subject to a lien;

(B) confirmation of a plan;

(C) modification of the plan after confirmation; or

(D) the sale of property of the estate;

(4) ensure that the debtor commences making timely payments required by a confirmed plan;

(5) if the debtor ceases to be a debtor in possession, perform the duties specified in sections 704(a)(8), 1106(a)(1), 1106(a)(2), 1106(a)(6), 1106(a)(7), and 1203; and

(6) if with respect to the debtor there is a claim for a domestic support obligation, provide the applicable notice specified in subsection (c).

(c) (1) In a case described in subsection (b)(6) to which subsection (b)(6) applies, the trustee shall—

(A) (i) provide written notice to the holder of the claim described in subsection (b)(6) of such claim and of the right of such holder to use the services of the State child support enforcement agency established under sections 464 and 466 of the Social Security Act for the State in which such holder resides, for assistance in collecting child support during and after the case under this title; and

(ii) include in the notice provided under clause (i) the address and telephone number of such State child support enforcement agency;

(B) (i) provide written notice to such State child support enforcement agency of such claim; and

(ii) include in the notice provided under clause (i) the name, address, and telephone number of such holder; and

(C) at such time as the debtor is granted a discharge under section 1228, provide written notice to such holder and to such State child support enforcement agency of—

(i) the granting of the discharge;

(ii) the last recent known address of the debtor;

(iii) the last recent known name and address of the debtor's employer; and

(iv) the name of each creditor that holds a claim that—

(I) is not discharged under paragraph (2), (4), or (14A) of section 523(a); or

(II) was reaffirmed by the debtor under section 524(c).

(2) (A) The holder of a claim described in subsection (b)(6) or the State child support enforcement agency of the State in which such holder resides may request from a creditor described in paragraph (1)(C)(iv) the last known address of the debtor.

(B) Notwithstanding any other provision of law, a creditor that makes a disclosure of a last known address of a debtor in connection with a request made under subparagraph (A) shall not be liable by reason of making that disclosure.

Bankruptcy Rule References: 2009, 2012, 2015 and 5002

## § 1203 Rights and powers of debtor

Subject to such limitations as the court may prescribe, a debtor in possession shall have all the rights, other than the right to compensation under section 330, and powers, and shall perform all the functions and duties, except the duties specified in paragraphs (3) and (4) of section 1106(a), of a trustee serving in a case under chapter 11, including operating the debtor's farm or commercial fishing operation.

Bankruptcy Rule References: 2015 and 6004

## § 1204 Removal of debtor as debtor in possession

(a) On request of a party in interest, and after notice and a hearing, the court shall order that the debtor shall not be a debtor in possession for cause, including fraud, dishonesty, incompetence, or gross mismanagement of the affairs of the debtor, either before or after the commencement of the case.

(b) On request of a party in interest, and after notice and a hearing, the court may reinstate the debtor in possession.

Bankruptcy Rule Reference: 2015

## § 1205 Adequate protection

(a) Section 361 does not apply in a case under this chapter.

(b) In a case under this chapter, when adequate protection is required under section 362, 363, or 364 of this title of an interest of an entity in property, such adequate protection may be provided by—

(1) requiring the trustee to make a cash payment or periodic cash payments to such entity, to the extent that the stay under section 362 of this title, use, sale, or lease under section 363 of this title, or any grant of a lien under section 364 of this title results in a decrease in the value of property securing a claim or of an entity's ownership interest in property;

(2) providing to such entity an additional or replacement lien to the extent that such stay, use, sale, lease, or grant results in a decrease in the value of property securing a claim or of an entity's ownership interest in property;

(3) paying to such entity for the use of farmland the reasonable rent customary in the community where the property is located, based upon the rental value, net income, and earning capacity of the property; or

(4) granting such other relief, other than entitling such entity to compensation allowable under section 503(b)(1) of this title as an administrative expense, as will adequately protect the value of property securing a claim or of such entity's ownership interest in property.

BANKRUPTCY RULE REFERENCE: 4001

## § 1206 Sales free of interests

After notice and a hearing, in addition to the authorization contained in section 363(f), the trustee in a case under this chapter may sell property under section 363(b) and (c) free and clear of any interest in such property of an entity other than the estate if the property is farmland, farm equipment, or property used to carry out a commercial fishing operation (including a commercial fishing vessel), except that the proceeds of such sale shall be subject to such interest.

BANKRUPTCY RULE REFERENCE: 6004

## § 1207 Property of the estate

(a) Property of the estate includes, in addition to the property specified in section 541 of this title—

(1) all property of the kind specified in such section that the debtor acquires after the commencement of the case but before the case is closed, dismissed, or converted to a case under chapter 7 of this title, whichever occurs first; and

(2) earnings from services performed by the debtor after the commencement of the case but before the case is closed, dismissed, or converted to a case under chapter 7 of this title, whichever occurs first.

(b) Except as provided in section 1204, a confirmed plan, or an order confirming a plan, the debtor shall remain in possession of all property of the estate.

## § 1208 Conversion or dismissal

(a) The debtor may convert a case under this chapter to a case under chapter 7 of this title at any time. Any waiver of the right to convert under this subsection is unenforceable.

(b) On request of the debtor at any time, if the case has not been converted under section 706 or 1112 of this title, the court shall dismiss a case under this chapter. Any waiver of the right to dismiss under this subsection is unenforceable.

(c) On request of a party in interest, and after notice and a hearing, the court may dismiss a case under this chapter for cause, including—

(1) unreasonable delay, or gross mismanagement, by the debtor that is prejudicial to creditors;

(2) nonpayment of any fees and charges required under chapter 123 of title 28;

(3) failure to file a plan timely under section 1221 of this title;

(4) failure to commence making timely payments required by a confirmed plan;

(5) denial of confirmation of a plan under section 1225 of this title and denial of a request made for additional time for filing another plan or a modification of a plan;

(6) material default by the debtor with respect to a term of a confirmed plan;

(7) revocation of the order of confirmation under section 1230 of this title, and denial of confirmation of a modified plan under section 1229 of this title;

(8) termination of a confirmed plan by reason of the occurrence of a condition specified in the plan;

(9) continuing loss to or diminution of the estate and absence of a reasonable likelihood of rehabilitation; and

(10) failure of the debtor to pay any domestic support obligation that first becomes payable after the date of the filing of the petition.

(d) On request of a party in interest, and after notice and a hearing, the court may dismiss a case under this chapter or convert a case under this chapter to a case under chapter 7 of this title upon a showing that the debtor has committed fraud in connection with the case.

(e) Notwithstanding any other provision of this section, a case may not be converted to a case under another chapter of this title unless the debtor may be a debtor under such chapter.

BANKRUPTCY RULE REFERENCES: 1017, 1019 and 2002

## Subchapter II
## The Plan

### § 1221 Filing of plan

The debtor shall file a plan not later than 90 days after the order for relief under this chapter, except that the court may extend such period if the need for an extension is attributable to circumstances for which the debtor should not justly be held accountable.

Bankruptcy Rule Reference: 3015

### § 1222 Contents of plan

(a) The plan shall–

(1) provide for the submission of all or such portion of future earnings or other future income of the debtor to the supervision and control of the trustee as is necessary for the execution of the plan;

(2) provide for the full payment, in deferred cash payments, of all claims entitled to priority under section 507, unless the holder of a particular claim agrees to a different treatment of that claim;

(3) if the plan classifies claims and interests, provide the same treatment for each claim or interest within a particular class unless the holder of a particular claim or interest agrees to less favorable treatment;

(4) notwithstanding any other provision of this section, a plan may provide for less than full payment of all amounts owed for a claim entitled to priority under section 507(a)(1)(B) only if the plan provides that all of the debtor's projected disposable income for a 5-year period beginning on the date that the first payment is due under the plan will be applied to make payments under the plan; and

(5) subject to section 1232, provide for the treatment of any claim by a governmental unit of a kind described in section 1232(a).

(b) Subject to subsections (a) and (c) of this section, the plan may–

(1) designate a class or classes of unsecured claims, as provided in section 1122 of this title, but may not discriminate unfairly against any class so designated; however, such plan may treat claims for a consumer debt of the debtor if an individual is liable on such consumer debt with the debtor differently than other unsecured claims;

(2) modify the rights of holders of secured claims, or of holders of unsecured claims, or leave unaffected the rights of holders of any class of claims;

(3) provide for the curing or waiving of any default;

(4) provide for payments on any unsecured claim to be made concurrently with payments on any secured claim or any other unsecured claim;

(5) provide for the curing of any default within a reasonable time and maintenance of payments while the case is pending on any unsecured claim or

secured claim on which the last payment is due after the date on which the final payment under the plan is due;

(6) subject to section 365 of this title, provide for the assumption, rejection, or assignment of any executory contract or unexpired lease of the debtor not previously rejected under such section;

(7) provide for the payment of all or part of a claim against the debtor from property of the estate or property of the debtor;

(8) provide for the sale of all or any part of the property of the estate or the distribution of all or any part of the property of the estate among those having an interest in such property;

(9) provide for payment of allowed secured claims consistent with section 1225(a)(5) of this title, over a period exceeding the period permitted under section 1222(c);

(10) provide for the vesting of property of the estate, on confirmation of the plan or at a later time, in the debtor or in any other entity;

(11) provide for the payment of interest accruing after the date of the filing of the petition on unsecured claims that are nondischargeable under section 1228(a), except that such interest may be paid only to the extent that the debtor has disposable income available to pay such interest after making provision for full payment of all allowed claims; and

(12) include any other appropriate provision not inconsistent with this title.

(c) Except as provided in subsections (b)(5) and (b)(9), the plan may not provide for payments over a period that is longer than three years unless the court for cause approves a longer period, but the court may not approve a period that is longer than five years.

(d) Notwithstanding subsection (b)(2) of this section and sections 506(b) and 1225(a)(5) of this title, if it is proposed in a plan to cure a default, the amount necessary to cure the default, shall be determined in accordance with the underlying agreement and applicable nonbankruptcy law.

Bankruptcy Rule References: 3012 and 3013

### § 1223 Modification of plan before confirmation

(a) The debtor may modify the plan at any time before confirmation, but may not modify the plan so that the plan as modified fails to meet the requirements of section 1222 of this title.

(b) After the debtor files a modification under this section, the plan as modified becomes the plan.

(c) Any holder of a secured claim that has accepted or rejected the plan is deemed to have accepted or rejected, as the case may be, the plan as modified, unless the modification provides for a change in the rights of such holder from what such rights were under the plan before modification, and such holder changes such holder's previous acceptance or rejection.

BANKRUPTCY RULE REFERENCES: 3015 and 3019

## § 1224 Confirmation hearing

After expedited notice, the court shall hold a hearing on confirmation of the plan. A party in interest, the trustee, or the United States trustee may object to the confirmation of the plan. Except for cause, the hearing shall be concluded not later than 45 days after the filing of the plan.

BANKRUPTCY RULE REFERENCES: 2002, 3015 and 9014

## § 1225 Confirmation of plan

(a) Except as provided in subsection (b), the court shall confirm a plan if—

(1) the plan complies with the provisions of this chapter and with the other applicable provisions of this title;

(2) any fee, charge, or amount required under chapter 123 of title 28, or by the plan, to be paid before confirmation, has been paid;

(3) the plan has been proposed in good faith and not by any means forbidden by law;

(4) the value, as of the effective date of the plan, of property to be distributed under the plan on account of each allowed unsecured claim is not less than the amount that would be paid on such claim if the estate of the debtor were liquidated under chapter 7 of this title on such date;

(5) with respect to each allowed secured claim provided for by the plan—

(A) the holder of such claim has accepted the plan;

(B) (i) the plan provides that the holder of such claim retain the lien securing such claim; and

(ii) the value, as of the effective date of the plan, of property to be distributed by the trustee or the debtor under the plan on account of such claim is not less than the allowed amount of such claim; or

(C) the debtor surrenders the property securing such claim to such holder;

(6) the debtor will be able to make all payments under the plan and to comply with the plan; and

(7) the debtor has paid all amounts that are required to be paid under a domestic support obligation and that first become payable after the date of the filing of the petition if the debtor is required by a judicial or administrative order, or by statute, to pay such domestic support obligation.

(b) (1) If the trustee or the holder of an allowed unsecured claim objects to the confirmation of the plan, then the court may not approve the plan unless, as of the effective date of the plan—

(A) the value of the property to be distributed under the plan on account of such claim is not less than the amount of such claim;

(B) the plan provides that all of the debtor's projected disposable income to be received in the three-year period, or such longer period as the court may approve under section 1222(c), beginning on the date that the first payment is due under the plan will be applied to make payments under the plan; or

(C) the value of the property to be distributed under the plan in the 3-year period, or such longer period as the court may approve under section 1222(c), beginning on the date that the first distribution is due under the plan is not less than the debtor's projected disposable income for such period.

(2) For purposes of this subsection, "disposable income" means income which is received by the debtor and which is not reasonably necessary to be expended-

(A) for the maintenance or support of the debtor or a dependent of the debtor or for a domestic support obligation that first becomes payable after the date of the filing of the petition; or

(B) for the payment of expenditures necessary for the continuation, preservation, and operation of the debtor's business.

(c) After confirmation of a plan, the court may order any entity from whom the debtor receives income to pay all or any part of such income to the trustee.

(d) Notwithstanding section 1222(a)(2) of this title and subsection (b)(1) of this section, a plan that provides for payment of a claim of a kind specified in section 503(b)(10) of this title may be confirmed if the plan proposes to make payments on account of such claim when due under the terms of the loan giving rise to such claim.[88]

Bankruptcy Rule References: 2002 and 3015

## § 1226 Payments

(a) Payments and funds received by the trustee shall be retained by the trustee

---

[88] Ed note: Underscored language enacted by the Consolidated Appropriations Act, 2021, Pub. L. No. 116-260, div. N, § 320(d). The amendment will:

(A) take effect on the date on which the Administrator submits to the Director of the Executive Office for United States Trustees a written determination that, subject to satisfying any other eligibility requirements, any debtor in possession or trustee that is authorized to operate the business of the debtor under section 1183, 1184, 1203, 1204, or 1304 of title 11, United States Code, would be eligible for a loan under paragraphs (36) and (37) of section 7(a) of the Small Business Act (15 U.S.C. 636(a)); and

(B) apply to any case pending on or commenced on or after the date described in subparagraph (A).

The amendment will sunset "effective on the date that is 2 years after the date of enactment" of the Act, which was December 27, 2020. Pub. L. No. 116-260, div. N, § 320(f). On April 8, 2021, the Small Business Administration issued a procedural notice stating that chapter 11, 12 and 13 debtors are eligible to receive Paycheck Protection Program loans after confirmation of a plan. *See* SBA, "Paycheck Protection Program Loans, FAQs," Q. 67 (July 29, 2021), https://www.sba.gov/sites/default/files/2021-07/FINAL%20FAQ%20Update%207.29.21-508.pdf.

until confirmation or denial of confirmation of a plan. If a plan is confirmed, the trustee shall distribute any such payment in accordance with the plan. If a plan is not confirmed, the trustee shall return any such payments to the debtor, after deducting—

(1) any unpaid claim allowed under section 503(b) of this title; and

(2) if a standing trustee is serving in the case, the percentage fee fixed for such standing trustee.

(b) Before or at the time of each payment to creditors under the plan, there shall be paid—

(1) any unpaid claim of the kind specified in section 507(a)(2) of this title; and

(2) if a standing trustee appointed under section 1202(c) of this title is serving in the case, the percentage fee fixed for such standing trustee under section 1202(d) of this title.

(c) Except as otherwise provided in the plan or in the order confirming the plan, the trustee shall make payments to creditors under the plan.

BANKRUPTCY RULE REFERENCES: 3010, 3011 and 3021

### § 1227 Effect of confirmation

(a) Except as provided in section 1228(a) of this title, the provisions of a confirmed plan bind the debtor, each creditor, each equity security holder, and each general partner in the debtor, whether or not the claim of such creditor, such equity security holder, or such general partner in the debtor is provided for by the plan, and whether or not such creditor, such equity security holder, or such general partner in the debtor has objected to, has accepted, or has rejected the plan.

(b) Except as otherwise provided in the plan or the order confirming the plan, the confirmation of a plan vests all of the property of the estate in the debtor.

(c) Except as provided in section 1228(a) of this title and except as otherwise provided in the plan or in the order confirming the plan, the property vesting in the debtor under subsection (b) of this section is free and clear of any claim or interest of any creditor provided for by the plan.

BANKRUPTCY RULE REFERENCE: 3015

### § 1228 Discharge

(a) Subject to subsection (d), as soon as practicable after completion by the debtor of all payments under the plan, and in the case of a debtor who is required by a judicial or administrative order, or by statute, to pay a domestic support obligation, after such debtor certifies that all amounts payable under such order or such statute that are due on or before the date of the certification (including amounts due before the petition was filed, but only to the extent provided for by the plan) have been paid, other than payments to holders of allowed claims provided for under section 1222(b)(5) or 1222(b)(9) of this title, unless the court approves a written waiver of discharge executed by the debtor after the order for relief under this chapter, the court shall grant the debtor a discharge of all debts provided for by the plan, allowed under section 503 of this title, or disallowed under section 502 of this title, except any debt—

(1) provided for under section 1222(b)(5) or 1222(b)(9) of this title; or

(2) of a kind specified in section 523(a) of this title, except as provided in section 1232(c).

(b) Subject to subsection (d), at any time after the confirmation of the plan and after notice and a hearing, the court may grant a discharge to a debtor that has not completed payments under the plan only if—

(1) the debtor's failure to complete such payments is due to circumstances for which the debtor should not justly be held accountable;

(2) the value, as of the effective date of the plan, of property actually distributed under the plan on account of each allowed unsecured claim is not less than the amount that would have been paid on such claim if the estate of the debtor had been liquidated under chapter 7 of this title on such date; and

(3) modification of the plan under section 1229 of this title is not practicable.

(c) A discharge granted under subsection (b) of this section discharges the debtor from all unsecured debts provided for by the plan or disallowed under section 502 of this title, except any debt—

(1) provided for under section 1222(b)(5) or 1222(b)(9) of this title; or

(2) of a kind specified in section 523(a) of this title, except as provided in section 1232(c).

(d) On request of a party in interest before one year after a discharge under this section is granted, and after notice and a hearing, the court may revoke such discharge only if—

(1) such discharge was obtained by the debtor through fraud; and

(2) the requesting party did not know of such fraud until after such discharge was granted.

(e) After the debtor is granted a discharge, the court shall terminate the services of any trustee serving in the case.

(f) The court may not grant a discharge under this chapter unless the court after notice and a hearing held not more than 10 days before the date of the entry of the order granting the discharge finds that there is no reasonable cause to believe that—

(1) section 522(q)(1) may be applicable to the debtor; and

(2) there is pending any proceeding in which the debtor may be found guilty of a felony of the kind described in section 522(q)(1)(A) or liable for a debt of the kind described in section 522(q)(1)(B).

BANKRUPTCY RULE REFERENCES: 1007-I, 4004, 4006, 4007 and 7001

## § 1229 Modification of plan after confirmation

(a) At any time after confirmation of the plan but before the completion of payments under such plan, the plan may be modified, on request of the debtor, the trustee, or the holder of an allowed unsecured claim, to—

(1) increase or reduce the amount of payments on claims of a particular class provided for by the plan;

(2) extend or reduce the time for such payments;

(3) alter the amount of the distribution to a creditor whose claim is provided for by the plan to the extent necessary to take account of any payment of such claim other than under the plan; or

(4) provide for the payment of a claim described in section 1232(a) that arose after the date on which the petition was filed.

(b) (1) Sections 1222(a), 1222(b), and 1223(c) of this title and the requirements of section 1225(a) of this title apply to any modification under subsection (a) of this section.

(2) The plan as modified becomes the plan unless, after notice and a hearing, such modification is disapproved.

(c) A plan modified under this section may not provide for payments over a period that expires after three years after the time that the first payment under the original confirmed plan was due, unless the court, for cause, approves a longer period, but the court may not approve a period that expires after five years after such time.

(d) A plan may not be modified under this section—

(1) to increase the amount of any payment due before the plan as modified becomes the plan;

(2) by anyone except the debtor, based on an increase in the debtor's disposable income, to increase the amount of payments to unsecured creditors required for a particular month so that the aggregate of such payments exceeds the debtor's disposable income for such month; or

(3) in the last year of the plan by anyone except the debtor, to require payments that would leave the debtor with insufficient funds to carry on the farming operation after the plan is completed.

BANKRUPTCY RULE REFERENCES: 2002, 3015 and 9014

## § 1230 Revocation of an order of confirmation

(a) On request of a party in interest at any time within 180 days after the date of the entry of an order of confirmation under section 1225 of this title, and after notice and a hearing, the court may revoke such order if such order was procured by fraud.

(b) If the court revokes an order of confirmation under subsection (a) of this section, the court shall dispose of the case under section 1207 of this title, unless, within the time fixed by the court, the debtor proposes and the court confirms a modification of the plan under section 1229 of this title.

Bankruptcy Rule References: 7001 and 9024

### § 1231 Special tax provisions

(a) The issuance, transfer, or exchange of a security, or the making or delivery of an instrument of transfer under a plan confirmed under section 1225 of this title, may not be taxed under any law imposing a stamp tax or similar tax.

(b) The court may authorize the proponent of a plan to request a determination, limited to questions of law, by any governmental unit charged with responsibility for collection or determination of a tax on or measured by income, of the tax effects, under section 346 of this title and under the law imposing such tax, of the plan. In the event of an actual controversy, the court may declare such effects after the earlier of—

(1) the date on which such governmental unit responds to the request under this subsection; or

(2) 270 days after such request.

### § 1232 Claim by a governmental unit based on the disposition of property used in a farming operation

(a) Any unsecured claim of a governmental unit against the debtor or the estate that arises before the filing of the petition, or that arises after the filing of the petition and before the debtor's discharge under section 1228, as a result of the sale, transfer, exchange, or other disposition of any property used in the debtor's farming operation—

(1) shall be treated as an unsecured claim arising before the date on which the petition is filed;

(2) shall not be entitled to priority under section 507;

(3) shall be provided for under a plan; and

(4) shall be discharged in accordance with section 1228.

(b) For purposes of applying sections 1225(a)(4), 1228(b)(2), and 1229(b)(1) to a claim described in subsection (a) of this section, the amount that would be paid on such claim if the estate of the debtor were liquidated in a case under chapter 7 of this title shall be the amount that would be paid by the estate in a chapter 7 case if the claim were an unsecured claim arising before the date on which the petition was filed and were not entitled to priority under section 507.

(c) For purposes of applying sections 523(a), 1228(a)(2), and 1228(c)(2) to a claim described in subsection (a) of this section, the claim shall not be treated as a claim of a kind specified in subparagraph (A) or (B) of section 523(a)(1).

(d) (1) A governmental unit may file a proof of claim for a claim described in subsection (a) that arises after the date on which the petition is filed.

(2) If a debtor files a tax return after the filing of the petition for a period in which a claim described in subsection (a) arises, and the claim relates to the tax return, the debtor shall serve notice of the claim on the governmental unit charged with the responsibility for the collection of the tax at the address and in the manner designated in section 505(b)(1). Notice under this paragraph shall state that the debtor has filed a petition under this chapter, state the name and location of the court in which the case under this chapter is pending, state the amount of the claim, and include a copy of the filed tax return and documentation supporting the calculation of the claim.

(3) If notice of a claim has been served on the governmental unit in accordance with paragraph (2), the governmental unit may file a proof of claim not later than 180 days after the date on which such notice was served. If the governmental unit has not filed a timely proof of the claim, the debtor or trustee may file proof of the claim that is consistent with the notice served under paragraph (2). If a proof of claim is filed by the debtor or trustee under this paragraph, the governmental unit may not amend the proof of claim.

(4) A claim filed under this subsection shall be determined and shall be allowed under subsection (a), (b), or (c) of section 502, or disallowed under subsection (d) or (e) of section 502, in the same manner as if the claim had arisen immediately before the date of the filing of the petition.

BANKRUPTCY RULE REFERENCE: 6004

# CHAPTER 13
# ADJUSTMENT OF DEBTS OF AN INDIVIDUAL WITH REGULAR INCOME

## SUBCHAPTER I
## Officers, Administration, and the Estate

### § 1301 Stay of action against codebtor

(a) Except as provided in subsections (b) and (c) of this section, after the order for relief under this chapter, a creditor may not act, or commence or continue any civil action, to collect all or any part of a consumer debt of the debtor from any individual that is liable on such debt with the debtor, or that secured such debt, unless—

(1) such individual became liable on or secured such debt in the ordinary course of such individual's business; or

(2) the case is closed, dismissed, or converted to a case under chapter 7 or 11 of this title.

(b) A creditor may present a negotiable instrument, and may give notice of dishonor of such an instrument.

(c) On request of a party in interest and after notice and a hearing, the court shall grant relief from the stay provided by subsection (a) of this section with respect to a creditor, to the extent that—

(1) as between the debtor and the individual protected under subsection (a) of this section, such individual received the consideration for the claim held by such creditor;

(2) the plan filed by the debtor proposes not to pay such claim; or

(3) such creditor's interest would be irreparably harmed by continuation of such stay.

(d) Twenty days after the filing of a request under subsection (c)(2) of this section for relief from the stay provided by subsection (a) of this section, such stay is terminated with respect to the party in interest making such request, unless the debtor or any individual that is liable on such debt with the debtor files and serves upon such party in interest a written objection to the taking of the proposed action.

BANKRUPTCY RULE REFERENCES: 4001, 9013 and 9014

### § 1302 Trustee

(a) If the United States trustee appoints an individual under section 586(b) of title 28 to serve as standing trustee in cases under this chapter and if such individual qualifies under section 322 of this title, then such individual shall serve as trustee in the case. Otherwise, the United States trustee shall appoint one disinterested person to serve as trustee in the case or the United States trustee may serve as a trustee in the case.

(b) The trustee shall—

(1) perform the duties specified in sections 704(a)(2), 704(a)(3), 704(a)(4), 704(a)(5), 704(a)(6), 704(a)(7), and 704(a)(9) of this title;

(2) appear and be heard at any hearing that concerns—

(A) the value of property subject to a lien;

(B) confirmation of a plan; or

(C) modification of the plan after confirmation;

(3) dispose of, under regulations issued by the Director of the Administrative Office of the United States Courts, moneys received or to be received in a case under chapter XIII of the Bankruptcy Act;

(4) advise, other than on legal matters, and assist the debtor in performance under the plan;

(5) ensure that the debtor commences making timely payments under section 1326 of this title; and

(6) if with respect to the debtor there is a claim for a domestic support obligation, provide the applicable notice specified in subsection (d).

(c) If the debtor is engaged in business, then in addition to the duties specified in subsection (b) of this section, the trustee shall perform the duties specified in sections 1106(a)(3) and 1106(a)(4) of this title.

(d) (1) In a case described in subsection (b)(6) to which subsection (b)(6) applies, the trustee shall—

(A) (i) provide written notice to the holder of the claim described in subsection (b)(6) of such claim and of the right of such holder to use the services of the State child support enforcement agency established under sections 464 and 466 of the Social Security Act for the State in which such holder resides, for assistance in collecting child support during and after the case under this title; and

(ii) include in the notice provided under clause (i) the address and telephone number of such State child support enforcement agency;

(B) (i) provide written notice to such State child support enforcement agency of such claim; and

(ii) include in the notice provided under clause (i) the name, address, and telephone number of such holder; and

(C) at such time as the debtor is granted a discharge under section 1328, provide written notice to such holder and to such State child support enforcement agency of—

(i) the granting of the discharge;

(ii) the last recent known address of the debtor;

(iii) the last recent known name and address of the debtor's employer;

and

(iv) the name of each creditor that holds a claim that—

(I) is not discharged under paragraph (2) or (4) of section 523(a); or

(II) was reaffirmed by the debtor under section 524(c).

(2) (A) The holder of a claim described in subsection (b)(6) or the State child support enforcement agency of the State in which such holder resides may request from a creditor described in paragraph (1)(C)(iv) the last known address of the debtor.

(B) Notwithstanding any other provision of law, a creditor that makes a disclosure of a last known address of a debtor in connection with a request made under subparagraph (A) shall not be liable by reason of making that disclosure.

Bankruptcy Rule References: 2008, 2009, 2010, 2011, 2012, 2013, 2014, 2015, 2016, 2017, 5002 and 6009

## § 1303 Rights and powers of debtor

Subject to any limitations on a trustee under this chapter, the debtor shall have, exclusive of the trustee, the rights and powers of a trustee under sections 363(b), 363(d), 363(e), 363(f), and 363(*l*), of this title.

Bankruptcy Rule References: 2002, 2015 and 6004

## § 1304 Debtor engaged in business

(a) A debtor that is self-employed and incurs trade credit in the production of income from such employment is engaged in business.

(b) Unless the court orders otherwise, a debtor engaged in business may operate the business of the debtor and, subject to any limitations on a trustee under sections 363(c) and 364 of this title and to such limitations or conditions as the court prescribes, shall have, exclusive of the trustee, the rights and powers of the trustee under such sections.

(c) A debtor engaged in business shall perform the duties of the trustee specified in section 704(a)(8) of this title.

Bankruptcy Rule Reference: 2015

## § 1305 Filing and allowance of postpetition claims

(a) A proof of claim may be filed by any entity that holds a claim against the debtor—

(1) for taxes that become payable to a governmental unit while the case is pending; or

(2) that is a consumer debt, that arises after the date of the order for relief under this chapter, and that is for property or services necessary for the debtor's performance under the plan.

(b) Except as provided in subsection (c) of this section, a claim filed under subsection (a) of this section shall be allowed or disallowed under section 502 of this title, but shall be determined as of the date such claim arises, and shall be allowed under section 502(a), 502(b), or 502(c) of this title, or disallowed under section 502(d) or 502(e) of this title, the same as if such claim had arisen before the date of the filing of the petition.

(c) A claim filed under subsection (a)(2) of this section shall be disallowed if the holder of such claim knew or should have known that prior approval by the trustee of the debtor's incurring the obligation was practicable and was not obtained.

Bankruptcy Rule References: 3001, 3002, 3004, 3005, 3006, 3007 and 3008

### § 1306 Property of the estate

(a) Property of the estate includes, in addition to the property specified in section 541 of this title–

(1) all property of the kind specified in such section that the debtor acquires after the commencement of the case but before the case is closed, dismissed, or converted to a case under chapter 7, 11, or 12 of this title, whichever occurs first; and

(2) earnings from services performed by the debtor after the commencement of the case but before the case is closed, dismissed, or converted to a case under chapter 7, 11, or 12 of this title, whichever occurs first.

(b) Except as provided in a confirmed plan or order confirming a plan, the debtor shall remain in possession of all property of the estate.

### § 1307 Conversion or dismissal

(a) The debtor may convert a case under this chapter to a case under chapter 7 of this title at any time. Any waiver of the right to convert under this subsection is unenforceable.

(b) On request of the debtor at any time, if the case has not been converted under section 706, 1112, or 1208 of this title, the court shall dismiss a case under this chapter. Any waiver of the right to dismiss under this subsection is unenforceable.

(c) Except as provided in subsection (f) of this section, on request of a party in interest or the United States trustee and after notice and a hearing, the court may convert a case under this chapter to a case under chapter 7 of this title, or may dismiss a case under this chapter, whichever is in the best interests of creditors and the estate, for cause, including–

(1) unreasonable delay by the debtor that is prejudicial to creditors;

(2) nonpayment of any fees and charges required under chapter 123 of title 28;

(3) failure to file a plan timely under section 1321 of this title;

(4) failure to commence making timely payments under section 1326 of this title;

(5) denial of confirmation of a plan under section 1325 of this title and denial of a request made for additional time for filing another plan or a modification of a plan;

(6) material default by the debtor with respect to a term of a confirmed plan;

(7) revocation of the order of confirmation under section 1330 of this title, and denial of confirmation of a modified plan under section 1329 of this title;

(8) termination of a confirmed plan by reason of the occurrence of a condition specified in the plan other than completion of payments under the plan;

(9) only on request of the United States trustee, failure of the debtor to file, within fifteen days, or such additional time as the court may allow, after the filing of the petition commencing such case, the information required by paragraph (1) of section 521(a);

(10) only on request of the United States trustee, failure to timely file the information required by paragraph (2) of section 521(a); or

(11) failure of the debtor to pay any domestic support obligation that first becomes payable after the date of the filing of the petition.

(d) Except as provided in subsection (f) of this section, at any time before the confirmation of a plan under section 1325 of this title, on request of a party in interest or the United States trustee and after notice and a hearing, the court may convert a case under this chapter to a case under chapter 11 or 12 of this title.

(e) Upon the failure of the debtor to file a tax return under section 1308, on request of a party in interest or the United States trustee and after notice and a hearing, the court shall dismiss a case or convert a case under this chapter to a case under chapter 7 of this title, whichever is in the best interest of the creditors and the estate.

(f) The court may not convert a case under this chapter to a case under chapter 7, 11, or 12 of this title if the debtor is a farmer, unless the debtor requests such conversion.

(g) Notwithstanding any other provision of this section, a case may not be converted to a case under another chapter of this title unless the debtor may be a debtor under such chapter.

BANKRUPTCY RULE REFERENCES: 1017, 1019, 2002, 9013 and 9014

### § 1308 Filing of prepetition tax returns

(a) Not later than the day before the date on which the meeting of the creditors is first scheduled to be held under section 341(a), if the debtor was required to file a tax return under applicable nonbankruptcy law, the debtor shall file with appropriate tax authorities all tax returns for all taxable periods ending during the 4-year period ending on the date of the filing of the petition.

(b) (1) Subject to paragraph (2), if the tax returns required by subsection (a) have not been filed by the date on which the meeting of creditors is first scheduled to be held under section 341(a), the trustee may hold open that meeting for a reasonable period of time to allow the debtor an additional period of time to file any unfiled returns, but such additional period of time shall not extend beyond—

(A) for any return that is past due as of the date of the filing of the petition, the date that is 120 days after the date of that meeting; or

(B) for any return that is not past due as of the date of the filing of the petition, the later of—

(i) the date that is 120 days after the date of that meeting; or

(ii) the date on which the return is due under the last automatic extension of time for filing that return to which the debtor is entitled, and for which request is timely made, in accordance with applicable nonbankruptcy law.

(2) After notice and a hearing, and order entered before the tolling of any applicable filing period determined under paragraph (1), if the debtor demonstrates by a preponderance of the evidence that the failure to file a return as required under paragraph (1) is attributable to circumstances beyond the control of the debtor, the court may extend the filing period established by the trustee under paragraph (1) for—

(A) a period of not more than 30 days for returns described in paragraph (1)(A); and

(B) a period not to extend after the applicable extended due date for a return described in paragraph (1)(B).

(c) For purposes of this section, the term "return" includes a return prepared pursuant to subsection (a) or (b) of section 6020 of the Internal Revenue Code of 1986, or a similar State or local law, or a written stipulation to a judgment or a final order entered by a nonbankruptcy tribunal.

Bankruptcy Rule Reference: 3002

## Subchapter II
## The Plan

### § 1321 Filing of plan

The debtor shall file a plan.

Bankruptcy Rule References: 3015 and 9006

### § 1322 Contents of plan

(a) The plan—

(1) shall provide for the submission of all or such portion of future earnings or other future income of the debtor to the supervision and control of the trustee as is necessary for the execution of the plan;

(2) shall provide for the full payment, in deferred cash payments, of all claims entitled to priority under section 507 of this title, unless the holder of a particular claim agrees to a different treatment of such claim;

(3) if the plan classifies claims, shall provide the same treatment for each claim within a particular class; and

(4) notwithstanding any other provision of this section, may provide for less than full payment of all amounts owed for a claim entitled to priority under section 507(a)(1)(B) only if the plan provides that all of the debtor's projected disposable income for a 5-year period beginning on the date that the first payment is due under the plan will be applied to make payments under the plan.

(b) Subject to subsections (a) and (c) of this section, the plan may—

(1) designate a class or classes of unsecured claims, as provided in section 1122 of this title, but may not discriminate unfairly against any class so designated; however, such plan may treat claims for a consumer debt of the debtor if an individual is liable on such consumer debt with the debtor differently than other unsecured claims;

(2) modify the rights of holders of secured claims, other than a claim secured only by a security interest in real property that is the debtor's principal residence, or of holders of unsecured claims, or leave unaffected the rights of holders of any class of claims;

(3) provide for the curing or waiving of any default;

(4) provide for payments on any unsecured claim to be made concurrently with payments on any secured claim or any other unsecured claim;

(5) notwithstanding paragraph (2) of this subsection, provide for the curing of any default within a reasonable time and maintenance of payments while the case is pending on any unsecured claim or secured claim on which the last payment is due after the date on which the final payment under the plan is due;

(6) provide for the payment of all or any part of any claim allowed under

section 1305 of this title;

(7) subject to section 365 of this title, provide for the assumption, rejection, or assignment of any executory contract or unexpired lease of the debtor not previously rejected under such section;

(8) provide for the payment of all or part of a claim against the debtor from property of the estate or property of the debtor;

(9) provide for the vesting of property of the estate, on confirmation of the plan or at a later time, in the debtor or in any other entity;

(10) provide for the payment of interest accruing after the date of the filing of the petition on unsecured claims that are nondischargeable under section 1328(a), except that such interest may be paid only to the extent that the debtor has disposable income available to pay such interest after making provision for full payment of all allowed claims; and

(11) include any other appropriate provision not inconsistent with this title.

(c) Notwithstanding subsection (b)(2) and applicable nonbankruptcy law—

(1) a default with respect to, or that gave rise to, a lien on the debtor's principal residence may be cured under paragraph (3) or (5) of subsection (b) until such residence is sold at a foreclosure sale that is conducted in accordance with applicable nonbankruptcy law; and

(2) in a case in which the last payment on the original payment schedule for a claim secured only by a security interest in real property that is the debtor's principal residence is due before the date on which the final payment under the plan is due, the plan may provide for the payment of the claim as modified pursuant to section 1325(a)(5) of this title.

(d) (1) If the current monthly income of the debtor and the debtor's spouse combined, when multiplied by 12, is not less than—

(A) in the case of a debtor in a household of 1 person, the median family income of the applicable State for 1 earner;

(B) in the case of a debtor in a household of 2, 3, or 4 individuals, the highest median family income of the applicable State for a family of the same number or fewer individuals; or

(C) in the case of a debtor in a household exceeding 4 individuals, the highest median family income of the applicable State for a family of 4 or fewer individuals, plus $750[89] per month for each individual in excess of 4,

the plan may not provide for payments over a period that is longer than 5 years.

(2) If the current monthly income of the debtor and the debtor's spouse combined, when multiplied by 12, is less than—

---

[89] Ed. Note: For cases commenced in the three-year period before April 1, 2019, the dollar amount is $700.

(A) in the case of a debtor in a household of 1 person, the median family income of the applicable State for 1 earner;

(B) in the case of a debtor in a household of 2, 3, or 4 individuals, the highest median family income of the applicable State for a family of the same number or fewer individuals; or

(C) in the case of a debtor in a household exceeding 4 individuals, the highest median family income of the applicable State for a family of 4 or fewer individuals, plus $750[90] per month for each individual in excess of 4,

the plan may not provide for payments over a period that is longer than 3 years, unless the court, for cause, approves a longer period, but the court may not approve a period that is longer than 5 years.

(e) Notwithstanding subsection (b)(2) of this section and sections 506(b) and 1325(a)(5) of this title, if it is proposed in a plan to cure a default, the amount necessary to cure the default, shall be determined in accordance with the underlying agreement and applicable nonbankruptcy law.

(f) A plan may not materially alter the terms of a loan described in section 362(b)(19) and any amounts required to repay such loan shall not constitute "disposable income" under section 1325.

BANKRUPTCY RULE REFERENCES: 3002.1, 3012 and 3013

## § 1323 Modification of plan before confirmation

(a) The debtor may modify the plan at any time before confirmation, but may not modify the plan so that the plan as modified fails to meet the requirements of section 1322 of this title.

(b) After the debtor files a modification under this section, the plan as modified becomes the plan.

(c) Any holder of a secured claim that has accepted or rejected the plan is deemed to have accepted or rejected, as the case may be, the plan as modified, unless the modification provides for a change in the rights of such holder from what such rights were under the plan before modification, and such holder changes such holder's previous acceptance or rejection.

BANKRUPTCY RULE REFERENCES: 3015 and 3019

## § 1324 Confirmation hearing

(a) Except as provided in subsection (b) and after notice, the court shall hold a hearing on confirmation of the plan. A party in interest may object to confirmation of the plan.

(b) The hearing on confirmation of the plan may be held not earlier than 20 days and not later than 45 days after the date of the meeting of creditors under section 341(a), unless the court determines that it would be in the best interests of the

[90] ED. NOTE: For cases commenced in the three-year period before April 1, 2019, the dollar amount is $700.

creditors and the estate to hold such hearing at an earlier date and there is no objection to such earlier date.

BANKRUPTCY RULE REFERENCES: 2002, 3015 and 9014

### § 1325 Confirmation of plan

(a) Except as provided in subsection (b), the court shall confirm a plan if—[91]

(1) the plan complies with the provisions of this chapter and with the other applicable provisions of this title;

(2) any fee, charge, or amount required under chapter 123 of title 28, or by the plan, to be paid before confirmation, has been paid;

(3) the plan has been proposed in good faith and not by any means forbidden by law;

(4) the value, as of the effective date of the plan, of property to be distributed under the plan on account of each allowed unsecured claim is not less than the amount that would be paid on such claim if the estate of the debtor were liquidated under chapter 7 of this title on such date;

(5) with respect to each allowed secured claim provided for by the plan—

(A) the holder of such claim has accepted the plan;

(B) (i) the plan provides that—

(I) the holder of such claim retain the lien securing such claim until the earlier of—

(aa) the payment of the underlying debt determined under nonbankruptcy law; or

(bb) discharge under section 1328; and

(II) if the case under this chapter is dismissed or converted without completion of the plan, such lien shall also be retained by such holder to the extent recognized by applicable nonbankruptcy law;

(ii) the value, as of the effective date of the plan, of property to be distributed under the plan on account of such claim is not less than the allowed amount of such claim; and

(iii) if—

(I) property to be distributed pursuant to this subsection is in the form of periodic payments, such payments shall be in equal monthly amounts; and

(II) the holder of the claim is secured by personal property, the

---

[91] ED. NOTE: Section 1228(b) of the 2005 Act provides: "CHAPTER 11 AND CHAPTER 13 CASES.—The court shall not confirm a plan of reorganization in the case of an individual under chapter 11 or 13 of title 11, United States Code, unless requested tax documents have been filed with the court."

amount of such payments shall not be less than an amount sufficient to provide to the holder of such claim adequate protection during the period of the plan; or

(C) the debtor surrenders the property securing such claim to such holder;

(6) the debtor will be able to make all payments under the plan and to comply with the plan;

(7) the action of the debtor in filing the petition was in good faith;

(8) the debtor has paid all amounts that are required to be paid under a domestic support obligation and that first become payable after the date of the filing of the petition if the debtor is required by a judicial or administrative order, or by statute, to pay such domestic support obligation; and

(9) the debtor has filed all applicable Federal, State, and local tax returns as required by section 1308.

For purposes of paragraph (5), section 506 shall not apply to a claim described in that paragraph if the creditor has a purchase money security interest securing the debt that is the subject of the claim, the debt was incurred within the 910-day period preceding the date of the filing of the petition, and the collateral for that debt consists of a motor vehicle (as defined in section 30102 of title 49) acquired for the personal use of the debtor, or if collateral for that debt consists of any other thing of value, if the debt was incurred during the 1-year period preceding that filing.

(b) (1) If the trustee or the holder of an allowed unsecured claim objects to the confirmation of the plan, then the court may not approve the plan unless, as of the effective date of the plan—

(A) the value of the property to be distributed under the plan on account of such claim is not less than the amount of such claim; or

(B) the plan provides that all of the debtor's projected disposable income to be received in the applicable commitment period beginning on the date that the first payment is due under the plan will be applied to make payments to unsecured creditors under the plan.

(2) For purposes of this subsection, the term "disposable income" means current monthly income received by the debtor (other than <u>payments made under Federal law relating to the national emergency declared by the President under the National Emergencies Act (50 U.S.C. 1601 et seq.) with respect to the coronavirus disease 2019 (COVID-19),</u>[92] child support payments, foster care payments, or disability payments for a dependent child made in accordance with applicable nonbankruptcy law to the extent reasonably necessary to be expended for such child) less amounts reasonably necessary to be expended—

---

[92] Ed. Note: Underscored material applies to cases commenced before, on or after March 27, 2020. *See* Coronavirus, Aid, Relief, and Economic Security Act, Pub. L. No. 116-136, § 1113(b)(D)(i) (2020). It will expire two years after March 27, 2020. *See* COVID-19 Bankruptcy Relief Extension Act of 2021, Pub. L. No. 117-5 (2021).

(A) (i) for the maintenance or support of the debtor or a dependent of the debtor, or for a domestic support obligation, that first becomes payable after the date the petition is filed; and

(ii) for charitable contributions (that meet the definition of "charitable contribution" under section 548(d)(3)) to a qualified religious or charitable entity or organization (as defined in section 548(d)(4)) in an amount not to exceed 15 percent of gross income of the debtor for the year in which the contributions are made; and

(B) if the debtor is engaged in business, for the payment of expenditures necessary for the continuation, preservation, and operation of such business.

(3) Amounts reasonably necessary to be expended under paragraph (2), other than subparagraph (A)(ii) of paragraph (2), shall be determined in accordance with subparagraphs (A) and (B) of section 707(b)(2) if the debtor has current monthly income, when multiplied by 12, greater than—

(A) in the case of a debtor in a household of 1 person, the median family income of the applicable State for 1 earner;

(B) in the case of a debtor in a household of 2, 3, or 4 individuals, the highest median family income of the applicable State for a family of the same number or fewer individuals; or

(C) in the case of a debtor in a household exceeding 4 individuals, the highest median family income of the applicable State for a family of 4 or fewer individuals, plus $750[93] per month for each individual in excess of 4.

(4) For purposes of this subsection, the "applicable commitment period"—

(A) subject to subparagraph (B), shall be—

(i) 3 years; or

(ii) not less than 5 years, if the current monthly income of the debtor and the debtor's spouse combined, when multiplied by 12, is not less than—

(I) in the case of a debtor in a household of 1 person, the median family income of the applicable State for 1 earner;

(II) in the case of a debtor in a household of 2, 3, or 4 individuals, the highest median family income of the applicable State for a family of the same number or fewer individuals; or

(III) in the case of a debtor in a household exceeding 4 individuals, the highest median family income of the applicable State for a family of 4 or fewer individuals, plus $750[94] per month for each individual in

---

[93] ED. NOTE: For cases commenced in the three-year period before April 1, 2019, the dollar amount is $700.

[94] ED. NOTE: For cases commenced in the three-year period before April 1, 2019, the dollar amount is $700.

excess of 4; and

(B) may be less than 3 or 5 years, whichever is applicable under subparagraph (A), but only if the plan provides for payment in full of all allowed unsecured claims over a shorter period.

(c) After confirmation of a plan, the court may order any entity from whom the debtor receives income to pay all or any part of such income to the trustee.

(d) Notwithstanding section 1322(a)(2) of this title and subsection (b)(1) of this section, a plan that provides for payment of a claim of a kind specified in section 503(b)(10) of this title may be confirmed if the plan proposes to make payments on account of such claim when due under the terms of the loan giving rise to such claim.[95]

Bankruptcy Rule References: 1007, 2002 and 3015

## § 1326 Payments

(a) (1) Unless the court orders otherwise, the debtor shall commence making payments not later than 30 days after the date of the filing of the plan or the order for relief, whichever is earlier, in the amount—

(A) proposed by the plan to the trustee;

(B) scheduled in a lease of personal property directly to the lessor for that portion of the obligation that becomes due after the order for relief, reducing the payments under subparagraph (A) by the amount so paid and providing the trustee with evidence of such payment, including the amount and date of payment; and

(C) that provides adequate protection directly to a creditor holding an allowed claim secured by personal property to the extent the claim is attributable to the purchase of such property by the debtor for that portion of the obligation that becomes due after the order for relief, reducing the payments under subparagraph (A) by the amount so paid and providing the

---

[95] Ed note: Underscored language enacted by the Consolidated Appropriations Act, 2021, Pub. L. No. 116-260, div. N, § 320(e). The amendment will:

(A) take effect on the date on which the Administrator submits to the Director of the Executive Office for United States Trustees a written determination that, subject to satisfying any other eligibility requirements, any debtor in possession or trustee that is authorized to operate the business of the debtor under section 1183, 1184, 1203, 1204, or 1304 of title 11, United States Code, would be eligible for a loan under paragraphs (36) and (37) of section 7(a) of the Small Business Act (15 U.S.C. 636(a)); and

(B) apply to any case pending on or commenced on or after the date described in subparagraph (A).

The amendment will sunset "effective on the date that is 2 years after the date of enactment of the Act," which was December 27, 2020. Pub. L. No. 116-260, div. N, § 320(f). On April 8, 2021, the Small Business Administration issued a procedural notice stating that chapter 11, 12 and 13 debtors are eligible to receive Paycheck Protection Program loans after confirmation of a plan. *See* SBA, "Paycheck Protection Program Loans, FAQs," Q. 67 (July 29, 2021), https://www.sba.gov/sites/default/files/2021-07/FINAL%20FAQ%20Update%207.29.21-508.pdf.

trustee with evidence of such payment, including the amount and date of payment.

(2) A payment made under paragraph (1)(A) shall be retained by the trustee until confirmation or denial of confirmation. If a plan is confirmed, the trustee shall distribute any such payment in accordance with the plan as soon as is practicable. If a plan is not confirmed, the trustee shall return any such payments not previously paid and not yet due and owing to creditors pursuant to paragraph (3) to the debtor, after deducting any unpaid claim allowed under section 503(b).

(3) Subject to section 363, the court may, upon notice and a hearing, modify, increase, or reduce the payments required under this subsection pending confirmation of a plan.

(4) Not later than 60 days after the date of filing of a case under this chapter, a debtor retaining possession of personal property subject to a lease or securing a claim attributable in whole or in part to the purchase price of such property shall provide the lessor or secured creditor reasonable evidence of the maintenance of any required insurance coverage with respect to the use or ownership of such property and continue to do so for so long as the debtor retains possession of such property.

(b) Before or at the time of each payment to creditors under the plan, there shall be paid—

(1) any unpaid claim of the kind specified in section 507(a)(2) of this title;

(2) if a standing trustee appointed under section 586(b) of title 28 is serving in the case, the percentage fee fixed for such standing trustee under section 586(e)(1)(B) of title 28; and

(3) if a chapter 7 trustee has been allowed compensation due to the conversion or dismissal of the debtor's prior case pursuant to section 707(b), and some portion of that compensation remains unpaid in a case converted to this chapter or in the case dismissed under section 707(b) and refiled under this chapter, the amount of any such unpaid compensation, which shall be paid monthly—

(A) by prorating such amount over the remaining duration of the plan; and

(B) by monthly payments not to exceed the greater of—

(i) $25;[96] or

(ii) the amount payable to unsecured nonpriority creditors, as provided by the plan, multiplied by 5 percent, and the result divided by the number of months in the plan.

(c) Except as otherwise provided in the plan or in the order confirming the plan,

---

[96] Ed. Note: For cases commenced in the three-year period before April 1, 2019, the dollar amount is also $25.

the trustee shall make payments to creditors under the plan.

(d) Notwithstanding any other provision of this title—

(1) compensation referred to in subsection (b)(3) is payable and may be collected by the trustee under that paragraph, even if such amount has been discharged in a prior case under this title; and

(2) such compensation is payable in a case under this chapter only to the extent permitted by subsection (b)(3).

BANKRUPTCY RULE REFERENCES: 3010, 3011, 3015, 3021 and 9006

## § 1327 Effect of confirmation

(a) The provisions of a confirmed plan bind the debtor and each creditor, whether or not the claim of such creditor is provided for by the plan, and whether or not such creditor has objected to, has accepted, or has rejected the plan.

(b) Except as otherwise provided in the plan or the order confirming the plan, the confirmation of a plan vests all of the property of the estate in the debtor.

(c) Except as otherwise provided in the plan or in the order confirming the plan, the property vesting in the debtor under subsection (b) of this section is free and clear of any claim or interest of any creditor provided for by the plan.

BANKRUPTCY RULE REFERENCE: 3015

## § 1328 Discharge

(a) Subject to subsection (d), as soon as practicable after completion by the debtor of all payments under the plan, and in the case of a debtor who is required by a judicial or administrative order, or by statute, to pay a domestic support obligation, after such debtor certifies that all amounts payable under such order or such statute that are due on or before the date of the certification (including amounts due before the petition was filed, but only to the extent provided for by the plan) have been paid, unless the court approves a written waiver of discharge executed by the debtor after the order for relief under this chapter, the court shall grant the debtor a discharge of all debts provided for by the plan or disallowed under section 502 of this title, except any debt—

(1) provided for under section 1322(b)(5);

(2) of the kind specified in section 507(a)(8)(C) or in paragraph (1)(B), (1)(C), (2), (3), (4), (5), (8), or (9) of section 523(a);

(3) for restitution, or a criminal fine, included in a sentence on the debtor's conviction of a crime; or

(4) for restitution, or damages, awarded in a civil action against the debtor as a result of willful or malicious injury by the debtor that caused personal injury to an individual or the death of an individual.

(b) Subject to subsection (d), at any time after the confirmation of the plan and after notice and a hearing, the court may grant a discharge to a debtor that has not completed payments under the plan only if—

(1) the debtor's failure to complete such payments is due to circumstances for which the debtor should not justly be held accountable;

(2) the value, as of the effective date of the plan, of property actually distributed under the plan on account of each allowed unsecured claim is not less than the amount that would have been paid on such claim if the estate of the debtor had been liquidated under chapter 7 of this title on such date; and

(3) modification of the plan under section 1329 of this title is not practicable.

(c) A discharge granted under subsection (b) of this section discharges the debtor from all unsecured debts provided for by the plan or disallowed under section 502 of this title, except any debt—

(1) provided for under section 1322(b)(5) of this title; or

(2) of a kind specified in section 523(a) of this title.

(d) Notwithstanding any other provision of this section, a discharge granted under this section does not discharge the debtor from any debt based on an allowed claim filed under section 1305(a)(2) of this title if prior approval by the trustee of the debtor's incurring such debt was practicable and was not obtained.

(e) On request of a party in interest before one year after a discharge under this section is granted, and after notice and a hearing, the court may revoke such discharge only if—

(1) such discharge was obtained by the debtor through fraud; and

(2) the requesting party did not know of such fraud until after such discharge was granted.

(f) Notwithstanding subsections (a) and (b), the court shall not grant a discharge of all debts provided for in the plan or disallowed under section 502, if the debtor has received a discharge—

(1) in a case filed under chapter 7, 11, or 12 of this title during the 4-year period preceding the date of the order for relief under this chapter, or

(2) in a case filed under chapter 13 of this title during the 2-year period preceding the date of such order.

(g)(1) The court shall not grant a discharge under this section to a debtor unless after filing a petition the debtor has completed an instructional course concerning personal financial management described in section 111.

(2) Paragraph (1) shall not apply with respect to a debtor who is a person described in section 109(h)(4) or who resides in a district for which the United States trustee (or the bankruptcy administrator, if any) determines that the approved instructional courses are not adequate to service the additional individuals who would otherwise be required to complete such instructional course by reason of the requirements of paragraph (1).

(3) The United States trustee (or the bankruptcy administrator, if any) who makes a determination described in paragraph (2) shall review such determi-

nation not later than 1 year after the date of such determination, and not less frequently than annually thereafter.

(h) The court may not grant a discharge under this chapter unless the court after notice and a hearing held not more than 10 days before the date of the entry of the order granting the discharge finds that there is no reasonable cause to believe that—

(1) section 522(q)(1) may be applicable to the debtor; and

(2) there is pending any proceeding in which the debtor may be found guilty of a felony of the kind described in section 522(q)(1)(A) or liable for a debt of the kind described in section 522(q)(1)(B).

(i) Subject to subsection (d), after notice and a hearing, the court may grant a discharge of debts dischargeable under subsection (a) to a debtor who has not completed payments to the trustee or a creditor holding a security interest in the principal residence of the debtor if—

(1) the debtor defaults on not more than 3 monthly payments due on a residential mortgage under section 1322(b)(5) on or after March 13, 2020, to the trustee or creditor caused by a material financial hardship due, directly or indirectly, by the coronavirus disease 2019 (COVID-19) pandemic; or

(2) (A) the plan provides for the curing of a default and maintenance of payments on a residential mortgage under section 1322(b)(5); and

(B) the debtor has entered into a forbearance agreement or loan modification agreement with the holder or servicer (as defined in section 6(i) of the Real Estate Settlement Procedures Act of 1974 (12 U.S.C. 2605(i)) of the mortgage described in subparagraph (A).[97]

## § 1329 Modification of plan after confirmation

(a) At any time after confirmation of the plan but before the completion of payments under such plan, the plan may be modified, upon request of the debtor, the trustee, or the holder of an allowed unsecured claim, to—

(1) increase or reduce the amount of payments on claims of a particular class provided for by the plan;

(2) extend or reduce the time for such payments;

(3) alter the amount of the distribution to a creditor whose claim is provided for by the plan to the extent necessary to take account of any payment of such claim other than under the plan; or

(4) reduce amounts to be paid under the plan by the actual amount expended by the debtor to purchase health insurance for the debtor (and for any dependent of the debtor if such dependent does not otherwise have health

[97] Ed. Note: Underscored material enacted by the Consolidated Appropriations Act, 2021, Pub. L. No. 116-260, div. FF, tit. X, § 1001(b)(1). The amendment will sunset one year after the date of enactment of the Act, which was December 27, 2020. Pub. L. No. 116-260, div. FF, tit. X, § 1001(b)(2).

insurance coverage) if the debtor documents the cost of such insurance and demonstrates that—

(A) such expenses are reasonable and necessary;

(B) (i) if the debtor previously paid for health insurance, the amount is not materially larger than the cost the debtor previously paid or the cost necessary to maintain the lapsed policy; or

(ii) if the debtor did not have health insurance, the amount is not materially larger than the reasonable cost that would be incurred by a debtor who purchases health insurance, who has similar income, expenses, age, and health status, and who lives in the same geographical location with the same number of dependents who do not otherwise have health insurance coverage; and

(C) the amount is not otherwise allowed for purposes of determining disposable income under section 1325(b) of this title;

and upon request of any party in interest, files proof that a health insurance policy was purchased.

(b) (1) Sections 1322(a), 1322(b), and 1323(c) of this title and the requirements of section 1325(a) of this title apply to any modification under subsection (a) of this section.

(2) The plan as modified becomes the plan unless, after notice and a hearing, such modification is disapproved.

(c) A plan modified under this section may not provide for payments over a period that expires after the applicable commitment period under section 1325(b)(1)(B) after the time that the first payment under the original confirmed plan was due, unless the court, for cause, approves a longer period, but the court may not approve a period that expires after five years after such time.

(d) (1) Subject to paragraph (3), for a plan confirmed prior to the date of enactment of the COVID-19 Bankruptcy Relief Extension Act of 2021, the plan may be modified upon the request of the debtor if—

(A) the debtor is experiencing or has experienced a material financial hardship due, directly or indirectly, to the coronavirus disease 2019 (COVID-19) pandemic; and

(B) the modification is approved after notice and a hearing.

(2) A plan modified under paragraph (1) may not provide for payments over a period that expires more than 7 years after the time that the first payment under the original confirmed plan was due.

(3) Sections 1322(a), 1322(b), 1323(c), and the requirements of section 1325(a) shall apply to any modification under paragraph (1).[98]

---

[98] Ed. Note: Underscored material (subsection (d)) applies to any case for which a plan has been confirmed under section 1325 before March 27, 2020. *See* Coronavirus, Aid, Relief, and Economic Security

(e) (1) A debtor of a case for which a creditor files a proof of claim under section 501(f) may file a request for a modification of the plan to provide for the proof of claim.

(2) If the debtor does not file a request for a modification of the plan under paragraph (1) on or before the date that is 30 days after the date on which a creditor files a claim under section 501(f), after notice, the court, on a motion of the court or on a motion of the United States trustee, the trustee, a bankruptcy administrator, or any party in interest, may request a modification of the plan to provide for the proof of claim.[99]

BANKRUPTCY RULE REFERENCES: 2001, 3015 and 9014

## § 1330 Revocation of an order of confirmation

(a) On request of a party in interest at any time within 180 days after the date of the entry of an order of confirmation under section 1325 of this title, and after notice and a hearing, the court may revoke such order if such order was procured by fraud.

(b) If the court revokes an order of confirmation under subsection (a) of this section, the court shall dispose of the case under section 1307 of this title, unless, within the time fixed by the court, the debtor proposes and the court confirms a modification of the plan under section 1329 of this title.

BANKRUPTCY RULE REFERENCES: 7001 and 9024

---

Act, Pub. L. No. 116-136, § 1113(b)(D)(ii) (2020). It will expire two years after March 27, 2020. *See* COVID-19 Bankruptcy Relief Extension Act of 2021, Pub. L. No. 117-5 (2021).

[99] ED. NOTE: Underscored material (subsection (e)) enacted by the Consolidated Appropriations Act, 2021, Pub. L. No. 116-260, div. FF, tit. X, § 1001(e)(1). The amendment will sunset one year after the date of enactment of the Act, which was December 27, 2020. Pub. L. No. 116-260, div. FF, tit. X, § 1001(e)(2).

## CHAPTER 15
## ANCILLARY AND OTHER CROSS-BORDER CASES

### § 1501 Purpose and scope of application

(a) The purpose of this chapter is to incorporate the Model Law on Cross-Border Insolvency so as to provide effective mechanisms for dealing with cases of cross-border insolvency with the objectives of—

(1) cooperation between—

(A) courts of the United States, United States trustees, trustees, examiners, debtors, and debtors in possession; and

(B) the courts and other competent authorities of foreign countries involved in cross-border insolvency cases;

(2) greater legal certainty for trade and investment;

(3) fair and efficient administration of cross-border insolvencies that protects the interests of all creditors, and other interested entities, including the debtor;

(4) protection and maximization of the value of the debtor's assets; and

(5) facilitation of the rescue of financially troubled businesses, thereby protecting investment and preserving employment.

(b) This chapter applies where—

(1) assistance is sought in the United States by a foreign court or a foreign representative in connection with a foreign proceeding;

(2) assistance is sought in a foreign country in connection with a case under this title;

(3) a foreign proceeding and a case under this title with respect to the same debtor are pending concurrently; or

(4) creditors or other interested persons in a foreign country have an interest in requesting the commencement of, or participating in, a case or proceeding under this title.

(c) This chapter does not apply to—

(1) a proceeding concerning an entity, other than a foreign insurance company, identified by exclusion in section 109(b);

(2) an individual, or to an individual and such individual's spouse, who have debts within the limits specified in section 109(e) and who are citizens of the United States or aliens lawfully admitted for permanent residence in the United States; or

(3) an entity subject to a proceeding under the Securities Investor Protection Act of 1970, a stockbroker subject to subchapter III of chapter 7 of this title, or a commodity broker subject to subchapter IV of chapter 7 of this title.

(d) The court may not grant relief under this chapter with respect to any deposit, escrow, trust fund, or other security required or permitted under any applicable State insurance law or regulation for the benefit of claim holders in the United States.

BANKRUPTCY RULE REFERENCES: 1007, 1010, 1011, 2002 and 2015

## Subchapter I
## General Provisions

### § 1502 Definitions

For the purposes of this chapter, the term—

(1) "debtor" means an entity that is the subject of a foreign proceeding;

(2) "establishment" means any place of operations where the debtor carries out a nontransitory economic activity;

(3) "foreign court" means a judicial or other authority competent to control or supervise a foreign proceeding;

(4) "foreign main proceeding" means a foreign proceeding pending in the country where the debtor has the center of its main interests;

(5) "foreign nonmain proceeding" means a foreign proceeding, other than a foreign main proceeding, pending in a country where the debtor has an establishment;

(6) "trustee" includes a trustee, a debtor in possession in a case under any chapter of this title, or a debtor under chapter 9 of this title;

(7) "recognition" means the entry of an order granting recognition of a foreign main proceeding or foreign nonmain proceeding under this chapter; and

(8) "within the territorial jurisdiction of the United States", when used with reference to property of a debtor, refers to tangible property located within the territory of the United States and intangible property deemed under applicable nonbankruptcy law to be located within that territory, including any property subject to attachment or garnishment that may properly be seized or garnished by an action in a Federal or State court in the United States.

### § 1503 International obligations of the United States

To the extent that this chapter conflicts with an obligation of the United States arising out of any treaty or other form of agreement to which it is a party with one or more other countries, the requirements of the treaty or agreement prevail.

### § 1504 Commencement of ancillary case

A case under this chapter is commenced by the filing of a petition for recognition of a foreign proceeding under section 1515.

Bankruptcy Rule Reference: 1002

### § 1505 Authorization to act in a foreign country

A trustee or another entity (including an examiner) may be authorized by the court to act in a foreign country on behalf of an estate created under section 541. An entity authorized to act under this section may act in any way permitted by the applicable foreign law.

### § 1506 Public policy exception

Nothing in this chapter prevents the court from refusing to take an action governed by this chapter if the action would be manifestly contrary to the public policy of the United States.

### § 1507 Additional assistance

(a) Subject to the specific limitations stated elsewhere in this chapter the court, if recognition is granted, may provide additional assistance to a foreign representative under this title or under other laws of the United States.

(b) In determining whether to provide additional assistance under this title or under other laws of the United States, the court shall consider whether such additional assistance, consistent with the principles of comity, will reasonably assure—

(1) just treatment of all holders of claims against or interests in the debtor's property;

(2) protection of claim holders in the United States against prejudice and inconvenience in the processing of claims in such foreign proceeding;

(3) prevention of preferential or fraudulent dispositions of property of the debtor;

(4) distribution of proceeds of the debtor's property substantially in accordance with the order prescribed by this title; and

(5) if appropriate, the provision of an opportunity for a fresh start for the individual that such foreign proceeding concerns.

### § 1508 Interpretation

In interpreting this chapter, the court shall consider its international origin, and the need to promote an application of this chapter that is consistent with the application of similar statutes adopted by foreign jurisdictions.

## Subchapter II
## Access of Foreign Representatives and Creditors to the Court

### § 1509 Right of direct access

(a) A foreign representative may commence a case under section 1504 by filing directly with the court a petition for recognition of a foreign proceeding under section 1515.

(b) If the court grants recognition under section 1517, and subject to any limitations that the court may impose consistent with the policy of this chapter—

(1) the foreign representative has the capacity to sue and be sued in a court in the United States;

(2) the foreign representative may apply directly to a court in the United States for appropriate relief in that court; and

(3) a court in the United States shall grant comity or cooperation to the foreign representative.

(c) A request for comity or cooperation by a foreign representative in a court in the United States other than the court which granted recognition shall be accompanied by a certified copy of an order granting recognition under section 1517.

(d) If the court denies recognition under this chapter, the court may issue any appropriate order necessary to prevent the foreign representative from obtaining comity or cooperation from courts in the United States.

(e) Whether or not the court grants recognition, and subject to sections 306 and 1510, a foreign representative is subject to applicable nonbankruptcy law.

(f) Notwithstanding any other provision of this section, the failure of a foreign representative to commence a case or to obtain recognition under this chapter does not affect any right the foreign representative may have to sue in a court in the United States to collect or recover a claim which is the property of the debtor.

### § 1510 Limited jurisdiction

The sole fact that a foreign representative files a petition under section 1515 does not subject the foreign representative to the jurisdiction of any court in the United States for any other purpose.

Bankruptcy Rule Reference: 1002

### § 1511 Commencement of case under section 301, 302, or 303

(a) Upon recognition, a foreign representative may commence—

(1) an involuntary case under section 303; or

(2) a voluntary case under section 301 or 302, if the foreign proceeding is a foreign main proceeding.

(b) The petition commencing a case under subsection (a) must be accompanied by a certified copy of an order granting recognition. The court where the petition for recognition has been filed must be advised of the foreign representative's intent to commence a case under subsection (a) prior to such commencement.

### § 1512 Participation of a foreign representative in a case under this title

Upon recognition of a foreign proceeding, the foreign representative in the recognized proceeding is entitled to participate as a party in interest in a case regarding the debtor under this title.

BANKRUPTCY RULE REFERENCE: 1002

### § 1513 Access of foreign creditors to a case under this title

(a) Foreign creditors have the same rights regarding the commencement of, and participation in, a case under this title as domestic creditors.

(b) (1) Subsection (a) does not change or codify present law as to the priority of claims under section 507 or 726, except that the claim of a foreign creditor under those sections shall not be given a lower priority than that of general unsecured claims without priority solely because the holder of such claim is a foreign creditor.

(2) (A) Subsection (a) and paragraph (1) do not change or codify present law as to the allowability of foreign revenue claims or other foreign public law claims in a proceeding under this title.

(B) Allowance and priority as to a foreign tax claim or other foreign public law claim shall be governed by any applicable tax treaty of the United States, under the conditions and circumstances specified therein.

### § 1514 Notification to foreign creditors concerning a case under this title

(a) Whenever in a case under this title notice is to be given to creditors generally or to any class or category of creditors, such notice shall also be given to the known creditors generally, or to creditors in the notified class or category, that do not have addresses in the United States. The court may order that appropriate steps be taken with a view to notifying any creditor whose address is not yet known.

(b) Such notification to creditors with foreign addresses described in subsection (a) shall be given individually, unless the court considers that, under the circumstances, some other form of notification would be more appropriate. No letter or other formality is required.

(c) When a notification of commencement of a case is to be given to foreign creditors, such notification shall—

(1) indicate the time period for filing proofs of claim and specify the place for filing such proofs of claim;

(2) indicate whether secured creditors need to file proofs of claim; and

(3) contain any other information required to be included in such notification to creditors under this title and the orders of the court.

(d) Any rule of procedure or order of the court as to notice or the filing of a proof of claim shall provide such additional time to creditors with foreign addresses as is reasonable under the circumstances.

BANKRUPTCY RULE REFERENCES: 2002 and 3002

## Subchapter III
## Recognition of a Foreign Proceeding and Relief

### § 1515 Application for recognition

(a) A foreign representative applies to the court for recognition of a foreign proceeding in which the foreign representative has been appointed by filing a petition for recognition.

(b) A petition for recognition shall be accompanied by–

(1) a certified copy of the decision commencing such foreign proceeding and appointing the foreign representative;

(2) a certificate from the foreign court affirming the existence of such foreign proceeding and of the appointment of the foreign representative; or

(3) in the absence of evidence referred to in paragraphs (1) and (2), any other evidence acceptable to the court of the existence of such foreign proceeding and of the appointment of the foreign representative.

(c) A petition for recognition shall also be accompanied by a statement identifying all foreign proceedings with respect to the debtor that are known to the foreign representative.

(d) The documents referred to in paragraphs (1) and (2) of subsection (b) shall be translated into English. The court may require a translation into English of additional documents.

### § 1516 Presumptions concerning recognition

(a) If the decision or certificate referred to in section 1515(b) indicates that the foreign proceeding is a foreign proceeding and that the person or body is a foreign representative, the court is entitled to so presume.

(b) The court is entitled to presume that documents submitted in support of the petition for recognition are authentic, whether or not they have been legalized.

(c) In the absence of evidence to the contrary, the debtor's registered office, or habitual residence in the case of an individual, is presumed to be the center of the debtor's main interests.

Bankruptcy Rule Reference: 1002

### § 1517 Order granting recognition

(a) Subject to section 1506, after notice and a hearing, an order recognizing a foreign proceeding shall be entered if–

(1) such foreign proceeding for which recognition is sought is a foreign main proceeding or foreign nonmain proceeding within the meaning of section 1502;

(2) the foreign representative applying for recognition is a person or body; and

(3) the petition meets the requirements of section 1515.

(b) Such foreign proceeding shall be recognized—

(1) as a foreign main proceeding if it is pending in the country where the debtor has the center of its main interests; or

(2) as a foreign nonmain proceeding if the debtor has an establishment within the meaning of section 1502 in the foreign country where the proceeding is pending.

(c) A petition for recognition of a foreign proceeding shall be decided upon at the earliest possible time. Entry of an order recognizing a foreign proceeding constitutes recognition under this chapter.

(d) The provisions of this subchapter do not prevent modification or termination of recognition if it is shown that the grounds for granting it were fully or partially lacking or have ceased to exist, but in considering such action the court shall give due weight to possible prejudice to parties that have relied upon the order granting recognition. A case under this chapter may be closed in the manner prescribed under section 350.

### § 1518 Subsequent information

From the time of filing the petition for recognition of a foreign proceeding, the foreign representative shall file with the court promptly a notice of change of status concerning—

(1) any substantial change in the status of such foreign proceeding or the status of the foreign representative's appointment; and

(2) any other foreign proceeding regarding the debtor that becomes known to the foreign representative.

Bankruptcy Rule Reference: 2015

### § 1519 Relief that may be granted upon filing petition for recognition

(a) From the time of filing a petition for recognition until the court rules on the petition, the court may, at the request of the foreign representative, where relief is urgently needed to protect the assets of the debtor or the interests of the creditors, grant relief of a provisional nature, including—

(1) staying execution against the debtor's assets;

(2) entrusting the administration or realization of all or part of the debtor's assets located in the United States to the foreign representative or another person authorized by the court, including an examiner, in order to protect and preserve the value of assets that, by their nature or because of other circumstances, are perishable, susceptible to devaluation or otherwise in jeopardy; and

(3) any relief referred to in paragraph (3), (4), or (7) of section 1521(a).

(b) Unless extended under section 1521(a)(6), the relief granted under this section terminates when the petition for recognition is granted.

(c) It is a ground for denial of relief under this section that such relief would interfere with the administration of a foreign main proceeding.

(d) The court may not enjoin a police or regulatory act of a governmental unit, including a criminal action or proceeding, under this section.

(e) The standards, procedures, and limitations applicable to an injunction shall apply to relief under this section.

(f) The exercise of rights not subject to the stay arising under section 362(a) pursuant to paragraph (6), (7), (17), or (27) of section 362(b) or pursuant to section 362(o) shall not be stayed by any order of a court or administrative agency in any proceeding under this chapter.

Bankruptcy Rule Reference: 1004.2

## § 1520 Effects of recognition of a foreign main proceeding

(a) Upon recognition of a foreign proceeding that is a foreign main proceeding—

(1) sections 361 and 362 apply with respect to the debtor and the property of the debtor that is within the territorial jurisdiction of the United States;

(2) sections 363, 549, and 552 apply to a transfer of an interest of the debtor in property that is within the territorial jurisdiction of the United States to the same extent that the sections would apply to property of an estate;

(3) unless the court orders otherwise, the foreign representative may operate the debtor's business and may exercise the rights and powers of a trustee under and to the extent provided by sections 363 and 552; and

(4) section 552 applies to property of the debtor that is within the territorial jurisdiction of the United States.

(b) Subsection (a) does not affect the right to commence an individual action or proceeding in a foreign country to the extent necessary to preserve a claim against the debtor.

(c) Subsection (a) does not affect the right of a foreign representative or an entity to file a petition commencing a case under this title or the right of any party to file claims or take other proper actions in such a case.

Bankruptcy Rule References: 1007 and 1010

## § 1521 Relief that may be granted upon recognition

(a) Upon recognition of a foreign proceeding, whether main or nonmain, where necessary to effectuate the purpose of this chapter and to protect the assets of the debtor or the interests of the creditors, the court may, at the request of the foreign representative, grant any appropriate relief, including—

(1) staying the commencement or continuation of an individual action or proceeding concerning the debtor's assets, rights, obligations or liabilities to the extent they have not been stayed under section 1520(a);

(2) staying execution against the debtor's assets to the extent it has not been stayed under section 1520(a);

(3) suspending the right to transfer, encumber or otherwise dispose of any assets of the debtor to the extent this right has not been suspended under section 1520(a);

(4) providing for the examination of witnesses, the taking of evidence or the delivery of information concerning the debtor's assets, affairs, rights, obligations or liabilities;

(5) entrusting the administration or realization of all or part of the debtor's assets within the territorial jurisdiction of the United States to the foreign representative or another person, including an examiner, authorized by the court;

(6) extending relief granted under section 1519(a); and

(7) granting any additional relief that may be available to a trustee, except for relief available under sections 522, 544, 545, 547, 548, 550, and 724(a).

(b) Upon recognition of a foreign proceeding, whether main or nonmain, the court may, at the request of the foreign representative, entrust the distribution of all or part of the debtor's assets located in the United States to the foreign representative or another person, including an examiner, authorized by the court, provided that the court is satisfied that the interests of creditors in the United States are sufficiently protected.

(c) In granting relief under this section to a representative of a foreign nonmain proceeding, the court must be satisfied that the relief relates to assets that, under the law of the United States, should be administered in the foreign nonmain proceeding or concerns information required in that proceeding.

(d) The court may not enjoin a police or regulatory act of a governmental unit, including a criminal action or proceeding, under this section.

(e) The standards, procedures, and limitations applicable to an injunction shall apply to relief under paragraphs (1), (2), (3), and (6) of subsection (a).

(f) The exercise of rights not subject to the stay arising under section 362(a) pursuant to paragraph (6), (7), (17), or (27) of section 362(b) or pursuant to section 362(o) shall not be stayed by any order of a court or administrative agency in any proceeding under this chapter.

### § 1522 Protection of creditors and other interested persons

(a) The court may grant relief under section 1519 or 1521, or may modify or terminate relief under subsection (c), only if the interests of the creditors and other interested entities, including the debtor, are sufficiently protected.

(b) The court may subject relief granted under section 1519 or 1521, or the operation of the debtor's business under section 1520(a)(3), to conditions it considers appropriate, including the giving of security or the filing of a bond.

(c) The court may, at the request of the foreign representative or an entity affected by relief granted under section 1519 or 1521, or at its own motion, modify or terminate such relief.

(d) Section 1104(d) shall apply to the appointment of an examiner under this chapter. Any examiner shall comply with the qualification requirements imposed on a trustee by section 322.

### § 1523 Actions to avoid acts detrimental to creditors

(a) Upon recognition of a foreign proceeding, the foreign representative has standing in a case concerning the debtor pending under another chapter of this title to initiate actions under sections 522, 544, 545, 547, 548, 550, 553, and 724(a).

(b) When a foreign proceeding is a foreign nonmain proceeding, the court must be satisfied that an action under subsection (a) relates to assets that, under United States law, should be administered in the foreign nonmain proceeding.

### § 1524 Intervention by a foreign representative

Upon recognition of a foreign proceeding, the foreign representative may intervene in any proceedings in a State or Federal court in the United States in which the debtor is a party.

## Subchapter IV
## Cooperation With Foreign Courts and Foreign Representatives

### § 1525 Cooperation and direct communication between the court and foreign courts or foreign representatives

(a) Consistent with section 1501, the court shall cooperate to the maximum extent possible with a foreign court or a foreign representative, either directly or through the trustee.

(b) The court is entitled to communicate directly with, or to request information or assistance directly from, a foreign court or a foreign representative, subject to the rights of a party in interest to notice and participation.

### § 1526 Cooperation and direct communication between the trustee and foreign courts or foreign representatives

(a) Consistent with section 1501, the trustee or other person, including an examiner, authorized by the court, shall, subject to the supervision of the court, cooperate to the maximum extent possible with a foreign court or a foreign representative.

(b) The trustee or other person, including an examiner, authorized by the court is entitled, subject to the supervision of the court, to communicate directly with a foreign court or a foreign representative.

### § 1527 Forms of cooperation

Cooperation referred to in sections 1525 and 1526 may be implemented by any appropriate means, including—

(1) appointment of a person or body, including an examiner, to act at the direction of the court;

(2) communication of information by any means considered appropriate by the court;

(3) coordination of the administration and supervision of the debtor's assets and affairs;

(4) approval or implementation of agreements concerning the coordination of proceedings; and

(5) coordination of concurrent proceedings regarding the same debtor.

## SUBCHAPTER V
## Concurrent Proceedings

### § 1528 Commencement of a case under this title after recognition of a foreign main proceeding

After recognition of a foreign main proceeding, a case under another chapter of this title may be commenced only if the debtor has assets in the United States. The effects of such case shall be restricted to the assets of the debtor that are within the territorial jurisdiction of the United States and, to the extent necessary to implement cooperation and coordination under sections 1525, 1526, and 1527, to other assets of the debtor that are within the jurisdiction of the court under sections 541(a) of this title, and 1334(e) of title 28, to the extent that such other assets are not subject to the jurisdiction and control of a foreign proceeding that has been recognized under this chapter.

### § 1529 Coordination of a case under this title and a foreign proceeding

If a foreign proceeding and a case under another chapter of this title are pending concurrently regarding the same debtor, the court shall seek cooperation and coordination under sections 1525, 1526, and 1527, and the following shall apply:

(1) If the case in the United States is pending at the time the petition for recognition of such foreign proceeding is filed—

(A) any relief granted under section 1519 or 1521 must be consistent with the relief granted in the case in the United States; and

(B) section 1520 does not apply even if such foreign proceeding is recognized as a foreign main proceeding.

(2) If a case in the United States under this title commences after recognition, or after the date of the filing of the petition for recognition, of such foreign proceeding—

(A) any relief in effect under section 1519 or 1521 shall be reviewed by the court and shall be modified or terminated if inconsistent with the case in the United States; and

(B) if such foreign proceeding is a foreign main proceeding, the stay and suspension referred to in section 1520(a) shall be modified or terminated if inconsistent with the relief granted in the case in the United States.

(3) In granting, extending, or modifying relief granted to a representative of a foreign nonmain proceeding, the court must be satisfied that the relief relates to assets that, under the laws of the United States, should be administered in the foreign nonmain proceeding or concerns information required in that proceeding.

(4) In achieving cooperation and coordination under sections 1528 and 1529, the court may grant any of the relief authorized under section 305.

## § 1530 Coordination of more than 1 foreign proceeding

In matters referred to in section 1501, with respect to more than 1 foreign proceeding regarding the debtor, the court shall seek cooperation and coordination under sections 1525, 1526, and 1527, and the following shall apply:

(1) Any relief granted under section 1519 or 1521 to a representative of a foreign nonmain proceeding after recognition of a foreign main proceeding must be consistent with the foreign main proceeding.

(2) If a foreign main proceeding is recognized after recognition, or after the filing of a petition for recognition, of a foreign nonmain proceeding, any relief in effect under section 1519 or 1521 shall be reviewed by the court and shall be modified or terminated if inconsistent with the foreign main proceeding.

(3) If, after recognition of a foreign nonmain proceeding, another foreign nonmain proceeding is recognized, the court shall grant, modify, or terminate relief for the purpose of facilitating coordination of the proceedings.

## § 1531 Presumption of insolvency based on recognition of a foreign main proceeding

In the absence of evidence to the contrary, recognition of a foreign main proceeding is, for the purpose of commencing a proceeding under section 303, proof that the debtor is generally not paying its debts as such debts become due.

## § 1532 Rule of payment in concurrent proceedings

Without prejudice to secured claims or rights in rem, a creditor who has received payment with respect to its claim in a foreign proceeding pursuant to a law relating to insolvency may not receive a payment for the same claim in a case under any other chapter of this title regarding the debtor, so long as the payment to other creditors of the same class is proportionately less than the payment the creditor has already received.

# Judicial Code—Selected Provisions

## BANKRUPTCY JUDGES; APPEALS (CHAPTER 6)

### 28 USC § 151 Designation of bankruptcy courts

In each judicial district, the bankruptcy judges in regular active service shall constitute a unit of the district court to be known as the bankruptcy court for that district. Each bankruptcy judge, as a judicial officer of the district court, may exercise the authority conferred under this chapter with respect to any action, suit, or proceeding and may preside alone and hold a regular or special session of the court, except as otherwise provided by law or by rule or order of the district court.

### 28 USC § 152 Appointment of bankruptcy judges

(a) (1) Each bankruptcy judge to be appointed for a judicial district, as provided in paragraph (2), shall be appointed by the court of appeals of the United States for the circuit in which such district is located Such appointments shall be made after considering the recommendations of the Judicial Conference submitted pursuant to subsection (b). Each bankruptcy judge shall be appointed for a term of fourteen years, subject to the provisions of subsection (e). However, upon the expiration of the term, a bankruptcy judge may, with the approval of the judicial council of the circuit, continue to perform the duties of the office until the earlier of the date which is 180 days after the expiration of the term or the date of the appointment of a successor. Bankruptcy judges shall serve as judicial officers of the United States district court established under Article III of the Constitution.

(2) The bankruptcy judges appointed pursuant to this section shall be appointed for the several judicial districts as follows:

| *Districts* | Judges |
|---|---|
| Alabama: | |
| Northern | 5 |
| Middle | 2 |
| Southern | 2 |
| Alaska | 2 |
| Arizona | 7 |
| Arkansas: | |
| Eastern and Western | 3 |
| California: | |
| Northern | 9 |
| Eastern | 6 |
| Central | 21 |
| Southern | 4 |
| Colorado | 5 |
| Connecticut | 3 |
| Delaware | 1 |
| District of Columbia | 1 |
| Florida: | |
| Northern | 1 |

| *Districts* | | Judges |
|---|---|---|
| | Middle | 8 |
| | Southern | 5 |
| Georgia: | | |
| | Northern | 8 |
| | Middle | 3 |
| | Southern | 2 |
| Hawaii | | 1 |
| Idaho | | 2 |
| Illinois: | | |
| | Northern | 10 |
| | Central | 3 |
| | Southern | 1 |
| Indiana: | | |
| | Northern | 3 |
| | Southern | 4 |
| Iowa: | | |
| | Northern | 2 |
| | Southern | 2 |
| Kansas | | 4 |
| Kentucky: | | |
| | Eastern | 2 |
| | Western | 3 |
| Louisiana: | | |
| | Eastern | 2 |
| | Middle | 1 |
| | Western | 3 |
| Maine | | 2 |
| Maryland | | 4 |
| Massachusetts | | 5 |
| Michigan: | | |
| | Eastern | 4 |
| | Western | 3 |
| Minnesota | | 4 |
| Mississippi: | | |
| | Northern | 1 |
| | Southern | 2 |
| Missouri: | | |
| | Eastern | 3 |
| | Western | 3 |
| Montana | | 1 |
| Nebraska | | 2 |
| Nevada | | 3 |
| New Hampshire | | 1 |
| New Jersey | | 8 |
| New Mexico | | 2 |

| *Districts* | | Judges |
|---|---|---|
| New York: | | |
| | Northern | 2 |
| | Southern | 9 |
| | Eastern | 6 |
| | Western | 3 |
| North Carolina: | | |
| | Eastern | 2 |
| | Middle | 2 |
| | Western | 2 |
| North Dakota | | 1 |
| Ohio: | | |
| | Northern | 8 |
| | Southern | 7 |
| Oklahoma: | | |
| | Northern | 2 |
| | Eastern | 1 |
| | Western | 3 |
| Oregon | | 5 |
| Pennsylvania: | | |
| | Eastern | 5 |
| | Middle | 2 |
| | Western | 4 |
| Puerto Rico | | 2 |
| Rhode Island | | 1 |
| South Carolina | | 2 |
| South Dakota | | 2 |
| Tennessee: | | |
| | Eastern | 3 |
| | Middle | 3 |
| | Western | 4 |
| Texas: | | |
| | Northern | 6 |
| | Eastern | 2 |
| | Southern | 6 |
| | Western | 4 |
| Utah | | 3 |
| Vermont | | 1 |
| Virginia: | | |
| | Eastern | 5 |
| | Western | 3 |
| Washington: | | |
| | Eastern | 2 |
| | Western | 5 |
| West Virginia: | | |
| | Northern | 1 |

| Districts | | Judges |
|---|---|---|
| | Southern | 1 |
| Wisconsin: | | |
| | Eastern | 4 |
| | Western | 2 |
| Wyoming | | 1 |

(3) Whenever a majority of the judges of any court of appeals cannot agree upon the appointment of a bankruptcy judge, the chief judge of such court shall make such appointment.

(4) The judges of the district courts for the territories shall serve as the bankruptcy judges for such courts. The United States court of appeals for the circuit within which such a territorial district court is located may appoint bankruptcy judges under this chapter for such district if authorized to do so by the Congress of the United States under this section.

(b) (1) The Judicial Conference of the United States shall, from time to time, and after considering the recommendations submitted by the Director of the Administrative Office of the United States Courts after such Director has consulted with the judicial council of the circuit involved, determine the official duty stations of bankruptcy judges and places of holding court.

(2) The Judicial Conference shall, from time to time, submit recommendations to the Congress regarding the number of bankruptcy judges needed and the districts in which such judges are needed.

(3) Not later than December 31, 1994, and not later than the end of each 2-year period thereafter, the Judicial Conference of the United States shall conduct a comprehensive review of all judicial districts to assess the continuing need for the bankruptcy judges authorized by this section, and shall report to the Congress its findings and any recommendations for the elimination of any authorized position which can be eliminated when a vacancy exists by reason of resignation, retirement, removal, or death.

(c) (1) Each bankruptcy judge may hold court at such places within the judicial district, in addition to the official duty station of such judge, as the business of the court may require.

(2) (A) Bankruptcy judges may hold court at such places within the United States outside the judicial district as the nature of the business of the court may require, and upon such notice as the court orders, upon a finding by either the chief judge of the bankruptcy court (or, if the chief judge is unavailable, the most senior available bankruptcy judge) or by the judicial council of the circuit that, because of emergency conditions, no location within the district is reasonably available where the bankruptcy judges could hold court.

(B) Bankruptcy judges may transact any business at special sessions of court held outside the district pursuant to this paragraph that might be transacted at a regular session.

(C) If a bankruptcy court issues an order exercising its authority under subparagraph (A), the court—

(i) through the Administrative Office of the United States Courts, shall—

(I) send notice of such order, including the reasons for the issuance of such order, to the Committee on the Judiciary of the Senate and the Committee on the Judiciary of the House of Representatives; and

(II) not later than 180 days after the expiration of such court order submit a brief report to the Committee on the Judiciary of the Senate and the Committee on the Judiciary of the House of Representatives describing the impact of such order, including—

(aa) the reasons for the issuance of such order;

(bb) the duration of such order;

(cc) the impact of such order on litigants; and

(dd) the costs to the judiciary resulting from such order; and

(ii) shall provide reasonable notice to the United States Marshals Service before the commencement of any special session held pursuant to such order.

(d) With the approval of the Judicial Conference and of each of the judicial councils involved, a bankruptcy judge may be designated to serve in any district adjacent to or near the district for which such bankruptcy judge was appointed.

(e) A bankruptcy judge may be removed during the term for which such bankruptcy judge is appointed, only for incompetence, misconduct, neglect of duty, or physical or mental disability and only by the judicial council of the circuit in which the judge's official duty station is located. Removal may not occur unless a majority of all of the judges of such council concur in the order of removal. Before any order of removal may be entered, a full specification of charges shall be furnished to such bankruptcy judge who shall be accorded an opportunity to be heard on such charges.

## 28 USC § 153 Salaries; Character of service

(a) Each bankruptcy judge shall serve on a full-time basis and shall receive as full compensation for his services a salary at an annual rate that is equal to 92 percent of the salary of a judge of the district court of the United States as determined pursuant to section 135, to be paid at such times as the Judicial Conference of the United States determines.

(b) A bankruptcy judge may not engage in the practice of law and may not engage in any other practice, business, occupation, or employment inconsistent with the expeditious, proper, and impartial performance of such bankruptcy judge's duties as a judicial officer. The Conference may promulgate appropriate rules and regulations to implement this subsection.

(c) Each individual appointed under this chapter shall take the oath or affirmation prescribed by section 453 of this title before performing the duties of the office of bankruptcy judge.

(d) A bankruptcy judge appointed under this chapter shall be exempt from the provisions of subchapter I of chapter 63 of title 5, United States Code.

**28 USC § 154 Division of businesses; chief judge**

(a) Each bankruptcy court for a district having more than one bankruptcy judge shall by majority vote promulgate rules for the division of business among the bankruptcy judges to the extent that the division of business is not otherwise provided for by the rules of the district court.

(b) In each district court having more than one bankruptcy judge the district court shall designate one judge to serve as chief judge of such bankruptcy court. Whenever a majority of the judges of such district court cannot agree upon the designation as chief judge, the chief judge of such district court shall make such designation. The chief judge of the bankruptcy court shall ensure that the rules of the bankruptcy court and of the district court are observed and that the business of the bankruptcy court is handled effectively and expeditiously.

**28 USC § 155 Temporary transfer of bankruptcy judges**

(a) A bankruptcy judge may be transferred to serve temporarily as a bankruptcy judge in any judicial district other than the judicial district for which such bankruptcy judge was appointed upon the approval of the judicial council of each of the circuits involved.

(b) A bankruptcy judge who has retired may, upon consent, be recalled to serve as a bankruptcy judge in any judicial district by the judicial council of the circuit within which such district is located. Upon recall, a bankruptcy judge may receive a salary for such service in accordance with regulations promulgated by the Judicial Conference of the United States, subject to the restrictions on the payment of an annuity in section 377 of this title or in subchapter III of chapter 83, and chapter 84, of title 5 which are applicable to such judge.

**28 USC § 156 Staff; expenses**

(a) Each bankruptcy judge may appoint a secretary, a law clerk, and such additional assistants as the Director of the Administrative Office of the United States Courts determines to be necessary. A law clerk appointed under this section shall be exempt from the provisions of subchapter I of chapter 63 of title 5, United States Code, unless specifically included by the appointing judge or by local rule of court.

(b) Upon certification to the judicial council of the circuit involved and to the Director of the Administrative Office of the United States Courts that the number of cases and proceedings pending within the jurisdiction under section 1334 of this title within a judicial district so warrants, the bankruptcy judges for such district may appoint an individual to serve as clerk of such bankruptcy court. The clerk may appoint, with the approval of such bankruptcy judges, and in such number as may be approved by the Director, necessary deputies, and may remove such deputies with the approval of such bankruptcy judges.

(c) Any court may utilize facilities or services, either on or off the court's premises, which pertain to the provision of notices, dockets, calendars, and other administrative information to parties in cases filed under the provisions of title 11, United States Code, where the costs of such facilities or services are paid for out of the assets of the estate and are not charged to the United States. The utilization of such facilities or services shall be subject to such conditions and limitations as the pertinent circuit council may prescribe.

(d) No office of the bankruptcy clerk of court may be consolidated with the district clerk of court office without the prior approval of the Judicial Conference and the Congress.

(e) In a judicial district where a bankruptcy clerk has been appointed pursuant to subsection (b), the bankruptcy clerk shall be the official custodian of the records and dockets of the bankruptcy court.

(f) For purposes of financial accountability in a district where a bankruptcy clerk has been certified, such clerk shall be accountable for and pay into the Treasury all fees, costs, and other monies collected by such clerk except uncollected fees not required by an Act of Congress to be prepaid. Such clerk shall make returns thereof to the Director of the Administrative Office of the United States Courts and the Director of the Executive Office For United States Trustees, under regulations prescribed by such Directors.

**28 USC § 157 Procedures**

(a) Each district court may provide that any or all cases under title 11 and any or all proceedings arising under title 11 or arising in or related to a case under title 11 shall be referred to the bankruptcy judges for the district.

(b) (1) Bankruptcy judges may hear and determine all cases under title 11 and all core proceedings arising under title 11, or arising in a case under title 11, referred under subsection (a) of this section, and may enter appropriate orders and judgments, subject to review under section 158 of this title.

(2) Core proceedings include, but are not limited to—

(A) matters concerning the administration of the estate;

(B) allowance or disallowance of claims against the estate or exemptions from property of the estate, and estimation of claims or interests for the purposes of confirming a plan under chapter 11, 12, or 13 of title 11 but not the liquidation or estimation of contingent or unliquidated personal injury tort or wrongful death claims against the estate for purposes of distribution in a case under title 11;

(C) counterclaims by the estate against persons filing claims against the estate;

(D) orders in respect to obtaining credit;

(E) orders to turn over property of the estate;

(F) proceedings to determine, avoid, or recover preferences;

(G) motions to terminate, annul, or modify the automatic stay;

(H) proceedings to determine, avoid, or recover fraudulent conveyances;

(I) determinations as to the dischargeability of particular debts;

(J) objections to discharges;

(K) determinations of the validity, extent, or priority of liens;

(L) confirmations of plans;

(M) orders approving the use or lease of property, including the use of cash collateral;

(N) orders approving the sale of property other than property resulting from claims brought by the estate against persons who have not filed claims against the estate;

(O) other proceedings affecting the liquidation of the assets of the estate or the adjustment of the debtor-creditor or the equity security holder relationship, except personal injury tort or wrongful death claims; and

(P) recognition of foreign proceedings and other matters under chapter 15 of title 11.

(3) The bankruptcy judge shall determine, on the judge's own motion or on timely motion of a party, whether a proceeding is a core proceeding under this subsection or is a proceeding that is otherwise related to a case under title 11. A determination that a proceeding is not a core proceeding shall not be made solely on the basis that its resolution may be affected by State law.

(4) Non-core proceedings under section 157(b)(2)(B) of title 28, United States Code, shall not be subject to the mandatory abstention provisions of section 1334(c)(2).

(5) The district court shall order that personal injury tort and wrongful death claims shall be tried in the district court in which the bankruptcy case is pending, or in the district court in the district in which the claim arose, as determined by the district court in which the bankruptcy case is pending.

(c) (1) A bankruptcy judge may hear a proceeding that is not a core proceeding but that is otherwise related to a case under title 11. In such proceeding, the bankruptcy judge shall submit proposed findings of fact and conclusions of law to the district court, and any final order or judgment shall be entered by the district judge after considering the bankruptcy judge's proposed findings and conclusions and after reviewing de novo those matters to which any party has timely and specifically objected.

(2) Notwithstanding the provisions of paragraph (1) of this subsection, the district court, with the consent of all the parties to the proceeding, may refer a proceeding related to a case under title 11 to a bankruptcy judge to hear and

determine and to enter appropriate orders and judgments, subject to review under section 158 of this title.

(d) The district court may withdraw, in whole or in part, any case or proceeding referred under this section, on its own motion or on timely motion of any party, for cause shown. The district court shall, on timely motion of a party, so withdraw a proceeding if the court determines that resolution of the proceeding requires consideration of both title 11 and other laws of the United States regulating organizations or activities affecting interstate commerce.

(e) If the right to a jury trial applies in a proceeding that may be heard under this section by a bankruptcy judge, the bankruptcy judge may conduct the jury trial if specially designated to exercise such jurisdiction by the district court and with the express consent of all the parties.



## 28 USC § 158 Appeals

(a) The district courts of the United States shall have jurisdiction to hear appeals

(1) from final judgments, orders, and decrees;

(2) from interlocutory orders and decrees issued under section 1121(d) of title 11 increasing or reducing the time periods referred to in section 1121 of such title; and

(3) with leave of the court, from other interlocutory orders and decrees;

and, with leave of the court, from interlocutory orders and decrees,[1] of bankruptcy judges entered in cases and proceedings referred to the bankruptcy judges under section 157 of this title. An appeal under this subsection shall be taken only to the district court for the judicial district in which the bankruptcy judge is serving.

(b) (1) The judicial council of a circuit shall establish a bankruptcy appellate panel service composed of bankruptcy judges of the districts in the circuit who are appointed by the judicial council in accordance with paragraph (3), to hear and determine, with the consent of all the parties, appeals under subsection (a) unless the judicial council finds that—

(A) there are insufficient judicial resources available in the circuit; or

(B) establishment of such service would result in undue delay or increased cost to parties in cases under title 11.

Not later than 90 days after making the finding, the judicial council shall submit to the Judicial Conference of the United States a report containing the factual basis of such finding.

---

[1] ED. NOTE: The intent of Congress regarding the eleven words preceding this footnote is unclear. Pub. L. No. 103-394 (1994) stated that "Section 158(a) of title 28, United States Code, is amended by striking 'from' the first place it appears and all that follows through 'decrees,' and inserting [paragraphs (1) through (3)]". Because "decrees," appeared twice in the affected sentence, the instance immediately preceding this footnote having been the second of the two, it cannot be determined with certitude that Congress intended for these eleven words to be removed.

(2) (A) A judicial council may reconsider, at any time, the finding described in paragraph (1).

(B) On the request of a majority of the district judges in a circuit for which a bankruptcy appellate panel service is established under paragraph (1), made after the expiration of the 1-year period beginning on the date such service is established, the judicial council of the circuit shall determine whether a circumstance specified in subparagraph (A) or (B) of such paragraph exists.

(C) On its own motion, after the expiration of the 3-year period beginning on the date a bankruptcy appellate panel service is established under paragraph (1), the judicial council of the circuit may determine whether a circumstance specified in subparagraph (A) or (B) of such paragraph exists.

(D) If the judicial council finds that either of such circumstances exists, the judicial council may provide for the completion of the appeals then pending before such service and the orderly termination of such service.

(3) Bankruptcy judges appointed under paragraph (1) shall be appointed and may be reappointed under such paragraph.

(4) If authorized by the Judicial Conference of the United States, the judicial councils of 2 or more circuits may establish a joint bankruptcy appellate panel comprised of bankruptcy judges from the districts within the circuits for which such panel is established, to hear and determine, upon the consent of all the parties, appeals under subsection (a) of this section.

(5) An appeal to be heard under this subsection shall be heard by a panel of 3 members of the bankruptcy appellate panel service, except that a member of such service may not hear an appeal originating in the district for which such member is appointed or designated under section 152 of this title.

(6) Appeals may not be heard under this subsection by a panel of the bankruptcy appellate panel service unless the district judges for the district in which the appeals occur, by majority vote, have authorized such service to hear and determine appeals originating in such district.

(c) (1) Subject to subsections (b) and (d)(2), each appeal under subsection (a) shall be heard by a 3-judge panel of the bankruptcy appellate panel service established under subsection (b)(1) unless—

(A) the appellant elects at the time of filing the appeal; or

(B) any other party elects, not later than 30 days after service of notice of the appeal;

to have such appeal heard by the district court.

(2) An appeal under subsections (a) and (b) of this section shall be taken in the same manner as appeals in civil proceedings generally are taken to the courts of appeals from the district courts and in the time provided by Rule 8002 of the Bankruptcy Rules.

(d) (1) The courts of appeals shall have jurisdiction of appeals from all final decisions, judgments, orders, and decrees entered under subsections (a) and (b) of this section.

(2) (A) The appropriate court of appeals shall have jurisdiction of appeals described in the first sentence of subsection (a) if the bankruptcy court, the district court, or the bankruptcy appellate panel involved, acting on its own motion or on the request of a party to the judgment, order, or decree described in such first sentence, or all the appellants and appellees (if any) acting jointly, certify that—

(i) the judgment, order, or decree involves a question of law as to which there is no controlling decision of the court of appeals for the circuit or of the Supreme Court of the United States, or involves a matter of public importance;

(ii) the judgment, order, or decree involves a question of law requiring resolution of conflicting decisions; or

(iii) an immediate appeal from the judgment, order, or decree may materially advance the progress of the case or proceeding in which the appeal is taken;

and if the court of appeals authorizes the direct appeal of the judgment, order, or decree.

(B) If the bankruptcy court, the district court, or the bankruptcy appellate panel—

(i) on its own motion or on the request of a party, determines that a circumstance specified in clause (i), (ii), or (iii) of subparagraph (A) exists; or

(ii) receives a request made by a majority of the appellants and a majority of the appellees (if any) to make the certification described in subparagraph (A);

then the bankruptcy court, the district court, or the bankruptcy appellate panel shall make the certification described in subparagraph (A).

(C) The parties may supplement the certification with a short statement of the basis for the certification.

(D) An appeal under this paragraph does not stay any proceeding of the bankruptcy court, the district court, or the bankruptcy appellate panel from which the appeal is taken, unless the respective bankruptcy court, district court, or bankruptcy appellate panel, or the court of appeals in which the appeal is pending, issues a stay of such proceeding pending the appeal.

(E) Any request under subparagraph (B) for certification shall be made not later than 60 days after the entry of the judgment, order, or decree.

**28 USC § 159 Bankruptcy statistics**

(a) The clerk of the district court, or the clerk of the bankruptcy court if one is certified pursuant to section 156(b) of this title, shall collect statistics regarding debtors who are individuals with primarily consumer debts seeking relief under chapter 7, 11, and 13 of title 11. Those statistics shall be in a standardized format prescribed by the Director of the Administrative Office of the United States Courts (referred to in this section as the "Director").

(b) The Director shall—

(1) compile the statistics referred to in subsection (a);

(2) make the statistics available to the public; and

(3) not later than July 1, 2008, and annually thereafter, prepare, and submit to Congress a report concerning the information collected under subsection (a) that contains an analysis of the information.

(c) The compilation required under subsection (b) shall—

(1) be itemized, by chapter, with respect to title 11;

(2) be presented in the aggregate and for each district; and

(3) include information concerning—

(A) the total assets and total liabilities of the debtors described in subsection (a), and in each category of assets and liabilities, as reported in the schedules prescribed pursuant to section 2075 of this title and filed by debtors;

(B) the current monthly income, average income, and average expenses of debtors as reported on the schedules and statements that each such debtor files under sections 521 and 1322 of title 11;

(C) the aggregate amount of debt discharged in cases filed during the reporting period, determined as the difference between the total amount of debt and obligations of a debtor reported on the schedules and the amount of such debt reported in categories which are predominantly nondischarge-able;

(D) the average period of time between the date of the filing of the petition and the closing of the case for cases closed during the reporting period;

(E) for cases closed during the reporting period—

(i) the number of cases in which a reaffirmation agreement was filed; and

(ii) (I) the total number of reaffirmation agreements filed;

(II) of those cases in which a reaffirmation agreement was filed, the number of cases in which the debtor was not represented by an attorney; and

(III) of those cases in which a reaffirmation agreement was filed, the number of cases in which the reaffirmation agreement was approved by the court;

(F) with respect to cases filed under chapter 13 of title 11, for the reporting period—

(i) (I) the number of cases in which a final order was entered determining the value of property securing a claim in an amount less than the amount of the claim; and

(II) the number of final orders entered determining the value of property securing a claim;

(ii) the number of cases dismissed, the number of cases dismissed for failure to make payments under the plan, the number of cases refiled after dismissal, and the number of cases in which the plan was completed, separately itemized with respect to the number of modifications make before completion of the plan, if any; and

(iii) the number of cases in which the debtor filed another case during the 6-year period preceding the filing;

(G) the number of cases in which creditors were fined for misconduct and any amount of punitive damages awarded by the court for creditor misconduct; and

(H) the number of cases in which sanctions under rule 9011 of the Federal Rules of Bankruptcy Procedure were imposed against the debtor's attorney or damages awarded under such Rule.

## UNITED STATES TRUSTEES (CHAPTER 39)

### 28 USC § 581 United States trustees

(a) The Attorney General shall appoint one United States trustee for each of the following regions composed of Federal judicial districts (without regard to section 451):

(1) The judicial districts established for the States of Maine, Massachusetts, New Hampshire, and Rhode Island.

(2) The judicial districts established for the States of Connecticut, New York, and Vermont.

(3) The judicial districts established for the States of Delaware, New Jersey, and Pennsylvania.

(4) The judicial districts established for the States of Maryland, North Carolina, South Carolina, Virginia, and West Virginia and for the District of Columbia.

(5) The judicial districts established for the States of Louisiana and Mississippi.

(6) The Northern District of Texas and the Eastern District of Texas.

(7) The Southern District of Texas and the Western District of Texas.

(8) The judicial districts established for the States of Kentucky and Tennessee.

(9) The judicial districts established for the States of Michigan and Ohio.

(10) The Central District of Illinois and the Southern District of Illinois; and the judicial districts established for the State of Indiana.

(11) The Northern District of Illinois; and the judicial districts established for the State of Wisconsin.

(12) The judicial districts established for the States of Minnesota, Iowa, North Dakota, and South Dakota.

(13) The judicial districts established for the States of Arkansas, Nebraska, and Missouri.

(14) The District of Arizona.

(15) The Southern District of California; and the judicial districts established for the State of Hawaii, and for Guam and the Commonwealth of the Northern Mariana Islands.

(16) The Central District of California.

(17) The Eastern District of California and the Northern District of California; and the judicial district established for the State of Nevada.

(18) The judicial districts established for the States of Alaska, Idaho (exclusive of Yellowstone National Park), Montana (exclusive of Yellowstone National Park), Oregon, and Washington.

(19) The judicial districts established for the States of Colorado, Utah, and Wyoming (including those portions of Yellowstone National Park situated in the States of Montana and Idaho).

(20) The judicial districts established for the States of Kansas, New Mexico, and Oklahoma.

(21) The judicial districts established for the States of Alabama, Florida, and Georgia and for the Commonwealth of Puerto Rico and the Virgin Islands of the United States.

(b) Each United States trustee shall be appointed for a term of five years. On the expiration of his term, a United States trustee shall continue to perform the duties of his office until his successor is appointed and qualifies.

(c) Each United States trustee is subject to removal by the Attorney General.



**28 USC § 582 Assistant United States trustees**

(a) The Attorney General may appoint one or more assistant United States trustees in any region when the public interest so requires.

(b) Each assistant United States trustee is subject to removal by the Attorney General.

**28 USC § 583 Oath of office**

Each United States trustee and assistant United States trustee, before taking office, shall take an oath to execute faithfully his duties.

**28 USC § 584 Official stations**

The Attorney General may determine the official stations of the United States trustees and assistant United States trustees within the regions for which they were appointed.

**28 USC § 585 Vacancies**

(a) The Attorney General may appoint an acting United States trustee for a region in which the office of the United States trustee is vacant. The individual so appointed may serve until the date on which the vacancy if filled by appointment under section 581 of this title or by designation under subsection (b) of this section.

(b) The Attorney General may designate a United States trustee to serve in not more than two regions for such time as the public interest requires.

**28 USC § 586 Duties; supervision by Attorney General**

(a) Each United States trustee, within the region for which such United States trustee is appointed, shall—

(1) establish, maintain, and supervise a panel of private trustees that are eligible and available to serve as trustees in cases under chapter 7 of title 11;

(2) serve as and perform the duties of a trustee in a case under title 11 when required under title 11 to serve as trustee in such a case;

(3) supervise the administration of cases and trustees in cases under chapter 7, 11 (including subchapter V of chapter 11), 12, 13, or 15 of title 11 by, whenever the United States trustee considers it to be appropriate—

(A) (i) reviewing, in accordance with procedural guidelines adopted by the Executive Office of the United States Trustee (which guidelines shall be applied uniformly by the United States trustee except when circumstances warrant different treatment), applications filed for compensation and reimbursement under section 330 of title 11; and

(ii) filing with the court comments with respect to such application and, if the United States Trustee considers it to be appropriate, objections to such application;

(B) monitoring plans and disclosure statements filed in cases under chapter 11 of title 11 and filing with the court, in connection with hearings under sections 1125 and 1128 of such title, comments with respect to such plans and disclosure statements;

(C) monitoring plans filed under chapters 12 and 13 of title 11 and filing with the court, in connection with hearings under sections 1224, 1229, 1324, and 1329 of such title, comments with respect to such plans;

(D) taking such action as the United States trustee deems to be appropriate to ensure that all reports, schedules, and fees required to be filed under title 11 and this title by the debtor are properly and timely filed;

(E) monitoring creditors' committees appointed under title 11;

(F) notifying the appropriate United States attorney of matters which relate to the occurrence of any action which may constitute a crime under the laws of the United States and, on the request of the United States attorney, assisting the United States attorney in carrying out prosecutions based on such action;

(G) monitoring the progress of cases under title 11 and taking such actions as the United States trustee deems to be appropriate to prevent undue delay in such progress;

(H) in small business cases (as defined in section 101 of title 11), performing the additional duties specified in title 11 pertaining to such cases; and

(I) monitoring applications filed under section 327 of title 11 and, whenever the United States trustee deems it to be appropriate, filing with the court comments with respect to the approval of such applications;

(4) deposit or invest under section 345 of title 11 money received as trustee in cases under title 11;

(5) perform the duties prescribed for the United States trustee under title 11 and this title, and such duties consistent with title 11 and this title as the Attorney General may prescribe;

(6) make such reports as the Attorney General directs, including the results of audits performed under section 603(a) of the Bankruptcy Abuse Prevention and Consumer Protection Act of 2005;[2]

(7) in each of such small business cases—

(A) conduct an initial debtor interview as soon as practicable after the date of the order for relief but before the first meeting scheduled under section 341(a) of title 11, at which time the United States trustee shall—

(i) begin to investigate the debtor's viability;

(ii) inquire about the debtor's business plan;

(iii) explain the debtor's obligations to file monthly operating reports and other required reports;

(iv) attempt to develop an agreed scheduling order; and

(v) inform the debtor of other obligations;

(B) if determined to be appropriate and advisable, visit the appropriate business premises of debtor, ascertain the state of the debtor's books and records, and verify that the debtor has filed its tax returns; and

(C) review and monitor diligently the debtor's activities, to determine as



---

[2] Ed. Note: Section 603(a) of the 2005 Act provides:

**Sec. 603 Audit Procedures**

(a) In General.—

(1) Establishment of procedures.— The Attorney General (in judicial districts served by United States trustees) and the Judicial Conference of the United States (in judicial districts served by bankruptcy administrators) shall establish procedures to determine the accuracy, veracity, and completeness of petitions, schedules, and other information that the debtor is required to provide under sections 521 and 1322 of title 11, United States Code, and, if applicable, section 111 of such title, in cases filed under chapter 7 or 13 of such title in which the debtor is an individual. Such audits shall be in accordance with generally accepted auditing standards and performed by independent certified public accountants or independent licensed public accountants, provided that the Attorney General and the Judicial Conference, as appropriate, may develop alternative auditing standards not later than 2 years after the date of enactment of this Act.

(2) Procedures.— Those procedures required by paragraph (1) shall—

(A) establish a method of selecting appropriate qualified persons to contract to perform those audits;

(B) establish a method of randomly selecting cases to be audited, except that not less than 1 out of every 250 cases in each Federal judicial district shall be selected for audit;

(C) require audits of schedules of income and expenses that reflect greater than average variances from the statistical norm of the district in which the schedules were filed if those variances occur by reason of higher income or higher expenses than the statistical norm of the district in which the schedules were filed; and

(D) establish procedures for providing, not less frequently than annually, public information concerning the aggregate results of such audits including the percentage of cases, by district, in which a material misstatement of income or expenditures is reported.

promptly as possible whether the debtor will be unable to confirm a plan; and

(8) in any case in which the United States trustee finds material grounds for any relief under section 1112 of title 11, apply promptly after making that finding to the court for relief.

(b) If the number of cases under subchapter V of chapter 11 or chapter 12 or 13 of title 11 commenced in a particular region so warrants, the United States trustee for such region may, subject to the approval of the Attorney General, appoint one or more individuals to serve as standing trustee, or designate one or more assistant United States trustees to serve in cases under such chapter. The United States trustee for such region shall supervise any such individual appointed as standing trustee in the performance of the duties of standing trustee.

(c) Each United States trustee shall be under the general supervision of the Attorney General, who shall provide general coordination and assistance to the United States trustees.

(d) (1) The Attorney General shall prescribe by rule qualifications for membership on the panels established by United States trustees under paragraph (a)(1) of this section, and qualifications for appointment under subsection (b) of this section to serve as standing trustee in cases under subchapter V of chapter 11 or chapter 12 or 13 of title 11. The Attorney General may not require that an individual be an attorney in order to qualify for appointment under subsection (b) of this section to serve as standing trustee in cases under subchapter V of chapter 11 or chapter 12 or 13 of title 11.

(2) A trustee whose appointment under subsection (a)(1) or under subsection (b) is terminated or who ceases to be assigned to cases filed under title 11, United States Code, may obtain judicial review of the final agency decision by commencing an action in the district court of the United States for the district for which the panel to which the trustee is appointed under subsection (a)(1), or in the district court of the United States for the district in which the trustee is appointed under subsection (b) resides, after first exhausting all available administrative remedies, which if the trustee elects, shall also include an administrative hearing on the record. Unless the trustee elects to have an administrative hearing on the record, the trustee shall be deemed to have exhausted all administrative remedies for purposes of this paragraph if the agency fails to make a final agency decision within 90 days after the trustee requests administrative remedies. The Attorney General shall prescribe procedures to implement this paragraph. The decision of the agency shall be affirmed by the district court unless it is unreasonable and without cause based on the administrative record before the agency.

(e) (1) The Attorney General, after consultation with a United States trustee that has appointed an individual under subsection (b) of this section to serve as standing trustee in cases under subchapter V of chapter 11 or chapter 12 or 13 of title 11, shall fix—

(A) a maximum annual compensation for such individual consisting of—

(i) an amount not to exceed the highest annual rate of basic pay in effect for level V of the Executive Schedule; and

(ii) the cash value of employment benefits comparable to the employment benefits provided by the United States to individuals who are employed by the United States at the same rate of basic pay to perform similar services during the same period of time; and

(B) a percentage fee not to exceed—

(i) in the case of a debtor who is not a family farmer, ten percent; or

(ii) in the case of a debtor who is a family farmer, the sum of—

(I) not to exceed ten percent of the payments made under the plan of such debtor, with respect to payments in an aggregate amount not to exceed $450,000; and

(II) three percent of payments made under the plan of such debtor, with respect to payments made after the aggregate amount of payments made under the plan exceeds $450,000;

based on such maximum annual compensation and the actual, necessary expenses incurred by such individual as standing trustee.

(2) Such individual shall collect such percentage fee from all payments received by such individual under plans in the cases under subchapter V of chapter 11 or chapter 12 or 13 of title 11 for which such individual serves as standing trustee. Such individual shall pay to the United States trustee, and the United States trustee shall deposit in the United States Trustee System Fund—

(A) any amount by which the actual compensation of such individual exceeds 5 per centum upon all payments received under plans in cases under subchapter V of chapter 11 or chapter 12 or 13 of title 11 for which such individual serves as standing trustee; and

(B) any amount by which the percentage for all such cases exceeds—

(i) such individual's actual compensation for such cases, as adjusted under subparagraph (A) of paragraph (1); plus

(ii) the actual, necessary expenses incurred by such individual as standing trustee in such cases. Subject to the approval of the Attorney General, any or all of the interest earned from the deposit of payments under plans by such individual may be utilized to pay actual, necessary expenses without regard to the percentage limitation contained in subparagraph (d)(1)(B) of this section.

(3) After first exhausting all available administrative remedies, an individual appointed under subsection (b) may obtain judicial review of final agency action to deny a claim of actual, necessary expenses under this subsection by commencing an action in the district court of the United States for the district where the individual resides. The decision of the agency shall be affirmed by the district court unless it is unreasonable and without cause based upon the

JUDICIAL CODE

administrative record before the agency.

(4) The Attorney General shall prescribe procedures to implement this subsection.

(5) In the event that the services of the trustee in a case under subchapter V of chapter 11 of title 11 are terminated by dismissal or conversion of the case, or upon substantial consummation of a plan under section 1183(c)(1) of that title, the court shall award compensation to the trustee consistent with services performed by the trustee and the limits on the compensation of the trustee established pursuant to paragraph (1) of this subsection.

(f) (1) The United States trustee for each district is authorized to contract with auditors to perform audits in cases designated by the United States trustee, in accordance with the procedures established under section 603(a) of the Bankruptcy Abuse Prevention and Consumer Protection Act of 2005.

(2) (A) The report of each audit referred to in paragraph (1) shall be filed with the court and transmitted to the United States trustee. Each report shall clearly and conspicuously specify any material misstatement of income or expenditures or of assets identified by the person performing the audit. In any case in which a material misstatement of income or expenditures or of assets has been reported, the clerk of the district court (or the clerk of the bankruptcy court if one is certified under section 156(b) of this title) shall give notice of misstatement to the creditors in the case.

(B) If a material misstatement of income or expenditures or of assets is reported, the United States trustee shall—

(i) report the material misstatement, if appropriate, to the United States Attorney pursuant to section 3057 of title 18; and

(ii) if advisable, take appropriate action, including but not limited to commencing an adversary proceeding to revoke the debtor's discharge pursuant to section 727(d) of title 11.

### 28 USC § 587 Salaries

Subject to sections 5315 through 5317 of title 5, the Attorney General shall fix the annual salaries of United States trustees and assistant United States trustees at rates of compensation not in excess of the rate of basic compensation provided for Executive Level IV of the Executive Schedule set forth in section 5315 of title 5, United States Code.

### 28 USC § 588 Expenses

Necessary office expenses of the United States trustee shall be allowed when authorized by the Attorney General.

### 28 USC § 589 Staff and other employees

The United States trustee may employ staff and other employees on approval of the Attorney General.

**28 USC § 589a United States Trustee System Fund**

(a) There is hereby established in the Treasury of the United States a special fund to be known as the "United States Trustee System Fund" (hereinafter in this section referred to as the "Fund"). Monies in the Fund shall be available to the Attorney General without fiscal year limitation in such amounts as may be specified in appropriations Acts for the following purposes in connection with the operations of United States trustees—

(1) salaries and related employee benefits;

(2) travel and transportation;

(3) rental of space;

(4) communication, utilities, and miscellaneous computer charges;

(5) security investigations and audits;

(6) supplies, books, and other materials for legal research;

(7) furniture and equipment;

(8) miscellaneous services, including those obtained by contract; and

(9) printing.

(b) the purpose of recovering the cost of services of the United States Trustee System, there shall be deposited as offsetting collections to the appropriation "United States Trustee System Fund", to remain available until expended, the following—

(1) (A) 40.46 percent of the fees collected under section 1930(a)(1)(A); and

(B) 28.33 percent of the fees collected under section 1930(a)(1)(B);

(2) 48.89 percent of the fees collected under section 1930(a)(3) of this title;

(3) one-half of the fees collected under section 1930(a)(4) of this title;

(4) one-half of the fees collected under section 1930(a)(5) of this title;

(5) 100 percent of the fees collected under section 1930(a)(6) of this title;

(6) three-fourths of the fees collected under the last sentence of section 1930(a) of this title;

(7) the compensation of trustees received under section 330(d) of title 11 by the clerks of the bankruptcy courts;

(8) excess fees collected under section 586(e)(2) of this title;

(9) interest earned on Fund investment; and

(10) fines imposed under section 110(l) of title 11, United States Code.

(c) Amounts in the Fund which are not currently needed for the purposes specified in subsection (a) shall be kept on deposit or invested in obligations of, or guaranteed by, the United States.

(d) The Attorney General shall transmit to the Congress, not later than 120 days after the end of each fiscal year, a detailed report on the amounts deposited in the Fund and a description of expenditures made under this section.

(e) There are authorized to be appropriated to the Fund for any fiscal year such sums as may be necessary to supplement amounts deposited under subsection (b) for the purposes specified in subsection (a).

(f) (1) During each of fiscal years 2021 through 2026 and notwithstanding subsections (b) and (c), the fees collected under section 1930(a)(6), less the amount specified in paragraph (2), shall be deposited as follows, in the following order:

(A) First, the amounts specified in the Department of Justice appropriations for that fiscal year, shall be deposited as discretionary offsetting collections to the "United States Trustee System Fund", pursuant to subsection (a), to remain available until expended.

(B) Second, the amounts determined annually by the Director of the Administrative Office of the United States Courts that are necessary to reimburse the judiciary for the costs of administering payments under section 330(e) of title 11, shall be deposited as mandatory offsetting collections to the "United States Trustee System Fund", and transferred and deposited into the special fund established under section 1931(a), and notwithstanding subsection (a), shall be available for expenditure without further appropriation.

(C) Third, the amounts determined annually by the Director of the Administrative Office of the United States Courts that are necessary to pay trustee compensation authorized by section 330(e)(2) of title 11, shall be deposited as mandatory offsetting collections to the "United States Trustee System Fund", and transferred and deposited into the Chapter 7 Trustee Fund established under section 330(e) of title 11 for payment to trustees serving in cases under chapter 7 of title 11 (in addition to the amounts paid under section 330(b) of title 11), in accordance with that section, and notwithstanding subsection (a), shall be available for expenditure without further appropriation.

(D) Fourth, any remaining amounts shall be deposited as discretionary offsetting collections to the "United States Trustee System Fund", to remain available until expended.

(2) Notwithstanding subsection (b), for each of fiscal years 2021 through 2026, $5,400,000 of the fees collected under section 1930(a)(6) shall be deposited in the general fund of the Treasury.

## 28 USC § 589b Bankruptcy data

(a) Rules. The Attorney General shall, within a reasonable time after the effective date of this section, issue rules requiring uniform forms for (and from time to time thereafter to appropriately modify and approve)—

(1) final reports by trustees in cases under subchapter V of chapter 11 and chapters 7, 12, and 13 of title 11; and

(2) periodic reports by debtors in possession or trustees in cases under chapter 11 of title 11.

(b) Reports. Each report referred to in subsection (a) shall be designed (and the requirements as to place and manner of filing shall be established) so as to facilitate compilation of data and maximum possible access of the public, both by physical inspection at one or more central filing locations, and by electronic access through the Internet or other appropriate media.



(c) Required Information. The information required to be filed in the reports referred to in subsection (b) shall be that which is in the best interests of debtors and creditors, and in the public interest in reasonable and adequate information to evaluate the efficiency and practicality of the Federal bankruptcy system. In issuing rules proposing the forms referred to in subsection (a), the Attorney General shall strike the best achievable practical balance between—

(1) the reasonable needs of the public information about the operational results of the Federal bankruptcy system;

(2) economy, simplicity, and lack of undue burden of persons with a duty to file reports; and

(3) appropriate privacy concerns and safeguards.

(d) Final Reports. The uniform forms for final reports required under subsection (a) for use by trustees under subchapter V of chapter 11 and chapters 7, 12, and 13 of title 11 shall, in addition to such other matters as are required by law or as the Attorney General in the discretion of the Attorney General shall propose, include with respect to a case under such title—

(1) information about the length of time the case was pending;

(2) assets abandoned;

(3) assets exempted;

(4) receipts and disbursements of the estate;

(5) expenses of administration, including for use under section 707(b), actual costs of administering cases under chapter 13 of title 11;

(6) claims asserted;

(7) claims allowed; and

(8) distributions to claimants and claims discharged without payment,

in each case by appropriate category and, in cases under subchapter V of chapter 11 and chapters 12 and 13 of title 11, date of confirmation of the plan, each modification thereto, and defaults by the debtor in performance under the plan.

(e) Periodic Reports. The uniform forms for periodic reports required under subsection (a) for use by trustees or debtors in possession under chapter 11 of title

11 shall, in addition to such other matters as are required by law or as the Attorney General in the discretion of the Attorney General shall propose, include–

(1) information about the industry classification, published by the Department of Commerce, for the business conducted by the debtor;

(2) the length of time the cases has been pending;

(3) number of full-time employees as of the date of the order for relief and at the end of each reporting period since the case was filed;

(4) cash receipts, cash disbursements and profitability of the debtor for the most recent period and cumulatively since the date of the order for relief;

(5) compliance with title 11, whether or not tax returns and tax payments since the date of the order for relief has been timely filed and made;

(6) all professional fees approved by the court in the case for the most recent period and cumulatively since the date of the order for relief (separately reported, for the professional fees incurred by or on behalf of the debtor, between those that would have been incurred absent a bankruptcy case and those not); and

(7) plans of reorganization filed and confirmed and, with respect thereto, by class, the recoveries of the holders, expressed in aggregate dollar values and, in the cases of claims, as a percentage of total claims of the class allowed.

## ARBITRATION (CHAPTER 44)

### 28 USC § 651 Authorization of alternative dispute resolution

(a) Definition. For purposes of this chapter, an alternative dispute resolution process includes any process or procedure, other than an adjudication by a presiding judge, in which a neutral third party participates to assist in the resolution of issues in controversy, through processes such as early neutral evaluation, mediation, minitrial, and arbitration as provided in sections 654 through 658.

(b) Authority. Each United States district court shall authorize, by local rule adopted under section 2071(a), the use of alternative dispute resolution processes in all civil actions, including adversary proceedings in bankruptcy, in accordance with this chapter, except that the use of arbitration may be authorized only as provided in section 654. Each United States district court shall devise and implement its own alternative dispute resolution program, by local rule adopted under section 2071(a), to encourage and promote the use of alternative dispute resolution in its district.

(c) Existing Alternative Dispute Resolution Programs. In those courts where an alternative dispute resolution program is in place on the date of the enactment of the Alternative Dispute Resolution Act of 1998, the court shall examine the effectiveness of that program and adopt such improvements to the program as are consistent with the provisions and purposes of this chapter.

(d) Administration of Alternative Dispute Resolution Programs. Each United States district court shall designate an employee, or a judicial officer, who is knowledgeable in alternative dispute resolution practices and processes to implement, administer, oversee, and evaluate the court's alternative dispute resolution program. Such person may also be responsible for recruiting, screening, and training attorneys to serve as neutrals and arbitrators in the court's alternative dispute resolution program.

(e) Title 9 Not Affected. This chapter shall not affect title 9, United States Code.

(f) Program Support. The Federal Judicial Center and the Administrative Office of the United States Courts are authorized to assist the district courts in the establishment and improvement of alternative dispute resolution programs by identifying particular practices employed in successful programs and providing additional assistance as needed and appropriate.

### 28 USC § 652 Jurisdiction

(a) Consideration of Alternative Dispute Resolution in Appropriate Cases. Notwithstanding any provision of law to the contrary and except as provided in subsections (b) and (c), each district court shall, by local rule adopted under section 2071(a), require that litigants in all civil cases consider the use of an alternative dispute resolution process at an appropriate stage in the litigation. Each district court shall provide litigants in all civil cases with at least one alternative dispute resolution process, including, but not limited to, mediation, early neutral evaluation, minitrial, and arbitration as authorized in sections 654 through 658. Any district court that elects to require the use of alternative dispute resolution in certain cases may do so only with respect to mediation, early neutral evaluation, and, if the parties consent, arbitration.

(b) Actions Exempted from Consideration of Alternative Dispute Resolution. Each district court may exempt from the requirements of this section specific cases or categories of cases in which use of alternative dispute resolution would not be appropriate. In defining these exemptions, each district court shall consult with members of the bar, including the United States Attorney for that district.

(c) Authority of the Attorney General. Nothing in this section shall alter or conflict with the authority of the Attorney General to conduct litigation on behalf of the United States, with the authority of any Federal agency authorized to conduct litigation in the United States courts, or with any delegation of litigation authority by the Attorney General.

(d) Confidentiality Provisions. Until such time as rules are adopted under chapter 131 of this title providing for the confidentiality of alternative dispute resolution processes under this chapter, each district court shall, by local rule adopted under section 2071(a), provide for the confidentiality of the alternative dispute resolution processes and to prohibit disclosure of confidential dispute resolution communications.

## 28 USC § 653 Neutrals

(a) Panel of Neutrals. Each district court that authorizes the use of alternative dispute resolution processes shall adopt appropriate processes for making neutrals available for use by the parties for each category of process offered. Each district court shall promulgate its own procedures and criteria for the selection of neutrals on its panels.

(b) Qualifications and Training. Each person serving as a neutral in an alternative dispute resolution process should be qualified and trained to serve as a neutral in the appropriate alternative dispute resolution process. For this purpose, the district court may use, among others, magistrate judges who have been trained to serve as neutrals in alternative dispute resolution processes, professional neutrals from the private sector, and persons who have been trained to serve as neutrals in alternative dispute resolution processes. Until such time as rules are adopted under chapter 131 of this title relating to the disqualification of neutrals, each district court shall issue rules under section 2071(a) relating to the disqualification of neutrals (including, where appropriate, disqualification under section 455 of this title, other applicable law, and professional responsibility standards).

## 28 USC § 654 Arbitration

(a) Referral of Actions to Arbitration. Notwithstanding any provision of law to the contrary and except as provided in subsections (a), (b), and (c) of section 652 and subsection (d) of this section, a district court may allow the referral to arbitration of any civil action (including any adversary proceeding in bankruptcy) pending before it when the parties consent, except that referral to arbitration may not be made where—

(1) the action is based on an alleged violation of a right secured by the Constitution of the United States;

(2) jurisdiction is based in whole or in part on section 1343 of this title; or

(3) the relief sought consists of money damages in an amount greater than $150,000.

(b) Safeguards in Consent Cases. Until such time as rules are adopted under chapter 131 of this title relating to procedures described in this subsection, the district court shall, by local rule adopted under section 2071(a), establish procedures to ensure that any civil action in which arbitration by consent is allowed under subsection (a)–

(1) consent to arbitration is freely and knowingly obtained; and

(2) no party or attorney is prejudiced for refusing to participate in arbitration.

(c) Presumptions. For purposes of subsection (a)(3), a district court may presume damages are not in excess of $150,000 unless counsel certifies that damages exceed such amount.

(d) Existing Programs. Nothing in this chapter is deemed to affect any program in which arbitration is conducted pursuant to section title IX of the Judicial Improvements and Access to Justice Act (Public Law 100-702), as amended by section 1 of Public Law 105-53.

**28 USC § 655 Arbitrators**

(a) Powers of Arbitrators. An arbitrator to whom an action is referred under section 654 shall have the power, within the judicial district of the district court which referred the action to arbitration–

(1) to conduct arbitration hearings;

(2) to administer oaths and affirmations; and

(3) to make awards.

(b) Standards for Certification. Each district court that authorizes arbitration shall establish standards for the certification of arbitrators and shall certify arbitrators to perform services in accordance with such standards and this chapter. The standards shall include provisions requiring that any arbitrator–

(1) shall take the oath or affirmation described in section 453; and

(2) shall be subject to the disqualification rules under section 455.

(c) Immunity. All individuals serving as arbitrators in an alternative dispute resolution program under this chapter are performing quasi-judicial functions and are entitled to the immunities and protections that the law accords to persons serving in such capacity.

**28 USC § 656 Subpoenas**

Rule 45 of the Federal Rules of Civil Procedure (relating to subpoenas) applies to subpoenas for the attendance of witnesses and the production of documentary evidence at an arbitration hearing under this chapter.

## 28 USC § 657 Arbitration award and judgment

(a) FILING AND EFFECT OF ARBITRATION AWARD. An arbitration award made by an arbitrator under this chapter, along with proof of service of such award on the other party by the prevailing party or by the plaintiff, shall be filed promptly after the arbitration hearing is concluded with the clerk of the district court that referred the case to arbitration. Such award shall be entered as the judgment of the court after the time has expired for requesting a trial de novo. The judgment so entered shall be subject to the same provisions of law and shall have the same force and effect as a judgment of the court in a civil action, except that the judgment shall not be subject to review in any other court by appeal or otherwise.

(b) SEALING OF ARBITRATION AWARD. The district court shall provide, by local rule adopted under section 2071(a), that the contents of any arbitration award made under this chapter shall not be made known to any judge who might be assigned to the case until the district court has entered final judgment in the action or the action has otherwise terminated.

(c) TRIAL DE NOVO OF ARBITRATION AWARDS.

(1) TIME FOR FILING DEMAND. Within 30 days after the filing of an arbitration award with a district court under subsection (a), any party may file a written demand for a trial de novo in the district court.

(2) ACTION RESTORED TO COURT DOCKET. Upon a demand for a trial de novo, the action shall be restored to the docket of the court and treated for all purposes as if it had not been referred to arbitration.

(3) EXCLUSION OF EVIDENCE OF ARBITRATION. The court shall not admit at the trial de novo any evidence that there has been an arbitration proceeding, the nature or amount of any award, or any other matter concerning the conduct of the arbitration proceeding, unless—

(A) the evidence would otherwise be admissible in the court under the Federal Rules of Evidence; or

(B) the parties have otherwise stipulated.

## 28 USC § 658 Compensation of arbitrators and neutrals

(a) COMPENSATION. The district court shall, subject to regulations approved by the Judicial Conference of the United States, establish the amount of compensation, if any, that each arbitrator or neutral shall receive for services rendered in each case under this chapter.

(b) TRANSPORTATION ALLOWANCES. Under regulations prescribed by the Director of the Administrative Office of the United States Courts, a district court may reimburse arbitrators and other neutrals for actual transportation expenses necessarily incurred in the performance of duties under this chapter.

## GENERAL PROVISIONS APPLICABLE TO COURT OFFICERS AND EMPLOYEES (CHAPTER 57)

### 28 USC § 959 Trustees and receivers suable; management; State laws

(a) Trustees, receivers or managers of any property, including debtors in possession, may be sued, without leave of the court appointing them, with respect to any of their acts or transactions in carrying on business connected with such property. Such actions shall be subject to the general equity power of such court so far as the same may be necessary to the ends of justice, but this shall not deprive a litigant of his right to trial by jury.

(b) Except as provided in section 1166 of title 11, a trustee, receiver or manager appointed in any cause pending in any court of the United States, including a debtor in possession, shall manage and operate the property in his possession as such trustee, receiver or manager according to the requirements of the valid laws of the State in which such property is situated, in the same manner that the owner or possessor thereof would be bound to do if in possession thereof.

### 28 USC § 960 Tax liability

(a) Any officers and agents conducting any business under authority of a United States court shall be subject to all Federal, State and local taxes applicable to such business to the same extent as if it were conducted by an individual or corporation.

(b) A tax under subsection (a) shall be paid on or before the due date of the tax under applicable nonbankruptcy law, unless—

(1) the tax is a property tax secured by a lien against property that is abandoned under section 554 of title 11, within a reasonable period of time after the lien attaches, by the trustee in a case under title 11; or

(2) payment of the tax is excused under a specific provision of title 11.

(c) In a case pending under chapter 7 of title 11, payment of a tax may be deferred until final distribution is made under section 726 of title 11, if—

(1) the tax was not incurred by a trustee duly appointed or elected under chapter 7 of title 11; or

(2) before the due date of the tax, an order of the court makes a finding of probable insufficiency of funds of the estate to pay in full the administrative expenses allowed under section 503(b) of title 11 that have the same priority in distribution under section 726(b) of title 11 as the priority of that tax.

## DISTRICT COURTS; JURISDICTION (CHAPTER 85)

### 28 USC § 1334 Bankruptcy cases and proceedings

(a) Except as provided in subsection (b) of this section, the district courts shall have original and exclusive jurisdiction of all cases under title 11.

(b) Except as provided in subsection (e)(2), and notwithstanding any Act of Congress that confers exclusive jurisdiction on a court or courts other than the district courts, the district courts shall have original but not exclusive jurisdiction of all civil proceedings arising under title 11, or arising in or related to cases under title 11.

(c) (1) Except with respect to a case under chapter 15 of title 11, nothing in this section prevents a district court in the interest of justice, or in the interest of comity with State courts or respect for State law, from abstaining from hearing a particular proceeding arising under title 11 or arising in or related to a case under title 11.

(2) Upon timely motion of a party in a proceeding based upon a State law claim or State law cause of action, related to a case under title 11 but not arising under title 11 or arising in a case under title 11, with respect to which an action could not have been commenced in a court of the United States absent jurisdiction under this section, the district court shall abstain from hearing such proceeding if an action is commenced, and can be timely adjudicated, in a State forum of appropriate jurisdiction.

(d) Any decision to abstain or not to abstain made under subsection *(c)* (other than a decision not to abstain in a proceeding described in subsection (c)(2)) is not reviewable by appeal or otherwise by the court of appeals under section 158(d), 1291, or 1292 of this title or by the Supreme Court of the United States under section 1254 of this title. Subsection (c) and this subsection shall not be construed to limit the applicability of the stay provided for by section 362 of title 11, United States Code, as such section applies to an action affecting the property of the estate in bankruptcy.

(e) The district court in which a case under title 11 is commenced or is pending shall have exclusive jurisdiction—

(1) of all of the property, wherever located, of the debtor as of the commencement of such case, and of property of the estate; and

(2) over all claims or causes of action that involve construction of section 327 of title 11, United States Code, or rules relating to disclosure requirements under section 327.

## DISTRICT COURTS; VENUE; JURY TRIALS (CHAPTER 87)

### 28 USC § 1404 Change of venue

(a) For the convenience of parties and witnesses, in the interest of justice, a district court may transfer any civil action to any other district or division where it might have been brought or to any district or division to which all parties have consented.

(b) Upon motion, consent or stipulation of all parties, any action, suit or proceeding of a civil nature or any motion or hearing thereof, may be transferred, in the discretion of the court, from the division in which pending to any other division in the same district. Transfer of proceedings in rem brought by or on behalf of the United States may be transferred under this section without the consent of the United States where all other parties request transfer.

(c) A district court may order any civil action to be tried at any place within the division in which it is pending.

(d) Transfers from a district court of the United States to the District Court of Guam, the District Court for the Northern Mariana Islands, or the District Court of the Virgin Islands shall not be permitted under this section. As otherwise used in this section, the term "district court" includes the District Court of Guam, the District Court for the Northern Mariana Islands, and the District Court of the Virgin Islands, and the term "district" includes the territorial jurisdiction of each such court.

### 28 USC § 1406 Cure or waiver of defects

(a) The district court of a district in which is filed a case laying venue in the wrong division or district shall dismiss, or if it be in the interest of justice, transfer such case to any district or division in which it could have been brought.

(b) Nothing in this chapter shall impair the jurisdiction of a district court of any matter involving a party who does not interpose timely and sufficient objection to the venue.

(c) As used in this section, the term "district court" includes the District Court of Guam, the District Court for the Northern Mariana Islands, and the District Court of the Virgin Islands, and the term "district" includes the territorial jurisdiction of each such court.

### 28 USC § 1408 Venue of cases under title 11

Except as provided in section 1410 of this title, a case under title 11 may be commenced in the district court for the district—

(1) in which the domicile, residence, principal place of business in the United States, or principal assets in the United States, of the person or entity that is the subject of such case have been located for the one hundred and eighty days immediately preceding such commencement, or for a longer portion of such one-hundred-and-eighty-day period than the domicile, residence, or principal place of business, in the United States, or principal assets in the United States, of such person were located in any other district; or

(2) in which there is pending a case under title 11 concerning such person's affiliate, general partner, or partnership.

## 28 USC § 1409 Venue of proceedings arising under title 11 or arising in or related to cases under title 11

(a) Except as otherwise provided in subsections (b) and (d), a proceeding arising under title 11 or arising in or related to a case under title 11 may be commenced in the district court in which such case is pending.

(b) Except as provided in subsection (d) of this section, a trustee in a case under title 11 may commence a proceeding arising in or related to such case to recover a money judgment of or property worth less than $1,375[3] or a consumer debt of less than $20,450,[4] or a debt (excluding a consumer debt) against a noninsider of less than $25,000,[5] only in the district court for the district in which the defendant resides.

(c) Except as provided in subsection (b) of this section, a trustee in a case under title 11 may commence a proceeding arising in or related to such case as statutory successor to the debtor or creditors under section 541 or 544(b) of title 11 in the district court for the district where the State or Federal court sits in which, under applicable nonbankruptcy venue provisions, the debtor or creditors, as the case may be, may have commenced an action on which such proceeding is based if the case under title 11 had not been commenced.

(d) A trustee may commence a proceeding arising under title 11 or arising in or related to a case under title 11 based on a claim arising after the commencement of such case from the operation of the business of the debtor only in the district court for the district where a State or Federal court sits in which, under applicable nonbankruptcy venue provisions, an action on such claim may have been brought.

(e) A proceeding arising under title 11 or arising in or related to a case under title 11, based on a claim arising after the commencement of such case from the operation of the business of the debtor, may be commenced against the representative of the estate in such case in the district court for the district where the State or Federal court sits in which the party commencing such proceeding may, under applicable nonbankruptcy venue provisions, have brought an action on such claim, or in the district court in which such case is pending.

---

[3] Ed. Note: For cases commenced in the three-year period before April 1, 2019, the dollar amount is $1,300. *See* 11 U.S.C. § 104(b).

[4] Ed. Note: For cases commenced in the three-year period before April 1, 2019, the dollar amount is $19,250. *See* 11 U.S.C. § 104(b).

[5] Ed. Note: For cases commenced in the three-year period before April 1, 2019, the dollar amount is $12,850. *See* 11 U.S.C. § 104(b). The dollar amount was increased to $13,650 effective April 1, 2019, and was subsequently increased to $25,000 by the Small Business Reorganization Act of 2019, Pub. L. No. 116-54, § 3(b) (2019), effective Feb. 19, 2020. *Id.* § 5.

## 28 USC § 1410 Venue of cases ancillary to foreign proceedings

A case under chapter 15 of title 11 may be commenced in the district court of the United States for the district

(1) in which the debtor has its principal place of business or principal assets in the United States;

(2) if the debtor does not have a place of business or assets in the United States, in which there is pending against the debtor an action or proceeding in a Federal or State court; or

(3) in a case other than those specified in paragraph (1) or (2), in which venue will be consistent with the interests of justice and convenience of the parties, having regard to the relief sought by the foreign representative.

## 28 USC § 1411 Jury trials

(a) Except as provided in subsection (b) of this section, this chapter and title 11 do not affect any right to trial by jury that an individual has under applicable nonbankruptcy law with regard to a personal injury or wrongful death tort claim.

(b) The district court may order the issues arising under section 303 of title 11 to be tried without a jury.

## 28 USC § 1412 Change of venue

A district court may transfer a case or proceeding under title 11 to a district court for another district, in the interest of justice or for the convenience of the parties.

## DISTRICT COURTS; REMOVAL OF CASES FROM STATE COURTS (CHAPTER 89)

### 28 USC § 1441 Removal of civil actions

(a) GENERALLY. Except as otherwise expressly provided by Act of Congress, any civil action brought in a State court of which the district courts of the United States have original jurisdiction, may be removed by the defendant or the defendants, to the district court of the United States for the district and division embracing the place where such action is pending.

(b) REMOVAL BASED ON DIVERSITY OF CITIZENSHIP.

(1) In determining whether a civil action is removable on the basis of the jurisdiction under section 1332(a) of this title, the citizenship of defendants sued under fictitious names shall be disregarded.

(2) A civil action otherwise removable solely on the basis of the jurisdiction under section 1332(a) of this title may not be removed if any of the parties in interest properly joined and served as defendants is a citizen of the State in which such action is brought.

(c) JOINDER OF FEDERAL LAW CLAIMS AND STATE LAW CLAIMS.

(1) If a civil action includes–

(A) a claim arising under the Constitution, laws, or treaties of the United States (within the meaning of section 1331 of this title, and

(B) a claim not within the original or supplemental jurisdiction of the district court or a claim that has been made nonremovable by statute, the entire action may be removed if the action would be removable without the inclusion of the claim described in subparagraph (B).

(2) Upon removal of an action described in paragraph (1), the district court shall sever from the action all claims described in paragraph (1)(B) and shall remand the severed claims to the State court from which the action was removed. Only defendants against whom a claim described in paragraph (1)(A) has been asserted are required to join in or consent to the removal under paragraph (1).

(d) ACTIONS AGAINST FOREIGN STATES. Any civil action brought in a State court against a foreign state as defined in section 1603(a) of this title may be removed by the foreign state to the district court of the United States for the district and division embracing the place where such action is pending. Upon removal the action shall be tried by the court without jury. Where removal is based upon this subsection, the time limitations of section 1446(b) of this chapter may be enlarged at any time for cause shown.

(e) MULTIPARTY, MULTIFORUM JURISDICTION.

(1) Notwithstanding the provisions of subsection (b) of this section, a defendant in a civil action in a State court may remove the action to the district

court of the United States for the district and division embracing the place where the action is pending if—

(A) the action could have been brought in a United States district court under section 1369 of this title; or

(B) the defendant is a party to an action which is or could have been brought, in whole or in part, under section 1369 in a United States district court and arises from the same accident as the action in State court, even if the action to be removed could not have been brought in a district court as an original matter.

The removal of an action under this subsection shall be made in accordance with section 1446 of this title, except that a notice of removal may also be filed before trial of the action in State court within 30 days after the date on which the defendant first becomes a party to an action under section 1369 in a United States district court that arises from the same accident as the action in State court, or at a later time with leave of the district court.

(2) Whenever an action is removed under this subsection and the district court to which it is removed or transferred under section 1407(j) has made a liability determination requiring further proceedings as to damages, the district court shall remand the action to the State court from which it had been removed for the determination of damages, unless the court finds that, for the convenience of parties and witnesses and in the interest of justice, the action should be retained for the determination of damages.

(3) Any remand under paragraph (2) shall not be effective until 60 days after the district court has issued an order determining liability and has certified its intention to remand the removed action for the determination of damages. An appeal with respect to the liability determination of the district court may be taken during that 60-day period to the court of appeals with appellate jurisdiction over the district court. In the event a party files such an appeal, the remand shall not be effective until the appeal has been finally disposed of. Once the remand has become effective, the liability determination shall not be subject to further review by appeal or otherwise.

(4) Any decision under this subsection concerning remand for the determination of damages shall not be reviewable by appeal or otherwise.

(5) An action removed under this subsection shall be deemed to be an action under section 1369 and an action in which jurisdiction is based on section 1369 of this title for purposes of this section and sections 1407, 1697, and 1785 of this title.

(6) Nothing in this subsection shall restrict the authority of the district court to transfer or dismiss an action on the ground of inconvenient forum.

(f) Derivative Removal Jurisdiction. The court to which a civil action is removed under this section is not precluded from hearing and determining any claim in such civil action because the State court from which such civil action is removed did not have jurisdiction over that claim.

## 28 USC § 1447 Procedure after removal generally

(a) In any case removed from a State court, the district court may issue all necessary orders and process to bring before it all proper parties whether served by process issued by the State court or otherwise.

(b) It may require the removing party to file with its clerk copies of all records and proceedings in such State court or may cause the same to be brought before it by writ of certiorari issued to such State court.

(c) A motion to remand the case on the basis of any defect other than lack of subject matter jurisdiction must be made within 30 days after the filing of the notice of removal under section 1446(a). If at any time before final judgment it appears that the district court lacks subject matter jurisdiction, the case shall be remanded. An order remanding the case may require payment of just costs and any actual expenses, including attorney fees, incurred as a result of the removal. A certified copy of the order of remand shall be mailed by the clerk to the clerk of the State court. The State court may thereupon proceed with such case.

(d) An order remanding a case to the State court from which it was removed is not reviewable on appeal or otherwise, except that an order remanding a case to the State court from which it was removed pursuant to 1442 or section 1443 of this title shall be reviewable by appeal or otherwise.

(e) If after removal the plaintiff seeks to join additional defendants whose joinder would destroy subject matter jurisdiction, the court may deny joinder, or permit joinder and remand the action to the State court.

## 28 USC § 1452 Removal of claims related to bankruptcy cases

(a) A party may remove any claim or cause of action in a civil action other than a proceeding before the United States Tax Court or a civil action by a governmental unit to enforce such governmental unit's police or regulatory power, to the district court for the district where such civil action is pending, if such district court has jurisdiction of such claim or cause of action under section 1334 of this title.

(b) The court to which such claim or cause of action is removed may remand such claim or cause of action on any equitable ground. An order entered under this subsection remanding a claim or cause of action, or a decision to not remand, is not reviewable by appeal or otherwise by the court of appeals under section 158(d), 1291, or 1292 of this title or by the Supreme Court of the United States under section 1254 of this title.

## EVIDENCE; WITNESSES (CHAPTER 119)

### 28 USC § 1826 Recalcitrant witnesses

(a) Whenever a witness in any proceeding before or ancillary to any court or grand jury of the United States refuses without just cause shown to comply with an order of the court to testify or provide other information, including any book, paper, document, record, recording or other material, the court, upon such refusal, or when such refusal is duly brought to its attention, may summarily order his confinement at a suitable place until such time as the witness is willing to give such testimony or provide such information. No period of such confinement shall exceed the life of—

(1) the court proceeding, or

(2) the term of the grand jury including extensions, before which such refusal to comply with the court order occurred, but in no event shall such confinement exceed eighteen months.

(b) No person confined pursuant to subsection (a) of this section shall be admitted to bail pending the determination of an appeal taken by him from the order for his confinement if it appears that the appeal is frivolous or taken for delay. Any appeal from an order of confinement under this section shall be disposed of as soon as practicable, but not later than thirty days from the filing of such appeal.

(c) Whoever escapes or attempts to escape from the custody of any facility or from any place in which or to which he is confined pursuant to this section or section 4243 of title 18, or whoever rescues or attempts to rescue or instigates, aids, or assists the escape or attempt to escape of such a person, shall be subject to imprisonment for not more than three years, or a fine of not more than $10,000, or both.

## FEES AND COSTS (CHAPTER 123)

### 28 USC § 1927 Counsel's liability for excessive costs

Any attorney or other person admitted to conduct cases in any court of the United States or any Territory thereof who so multiplies the proceedings in any case unreasonably and vexatiously may be required by the court to satisfy personally the excess costs, expenses, and attorneys' fees reasonably incurred because of such conduct.

### 28 USC § 1930 Bankruptcy fees

(a) The parties commencing a case under title 11 shall pay to the clerk of the district court or the clerk of the bankruptcy court, if one has been certified pursuant to section 156(b) of this title, the following filing fees:

(1) For a case commenced under–

(A) chapter 7 of title 11, $245, and

(B) chapter 13 of title 11, $235.

(2) For a case commenced under chapter 9 of title 11, equal to the fee specified in paragraph (3) for filing a case under chapter 11 of title 11. The amount by which the fee payable under this paragraph exceeds $300 shall be deposited in the fund established under section 1931 of this title.

(3) For a case commenced under chapter 11 of title 11 that does not concern a railroad, as defined in section 101 of title 11, $1,167.

(4) For a case commenced under chapter 11 of title 11 concerning a railroad, as so defined, $1,000.

(5) For a case commenced under chapter 12 of title 11, $200.

(6) (A) Except as provided in subparagraph (B), in addition to the filing fee paid to the clerk, a quarterly fee shall be paid to the United States trustee, for deposit in the Treasury, in each case under chapter 11 of title 11, other than under subchapter V, for each quarter (including any fraction thereof) until the case is converted or dismissed, whichever occurs first. The fee shall be $325 for each quarter in which disbursements total less than $15,000; $650 for each quarter in which disbursements total $15,000 or more but less than $75,000; $975 for each quarter in which disbursements total $75,000 or more but less than $150,000; $1,625 for each quarter in which disbursements total $150,000 or more but less than $225,000; $1,950 for each quarter in which disbursements total $225,000 or more but less than $300,000; $4,875 for each quarter in which disbursements total $300,000 or more but less than $1,000,000; $6,500 for each quarter in which disbursements total $1,000,000 or more but less than $2,000,000; $9,750 for each quarter in which disbursements total $2,000,000 or more but less than $3,000,000; $10,400 for each quarter in which disbursements total $3,000,000 or more but less than $5,000,000; $13,000 for each quarter in which disbursements total $5,000,000 or more but less than $15,000,000; $20,000 for each quarter in which disbursements total $15,000,000 or more but less

than $30,000,000; $30,000 for each quarter in which disbursements total more than $30,000,000. The fee shall be payable on the last day of the calendar month following the calendar quarter for which the fee is owed.

(B) (i) During the 5-year period beginning on January 1, 2021, in addition to the filing fee paid to the clerk, a quarterly fee shall be paid to the United States trustee, for deposit in the Treasury, in each open and reopened case under chapter 11 of title 11, other than under subchapter V, for each quarter (including any fraction thereof) until the case is closed, converted, or dismissed, whichever occurs first.

(ii) The fee shall be the greater of—

(I) 0.4 percent of disbursements or $250 for each quarter in which disbursements total less than $1,000,000; and

(II) 0.8 percent of disbursements but not more than $250,000 for each quarter in which disbursements total at least $1,000,000.

(iii) The fee shall be payable on the last day of the calendar month following the calendar quarter for which the fee is owed.

(7) In districts that are not part of a United States trustee region as defined in section 581 of this title, the Judicial Conference of the United States shall require the debtor in a case under chapter 11 of title 11 to pay fees equal to those imposed by paragraph (6) of this subsection. Such fees shall be deposited as offsetting receipts to the fund established under section 1931 of this title and shall remain available until expended.

An individual commencing a voluntary case or a joint case under title 11 may pay such fee in installments. For converting, on request of the debtor, a case under chapter 7, or 13 of title 11, to a case under chapter 11 of title 11, the debtor shall pay to the clerk of the district court or the clerk of the bankruptcy court, if one has been certified pursuant to section 156(b) of this title, a fee of the amount equal to the difference between the fee specified in paragraph (3) and the fee specified in paragraph (1).

(b) The Judicial Conference of the United States may prescribe additional fees in cases under title 11 of the same kind as the Judicial Conference prescribes under section 1914(b) of this title.

(c) Upon the filing of any separate or joint notice of appeal or application for appeal or upon the receipt of any order allowing, or notice of the allowance of, an appeal or a writ of certiorari $5 shall be paid to the clerk of the court, by the appellant or petitioner.

(d) Whenever any case or proceeding is dismissed in any bankruptcy court for want of jurisdiction, such court may order the payment of just costs.

(e) The clerk of the court may collect only the fees prescribed under this section.

(f) (1) Under the procedures prescribed by the Judicial Conference of the United States, the district court or bankruptcy court may waive the filing fee in a case under chapter 7 of title 11 for an individual if the court determines that such individual has income less than 150 percent of the income official poverty line (as defined by the Office of Management and Budget, and revised annually in accordance with section 673(2) of the Omnibus Budget Reconciliation Act of 1981) applicable to a family of the size involved and is unable to pay that fee in installments. For purposes of this paragraph, the term "filing fee" means the filing fee required by subsection (a), or any other fee prescribed by the Judicial Conference under subsections (b) and (c) that is payable to the clerk upon the commencement of a case under chapter 7.

(2) The district court or the bankruptcy court may waive for such debtors other fees prescribed under subsections (b) and (c).

(3) This subsection does not restrict the district court or the bankruptcy court from waiving, in accordance with Judicial Conference policy, fees prescribed under this section for other debtors and creditors.

**EDITORS' NOTE:** The Bankruptcy Court Miscellaneous Fee Schedule, effective December 1, 2020, is as follows:

BANKRUPTCY COURT MISCELLANEOUS FEE SCHEDULE

The fees included in the Bankruptcy Court Miscellaneous Fee Schedule are to be charged for services provided by the bankruptcy courts.

- The United States should not be charged fees under this schedule, with the exception of those specifically prescribed in Items 1, 3 and 5 when the information requested is available through remote electronic access.
- Federal agencies or programs that are funded from judiciary appropriations (agencies, organizations, and individuals providing services authorized by the Criminal Justice Act, 18 U.S.C. § 3006A, and bankruptcy administrators) should not be charged any fees under this schedule.

1. a. For reproducing any document, and providing a copy in paper form, $.50 per page. This fee applies to services rendered on behalf of the United States if the document requested is available through electronic access.

   b. For reproducing and transmitting in any matter a copy of an electronic record stored outside of the court's electronic case management system, including but not limited to, document files, audio recordings, and video recordings, $31 per record provided. Audio recordings of court proceedings continue to be governed by a separate fee under item 3 of this schedule.

2. For certification of any document, $11.

   For exemplification of any document, $23.

3. For reproduction of an audio recording of a court proceeding, $32. This fee applies to services rendered on behalf of the United States if the recording is available electronically.

4. For filing an amendment to the debtor's schedules of creditors, lists of creditors, or mailing list, $32, except:

   - The bankruptcy judge may, for good cause, waive the charge in any case.

- This fee must not be charged if—
  - the amendment is to change the address of a creditor or an attorney for a creditor listed on the schedules; or
  - the amendment is to add the name and address of an attorney for a creditor listed on the schedules.

5. For conducting a search of the bankruptcy court records, $32 per name or item searched. This fee applies to services rendered on behalf of the United States if the information requested is available through electronic access.
6. For filing a complaint, $350, except:
   - If the trustee or debtor-in-possession files the complaint, the fee must be paid only by the estate, to the extent there is an estate.
   - This fee must not be charged if—
     - the debtor is the plaintiff; or
     - a child support creditor or representative files the complaint and submits the form required by § 304(g) of the Bankruptcy Reform Act of 1994.
7. For filing any document that is not related to a pending case or proceeding, $49.
8. Administrative fee:
   - For filing a petition under Chapter 7, 12, or 13, $78.
   - For filing a petition under Chapter 9, 11, or 15, $571.
   - When a motion to divide a joint case under Chapter 7, 12, or 13 is filed, $78.
   - When a motion to divide a joint case under Chapter 11 is filed, $571.
9. For payment to trustees pursuant to 11 U.S.C. § 330(b)(2), a $15 fee applies in the following circumstances:
   - For filing a petition under Chapter 7.
   - For filing a notice of conversion to a Chapter 7 case.
   - For filing a motion to convert a case to a Chapter 7 case.
   - For filing a motion to divide a joint Chapter 7 case.
   - For filing a motion to reopen a Chapter 7 case.
10. In addition to any fees imposed under Item 9, above, the following fees must be collected:
    - For filing a motion to convert a Chapter 12 case to a Chapter 7 case or a notice of conversion pursuant to 11 U.S.C. § 1208(a), $45.
    - For filing a motion to convert a Chapter 13 case to a Chapter 7 case or a notice of conversion pursuant to 11 U.S.C. § 1307(a), $10.

JUDICIAL CODE

The fee amounts in this item are derived from the fees prescribed in 28 U.S.C. § 1930(a).

If the trustee files the motion to convert, the fee is payable only from the estate that exists prior to conversion.

If the filing fee for the chapter to which the case is requested to be converted is less than the fee paid at the commencement of the case, no refund may be provided.

11. For filing a motion to reopen, the following fees apply:
    - For filing a motion to reopen a Chapter 7 case, $245.
    - For filing a motion to reopen a Chapter 9 case, $1167.
    - For filing a motion to reopen a Chapter 11 case, $1167.
    - For filing a motion to reopen a Chapter 12 case, $200.
    - For filing a motion to reopen a Chapter 13 case, $235.
    - For filing a motion to reopen a Chapter 15 case, $1167.

    The fee amounts in this item are derived from the fees prescribed in 28 U.S.C. § 1930(a).

    The reopening fee must be charged when a case has been closed without a discharge being entered.

    The court may waive this fee under appropriate circumstances or may defer payment of the fee from trustees pending discovery of additional assets. If payment is deferred, the fee should be waived if no additional assets are discovered.

    The reopening fee must not be charged in the following situations:
    - to permit a party to file a complaint to obtain a determination under Rule 4007(b);
    - when a debtor files a motion to reopen a case based upon an alleged violation of the terms of the discharge under 11 U.S.C. § 524;
    - when the reopening is to correct an administrative error;
    - to redact a record already filed in a case, pursuant to Fed. R. Bankr. P. 9037, if redaction is the only reason for reopening; or
    - when a party files a motion to reopen a case to request to withdraw unclaimed funds, unless the court orders otherwise.

12. For retrieval of one box of records from a Federal Records Center, National Archives, or other storage location removed from the place of business of the court, $64. For retrievals involving multiple boxes, $39 for each additional box. For electronic retrievals, $10 plus any charges assessed by the Federal Records Center, National Archives, or other storage location removed from the place of business of the courts.

13. For any payment returned or denied for insufficient funds, or reversed due to a chargeback, $53.
14. For filing an appeal or cross appeal from a judgment, order, or decree, $293.

    This fee is collected in addition to the statutory fee of $5 that is collected under 28 U.S.C. § 1930(c) when a notice of appeal is filed.

    Parties filing a joint notice of appeal should pay only one fee.

    If a trustee or debtor-in-possession is the appellant, the fee must be paid only by the estate, to the extent there is an estate.

    Upon notice from the court of appeals that a direct appeal or direct cross appeal has been authorized, an additional fee of $207 must be collected.
15. For filing a case under Chapter 15 of the Bankruptcy Code, $1167.

    This fee is derived from and equal to the fee prescribed in 28 U.S.C. § 1930(a)(3) for filing a case commenced under Chapter 11 of Title 11.
16. The court may charge and collect fees commensurate with the cost of providing copies of the local rules of court. The court may also distribute copies of the local rules without charge.
17.
    - For handling registry funds deposited with and held by the court, the clerk shall assess a charge from interest earnings, in accordance with the detailed fee schedule issued by the Director of the Administrative Office of the United States Courts.
    - For management of registry funds invested through the Court Registry Investment System, a fee at an annual rate of 10 basis points of assets on deposit shall be assessed from interest earnings, excluding registry funds from disputed ownership interpleader cases deposited under 28 U.S.C. § 1335 and held in a Court Registry Investment System Disputed Ownership Fund.
    - For management of funds deposited under 28 U.S.C. § 1335 and invested in a Disputed Ownership Fund through the Court Registry Investment System, a fee at an annual rate of 20 basis points of assets on deposit shall be assessed from interest earnings.
    - The Director of the Administrative Office has the authority to waive these fees for cause.
18. For a motion filed by the debtor to divide a joint case filed under 11 U.S.C. § 302, the following fees apply:
    - For filing a motion to divide a joint Chapter 7 case, $245.
    - For filing a motion to divide a joint Chapter 11 case, $1167.
    - For filing a motion to divide a joint Chapter 12 case, $200.

- For filing a motion to divide a joint Chapter 13 case, $235.

These fees are derived from and equal to the filing fees prescribed in 28 U.S.C. § 1930(a).

19. For filing the following motions, $188:
    - To terminate, annul, modify or condition the automatic stay;
    - To compel abandonment of property of the estate pursuant to Rule 6007(b) of the Federal Rules of Bankruptcy Procedure;
    - To withdraw the reference of a case or proceeding under 28 U.S.C. § 157(d); or
    - To sell property of the estate free and clear of liens under 11 U.S.C. § 363(f).

    This fee must not be collected in the following situations:
    - For a motion for relief from the co-debtor stay;
    - For a stipulation for court approval of an agreement for relief from a stay; or
    - For a motion filed by a child support creditor or its representative, if the form required by § 304(g) of the Bankruptcy Reform Act of 1994 is filed.
20. For filing a transfer of claim, $26 per claim transferred.
21. For filing a motion to redact a record, $26 per affected case. The court may waive this fee under appropriate circumstances.

## BANKRUPTCY RULES (CHAPTER 131)

### 28 USC § 2075 Bankruptcy rules

The Supreme Court shall have the power to prescribe by general rules, the forms of process, writs, pleadings, and motions, and the practice and procedure in cases under title 11.

Such rules shall not abridge, enlarge, or modify any substantive right.

The Supreme Court shall transmit to Congress not later than May 1 of the year in which a rule prescribed under this section is to become effective a copy of the proposed rule. The rule shall take effect no earlier than December 1 of the year in which it is transmitted to Congress unless otherwise provided by law.

The bankruptcy rules promulgated under this section shall prescribe a form for the statement required under section 707(b)(2)(C) of title 11 and may provide general rules on the content of such statement.

# Additional Statutory Provisions

**Limitations—Bankruptcy-Related Provision**



**Postsentence Administration**



**Immunity of Witnesses**



**Indian Health Professional Personnel**



**Internal Revenue Code**



**Navigation and Navigable Waters**



**Pay and Allowances of the Uniformed Services**

**Uncodified Provision Relating to Child Support Creditors (Bankruptcy Reform Act of 1994)**



**Uncodified Discharge Provision Relating to the Troops-to-Teachers Program (Pub. L. No. 106-65)**



**Selected Uncodified Provisions Relating to the Bankruptcy Administrator Program and the North Carolina and Alabama Exemption From the U.S. Trustee Program**

**(Bankruptcy Judges, U.S. Trustees & Family Farmer Bankruptcy Act of 1986)**



**Judicial Improvements Act of 1990**



**Bankruptcy Reform Act of 1994**



**Federal Courts Improvement Act of 2000**



**Selected Uncodified Provisions of the Bankruptcy Abuse Prevention and Consumer Protection Act of 2005 (Pub. L. No. 109-8)**



ADDITIONAL STATUTES

## TITLE 10 ARMED FORCES
## Enlistments (Chapter 31)

### 10 USC § 510 Enlistment incentives for pursuit of skills to facilitate national service.

* * *

(b) National Call to Service Participant. In this section, the term "National Call to Service participant" means a person who has not previously served in the armed forces who enters into an original enlistment pursuant to a written agreement with the Secretary of a military department (in such form and manner as may be prescribed by that Secretary) under which the person agrees to perform a period of national service as specified in subsection (c).

* * *

(i) Repayment. If a National Call to Service participant who has entered into an agreement under subsection (b) and received or benefitted from an incentive under paragraph (1) or (2) of subsection (e) fails to complete the total period of service specified in the agreement, the National Call to Service participant shall be subject to the repayment provisions of section 303a(e) or 373 of title 37.

* * *

### 10 USC § 511 College First Program.

(a) Program Authority. The Secretary of each military department may establish a program to increase the number of, and the level of the qualifications of, persons entering the armed forces as enlisted members by encouraging recruits to pursue higher education or vocational or technical training before entry into active service.

* * *

(e) Recoupment of Allowance.

* * *

(3) A discharge of a person in bankruptcy under title 11 that is entered less than five years after the date on which the person was, or was to be, enlisted in the regular Army pursuant to the delayed entry authority under section 513 [of this title] does not discharge that person from a debt arising under paragraph (1).

* * *

## Training Generally (Chapter 101)

### 10 USC § 2005 Advanced education assistance: active duty agreement; reimbursement requirements.

(a) The Secretary concerned may require, as a condition to the Secretary providing advanced education assistance to any person, that such person enter into a written agreement with the Secretary concerned under the terms of which such person shall agree—

(1) to complete the educational requirements specified in the agreement and to serve on active duty for a period specified in the agreement;

(2) that if such person fails to complete the education requirements specified in the agreement, such person will serve on active duty for a period specified in the agreement;

(3) that if such person does not complete the period of active duty specified in the agreement, or does not fulfill any term or condition prescribed pursuant to paragraph (4), such person shall be subject to the repayment provisions of section 303a(e) or 373 of title 37; and

(4) to such other terms and conditions as the Secretary concerned may prescribe to protect the interest of the United States.

* * *

(c) As a condition of the Secretary concerned providing financial assistance under section 2107 or 2107a of this title to any person, the Secretary concerned shall require that the person enter into the agreement described in subsection (a). In addition to the requirements of paragraphs (1) through (4) of such subsection, the agreement shall specify that, if the person does not complete the education requirements specified in the agreement or does not fulfill any term or condition prescribed pursuant to paragraph (4) of such subsection, the person shall be subject to the repayment provisions of section 303a(e) or 373 of title 37 without the Secretary first ordering such person to active duty as provided for under subsection (a)(2) and sections 2107(f) and 2107a(f) of this title.

* * *

## Armed Forces Health Professions Financial Assistance Programs (Chapter 105)

### 10 USC § 2130a Financial assistance: nurse officer candidates.

(a) Bonus Authorized.

(1) A person described in subsection (b) who, during the period beginning on November 29, 1989, and ending on December 31, 2021, executes a written agreement in accordance with subsection (c) to accept an appointment as a nurse officer may, upon the acceptance of the agreement by the Secretary concerned, be paid an accession bonus of not more than $20,000. The bonus shall be paid in periodic installments, as determined by the Secretary concerned at the time the agreement is accepted, except that the first installment may not exceed $10,000.

(2) In addition to the accession bonus payable under paragraph (1), a person selected under such paragraph shall be entitled to a monthly stipend in an amount not to exceed the stipend rate in effect under section 2121(d) of this title for each month the individual is enrolled as a full-time student in an accredited baccalaureate degree program in nursing at a civilian educational institution by the Secretary selecting the person. The continuation bonus may be paid for not more than 24 months.

* * *

(d) Repayment. A person who does not complete a nursing degree program in which the person is enrolled in accordance with the agreement entered into under subsection (a), or having completed the nursing degree program, does not become an officer in the Nurse Corps of the Army or the Navy or an officer designated as a nurse officer of the Air Force or commissioned corps of the Public Health Service or does not complete the period of obligated active service required under the agreement, shall be subject to the repayment provisions of section 303a(e) of title 37.

* * *

## Information Security Scholarship Program (Chapter 112)

### 10 USC § 2200a Scholarship program.

(a) Authority. The Secretary of Defense may, subject to subsection (f), provide financial assistance in accordance with this section to a person—

(1) who is pursuing an associate, baccalaureate, or advanced degree, or a certification, in a cyber discipline referred to in section 2200(a) of this title at an institution of higher education; and

(2) who enters into an agreement with the Secretary as described in subsection (b).

* * *

(e) Repayment for Period of Unserved Obligated Service.

(1) A member of an armed force who does not complete the period of active duty specified in the service agreement under subsection (b) shall be subject to the repayment provisions of section 303a(e) or 373 of title 37.

(2) A civilian employee of the Department of Defense who voluntarily terminates service before the end of the period of obligated service required under an agreement entered into under subsection (b) shall be subject to the repayment provisions of section 303a(e) or 373 of title 37 in the same manner and to the same extent as if the civilian employee were a member of the armed forces.

* * *

## Educational Assistance for Members of the Selected Reserve (Chapter 1606)

### 10 USC § 16135 Failure to participate satisfactorily; penalties.

(a) Penalties. At the option of the Secretary concerned, a member of the Selected Reserve of an armed force who does not participate satisfactorily in required training as a member of the Selected Reserve during a term of enlistment or other period of obligated service that created entitlement of the member to educational assistance under this chapter, and during which the member has received such assistance, may—

(1) be ordered to active duty for a period of two years or the period of obligated service the person has remaining under section 16132 of this title, whichever is less; or

(2) be subject to the repayment provisions under section 303a(e) or 373 of title 37.

(b) Effect of Repayment. Any repayment under section 303a(e) or 373 of title 37 shall not affect the period of obligation of a member to serve as a Reserve in the Selected Reserve.

## TITLE 14 COAST GUARD

### 14 USC § 3710 Reserve student pre-commissioning assistance program.

(a) The Secretary may provide financial assistance to an eligible enlisted member of the Coast Guard Reserve, not on active duty, for expenses of the member while the member is pursuing on a full-time basis at an institution of higher education a program of education approved by the Secretary that leads to—

(1) a baccalaureate degree in not more than 5 academic years; or

(2) a post-baccalaureate degree.

* * *

(g) (1) If a member requests to be released from the program and the request is accepted by the Secretary, or if the member fails because of misconduct to complete the period of active duty specified, or if the member fails to fulfill any term or condition of the written agreement required to be eligible for financial assistance under this section, the financial assistance shall be terminated. The Secretary may request the member to reimburse the United States in an amount that bears the same ratio to the total costs of the education provided to that member as the unserved portion of active duty bears to the total period of active duty the member agreed to serve. The Secretary shall have the option to order such reimbursement without first ordering the member to active duty. An obligation to reimburse the United States imposed under this paragraph is a debt owed to the United States.

* * *

(3) A discharge in bankruptcy under title 11 that is entered less than 5 years after the termination of a written agreement entered into under subsection (b) does not discharge the individual signing the agreement from a debt arising under such agreement or under paragraph (1).

* * *

ADDITIONAL STATUTES

## TITLE 18 CRIMES AND CRIMINAL PROCEDURE
## Bankruptcy Crimes (Chapter 9)

### 18 USC § 151 Definition.

As used in this chapter, the term "debtor" means a debtor concerning whom a petition has been filed under title 11.

### 18 USC § 152 Concealment of assets; false oaths and claims; bribery.

A person who—

(1) knowingly and fraudulently conceals from a custodian, trustee, marshal, or other officer of the court charged with the control or custody of property, or, in connection with a case under title 11, from creditors or the United States Trustee, any property belonging to the estate of a debtor;

(2) knowingly and fraudulently makes a false oath or account in or in relation to any case under title 11;

(3) knowingly and fraudulently makes a false declaration, certificate, verification, or statement under penalty of perjury as permitted under section 1746 of title 28, in or in relation to any case under title 11;

(4) knowingly and fraudulently presents any false claim for proof against the estate of a debtor, or uses any such claim in any case under title 11, in a personal capacity or as or through an agent, proxy, or attorney;

(5) knowingly and fraudulently receives any material amount of property from a debtor after the filing of a case under title 11, with intent to defeat the provisions of title 11;

(6) knowingly and fraudulently gives, offers, receives, or attempts to obtain any money or property, remuneration, compensation, reward, advantage, or promise thereof for acting or forbearing to act in any case under title 11;

(7) in a personal capacity or as an agent or officer of any person or corporation, in contemplation of a case under title 11 by or against the person or any other person or corporation, or with intent to defeat the provisions of title 11, knowingly and fraudulently transfers or conceals any of his property or the property of such other person or corporation;

(8) after the filing of a case under title 11 or in contemplation thereof, knowingly and fraudulently conceals, destroys, mutilates, falsifies, or makes a false entry in any recorded information (including books, documents, records, and papers) relating to the property or financial affairs of a debtor; or

(9) after the filing of a case under title 11, knowingly and fraudulently withholds from a custodian, trustee, marshal, or other officer of the court or a United States Trustee entitled to its possession, any recorded information (including books, documents, records, and papers) relating to the property or financial affairs of a debtor,

shall be fined under this title, imprisoned not more than 5 years, or both.

**18 USC § 153 Embezzlement against estate.**

(a) Offense. A person described in subsection (b) who knowingly and fraudulently appropriates to the person's own use, embezzles, spends, or transfers any property or secretes or destroys any document belonging to the estate of a debtor shall be fined under this title, imprisoned not more than 5 years, or both.

(b) Person to Whom Section Applies. A person described in this subsection is one who has access to property or documents belonging to an estate by virtue of the person's participation in the administration of the estate as a trustee, custodian, marshal, attorney, or other officer of the court or as an agent, employee, or other person engaged by such an officer to perform a service with respect to the estate.

**18 USC § 154 Adverse interest and conduct of officers.**

A person who, being a custodian, trustee, marshal, or other officer of the court—

(1) knowingly purchases, directly or indirectly, any property of the estate of which the person is such an officer in a case under title 11;

(2) knowingly refuses to permit a reasonable opportunity for the inspection by parties in interest of the documents and accounts relating to the affairs of estates in the person's charge by parties when directed by the court to do so; or

(3) knowingly refuses to permit a reasonable opportunity for the inspection by the United States Trustee of the documents and accounts relating to the affairs of an estate in the person's charge,

shall be fined under this title and shall forfeit the person's office, which shall thereupon become vacant.

**18 USC § 155 Fee agreements in cases under title 11 and receiverships.**

Whoever, being a party in interest, whether as a debtor, creditor, receiver, trustee or representative of any of them, or attorney for any such party in interest, in any receivership or case under title 11 in any United States court or under its supervision, knowingly and fraudulently enters into any agreement, express or implied, with another such party in interest or attorney for another such party in interest, for the purpose of fixing the fees or other compensation to be paid to any party in interest or to any attorney for any party in interest for services rendered in connection therewith, from the assets of the estate shall be fined under this title or imprisoned not more than one year, or both.

**18 USC § 156 Knowing disregard of bankruptcy law or rule.**

(a) Definitions. In this section—

(1) the term "bankruptcy petition preparer" means a person, other than the debtor's attorney or an employee of such an attorney, who prepares for compensation a document for filing; and

(2) the term "document for filing" means a petition or any other document prepared for filing by a debtor in a United States bankruptcy court or a United

ADDITIONAL STATUTES

States district court in connection with a case under title 11.

(b) OFFENSE. If a bankruptcy case or related proceeding is dismissed because of a knowing attempt by a bankruptcy petition preparer in any manner to disregard the requirements of title 11, United States Code, or the Federal Rules of Bankruptcy Procedure, the bankruptcy petition preparer shall be fined under this title, imprisoned not more than 1 year, or both.

**18 USC § 157 Bankruptcy fraud.**[1]

A person who, having devised or intending to devise a scheme or artifice to defraud and for the purpose of executing or concealing such a scheme or artifice or attempting to do so—

(1) files a petition under title 11, including a fraudulent involuntary petition under section 303 of such title;

(2) files a document in a proceeding under title 11; or

(3) makes a false or fraudulent representation, claim, or promise concerning or in relation to a proceeding under title 11, at any time before or after the filing of the petition, or in relation to a proceeding falsely asserted to be pending under such title,

shall be fined under this title, imprisoned not more than 5 years, or both.

**18 USC § 158 Designation of United States attorneys and agents of the Federal Bureau of Investigation to address abusive reaffirmations of debt and materially fraudulent statements in bankruptcy schedules.**

(a) IN GENERAL. The Attorney General of the United States shall designate the individuals described in subsection (b) to have primary responsibility in carrying out enforcement activities in addressing violations of section 152 or 157 relating to abusive reaffirmations of debt. In addition to addressing the violations referred to in the preceding sentence, the individuals described under subsection (b) shall address violations of section 152 or 157 relating to materially fraudulent statements in bankruptcy schedules that are intentionally false or intentionally misleading.

(b) UNITED STATES ATTORNEYS AND AGENTS OF THE FEDERAL BUREAU OF INVESTIGATION. The individuals referred to in subsection (a) are—

(1) the United States attorney for each judicial district of the United States; and

(2) an agent of the Federal Bureau of Investigation for each field office of the Federal Bureau of Investigation.

(c) BANKRUPTCY INVESTIGATIONS. Each United States attorney designated under this section shall, in addition to any other responsibilities, have primary responsibility

---

[1] ED. NOTE: Pub. L. No. 109-8, which directed insertion of "including a fraudulent involuntary bankruptcy petition under section 303 of such title" after "title 11," was executed by making the insertion after "title 11" wherever appearing, to reflect the probable intent of Congress.

for carrying out the duties of a United States attorney under section 3057.

(d) BANKRUPTCY PROCEDURES. The bankruptcy courts shall establish procedures for referring any case that may contain a materially fraudulent statement in a bankruptcy schedule to the individuals designated under this section.

## Obstruction of Justice (Chapter 73)

### 18 USC § 1519 Destruction, alteration, or falsification of records in Federal investigations and bankruptcy.

Whoever knowingly alters, destroys, mutilates, conceals, covers up, falsifies, or makes a false entry in any record, document, or tangible object with the intent to impede, obstruct, or influence the investigation or proper administration of any matter within the jurisdiction of any department or agency of the United States or any case filed under title 11, or in relation to or contemplation of any such matter or case, shall be fined under this title, imprisoned not more than 20 years, or both.

**Wire and Electronic Communications**
**Interception and Interception of Oral Communications**
**(Chapter 119)**

## 18 USC § 2516 Authorization for interception of wire, oral, or electronic communications.

(1) The Attorney General, Deputy Attorney General, Associate Attorney General, or any Assistant Attorney General, any acting Assistant Attorney General, or any Deputy Assistant Attorney General or acting Deputy Assistant Attorney General in the Criminal Division or National Security Division specially designated by the Attorney General, may authorize an application to a Federal judge of competent jurisdiction for, and such judge may grant in conformity with section 2518 of this chapter an order authorizing or approving the interception of wire or oral communications by the Federal Bureau of Investigation, or a Federal agency having responsibility for the investigation of the offense as to which the application is made, when such interception may provide or has provided evidence of–

* * *

(e) any offense involving fraud connected with a case under title 11 or the manufacture, importation, receiving, concealment, buying, selling, or otherwise dealing in narcotic drugs, marihuana, or other dangerous drugs, punishable under any law of the United States;

* * *

## Arrest and Commitment (Chapter 203)

### 18 USC § 3057 Bankruptcy investigations.

(a) Any judge, receiver,[2] or trustee having reasonable grounds for believing that any violation under chapter 9 of this title or other laws of the United States relating to insolvent debtors, receiverships or reorganization plans has been committed, or that an investigation should be had in connection therewith, shall report to the appropriate United States attorney all the facts and circumstances of the case, the names of the witnesses and the offense or offenses believed to have been committed. Where one of such officers has made such report, the others need not do so.

(b) The United States attorney thereupon shall inquire into the facts and report thereon to the judge and if it appears probable that any such offense has been committed, shall without delay, present the matter to the grand jury, unless upon inquiry and examination he decides that the ends of public justice do not require investigation or prosecution, in which case he shall report the facts to the Attorney General for his direction.

---

[2] Ed. Note: The Code abolishes the office of "receiver." In lieu thereof, an "interim trustee" is appointed at the outset of a chapter 7 case.

## Limitations (Chapter 213)

### 18 USC § 3284 Concealment of bankrupt's assets.

The concealment of assets of a debtor in a case under title 11 shall be deemed to be a continuing offense until the debtor shall have been finally discharged or a discharge denied, and the period of limitations shall not begin to run until such final discharge or denial of discharge.

## Postsentence Administration (Chapter 229)

### 18 USC § 3613 Civil remedies for satisfaction of an unpaid fine.

(a) ENFORCEMENT. The United States may enforce a judgment imposing a fine in accordance with the practices and procedures for the enforcement of a civil judgment under Federal law or State law. Notwithstanding any other Federal law (including section 207 of the Social Security Act), a judgment imposing a fine may be enforced against all property or rights to property of the person fined, except that—

(1) property exempt from levy for taxes pursuant to section 6334(a) (1), (2), (3), (4), (5), (6), (7), (8), (10), and (12) of the Internal Revenue Code of 1986 shall be exempt from enforcement of the judgment under Federal law;

(2) section 3014 of chapter 176 of title 28 shall not apply to enforcement under Federal law; and

(3) the provisions of section 303 of the Consumer Credit Protection Act (15 U.S.C. 1673) shall apply to enforcement of the judgment under Federal law or State law.

* * *

(c) LIEN. A fine imposed pursuant to the provisions of subchapter C of chapter 227 of this title, an assessment imposed pursuant to section 2259A of this title, or an order of restitution made pursuant to sections [section] 2248, 2259, 2264, 2327, 3663, 3663A, or 3664 of this title, is a lien in favor of the United States on all property and rights to property of the person fined as if the liability of the person fined were a liability for a tax assessed under the Internal Revenue Code of 1986. The lien arises on the entry of judgment and continues for 20 years or until the liability is satisfied, remitted, set aside, or is terminated under subsection (b).

* * *

(e) DISCHARGE OF DEBT INAPPLICABLE. No discharge of debts in a proceeding pursuant to any chapter of title 11, United States Code, shall discharge liability to pay a fine pursuant to this section, and a lien filed as prescribed by this section shall not be voided in a bankruptcy proceeding.

* * *

## Immunity of Witnesses (Chapter 601)

### 18 USC § 6001 Definitions.

As used in this chapter [18 U.S.C. § 6001 *et seq.*]—

(1) "agency of the United States" means any executive department as defined in section 101 of title 5, United States Code, a military department as defined in section 102 of title 5, United States Code, the Nuclear Regulatory Commission, the Board of Governors of the Federal Reserve System, the China Trade Act registrar appointed under 53 Stat. 1432 (15 U.S.C. § 143), the Commodity Futures Trading Commission, the Federal Communications Commission, the Federal Deposit Insurance Corporation, the Federal Maritime Commission, the Federal Power Commission, the Federal Trade Commission, the Surface Transportation Board, the National Labor Relations Board, the National Transportation Safety Board, the Railroad Retirement Board, an arbitration board established under 48 Stat. 1193 (45 U.S.C. § 157), the Securities and Exchange Commission, or a board established under 49 Stat. 31 (15 U.S.C. § 715d);

(2) "other information" includes any book, paper, document, record, recording, or other material;

(3) "proceeding before an agency of the United States" means any proceeding before such an agency with respect to which it is authorized to issue subpenas and to take testimony or receive other information from witnesses under oath; and

(4) "court of the United States" means any of the following courts: the Supreme Court of the United States, a United States court of appeals, a United States district court established under chapter 5, title 28, United States Code, a United States bankruptcy court established under chapter 6, title 28, United States Code, the District of Columbia Court of Appeals, the Superior Court of the District of Columbia, the District Court of Guam, the District Court of the Virgin Islands, the United States Claims Court [United States Court of Federal Claims], the Tax Court of the United States, the Court of International Trade, and the Court of Appeals for the Armed Forces.

## TITLE 25 INDIANS

### 25 USC § 1613a Indian health professions scholarships.

(a) General Authority. In order to provide health professionals to Indians, Indian tribes, tribal organizations, and urban Indian organizations, the Secretary, acting through the Service and in accordance with this section, shall make scholarship grants to Indians who are enrolled full or part time in appropriately accredited schools and pursuing courses of study in the health professions. Such scholarships shall be designated Indian Health Scholarships and shall be made in accordance with section 338A of the Public Health Service Act (42 U.S.C. 254l), except as provided in subsection (b) of this section.

(b) Recipients; Active Duty Service Obligation.

* * *

(5) (A) An individual who has, on or after the date of the enactment of this paragraph [enacted Oct. 29, 1992], entered into a written contract with the Secretary under this section and who—

(i) fails to maintain an acceptable level of academic standing in the educational institution in which he is enrolled (such level determined by the educational institution under regulations of the Secretary),

(ii) is dismissed from such educational institution for disciplinary reasons,

(iii) voluntarily terminates the training in such an educational institution for which he is provided a scholarship under such contract before the completion of such training, or

(iv) fails to accept payment, or instructs the educational institution in which he is enrolled not to accept payment, in whole or in part, of a scholarship under such contract,

in lieu of any service obligation arising under such contract, shall be liable to the United States for the amount which has been paid to him, or on his behalf, under the contract.

* * *

(F) Notwithstanding any other provision of law, with respect to a recipient of an Indian Health Scholarship, no obligation for payment may be released by a discharge in bankruptcy under title 11, United States Code, unless that discharge is granted after the expiration of the 5-year period beginning on the initial date on which that payment is due, and only if the bankruptcy court finds that the nondischarge of the obligation would be unconscionable.

* * *

## 25 USC § 1616a Indian Health Service Loan Repayment Program.

(a) Establishment.

(1) The Secretary, acting through the Service, shall establish a program to be known as the Indian Health Service Loan Repayment Program (hereinafter referred to as the "Loan Repayment Program") in order to assure an adequate supply of trained health professionals necessary to maintain accreditation of, and provide health care services to Indians through, Indian health programs.

* * *

(m) Cancellation or Waiver of Obligations; Bankruptcy Discharge.

* * *

(4) Any obligation of an individual under the Loan Repayment Program for payment of damages may be released by a discharge in bankruptcy under title 11 of the United States Code only if such discharge is granted after the expiration of the 5-year period beginning on the first date that payment of such damages is required, and only if the bankruptcy court finds that nondischarge of the obligation would be unconscionable.

* * *

## TITLE 26 INTERNAL REVENUE CODE

### 26 USC § 108 Income from discharge of indebtedness.

(a) Exclusion From Gross Income.

(1) In General. Gross income does not include any amount which (but for this subsection) would be includible in gross income by reason of the discharge (in whole or in part) of indebtedness of the taxpayer if—

(A) the discharge occurs in a title 11 case,

(B) the discharge occurs when the taxpayer is insolvent,

(C) the indebtedness discharged is qualified farm indebtedness,

(D) in the case of a taxpayer other than a C corporation, the indebtedness discharged is qualified real property business indebtedness, or

(E) the indebtedness discharged is qualified principal residence indebtedness which is discharged—

(i) before January 1, 2026, or

(ii) subject to an arrangement that is entered into and evidenced in writing before January 1, 2026.

(2) Coordination of Exclusions.

(A) Title 11 exclusion takes precedence. Subparagraphs (B), (C), and (D) of paragraph (1) shall not apply to a discharge which occurs in a title 11 case.

(B) Insolvency exclusion takes precedence over qualified farm exclusion and qualified real property business exclusion. Subparagraphs (C) and (D) of paragraph (1) shall not apply to a discharge to the extent the taxpayer is insolvent.

(3) Insolvency Exclusion Limited to Amount of Insolvency. In the case of a discharge to which paragraph (1)(B) applies, the amount excluded under paragraph (1)(B) shall not exceed the amount by which the taxpayer is insolvent.

(b) Reduction of Tax Attributes.

(1) In General. The amount excluded from gross income under subparagraph (A), (B), or (C) of subsection (a)(1) shall be applied to reduce the tax attributes of the taxpayer as provided in paragraph (2).

(2) Tax Attributes Affected; Order of Reduction. Except as provided in paragraph (5), the reduction referred to in paragraph (1) shall be made in the following tax attributes in the following order:

(A) NOL. Any net operating loss for the taxable year of the discharge, and any net operating loss carryover to such taxable year.

(B) General Business Credit. Any carryover to or from the taxable year of a discharge of an amount for purposes for determining the amount allowable as a credit under section 38 (relating to general business credit).

(C) Minimum Tax Credit. The amount of the minimum tax credit available under section 53(b) as of the beginning of the taxable year immediately following the taxable year of the discharge.

(D) Capital Loss Carryovers. Any net capital loss for the taxable year of the discharge, and any capital loss carryover to such taxable year under section 1212.

(E) Basis Reduction.

(i) In General. The basis of the property of the taxpayer.

(ii) Cross Reference. For provisions for making the reduction described in clause (i), see section 1017.

(F) Passive Activity Loss and Credit Carryovers. Any passive activity loss or credit carryover of the taxpayer under section 469(b) from the taxable year of the discharge.

(G) Foreign Tax Credit Carryovers. Any carryover to or from the taxable year of the discharge for purposes of determining the amount of the credit allowable under section 27.

(3) Amount of Reduction.

(A) In General. Except as provided in subparagraph (B), the reductions described in paragraph (2) shall be one dollar for each dollar excluded by subsection (a).

(B) Credit Carryover Reduction. The reductions described in subparagraphs (B), (C), and (G) shall be 33 ⅓ cents for each dollar excluded by subsection (a). The reduction described in subparagraph (F) in any passive activity credit carryover shall be 33 ⅓ cents for each dollar excluded by subsection (a).

(4) Ordering Rules.

(A) Reductions Made After Determination of Tax for Year. The reductions described in paragraph (2) shall be made after the determination of the tax imposed by this chapter for the taxable year of the discharge.

(B) Reductions Under Subparagraph (A) or (D) of Paragraph (2). The reductions described in subparagraph (A) or (D) of paragraph (2) (as the case may be) shall be made first in the loss for the taxable year of the discharge and then in the carryovers to such taxable year in the order of the taxable years from which each such carryover arose.

(C) Reductions Under Subparagraphs (B) and (G) of Paragraph (2). The reductions described in subparagraphs (B) and (G) of paragraph (2) shall be made in the order in which carryovers are taken into account under this chapter for the taxable year of the discharge.

(5) Election to Apply Reduction First Against Depreciable Property.

(A) In General. The taxpayer may elect to apply any portion of the

ADDITIONAL STATUTES

reduction referred to in paragraph (1) to the reduction under section 1017 of the basis of the depreciable property of the taxpayer.

(B) Limitation. The amount to which an election under subparagraph (A) applies shall not exceed the aggregate adjusted bases of the depreciable property held by the taxpayer as of the beginning of the taxable year following the taxable year in which the discharge occurs.

(C) Other Tax Attributes Not Reduced. Paragraph (2) shall not apply to any amount to which an election under this paragraph applies.

(c) Treatment of Discharge of Qualified Real Property Business Indebtedness.

(2) Limitations.

(A) Indebtedness in Excess of Value. The amount excluded under subparagraph (D) of subsection (a)(1) with respect to any qualified real property business indebtedness shall not exceed the excess (if any) of—

(i) the outstanding principal amount of such indebtedness (immediately before the discharge), over

(ii) the fair market value of the real property described in paragraph (3)(A) (as of such time), reduced by the outstanding principal amount of any other qualified real property business indebtedness secured by such property (as of such time).

(B) Overall Limitation. The amount excluded under subparagraph (D) of subsection (a)(1) shall not exceed the aggregate adjusted bases of depreciable real property (determined after any reductions under subsections (b) and (g)) held by the taxpayer immediately before the discharge (other than depreciable real property acquired in contemplation of such discharge).

(3) Qualified Real Property Business Indebtedness. The term "qualified real property business indebtedness" means indebtedness which—

(A) was incurred or assumed by the taxpayer in connection with real property used in a trade or business and is secured by such real property,

(B) was incurred or assumed before January 1, 1993, or if incurred or assumed on or after such date, is qualified acquisition indebtedness, and

(C) with respect to which such taxpayer makes an election to have this paragraph apply.

Such term shall not include qualified farm indebtedness. Indebtedness under subparagraph (B) shall include indebtedness resulting from the refinancing of indebtedness under subparagraph (B) (or this sentence), but only to the extent it does not exceed the amount of the indebtedness being refinanced.

(4) Qualified Acquisition Indebtedness. For purposes of paragraph (3)(B), the term "qualified acquisition indebtedness" means, with respect to any real property described in paragraph (3)(A), indebtedness incurred or assumed to acquire, construct, reconstruct, or substantially improve such property.

(5) Regulations. The Secretary shall issue such regulations as are necessary to carry out this subsection, including regulations preventing the abuse of this subsection through cross-collateralization or other means.

(d) Meaning of Terms; Special Rules Relating to Certain Provisions.

(1) Indebtedness of Taxpayer. For purposes of this section, the term "indebtedness of the taxpayer" means any indebtedness—

(A) for which the taxpayer is liable, or

(B) subject to which the taxpayer holds property.

(2) Title 11 Case. For purposes of this section, the term "title 11 case" means a case under title 11 of the United States Code (relating to bankruptcy), but only if the taxpayer is under the jurisdiction of the court in such case and the discharge of indebtedness is granted by the court or is pursuant to a plan approved by the court.

(3) Insolvent. For purposes of this section, the term "insolvent" means the excess of liabilities over the fair market value of assets. With respect to any discharge, whether or not the taxpayer is insolvent, and the amount by which the taxpayer is insolvent, shall be determined on the basis of the taxpayer's assets and liabilities immediately before the discharge.

(4) [Repealed.]

(5) Depreciable Property. The term "depreciable property" has the same meaning as when used in section 1017.

(6) Certain Provisions to Be Applied at Partner Level. In the case of a partnership, subsections (a), (b), (c), and (g) shall be applied at the partner level.

(7) Special Rules for S Corporation.

(A) Certain Provisions to Be Applied at Corporate Level. In the case of an S corporation, subsections (a), (b), (c), and (g) shall be applied at the corporate level, including by not taking into account under section 1366(a) any amount excluded under subsection (a) of this section.

(B) Reduction in Carryover of Disallowed Losses and Deductions. In the case of an S corporation, for purposes of subparagraph (A) of subsection (b)(2), any loss or deduction which is disallowed for the taxable year of the discharge under section 1366(d)(1) shall be treated as a net operating loss for such taxable year. The preceding sentence shall not apply to any discharge to the extent that subsection (a)(1)(D) applies to such discharge.

(C) Coordination with Basis Adjustments Under Section 1367(b)(2). For purposes of subsection (e)(6), a shareholder's adjusted basis in indebtedness of an S corporation shall be determined without regard to any adjustments made under section 1367(b)(2).

(8) Reductions of Tax Attributes in Title 11 Cases of Individuals to Be Made by Estate. In any case under chapter 7 or 11 of title 11 of the United States Code to which

section 1398 applies, for purposes of paragraphs (1) and (5) of subsection (b) the estate (and not the individual) shall be treated as the taxpayer. The preceding sentence shall not apply for purposes of applying section 1017 to property transferred by the estate to the individual.

(9) Time for Making Election, etc.

(A) Time. An election under paragraph (5) of subsection (b) or under paragraph (3)(C) of subsection (c) shall be made on the taxpayer's return for the taxable year in which the discharge occurs or at such other time as may be permitted in regulations prescribed by the Secretary.

(B) Revocation Only with Consent. An election referred to in subparagraph (A), once made, may be revoked only with the consent of the Secretary.

(C) Manner. An election referred to in subparagraph (A) shall be made in such manner as the Secretary may by regulations prescribe.

(10) Cross Reference. For provision that no reduction is to be made in the basis of exempt property of an individual debtor, see section 1017(c)(1).

(e) General Rules for Discharge of Indebtedness (Including Discharges Not in Title 11 Cases or Insolvency). For purposes of this title—

(1) No Other Insolvency Exception. Except as otherwise provided in this section, there shall be no insolvency exception from the general rule that gross income includes income from the discharge of indebtedness.

(2) Income Not Realized to Extent of Lost Deductions. No income shall be realized from the discharge of indebtedness to the extent that payment of the liability would have given rise to a deduction.

(3) Adjustments for Unamortized Premium and Discount. The amount taken into account with respect to any discharge shall be properly adjusted for unamortized premium and unamortized discount with respect to the indebtedness discharged.

(4) Acquisition of Indebtedness by Person Related to Debtor.

(A) Treated as Acquisition by Debtor. For purposes of determining income of the debtor from discharge of indebtedness, to the extent provided in regulations prescribed by the Secretary, the acquisition of outstanding indebtedness by a person bearing a relationship to the debtor specified in section 267(b) or 707(b)(1) from a person who does not bear such a relationship to the debtor shall be treated as the acquisition of such indebtedness by the debtor. Such regulations shall provide for such adjustments in the treatment of any subsequent transactions involving the indebtedness as may be appropriate by reason of the application of the preceding sentence.

(B) Members of Family. For purposes of this paragraph, sections 267(b) and 707(b)(1) shall be applied as if section 267(c)(4) provided that the family of an individual consists of the individual's spouse, the individual's children, grandchildren, and parents, and any spouse of the individual's children or grandchildren.

(C) Entities Under Common Control Treated as Related. For purposes of this paragraph, two entities which are treated as a single employer under subsection (b) or (c) of section 414 shall be treated as bearing a relationship to each other which is described in section 267(b).

(5) Purchase-Money Debt Reduction for Solvent Debtor Treated as Price Reduction. If—

(A) the debt of a purchaser of property to the seller of such property which arose out of the purchase of such property is reduced,

(B) such reduction does not occur—

(i) in a title 11 case, or

(ii) when the purchaser is insolvent, and

(C) but for this paragraph, such reduction would be treated as income to the purchaser from the discharge of indebtedness,

then such reduction shall be treated as a purchase price adjustment.

(6) Indebtedness Contributed to Capital. Except as provided in regulations, for purposes of determining income of the debtor from discharge of indebtedness, if a debtor corporation acquires its indebtedness from a shareholder as a contribution to capital—

(A) section 118 shall not apply, but

(B) such corporation shall be treated as having satisfied the indebtedness with an amount of money equal to the shareholder's adjusted basis in the indebtedness.

(7) Recapture of Gain on Subsequent Sale of Stock.

(A) In General. If a creditor acquires stock of a debtor corporation in satisfaction of such corporation's indebtedness, for purposes of section 1245—

(i) such stock (and any other property the basis of which is determined in whole or in part by reference to the adjusted basis of such stock) shall be treated as section 1245 property,

(ii) the aggregate amount allowed to the creditor—

(I) as deductions under subsection (a) or (b) of section 166 (by reason of the worthlessness or partial worthlessness of the indebtedness), or

(II) as an ordinary loss on the exchange,

shall be treated as an amount allowed as a deduction for depreciation, and

(iii) an exchange of such stock qualifying under section 354(a),

355(a), or 356(a) shall be treated as an exchange to which section 1245(b)(3) applies.

The amount determined under clause (ii) shall be reduced by the amount (if any) included in the creditor's gross income on the exchange.

(B) Special Rule for Cash Basis Taxpayers. In the case of any creditor who computes his taxable income under the cash receipts and disbursements method, proper adjustment shall be made in the amount taken into account under clause (ii) of subparagraph (A) for any amount which was not included in the creditor's gross income but which would have been included in such gross income if such indebtedness had been satisfied in full.

(C) Stock of Parent Corporation. For purposes of this paragraph, stock of a corporation in control (within the meaning of section 368(c)) of the debtor corporation shall be treated as stock of the debtor corporation.

(D) Treatment of Successor Corporation. For purposes of this paragraph, the term "debtor corporation" includes a successor corporation.

(E) Partnership Rule. Under regulations prescribed by the Secretary, rules similar to the rules of the foregoing subparagraphs of this paragraph shall apply with respect to the indebtedness of a partnership.

(8) Indebtedness Satisfied by Corporate Stock or Partnership Interest. For purposes of determining income of a debtor from discharge of indebtedness, if—

(A) a debtor corporation transfers stock, or

(B) a debtor partnership transfers a capital or profits interest in such partnership,

to a creditor in satisfaction of its recourse or nonrecourse indebtedness, such corporation or partnership shall be treated as having satisfied the indebtedness with an amount of money equal to the fair market value of the stock or interest. In the case of any partnership, any discharge of indebtedness income recognized under this paragraph shall be included in the distributive shares of taxpayers which were the partners in the partnership immediately before such discharge.

(9) Discharge of Indebtedness Income Not Taken into Account in Determining Whether Entity Meets REIT Qualifications. Any amount included in gross income by reason of the discharge of indebtedness shall not be taken into account for purposes of paragraphs (2) and (3) of section 856(c).

(10) Indebtedness Satisfied by Issuance of Debt Instrument.

(A) In General. For purposes of determining income of a debtor from discharge of indebtedness, if a debtor issues a debt instrument in satisfaction of indebtedness, such debtor shall be treated as having satisfied the indebtedness with an amount of money equal to the issue price of such debt instrument.

(B) Issue Price. For purposes of subparagraph (A), the issue price of any debt instrument shall be determined under sections 1273 and 1274. For purposes of the preceding sentence, section 1273(b)(4) shall be applied by reducing the stated redemption price of any instrument by the portion of such stated redemption price which is treated as interest for purposes of this chapter.

(11) [*Redesignated*]

(f) Student Loans.

(1) In General. In the case of an individual, gross income does not include any amount which (but for this subsection) would be includible in gross income by reason of the discharge (in whole or in part) of any student loan if such discharge was pursuant to a provision of such loan under which all or part of the indebtedness of the individual would be discharged if the individual worked for a certain period of time in certain professions for any of a broad class of employers.

(2) Student Loan. For purposes of this subsection, the term "student loan" means any loan to an individual to assist the individual in attending an educational organization described in section 170(b)(1)(A)(ii) made by—

(A) the United States, or an instrumentality or agency thereof,

(B) a State, territory, or possession of the United States, or the District of Columbia, or any political subdivision thereof,

(C) a public benefit corporation—

(i) which is exempt from taxation under section 501(c)(3),

(ii) which has assumed control over a State, county, or municipal hospital, and

(iii) whose employees have been deemed to be public employees under State law, or

(D) any educational organization described in section 170(b)(1)(A)(ii) if such loan is made—

(i) pursuant to an agreement with any entity described in subparagraph (A), (B), or (C) under which the funds from which the loan was made were provided to such educational organization, or

(ii) pursuant to a program of such educational organization which is designed to encourage its students to serve in occupations with unmet needs or in areas with unmet needs and under which the services provided by the students (or former students) are for or under the direction of a governmental unit or an organization described in section 501(c)(3) and exempt from tax under section 501(a).

The term "student loan" includes any loan made by an educational organization described in section 170(b)(1)(A)(ii) or by an organization exempt from tax under section 501(a) to refinance a loan to an individual to assist the individual in attending any such educational organization but only if the refinancing loan is pursuant to a program of the refinancing organization which is designed as described in subparagraph (D)(ii).

(3) Exception for Discharges on Account of Services Performed for Certain Lenders. Paragraph (1) shall not apply to the discharge of a loan made by an organization described in paragraph (2)(D) if the discharge is on account of services performed for either such organization.

(4) Payments under National Health Service Corps Loan Repayment Program and Certain State Loan Repayment Programs. In the case of an individual, gross income shall not include any amount received under section 338B(g) of the Public Health Service Act or under a State program described in section 338I of such Act, or under any other State loan repayment or loan forgiveness program that is intended to provide for the increased availability of health care services in underserved or health professional shortage areas (as determined by such State).

(5) Special rule for discharges in 2021 through 2025. Gross income does not include any amount which (but for this subsection) would be includible in gross income by reason of the discharge (in whole or in part) after December 31, 2020, and before January 1, 2026, of—

(A) any loan provided expressly for postsecondary educational expenses, regardless of whether provided through the educational institution or directly to the borrower, if such loan was made, insured, or guaranteed by—

(i) the United States, or an instrumentality or agency thereof,

(ii) a State, territory, or possession of the United States, or the District of Columbia, or any political subdivision thereof, or

(iii) an eligible educational institution (as defined in section 25A),

(B) any private education loan (as defined in section 140(a)(7) of the Truth in Lending Act,

(C) any loan made by any educational organization described in section 170(b)(1)(A)(ii) if such loan is made—

(i) pursuant to an agreement with any entity described in subparagraph (A) or any private education lender (as defined in section 140(a) of the Truth in Lending Act under which the funds from which the loan was made were provided to such educational organization, or

(ii) pursuant to a program of such educational organization which is designed to encourage its students to serve in occupations with unmet needs or in areas with unmet needs and under which the services provided by the students (or former students) are for or under the direction of a governmental unit or an organization described in section 501(c)(3) and exempt from tax under section 501(a), or

(D) any loan made by an educational organization described in section

170(b)(1)(A)(ii) or by an organization exempt from tax under section 501(a) to refinance a loan to an individual to assist the individual in attending any such educational organization but only if the refinancing loan is pursuant to a program of the refinancing organization which is designed as described in subparagraph (C)(ii).

The preceding sentence shall not apply to the discharge of a loan made by an organization described in subparagraph (C) or made by a private education lender (as defined in section 140(a)(7) of the Truth in Lending Act) if the discharge is on account of services performed for either such organization or for such private education lender.

(g) SPECIAL RULES FOR DISCHARGE OF QUALIFIED FARM INDEBTEDNESS.

(1) DISCHARGE MUST BE BY QUALIFIED PERSON.

(A) IN GENERAL. Subparagraph (C) of subsection (a)(1) shall apply only if the discharge is by a qualified person.

(B) QUALIFIED PERSON. For purposes of subparagraph (A), the term "qualified person" has the meaning given to such term by section 49(a)(1)(D)(iv); except that such term shall include any Federal, State, or local government or agency or instrumentality thereof.

(2) QUALIFIED FARM INDEBTEDNESS. For purposes of this section, indebtedness of a taxpayer shall be treated as qualified farm indebtedness if–

(A) such indebtedness was incurred directly in connection with the operation by the taxpayer of the trade or business of farming, and

(B) 50 percent or more of the aggregate gross receipts of the taxpayer for the 3 taxable years preceding the taxable year in which the discharge of such indebtedness occurs is attributable to the trade or business of farming.

(3) AMOUNT EXCLUDED CANNOT EXCEED SUM OF TAX ATTRIBUTES AND BUSINESS AND INVESTMENT ASSETS.

(A) IN GENERAL. The amount excluded under subparagraph (C) of subsection (a)(1) shall not exceed the sum of–

(i) the adjusted tax attributes of the taxpayer, and

(ii) the aggregate adjusted bases of qualified property held by the taxpayer as of the beginning of the taxable year following the taxable year in which the discharge occurs.

(B) ADJUSTED TAX ATTRIBUTES. For purposes of subparagraph (A), the term "adjusted tax attributes" means the sum of the tax attributes described in subparagraphs (A), (B), (C), (D), (F), and (G) of subsection (b)(2) determined by taking into account $3 for each $1 of the attributes described in subparagraphs (B), (C), and (G) of subsection (b)(2) and the attribute described in subparagraph (F) of subsection (b)(2) to the extent attributable to any passive activity credit carryover.

(C) QUALIFIED PROPERTY. For purposes of this paragraph, the term "qualified property" means any property which is used or is held for use in a trade or business or for the production of income.

(D) Coordination with Insolvency Exclusion. For purposes of this paragraph, the adjusted basis of any qualified property and the amount of the adjusted tax attributes shall be determined after any reduction under subsection (b) by reason of amounts excluded from gross income under subsection (a)(1)(B).

(h) Special Rules Relating to Qualified Principal Residence Indebtedness.

(1) Basis Reduction. The amount excluded from gross income by reason of subsection (a)(1)(E) shall be applied to reduce (but not below zero) the basis of the principal residence of the taxpayer.

(2) Qualified Principal Residence Indebtedness. For purposes of this section, the term "qualified principal residence indebtedness" means acquisition indebtedness (within the meaning of section 163(h)(3)(B), applied by substituting "$750,000 ($375,000" for "$1,000,000 ($500,000" in clause (ii) thereof and determined without regard to the substitution described in section 163(h)(3)(F)(i)(II)) with respect to the principal residence of the taxpayer.

(3) Exception for Certain Discharges Not Related to Taxpayer's Financial Condition. Subsection (a)(1)(E) shall not apply to the discharge of a loan if the discharge is on account of services performed for the lender or any other factor not directly related to a decline in the value of the residence or to the financial condition of the taxpayer.

(4) Ordering Rule. If any loan is discharged, in whole or in part, and only a portion of such loan is qualified principal residence indebtedness, subsection (a)(1)(E) shall apply only to so much of the amount discharged as exceeds the amount of the loan (as determined immediately before such discharge) which is not qualified principal residence indebtedness.

(5) Principal Residence. For purposes of this subsection, the term "principal residence" has the same meaning as when used in section 121.

(i) Deferral and Ratable Inclusion of Income Arising From Business Indebtedness Discharged by the Reacquisition of a Debt Instrument.

(1) In General. At the election of the taxpayer, income from the discharge of indebtedness in connection with the reacquisition after December 31, 2008, and before January 1, 2011, of an applicable debt instrument shall be includible in gross income ratably over the 5-taxable-year period beginning with—

(A) in the case of a reacquisition occurring in 2009, the fifth taxable year following the taxable year in which the reacquisition occurs, and

(B) in the case of a reacquisition occurring in 2010, the fourth taxable year following the taxable year in which the reacquisition occurs.

(2) Deferral of Deduction for Original Issue Discount in Debt for Debt Exchanges.

(A) In General. If, as part of a reacquisition to which paragraph (1) applies, any debt instrument is issued for the applicable debt instrument being reacquired (or is treated as so issued under subsection (e)(4) and the regulations thereunder) and there is any original issue discount determined under subpart A of part V of subchapter P of this chapter with respect to the debt instrument so issued—

(i) except as provided in clause (ii), no deduction otherwise allowable under this chapter shall be allowed to the issuer of such debt instrument with respect to the portion of such original issue discount which—

(I) accrues before the 1st taxable year in the 5-taxable-year period in which income from the discharge of indebtedness attributable to the reacquisition of the debt instrument is includible under paragraph (1), and

(II) does not exceed the income from the discharge of indebtedness with respect to the debt instrument being reacquired, and

(ii) the aggregate amount of deductions disallowed under clause (i) shall be allowed as a deduction ratably over the 5-taxable-year period described in clause (i)(I).

If the amount of the original issue discount accruing before such 1st taxable year exceeds the income from the discharge of indebtedness with respect to the applicable debt instrument being reacquired, the deductions shall be disallowed in the order in which the original issue discount is accrued.

(B) Deemed Debt for Debt Exchanges. For purposes of subparagraph (A), if any debt instrument is issued by an issuer and the proceeds of such debt instrument are used directly or indirectly by the issuer to reacquire an applicable debt instrument of the issuer, the debt instrument so issued shall be treated as issued for the debt instrument being reacquired. If only a portion of the proceeds from a debt instrument are so used, the rules of subparagraph (A) shall apply to the portion of any original issue discount on the newly issued debt instrument which is equal to the portion of the proceeds from such instrument used to reacquire the outstanding instrument.

(3) Applicable Debt Instrument. For purposes of this subsection—

(A) Applicable Debt Instrument. The term "applicable debt instrument" means any debt instrument which was issued by—

(i) a C corporation, or

(ii) any other person in connection with the conduct of a trade or business by such person.

(B) Debt Instrument. The term "debt instrument" means a bond, debenture, note, certificate, or any other instrument or contractual arrangement constituting indebtedness (within the meaning of section 1275(a)(1)).

(4) Reacquisition. For purposes of this subsection—

(A) In General. The term "reacquisition" means, with respect to any

ADDITIONAL STATUTES

applicable debt instrument, any acquisition of the debt instrument by—

(i) the debtor which issued (or is otherwise the obligor under) the debt instrument, or

(ii) a related person to such debtor.

(B) ACQUISITION. The term "acquisition" shall, with respect to any applicable debt instrument, include an acquisition of the debt instrument for cash, the exchange of the debt instrument for another debt instrument (including an exchange resulting from a modification of the debt instrument), the exchange of the debt instrument for corporate stock or a partnership interest, and the contribution of the debt instrument to capital. Such term shall also include the complete forgiveness of the indebtedness by the holder of the debt instrument.

(5) OTHER DEFINITIONS AND RULES. For purposes of this subsection—

(A) RELATED PERSON. The determination of whether a person is related to another person shall be made in the same manner as under subsection (e)(4).

(B) ELECTION.

(i) IN GENERAL. An election under this subsection with respect to any applicable debt instrument shall be made by including with the return of tax imposed by chapter 1 for the taxable year in which the reacquisition of the debt instrument occurs a statement which—

(I) clearly identifies such instrument, and

(II) includes the amount of income to which paragraph (1) applies and such other information as the Secretary may prescribe.

(ii) ELECTION IRREVOCABLE. Such election, once made, is irrevocable.

(iii) PASS-THRU ENTITIES. In the case of a partnership, S corporation, or other pass-thru entity, the election under this subsection shall be made by the partnership, the S corporation, or other entity involved.

(C) COORDINATION WITH OTHER EXCLUSIONS. If a taxpayer elects to have this subsection apply to an applicable debt instrument, subparagraphs (A), (B), (C), and (D) of subsection (a)(1) shall not apply to the income from the discharge of such indebtedness for the taxable year of the election or any subsequent taxable year.

(D) ACCELERATION OF DEFERRED ITEMS.

(i) IN GENERAL. In the case of the death of the taxpayer, the liquidation or sale of substantially all the assets of the taxpayer (including in a title 11 or similar case), the cessation of business by the taxpayer, or similar circumstances, any item of income or deduction which is deferred under this subsection (and has not previously been taken into account) shall be taken into account in the taxable year in which such event occurs (or in the case of a title 11 or similar case, the day before the petition is filed).

(ii) Special Rule for Pass-Thru Entities. The rule of clause (i) shall also apply in the case of the sale or exchange or redemption of an interest in a partnership, S corporation, or other pass-thru entity by a partner, shareholder, or other person holding an ownership interest in such entity.

(6) Special Rule for Partnerships. In the case of a partnership, any income deferred under this subsection shall be allocated to the partners in the partnership immediately before the discharge in the manner such amounts would have been included in the distributive shares of such partners under section 704 if such income were recognized at such time. Any decrease in a partner's share of partnership liabilities as a result of such discharge shall not be taken into account for purposes of section 752 at the time of the discharge to the extent it would cause the partner to recognize gain under section 731. Any decrease in partnership liabilities deferred under the preceding sentence shall be taken into account by such partner at the same time, and to the extent remaining in the same amount, as income deferred under this subsection is recognized.

(7) Secretarial Authority. The Secretary may prescribe such regulations, rules, or other guidance as may be necessary or appropriate for purposes of applying this subsection, including—

(A) extending the application of the rules of paragraph (5)(D) to other circumstances where appropriate,

(B) requiring reporting of the election (and such other information as the Secretary may require) on returns of tax for subsequent taxable years, and

(C) rules for the application of this subsection to partnerships, S corporations, and other pass-thru entities, including for the allocation of deferred deductions.

## 26 USC § 1017 Discharge of indebtedness.

(a) General Rule. If—

(1) an amount is excluded from gross income under subsection (a) of section 108 (relating to discharge of indebtedness), and

(2) under subsection (b)(2)(E), (b)(5), or (c)(1) of section 108, any portion of such amount is to be applied to reduce basis, then such portion shall be applied in reduction of the basis of any property held by the taxpayer at the beginning of the taxable year following the taxable year in which the discharge occurs.

(b) Amount and Properties Determined Under Regulations.

(1) In General. The amount of reduction to be applied under subsection (a) (not in excess of the portion referred to in subsection (a)), and the particular properties the bases of which are to be reduced, shall be determined under regulations prescribed by the Secretary.

(2) Limitation in Title 11 Case or Insolvency. In the case of a discharge to which

subparagraph (A) or (B) of section 108(a)(1) applies, the reduction in basis under subsection (a) of this section shall not exceed the excess of–

(A) the aggregate of the bases of the property held by the taxpayer immediately after the discharge, over

(B) the aggregate of the liabilities of the taxpayer immediately after the discharge.

The preceding sentence shall not apply to any reduction in basis by reason of an election under section 108(b)(5).

(3) Certain Reductions May Only Be Made in the Basis of Depreciable Property.

(A) In General. Any amount which under subsection (b)(5) or (c)(1) of section 108 is to be applied to reduce basis shall be applied only to reduce the basis of depreciable property held by the taxpayer.

(B) Depreciable Property. For purposes of this section, the term "depreciable property" means any property of a character subject to the allowance for depreciation, but only if a basis reduction under subsection (a) will reduce the amount of depreciation or amortization which otherwise would be allowable for the period immediately following such reduction.

(C) Special Rule for Partnership Interests. For purposes of this section, any interest of a partner in a partnership shall be treated as depreciable property to the extent of such partner's proportionate interest in the depreciable property held by such partnership. The preceding sentence shall apply only if there is a corresponding reduction in the partnership's basis in depreciable property with respect to such partner.

(D) Special Rule in Case of Affiliated Group. For purposes of this section, if–

(i) a corporation holds stock in another corporation (hereinafter in this subparagraph referred to as the "subsidiary"), and

(ii) such corporations are members of the same affiliated group which file a consolidated return under section 1501 for the taxable year in which the discharge occurs,

then such stock shall be treated as depreciable property to the extent that such subsidiary consents to a corresponding reduction in the basis of its depreciable property.

(E) Election to Treat Certain Inventory as Depreciable Property.

(i) In General. At the election of the taxpayer, for purposes of this section, the term "depreciable property" includes any real property which is described in section 1221(a)(1).

(ii) Election. An election under clause (i) shall be made on the taxpayer's return for the taxable year in which the discharge occurs or at such other time as may be permitted in regulations prescribed by the Secretary. Such an election, once made, may be revoked only with the consent of the Secretary.

(F) Special Rules for Qualified Real Property Business Indebtedness. In the case of any amount which under section 108(c)(1) is to be applied to reduce basis—

(i) depreciable property shall only include depreciable real property for purposes of subparagraphs (A) and (C),

(ii) subparagraph (E) shall not apply, and

(iii) in the case of property taken into account under section 108(c)(2)(B), the reduction with respect to such property shall be made as of the time immediately before disposition if earlier than the time under subsection (a).

(4) Special Rules for Qualified Farm Indebtedness.

(A) In General. Any amount which under subsection (b)(2)(E) of section 108 is to be applied to reduce basis and which is attributable to an amount excluded under subsection (a)(1)(C) of section 108—

(i) shall be applied only to reduce the basis of qualified property held by the taxpayer, and

(ii) shall be applied to reduce the basis of qualified property in the following order:

(I) First the basis of qualified property which is depreciable property.

(II) Second the basis of qualified property which is land used or held for use in the trade or business of farming.

(III) Then the basis of other qualified property.

(B) Qualified Property. For purposes of this paragraph, the term "qualified property" has the meaning given to such term by section 108(g)(3)(C).

(C) Certain Rules Made Applicable. Rules similar to the rules of subparagraphs (C), (D), and (E) of paragraph (3) shall apply for purposes of this paragraph and section 108(g).

(c) Special Rules.

(1) Reduction Not to Be Made in Exempt Property. In the case of an amount excluded from gross income under section 108(a)(1)(A), no reduction in basis shall be made under this section in the basis of property which the debtor treats as exempt property under section 522 of title 11 of the United States Code.

(2) Reductions in Basis Not Treated as Dispositions. For purposes of this title, a reduction in basis under this section shall not be treated as a disposition.

(d) Recapture of Reductions.

(1) In General. For purposes of sections 1245 and 1250—

(A) any property the basis of which is reduced under this section and which is neither section 1245 property nor section 1250 property shall be treated as section 1245 property, and

(B) any reduction under this section shall be treated as a deduction allowed for depreciation.

(2) Special Rule for Section 1250. For purposes of section 1250(b), the determination of what would have been the depreciation adjustments under the straight line method shall be made as if there had been no reduction under this section.

**26 USC § 1398 Rules relating to individuals' title 11 cases.**

(a) Cases to Which Section Applies. Except as provided in subsection (b), this section shall apply to any case under chapter 7 (relating to liquidations) or chapter 11 (relating to reorganizations) of title 11 of the United States Code in which the debtor is an individual.

(b) Exceptions Where Case Is Dismissed, etc.

(1) Section Does Not Apply Where Case Is Dismissed. This section shall not apply if the case under chapter 7 or 11 of title 11 of the United States Code is dismissed.

(2) Section Does Not Apply at Partnership Level. For purposes of subsection (a), a partnership shall not be treated as an individual, but the interest in a partnership of a debtor who is an individual shall be taken into account under this section in the same manner as any other interest of the debtor.

(c) Computation and Payment of Tax; Basic Standard Deduction.

(1) Computation and Payment of tax. Except as otherwise provided in this section, the taxable income of the estate shall be computed in the same manner as for an individual. The tax shall be computed on such taxable income and shall be paid by the trustee.

(2) Tax Rates. The tax on the taxable income of the estate shall be determined under subsection (d) of section 1.

(3) Basic Standard Deduction. In the case of an estate which does not itemize deductions, the basic standard deduction for the estate for the taxable year shall be the same as for a married individual filing a separate return for such year.

(d) Taxable Year of Debtors.

(1) General Rule. Except as provided in paragraph (2), the taxable year of the debtor shall be determined without regard to the case under title 11 of the United States Code to which this section applies.

(2) Election to Terminate Debtor' s Year When Case Commences.

(A) In General. Notwithstanding section 442, the debtor may (without the approval of the Secretary) elect to treat the debtor's taxable year which includes the commencement date as 2 taxable years—

(i) the first of which ends on the day before the commencement date, and

(ii) the second of which begins on the commencement date.

(B) Spouse May Join in Election. In the case of a married individual (within the meaning of section 7703), the spouse may elect to have the debtor's election under subparagraph (A) also apply to the spouse, but only if the debtor and the spouse file a joint return for the taxable year referred to in subparagraph (A)(i).

(C) No Election Where Debtor Has No Assets. No election may be made under subparagraph (A) by a debtor who has no assets other than property which the debtor may treat as exempt property under section 522 of title 11 of the United States Code.

(D) Time for Making Election. An election under subparagraph (A) or (B) may be made only on or before the due date for filing the return for the taxable year referred to in subparagraph (A)(i). Any such election, once made, shall be irrevocable.

(E) Returns. A return shall be made for each of the taxable years specified in subparagraph (A).

(F) Annualization. For purposes of subsections (b), (c), and (d) of section 443, a return filed for either of the taxable years referred to in subparagraph (A) shall be treated as a return made under paragraph (1) of subsection (a) of section 443.

(3) Commencement Date Defined. For purposes of this subsection, the term "commencement date" means the day on which the case under title 11 of the United States Code to which this section applies commences.

(e) Treatment of Income, Deductions, and Credits.

(1) Estate's Share of Debtor's Income. The gross income of the estate for each taxable year shall include the gross income of the debtor to which the estate is entitled under title 11 of the United States Code. The preceding sentence shall not apply to any amount received or accrued by the debtor before the commencement date (as defined in subsection (d)(3)).

(2) Debtor's Share of Debtor's Income. The gross income of the debtor for any taxable year shall not include any item to the extent that such item is included in the gross income of the estate by reason of paragraph (1).

(3) Rule for Making Determinations with Respect to Deductions, Credits, and Employment Taxes. Except as otherwise provided in this section, the determination of whether or not any amount paid or incurred by the estate—

(A) is allowable as a deduction or credit under this chapter, or

(B) is wages for purposes of subtitle C,

shall be made as if the amount were paid or incurred by the debtor and as if the debtor were still engaged in the trades and businesses, and in the

ADDITIONAL STATUTES

activities, the debtor was engaged in before the commencement of the case.

(f) Treatment of Transfers Between Debtor and Estate.

(1) Transfer to Estate Not Treated as Disposition. A transfer (other than by sale or exchange) of an asset from the debtor to the estate shall not be treated as a disposition for purposes of any provision of this title assigning tax consequences to a disposition, and the estate shall be treated as the debtor would be treated with respect to such asset.

(2) Transfer from Estate to Debtor Not Treated as Disposition. In the case of a termination of the estate, a transfer (other than by sale or exchange) of an asset from the estate to the debtor shall not be treated as a disposition for purposes of any provision of this title assigning tax consequences to a disposition, and the debtor shall be treated as the estate would be treated with respect to such asset.

(g) Estate Succeeds to Tax Attributes of Debtor. The estate shall succeed to and take into account the following items (determined as of the first day of the debtor's taxable year in which the case commences) of the debtor—

(1) Net Operating Loss Carryovers. The net operating loss carryovers determined under section 172.

(2) Charitable Contributions Carryovers. The carryover of excess charitable contributions determined under section 170(d)(1).

(3) Recovery of Tax Benefit Items. Any amount to which section 111 (relating to recovery of tax benefit items) applies.

(4) Credit Carryovers, etc. The carryovers of any credit, and all other items which, but for the commencement of the case, would be required to be taken into account by the debtor with respect to any credit.

(5) Capital Loss Carryovers. The capital loss carryover determined under section 1212.

(6) Basis, Holding Period, and Character of Assets. In the case of any asset acquired (other than by sale or exchange) by the estate from the debtor, the basis, holding period, and character it had in the hands of the debtor.

(7) Method of Accounting. The method of accounting used by the debtor.

(8) Other Attributes. Other tax attributes of the debtor, to the extent provided in regulations prescribed by the Secretary as necessary or appropriate to carry out the purposes of this section.

(h) Administration, Liquidation, and Reorganization Expenses; Carryovers and Carrybacks of Certain Excess Expenses.

(1) Administration, Liquidation, and Reorganization Expenses. Any administrative expense allowed under section 503 of title 11 of the United States Code, and any fee or charge assessed against the estate under chapter 123 of title 28 of the United States Code, to the extent not disallowed under any other provision of

this title, shall be allowed as a deduction.

(2) CARRYBACK AND CARRYOVER OF EXCESS ADMINISTRATIVE COSTS, ETC., TO ESTATE TAXABLE YEARS.

(A) DEDUCTION ALLOWED. There shall be allowed as a deduction for the taxable year an amount equal to the aggregate of (i) the administrative expense carryovers to such year, plus (ii) the administrative expense carrybacks to such year.

(B) ADMINISTRATIVE EXPENSE LOSS, ETC. If a net operating loss would be created or increased for any estate taxable year if section 172(c) were applied without the modification contained in paragraph (4) of section 172(d), then the amount of the net operating loss so created (or the amount of the increase in the net operating loss) shall be an administrative expense loss for such taxable year which shall be an administrative expense carryback to each of the 3 preceding taxable years and an administrative expense carryover to each of the 7 succeeding taxable years.

(C) DETERMINATION OF AMOUNT CARRIED TO EACH TAXABLE YEAR. The portion of any administrative expense loss which may be carried to any other taxable year shall be determined under section 172(b)(2), except that for each taxable year the computation under section 172(b)(2) with respect to the net operating loss shall be made before the computation under this paragraph.

(D) ADMINISTRATIVE EXPENSE DEDUCTIONS ALLOWED ONLY TO ESTATE. The deductions allowable under this chapter solely by reason of paragraph (1), and the deduction provided by subparagraph (A) of this paragraph, shall be allowable only to the estate.

(i) DEBTOR SUCCEEDS TO TAX ATTRIBUTES OF ESTATE. In the case of a termination of an estate, the debtor shall succeed to and take into account the items referred to in paragraphs (1), (2), (3), (4), (5), and (6) of subsection (g) in a manner similar to that provided in such paragraphs (but taking into account that the transfer is from the estate to the debtor instead of from the debtor to the estate). In addition, the debtor shall succeed to and take into account the other tax attributes of the estate, to the extent provided in regulations prescribed by the Secretary as necessary or appropriate to carry out the purposes of this section.

(j) OTHER SPECIAL RULES.

(1) CHANGE OF ACCOUNTING PERIOD WITHOUT APPROVAL. Notwithstanding section 442, the estate may change its annual accounting period one time without the approval of the Secretary.

(2) TREATMENT OF CERTAIN CARRYBACKS.

(A) CARRYBACKS FROM ESTATE. If any carryback year of the estate is a taxable year before the estate's first taxable year, the carryback to such carryback year shall be taken into account for the debtor's taxable year corresponding to the carryback year.

(B) CARRYBACKS FROM DEBTOR' S ACTIVITIES. The debtor may not carry back to a

ADDITIONAL STATUTES

taxable year before the debtor's taxable year in which the case commences any carryback from a taxable year ending after the case commences.

(C) CARRYBACK AND CARRYBACK YEAR DEFINED. For purposes of this paragraph—

(i) CARRYBACK. The term "carryback" means a net operating loss carryback under section 172 or a carryback of any credit provided by part IV of subchapter A.

(ii) CARRYBACK YEAR. The term "carryback year" means the taxable year to which a carryback is carried.

**26 USC § 1399 No separate taxable entities for partnerships, corporations, etc.**

Except in any case to which section 1398 applies, no separate taxable entity shall result from the commencement of a case under title 11 of the United States Code.

**26 USC § 6012 Persons required to make returns of income.**

(a) GENERAL RULE. Returns with respect to income taxes under subtitle A shall be made by the following:

(1) (A) Every individual having for the taxable year gross income which equals or exceeds the exemption amount, except that a return shall not be required of an individual—

(i) who is not married (determined by applying section 7703), is not a surviving spouse (as defined in section 2(a)), is not a head of a household (as defined in section 2(b)), and for the taxable year has gross income of less than the sum of the exemption amount plus the basic standard deduction applicable to such an individual,

(ii) who is a head of a household (as so defined) and for the taxable year has gross income of less than the sum of the exemption amount plus the basic standard deduction applicable to such an individual,

(iii) who is a surviving spouse (as so defined) and for the taxable year has gross income of less than the sum of the exemption amount plus the basic standard deduction applicable to such an individual, or

(iv) who is entitled to make a joint return and whose gross income, when combined with the gross income of his spouse, is, for the taxable year, less than the sum of twice the exemption amount plus the basic standard deduction applicable to a joint return, but only if such individual and his spouse, at the close of the taxable year, had the same household as their home.

Clause (iv) shall not apply if for the taxable year such spouse makes a separate return or any other taxpayer is entitled to an exemption for such spouse under section 151(c).

(B) The amount specified in clause (i), (ii), or (iii) of subparagraph (A) shall be increased by the amount of 1 additional standard deduction (within the meaning of section 63(c)(3)) in the case of an individual entitled to such deduction by reason of section 63(f)(1)(A) (relating to individuals age 65 or more), and the amount specified in clause (iv) of subparagraph (A) shall be increased by the amount of the additional standard deduction for each additional standard deduction to which the individual or his spouse is entitled by reason of section 63(f)(1).

(C) The exception under subparagraph (A) shall not apply to any individual—

(i) who is described in section 63(c)(5) and who has—

(I) income (other than earned income) in excess of the sum of the amount in effect under section 63(c)(5)(A) plus the additional standard deduction (if any) to which the individual is entitled, or

(II) total gross income in excess of the standard deduction, or

(ii) for whom the standard deduction is zero under section 63(c)(6).

(D) For purposes of this subsection—

(i) The terms "standard deduction", "basic standard deduction" and "additional standard deduction" have the respective meanings given such terms by section 63(c).

(ii) The term "exemption amount" has the meaning given such term by section 151(d). In the case of an individual described in section 151(d)(2), the exemption amount shall be zero.

(2) Every corporation subject to taxation under subtitle A;

(3) Every estate the gross income of which for the taxable year is $600 or more;

(4) Every trust having for the taxable year any taxable income, or having gross income of $600 or over, regardless of the amount of taxable income;

(5) Every estate or trust of which any beneficiary is a nonresident alien;

(6) Every political organization (within the meaning of section 527(e)(1)), and every fund treated under section 527(g) as if it constituted a political organization, which has political organization taxable income (within the meaning of section 527(c)(1)) for the taxable year;

(7) Every homeowners association (within the meaning of section 528(c)(1)) which has homeowners association taxable income (within the meaning of section 528(d)) for the taxable year;

(8) Every estate of an individual under chapter 7 or 11 of title 11 of the United States Code (relating to bankruptcy) the gross income of which for the taxable year is not less than the sum of the exemption amount plus the basic standard deduction under section 63(c)(2)(C);

except that subject to such conditions, limitations, and exceptions and under such regulations as may be prescribed by the Secretary, nonresident alien individuals subject to the tax imposed by section 871 and foreign corporations subject to the tax imposed by section 881 may be exempted from the requirement of making returns under this section.

(b) Returns Made by Fiduciaries and Receivers.

(1) Returns of Decedents. If an individual is deceased, the return of such individual required under subsection (a) shall be made by his executor, administrator, or other person charged with the property of such decedent.

(2) Persons Under a Disability. If an individual is unable to make a return required under subsection (a), the return of such individual shall be made by a duly authorized agent, his committee, guardian, fiduciary or other person charged with the care of the person or property of such individual. The preceding sentence shall not apply in the case of a receiver appointed by authority of law in possession of only a part of the property of an individual.

(3) Receivers, Trustees and Assignees for Corporations. In a case where a receiver, trustee in a case under title 11 of the United States Code, or assignee, by order of a court of competent jurisdiction, by operation of law or otherwise, has possession of or holds title to all or substantially all the property or business of a corporation, whether or not such property or business is being operated, such receiver, trustee, or assignee shall make the return of income for such corporation in the same manner and form as corporations are required to make such returns.

(4) Returns of Estates and Trusts. Returns of an estate, a trust, or an estate of an individual under chapter 7 or 11 of title 11 of the United States Code shall be made by the fiduciary thereof.

(5) Joint Fiduciaries. Under such regulations as the Secretary may prescribe, a return made by one of two or more joint fiduciaries shall be sufficient compliance with the requirements of this section. A return made pursuant to this paragraph shall contain a statement that the fiduciary has sufficient knowledge of the affairs of the person for whom the return is made to enable him to make the return, and that the return is, to the best of his knowledge and belief, true and correct.

(6) IRA Share of Partnership Income. In the case of a trust which is exempt from taxation under section 408(e), for purposes of this section, the trust's distributive share of items of gross income and gain of any partnership to which subchapter C or D of chapter 63 applies shall be treated as equal to the trust's distributive share of the taxable income of such partnership.

(c) Certain Income Earned Abroad or from Sale of Residence. For purposes of this section, gross income shall be computed without regard to the exclusion provided for in section 121 (relating to gain from sale of principal residence) and without regard to the exclusion provided for in section 911 (relating to citizens or residents of the United States living abroad).

(d) Tax-Exempt Interest Required to Be Shown on Return. Every person required to file a return under this section for the taxable year shall include on such return the amount of interest received or accrued during the taxable year which is exempt from the tax imposed by chapter 1.

(e) Consolidated Returns. For provisions relating to consolidated returns by affiliated corporations, see chapter 6.

(f) Special Rule for Taxable Years 2018 Through 2025. In the case of a taxable year beginning after December 31, 2017, and before January 1, 2026, subsection (a)(1) shall not apply, and every individual who has gross income for the taxable year shall be required to make returns with respect to income taxes under subtitle A, except that a return shall not be required of—

(1) an individual who is not married (determined by applying section 7703) and who has gross income for the taxable year which does not exceed the standard deduction applicable to such individual for such taxable year under section 63, or

(2) an individual entitled to make a joint return if—

(A) the gross income of such individual, when combined with the gross income of such individual's spouse, for the taxable year does not exceed the standard deduction which would be applicable to the taxpayer for such taxable year under section 63 if such individual and such individual's spouse made a joint return,

(B) such individual and such individual's spouse have the same household as their home at the close of the taxable year,

(C) such individual's spouse does not make a separate return, and

(D) neither such individual nor such individual's spouse is an individual described in section 63(c)(5) who has income (other than earned income) in excess of the amount in effect under section 63(c)(5)(A).

**26 USC § 6062 Signing of corporation returns.**

The return of a corporation with respect to income shall be signed by the president, vice-president, treasurer, assistant treasurer, chief accounting officer or any other officer duly authorized so to act. In the case of a return made for a corporation by a fiduciary pursuant to the provisions of section 6012(b)(3), such fiduciary shall sign the return. The fact that an individual's name is signed on the return shall be prima facie evidence that such individual is authorized to sign the return on behalf of the corporation.

**26 USC § 6213 Restrictions applicable to deficiencies; petition to Tax Court.**

(a) Time for Filing Petition and Restriction on Assessment. Within 90 days, or 150 days if the notice is addressed to a person outside the United States, after the notice of deficiency authorized in section 6212 is mailed (not counting Saturday, Sunday, or a legal holiday in the District of Columbia as the last day), the taxpayer may file a petition with the Tax Court for a redetermination of the deficiency. Except as otherwise provided in section 6851, 6852, or 6861 no assessment of a deficiency in respect of any tax imposed by subtitle A or B, chapter 41, 42, 43, or 44 and no levy or proceeding in court for its collection shall be made, begun, or prosecuted

ADDITIONAL STATUTES

until such notice has been mailed to the taxpayer, nor until the expiration of such 90-day or 150-day period, as the case may be, nor, if a petition has been filed with the Tax Court, until the decision of the Tax Court has become final. Notwithstanding the provisions of section 7421(a), the making of such assessment or the beginning of such proceeding or levy during the time such prohibition is in force may be enjoined by a proceeding in the proper court, including the Tax Court, and a refund may be ordered by such court of any amount collected within the period during which the Secretary is prohibited from collecting by levy or through a proceeding in court under the provisions of this subsection. The Tax Court shall have no jurisdiction to enjoin any action or proceeding or order any refund under this subsection unless a timely petition for a redetermination of the deficiency has been filed and then only in respect of the deficiency that is the subject of such petition. Any petition filed with the Tax Court on or before the last date specified for filing such petition by the Secretary in the notice of deficiency shall be treated as timely filed.

(b) Exceptions to Restrictions on Assessment.

(1) Assessments Arising out of Mathematical or Clerical Errors. If the taxpayer is notified that, on account of a mathematical or clerical error appearing on the return, an amount of tax in excess of that shown on the return is due, and that an assessment of the tax has been or will be made on the basis of what would have been the correct amount of tax but for the mathematical or clerical error, such notice shall not be considered as a notice of deficiency for the purposes of subsection (a) (prohibiting assessment and collection until notice of the deficiency has been mailed), or of section 6212(c)(1) (restricting further deficiency letters), or of section 6512(a) (prohibiting credits or refunds after petition to the Tax Court), and the taxpayer shall have no right to file a petition with the Tax Court based on such notice, nor shall such assessment or collection be prohibited by the provisions of subsection (a) of this section. Each notice under this paragraph shall set forth the error alleged and an explanation thereof.

(2) Abatement of Assessment of Mathematical or Clerical Errors.

(A) Request for Abatement. Notwithstanding section 6404(b), a taxpayer may file with the Secretary within 60 days after notice is sent under paragraph (1) a request for an abatement of any assessment specified in such notice, and upon receipt of such request, the Secretary shall abate the assessment. Any reassessment of the tax with respect to which an abatement is made under this subparagraph shall be subject to the deficiency procedures prescribed by this subchapter.

(B) Stay of Collection. In the case of any assessment referred to in paragraph (1), notwithstanding paragraph (1), no levy or proceeding in court for the collection of such assessment shall be made, begun, or prosecuted during the period in which such assessment may be abated under this paragraph.

(3) Assessments Arising out of Tentative Carryback or Refund Adjustments. If the Secretary determines that the amount applied, credited, or refunded under section 6411 is in excess of the overassessment attributable to the carryback or

the amount described in section 1341(b)(1) with respect to which such amount was applied, credited, or refunded, he may assess without regard to the provisions of paragraph (2) the amount of the excess as a deficiency as if it were due to a mathematical or clerical error appearing on the return.

(4) Assessment of Amount Paid. Any amount paid as a tax or in respect of a tax may be assessed upon the receipt of such payment notwithstanding the provisions of subsection (a). In any case where such amount is paid after the mailing of a notice of deficiency under section 6212, such payment shall not deprive the Tax Court of jurisdiction over such deficiency determined under section 6211 without regard to such assessment.

(5) Certain Orders of Criminal Restitution. If the taxpayer is notified that an assessment has been or will be made pursuant to section 6201(a)(4)

(A) such notice shall not be considered as a notice of deficiency for the purposes of subsection (a) (prohibiting assessment and collection until notice of the deficiency has been mailed), section 6212(c)(1) (restricting further deficiency letters), or section 6512(a) (prohibiting credits or refunds after petition to the Tax Court), and

(B) subsection (a) shall not apply with respect to the amount of such assessment.

(c) Failure to File Petition. If the taxpayer does not file a petition with the Tax Court within the time prescribed in subsection (a), the deficiency, notice of which has been mailed to the taxpayer, shall be assessed, and shall be paid upon notice and demand from the Secretary.

(d) Waiver of Restrictions. The taxpayer shall at any time (whether or not a notice of deficiency has been issued) have the right, by a signed notice in writing filed with the Secretary, to waive the restrictions provided in subsection (a) on the assessment and collection of the whole or any part of the deficiency.

(e) Suspension of Filing Period for Certain Excise Taxes. The running of the time prescribed by subsection (a) for filing a petition in the Tax Court with respect to the taxes imposed by section 4941 (relating to taxes on self-dealing), 4942 (relating to taxes on failure to distribute income), 4943 (relating to taxes on excess business holdings), 4944 (relating to investments which jeopardize charitable purpose), 4945 (relating to taxes on taxable expenditures), 4951 (relating to taxes on self-dealing), or 4952 (relating to taxes on taxable expenditures), 4955 (relating to taxes on political expenditures), 4958 (relating to private excess benefit), 4971 (relating to excise taxes on failure to meet minimum funding standard), 4975 (relating to excise taxes on prohibited transactions) shall be suspended for any period during which the Secretary has extended the time allowed for making correction under section 4963(e).

(f) Coordination with Title 11.

(1) Suspension of Running of Period for Filing Petition in Title 11 Cases. In any case under title 11 of the United States Code, the running of the time prescribed by subsection (a) for filing a petition in the Tax Court with respect to any

deficiency shall be suspended for the period during which the debtor is prohibited by reason of such case from filing a petition in the Tax Court with respect to such deficiency, and for 60 days thereafter.

(2) Certain Action Not Taken into Account. For purposes of the second and third sentences of subsection (a), the filing of a proof of claim or request for payment (or the taking of any other action) in a case under title 11 of the United States Code shall not be treated as action prohibited by such second sentence.

(g) Definitions. For purposes of this section—

(1) Return. The term "return" includes any return, statement, schedule, or list, and any amendment or supplement thereto, filed with respect to any tax imposed by subtitle A or B, or chapter 41, 42, 43, or 44.

(2) Mathematical or Clerical Error. The term "mathematical or clerical error" means—

(A) an error in addition, subtraction, multiplication, or division shown on any return,

(B) an incorrect use of any table provided by the Internal Revenue Service with respect to any return if such incorrect use is apparent from the existence of other information on the return,

(C) an entry on a return of an item which is inconsistent with another entry of the same or another item on such return,

(D) an omission of information which is required to be supplied on the return to substantiate an entry on the return,

(E) an entry on a return of a deduction or credit in an amount which exceeds a statutory limit imposed by subtitle A or B, or chapter 41, 42 43, or 44, if such limit is expressed—

(i) as a specified monetary amount, or

(ii) as a percentage, ratio, or fraction,

and if the items entering into the application of such limit appear on such return,

(F) an omission of a correct taxpayer identification number required under section 32 (relating to the earned income credit) to be included on a return,

(G) an entry on a return claiming the credit under section 32 with respect to net earnings from self-employment described in section 32(c)(2)(A) to the extent the tax imposed by section 1401 (relating to self-employment tax) on such net earnings has not been paid,

(H) an omission of a correct TIN required under section 21 (relating to expenses for household and dependent care services necessary for gainful employment) or section 151 (relating to allowance of deductions for personal exemptions),

(I) an omission of a correct TIN required under section 24(e) (relating to child tax credit) to be included on a return,

(J) an omission of a correct TIN required under section 25A(g)(1) (relating to higher education tuition and related expenses) to be included on a return,

(K) an omission of information required by section 32(k)(2) (relating to taxpayers making improper prior claims of earned income credit) or an entry on the return claiming the credit under section 32 for a taxable year for which the credit is disallowed under subsection (k)(1) thereof,

(L) the inclusion on a return of a TIN required to be included on the return under section 21, 24, 32, 6428, or 6428A if–

(i) such TIN is of an individual whose age affects the amount of the credit under such section, and

(ii) the computation of the credit on the return reflects the treatment of such individual as being of an age different from the individual's age based on such TIN[.]

. . . .

A taxpayer shall be treated as having omitted a correct TIN for purposes of the preceding sentence if information provided by the taxpayer on the return with respect to the individual whose TIN was provided differs from the information the Secretary obtains from the person issuing the TIN.

(h) Cross References.

(1) For assessment as if a mathematical error on the return, in the case of erroneous claims for income tax prepayment credits, see section 6201(a)(3).

(2) For assessments without regard to restrictions imposed by this section in the case of–

(A) Recovery of foreign income taxes, see section 905(c).

(B) Recovery of foreign estate tax, see section 2016.

(3) For provisions relating to application of this subchapter in the case of certain partnership items, etc., see section 6230(a).[3]

**26 USC § 6321 Lien for taxes.**

If any person liable to pay any tax neglects or refuses to pay the same after demand, the amount (including any interest, additional amount, addition to tax, or assessable penalty, together with any costs that may accrue in addition thereto) shall be a lien in favor of the United States upon all property and rights to property, whether real or personal, belonging to such person.

---

[3] Ed. note: **Sunset of amendments made by Economic Growth and Tax Relief Reconciliation Act of 2001 (Pub. L. No. 107-16).** Pursuant to § 901(a)(1), (b) of Act June 7, 2001, Pub. L. No. 107-16 (26 U.S.C. § 1 note), the amendments made to this section by such Act shall not apply to taxable, plan or limitation years beginning after December 31, 2010, and the Internal Revenue Code of 1986 shall be applied and administered to such years as if the amendments had never been enacted.

ADDITIONAL STATUTES

**26 USC § 6322 Period of lien.**

Unless another date is specifically fixed by law, the lien imposed by section 6321 shall arise at the time the assessment is made and shall continue until the liability for the amount so assessed (or a judgment against the taxpayer arising out of such liability) is satisfied or becomes unenforceable by reason of lapse of time.

**26 USC § 6323 Validity and priority against certain persons.**

(a) Purchasers, Holders of Security Interests, Mechanic' s Lienors, and Judgment Lien Creditors. The lien imposed by section 6321 shall not be valid as against any purchaser, holder of a security interest, mechanic's lienor, or judgment lien creditor until notice thereof which meets the requirements of subsection (f) has been filed by the Secretary.

(b) Protection for Certain Interests Even Though Notice Filed. Even though notice of a lien imposed by section 6321 has been filed, such lien shall not be valid—

(1) Securities. With respect to a security (as defined in subsection (h)(4))—

(A) as against a purchaser of such security who at the time of purchase did not have actual notice or knowledge of the existence of such lien; and

(B) as against a holder of a security interest in such security who, at the time such interest came into existence, did not have actual notice or knowledge of the existence of such lien.

(2) Motor Vehicles. With respect to a motor vehicle (as defined in subsection (h)(3)), as against a purchaser of such motor vehicle, if—

(A) at the time of the purchase such purchaser did not have actual notice or knowledge of the existence of such lien, and

(B) before the purchaser obtains such notice or knowledge, he has acquired possession of such motor vehicle and has not thereafter relinquished possession of such motor vehicle to the seller or his agent.

(3) Personal Property Purchased at Retail. With respect to tangible personal property purchased at retail, as against a purchaser in the ordinary course of the seller's trade or business, unless at the time of such purchase such purchaser intends such purchase to (or knows such purchase will) hinder, evade, or defeat the collection of any tax under this title.

(4) Personal Property Purchased in Casual Sale. With respect to household goods, personal effects, or other tangible personal property described in section 6334(a) purchased (not for resale) in a casual sale for less than $1,000, as against the purchaser, but only if such purchaser does not have actual notice or knowledge (A) of the existence of such lien, or (B) that this sale is one of a series of sales.

(5) Personal Property Subject to Possessory Lien. With respect to tangible personal property subject to a lien under local law securing the reasonable price of the repair or improvement of such property, as against a holder of such a lien, if

such holder is, and has been, continuously in possession of such property from the time such lien arose.

(6) Real Property Tax and Special Assessment Liens. With respect to real property, as against a holder of a lien upon such property, if such lien is entitled under local law to priority over security interests in such property which are prior in time, and such lien secures payment of—

(A) a tax of general application levied by any taxing authority based upon the value of such property;

(B) a special assessment imposed directly upon such property by any taxing authority, if such assessment is imposed for the purpose of defraying the cost of any public improvement; or

(C) charges for utilities or public services furnished to such property by the United States, a State or political subdivision thereof, or an instrumentality of any one or more of the foregoing.

(7) Residential Property Subject to a Mechanic's Lien for Certain Repairs and Improvements. With respect to real property subject to a lien for repair or improvement of a personal residence (containing not more than four dwelling units) occupied by the owner of such residence, as against a mechanic's lienor, but only if the contract price on the contract with the owner is not more than $5,000.

(8) Attorneys' Liens. With respect to a judgment or other amount in settlement of a claim or of a cause of action, as against an attorney who, under local law, holds a lien upon or a contract enforceable against such judgment or amount, to the extent of his reasonable compensation for obtaining such judgment or procuring such settlement, except that this paragraph shall not apply to any judgment or amount in settlement of a claim or of a cause of action against the United States to the extent that the United States offsets such judgment or amount against any liability of the taxpayer to the United States.

(9) Certain Insurance Contracts. With respect to a life insurance, endowment, or annuity contract, as against the organization which is the insurer under such contract, at any time—

(A) before such organization had actual notice or knowledge of the existence of such lien;

(B) after such organization had such notice or knowledge, with respect to advances required to be made automatically to maintain such contract in force under an agreement entered into before such organization had such notice or knowledge; or

(C) after satisfaction of a levy pursuant to section 6332(b), unless and until the Secretary delivers to such organization a notice, executed after the date of such satisfaction, of the existence of such lien.

(10) Deposit-Secured Loans. With respect to a savings deposit, share, or other account with an institution described in section 581 or 591, to the extent of any

loan made by such institution without actual notice or knowledge of the existence of such lien, as against such institution, if such loan is secured by such account.

(c) PROTECTION FOR CERTAIN COMMERCIAL TRANSACTIONS FINANCING AGREEMENTS, ETC.

(1) IN GENERAL. To the extent provided in this subsection, even though notice of a lien imposed by section 6321 has been filed, such lien shall not be valid with respect to a security interest which came into existence after tax lien filing but which–

(A) is in qualified property covered by the terms of a written agreement entered into before tax lien filing and constituting–

(i) a commercial transactions financing agreement,

(ii) a real property construction or improvement financing agreement, or

(iii) an obligatory disbursement agreement, and

(B) is protected under local law against a judgment lien arising, as of the time of tax lien filing, out of an unsecured obligation.

(2) COMMERCIAL TRANSACTIONS FINANCING AGREEMENT. For purposes of this subsection–

(A) DEFINITION. The term "commercial transactions financing agreement" means an agreement (entered into by a person in the course of his trade or business)–

(i) to make loans to the taxpayer to be secured by commercial financing security acquired by the taxpayer in the ordinary course of his trade or business, or

(ii) to purchase commercial financing security (other than inventory) acquired by the taxpayer in the ordinary course of his trade or business;

but such an agreement shall be treated as coming within the term only to the extent that such loan or purchase is made before the 46th day after the date of tax lien filing or (if earlier) before the lender or purchaser had actual notice or knowledge of such tax lien filing.

(B) LIMITATION ON QUALIFIED PROPERTY. The term "qualified property", when used with respect to a commercial transactions financing agreement, includes only commercial financing security acquired by the taxpayer before the 46th day after the date of tax lien filing.

(C) COMMERCIAL FINANCING SECURITY DEFINED. The term "commercial financing security" means (i) paper of a kind ordinarily arising in commercial transactions, (ii) accounts receivable, (iii) mortgages on real property, and (iv) inventory.

(D) PURCHASER TREATED AS ACQUIRING SECURITY INTEREST. A person who satisfies subparagraph (A) by reason of clause (ii) thereof shall be treated as having acquired a security interest in commercial financing security.

(3) Real Property Construction or Improvement Financing Agreement. For purposes of this subsection—

(A) Definition. The term "real property construction or improvement financing agreement" means an agreement to make cash disbursements to finance—

(i) the construction or improvement of real property,

(ii) a contract to construct or improve real property, or

(iii) the raising or harvesting of a farm crop or the raising of livestock or other animals.

For purposes of clause (iii), the furnishing of goods and services shall be treated as the disbursement of cash.

(B) Limitation on Qualified Property. The term "qualified property", when used with respect to a real property construction or improvement financing agreement, includes only—

(i) in the case of subparagraph (A)(i), the real property with respect to which the construction or improvement has been or is to be made,

(ii) in the case of subparagraph (A)(ii), the proceeds of the contract described therein, and

(iii) in the case of subparagraph (A)(iii), property subject to the lien imposed by section 6321 at the time of tax lien filing and the crop or the livestock or other animals referred to in subparagraph (A)(iii).

(4) Obligatory Disbursement Agreement. For purposes of this subsection—

(A) Definition. The term "obligatory disbursement agreement" means an agreement (entered into by a person in the course of his trade or business) to make disbursements, but such an agreement shall be treated as coming within the term only to the extent of disbursements which are required to be made by reason of the intervention of the rights of a person other than the taxpayer.

(B) Limitation on Qualified Property. The term "qualified property", when used with respect to an obligatory disbursement agreement, means property subject to the lien imposed by section 6321 at the time of tax lien filing and (to the extent that the acquisition is directly traceable to the disbursements referred to in subparagraph (A)) property acquired by the taxpayer after tax lien filing.

(C) Special Rules for Surety Agreements. Where the obligatory disbursement agreement is an agreement ensuring the performance of a contract between the taxpayer and another person—

(i) the term "qualified property" shall be treated as also including the proceeds of the contract the performance of which was ensured, and

(ii) If the contract the performance of which was ensured was a

ADDITIONAL STATUTES

contract to construct or improve real property, to produce goods, or to furnish services, the term "qualified property" shall be treated as also including any tangible personal property used by the taxpayer in the performance of such ensured contract.

(d) 45-Day Period for Making Disbursements. Even though notice of a lien imposed by section 6321 has been filed, such lien shall not be valid with respect to a security interest which came into existence after tax lien filing by reason of disbursements made before the 46th day after the date of tax lien filing, or (if earlier) before the person making such disbursements had actual notice or knowledge of tax lien filing, but only if such security interest—

(1) is in property (A) subject, at the time of tax lien filing, to the lien imposed by section 6321, and (B) covered by the terms of a written agreement entered into before tax lien filing, and

(2) is protected under local law against a judgment lien arising, as of the time of tax lien filing, out of an unsecured obligation.

(e) Priority of Interest and Expenses. If the lien imposed by section 6321 is not valid as against a lien or security interest, the priority of such lien or security interest shall extend to—

(1) any interest or carrying charges upon the obligation secured,

(2) the reasonable charges and expenses of an indenture trustee or agent holding the security interest for the benefit of the holder of the security interest,

(3) the reasonable expenses, including reasonable compensation for attorneys, actually incurred in collecting or enforcing the obligation secured,

(4) the reasonable costs of insuring, preserving, or repairing the property to which the lien or security interest relates,

(5) the reasonable costs of insuring payment of the obligation secured, and

(6) amounts paid to satisfy any lien on the property to which the lien or security interest relates, but only if the lien so satisfied is entitled to priority over the lien imposed by section 6321,

to the extent that, under local law, any such item has the same priority as the lien or security interest to which it relates.

(f) Place for Filing Notice; Form.

(1) Place for Filing. The notice referred to in subsection (a) shall be filed—

(A) Under State Laws.

(i) Real Property. In the case of real property, in one office within the State (or the county, or other governmental subdivision), as designated by the laws of such State, in which the property subject to the lien is situated; and

(ii) Personal Property. In the case of personal property, whether tangible or intangible, in one office within the State (or the county, or other governmental subdivision), as designated by the laws of such State, in which the property subject to the lien is situated, except that State law merely conforming to or reenacting Federal law establishing a national filing system does not constitute a second office for filing as designated by the laws of such State; or

(B) With Clerk of District Court. In the office of the clerk of the United States district court for the judicial district in which the property subject to the lien is situated, whenever the State has not by law designated one office which meets the requirements of subparagraph (A); or

(C) With Recorder of Deeds of the District of Columbia. In the office of the Recorder of Deeds of the District of Columbia, if the property subject to the lien is situated in the District of Columbia.

(2) Situs of Property Subject to Lien. For purposes of paragraphs (1) and (4), property shall be deemed to be situated—

(A) Real Property. In the case of real property, at its physical location; or

(B) Personal Property. In the case of personal property, whether tangible or intangible, at the residence of the taxpayer at the time the notice of lien is filed.

For purposes of paragraph (2)(B), the residence of a corporation or partnership shall be deemed to be the place at which the principal executive office of the business is located, and the residence of a taxpayer whose residence is without the United States shall be deemed to be in the District of Columbia.

(3) Form. The form and content of the notice referred to in subsection (a) shall be prescribed by the Secretary. Such notice shall be valid notwithstanding any other provision of law regarding the form or content of a notice of lien.

(4) Indexing Required with Respect to Certain Real Property. In the case of real property, if—

(A) under the laws of the State in which the real property is located, a deed is not valid as against a purchaser of the property who (at the time of purchase) does not have actual notice or knowledge of the existence of such deed unless the fact of filing of such deed has been entered and recorded in a public index at the place of filing in such a manner that a reasonable inspection of the index will reveal the existence of the deed, and

(B) there is maintained (at the applicable office under paragraph (1)) an adequate system for the public indexing of Federal tax liens,

then the notice of lien referred to in subsection (a) shall not be treated as meeting the filing requirements under paragraph (1) unless the fact of filing is entered and recorded in the index referred to in subparagraph (B) in such

ADDITIONAL STATUTES

a manner that a reasonable inspection of the index will reveal the existence of the lien.

(5) National Filing Systems. The filing of a notice of lien shall be governed solely by this title and shall not be subject to any other Federal law establishing a place or places for the filing of liens or encumbrances under a national filing system.

(g) Refiling of Notice. For purposes of this section—

(1) General Rule. Unless notice of lien is refiled in the manner prescribed in paragraph (2) during the required refiling period, such notice of lien shall be treated as filed on the date on which it is filed (in accordance with subsection (f)) after the expiration of such refiling period.

(2) Place for Filing. A notice of lien refiled during the required refiling period shall be effective only—

(A) if—

(i) such notice of lien is refiled in the office in which the prior notice of lien was filed, and

(ii) in the case of real property, the fact of refiling is entered and recorded in an index to the extent required by subsection (f)(4); and

(B) in any case in which, 90 days or more prior to the date of a refiling of notice of lien under subparagraph (A), the Secretary received written information (in the manner prescribed in regulations issued by the Secretary) concerning a change in the taxpayer's residence, if a notice of such lien is also filed in accordance with subsection (f) in the State in which such residence is located.

(3) Required Refiling Period. In the case of any notice of lien, the term "required refiling period" means—

(A) the one-year period ending 30 days after the expiration of 10 years after the date of the assessment of the tax, and

(B) the one-year period ending with the expiration of 10 years after the close of the preceding required refiling period for such notice of lien.

(4) Transitional Rule. Notwithstanding paragraph (3), if the assessment of the tax was made before January 1, 1962, the first required refiling period shall be the calendar year 1967.

(h) Definitions. For purposes of this section and section 6324—

(1) Security Interest. The term "security interest" means any interest in property acquired by contract for the purpose of securing payment or performance of an obligation or indemnifying against loss or liability. A security interest exists at any time (A) if, at such time, the property is in existence and the interest has become protected under local law against a subsequent judgment lien arising out of an unsecured obligation, and (B) to the extent that,

at such time, the holder has parted with money or money's worth.

(2) Mechanic' s Lienor. The term "mechanic's lienor" means any person who under local law has a lien on real property (or on the proceeds of a contract relating to real property) for services, labor, or materials furnished in connection with the construction or improvement of such property. For purposes of the preceding sentence, a person has a lien on the earliest date such lien becomes valid under local law against subsequent purchasers without actual notice, but not before he begins to furnish the services, labor, or materials.

(3) Motor Vehicle. The term "motor vehicle" means a self-propelled vehicle which is registered for highway use under the laws of any State or foreign country.

(4) Security. The term "security" means any bond, debenture, note, or certificate or other evidence of indebtedness, issued by a corporation or a government or political subdivision thereof, with interest coupons or in registered form, share of stock, voting trust certificate, or any certificate of interest or participation in, certificate of deposit or receipt for, temporary or interim certificate for, or warrant or right to subscribe to or purchase, any of the foregoing; negotiable instrument; or money.

(5) Tax Lien Filing. The term "tax lien filing" means the filing of notice (referred to in subsection (a)) of the lien imposed by section 6321.

(6) Purchaser. The term "purchaser" means a person who, for adequate and full consideration in money or money's worth, acquires an interest (other than a lien or security interest) in property which is valid under local law against subsequent purchasers without actual notice. In applying the preceding sentence for purposes of subsection (a) of this section, and for purposes of section 6324–

(A) a lease of property,

(B) a written executory contract to purchase or lease property,

(C) an option to purchase or lease property or any interest therein, or

(D) an option to renew or extend a lease of property,

which is not a lien or security interest shall be treated as an interest in property.

(i) Special Rules.

(1) Actual Notice or Knowledge. For purposes of this subchapter, an organization shall be deemed for purposes of a particular transaction to have actual notice or knowledge of any fact from the time such fact is brought to the attention of the individual conducting such transaction, and in any event from the time such fact would have been brought to such individual's attention if the organization had exercised due diligence. An organization exercises due diligence if it maintains reasonable routines for communicating significant information to the person conducting the transaction and there is reasonable compliance with the routines. Due diligence does not require an individual

ADDITIONAL STATUTES

acting for the organization to communicate information unless such communication is part of his regular duties or unless he has reason to know of the transaction and that the transaction would be materially affected by the information.

(2) Subrogation. Where, under local law, one person is subrogated to the rights of another with respect to a lien or interest, such person shall be subrogated to such rights for purposes of any lien imposed by section 6321 or 6324.

(3) Forfeitures. For purposes of this subchapter, a forfeiture under local law of property seized by a law enforcement agency of a State, county, or other local governmental subdivision shall relate back to the time of seizure, except that this paragraph shall not apply to the extent that under local law the holder of an intervening claim or interest would have priority over the interest of the State, county, or other local governmental subdivision in the property.

(4) Cost-of-Living Adjustment. In the case of notices of liens imposed by section 6321 which are filed in any calendar year after 1998, each of the dollar amounts under paragraph (4) or (7) of subsection (b) shall be increased by an amount equal to—

(A) such dollar amount, multiplied by

(B) the cost-of-living adjustment determined under section 1(f)(3) for the calendar year, determined by substituting "calendar year 1996" for "calendar year 2016" in subparagraph (A)(ii) thereof

If any amount as adjusted under the preceding sentence is not a multiple of $10, such amount shall be rounded to the nearest multiple of $10.

(j) Withdrawal of Notice in Certain Circumstances.

(1) In General. The Secretary may withdraw a notice of a lien filed under this section and this chapter shall be applied as if the withdrawn notice had not been filed, if the Secretary determines that—

(A) the filing of such notice was premature or otherwise not in accordance with administrative procedures of the Secretary,

(B) the taxpayer has entered into an agreement under section 6159 to satisfy the tax liability for which the lien was imposed by means of installment payments, unless such agreement provides otherwise,

(C) the withdrawal of such notice will facilitate the collection of the tax liability, or

(D) with the consent of the taxpayer or the National Taxpayer Advocate, the withdrawal of such notice would be in the best interests of the taxpayer (as determined by the National Taxpayer Advocate) and the United States.

Any such withdrawal shall be made by filing notice at the same office as the withdrawn notice. A copy of such notice of withdrawal shall be provided to the taxpayer.

(2) Notice to Credit Agencies, etc. Upon written request by the taxpayer with respect to whom a notice of a lien was withdrawn under paragraph (1), the Secretary shall promptly make reasonable efforts to notify credit reporting agencies, and any financial institution or creditor whose name and address is specified in such request, of the withdrawal of such notice. Any such request shall be in such form as the Secretary may prescribe.

## 26 USC § 6503 Suspension of running of period of limitation.

(a) Issuance of Statutory Notice of Deficiency.

(1) General Rule.[4] The running of the period of limitations provided in section 6501 or 6502 on the making of assessments or the collection by levy or a proceeding in court, in respect of any deficiency as defined in section 6211 (relating to income, estate, gift and certain excise taxes), shall (after the mailing of a notice under section 6212(a)) be suspended for the period during which the Secretary is prohibited from making the assessment or from collecting by levy or a proceeding in court (and in any event, if a proceeding in respect of the deficiency is placed on the docket of the Tax Court, until the decision of the Tax Court becomes final), and for 60 days thereafter.

(2) Corporation Joining in Consolidated Income Tax Return. If a notice under section 6212(a) in respect of a deficiency in tax imposed by subtitle A for any taxable year is mailed to a corporation, the suspension of the running of the period of limitations provided in paragraph (1) of this subsection shall apply in the case of corporations with which such corporation made a consolidated income tax return for such taxable year.

(b) Assets of Taxpayer in Control or Custody of Court. The period of limitations on collection after assessment prescribed in section 6502 shall be suspended for the period the assets of the taxpayer are in the control or custody of the court in any proceeding before any court of the United States or of any State or of the District of Columbia, and for 6 months thereafter.

(c) Taxpayer Outside United States. The running of the period of limitations on collection after assessment prescribed in section 6502 shall be suspended for the period during which the taxpayer is outside the United States if such period of absence is for a continuous period of at least 6 months. If the preceding sentence applies and at the time of the taxpayer's return to the United States the period of limitations on collection after assessment prescribed in section 6502 would expire before the expiration of 6 months from the date of his return, such period shall not expire before the expiration of such 6 months.

(d) Extensions of Time for Payment of Estate Tax. The running of the period of limitation for collection of any tax imposed by chapter 11 shall be suspended for the period of any extension of time for payment granted under the provisions of

---

[4] Ed. note: **Amendment of subsec. (a)(1), applicable to partnership taxable years beginning after Dec. 31, 2017.** Act Nov. 2, 2015, P.L. 114-74, Title XI, § 1101(f)(4), 129 Stat. 638 (applicable to partnership taxable years beginning after Dec. 31, 2017, as provided by § 1101(g) of Act Nov. 2, 2015, P.L. 114-74, which appears as 26 U.S.C. § 6221 note), provides: "Section 6503(a)(1) of such Code is amended by striking '(or section 6229' and all that follows through'of section 6230(a))'.".

ADDITIONAL STATUTES

section 6161(a)(2) or (b)(2) or under the provisions of section 6163 or 6166.

(e) Extensions of Time for Payment of Tax Attributable to Recoveries of Foreign Expropriation Losses. The running of the period of limitations for collection of the tax attributable to a recovery of a foreign expropriation loss (within the meaning of section 6167(f)) shall be suspended for the period of any extension of time for payment under subsection (a) or (b) of section 6167.

(f) Wrongful Seizure of or Lien on Property of Third Party.

(1) Wrongful Seizure. The running of the period under section 6502 shall be suspended for a period equal to the period from the date property (including money) of a third party is wrongfully seized or received by the Secretary to the date the Secretary returns property pursuant to section 6343(b) or the date on which a judgment secured pursuant to section 7426 with respect to such property becomes final, and for 30 days thereafter. The running of such period shall be suspended under this paragraph only with respect to the amount of such assessment equal to the amount of money or the value of specific property returned.

(2) Wrongful Lien. In the case of any assessment for which a lien was made on any property, the running of the period under section 6502 shall be suspended for a period equal to the period beginning on the date any person becomes entitled to a certificate under section 6325(b)(4) with respect to such property and ending on the date which is 30 days after the earlier of–

(A) the earliest date on which the Secretary no longer holds any amount as a deposit or bond provided under section 6325(b)(4) by reason of such deposit or bond being used to satisfy the unpaid tax or being refunded or released; or

(B) the date that the judgment secured under section 7426(b)(5) becomes final.

The running of such period shall be suspended under this paragraph only with respect to the amount of such assessment equal to the value of the interest of the United States in the property plus interest, penalties, additions to the tax, and additional amounts attributable thereto.

(g) Suspension Pending Correction. The running of the periods of limitations provided in sections 6501 and 6502 on the making of assessments or the collection by levy or a proceeding in court in respect of any tax imposed by chapter 42 or section 507, 4971, or 4975 shall be suspended for any period described in section 507(g)(2) or during which the Secretary has extended the time for making correction under section 4963(e).

(h) Cases Under Title 11 of the United States Code. The running of the period of limitations provided in section 6501 or 6502 on the making of assessments or collection shall, in a case under title 11 of the United States Code, be suspended for the period during which the Secretary is prohibited by reason of such case from making the assessment or from collecting and—

(1) for assessment, 60 days thereafter, and

(2) for collection, 6 months thereafter.

(i) Extension of Time for Payment of Undistributed PFIC Earnings Tax Liability. The running of any period of limitations for collection of any amount of undistributed PFIC earnings tax liability (as defined in section 1294(b)) shall be suspended for the period of any extension of time under section 1294 for payment of such amount.

(j) Extension in Case of Certain Summonses.

(1) In General. If any designated summons is issued by the Secretary to a corporation (or to any other person to whom the corporation has transferred records) with respect to any return of tax by such corporation for a taxable year (or other period) for which such corporation is being examined under the coordinated industry case program (or any successor program) of the Internal Revenue Service, the running of any period of limitations provided in section 6501 on the assessment of such tax shall be suspended—

(A) during any judicial enforcement period—

(i) with respect to such summons, or

(ii) with respect to any other summons which is issued during the 30-day period which begins on the date on which such designated summons is issued and which relates to the same return as such designated summons, and

(B) if the court in any proceeding referred to in paragraph (3) requires any compliance with a summons referred to in subparagraph (A), during the 120-day period beginning with the 1st day after the close of the suspension under subparagraph (A).

If subparagraph (B) does not apply, such period shall in no event expire before the 60th day after the close of the suspension under subparagraph (A).

(2) Designated Summons. For purposes of this subsection—

(A) In General. The term "designated summons" means any summons issued for purposes of determining the amount of any tax imposed by this title if—

(i) the issuance of such summons is preceded by a review and written approval of such issuance by the Commissioner of the relevant operating division of the Internal Revenue Service and the Chief Counsel which—

(I) states facts clearly establishing that the Secretary has made reasonable requests for the information that is the subject of the summons, and

(II) is attached to such summons,

(ii) such summons is issued at least 60 days before the day on which the period prescribed in section 6501 for the assessment of such tax expires (determined with regard to extensions), and

(iii) such summons clearly states that it is a designated summons for purposes of this subsection.

(B) Limitation. A summons which relates to any return shall not be treated as a designated summons if a prior summons which relates to such return was treated as a designated summons for purposes of this subsection.

(3) Judicial Enforcement Period. For purposes of this subsection, the term "judicial enforcement period" means, with respect to any summons, the period–

(A) which begins on the day on which a court proceeding with respect to such summons is brought, and

(B) which ends on the day on which there is a final resolution as to the summoned person's response to such summons.

(4) Establishment that reasonable requests for information were made. In any court proceeding described in paragraph (3), the Secretary shall establish that reasonable requests were made for the information that is the subject of the summons.

(k) Cross References. For suspension in case of–

(1) Deficiency dividends of a personal holding company, see section 547(f).

(2) Receiverships, see subchapter B of chapter 70.

(3) Claims against transferees and fiduciaries, see chapter 71.

(4) Tax return preparers, see section 6694(c)(3).

(5) Deficiency dividends in the case of a regulated investment company or a real estate investment trust, see section 860(h).

## 26 USC § 6658 Coordination with title 11.

(a) Certain Failures to Pay Tax. No addition to the tax shall be made under section 6651, 6654, or 6655 for failure to make timely payment of tax with respect to a period during which a case is pending under title 11 of the United States Code–

(1) if such tax was incurred by the estate and the failure occurred pursuant to an order of the court finding probable insufficiency of funds of the estate to pay administrative expenses, or

(2) if–

(A) such tax was incurred by the debtor before the earlier of the order for relief or (in the involuntary case) the appointment of a trustee, and

(B) (i) the petition was filed before the due date prescribed by law (including extensions) for filing a return of such tax, or

(ii) the date for making the addition to the tax occurs on or after the day on which the petition was filed.

(b) Exception for Collected Taxes. Subsection (a) shall not apply to any liability for an addition to the tax which arises from the failure to pay or deposit a tax withheld or collected from others and required to be paid to the United States.

**26 USC § 6672 Failure to collect and pay over tax, or attempt to evade or defeat tax.**

(a) GENERAL RULE. Any person required to collect, truthfully account for, and pay over any tax imposed by this title who willfully fails to collect such tax, or truthfully account for and pay over such tax, or willfully attempts in any manner to evade or defeat any such tax or the payment thereof, shall, in addition to other penalties provided by law, be liable to a penalty equal to the total amount of the tax evaded, or not collected, or not accounted for and paid over. No penalty shall be imposed under section 6653 or part II of subchapter A of chapter 68 for any offense to which this section is applicable.

(b) PRELIMINARY NOTICE REQUIREMENT.

(1) IN GENERAL. No penalty shall be imposed under subsection (a) unless the Secretary notifies the taxpayer in writing by mail to an address as determined under section 6212(b) or in person that the taxpayer shall be subject to an assessment of such penalty.

(2) TIMING OF NOTICE. The mailing of the notice described in paragraph (1) (or, in the case of such a notice delivered in person, such delivery) shall precede any notice and demand of any penalty under subsection (a) by at least 60 days.

(3) STATUTE OF LIMITATIONS. If a notice described in paragraph (1) with respect to any penalty is mailed or delivered in person before the expiration of the period provided by section 6501 for the assessment of such penalty (determined without regard to this paragraph), the period provided by such section for the assessment of such penalty shall not expire before the later of—

(A) the date 90 days after the date on which such notice was mailed or delivered in person, or

(B) if there is a timely protest of the proposed assessment, the date 30 days after the Secretary makes a final administrative determination with respect to such protest.

(4) EXCEPTION FOR JEOPARDY. This subsection shall not apply if the Secretary finds that the collection of the penalty is in jeopardy.

(c) EXTENSION OF PERIOD OF COLLECTION WHERE BOND IS FILED.

(1) IN GENERAL. If, within 30 days after the day on which notice and demand of any penalty under subsection (a) is made against any person, such person—

(A) pays an amount which is not less than the minimum amount required to commence a proceeding in court with respect to his liability for such penalty,

(B) files a claim for refund of the amount so paid, and

(C) furnishes a bond which meets the requirements of paragraph (3),

ADDITIONAL STATUTES

no levy or proceeding in court for the collection of the remainder of such penalty shall be made, begun, or prosecuted until a final resolution of a proceeding begun as provided in paragraph (2). Notwithstanding the provisions of section 7421(a), the beginning of such proceeding or levy during the time such prohibition is in force may be enjoined by a proceeding in the proper court. Nothing in this paragraph shall be construed to prohibit any counterclaim for the remainder of such penalty in a proceeding begun as provided in paragraph (2).

(2) Suit Must Be Brought to Determine Liability for Penalty. If, within 30 days after the day on which his claim for refund with respect to any penalty under subsection (a) is denied, the person described in paragraph (1) fails to begin a proceeding in the appropriate United States district court (or in the Court of Federal Claims) for the determination of his liability for such penalty, paragraph (1) shall cease to apply with respect to such penalty, effective on the day following the close of the 30-day period referred to in this paragraph.

(3) Bond. The bond referred to in paragraph (1) shall be in such form and with such sureties as the Secretary may by regulations prescribe and shall be in an amount equal to 1 ½ times the amount of excess of the penalty assessed over the payment described in paragraph (1).

(4) Suspension of Running of Period of Limitations on Collection. The running of the period of limitations provided in section 6502 on the collection by levy or by a proceeding in court in respect of any penalty described in paragraph (1) shall be suspended for the period during which the Secretary is prohibited from collecting by levy or a proceeding in court.

(5) Jeopardy Collection. If the Secretary makes a finding that the collection of the penalty is in jeopardy, nothing in this subsection shall prevent the immediate collection of such penalty.

(d) Right of Contribution Where More than 1 Person Liable for Penalty. If more than 1 person is liable for the penalty under subsection (a) with respect to any tax, each person who paid such penalty shall be entitled to recover from other persons who are liable for such penalty an amount equal to the excess of the amount paid by such person over such person's proportionate share of the penalty. Any claim for such a recovery may be made only in a proceeding which is separate from, and is not joined or consolidated with—

(1) an action for collection of such penalty brought by the United States, or

(2) a proceeding in which the United States files a counterclaim or third-party complaint for the collection of such penalty.

(e) Exception for Voluntary Board Members of Tax-Exempt Organizations. No penalty shall be imposed by subsection (a) on any unpaid, volunteer member of any board of trustees or directors of an organization exempt from tax under subtitle A if such member—

(1) is solely serving in an honorary capacity,

(2) does not participate in the day-to-day or financial operations of the organization, and

(3) does not have actual knowledge of the failure on which such penalty is imposed.

The preceding sentence shall not apply if it results in no person being liable for the penalty imposed by subsection (a).

## 26 USC § 7433 Civil damages for certain unauthorized collection actions.

* * *

(e) Actions for Violations of Certain Bankruptcy Procedures.

(1) In General. If, in connection with any collection of Federal tax with respect to a taxpayer, any officer or employee of the Internal Revenue Service willfully violates any provision of section 362 (relating to automatic stay) or 524 (relating to effect of discharge) of title 11, United States Code (or any successor provision), or any regulation promulgated under such provision, such taxpayer may petition the bankruptcy court to recover damages against the United States.

(2) Remedy to Be Exclusive.

(A) In General. Except as provided in subparagraph (B), notwithstanding section 105 of such title 11, such petition shall be the exclusive remedy for recovering damages resulting from such actions.

(B) Certain Other Actions Permitted. Subparagraph (A) shall not apply to an action under section 362(h) of such title 11[5] for a violation of a stay provided by section 362 of such title; except that—

(i) administrative and litigation costs in connection with such an action may only be awarded under section 7430; and

(ii) administrative costs may be awarded only if incurred on or after the date that the bankruptcy petition is filed.

---

[5] Ed. Note: The 2005 Act renumbered Code section 362(h) as section 362(k)(1) and revised the renumbered section 362(k)(1).

## TITLE 33 NAVIGATION AND NAVIGABLE WATERS

### 33 USC § 775 Payments nonassignable and exempt from process

No payment under sections 771 to 775 of this title shall be assignable, either in law or in equity, or be subject to execution, levy, lien, attachment, garnishment, or other legal process.

# TITLE 37 PAY AND ALLOWANCES OF THE UNIFORMED SERVICES

## 37 USC § 301b Special pay: aviation career officers extending period of active duty.

(a) Bonus Authorized. An aviation officer described in subsection (b) who, during the period beginning on January 1, 1989, and ending on December 31, 2018, executes a written agreement to remain on active duty in aviation service for at least one year may, upon the acceptance of the agreement by the Secretary concerned, be paid a retention bonus as provided in this section.

* * *

(g) Repayment. An officer who does not complete the period of active duty specified in the agreement entered into under subsection (a) shall be subject to the repayment provisions of section 303a(e) of this title.

* * *

## 37 USC § 301d Multiyear retention bonus: medical officers of the armed forces.

(a) Bonus Authorized.

(1) A medical officer described in subsection (b) who executes a written agreement to remain on active duty for two, three, or four years after completion of any other active-duty service commitment may, upon acceptance of the written agreement by the Secretary of the military department concerned, be paid a retention bonus as provided in this section.

(2) The amount of a retention bonus under paragraph (1) may not exceed $75,000 for each year covered by a four-year agreement. The maximum yearly retention bonus for two-year and three-year agreements shall be reduced to reflect the shorter service commitment.

* * *

(c) Repayment. An officer who does not complete the period of active duty specified in the agreement entered into under subsection (a) shall be subject to the repayment provisions of section 303a(e) of this title.

## 37 USC § 301e Multiyear retention bonus: dental officers of the armed forces.

(a) Bonus Authorized.

(1) A dental officer described in subsection (b) who executes a written agreement to remain on active duty for two, three, or four years after completion of any other active-duty service commitment may, upon acceptance of the written agreement by the Secretary of the military department concerned, be paid a retention bonus as provided in this section.

(2) The amount of a retention bonus under paragraph (1) may not exceed 50,000 for each year covered by a four-year agreement. The maximum yearly retention bonus for two-year and three-year agreements shall be reduced to

reflect the shorter service commitment.

* * *

(d) Repayment. An officer who does not complete the period of active duty specified in the agreement entered into under subsection (a) shall be subject to the repayment provisions of section 303a(e) of this title.

**37 USC § 302 Special pay: medical officers of the armed forces.**

(a) Variable, Additional, and Board Certification Special Pay.

(1) An officer who is an officer of the Medical Corps of the Army or the Navy or an officer of the Air Force designated as a medical officer and who is on active duty under a call or order to active duty for a period of not less than one year is entitled to special pay in accordance with this subsection.

* * *

(f) Repayment. An officer who does not complete the period for which the payment was made under subsection (a)(4) or subsection (b)(1) shall be subject to the repayment provisions of section 303a(e) of this title.

* * *

(i) Effect of Discharge in Bankruptcy. A discharge in bankruptcy under title 11 that is entered less than 5 years after the termination of an agreement under this section does not discharge the person signing such agreement from a debt arising under such agreement or under subsection (c)(2) or (f). This paragraph applies to any case commenced under title 11 after September 30, 1985.

**37 USC § 302b Special pay: dental officers of the armed forces.**

(a) Variable, Additional, Board Certification, and Incentive Special Pay.

(1) An officer who–

(A) is an officer of the Dental Corps of the Army or the Navy or an officer of the Air Force designated as a dental officer; and

(B) is on active duty under a call or order to active duty for a period of not less than one year, is entitled to special pay in accordance with this subsection.

* * *

(b) Active-Duty Agreement.

(1) An officer may not be paid additional special pay under paragraph (4) or (6) of subsection (a) for any 12-month period unless the officer first executes a written agreement under which the officer agrees to remain on active duty for a period of not less than one year beginning on the date the officer accepts the award of such special pay.

(2) Under regulations prescribed by the Secretary of Defense under section

303a(a) of this title [37 U.S.C. § 303a(a)], the Secretary of the military department concerned may terminate at any time an officer's entitlement to the special pay authorized by paragraph (4) or (6) of subsection (a). If such entitlement is terminated, the officer concerned shall be subject to the repayment provisions of section 303a(e) of this title.

* * *

(e) Repayment. An officer who does not complete the period of active duty specified in the agreement referred to in subsection (b) shall be subject to the repayment provisions of section 303a(e) of this title.

* * *

**37 USC § 302d Special pay: accession bonus for registered nurses.**

(a) Accession Bonus Authorized.

(1) A person who is a registered nurse and who, during the period beginning on November 29, 1989 and ending on December 31, 2018, executes a written agreement described in subsection (c) to accept a commission as an officer and remain on active duty for a period of not less than three years may, upon the acceptance of the agreement by the Secretary concerned, be paid an accession bonus in an amount determined by the Secretary concerned.

* * *

(c) Agreement. The agreement referred to in subsection (a) shall provide that, consistent with the needs of the uniformed service concerned, the person executing the agreement will be assigned to duty, for the period of obligated service covered by the agreement, as an officer of the Nurse Corps of the Army or Navy, an officer of the Air Force designated as a nurse, or an officer designated as a nurse in the commissioned corps of the Public Health Service.

(d) Repayment. An officer who does not become and remain licensed as a registered nurse during the period for which the payment is made, or who does not complete the period of active duty specified in the agreement entered into under subsection (a), shall be subject to the repayment provisions of section 303a(e) of this title.

**37 USC § 302e Special pay: nurse anesthetists.**

(a) Special Pay Authorized.

(1) An officer described in subsection (b)(1) who, during the period beginning on November 29, 1989, and ending on December 31, 2018, executes a written agreement to remain on active duty for a period of one year or more may, upon the acceptance of the agreement by the Secretary concerned, be paid incentive special pay in an amount not to exceed $50,000 for any 12-month period.

* * *

(b) COVERED OFFICERS.

(1) An officer referred to in subsection (a) is an officer of a uniformed service who—

(A) is an officer of the Nurse Corps of the Army or Navy, an officer of the Air Force designated as a nurse, or an officer designated as a nurse in the commissioned corps of the Public Health Service;

(B) is a qualified certified registered nurse anesthetist; and

(C) is on active duty under a call or order to active duty for a period of not less than one year.

* * *

(e) REPAYMENT. An officer who does not complete the period of active duty specified in the agreement entered into under subsection (a) shall be subject to the repayment provisions of section 303a(e) of this title.

### 37 USC § 302g Special pay: Selected Reserve health care professionals in critically short wartime specialties.

(a) SPECIAL PAY AUTHORIZED. An officer of a reserve component of the armed forces described in subsection (b) who executes a written agreement under which the officer agrees to serve in the Selected Reserve of an armed force for a period of not less than one year nor more than three years, beginning on the date the officer accepts the award of special pay under this section, may be paid special pay at an annual rate not to exceed $25,000.

(b) ELIGIBLE OFFICERS. An officer referred to in subsection (a) is an officer in a health care profession who is qualified in a specialty designated by regulations as a critically short wartime specialty.

* * *

(d) REPAYMENT. An officer who does not complete the period of service in the Selected Reserve specified in the agreement entered into under subsection (a) shall be subject to the repayment provisions of section 303a(e) of this title.

* * *

### 37 USC § 302h Special pay: accession bonus for dental officers.

(a) ACCESSION BONUS AUTHORIZED.

(1) A person who is a graduate of an accredited dental school and who, during the period beginning on September 23, 1996, and ending on December 31, 2018, executes a written agreement described in subsection (c) to accept a commission as an officer of the armed forces and remain on active duty for a period of not less than four years may, upon the acceptance of the agreement by the Secretary concerned, be paid an accession bonus in an amount determined by the Secretary concerned.

* * *

(d) Repayment. A person who, after signing an agreement under subsection (a), is not commissioned as an officer of the armed forces, does not become licensed as a dentist, or does not complete the period of active duty specified in the agreement shall be subject to the repayment provisions of section 303a(e) of this title.

**37 USC § 302j Special pay: accession bonus for pharmacy officers.**

(a) Accession Bonus Authorized. A person who is a graduate of an accredited pharmacy school and who, during the period beginning on October 30, 2000, and ending on December 31, 2018, executes a written agreement described in subsection (d) to accept a commission as an officer of a uniformed service and remain on active duty for a period of not less than 4 years may, upon acceptance of the agreement by the Secretary concerned, be paid an accession bonus in an amount determined by the Secretary concerned.

* * *

(e) Repayment. A person who, after signing an agreement under subsection (a), is not commissioned as an officer of the armed forces, does not become and remain certified or licensed as a pharmacist, or does not complete the period of active duty specified in the agreement shall be subject to the repayment provisions of section 303a(e) of this title.

**37 USC § 303a Special pay: general provisions.**

* * *

(e) Repayment of Unearned Portion of Bonuses and Other Benefits When Conditions of Payment Not Met; Termination of Entitlement to Unpaid Amounts.

(1) (A) Except as provided in paragraphs (2) and (3), a member of the uniformed services who receives a bonus or similar benefit and whose receipt of the bonus or similar benefit is subject to the condition that the member continue to satisfy certain eligibility requirements shall repay to the United States an amount equal to the unearned portion of the bonus or similar benefit if the member fails to satisfy the eligibility requirements and may not receive any unpaid amounts of the bonus or similar benefit after the member fails to satisfy the requirements, unless the Secretary concerned determines that the imposition of the repayment requirement and termination of the payment of unpaid amounts of the bonus or similar benefit with regard to the member would be contrary to a personnel policy or management objective, would be against equity and good conscience, or would be contrary to the best interests of the United States.

(B) The Secretary concerned may establish, by regulations, procedures for determining the amount of the repayment required under this subsection and the circumstances under which an exception to the required repayment may be granted. The Secretary concerned may specify in the regulations the conditions under which an installment payment of a bonus or similar benefit to be paid to a member of the uniformed services will not be made if the member no longer satisfies the eligibility requirements for the bonus or similar benefit. For the military departments, this subsection shall be administered under regulations prescribed by the Secretary of Defense.

(2) (A) If a member of the uniformed services receives a sole survivorship discharge, the Secretary concerned—

(i) shall not require repayment by the member of the unearned portion of any bonus, incentive pay, or similar benefit previously paid to the member; and

(ii) may grant an exception to the requirement to terminate the payment of any unpaid amounts of a bonus, incentive pay, or similar benefit if the Secretary concerned determines that termination of the payment of the unpaid amounts would be contrary to a personnel policy or management objective, would be against equity and good conscience, or would be contrary to the best interests of the United States.

(B) In this paragraph, the term "sole survivorship discharge" means the separation of a member from the Armed Forces, at the request of the member, pursuant to the Department of Defense policy permitting the early separation of a member who is the only surviving child in a family in which—

(i) the father or mother or one or more siblings—

(I) served in the Armed Forces; and

(II) was killed, died as a result of wounds, accident, or disease, is in a captured or missing in action status, or is permanently 100 percent disabled or hospitalized on a continuing basis (and is not employed gainfully because of the disability or hospitalization); and

(ii) the death, status, or disability did not result from the intentional misconduct or willful neglect of the parent or sibling and was not incurred during a period of unauthorized absence.

(3) (A) If a member of the uniformed services dies or is retired or separated with a combat-related disability, the Secretary concerned—

(i) shall not require repayment by the member or the member's estate of the unearned portion of any bonus or similar benefit previously paid to the member; and

(ii) shall require the payment to the member or the member's estate of the remainder of any bonus or similar benefit that was not yet paid to the member, but to which the member was entitled immediately before the death, retirement, or separation of the member, and would be paid if not for the death, retirement, or separation of the member.

(B) Subparagraph (A) does not apply if the death or disability of the member is the result of the member's misconduct.

(C) The amount to be paid under subparagraph (A)(ii) shall be equal to the full amount specified by the agreement or contract applicable to the bonus or similar benefit as if the member continued to be entitled to the bonus or similar benefit following the death, retirement, or separation.

(D) Amounts to be paid to a member or the member's estate under subparagraph (A)(ii) shall be paid in a lump sum not later than 90 days after the date of the death, retirement, or separation of the member, whichever applies.

(E) In this paragraph, the term "combat-related disability" has the meaning given that term in section 1413a(e) of title 10.

(4) An obligation to repay the United States under this subsection is, for all purposes, a debt owed the United States. A discharge in bankruptcy under title 11 does not discharge a person from such debt if the discharge order is entered less than five years after—

(A) the date of the termination of the agreement or contract on which the debt is based; or

(B) in the absence of such an agreement or contract, the date of the termination of the service on which the debt is based.

(5) In this subsection:

(A) The term "bonus or similar benefit" means a bonus, incentive pay, special pay, or similar payment, or an educational benefit or stipend, paid to a member of the uniformed services under a provision of law that refers to the repayment requirements of this subsection.

(B) The term "service", as used in paragraph (4)(B), refers to an obligation willingly undertaken by a member of the uniformed services, in exchange for a bonus or similar benefit offered by the Secretary of Defense or the Secretary concerned—

(i) to remain on active duty or in an active status in a reserve component;

(ii) to perform duty in a specified skill, with or without a specified qualification or credential;

(iii) to perform duty at a specified location; or

(iv) to perform duty for a specified period of time.

**37 USC § 308g Special pay: bonus for enlistment in elements of the Ready Reserve other than the Selected Reserve.**

(a) An eligible person who enlists in a combat or combat support skill of an element (other than the Selected Reserve) of the Ready Reserve of an armed force for a term of enlistment of not less than six years, and who has not previously served in an armed force, may be paid a bonus as provided in subsection (b).

* * *

(d) A person who does not serve satisfactorily in the element of the Ready Reserve in the combat or combat support skill for the period for which the bonus was paid under this section shall be subject to the repayment provisions of section 303a(e) of this title.

* * *

**37 USC § 308h Special pay: bonus for reenlistment, enlistment, or voluntary extension of enlistment in elements of the Ready Reserve other than the Selected Reserve.**

(a) Authority and Eligibility Requirements.

(1) The Secretary concerned may pay a bonus as provided in subsection (b) to an eligible person who reenlists, enlists, or voluntarily extends an enlistment in a reserve component of an armed force for assignment to an element (other than the Selected Reserve) of the Ready Reserve of that armed force if the reenlistment, enlistment, or extension is for a period of three years, or for a period of six years, beyond any other period the person is obligated to serve.

(2) A person is eligible for a bonus under this section if the person—

(A) is or has been a member of an armed force;

(B) is qualified in a skill or specialty designated by the Secretary concerned as a critically short wartime skill or critically short wartime specialty; and

(C) has not failed to complete satisfactorily any original term of enlistment in the armed forces.

(3) For the purposes of this section, the Secretary concerned may designate a skill or specialty as a critically short wartime skill or critically short wartime specialty for an armed force under the jurisdiction of the Secretary if the Secretary determines that—

(A) the skill or specialty is critical to meet wartime requirements of the armed force; and

(B) there is a critical shortage of personnel in that armed force who are qualified in that skill or specialty.

(4) The Secretary concerned may waive the eligibility requirement in paragraph (2)(B) in the case of a reenlistment or voluntary extension of enlistment by a member of the armed forces that is entered into as described in this subsection while the member is serving on active duty in Afghanistan, Iraq, or Kuwait in support of Operation Enduring Freedom and Operation Iraqi Freedom.

* * *

(c) Repayment. A person who does not complete the period of enlistment or extension of enlistment for which the bonus was paid under this section shall be subject to the repayment provisions of section 303a(e) of this title.

* * *

**37 USC § 308i Special pay: prior service enlistment bonus.**

(a) Authority and Eligibility Requirements.

(1) A person who is a former enlisted member of an armed force who enlists in the Selected Reserve of the Ready Reserve of an armed force for a period of three or six years in a critical military skill designated for such a bonus by the Secretary concerned and who meets the requirements of paragraph (2) may be paid a bonus as prescribed in subsection (b).

* * *

(d) Repayment. A person who receives a bonus payment under this section and who, during the period for which the bonus was paid, does not serve satisfactorily in the element of the Selected Reserve with respect to which the bonus was paid shall be subject to the repayment provisions of section 303a(e) of this title.

* * *

**37 USC § 308j Special pay: affiliation bonus for officers in the Selected Reserve.**

(a) Affiliation Bonus.

(1) The Secretary concerned may pay an affiliation bonus under this section to an eligible officer in any of the armed forces who enters into an agreement with the Secretary to serve, for the period specified in the agreement, in the Selected Reserve of the Ready Reserve of an armed force under the Secretary's jurisdiction—

(A) in a critical officer skill designated under paragraph (3); or

(B) to meet a manpower shortage in—

(i) a unit of that Selected Reserve; or

(ii) a particular pay grade in that armed force.

* * *

(b) Accession Bonus.

(1) The Secretary concerned may pay an accession bonus under this section to an eligible person who enters into an agreement with the Secretary—

(A) to accept an appointment as an officer in the armed forces; and

(B) to serve in the Selected Reserve of the Ready Reserve in a skill designated under paragraph (2) for a period specified in the agreement.

* * *

(g) Repayment. A person who enters into an agreement under this section and receives all or a part of a bonus under this agreement, but who does not accept a commission or an appointment as an officer or does not commence to participate

ADDITIONAL STATUTES

or does not satisfactorily participate in the Selected Reserve for the total period of service specified in the agreement, shall be subject to the repayment provisions of section 303a(e) of this title.

**37 USC § 309 Special pay: enlistment bonus.**

(a) Bonus Authorized; Bonus Amount. A person who enlists in an armed force for a period of at least 2 years may be paid a bonus in an amount not to exceed $40,000. The bonus may be paid in a single lump sum or in periodic installments.

(b) Repayment. A member who does not complete the term of enlistment for which a bonus was paid to the member under this section, or a member who is not technically qualified in the skill for which a bonus was paid to the member under this section, shall be subject to the repayment provisions of section 303a(e) of this title.

* * *

**37 USC § 314 Special pay or bonus: qualified members extending duty at designated locations overseas.**

(a) Covered Members. This section applies with respect to a member of an armed force who–

(1) is entitled to basic pay;

(2) has a specialty that is designated by the Secretary concerned for the purposes of this section;

(3) has completed a tour of duty (as defined in accordance with regulations prescribed by the Secretary concerned) at a location outside the continental United States that is designated by the Secretary concerned for the purposes of this section; and

(4) at the end of that tour of duty executes an agreement to extend that tour for a period of not less than one year.

* * *

(d) Repayment. A member who, having entered into a written agreement to extend a tour of duty for a period under subsection (a), receives a bonus payment under subsection (b)(2) for a 12-month period covered by the agreement and ceases during that 12-month period to perform the agreed tour of duty shall be subject to the repayment provisions of section 303a(e) of this title.

* * *

**37 USC § 315 Special pay: engineering and scientific career continuation pay.**

* * *

(b) Under regulations prescribed by the Secretary concerned, an officer of a uniformed service who–

(1) is entitled to basic pay;

(2) is below the pay grade of O-7;

(3) holds a degree in engineering or science from an accredited college or university;

(4) has been certified by the Secretary concerned as having the technical qualifications for detail to engineering or scientific duty;

(5) has completed at least three but less than nineteen years of engineering or scientific duty as an officer; and

(6) executes a written agreement to remain on active duty for detail to engineering or scientific duty for at least one year, but not more than four years;

may, upon acceptance of the written agreement by the Secretary concerned, be paid, in addition to all other compensation to which the officer is entitled, an amount not to exceed $3,000 multiplied by the number of years, or monthly fraction thereof, of obligated service to which the officer agrees under the agreement. The total amount payable may be paid in a lump sum or in equal periodic installments, as determined by the Secretary concerned.

(c) An officer who, having entered into a written agreement under subsection (b) and having received all or part of a bonus under this section, does not complete the period of active duty as specified in the agreement shall be subject to the repayment provisions of section 303a(e) of this title.



**37 USC § 316 Special pay: bonus for members with foreign language proficiency.**

(a) Availability of Bonus. Subject to subsection (c), the Secretary concerned may pay a bonus under this section to a member of the uniformed services who—

(1) is qualified in a uniformed services specialty requiring proficiency in a foreign language identified by the Secretary concerned as a foreign language in which it is necessary to have personnel proficient because of national defense or public health considerations;

(2) received training, under regulations prescribed by the Secretary concerned, designed to develop a proficiency in such a foreign language;

(3) is assigned to duties requiring a proficiency in such a foreign language; or

(4) is proficient in a foreign language for which the uniformed service may have a critical need, as determined by the Secretary concerned.

* * *

(e) Repayment. A member who receives a bonus under this section, but who does not satisfy an eligibility requirement specified in paragraph (1), (2), (3), or (4) of subsection (a) for the entire certification period, shall be subject to the repayment provisions of section 303a(e) of this title.

* * *

## 37 USC § 317 Special pay: officers in critical acquisition positions extending period of active duty.

(a) Bonus Authorized. An officer described in subsection (b) who executes a written agreement to remain on active duty in a critical acquisition position for at least one year may, upon the acceptance of the agreement by the Secretary concerned, be paid a retention bonus as provided in this section.

(b) Covered Officers. An officer referred to in subsection (a) is an officer of the Army, Navy, Air Force, or Marine Corps who—

(1) is a member of the acquisition workforce selected to serve in, or serving in, a critical acquisition position designated under section 1731 of title 10.[6]

(2) is eligible to retire, or is assigned to such position for a period that will extend beyond the date on which the officer will be eligible to retire, under any provision of law.

* * *

(f) Repayment. An officer who, having entered into a written agreement under subsection (a) and having received all or part of a bonus under this section, does not complete the period of active duty as specified in the agreement shall be subject to the repayment provisions of section 303a(e) of this title.

* * *

## 37 USC § 318 Special pay: special warfare officers extending period of active duty.

* * *

(b) Retention Bonus Authorized. A special warfare officer who meets the eligibility requirements specified in subsection (c) and who executes a written agreement to remain on active duty in special warfare service for at least one year may, upon the acceptance of the agreement by the Secretary concerned, be paid a retention bonus as provided in this section.

* * *

(h) Repayment. An officer who, having entered into a written agreement under subsection (b) and having received all or part of a bonus under this section, does not complete the period of active duty in special warfare service as specified in the agreement shall be subject to the repayment provisions of section 303a(e) of this title.

* * *

---

[6] Ed. note: So in original. The period probably should be "; and".

**37 USC § 319 Special pay: surface warfare officer continuation pay.**

* * *

(b) Special Pay Authorized. An eligible surface warfare officer who executes a written agreement to remain on active duty to complete one or more tours of duty to which the officer may be ordered as a department head on a surface vessel may, upon the acceptance of the agreement by the Secretary of the Navy, be paid an amount not to exceed $50,000.

* * *

(f) Repayment. An officer who, having entered into a written agreement under subsection (b) and having received all or part of a bonus under this section, does not complete the period of active duty as a department head on a surface vessel as specified in the agreement, shall be subject to the repayment provisions of section 303a(e) of this title.

* * *

**37 USC § 321 Special pay: judge advocate continuation pay.**

* * *

(b) Special Pay Authorized. An eligible judge advocate who executes a written agreement to remain on active duty for a period of obligated service specified in the agreement may, upon the acceptance of the agreement by the Secretary concerned, be paid continuation pay under this section. The total amount paid to an officer under one or more agreements under this section may not exceed $60,000.

* * *

(f) Repayment. An officer who has entered into a written agreement under subsection (b) and has received all or part of the amount payable under the agreement but who does not complete the total period of active duty specified in the agreement, shall be subject to the repayment provisions of section 303a(e) of this title.

* * *

**37 USC § 324 Special pay: accession bonus for new officers in critical skills.**

(a) Accession Bonus Authorized. Under regulations prescribed by the Secretary concerned, a person who executes a written agreement to accept a commission or an appointment as an officer of the armed forces and serve on active duty in a designated critical officer skill for the period specified in the agreement may, upon acceptance of the agreement by the Secretary concerned, be paid an accession bonus in an amount determined by the Secretary concerned.

* * *

(f) Repayment. An individual who, having received all or part of the bonus under

ADDITIONAL STATUTES

an agreement referred to in subsection (a), is not thereafter commissioned as an officer or does not commence or complete the total period of active duty service specified in the agreement shall be subject to the repayment provisions of section 303a(e) of this title.

* * *

**37 USC § 325 Incentive bonus: savings plan for education expenses and other contingencies.**

(a) Benefit and Eligibility. The Secretary concerned may purchase United States savings bonds under this section for a member of the armed forces who is eligible as follows:

(1) A member who, before completing three years of service on active duty, enters into a commitment to perform qualifying service.

(2) A member who, after completing three years of service on active duty, but not more than nine years of service on active duty, enters into a commitment to perform qualifying service.

(3) A member who, after completing nine years of service on active duty, enters into a commitment to perform qualifying service.

* * *

(g) Repayment. If a person does not complete the qualifying service for which the person is obligated under a commitment for which a benefit has been paid under this section, the person shall be subject to the repayment provisions of section 303a(e) of this title.

* * *

**37 USC § 326 Incentive bonus: conversion to military occupational specialty to ease personnel shortage.**

(a) Incentive Bonus Authorized. The Secretary concerned may pay a bonus under this section to an eligible member of a regular or reserve component of the armed forces who executes a written agreement to convert to, and serve for a period of not less than three years in, a military occupational specialty for which there is a shortage of trained and qualified personnel.

* * *

(e) Repayment. A member who does not convert to and complete the period of service in the military occupational specialty specified in the agreement executed under subsection (a) shall be subject to the repayment provisions of section 303a(e) of this title.

* * *

**37 USC § 354 Special pay: 15-year career status bonus for members entering service on or after August 1, 1986.**

(a) Availability of Bonus. The Secretary concerned shall pay a bonus under this section to an eligible career bonus member if the member–

(1) elects to receive the bonus under this section; and

(2) executes a written agreement (prescribed by the Secretary concerned) to remain continuously on active duty until the member has completed 20 years of active-duty service creditable under section 1405 of title 10.

* * *

(f) Repayment.[7] If a person paid a bonus under this section does not complete a period of active duty beginning on the date on which the election of the person under paragraph (1) of subsection (a) is received and ending on the date on which the person completes 20 years of active duty service as described in paragraph (2) of such subsection, the person shall be subject to the repayment provisions of section 373 of this title.

**37 USC § 355 Special pay: retention incentives for members qualified in critical military skills or assigned to high priority units.**

(a) Retention Bonus Authorized. An officer or enlisted member of the armed forces who is serving on active duty in a regular component or in an active status in a reserve component and who is qualified in a critical military skill designated under subsection (b) or accepts an assignment to a high priority unit designated under such subsection may be paid a retention bonus as provided in this section if–

(1) in the case of an officer, the member executes a written agreement to remain on active duty for at least one year or to remain in an active status in a reserve component for at least one year;

(2) in the case of an enlisted member, other than an enlisted member referred to in paragraph (3), the member reenlists or voluntarily extends the

ADDITIONAL STATUTES

---

[7] Ed Note: **Amendment of subsec. (f), effective Jan. 1, 2018.** Act Nov. 25, 2015, P.L. 114-92, Div A, Title VI, Subtitle D, Part I, § 631(c)(2), 129 Stat. 844 (effective on 1/1/2018, as provided by § 635 of such Act, which appears as 5 U.S.C. § 8432 note), provides that subsec. (f) of this section is amended to read as follows:

"(A) in subsection (f)–

"(ii) by adding at the end the following new paragraph:

" '(2) If a person who is paid a bonus under this section subsequently makes an election described in section 1409(b)(4)(B) of title 10, the person shall repay any bonus payments received under this section in the same manner as repayments are made under section 373 of this title.'; and

"(B) by adding at the end the following new subsection:

" '(g) Sunset and continuation of payments.

(1) A Secretary concerned may not pay a new bonus under this section after December 31, 2017.

" '(2) Subject to subsection (f)(2), the Secretary concerned may continue to make payments for bonuses that were awarded under this section on or before the date specified in paragraph (1).' ".

member's enlistment for a period of at least one year; or

(3) in the case of an enlisted member serving pursuant to an indefinite reenlistment, the member executes a written agreement to remain on active duty for a period of at least one year or to remain in an active status in a reserve component for a period of at least one year.

* * *

(g) Repayment. A member paid a bonus under this section who fails, during the period of service covered by the member's agreement, reenlistment, or voluntary extension of enlistment under subsection (a), to remain qualified in the critical military skill or to satisfy the other eligibility criteria for which the bonus was paid shall be subject to the repayment provisions of section 373 of this title.

* * *

## TITLE 38 VETERANS' BENEFITS

### 38 USC § 7634 Breach of agreement; waiver of liability.

* * *

(c) An obligation of a participant under the Educational Assistance Program (or an agreement thereunder) for payment of damages may not be released by a discharge in bankruptcy under title 11 before the expiration of the five-year period beginning on the first date the payment of such damages is due.

## TITLE 42 THE PUBLIC HEALTH AND WELFARE

### 42 USC § 254o Breach of scholarship contract or loan repayment contract.

* * *

(d) CANCELLATION OF OBLIGATION UPON DEATH OF INDIVIDUAL; WAIVER OR SUSPENSION OF OBLIGATION FOR IMPOSSIBILITY, HARDSHIP, OR UNCONSCIONABILITY; RELEASE OF DEBT BY DISCHARGE IN BANKRUPTCY, TIME LIMITATIONS.

(3) (A) Any obligation of an individual under the Scholarship Program (or a contract thereunder) or the Loan Repayment Program (or a contract thereunder) for payment of damages may be released by a discharge in bankruptcy under title 11 of the United States Code only if such discharge is granted after the expiration of the 7-year period beginning on the first date that payment of such damages is required, and only if the bankruptcy court finds that nondischarge of the obligation would be unconscionable.

(B) (i) Subparagraph (A) shall apply to any financial obligation of an individual under the provision of law specified in clause (ii) to the same extent and in the same manner as such subparagraph applies to any obligation of an individual under the Scholarship or Loan Repayment Program (or contract thereunder) for payment of damages.

(ii) The provision of law referred to in clause (i) is subsection (f) of section 225 of this Act, as in effect prior to the repeal of such section by section 408(b)(1) of Public Law 94-484.

* * *

### 42 USC § 292f Default of borrower.

* * *

(g) CONDITIONS FOR DISCHARGE OF DEBT IN BANKRUPTCY. Notwithstanding any other provision of Federal or State law, a debt that is a loan insured under the authority of this subpart may be released by a discharge in bankruptcy under any chapter of title 11, United States Code, only if such discharge is granted—

(1) after the expiration of the seven-year period beginning on the first date when repayment of such loan is required, exclusive of any period after such date in which the obligation to pay installments on the loan is suspended;

(2) upon a finding by the Bankruptcy Court that the nondischarge of such debt would be unconscionable; and

(3) upon the condition that the Secretary shall not have waived the Secretary's rights to apply subsection (f) to the borrower and the discharged debt.

* * *

**42 USC § 297a Student loan fund.**

* * *

(c) Regulatory Standards Applicable to Collection of Loans.

(1) Any standard established by the Secretary by regulation for the collection by schools of nursing of loans made pursuant to loan agreements under this part shall provide that the failure of any such school to collect such loans shall be measured in accordance with this subsection. With respect to the student loan fund established pursuant to such agreements, this subsection may not be construed to require such schools to reimburse such loan fund for loans that became uncollectable prior to 1983.

(2) The measurement of a school's failure to collect loans made under this part shall be the ratio (stated as a percentage) that the defaulted principal amount outstanding of such school bears to the matured loans of such school.

(3) For purposes of this subsection—

(A) the term "default" means the failure of a borrower of a loan made under this part to—

(i) make an installment payment when due; or

(ii) comply with any other term of the promissory note for such loan,

except that a loan made under this part shall not be considered to be in default if the loan is discharged in bankruptcy or if the school reasonably concludes from written contacts with the borrower that the borrower intends to repay the loan;

(B) the term "defaulted principal amount outstanding" means the total amount borrowed from the loan fund of a school that has reached the repayment stage (minus any principal amount repaid or cancelled) on loans—

(i) repayable monthly and in default for at least 120 days; and

(ii) repayable less frequently than monthly and in default for at least 180 days;

(C) the term "grace period" means the period of nine months beginning on the date on which the borrower ceases to pursue a full-time or half-time course of study at a school of nursing; and

(D) the term "matured loans" means the total principal amount of all loans made by a school of nursing under this part minus the total principal amount of loans made by such school to students who are—

(i) enrolled in a full-time or half-time course of study at such school; or

(ii) in their grace period.

ADDITIONAL STATUTES

## 42 USC § 656 Support obligation as obligation to State; amount; discharge in bankruptcy.

* * *

(b) Nondischargeability. A debt (as defined in section 101 of title 11 of the United States Code) owed under State law to a State (as defined in such section) or municipality (as defined in such section) that is in the nature of [child] support and that is enforceable under this part is not released by a discharge in bankruptcy under title 11 of the United States Code.

## TITLE 46 SHIPPING

## SUBTITLE V MERCHANT MARINE

Section 334 of the Bankruptcy Reform Act of 1978, Pub. L. 95-598, amended title 9 of the Merchant Marine Act, 1936 (46 U.S.C. Appx. § 1241 *et seq.*) by adding section 908 (46 U.S.C. Appx. § 1247). This provision was chapter XIV of the Bankruptcy Act. Because it does not govern bankruptcy proceedings it was placed in the Merchant Marine Act rather than the 1978 Bankruptcy Code. Only minor stylistic changes were made.

To complete the codification of Title 46, United States Code, "Shipping," the laws that were in the appendix to title 46 were reorganized and restated. *See* Pub. L. No. 109-304, § 8(b), 120 Stat. 1565 (Oct. 6, 2006).

### 46 USC § 50305 Appointment of trustee or receiver and operation of vessels.

(a) Appointment of Trustees and Receivers

(1) Appointment of Secretary. In a proceeding in a court of the United States in which a trustee or receiver may be appointed for a corporation operating a vessel of United States registry between the United States and a foreign country, on which the United States Government holds a mortgage, the court may appoint the Secretary of Transportation as the sole trustee or receiver (subject to the direction of the court) if–

(A) the court finds that the appointment will–

(i) inure to the advantage of the estate and the parties in interest; and

(ii) tend to carry out the purposes of this subtitle; and

(B) the Secretary expressly consents to the appointment.

(2) Appointment of Other Person. The appointment of another person as trustee or receiver without a hearing becomes effective when ratified by the Secretary, but the Secretary may demand a hearing.

(b) Operation of Vessels.

(1) In General. If the court is unwilling to allow the trustee or receiver to operate the vessel in foreign commerce without financial aid from the Government pending termination of the proceeding, and the Secretary certifies to the court that the continued operation of the vessel is essential to the foreign commerce of the United States and is reasonably calculated to carry out the purposes of this subtitle, the court may allow the Secretary to operate the vessel, either directly or through a managing agent or operator employed by the Secretary. The Secretary must agree to comply with terms imposed by the court sufficient to protect the parties in interest. The Secretary also must agree to pay all operating losses resulting from the operation. The operation shall be for the account of the trustee or receiver.

(2) Payment of Operating Losses and Other Amounts. The Secretary has no claim against the corporation, its estate, or its assets for operating losses paid by the Secretary, but the Secretary may pay amounts for depreciation the Secretary

ADDITIONAL STATUTES

considers reasonable and other amounts the court considers just. The payment of operating losses and the other amounts and compliance with terms imposed by the court shall be in satisfaction of any claim against the Secretary resulting from the operation of the vessel.

(3) Deemed Operation by Government. A vessel operated by the Secretary under this subsection is deemed to be a vessel operated by the United States under chapter 309 of this title.

# TITLE 50 SERVICEMEMBERS CIVIL RELIEF ACT

50 U.S.C. § 3931 *et seq.* provides special relief in civil proceedings for members of the United States Armed Forces and its provisions apply in bankruptcy cases. This Act, formerly known as the Soldiers' and Sailors' Civil Relief Act of 1940, was completely revised at Public Law 108-189 (Dec. 19, 2003) and retitled the Servicemembers Civil Relief Act. Title II ("General Relief") of the Act is reprinted below as amended.

## 50 USC § 3931 Protection of servicemembers against default judgments.

(a) Applicability of Section. This section applies to any civil action or proceeding, including any child custody proceeding, in which the defendant does not make an appearance.

(b) Affidavit Requirement.

(1) Plaintiff to File Affidavit. In any action or proceeding covered by this section, the court, before entering judgment for the plaintiff, shall require the plaintiff to file with the court an affidavit–

(A) stating whether or not the defendant is in military service and showing necessary facts to support the affidavit; or

(B) if the plaintiff is unable to determine whether or not the defendant is in military service, stating that the plaintiff is unable to determine whether or not the defendant is in military service.

(2) Appointment of Attorney to Represent Defendant in Military Service. If in an action covered by this section it appears that the defendant is in military service, the court may not enter a judgment until after the court appoints an attorney to represent the defendant. If an attorney appointed under this section to represent a servicemember cannot locate the servicemember, actions by the attorney in the case shall not waive any defense of the servicemember or otherwise bind the servicemember.

(3) Defendant' s Military Status Not Ascertained by Affidavit. If based upon the affidavits filed in such an action, the court is unable to determine whether the defendant is in military service, the court, before entering judgment, may require the plaintiff to file a bond in an amount approved by the court. If the defendant is later found to be in military service, the bond shall be available to indemnify the defendant against any loss or damage the defendant may suffer by reason of any judgment for the plaintiff against the defendant, should the judgment be set aside in whole or in part. The bond shall remain in effect until expiration of the time for appeal and setting aside of a judgment under applicable Federal or State law or regulation or under any applicable ordinance of a political subdivision of a State. The court may issue such orders or enter such judgments as the court determines necessary to protect the rights of the defendant under this Act [50 U.S.C. Appx. §§ 501 et seq.].

(4) Satisfaction of Requirement for Affidavit. The requirement for an affidavit under paragraph (1) may be satisfied by a statement, declaration, verification,

or certificate, in writing, subscribed and certified or declared to be true under penalty of perjury.

(c) Penalty for Making or Using False Affidavit. A person who makes or uses an affidavit permitted under subsection (b) (or a statement, declaration, verification, or certificate as authorized under subsection (b)(4)) knowing it to be false, shall be fined as provided in title 18, United States Code, or imprisoned for not more than one year, or both.

(d) Stay of Proceedings. In an action covered by this section in which the defendant is in military service, the court shall grant a stay of proceedings for a minimum period of 90 days under this subsection upon application of counsel, or on the court's own motion, if the court determines that—

(1) there may be a defense to the action and a defense cannot be presented without the presence of the defendant; or

(2) after due diligence, counsel has been unable to contact the defendant or otherwise determine if a meritorious defense exists.

(e) Inapplicability of Section 202 [50 U.S.C. Appx. § 522] Procedures. A stay of proceedings under subsection (d) shall not be controlled by procedures or requirements under section 202 [50 U.S.C. Appx. § 522].

(f) Section 202 [50 U.S.C. Appx. § 522] Protection. If a servicemember who is a defendant in an action covered by this section receives actual notice of the action, the servicemember may request a stay of proceeding under section 202 [50 U.S.C. Appx. § 522].

(g) Vacation or Setting Aside of Default Judgments.

(1) Authority for Court to Vacate or Set Aside Judgment. If a default judgment is entered in an action covered by this section against a servicemember during the servicemember's period of military service (or within 60 days after termination of or release from such military service), the court entering the judgment shall, upon application by or on behalf of the servicemember, reopen the judgment for the purpose of allowing the servicemember to defend the action if it appears that—

(A) the servicemember was materially affected by reason of that military service in making a defense to the action; and

(B) the servicemember has a meritorious or legal defense to the action or some part of it.

(2) Time for Filing Application. An application under this subsection must be filed not later than 90 days after the date of the termination of or release from military service.

(h) Protection of Bona Fide Purchaser. If a court vacates, sets aside, or reverses a default judgment against a servicemember and the vacating, setting aside, or reversing is because of a provision of this Act [50 U.S.C. Appx. §§ 501 et seq.], that action shall not impair a right or title acquired by a bona fide purchaser for value under the default judgment.

**50 USC § 3932 Stay of proceedings when servicemember has notice.**

(a) Applicability of Section. This section applies to any civil action or proceeding, including any child custody proceeding, in which the plaintiff or defendant at the time of filing an application under this section—

(1) is in military service or is within 90 days after termination of or release from military service; and

(2) has received notice of the action or proceeding.

(b) Stay of Proceedings.

(1) Authority for Stay. At any stage before final judgment in a civil action or proceeding in which a servicemember described in subsection (a) is a party, the court may on its own motion and shall, upon application by the servicemember, stay the action for a period of not less than 90 days, if the conditions in paragraph (2) are met.

(2) Conditions for Stay. An application for a stay under paragraph (1) shall include the following:

(A) A letter or other communication setting forth facts stating the manner in which current military duty requirements materially affect the servicemember's ability to appear and stating a date when the servicemember will be available to appear.

(B) A letter or other communication from the servicemember's commanding officer stating that the servicemember's current military duty prevents appearance and that military leave is not authorized for the servicemember at the time of the letter.

(c) Application Not a Waiver of Defenses. An application for a stay under this section does not constitute an appearance for jurisdictional purposes and does not constitute a waiver of any substantive or procedural defense (including a defense relating to lack of personal jurisdiction).

(d) Additional Stay.

(1) Application. A servicemember who is granted a stay of a civil action or proceeding under subsection (b) may apply for an additional stay based on continuing material affect of military duty on the servicemember's ability to appear. Such an application may be made by the servicemember at the time of the initial application under subsection (b) or when it appears that the servicemember is unavailable to prosecute or defend the action. The same information required under subsection (b)(2) shall be included in an application under this subsection.

(2) Appointment of Counsel When Additional Stay Refused. If the court refuses to grant an additional stay of proceedings under paragraph (1), the court shall appoint counsel to represent the servicemember in the action or proceeding.

ADDITIONAL STATUTES

(e) Coordination with Section 201. A servicemember who applies for a stay under this section and is unsuccessful may not seek the protections afforded by section 201 [50 U.S.C. Appx. § 521].

(f) Inapplicability to Section 301. The protections of this section do not apply to section 301 [50 U.S.C. Appx. § 531].

**50 USC § 3933 Fines and penalties under contracts.**

(a) Prohibition of Penalties. When an action for compliance with the terms of a contract is stayed pursuant to this Act [50 U.S.C. Appx. §§ 501 et seq.], a penalty shall not accrue for failure to comply with the terms of the contract during the period of the stay.

(b) Reduction or Waiver of Fines or Penalties. If a servicemember fails to perform an obligation arising under a contract and a penalty is incurred arising from that nonperformance, a court may reduce or waive the fine or penalty if—

(1) the servicemember was in military service at the time the fine or penalty was incurred; and

(2) the ability of the servicemember to perform the obligation was materially affected by such military service.

**50 USC § 3934 Stay or vacation of execution of judgments, attachments, and garnishments.**

(a) Court Action upon Material Affect Determination. If a servicemember, in the opinion of the court, is materially affected by reason of military service in complying with a court judgment or order, the court may on its own motion and shall on application by the servicemember—

(1) stay the execution of any judgment or order entered against the servicemember; and

(2) vacate or stay an attachment or garnishment of property, money, or debts in the possession of the servicemember or a third party, whether before or after judgment.

(b) Applicability. This section applies to an action or proceeding commenced in a court against a servicemember before or during the period of the servicemember's military service or within 90 days after such service terminates.

**50 USC § 3935 Duration and term of stays; codefendants not in service.**

(a) Period of Stay. A stay of an action, proceeding, attachment, or execution made pursuant to the provisions of this Act [50 U.S.C. Appx. §§ 501 et seq.] by a court may be ordered for the period of military service and 90 days thereafter, or for any part of that period. The court may set the terms and amounts for such installment payments as is considered reasonable by the court.

(b) Codefendants. If the servicemember is a codefendant with others who are not in military service and who are not entitled to the relief and protections provided under this Act [50 U.S.C. Appx. §§ 501 et seq.], the plaintiff may proceed against those other defendants with the approval of the court.

(c) Inapplicability of Section. This section does not apply to sections 202 and 701 [50 U.S.C. Appx. §§ 522 and 591].

**50 USC § 3936 Statute of limitations.**

(a) Tolling of Statutes of Limitation During Military Service. The period of a servicemember's military service may not be included in computing any period limited by law, regulation, or order for the bringing of any action or proceeding in a court, or in any board, bureau, commission, department, or other agency of a State (or political subdivision of a State) or the United States by or against the servicemember or the servicemember's heirs, executors, administrators, or assigns.

(b) Redemption of Real Property. A period of military service may not be included in computing any period provided by law for the redemption of real property sold or forfeited to enforce an obligation, tax, or assessment.

(c) Inapplicability to Internal Revenue Laws. This section does not apply to any period of limitation prescribed by or under the internal revenue laws of the United States.

**50 USC § 3937 Maximum rate of interest on debts incurred before military service.**

(a) Interest Rate Limitation.

(1) Limitation to 6 Percent. An obligation or liability bearing interest at a rate in excess of 6 percent per year that is incurred by a servicemember, or the servicemember and the servicemember's spouse jointly, before the servicemember enters military service shall not bear interest at a rate in excess of 6 percent—

(A) during the period of military service and one year thereafter, in the case of an obligation or liability consisting of a mortgage, trust deed, or other security in the nature of a mortgage; or

(B) during the period of military service, in the case of any other obligation or liability.

(2) Forgiveness of Interest in Excess of 6 Percent. Interest at a rate in excess of 6 percent per year that would otherwise be incurred but for the prohibition in paragraph (1) is forgiven.

(3) Prevention of Acceleration of Principal. The amount of any periodic payment due from a servicemember under the terms of the instrument that created an obligation or liability covered by this section shall be reduced by the amount of the interest forgiven under paragraph (2) that is allocable to the period for which such payment is made.

(b) Implementation of Limitation.

(1) Proof of Military Service.

(A) In General. Not later than 180 days after the date of a servicemember's termination or release from military service, in order for an obligation or liability of the servicemember to be subject to the interest rate limitation in subsection (a), the servicemember shall provide to the creditor written notice and a copy of—

(i) the military orders calling the servicemember to military service and any orders further extending military service; or

(ii) any other appropriate indicator of military service, including a certified letter from a commanding officer.

(B) Independent Verification by Creditor.

(i) In General. A creditor may use, in lieu of notice and documentation under subparagraph (A), information retrieved from the Defense Manpower Data Center through the creditor's normal business reviews of such Center for purposes of obtaining information indicating that the servicemember is on active duty.

(ii) Safe Harbor. A creditor that uses the information retrieved from the Defense Manpower Data Center under clause (i) with respect to a servicemember has not failed to treat the debt of the servicemember in accordance with subsection (a) if—

(I) such information indicates that, on the date the creditor retrieves such information, the servicemember is not on active duty; and

(II) the creditor has not, by the end of the 180-day period under subparagraph (A), received the written notice and documentation required under that subparagraph with respect to the servicemember.

(2) Limitation Effective as of Date of Order to Active Duty. Upon receipt of written notice and a copy of orders calling a servicemember to military service, the creditor shall treat the debt in accordance with subsection (a), effective as of the date on which the servicemember is called to military service.

(c) Creditor Protection. A court may grant a creditor relief from the limitations of this section if, in the opinion of the court, the ability of the servicemember to pay interest upon the obligation or liability at a rate in excess of 6 percent per year is not materially affected by reason of the servicemember's military service.

(d) Definitions. In this section—

(1) Interest. The term "interest" includes service charges, renewal charges, fees, or any other charges (except bona fide insurance) with respect to an obligation or liability.

(2) Obligation or Liability. The term "obligation or liability" includes an obligation or liability consisting of a mortgage, trust deed, or other security in the nature of a mortgage.

(e) Penalty. Whoever knowingly violates subsection (a) shall be fined as provided in title 18, United States Code, imprisoned for not more than one year, or both.

## BANKRUPTCY REFORM ACT OF 1994
## (Pub. L. No. 103-394)

### Sec. 111 Supplemental injunctions.

(a) Supplemental Injunctions. * * *

(b) Rule of construction. Nothing in subsection (a), or in the amendments made by subsection (a),[8] shall be construed to modify, impair, or supersede any other authority the court has to issue injunctions in connection with an order confirming a plan of reorganization.

---

[8] Ed. note: Subsection (a) of section 111 of the Bankruptcy Reform Act of 1994, Pub. L. No. 103-394, added subsections (g) and (h), on supplemental injunctions, to section 524 of the Bankruptcy Code. Those subsections have not been amended since the enactment of the 1994 Act.

## BANKRUPTCY REFORM ACT OF 1994
## (Pub. L. No. 103-394)

### Sec. 304 Protection of child support and alimony.

* * *

(g) APPEARANCE BEFORE COURT. Child support creditors or their representatives shall be permitted to appear and intervene without charge, and without meeting any special local court rule requirement for attorney appearances, in any bankruptcy case or proceeding in any bankruptcy court or district court of the United States if such creditors or representatives file a form in such court that contains information detailing the child support debt, its status, and other characteristics.

* * *

## NATIONAL DEFENSE AUTHORIZATION ACT FOR FISCAL YEAR 2000—Uncodified Discharge Provision Relating to the Troops-to-Teachers Program (Pub. L. No. 106-65)

### Sec. 1705 Stipend and bonus for participants.

(a) Stipend Authorized.

(1) Subject to paragraph (2), the administering Secretary shall pay to each participant in the Troops-to-Teachers Program a stipend in an amount equal to $5,000.

(2) The total number of stipends that may be paid under paragraph (1) in any fiscal year may not exceed 3,000.

(b) Bonus Authorized.

(1) Subject to paragraph (2), the administering Secretary may, in lieu of paying a stipend under subsection (a), pay a bonus of $10,000 to each participant in the Troops-to-Teachers Program who agrees under section 1704(e)[9] to accept full-time employment as an elementary or secondary school teacher or vocational or technical teacher for not less than four years in a high need school.

(2) The total number of bonuses that may be paid under paragraph (1) in any fiscal year may not exceed 1,000.

(3) In this subsection, the term "high need school" means an elementary school or secondary school that meets one or more of the following criteria:

---

[9] Ed. note: Subsection (e) of section 1704 of the 2000 Act ("Selection of Participants") provides as follows:

(e) Participation Agreement. A member of the Armed Forces selected to participate in the Troops-to-Teachers Program shall be required to enter into an agreement with the administering Secretary in which the member agrees—

(1) to obtain, within such time as the administering Secretary may require, certification or licensure as an elementary or secondary school teacher or vocational or technical teacher; and

(2) to accept an offer of full-time employment as an elementary or secondary school teacher or vocational or technical teacher for not less than four school years with a local educational agency identified under section 1702, to begin the school year after obtaining that certification or licensure.

Section 1702 of the Act ("Authorization of Troops-to-Teachers Program") provides, in pertinent part:

(b) Identification of Local Educational Agencies With Teacher Shortages.

(1) In carrying out the Troops-to-Teachers Program, the administering Secretary shall periodically identify local educational agencies that—

(A) are receiving grants under title I of the Elementary and Secondary Education Act of 1965 (20 U.S.C. 6301 et seq.) as a result of having within their jurisdictions concentrations of children from low-income families; or

(B) are experiencing a shortage of qualified teachers, in particular a shortage of science, mathematics, special education, or vocational or technical teachers.

(2) The administering Secretary may identify local educational agencies under paragraph (1) through surveys conducted for that purpose or by using information on local educational agencies that is available to the administering Secretary from other sources.

(A) The school has a drop out rate that exceeds the national average school drop out rate.

(B) The school has a large percentage of students (as determined by the Secretary of Education in consultation with the National Assessment Governing Board) who speak English as a second language.

(C) The school has a large percentage of students (as so determined) who are at risk of educational failure by reason of limited proficiency in English, poverty, race, geographic location, or economic circumstances.

(D) At least one-half of the students of the school are from families with an income below the poverty line (as that term is defined by the Office of Management and Budget and revised annually in accordance with section 673(2) of the Community Services Block Grant Act (42 U.S.C. 9902(2)) applicable to a family of the size involved.

(E) The school has a large percentage of students (as so determined) who qualify for assistance under part B of the Individuals with Disabilities Education Act (20 U.S.C. 1411 et seq.).

(F) The school meets any other criteria established by the administering Secretary in consultation with the National Assessment Governing Board.

* * *

(d) Reimbursement Under Certain Circumstances.

(1) If a participant in the Troops-to-Teachers Program fails to obtain teacher certification or licensure or employment as an elementary or secondary school teacher or vocational or technical teacher as required by the agreement under section 1704(e) or voluntarily leaves, or is terminated for cause, from the employment during the four years of required service in violation of the agreement, the participant shall be required to reimburse the administering Secretary for any stipend paid to the participant under subsection (a) in an amount that bears the same ratio to the amount of the stipend as the unserved portion of required service bears to the four years of required service.

(2) If a participant in the Troops-to-Teachers Program who is paid a bonus under subsection (b) fails to obtain employment for which the bonus was paid as required by the agreement under section 1704(e), or voluntarily leaves or is terminated for cause from the employment during the four years of required service in violation of the agreement, the participant shall be required to reimburse the administering Secretary for any bonus paid to the participant under that subsection in an amount that bears the same ratio to the amount of the bonus as the unserved portion of required service bears to the four years of required service.

(3) The obligation to reimburse the administering Secretary under this subsection is, for all purposes, a debt owing the United States. A discharge in bankruptcy under title 11, United States Code, shall not release a participant from the obligation to reimburse the administering Secretary.

(4) Any amount owed by a participant under this subsection shall bear interest at the rate equal to the highest rate being paid by the United States on the day on which the reimbursement is determined to be due for securities having maturities of ninety days or less and shall accrue from the day on which the participant is first notified of the amount due.

* * *

## BANKRUPTCY JUDGES, U.S. TRUSTEES & FAMILY FARMER BANKRUPTCY ACT OF 1986 (Pub. L. No. 99-554)

### Sec. 302 Effective dates: Application of amendments.

* * *

(d) Application of Amendments to Judicial Districts.

* * *

(3) Judicial Districts for the States of Alabama and North Carolina.

(A) Notwithstanding paragraphs (1) and (2),[10] and any other provision of law, the amendments made by subtitle A of title II of this Act,[11] and section 1930(a)(6) of title 28 of the United States Code (as added by section 117(4) of this Act), shall not–

(i) become effective in or with respect to a judicial district specified in subparagraph (E) until, or

(ii) apply to cases while pending in such district before, such district elects to be included in a bankruptcy region established in section 581(a) of title 28, United States Code, as amended by section 111(a) of this Act, or October 1, 1992, whichever occurs first.

(B) Any election under subparagraph (A) shall be made upon a majority vote of the chief judge of such district and each bankruptcy judge in such judicial district in favor of such election.

(C) Notice that an election has been made under subparagraph (A) shall be given, not later than 10 days after such election, to the Attorney General and the appropriate Federal Circuit Court of Appeals for such district.

(D) Any election made under subparagraph (A) shall become effective on the date the amendments made by subtitle A of title II of this Act become effective in the region that includes such district or 30 days after the Attorney General receives the notice required under subparagraph (C), whichever occurs later.

(E) Subparagraph (A) applies to the following:

---

[10] Ed. Note: Paragraphs (1) and (2) of section 302(d) of the Bankruptcy Judges, U.S. Trustees & Family Farmer Bankruptcy Act of 1986 (the "1986 Act"), Pub. L. No. 99-554 (1986) listed judicial districts that were not yet served by United States trustees and set forth time limits by which the United States trustee provisions would become effective in those districts.

[11] Ed. Note: Subtitle A of title II of the 1986 Act was entitled "Activities of United States Trustees." This Act amended the Bankruptcy Code and related statutes to provide that the United States trustee pilot program, which had been introduced under the Bankruptcy Reform Act of 1978, be made permanent and phased in over time. Subsequently, provisions exempting the judicial districts of North Carolina and Alabama from participation in the U.S. trustee system were extended, and current law no longer sets a specific requirement for those districts to join the U.S. trustee system. *See* Federal Courts Improvement Act of 2000, Pub. L. No. 106-518, § 501, reprinted *infra*.

(i) The judicial districts established for the State of Alabama.

(ii) The judicial districts established for the State of North Carolina.

(F) (i) Subject to clause (ii), with respect to cases under chapters 7, 11, 12, and 13 of title 11, United States Code—

(I) commenced before the effective date of this Act and

(II) pending in a judicial district in the State of Alabama or the State of North Carolina before any election made under subparagraph (A) by such district becomes effective or October 1, 1992, whichever occurs first.

the amendments made by section 113[12] and subtitle A of title II of this Act,[13] and section 1930(a)(6) of title 28 of the United States Code (as added by section 117(4) of this Act), shall not apply until October 1, 1993, or the expiration of the 1-year period beginning on the date such election becomes effective, whichever occurs first.

(ii) For purposes of clause (i), the amendments made by section 113[14] and subtitle A of title II of this Act,[15] and section 1930(a)(6) of title 28 of the United States Code (as added by section 117(4) of this Act), shall not apply with respect to a case under chapter 7, 11, 12, or 13 of title 11, United States Code, if—

(I) the trustee in the case files the final report and account of administration of the estate, required under section 704 of such title, or

(II) a plan is confirmed under section 1129, 1225, or 1325 of such title,

before October 1, 1993, or the expiration of the 1-year period beginning on the date such election becomes effective, whichever occurs first.

(G) Notwithstanding section 589a of title 28, United States Code, as added by section 115 of this Act, funds collected as a result of the amendments made by section 117 of this Act[16] in a judicial district in the State of Alabama or the State of North Carolina under section 1930(a) of title 28, United States Code, before the date the amendments made by subtitle A of title II of this Act[17] take effect in such district shall be deposited in the general receipts of the Treasury.

---

[12] Ed. Note: Section 113 of the 1986 Act was entitled "Duties of United States Trustees" and contained amendments to 28 U.S.C. § 586.

[13] Ed. Note: *See* note 11 *supra.*

[14] Ed. Note: *See* note 12 *supra.*

[15] Ed. Note: *See* note 11 *supra.*

[16] Ed. Note: Section 117 of the 1986 Act was entitled "Fees" and amended 28 U.S.C. § 1930(a).

[17] Ed. Note: *See* note 11 *supra.*

ADDITIONAL STATUTES

(H) The repeal made by section 231 of this Act[18] shall not apply in or with respect to the Northern District of Alabama until March 1, 1987, or the effective date of any election made under subparagraph (A) by such district, whichever occurs first.

(I) In any judicial district in the State of Alabama or the State of North Carolina that has not made the election described in subparagraph (A), any person who is appointed under regulations issued by the Judicial Conference of the United States to administer estates in cases under title 11 of the United States Code may—

(i) establish, maintain, and supervise a panel of private trustees that are eligible and available to serve as trustees in cases under title 11, United States Code, and

(ii) supervise the administration of cases and trustees in cases under chapters 7, 11, 12, and 13 of title 11, United States Code,

until the amendments made by subtitle A of title II take effect in such district.

* * *

[18] Ed. Note: Section 231 of the 1986 Act repealed former chapter 15 of the Bankruptcy Code, which set forth the provisions governing the United States trustee pilot program.

## JUDICIAL IMPROVEMENTS ACT OF 1990
## (Pub. L. No. 101-650)

### Sec. 317 Bankruptcy administrator program.

(a) EXTENSION. Section 302(d)(3) of the Bankruptcy Judges, United States Trustees, and Family Farmer Bankruptcy Act of 1986 (Public Law 99-554; 28 U.S.C. 581 note) is amended—

(1) in subparagraph (A)(ii), by striking out "October 1, 1992" and inserting in lieu thereof "October 1, 2002";

(2) in subparagraph (F)(i)(II), by striking out "October 1, 1992" and inserting in lieu thereof "October 1, 2002";

(3) in subparagraph (F)(i), by striking out "October 1, 1993" and inserting in lieu thereof "October 1, 2003"; and

(4) in subparagraph (F)(ii), by striking out "October 1, 1993" and inserting in lieu thereof "October 1, 2003".

(b) STANDING. A bankruptcy administrator may raise and may appear and be heard on any issue in any case under title 11, United States Code, but may not file a plan pursuant to section 1121(c) of such title.

* * *

## BANKRUPTCY REFORM ACT OF 1994
## (Pub. L. No. 103-394)

### Sec. 105 Participation by bankruptcy administrator at meetings of creditors and equity security holders.

(a) PRESIDING OFFICER. A bankruptcy administrator appointed under section 302(d)(3)(I) of the Bankruptcy Judges, United States Trustees, and Family Farmer Bankruptcy Act of 1986 (28 U.S.C. 581 note; Public Law 99-554; 100 Stat. 3123), as amended by section 317(a) of the Federal Courts Study Committee Implementation Act of 1990 (Public Law 101-650; 104 Stat. 5115), or the bankruptcy administrator's designee may preside at the meeting of creditors convened under section 341(a) of title 11, United States Code. The bankruptcy administrator or the bankruptcy administrator's designee may preside at any meeting of equity security holders convened under section 341(b) of title 11, United States Code.

(b) EXAMINATION OF THE DEBTOR. The bankruptcy administrator or the bankruptcy administrator's designee may examine the debtor at the meeting of creditors and may administer the oath required under section 343 of title 11, United States Code.

## FEDERAL COURTS IMPROVEMENT ACT OF 2000
## (Pub. L. No. 106-518)

### Sec. 501 Extensions relating to bankruptcy administrator program.

Section 302(d)(3) of the Bankruptcy Judges, United States Trustees, and Family Farmer Bankruptcy Act of 1986 (28 U.S.C. 581 note) is amended–

(1) in subparagraph (A), in the matter following clause (ii), by striking "or October 1, 2002, whichever occurs first,"; and

(2) in subparagraph (F)–

(A) in clause (i)–

(i) in subclause (II), by striking "or October 1, 2002, whichever occurs first"; and

(ii) in the matter following subclause (II)–

(I) by striking "October 1, 2003, or"; and

(II) by striking, "whichever occurs first"; and

(B) in clause (ii), in the matter following subclause (II)–

(i) by striking "October 1, 2003, or"; and

(ii) by striking, "whichever occurs first".

## BANKRUPTCY ABUSE PREVENTION AND CONSUMER PROTECTION ACT OF 2005 (Pub. L. No. 109-8)

### Sec. 103 Sense of Congress and study.

(a) Sense of Congress. It is the sense of Congress that the Secretary of the Treasury has the authority to alter the Internal Revenue Service standards established to set guidelines for repayment plans as needed to accommodate their use under section 707(b) of title 11, United States Code.

(b) Study.

(1) In General. Not later than 2 years after the date of enactment of this Act [enacted Apr. 20, 2005], the Director of the Executive Office for United States Trustees shall submit a report to the Committee on the Judiciary of the Senate and the Committee on the Judiciary of the House of Representatives containing the findings of the Director regarding the utilization of Internal Revenue Service standards for determining—

(A) the current monthly expenses of a debtor under section 707(b) of title 11, United States Code; and

(B) the impact that the application of such standards has had on debtors and on the bankruptcy courts.

(2) Recommendation. The report under paragraph (1) may include recommendations for amendments to title 11, United States Code, that are consistent with the findings of the Director under paragraph (1).

### Sec. 105 Debtor financial management training test program.

(a) Development of Financial Management and Training Curriculum and Materials. The Director of the Executive Office for United States Trustees (in this section referred to as the "Director") shall consult with a wide range of individuals who are experts in the field of debtor education, including trustees who serve in cases under chapter 13 of title 11, United States Code, and who operate financial management education programs for debtors, and shall develop a financial management training curriculum and materials that can be used to educate debtors who are individuals on how to better manage their finances.

(b) Test.

(1) Selection of Districts. The Director shall select 6 judicial districts of the United States in which to test the effectiveness of the financial management training curriculum and materials developed under subsection (a).

(2) Use. For an 18-month period beginning not later than 270 days after the date of the enactment of this Act [enacted Apr. 20, 2005], such curriculum and materials shall be, for the 6 judicial districts selected under paragraph (1), used as the instructional course concerning personal financial management for purposes of section 111 of title 11, United States Code.

(c) Evaluation.

(1) IN GENERAL. During the 18-month period referred to in subsection (b), the Director shall evaluate the effectiveness of—

(A) the financial management training curriculum and materials developed under subsection (a); and

(B) a sample of existing consumer education programs such as those described in the Report of the National Bankruptcy Review Commission (October 20, 1997) that are representative of consumer education programs carried out by the credit industry, by trustees serving under chapter 13 of title 11, United States Code, and by consumer counseling groups.

(2) REPORT. Not later than 3 months after concluding such evaluation, the Director shall submit a report to the Speaker of the House of Representatives and the President pro tempore of the Senate, for referral to the appropriate committees of the Congress, containing the findings of the Director regarding the effectiveness of such curriculum, such materials, and such programs and their costs.

**Sec. 107 Schedules of reasonable and necessary expenses.**

For purposes of section 707(b) of title 11, United States Code, as amended by this Act, the Director of the Executive Office for United States Trustees shall, not later than 180 days after the date of enactment of this Act [enacted Apr. 20, 2005], issue schedules of reasonable and necessary administrative expenses of administering a chapter 13 plan for each judicial district of the United States.

**Sec. 315 Giving creditors fair notice in chapters 7 and 13 cases.**

* * *

(c) (1) Not later than 180 days after the date of the enactment of this Act [enacted Apr. 20, 2005], the Director of the Administrative Office of the United States Courts shall establish procedures for safeguarding the confidentiality of any tax information required to be provided under this section.

(2) The procedures under paragraph (1) shall include restrictions on creditor access to tax information that is required to be provided under this section.

(3) Not later than 540 days after the date of enactment of this Act [enacted Apr. 20, 2005], the Director of the Administrative Office of the United States Courts shall prepare and submit to the President pro tempore of the Senate and the Speaker of the House of Representatives a report that—

(A) assesses the effectiveness of the procedures established under paragraph (1); and

(B) if appropriate, includes proposed legislation to—

(i) further protect the confidentiality of tax information; and

(ii) provide penalties for the improper use by any person of the tax information required to be provided under this section.

## Sec. 603 Audit procedures.

(a) In General.

(1) Establishment of Procedures. The Attorney General (in judicial districts served by United States trustees) and the Judicial Conference of the United States (in judicial districts served by bankruptcy administrators) shall establish procedures to determine the accuracy, veracity, and completeness of petitions, schedules, and other information that the debtor is required to provide under sections 521 and 1322 of title 11, United States Code, and, if applicable, section 111 of such title, in cases filed under chapter 7 or 13 of such title in which the debtor is an individual. Such audits shall be in accordance with generally accepted auditing standards and performed by independent certified public accountants or independent licensed public accountants, provided that the Attorney General and the Judicial Conference, as appropriate, may develop alternative auditing standards not later than 2 years after the date of enactment of this Act [enacted Apr. 20, 2005].

(2) Procedures. Those procedures required by paragraph (1) shall—

(A) establish a method of selecting appropriate qualified persons to contract to perform those audits;

(B) establish a method of randomly selecting cases to be audited, except that not less than 1 out of every 250 cases in each Federal judicial district shall be selected for audit;

(C) require audits of schedules of income and expenses that reflect greater than average variances from the statistical norm of the district in which the schedules were filed if those variances occur by reason of higher income or higher expenses than the statistical norm of the district in which the schedules were filed; and

(D) establish procedures for providing, not less frequently than annually, public information concerning the aggregate results of such audits including the percentage of cases, by district, in which a material misstatement of income or expenditures is reported.

* * *

## Sec. 1221 Transfers made by nonprofit charitable corporations.

(a) Sale of Property of Estate. —Section 363(d) of title 11, United States Code, is amended by striking "only" and all that follows through the end of the subsection and inserting "only—

"(1) in accordance with applicable nonbankruptcy law that governs the transfer of property by a corporation or trust that is not a moneyed, business, or commercial corporation or trust; and

"(2) to the extent not inconsistent with any relief granted under subsection (c), (d), (e), or (f) of section 362.".

(b) Confirmation of Plan of Reorganization. —Section 1129(a) of title 11, United

States Code, as amended by sections 213 and 321, is amended by adding at the end the following:

"(16) All transfers of property of the plan shall be made in accordance with any applicable provisions of nonbankruptcy law that govern the transfer of property by a corporation or trust that is not a moneyed, business, or commercial corporation or trust.".

(c) Transfer of Property. —Section 541 of title 11, United States Code, as amended by section 225, is amended by adding at the end the following:

"(f) Notwithstanding any other provision of this title, property that is held by a debtor that is a corporation described in section 501(c)(3) of the Internal Revenue Code of 1986 and exempt from tax under section 501(a) of such Code may be transferred to an entity that is not such a corporation, but only under the same conditions as would apply if the debtor had not filed a case under this title.".

(d) Applicability. —The amendments made by this section shall apply to a case pending under title 11, United States Code, on the date of enactment of this Act, or filed under that title on or after that date of enactment, except that the court shall not confirm a plan under chapter 11 of title 11, United States Code, without considering whether this section would substantially affect the rights of a party in interest who first acquired rights with respect to the debtor after the date of the filing of the petition. The parties who may appear and be heard in a proceeding under this section include the attorney general of the State in which the debtor is incorporated, was formed, or does business.



(e) Rule of Construction. —Nothing in this section shall be construed to require the court in which a case under chapter 11 of title 11, United States Code, is pending to remand or refer any proceeding, issue, or controversy to any other court or to require the approval of any other court for the transfer of property.

## Sec. 1228 Providing requested tax documents to the court.

(a) Chapter 7 Cases. The court shall not grant a discharge in the case of an individual who is a debtor in a case under chapter 7 of title 11, United States Code, unless requested tax documents have been provided to the court.

(b) Chapter 11 and Chapter 13 Cases. The court shall not confirm a plan of reorganization in the case of an individual under chapter 11 or 13 of title 11, United States Code, unless requested tax documents have been filed with the court.

(c) Document Retention. The court shall destroy documents submitted in support of a bankruptcy claim not sooner than 3 years after the date of the conclusion of a case filed by an individual under chapter 7, 11, or 13 of title 11, United States Code. In the event of a pending audit or enforcement action, the court may extend the time for destruction of such requested tax documents.

## Sec. 1233 Direct appeals of bankruptcy matters to courts of appeals.

* * *

(b) PROCEDURAL RULES.

(1) TEMPORARY APPLICATION. A provision of this subsection shall apply to appeals under section 158(d)(2) of title 28, United States Code, until a rule of practice and procedure relating to such provision and such appeals is promulgated or amended under chapter 131 of such title.

(2) CERTIFICATION. A district court, a bankruptcy court, or a bankruptcy appellate panel may make a certification under section 158(d)(2) of title 28, United States Code, only with respect to matters pending in the respective bankruptcy court, district court, or bankruptcy appellate panel.

(3) PROCEDURE. Subject to any other provision of this subsection, an appeal authorized by the court of appeals under section 158(d)(2)(A) of title 28, United States Code, shall be taken in the manner prescribed in subdivisions (a)(1), (b), (c), and (d) of rule 5 of the Federal Rules of Appellate Procedure. For purposes of subdivision (a)(1) of rule 5—

(A) a reference in such subdivision to a district court shall be deemed to include a reference to a bankruptcy court and a bankruptcy appellate panel, as appropriate; and

(B) a reference in such subdivision to the parties requesting permission to appeal to be served with the petition shall be deemed to include a reference to the parties to the judgment, order, or decree from which the appeal is taken.

(4) FILING OF PETITION WITH ATTACHMENT. A petition requesting permission to appeal, that is based on a certification made under subparagraph (A) or (B) of section 158(d)(2) shall—

(A) be filed with the circuit clerk not later than 10 days after the certification is entered on the docket of the bankruptcy court, the district court, or the bankruptcy appellate panel from which the appeal is taken; and

(B) have attached a copy of such certification.

(5) REFERENCES IN RULE 5. For purposes of rule 5 of the Federal Rules of Appellate Procedure—

(A) a reference in such rule to a district court shall be deemed to include a reference to a bankruptcy court and to a bankruptcy appellate panel; and

(B) a reference in such rule to a district clerk shall be deemed to include a reference to a clerk of a bankruptcy court and to a clerk of a bankruptcy appellate panel.

(6) APPLICATION OF RULES. The Federal Rules of Appellate Procedure shall apply in the courts of appeals with respect to appeals authorized under section 158(d)(2)(A), to the extent relevant and as if such appeals were taken from final

judgments, orders, or decrees of the district courts or bankruptcy appellate panels exercising appellate jurisdiction under subsection (a) or (b) of section 158 of title 28, United States Code.

# Federal Rules of Bankruptcy Procedure

## Rule 1001

## Scope of Rules and Forms; Short Title

The Bankruptcy Rules and Forms govern procedure in cases under title 11 of the United States Code. The rules shall be cited as the Federal Rules of Bankruptcy Procedure and the forms as the Official Bankruptcy Forms. These rules shall be construed, administered, and employed by the court and the parties to secure the just, speedy, and inexpensive determination of every case and proceeding.

# PART I

# COMMENCEMENT OF CASE; PROCEEDINGS RELATING TO PETITION AND ORDER FOR RELIEF

## Rule 1002 Commencement of Case

(*a*) *Petition.* A petition commencing a case under the Code shall be filed with the clerk.

(*b*) *Transmission to United States Trustee.* The clerk shall forthwith transmit to the United States trustee a copy of the petition filed pursuant to subdivision (a) of this rule.

BANKRUPTCY CODE REFERENCES: §§ 109, 301, 302 and 303; chapter 15

## Rule 1003 Involuntary Petition

(*a*) *Transferor or Transferee of Claim.* A transferor or transferee of a claim shall annex to the original and each copy of the petition a copy of all documents evidencing the transfer, whether transferred unconditionally, for security, or otherwise, and a signed statement that the claim was not transferred for the purpose of commencing the case and setting forth the consideration for and terms of the transfer. An entity that has transferred or acquired a claim for the purpose of commencing a case for liquidation under chapter 7 or for reorganization under chapter 11 shall not be a qualified petitioner.

(*b*) *Joinder of Petitioners After Filing.* If the answer to an involuntary petition filed by fewer than three creditors avers the existence of 12 or more creditors, the debtor shall file with the answer a list of all creditors with their addresses, a brief statement of the nature of their claims, and the amounts thereof. If it appears that there are 12 or more creditors as provided in § 303(b) of the Code, the court shall afford a reasonable opportunity for other creditors to join in the petition before a hearing is held thereon.

BANKRUPTCY CODE REFERENCE: § 303

## Rule 1004 Involuntary Petition Against a Partnership

After filing of an involuntary petition under § 303(b)(3) of the Code, (1) the petitioning partners or other petitioners shall promptly send to or serve on each general partner who is not a petitioner a copy of the petition; and (2) the clerk shall promptly issue a summons for service on each general partner who is not a petitioner. Rule 1010 applies to the form and service of the summons.

BANKRUPTCY CODE REFERENCES:
§§ 301 and 303

## Rule 1004.1 Petition for an Infant or Incompetent Person

If an infant or incompetent person has a representative, including a general guardian, committee, conservator, or similar fiduciary, the representative may file a voluntary petition on behalf of the infant or incompetent person. An infant or incompetent person who does not have a duly appointed representative may file a voluntary petition by next friend or guardian ad litem. The court shall appoint a guardian ad litem for an infant or incompetent person who is a debtor and is not otherwise represented or shall make any other order to protect the infant or incompetent debtor.

BANKRUPTCY CODE REFERENCES:
§§ 109, 112, 301 and 302

**Rule 1004.2 Petition in Chapter 15 Cases**

(*a*) *Designating Center of Main Interests.* A petition for recognition of a foreign proceeding under chapter 15 of the Code shall state the country where the debtor has its center of main interests. The petition shall also identify each country in which a foreign proceeding by, regarding, or against the debtor is pending.

(*b*) *Challenging Designation.* The United States trustee or a party in interest may file a motion for a determination that the debtor's center of main interests is other than as stated in the petition for recognition commencing the chapter 15 case. Unless the court orders otherwise, the motion shall be filed no later than seven days before the date set for the hearing on the petition. The motion shall be transmitted to the United States trustee and served on the debtor, all persons or bodies authorized to administer foreign proceedings of the debtor, all entities against whom provisional relief is being sought under § 1519 of the Code, all parties to litigation pending in the United States in which the debtor was a party as of the time the petition was filed, and such other entities as the court may direct.

**Rule 1005 Caption of Petition**

The caption of a petition commencing a case under the;Code shall contain the name of the court, the title of the case, and the docket number. The title of the case shall include the following information about the debtor: name, employer identification number, last four digits of the social-security number or individual debtor's taxpayer-identification number, any other federal taxpayer-identification number, and all other names used within eight years before filing the petition. If the petition is not filed by the debtor, it shall include all names used by the debtor which are known to the petitioners.

BANKRUPTCY CODE REFERENCE:
§ 342

**Rule 1006 Filing Fee**

(*a*) *General Requirement.* Every petition shall be accompanied by the filing fee except as provided in subdivisions (b) and (c) of this rule. For the purpose of this rule, "filing fee" means the filing fee prescribed by 28 U.S.C. § 1930(a)(1)–(a)(5) and any other fee prescribed by the Judicial Conference of the United States under 28 U.S.C. § 1930(b) that is payable to the clerk upon the commencement of a case under the Code.

(*b*) *Payment of Filing Fee in Installments.*

(*1*) *Application to Pay Filing Fee in Installments.* A voluntary petition by an individual shall be accepted for filing, regardless of whether any portion of the filing fee is paid, if accompanied by the debtor's signed application, prepared as

BANKRUPTCY RULES

prescribed by the appropriate Official Form, stating that the debtor is unable to pay the filing fee except in installments.

(2) *Action on Application.* Prior to the meeting of creditors, the court may order the filing fee paid to the clerk or grant leave to pay in installments and fix the number, amount and dates of payment. The number of installments shall not exceed four, and the final installment shall be payable not later than 120 days after filing the petition. for cause shown, the court may extend the time of any installment, provided the last installment is paid not later than 180 days after filing the petition.

(3) *Postponement of Attorney's Fees.* All installments of the filing fee must be paid in full before the debtor or chapter 13 trustee may make further payments to an attorney or any other person who renders services to the debtor in connection with the case.

(c) *Waiver of Filing Fee.* A voluntary chapter 7 petition filed by an individual shall be accepted for filing if accompanied by the debtor's application requesting a waiver under 28 U.S.C. § 1930(f), prepared as prescribed by the appropriate Official Form.

Bankruptcy Code References:

§§ 707, 1112, 1208 and 1307

Bankruptcy Statutory Reference:

28 U.S.C. § 1930

## Rule 1007 Lists, Schedules, Statements, and Other Documents; Time Limits

(a) *Corporate Ownership Statement, List of Creditors and Equity Security Holders, and Other Lists.*

(1) *Voluntary Case.* In a voluntary case, the debtor shall file with the petition a list containing the name and address of each entity included or to be included on Schedules D, E/F, G, and H as prescribed by the Official Forms. If the debtor is a corporation, other than a governmental unit, the debtor shall file with the petition a corporate ownership statement containing the information described in Rule 7007.1. The debtor shall file a supplemental statement promptly upon any change in circumstances that renders the corporate ownership statement inaccurate.

(2) *Involuntary Case.* In an involuntary case, the debtor shall file within seven days after entry of the order for relief, a list containing the name and address of each entity included or to be included on Schedules D, E/F, G, and H as prescribed by the Official Forms.

(3) *Equity Security Holders.* In a chapter 11 reorganization case, unless the court orders otherwise, the debtor shall file within 14 days after entry of the order for relief a list of the debtor's equity security holders of each class showing the number and kind of interests registered in the name of each holder, and the last known address or place of business of each holder.

(4) *Chapter 15 Case.* In addition to the documents required under § 1515 of

the Code, a foreign representative filing a petition for recognition under chapter 15 shall file with the petition: (A) a corporate ownership statement containing the information described in Rule 7007.1; and (B) unless the court orders otherwise, a list containing the names and addresses of all persons or bodies authorized to administer foreign proceedings of the debtor, all parties to litigation pending in the United States in which the debtor is a party at the time of the filing of the petition, and all entities against whom provisional relief is being sought under § 1519 of the Code.

(5) *Extension of Time.* Any extension of time for the filing of the lists required by this subdivision may be granted only on motion for cause shown and on notice to the United States trustee and to any trustee, committee elected under § 705 or appointed under § 1102 of the Code, or other party as the court may direct.

(*b*) *Schedules, Statements, and Other Documents Required.*

(*1*) Except in a chapter 9 municipality case, the debtor, unless the court orders otherwise, shall file the following schedules, statements, and other documents, prepared as prescribed by the appropriate Official Forms, if any:

(*A*) schedules of assets and liabilities;

(*B*) a schedule of current income and expenditures;

(*C*) a schedule of executory contracts and unexpired leases;

(*D*) a statement of financial affairs;

(*E*) copies of all payment advices or other evidence of payment, if any, received by the debtor from an employer within 60 days before the filing of the petition, with redaction of all but the last four digits of the debtor's social-security number or individual taxpayer-identification number; and

(*F*) a record of any interest that the debtor has in an account or program of the type specified in § 521(c) of the Code.

(*2*) An individual debtor in a chapter 7 case shall file a statement of intention as required by § 521(a) of the Code, prepared as prescribed by the appropriate Official Form. A copy of the statement of intention shall be served on the trustee and the creditors named in the statement on or before the filing of the statement.

(*3*) Unless the United States trustee has determined that the credit counseling requirement of § 109(h) does not apply in the district, an individual debtor must file a statement of compliance with the credit counseling requirement, prepared as prescribed by the appropriate Official Form which must include one of the following:

(*A*) an attached certificate and debt repayment plan, if any, required by § 521(b);

(*B*) a statement that the debtor has received the credit counseling briefing required by § 109(h)(1) but does not have the certificate required by § 521(b);

(*C*) a certification under § 109(h)(3); or

(*D*) a request for a determination by the court under § 109(h)(4).

(*4*) Unless § 707(b)(2)(D) applies, an individual debtor in a chapter 7 case shall file a statement of current monthly income prepared as prescribed by the appropriate Official Form, and, if the current monthly income exceeds the median family income for the applicable state and household size, the information, including calculations, required by § 707(b), prepared as prescribed by the appropriate Official Form.

(*5*) An individual debtor in a chapter 11 case shall file a statement of current monthly income, prepared as prescribed by the appropriate Official Form.

(*6*) A debtor in a chapter 13 case shall file a statement of current monthly income, prepared as prescribed by the appropriate Official Form, and, if the current monthly income exceeds the median family income for the applicable state and household size, a calculation of disposable income made in accordance with § 1325(b)(3), prepared as prescribed by the appropriate Official Form.

(*7*) Unless an approved provider of an instructional course concerning personal financial management has notified the court that a debtor has completed the course after filing the petition:

(*A*) An individual debtor in a chapter 7 or chapter 13 case shall file a statement of completion of the course, prepared as prescribed by the appropriate Official Form; and

(*B*) An individual debtor in a chapter 11 case shall file the statement if § 1141(d)(3) applies.

(*8*) If an individual debtor in a chapter 11, 12, or 13 case has claimed an exemption under § 522(b)(3)(A) in property of the kind described in § 522(p)(1) with a value in excess of the amount set out in § 522(q)(1), the debtor shall file a statement as to whether there is any proceeding pending in which the debtor may be found guilty of a felony of a kind described in § 522(q)(1)(A) or found liable for a debt of the kind described in § 522(q)(1)(B).

(c) *Time Limits.* In a voluntary case, the schedules, statements, and other documents required by subdivision (b)(1), (4), (5), and (6) shall be filed with the petition or within 14 days thereafter, except as otherwise provided in subdivisions (d), (e), (f), and (h) of this rule. In an involuntary case, the schedules, statements, and other documents required by subdivision (b)(1) shall be filed by the debtor within 14 days after the entry of the order for relief. In a voluntary case, the documents required by paragraphs (A), (C), and (D) of subdivision (b)(3) shall be filed with the petition. Unless the court orders otherwise, a debtor who has filed a statement under subdivision (b)(3)(B), shall file the documents required by subdivision (b)(3)(A) within 14 days of the order for relief. In a chapter 7 case, the debtor shall file the statement required by subdivision (b)(7) within 60 days after the first date set for the meeting of creditors under § 341 of the Code, and in a chapter 11 or 13 case no later than the date when the last payment was made by the debtor as required by the plan or the filing of a motion for a discharge under § 1141(d)(5)(B) or § 1328(b) of the Code. The court may, at any time and in its discretion, enlarge the time to file the statement required by subdivision (b)(7). The debtor shall file the statement required by subdivision (b)(8) no earlier than the date of the last payment made under the plan or the date of the filing of a motion for a discharge under §§ 1141(d)(5)(B), 1228(b), or 1328(b) of the Code. Lists, schedules, statements, and other documents filed prior to the conversion of a case to another chapter shall be deemed filed in the converted case unless the court directs otherwise. Except as provided in § 1116(3), any extension of time to file schedules, statements, and other documents required under this rule may be granted only on motion for cause shown and on notice to the United States trustee, any committee elected under § 705 or appointed under § 1102 of the Code, trustee, examiner, or other party as the court may direct. Notice of an extension shall be given to the United States trustee and to any committee, trustee, or other party as the court may direct.

(d) *List of 20 Largest Creditors in Chapter 9 Municipality Case or Chapter 11 Reorganization Case.* In addition to the list required by subdivision (a) of this rule, a debtor in a chapter 9 municipality case or a debtor in a voluntary chapter 11 reorganization case shall file with the petition a list containing the name, address and claim of the creditors that hold the 20 largest unsecured claims, excluding insiders, as prescribed by the appropriate Official Form. In an involuntary chapter 11 reorganization case, such list shall be filed by the debtor within 2 days after entry of the order for relief under § 303(h) of the Code.

(e) *List in Chapter 9 Municipality Cases.* The list required by subdivision (a) of this rule shall be filed by the debtor in a chapter 9 municipality case within such time as the court shall fix. If a proposed plan requires a revision of assessments so that the proportion of special assessments or special taxes to be assessed against some real property will be different from the proportion in effect at the date the petition is filed, the debtor shall also file a list showing the name and address of each known holder of title, legal or equitable, to real property adversely affected. On motion for cause shown, the court may modify the requirements of this subdivision and subdivision (a) of this rule.

(f) *Statement of Social Security Number.* An individual debtor shall submit a verified statement that sets out the debtor's social security number, or states that the debtor does not have a social security number. In a voluntary case, the debtor shall submit the statement with the petition. In an involuntary case, the debtor shall submit the statement within 14 days after the entry of the order for relief.

(g) *Partnership and Partners.* The general partners of a debtor partnership shall prepare and file the list required under subdivision (a), the schedules of the assets and liabilities, schedule of current income and expenditures, schedule of executory contracts and unexpired leases, and statement of financial affairs of the partnership. The court may order any general partner to file a statement of personal assets and liabilities within such time as the court may fix.

(*h*) *Interests Acquired or Arising After Petition.* If, as provided by § 541(a)(5) of the Code, the debtor acquires or becomes entitled to acquire any interest in property, the debtor shall within 14 days after the information comes to the debtor's knowledge or within such further time the court may allow, file a supplemental schedule in the chapter 7 liquidation case, chapter 11 reorganization case, chapter 12 family farmer's debt adjustment case, or chapter 13 individual debt adjustment case. If any of the property required to be reported under this subdivision is claimed by the debtor as exempt, the debtor shall claim the exemptions in the supplemental schedule. The duty to file a supplemental schedule in accordance with this subdivision continues notwithstanding the closing of the case, except that the schedule need not be filed in a chapter 11, chapter 12, or chapter 13 case with respect to property acquired after entry of the order confirming a chapter 11 plan or discharging the debtor in a chapter 12 or chapter 13 case.

(*i*) *Disclosure of List of Security Holders.* After notice and hearing and for cause shown, the court may direct an entity other than the debtor or trustee to disclose any list of security holders of the debtor in its possession or under its control, indicating the name, address and security held by any of them. The entity possessing this list may be required either to produce the list or a true copy thereof, or permit inspection or copying, or otherwise disclose the information contained on the list.

(*j*) *Impounding of Lists.* On motion of a party in interest and for cause shown the court may direct the impounding of the lists filed under this rule, and may refuse to permit inspection by any entity. The court may permit inspection or use of the lists, however, by any party in interest on terms prescribed by the court.

(*k*) *Preparation of List, Schedules, or Statements on Default of Debtor.* If a list, schedule, or statement, other than a statement of intention, is not prepared and filed as required by this rule, the court may order the trustee, a petitioning creditor, committee, or other party to prepare and file any of these papers within a time fixed by the court. The court may approve reimbursement of the cost incurred in complying with such an order as an administrative expense.

(*l*) *Transmission to United States Trustee.* The clerk shall forthwith transmit to the United States trustee a copy of every list, schedule, and statement filed pursuant to subdivision (a)(1), (a)(2), (b), (d), or (h) of this rule.

(*m*) *Infants and Incompetent Persons.* If the debtor knows that a person on the list of creditors or schedules is an infant or incompetent person, the debtor also shall include the name, address, and legal relationship of any person upon whom process would be served in an adversary proceeding against the infant or incompetent in accordance with Rule 7004(b)(2).

Bankruptcy Code References:

§§ 107, 521, 541 and 723

## Interim Rule 1007 Lists, Schedules, Statements, and Other Documents; Time Limits[1]

* * * * *

(*b*) *Schedules, Statements, and Other Documents Required.*

* * * * *

(*5*) An individual debtor in a chapter 11 case (unless under subchapter V) shall file a statement of current monthly income, prepared as prescribed by the appropriate Official Form.

* * * * *

(*h*) *Interests Acquired or Arising After Petition.* If, as provided by § 541(a)(5) of the Code, the debtor acquires or becomes entitled to acquire any interest in property, the debtor shall within 14 days after the information comes to the debtor's knowledge or within such further time the court may allow, file a supplemental schedule in the chapter 7 liquidation case, chapter 11 reorganization case, chapter 12 family farmer's debt adjustment case, or chapter 13 individual debt adjustment case. If any of the property required to be reported under this subdivision is claimed by the debtor as exempt, the debtor shall claim the exemptions in the supplemental schedule. ~~The~~ This duty to file a supplemental schedule ~~in accordance with this subdivision~~ continues even after the case is closed, except for property acquired after an order is entered: ~~notwithstanding the closing of the case, except that the schedule need not be filed in a chapter 11, chapter 12, or chapter 13 case with respect to property acquired after entry of the order~~

(*1*) confirming a chapter 11 plan (other than one confirmed under § 1191(b)); or

(*2*) discharging the debtor in a chapter 12 case, or a chapter 13 case, or a case under subchapter V of chapter 11 in which the plan is confirmed under § 1191(b).

* * * * *

[1] Ed. note: Interim Rule 1007 has been adopted by the bankruptcy courts to implement the Small Business Reorganization Act of 2019, Pub. L. No. 116-54 (2019). Changes from the existing rule are indicated with strikeouts and underscoring.

BANKRUPTCY RULES

## Interim Rule 1007-I Lists, Schedules, Statements and Other Documents; Time Limits; Expiration of Temporary Means Testing Exclusion[2]

(*b*) *Schedules, Statements, and Other Documents Required.*

* * * * *

(*4*) Unless either: (A) § 707(b)(2)(D)(i) applies, or (B) § 707(b)(2)(D)(ii) applies and the exclusion from means testing granted therein extends beyond the period specified by Rule 1017(e), an individual debtor in a chapter 7 case shall file a statement of current monthly income prepared as prescribed by the appropriate Official Form, and, if the current monthly income exceeds the median family income for the applicable state and household size, the information, including calculations, required by § 707(b), prepared as prescribed by the appropriate Official Form.

* * * * *

(*c*) *Time Limits.* In a voluntary case, the schedules, statements, and other documents required by subdivision (b)(1), (4), (5), and (6) shall be filed with the petition or within 14 days thereafter, except as otherwise provided in subdivisions (d), (e), (f), (h), and (n) of this rule. In an involuntary case, the schedules, statements, and other documents required by subdivision (b)(1) shall be filed by the debtor within 14 days after the entry of the order for relief. In a voluntary case, the documents required by paragraphs (A), (C), and (D) of subdivision (b)(3) shall be filed with the petition. Unless the court orders otherwise, a debtor who has filed a statement under subdivision (b)(3)(B), shall file the documents required by subdivision (b)(3)(A) within 14 days of the order for relief. In a chapter 7 case, the debtor shall file the statement required by subdivision (b)(7) within 60 days after the first date set for the meeting of creditors under § 341 of the Code, and in a chapter 11 or 13 case no later than the date when the last payment was made by the debtor as required by the plan or the filing of a motion for a discharge under § 1141(d)(5)(B) or § 1328(b) of the Code. The court may, at any time and in its discretion, enlarge the time to file the statement required by subdivision (b)(7). The debtor shall file the statement required by subdivision (b)(8) no earlier than the date of the last payment made under the plan or the date of the filing of a motion for a discharge under §§ 1141(d)(5)(B), 1228(b), or 1328(b) of the Code. Lists, schedules, statements, and other documents filed prior to the conversion of a case to another chapter shall be deemed filed in the converted case unless the court directs otherwise. Except as provided in § 1116(3), any extension of time to

---

[2] Interim Rule 1007-I has been adopted by the bankruptcy courts to implement the National Guard and Reservists Debt Relief Act of 2008, Public Law No. 110-438, as amended by Public Law No. 112-64. The amended Act, which provides a temporary exclusion from the application of the means test for certain members of the National Guard and reserve components of the Armed Forces, applies to bankruptcy cases commenced in the seven-year period beginning December 19, 2008. The rule iIncorporates (1) time amendments to Rule 1007 which took effect on December 1, 2009, (2) an amendment, effective December 1, 2010, which extended the time to file the statement of completion of a course in personal financial management in a chapter 7 case filed by an individual debtor, and (3) a conforming amendment, effective December 1, 2012, which removed an inconsistency created by the 2010 amendment.

file schedules, statements, and other documents required under this rule may be granted only on motion for cause shown and on notice to the United States trustee, any committee elected under § 705 or appointed under § 1102 of the Code, trustee, examiner, or other party as the court may direct. Notice of an extension shall be given to the United States trustee and to any committee, trustee, or other party as the court may direct.

* * * * *

(*n*) *Time Limits for, and Notice to, Debtors Temporarily Excluded from Means Testing*

(*1*) An individual debtor who is temporarily excluded from means testing pursuant to § 707(b)(2)(D)(ii) of the Code shall file any statement and calculations required by subdivision (b)(4) no later than14 days after the expiration of the temporary exclusion if the expiration occurs within the time specified by Rule 1017(e) for filing a motion pursuant to § 707(b)(2).

(*2*) If the temporary exclusion from means testing under § 707(b)(2)(D)(ii) terminates due to the circumstances specified in subdivision (n)(1), and if the debtor has not previously filed a statement and calculations required by subdivision (b)(4), the clerk shall promptly notify the debtor that the required statement and calculations must be filed within the time specified in subdivision (n)(1).

Bankruptcy Code References:
§§ 341, 707, 1102, 1116, 1141, 1228 and 1328

## Rule 1008 Verification of Petitions and Accompanying Papers

All petitions, lists, schedules, statements and amendments thereto shall be verified or contain an unsworn declaration as provided in 28 U.S.C. § 1746.

Bankruptcy Code Reference: § 110

Bankruptcy Statutory Reference: 28 U.S.C. § 1746

BANKRUPTCY RULES

## Rule 1009 Amendments of Voluntary Petitions, Lists, Schedules and Statements

(*a*) *General Right to Amend.* A voluntary petition, list, schedule, or statement may be amended by the debtor as a matter of course at any time before the case is closed. The debtor shall give notice of the amendment to the trustee and to any entity affected thereby. On motion of a party in interest, after notice and a hearing, the court may order any voluntary petition, list, schedule, or statement to be amended and the clerk shall give notice of the amendment to entities designated by the court.

(*b*) *Statement of Intention.* The statement of intention may be amended by the debtor at any time before the expiration of the period provided in § 521(a) of the Code. The debtor shall give notice of the amendment to the trustee and to any entity affected thereby.

(*c*) *Statement of Social Security Number.* If a debtor becomes aware that the statement of social security number submitted under Rule 1007(f) is incorrect, the debtor shall promptly submit an amended verified statement setting forth the correct social security number. The debtor shall give notice of the amendment to all of the entities required to be included on the list filed under Rule 1007(a)(1) or (a)(2).

(*d*) *Transmission to United States Trustee.* The clerk shall promptly transmit to the United States trustee a copy of every amendment filed or submitted under subdivision (a), (b), or (c) of this rule.

BANKRUPTCY CODE REFERENCES: §§ 105, 342 and 521

### Rule 1010 Service of Involuntary Petition and Summons

(*a*) *Service of Involuntary Petition and Summons.* On the filing of an involuntary petition, the clerk shall forthwith issue a summons for service. When an involuntary petition is filed, service shall be made on the debtor. The summons shall be served with a copy of the petition in the manner provided for service of a summons and complaint by Rule 7004(a) or (b). If service cannot be so made, the court may order that the summons and petition be served by mailing copies to the party's last known address, and by at least one publication in a manner and form directed by the court. The summons and petition may be served on the party anywhere. Rule 7004(e) and Rule 4(*l*) F.R.Civ.P. apply when service is made or attempted under this rule.

(*b*) *Corporate Ownership Statement.* Each petitioner that is a corporation shall file with the involuntary petition a corporate ownership statement containing the information described in Rule 7007.1

## CIVIL RULE:

Federal Rule of Civil Procedure 4(*l*), which was last amended effective December 1, 2007, provides:

**Rule 4 Summons**

(*l*) PROVING SERVICE.

* * *

(1) *Affidavit Required.* Unless service is waived, proof of service must be made to the court. Except for service by a United States marshal or deputy marshal, proof must be by the server's affidavit.

(2) *Service Outside the United States.* Service not within any judicial district of the United States must be proved as follows:

(A) if made under Rule 4(f)(1), as provided in the applicable treaty or convention; or

(B) if made under Rule 4(f)(2) or (f)(3), by a receipt signed by the addressee, or by other evidence satisfying the court that the summons and complaint were delivered to the addressee.

(3) *Validity of Service; Amending Proof.* Failure to prove service does not affect the validity of service. The court may permit proof of service to be amended.

* * *

Bankruptcy Code References: § 303

## Rule 1011 Responsive Pleading or Motion in Involuntary Cases

(*a*) *Who May Contest Petition.* The debtor named in an involuntary petition may contest the petition. In the case of a petition against a partnership under Rule 1004, a nonpetitioning general partner, or a person who is alleged to be a general partner but denies the allegation, may contest the petition.

(*b*) *Defenses and Objections; When Presented.* Defenses and objections to the petition shall be presented in the manner prescribed by Rule 12 F.R.Civ.P.[3] and shall be filed and served within 21 days after service of the summons, except that if service is made by publication on a party or partner not residing or found within the state in which the court sits, the court shall prescribe the time for filing and serving the response.

(*c*) *Effect of Motion.* Service of a motion under Rule 12(b) F.R.Civ.P. shall extend the time for filing and serving a responsive pleading as permitted by Rule 12(a) F.R.Civ.P.

(*d*) *Claims Against Petitioners.* A claim against a petitioning creditor may not be asserted in the answer except for the purpose of defeating the petition.

(*e*) *Other Pleadings.* No other pleadings shall be permitted, except that the court may order a reply to an answer and prescribe the time for filing and service.

(*f*) *Corporate Ownership Statement.* If the entity responding to the involuntary petition is a corporation, the entity shall file with its first appearance, pleading, motion, response, or other request addressed to the court a corporate ownership statement containing the information described in Rule 7007.1.

Bankruptcy Code References: § 303

## Rule 1012 Responsive Pleading in Cross-Border Cases

(*a*) *Who May Contest Petition.* The debtor or any party in interest may contest a petition for recognition of a foreign proceeding.

(*b*) *Objections and Responses; When Presented.* Objections and other responses to the petition shall be presented no later than seven days before the date set for the hearing on the petition, unless the court prescribes some other time or manner for responses.

(*c*) *Corporate Ownership Statement.* If the entity responding to the petition is a corporation, then the entity shall file a corporate ownership statement containing the information described in Rule 7007.1 with its first appearance, pleading, motion, response, or other request addressed to the court.

Bankruptcy Code References: §§ 1501–1532

## Rule 1013 Hearing and Disposition of a Petition in an Involuntary Case

(*a*) *Contested Petition.* The court shall determine the issues of a contested petition at the earliest practicable time and forthwith enter an order for relief,

---

[3] Ed. note: For the text of Fed. R. Civ. P. 12, *see* Fed. R. Bankr. P. 7012 *infra*.

dismiss the petition, or enter any other appropriate order.

(*b*) *Default.* If no pleading or other defense to a petition is filed within the time provided by Rule 1011, the court, on the next day, or as soon thereafter as practicable, shall enter an order for the relief requested in the petition.

(*c*) [*Abrogated.*]

BANKRUPTCY CODE REFERENCE: § 303

## Rule 1014 Dismissal and Change of Venue

(*a*) *Dismissal and Transfer of Cases.*

(*1*) *Cases Filed in Proper District.* If a petition is filed in the proper district, the court, on the timely motion of a party in interest or on its own motion, and after hearing on notice to the petitioners, the United States trustee, and other entities as directed by the court, may transfer the case to any other district if the court determines that the transfer is in the interest of justice or for the convenience of the parties.

(*2*) *Cases Filed in Improper District.* If a petition is filed in an improper district, the court, on the timely motion of a party in interest or on its own motion, and after hearing on notice to the petitioners, the United States trustee, and other entities as directed by the court, may dismiss the case or transfer it to any other district if the court determines that transfer is in the interest of justice or for the convenience of the parties.

(*b*) *Procedure When Petitions Involving the Same Debtor or Related Debtors Are Filed in Different Courts.* If petitions commencing cases under the Code or seeking recognition under chapter 15 are filed in different districts by, regarding, or against (1) the same debtor, (2) a partnership and one or more of its general partners, (3) two or more general partners, or (4) a debtor and an affiliate, the court in the district in which the first-filed petition is pending may determine, in the interest of justice or for the convenience of the parties, the district or districts in which any of the cases should proceed. The court may so determine on motion and after a hearing, with notice to the following entities in the affected cases: the United States trustee, entities entitled to notice under Rule 2002(a), and other entities as the court directs. The court may order the parties to the later-filed cases not to proceed further until it makes the determination.

BANKRUPTCY CODE REFERENCES: §§ 349, 707, 1112, 1208 and 1307

BANKRUPTCY STATUTORY REFERENCES: 28 U.S.C. §§ 1408, 1409, 1410 and 1412

## Rule 1015 Consolidation or Joint Administration of Cases Pending in Same Court

(*a*) *Cases Involving Same Debtor.* If two or more petitions by, regarding, or against the same debtor are pending in the same court, the court may order consolidation of the cases.

(*b*) *Cases Involving Two or More Related Debtors.* If a joint petition or two or more petitions are pending in the same court by or against (1) spouses, or (2) a partnership and one or more of its general partners, or (3) two or more general partners, or (4) a debtor and an affiliate, the court may order a joint administration of the estates. Prior to entering an order the court shall give consideration to protecting creditors of different estates against potential conflicts of interest. An order directing joint administration of individual cases of spouses shall, if one spouse has elected the exemptions under § 522(b)(2) of the Code and the other has elected the exemptions under § 522(b)(3), fix a reasonable time within which either may amend the election so that both shall have elected the same exemptions. The order shall notify the debtors that unless they elect the same exemptions within the time fixed by the court, they will be deemed to have elected the exemptions provided by § 522(b)(2).

(c) *Expediting and Protective Orders.* When an order for consolidation or joint administration of a joint case or two or more cases is entered pursuant to this rule, while protecting the rights of the parties under the Code, the court may enter orders as may tend to avoid unnecessary costs and delay.

BANKRUPTCY CODE REFERENCES: §§ 101, 302 and 522

## Rule 1016 Death or Incompetency of Debtor

Death or incompetency of the debtor shall not abate a liquidation case under chapter 7 of the Code. In such event the estate shall be administered and the case concluded in the same manner, so far as possible, as though the death or incompetency had not occurred. If a reorganization, family farmer's debt adjustment, or individual's debt adjustment case is pending under chapter 11, chapter 12, or chapter 13, the case may be dismissed; or if further administration is possible and in the best interest of the parties, the case may proceed and be concluded in the same manner, so far as possible, as though the death or incompetency had not occurred.

BANKRUPTCY CODE REFERENCES: §§ 101 and 109

## Rule 1017 Dismissal or Conversion of Case; Suspension

(a) *Voluntary Dismissal; Dismissal for Want of Prosecution or Other Cause.* Except as provided in §§ 707(a)(3), 707(b), 1208(b), and 1307(b) of the Code, and in Rule 1017(b), (c), and (e), a case shall not be dismissed on motion of the petitioner, for want of prosecution or other cause, or by consent of the parties, before a hearing on notice as provided in Rule 2002. For the purpose of the notice, the debtor shall file a list of creditors with their addresses within the time fixed by the court unless the list was previously filed. If the debtor fails to file the list, the court may order the debtor or another entity to prepare and file it.

(b) *Dismissal for Failure to Pay Filing Fee.*

(1) If any installment of the filing fee has not been paid, the court may, after a hearing on notice to the debtor and the trustee, dismiss the case.

(2) If the case is dismissed or closed without full payment of the filing fee, the installments collected shall be distributed in the same manner and proportions as if the filing fee had been paid in full.

(c) *Dismissal of Voluntary Chapter 7 or Chapter 13 Case for Failure to Timely File List of Creditors, Schedules, and Statement of Financial Affairs.* The court may dismiss a

BANKRUPTCY RULES

voluntary chapter 7 or chapter 13 case under § 707(a)(3) or § 1307(c)(9) after a hearing on notice served by the United States trustee on the debtor, the trustee, and any other entities as the court directs.

(*d*) *Suspension.* The court shall not dismiss a case or suspend proceedings under § 305 before a hearing on notice as provided in Rule 2002(a).

(*e*) *Dismissal of an Individual Debtor's Chapter 7 Case, or Conversion to a Case under Chapter 11 or 13, for Abuse.* The court may dismiss or, with the debtor's consent, convert an individual debtor's case for abuse under § 707(b) only on motion and after a hearing on notice to the debtor, the trustee, the United States trustee, and any other entity as the court directs.

(*1*) Except as otherwise provided in § 704(b)(2), a motion to dismiss a case for abuse under § 707(b) or (c) may be filed only within 60 days after the first date set for the meeting of creditors under § 341(a), unless, on request filed before the time has expired, the court for cause extends the time for filing the motion to dismiss. The party filing the motion shall set forth in the motion all matters to be considered at the hearing. In addition, a motion to dismiss under § 707(b)(1) and (3) shall state with particularity the circumstances alleged to constitute abuse.

(*2*) If the hearing is set on the court's own motion, notice of the hearing shall be served on the debtor no later than 60 days after the first date set for the meeting of creditors under § 341(a). The notice shall set forth all matters to be considered by the court at the hearing.

(*f*) *Procedure for Dismissal, Conversion, or Suspension.*

(*1*) Rule 9014 governs a proceeding to dismiss or suspend a case, or to convert a case to another chapter, except under §§ 706(a), 1112(a), 1208(a) or (b), or 1307(a) or (b).

(*2*) Conversion or dismissal under §§ 706(a), 1112(a), 1208(b), or 1307(b) shall be on motion filed and served as required by Rule 9013.

(*3*) A chapter 12 or chapter 13 case shall be converted without court order when the debtor files a notice of conversion under §§ 1208(a) or 1307(a). The filing date of the notice becomes the date of the conversion order for the purposes of applying § 348(c) and Rule 1019. The clerk shall promptly transmit a copy of the notice to the United States trustee.

BANKRUPTCY CODE REFERENCES: §§ 102, 348, 349, 706, 707, 1112, 1208 and 1307

### Rule 1018 Contested Involuntary Petitions; Contested Petitions Commencing Chapter 15 Cases; Proceedings to Vacate Order for Relief; Applicability of Rules in Part VII Governing Adversary Proceedings

Unless the court otherwise directs and except as otherwise prescribed in Part I of these rules, the following rules in Part VII apply to all proceedings contesting an involuntary petition or a chapter 15 petition for recognition, and to all proceedings to vacate an order for relief: Rules 7005, 7008–7010, 7015, 7016, 7024–7026, 7028–7037, 7052, 7054, 7056, and 7062. The court may direct that other rules in Part VII shall also apply. For the purposes of this rule a reference in the Part VII rules to adversary proceedings shall be read as a reference to proceedings contesting an involuntary petition or a chapter 15 petition for recognition, or proceedings to vacate an order for relief. Reference in the Federal Rules of Civil Procedure to the complaint shall be read as a reference to the petition.

Bankruptcy Code References: §§ 303, 1501–1532

## Rule 1019 Conversion of a Chapter 11 Reorganization Case, Chapter 12 Family Farmer's Debt Adjustment Case, or Chapter 13 Individual's Debt Adjustment Case to a Chapter 7 Liquidation Case

When a chapter 11, chapter 12, or chapter 13 case has been converted or reconverted to a chapter 7 case:

(1) *Filing of Lists, Inventories, Schedules, Statements.*

(*A*) Lists, inventories, schedules, and statements of financial affairs theretofore filed shall be deemed to be filed in the chapter 7 case, unless the court directs otherwise. If they have not been previously filed, the debtor shall comply with Rule 1007 as if an order for relief had been entered on an involuntary petition on the date of the entry of the order directing that the case continue under chapter 7.

(*B*) If a statement of intention is required, it shall be filed within 30 days after entry of the order of conversion or before the first date set for the meeting of creditors, whichever is earlier. The court may grant an extension of time for cause only on written motion filed, or oral request made during a hearing, before the time has expired. Notice of an extension shall be given to the United States trustee and to any committee, trustee, or other party as the court may direct.

(2) *New Filing Periods.*

(*A*) A new time period for filing a motion under § 707(b) or (c), a claim, a complaint objecting to discharge, or a complaint to obtain a determination of dischargeability of any debt shall commence under Rules 1017, 3002, 4004, or 4007, but a new time period shall not commence if a chapter 7 case had been converted to a chapter 11, 12, or 13 case and thereafter reconverted to a chapter 7 case and the time for filing a motion under § 707(b) or (c), a claim, a complaint objecting to discharge, or a complaint to obtain a determination of the dischargeability of any debt, or any extension thereof, expired in the original chapter 7 case.

(*B*) A new time period for filing an objection to a claim of exemptions shall commence under Rule 4003(b) after conversion of a case to a chapter 7 cases unless:

(*i*) the case was converted to chapter 7 more than one year after the entry of the first order confirming a plan under chapter 11, 12 or 13; or

(*ii*) the case was previously pending in chapter 7 and the time to object to a claimed exemption had expired in the original chapter 7 case.

(3) *Claims Filed Before Conversion.* All claims actually filed by a creditor before conversion of the case are deemed filed in the chapter 7 case.

(4) *Turnover of Records and Property.* After qualification of, or assumption of duties by the chapter 7 trustee, any debtor in possession or trustee previously acting in the chapter 11, 12, or 13 case shall, forthwith, unless otherwise ordered, turn over to the chapter 7 trustee all records and property of the estate in the possession or control of the debtor in possession or trustee.

(5) *Filing Final Report and Schedule of Postpetition Debts.*

(*A*) *Conversion of Chapter 11 or Chapter 12 Case.* Unless the court directs otherwise, if a chapter 11 or chapter 12 case is converted to chapter 7, the debtor in possession or, if the debtor is not a debtor in possession, the trustee serving at the time of conversion, shall:

(*i*) not later than 14 days after conversion of the case, file a schedule of unpaid debts incurred after the filing of the petition and before conversion of the case, including the name and address of each holder of a claim; and

(*ii*) not later than 30 days after conversion of the case, file and transmit to the United States trustee a final report and account;

(*B*) *Conversion of Chapter 13 Case.* Unless the court directs otherwise, if a chapter 13 case is converted to chapter 7,

(*i*) the debtor, not later than 14 days after conversion of the case, shall file a schedule of unpaid debts incurred after the filing of the petition and before conversion of the case, including the name and address of each holder of a claim; and

(*ii*) the trustee, not later than 30 days after conversion of the case, shall file and transmit to the United States trustee a final report and account;

(*C*) *Conversion After Confirmation of a Plan.* Unless the court orders otherwise, if a chapter 11, chapter 12, or chapter 13 case is converted to chapter 7 after confirmation of a plan, the debtor shall file:

(*i*) a schedule of property not listed in the final report and account acquired after the filing of the petition but before conversion, except if the case is converted from chapter 13 to chapter 7 and § 348(f)(2) does not apply;

(*ii*) a schedule of unpaid debts not listed in the final report and account incurred after confirmation but before the conversion; and

(*iii*) a schedule of executory contracts and unexpired leases entered into or assumed after the filing of the petition but before conversion.

(*D*) *Transmission to United States Trustee.* The clerk shall forthwith transmit to the United States trustee a copy of every schedule filed pursuant to Rule

1019(5).

(6) *Postpetition Claims; Preconversion Administration Expenses; Notice.* A request for payment of an administrative expense incurred before conversion of the case is timely filed under § 503(a) of the Code if it is filed before conversion or a time fixed by the court. If the request is filed by a governmental unit, it is timely if it is filed before conversion or within the later of a time fixed by the court or 180 days after the date of the conversion. A claim of a kind specified in § 348(d) may be filed in accordance with Rules 3001(a)–(d) and 3002. Upon the filing of the schedule of unpaid debts incurred after commencement of the case and before conversion, the clerk, or some other person as the court may direct, shall give notice to those entities listed on the schedule of the time for filing a request for payment of an administrative expense and, unless a notice of insufficient assets to pay a dividend is mailed in accordance with Rule 2002(e), the time for filing a claim of a kind specified in § 348(d).

Bankruptcy Code References: §§ 348, 501, 502, 503, 521, 523, 727, 1112, 1208 and 1307

## Rule 1020 Small Business Chapter 11 Reorganization Case

(*a*) *Small Business Debtor Designation.* In a voluntary chapter 11 case, the debtor shall state in the petition whether the debtor is a small business debtor. In an involuntary chapter 11 case, the debtor shall file within 14 days after entry of the order for relief a statement as to whether the debtor is a small business debtor. Except as provided in subdivision (c), the status of the case as a small business case shall be in accordance with the debtor's statement under this subdivision, unless and until the court enters an order finding that the debtor's statement is incorrect.

(*b*) *Objecting to Designation.* Except as provided in subdivision (c), the United States trustee or a party in interest may file an objection to the debtor's statement under subdivision (a) no later than 30 days after the conclusion of the meeting of creditors held under § 341(a) of the Code, or within 30 days after any amendment to the statement, whichever is later.

(*c*) *Appointment of Committee of Unsecured Creditors.* If a committee of unsecured creditors has been appointed under § 1102(a)(1), the case shall proceed as a small business case only if, and from the time when, the court enters an order determining that the committee has not been sufficiently active and representative to provide effective oversight of the debtor and that the debtor satisfies all the other requirements for being a small business. A request for a determination under this subdivision may be filed by the United States trustee or a party in interest only within a reasonable time after the failure of the committee to be sufficiently active and representative. The debtor may file a request for a determination at any time as to whether the committee has been sufficiently active and representative.

(*d*) *Procedure for Objection or Determination.* Any objection or request for a determination under this rule shall be governed by Rule 9014 and served on: the debtor; the debtor's attorney; the United States trustee; the trustee; any committee appointed under § 1102 or its authorized agent, or, if no committee of unsecured creditors has been appointed under § 1102, the creditors included on

BANKRUPTCY RULES

the list filed under Rule 1007(d); and any other entity as the court directs.

BANKRUPTCY CODE REFERENCES: §§ 101, 1102, 1116, 1121 and 1125

### Interim Rule 1020 ~~Small Business~~ Chapter 11 Reorganization Case for Small Business Debtors[4]

(*a*) *Small Business Debtor Designation.* In a voluntary chapter 11 case, the debtor shall state in the petition whether the debtor is a small business debtor and, if so, whether the debtor elects to have subchapter V of chapter 11 apply. In an involuntary chapter 11 case, the debtor shall file within 14 days after entry of the order for relief a statement as to whether the debtor is a small business debtor and, if so, whether the debtor elects to have subchapter V of chapter 11 apply. ~~Except as provided in subdivision (c), the~~ The status of the case as a small business case or a case under subchapter V of chapter 11 shall be in accordance with the debtor's statement under this subdivision, unless and until the court enters an order finding that the debtor's statement is incorrect.

(*b*) *Objecting to Designation.* ~~Except as provided in subdivision (c), the~~ The United States trustee or a party in interest may file an objection to the debtor's statement under subdivision (a) no later than 30 days after the conclusion of the meeting of creditors held under § 341(a) of the Code, or within 30 days after any amendment to the statement, whichever is later.

~~(*c*) *Appointment of Committee of Unsecured Creditors.* If a committee of unsecured creditors has been appointed under § 1102(a)(1) [11 USCS § 1102(a)(1)], the case shall proceed as a small business case only if, and from the time when, the court enters an order determining that the committee has not been sufficiently active and representative to provide effective oversight of the debtor and that the debtor satisfies all the other requirements for being a small business. A request for a determination under this subdivision may be filed by the United States trustee or a party in interest only within a reasonable time after the failure of the committee to be sufficiently active and representative. The debtor may file a request for a determination at any time as to whether the committee has been sufficiently active and representative.~~

(~~*d*~~*c*) *Procedure for Objection or Determination.* Any objection or request for a determination under this rule shall be governed by Rule 9014 and served on: the debtor; the debtor's attorney; the United States trustee; the trustee; the creditors included on the list filed under Rule 1007(d) or, if ~~any~~ a committee has been appointed under § 1102(a)(3), the committee or its authorized agent~~, or, if no committee of unsecured creditors has been appointed under § 1102, the creditors included on the list filed under Rule 1007(d)~~; and any other entity as the court directs.

### Rule 1021 Health Care Business Case

(*a*) *Health Care Business Designation.* Unless the court orders otherwise, if a

[4] ED. NOTE: Interim Rule 1020 has been adopted by the bankruptcy courts to implement the Small Business Reorganization Act of 2019, Pub. L. No. 116-54 (2019). Changes from the existing rule are indicated with strikeouts and underscoring.

petition in a case under chapter 7, chapter 9, or chapter 11 states that the debtor is a health care business, the case shall proceed as a case in which the debtor is a health care business.

(*b*) *Motion.* The United States trustee or a party in interest may file a motion to determine whether the debtor is a health care business. The motion shall be transmitted to the United States trustee and served on: the debtor; the trustee; any committee elected under § 705 or appointed under § 1102 of the Code or its authorized agent, or, if the case is a chapter 9 municipality case or a chapter 11 reorganization case and no committee of unsecured creditors has been appointed under § 1102, the creditors included on the list filed under Rule 1007(d); and any other entity as the court directs. The motion shall be governed by Rule 9014.

Bankruptcy Code Reference: § 101(27A)

# PART II

# OFFICERS AND ADMINISTRATION; NOTICES; MEETINGS; EXAMINATIONS; ELECTIONS; ATTORNEYS AND ACCOUNTANTS

## Rule 2001 Appointment of Interim Trustee Before Order for Relief in a Chapter 7 Liquidation Case

(*a*) *Appointment.* At any time following the commencement of an involuntary liquidation case and before an order for relief, the court on written motion of a party in interest may order the appointment of an interim trustee under § 303(g) of the Code. The motion shall set forth the necessity for the appointment and may be granted only after hearing on notice to the debtor, the petitioning creditors, the United States trustee, and other parties in interest as the court may designate.

(*b*) *Bond of Movant.* An interim trustee may not be appointed under this rule unless the movant furnishes a bond in an amount approved by the court, conditioned to indemnify the debtor for costs, attorney's fee, expenses, and damages allowable under § 303(i) of the Code.

(*c*) *Order of Appointment.* The order directing the appointment of an interim trustee shall state the reason the appointment is necessary and shall specify the trustee's duties.

(*d*) *Turnover and Report.* Following qualification of the trustee selected under § 702 of the Code, the interim trustee, unless otherwise ordered, shall (1) forthwith deliver to the trustee all the records and property of the estate in possession or subject to control of the interim trustee and, (2) within 30 days thereafter file a final report and account.

BANKRUPTCY CODE REFERENCES: §§ 105, 303, 701 and 702

## Rule 2002 Notices to Creditors, Equity Security Holders, Administrators in Foreign Proceedings, Persons Against Whom Provisional Relief is Sought in Ancillary and Other Cross-Border Cases, United States, and United States Trustee

(*a*) *Twenty-One-Day Notices to Parties in Interest.* Except as provided in subdivisions (h), (i), (*l*), (p), and (q) of this rule, the clerk, or some other person as the court may direct, shall give the debtor, the trustee, all creditors and indenture trustees at least 21 days' notice by mail of:

(*1*) the meeting of creditors under § 341 or § 1104(b) of the Code, which notice, unless the court orders otherwise, shall include the debtor's employer identification number, social security number, and any other federal taxpayer identification number;

(*2*) a proposed use, sale, or lease of property of the estate other than in the ordinary course of business, unless the court for cause shown shortens the time or directs another method of giving notice;

(3) the hearing on approval of a compromise or settlement of a controversy

other than approval of an agreement pursuant to Rule 4001(d), unless the court for cause shown directs that notice not be sent;

(*4*) in a chapter 7 liquidation, a chapter 11 reorganization case, or a chapter 12 family farmer debt adjustment case, the hearing on the dismissal of the case or the conversion of the case to another chapter, unless the hearing is under § 707(a)(3) or § 707(b) or is on dismissal of the case for failure to pay the filing fee;

(*5*) the time fixed to accept or reject a proposed modification of a plan;

(*6*) a hearing on any entity's request for compensation or reimbursement of expenses if the request exceeds $1,000;

(*7*) the time fixed for filing proofs of claims pursuant to Rule 3003(c);

(*8*) the time fixed for filing objections and the hearing to consider confirmation of a chapter 12 plan; and

(*9*) the time fixed for filing objections to confirmation of a chapter 13 plan.

(*b*) *Twenty-Eight-Day Notices to Parties in Interest.* Except as provided in subdivision (l) of this rule, the clerk, or some other person as the court may direct, shall give the debtor, the trustee, all creditors and indenture trustees not less than 28 days' notice by mail of the time fixed (1) for filing objections and the hearing to consider approval of a disclosure statement or, under § 1125(f), to make a final determination whether the plan provides adequate information so that a separate disclosure statement is not necessary; (2) for filing objections and the hearing to consider confirmation of a chapter 9 or chapter 11 plan; and (3) for the hearing to consider confirmation of a chapter 13 plan.

(*c*) *Content of Notice.*

(*1*) *Proposed Use, Sale, or Lease of Property.* Subject to Rule 6004, the notice of a proposed use, sale, or lease of property required by subdivision (a)(2) of this rule shall include the time and place of any public sale, the terms and conditions of any private sale and the time fixed for filing objections. The notice of a proposed use, sale, or lease of property, including real estate, is sufficient if it generally describes the property. The notice of a proposed sale or lease of personally identifiable information under § 363(b)(1) of the Code shall state whether the sale is consistent with any policy prohibiting the transfer of the information.

(*2*) *Notice of Hearing on Compensation.* The notice of a hearing on an application for compensation or reimbursement of expenses required by subdivision (a)(6) of this rule shall identify the applicant and the amounts requested.

(*3*) *Notice of Hearing on Confirmation When Plan Provides for an Injunction.* If a plan provides for an injunction against conduct not otherwise enjoined under the Code, the notice required under Rule 2002(b)(2) shall:

(*A*) include in conspicuous language (bold, italic, or underlined text) a statement that the plan proposes an injunction;

(*B*) describe briefly the nature of the injunction; and

(*C*) identify the entities that would be subject to the injunction.

(*d*) *Notice to Equity Security Holders.* In a chapter 11 reorganization case, unless otherwise ordered by the court, the clerk, or some other person as the court may direct, shall in the manner and form directed by the court give notice to all equity security holders of (1) the order for relief; (2) any meeting of equity security holders held pursuant to § 341 of the Code; (3) the hearing on the proposed sale of all or substantially all of the debtor's assets; (4) the hearing on the dismissal or conversion of a case to another chapter; (5) the time fixed for filing objections to and the hearing to consider approval of a disclosure statement; (6) the time fixed for filing objections to and the hearing to consider confirmation of a plan; and (7) the time fixed to accept or reject a proposed modification of a plan.

(*e*) *Notice of No Dividend.* In a chapter 7 liquidation case, if it appears from the schedules that there are no assets from which a dividend can be paid, the notice of the meeting of creditors may include a statement to that effect; that it is unnecessary to file claims; and that if sufficient assets become available for the payment of a dividend, further notice will be given for the filing of claims.

(*f*) *Other Notices.* Except as provided in subdivision (*l*) of this rule, the clerk, or some other person as the court may direct, shall give the debtor, all creditors, and indenture trustees notice by mail of:

(*1*) the order for relief;

(*2*) the dismissal or the conversion of the case to another chapter, or the suspension of proceedings under § 305;

(*3*) the time allowed for filing claims pursuant to Rule 3002;

(*4*) the time fixed for filing a complaint objecting to the debtor's discharge pursuant to § 727 of the Code as provided in Rule 4004;

(*5*) the time fixed for filing a complaint to determine the dischargeability of a debt pursuant to § 523 of the Code as provided in Rule 4007;

(*6*) the waiver, denial, or revocation of a discharge as provided in Rule 4006;

(*7*) entry of an order confirming a chapter 9, 11, 12, or 13 plan;

(*8*) a summary of the trustee's final report in a chapter 7 case if the net proceeds realized exceed $1,500;

(*9*) a notice under Rule 5008 regarding the presumption of abuse;

(*10*) a statement under § 704(b)(1) as to whether the debtor's case would be presumed to be an abuse under § 707(b); and

(*11*) the time to request a delay in the entry of the discharge under §§ 1141(d)(5)(C), 1228(f), and 1328(h). Notice of the time fixed for accepting or rejecting a plan pursuant to Rule 3017(c) shall be given in accordance with Rule

3017(d).

(*g*) *Addressing Notices.*

(*1*) Notices required to be mailed under Rule 2002 to a creditor, indenture trustee, or equity security holder shall be addressed as such entity or an authorized agent has directed in its last request filed in the particular case. For the purpose of this subdivision—

(*A*) a proof of claim filed by a creditor or indenture trustee that designates a mailing address constitutes a filed request to mail notices to that address, unless a notice of no dividend has been given under Rule 2002(e) and a later notice of possible dividend under Rule 3002(c)(5) has not been given; and

(*B*) a proof of interest filed by an equity security holder that designates a mailing address constitutes a filed request to mail notices to that address.

(*2*) Except as provided in § 342(f) of the Code, if a creditor or indenture trustee has not filed a request designating a mailing address under Rule 2002(g)(1) or Rule 5003(e), the notices shall be mailed to the address shown on the list of creditors or schedule of liabilities, whichever is filed later. If an equity security holder has not filed a request designating a mailing address under Rule 2002(g)(1) or Rule 5003(e), the notices shall be mailed to the address shown on the list of equity security holders.

(*3*) If a list or schedule filed under Rule 1007 includes the name and address of a legal representative of an infant or incompetent person, and a person other than that representative files a request or proof of claim designating a name and mailing address that differs from the name and address of the representative included in the list or schedule, unless the court orders otherwise, notices under Rule 2002 shall be mailed to the representative included in the list or schedules and to the name and address designated in the request or proof of claim.

(*4*) Notwithstanding Rule 2002(g)(1)–(3), an entity and a notice provider may agree that when the notice provider is directed by the court to give a notice, the notice provider shall give the notice to the entity in the manner agreed to and at the address or addresses the entity supplies to the notice provider. That address is conclusively presumed to be a proper address for the notice. The notice provider's failure to use the supplied address does not invalidate any notice that is otherwise effective under applicable law.

(*5*) A creditor may treat a notice as not having been brought to the creditor's attention under § 342(g)(1) only if, prior to issuance of the notice, the creditor has filed a statement that designates the name and address of the person or organizational subdivision of the creditor responsible for receiving notices under the Code, and that describes the procedures established by the creditor to cause such notices to be delivered to the designated person or subdivision.

(*h*) *Notices to Creditors Whose Claims Are Filed.*

(*1*) *Voluntary Case.* In a voluntary chapter 7 case, chapter 12 case, or chapter 13 case, after 70 days following the order for relief under that chapter or the date of the order converting the case to chapter 12 or chapter 13, the court may direct that all notices required by subdivision (a) of this rule be mailed only to:

- the debtor;
- the trustee;
- all indenture trustees;
- creditors that hold claims for which proofs of claim have been filed; and
- creditors, if any, that are still permitted to file claims because an extension was granted under Rule 3002(c)(1) or (c)(2).

(2) *Involuntary Case.* In an involuntary chapter 7 case, after 90 days following the order for relief under that chapter, the court may direct that all notices required by subdivision (a) of this rule be mailed only to:

- the debtor;
- the trustee;
- all indenture trustees;
- creditors that hold claims for which proofs of claim have been filed; and
- creditors, if any, that are still permitted to file claims because an extension was granted under Rule 3002(c)(1) or (c)(2).

(3) *Insufficient Assets.* In a case where notice of insufficient assets to pay a dividend has been given to creditors under subdivision (e) of this rule, after 90 days following the mailing of a notice of the time for filing claims under Rule 3002(c)(5), the court may direct that notices be mailed only to the entities specified in the preceding sentence.

(*i*) *Notices to Committees.* Copies of all notices required to be mailed pursuant to this rule shall be mailed to the committees elected under § 705 or appointed under § 1102 of the Code or to their authorized agents. Notwithstanding the foregoing subdivisions, the court may order that notices required by subdivision (a)(2), (3) and (6) of this rule be transmitted to the United States trustee and be mailed only to the committees elected under § 705 or appointed under § 1102 of the Code or to their authorized agents and to the creditors and equity security holders who serve on the trustee or debtor in possession and file a request that all notices be mailed to them. A committee appointed under § 1114 shall receive copies of all notices required by subdivisions (a)(1), (a)(5), (b), (f)(2), and (f)(7), and such other notices as the court may direct.

(*j*) *Notices to the United States.* Copies of notices required to be mailed to all creditors under this rule shall be mailed (1) in a chapter 11 reorganization case, to the Securities and Exchange Commission at any place the Commission designates, if the Commission has filed either a notice of appearance in the case or a written request to receive notices; (2) in a commodity broker case, to the Commodity Futures Trading Commission at Washington, D.C.; (3) in a chapter 11 case to the Internal Revenue Service at its address set out in the register maintained under

Rule 5003(e) for the district in which the case is pending; (4) if the papers in the case disclose a debt to the United States other than for taxes, to the United States attorney for the district in which the case is pending and to the department, agency, or instrumentality of the United States through which the debtor became indebted; or (5) if the filed papers disclose a stock interest of the United States, to the Secretary of the Treasury at Washington, D.C.

(*k*) *Notices to United States Trustee.* Unless the case is a chapter 9 municipality case or unless the United States trustee requests otherwise, the clerk, or some other person as the court may direct, shall transmit to the United States trustee notice of the matters described in subdivisions (a)(2), (a)(3), (a)(4), (a)(8), (a)(9), (b), (f)(1), (f)(2), (f)(4), (f)(6), (f)(7), (f)(8), and (q) of this rule and notice of hearings on all applications for compensation or reimbursement of expenses. Notices to the United States trustee shall be transmitted within the time prescribed in subdivision (a) or (b) of this rule. The United States trustee shall also receive notice of any other matter if such notice is requested by the United States trustee or ordered by the court. Nothing in these rules requires the clerk or any other person to transmit to the United States trustee any notice, schedule, report, application or other document in a case under the Securities Investor Protection Act, 15 U.S.C. § 78aaa *et seq.*

(*l*) *Notice by Publication.* The court may order notice by publication if it finds that notice by mail is impracticable or that it is desirable to supplement the notice.

(*m*) *Orders Designating Matter of Notices.* The court may from time to time enter orders designating the matters in respect to which, the entity to whom, and the form and manner in which notices shall be sent except as otherwise provided by these rules.

(*n*) *Caption.* The caption of every notice given under this rule Shall comply with Rule 1005. The caption of every notice required to be given by the debtor to a creditor shall include the information required to be in the notice by § 342(c) of the Code.

(*o*) *Notice of Order for Relief in Consumer Case.* In a voluntary case commenced by an individual debtor whose debts are primarily consumer debts, the clerk, or some other person as the court may direct, shall give the trustee and all creditors notice by mail of the order for relief within 21 days from the date thereof.

(*p*) *Notice to a Creditor with a Foreign Address.*

(*1*) If, at the request of the United States trustee or a party in interest, or on its own initiative, the court finds that a notice mailed within the time prescribed by these rules would not be sufficient to give a creditor with a foreign address to which notices under these rules are mailed reasonable notice under the circumstances, the court may order that the notice be supplemented with notice by other means or that the time prescribed for the notice by mail be enlarged.

(*2*) Unless the court for cause orders otherwise, a creditor with a foreign address to which notices under this rule are mailed shall be given at least 30 days' notice of the time fixed for filing a proof of claim under Rule 3002(c) or Rule 3003(c).

(3) Unless the court for cause orders otherwise, the mailing address of a creditor with a foreign address shall be determined under Rule 2002(g).

(*q*) *Notice of Petition for Recognition of Foreign Proceeding and of Court's Intention to Communicate with Foreign Courts and Foreign Representatives.*

(1) *Notice of Petition for Recognition.* After the filing of a petition for recognition of a foreign proceeding, the court shall promptly schedule and hold a hearing on the petition. The clerk, or some other person as the court may direct, shall forthwith give the debtor, all persons or bodies authorized to administer foreign proceedings of the debtor, all entities against whom provisional relief is being sought under § 1519 of the Code, all parties to litigation pending in the United States in which the debtor is a party at the time of the filing of the petition, and such other entities as the court may direct, at least 21 days' notice by mail of the hearing. The notice shall state whether the petition seeks recognition as a foreign main proceeding or foreign nonmain proceeding and shall include the petition and any other document the court may require. If the court consolidates the hearing on the petition with the hearing on a request for provisional relief, the court may set a shorter notice period, with notice to the entities listed in this subdivision.

(2) *Notice of Court's Intention to Communicate with Foreign Courts and Foreign Representatives.* The clerk, or some other person as the court may direct, shall give the debtor, all persons or bodies authorized to administer foreign proceedings of the debtor, all entities against whom provisional relief is being sought under § 1519 of the Code, all parties to litigation pending in the United States in which the debtor is a party at the time of the filing of the petition, and such other entities as the court may direct, notice by mail of the court's intention to communicate with a foreign court or foreign representative.

BANKRUPTCY CODE REFERENCES: §§ 102, 322, 341, 342, 502, 705, 706, 707, 1102, 1112, 1114, 1208 and 1307

## Rule 2003 Meeting of Creditors or Equity Security Holders

(*a*) *Date and Place.* Except as otherwise provided in § 341(e) of the Code, in a chapter 7 liquidation or a chapter 11 reorganization case, the United States trustee shall call a meeting of creditors to be held no fewer than 21 and no more than 40 days after the order for relief. In a chapter 12 family farmer's debt adjustment case, the United States trustee shall call a meeting of creditors to be held no fewer than 21 and no more than 35 days after the order for relief. In a chapter 13 individual's debt adjustment case, the United States trustee shall call a meeting of creditors to be held no fewer than 21 and no more than 50 days after the order for relief. If there is an appeal from or a motion to vacate the order for relief, or if there is a motion to dismiss the case, the United States trustee may set a later date for the meeting. The meeting may be held at a regular place for holding court or at any other place designated by the United States trustee within the district convenient for the parties in interest. If the United States trustee designates a place for the meeting which is not regularly staffed by the United States trustee or an assistant who may preside at the meeting, the meeting may be held not more than 60 days after the order for relief.

(*b*) *Order of Meeting.*

(*1*) *Meeting of Creditors.* The United States trustee shall preside at the meeting of creditors. The business of the meeting shall include the examination of the debtor under oath and, in a chapter 7 liquidation case, may include the election of a creditors' committee and, if the case is not under subchapter V of chapter 7, the election of a trustee. The presiding officer shall have the authority to administer oaths.

(*2*) *Meeting of Equity Security Holders.* If the United States trustee convenes a meeting of equity security holders pursuant to § 341(b) of the Code, the United States trustee shall fix a date for the meeting and shall preside.

(*3*) *Right to Vote.* In a chapter 7 liquidation case, a creditor is entitled to vote at a meeting if, at or before the meeting, the creditor has filed a proof of claim or a writing setting forth facts evidencing a right to vote pursuant to § 702(a) of the Code unless objection is made to the claim or the proof of claim is insufficient on its face. A creditor of a partnership may file a proof of claim or writing evidencing a right to vote for the trustee for the estate of a general partner notwithstanding that a trustee for the estate of the partnership has previously qualified. In the event of an objection to the amount or allowability of a claim for the purpose of voting, unless the court orders otherwise, the United States trustee shall tabulate the votes for each alternative presented by the dispute and, if resolution of such dispute is necessary to determine the result of the election, the tabulations for each alternative shall be reported to the court.

(*c*) *Record of Meeting.* Any examination under oath at the meeting of creditors held pursuant to § 341(a) of the Code shall be recorded verbatim by the United States trustee using electronic sound recording equipment or other means of recording, and such record shall be preserved by the United States trustee and available for public access until two years after the conclusion of the meeting of creditors. Upon request of any entity, the United States trustee shall certify and provide a copy or transcript of such recording at the entity's expense.

(*d*) *Report of Election and Resolution of Disputes in a Chapter 7 Case.*

(*1*) *Report of Undisputed Election.* In a chapter 7 case, if the election of a trustee or a member of a creditors' committee is not disputed, the United States trustee shall promptly file a report of the election, including the name and address of the person or entity elected and a statement that the election is undisputed.

(*2*) *Disputed Election.* If the election is disputed, the United States trustee shall promptly file a report stating that the election is disputed, informing the court of the nature of the dispute, and listing the name and address of any candidate elected under any alternative presented by the dispute. No later than the date on which the report is filed, the United States trustee shall mail a copy of the report to any party in interest that has made a request to receive a copy of the report. Pending disposition by the court of a disputed election for trustee, the interim trustee shall continue in office. Unless a motion for the resolution of the dispute is filed no later than 14 days after the United States trustee files a report of a disputed election for trustee, the interim trustee shall serve as trustee in the case.

(*e*) *Adjournment.* The meeting may be adjourned from time to time by announcement at the meeting of the adjourned date and time. The presiding official shall promptly file a statement specifying the date and time to which the meeting is adjourned.

(*f*) *Special Meetings.* The United States trustee may call a special meeting of creditors on request of a party in interest or on the United States trustee's own initiative.

(*g*) *Final Meeting.* If the United States trustee calls a final meeting of creditors in a case in which the net proceeds realized exceed $1,500, the clerk shall mail a summary of the trustee's final account to the creditors with a notice of the meeting, together with a statement of the amount of the claims allowed. The trustee shall attend the final meeting and shall, if requested, report on the administration of the estate.

BANKRUPTCY CODE REFERENCES: §§ 341, 343, 702, 703 and 1102

## Rule 2004 Examination

(*a*) *Examination on Motion.* On motion of any party in interest, the court may order the examination of any entity.

(*b*) *Scope of Examination.* The examination of an entity under this rule or of the debtor under § 343 of the Code may relate only to the acts, conduct, or property or to the liabilities and financial condition of the debtor, or to any matter which may affect the administration of the debtor's estate, or to the debtor's right to a discharge. In a family farmer's debt adjustment case under chapter 12, an individual's debt adjustment case under chapter 13, or a reorganization case under chapter 11 of the Code, other than for the reorganization of a railroad, the examination may also relate to the operation of any business and the desirability of its continuance, the source of any money or property acquired or to be acquired by the debtor for purposes of consummating a plan and the consideration given or offered therefor, and any other matter relevant to the case or to the formulation of a plan.

(*c*) *Compelling Attendance and Production of Documents or Electronically Stored Information.* The attendance of an entity for examination and for the production of documents or electronically stored information, whether the examination is to be conducted within or without the district in which the case is pending, may be compelled as provided in Rule 9016 for the attendance of a witness at a hearing or trial. As an officer of the court, an attorney may issue and sign a subpoena on behalf of the court where the case is pending if the attorney is admitted to practice in that court.

(*d*) *Time and Place of Examination of Debtor.* The court may for cause shown and on terms as it may impose order the debtor to be examined under this rule at any time or place it designates, whether within or without the district wherein the case is pending.

(*e*) *Mileage.* An entity other than a debtor shall not be required to attend as a witness unless lawful mileage and witness fee for one day's attendance shall be first tendered. If the debtor resides more than 100 miles from the place of examination when required to appear for an examination under this rule, the mileage allowed by law to a witness shall be tendered for any distance more than 100 miles from the debtor's residence at the date of the filing of the first petition commencing a case under the Code or the residence at the time the debtor is required to appear for the examination, whichever is the lesser.

Bankruptcy Code References: §§ 341, 343, 344 and 542

## Rule 2005 Apprehension and Removal of Debtor to Compel Attendance for Examination

(*a*) *Order to Compel Attendance for Examination.* On motion of any party in interest supported by an affidavit alleging (1) that the examination of the debtor is necessary for the proper administration of the estate and that there is reasonable cause to believe that the debtor is about to leave or has left the debtor's residence or principal place of business to avoid examination, or (2) that the debtor has evaded service of a subpoena or of an order to attend for examination, or (3) that the debtor has willfully disobeyed a subpoena or order to attend for examination, duly served, the court may issue to the marshal, or some other officer authorized by law, an order directing the officer to bring the debtor before the court without unnecessary delay. If, after hearing, the court finds the allegations to be true, the court shall thereupon cause the debtor to be examined forthwith. If necessary, the court shall fix conditions for further examination and for the debtor's obedience to all orders made in reference thereto.

(*b*) *Removal.* Whenever any order to bring the debtor before the court is issued under this rule and the debtor is found in a district other than that of the court issuing the order, the debtor may be taken into custody under the order and removed in accordance with the following rules:

(*1*) If the debtor is taken into custody under the order at a place less than 100 miles from the place of issue of the order, the debtor shall be brought forthwith before the court that issued the order.

(*2*) If the debtor is taken into custody under the order at a place 100 miles or more from the place of issue of the order, the debtor shall be brought without unnecessary delay before the nearest available United States magistrate judge, bankruptcy judge, or district judge. If, after hearing, the magistrate judge, bankruptcy judge, or district judge finds that an order has issued under this rule and that the person in custody is the debtor, or if the person in custody waives a hearing, the magistrate judge, bankruptcy judge, or district judge shall order removal, and the person in custody shall be released on conditions ensuring prompt appearance before the court that issued the order to compel the attendance.

(*c*) *Conditions of Release.* In determining what conditions will reasonably assure attendance or obedience under subdivision (a) of this rule or appearance under subdivision (b) of this rule, the court shall be governed by the relevant provisions and policies of title 18 U.S.C. § 3142.

BANKRUPTCY CODE REFERENCES: §§ 341, 343 and 521

## Rule 2006 Solicitation and Voting of Proxies in Chapter 7 Liquidation Cases

(*a*) *Applicability.* This rule applies only in a liquidation case pending under chapter 7 of the Code.

(*b*) *Definitions.*

(*1*) *Proxy.* A proxy is a written power of attorney authorizing any entity to vote the claim or otherwise act as the owner's attorney in fact in connection with the administration of the estate.

(*2*) *Solicitation of Proxy.* The solicitation of a proxy is any communication, other than one from an attorney to a regular client who owns a claim or from an attorney to the owner of a claim who has requested the attorney to represent the owner, by which a creditor is asked, directly or indirectly, to give a proxy after or in contemplation of the filing of a petition by or against the debtor.

(*c*) *Authorized Solicitation.*

(*1*) A proxy may be solicited only by (A) a creditor owning an allowable unsecured claim against the estate on the date of the filing of the petition; (B) a committee elected pursuant to § 705 of the Code; (C) a committee of creditors selected by a majority in number and amount of claims of creditors (i) whose claims are not contingent or unliquidated, (ii) who are not disqualified from voting under § 702(a) of the Code, and (iii) who were present or represented at a meeting of which all creditors having claims of over $500 or the 100 creditors having the largest claims had at least seven days notice in writing and of which meeting written minutes were kept and are available reporting the names of the creditors present or represented and voting and the amounts of their claims; or (D) a bona fide trade or credit association, but such association may solicit only creditors who were its members or subscribers in good standing and had allowable unsecured claims on the date of the filing of the petition.

(*2*) A proxy may be solicited only in writing.

(*d*) *Solicitation Not Authorized.* This rule does not permit solicitation (1) in any interest other than that of general creditors; (2) by or on behalf of any custodian; (3) by the interim trustee or by or on behalf of any entity not qualified to vote under § 702(a) of the Code; (4) by or on behalf of an attorney at law; or (5) by or on behalf of a transferee of a claim for collection only.

(*e*) *Data Required from Holders of Multiple Proxies.* At any time before the voting commences at any meeting of creditors pursuant to § 341 of the Code, or at any other time as the court may direct, a holder of two or more proxies shall file and transmit to the United States trustee a verified list of the proxies to be voted and a verified statement of the pertinent facts and circumstances in connection with the execution and delivery of each proxy, including:

(*1*) a copy of the solicitation;

(*2*) identification of the solicitor, the forwarder, if the forwarder is neither the solicitor nor the owner of the claim, and the proxyholder, including their connections with the debtor and with each other. If the solicitor, forwarder, or proxyholder is an association, there shall also be included a statement that the creditors whose claims have been solicited and the creditors whose claims are to be voted were members or subscribers in good standing and had allowable unsecured claims on the date of the filing of the petition. If the solicitor, forwarder, or proxyholder is a committee of creditors, the statement shall also set forth the date and place the committee was organized, that the committee was organized in accordance with clause (B) or (C) of paragraph (c)(1) of this rule, the members of the committee, the amounts of their claims, when the claims were acquired, the amounts paid therefor, and the extent to which the claims of the committee members are secured or entitled to priority;

(*3*) a statement that no consideration has been paid or promised by the proxyholder for the proxy;

(*4*) a statement as to whether there is any agreement and, if so, the particulars thereof, between the proxyholder and any other entity for the payment of any consideration in connection with voting the proxy, or for the sharing of compensation with any entity, other than a member or regular associate of the proxyholder's law firm, which may be allowed the trustee or any entity for services rendered in the case, or for the employment of any person as attorney, accountant, appraiser, auctioneer, or other employee for the estate;

(*5*) if the proxy was solicited by an entity other than the proxyholder, or forwarded to the holder by an entity who is neither a solicitor of the proxy nor the owner of the claim, a statement signed and verified by the solicitor or forwarder that no consideration has been paid or promised for the proxy, and whether there is any agreement, and, if so, the particulars thereof, between the solicitor or forwarder and any other entity for the payment of any consideration in connection with voting the proxy, or for sharing compensation with any entity other than a member or regular associate of the solicitor's or forwarder's law firm which may be allowed the trustee or any entity for services rendered in the case, or for the employment of any person as attorney, accountant, appraiser, auctioneer, or other employee for the estate;

(*6*) if the solicitor, forwarder, or proxyholder is a committee, a statement signed and verified by each member as to the amount and source of any consideration paid or to be paid to such member in connection with the case other than by way of dividend on the member's claim.

(*f*) *Enforcement of Restrictions on Solicitation.* On motion of any party in interest or on its own initiative, the court may determine whether there has been a failure to comply with the provisions of this rule or any other impropriety in connection with the solicitation or voting of a proxy. After notice and a hearing the court may reject any proxy for cause, vacate any order entered in consequence of the voting of any proxy which should have been rejected, or take any other appropriate action.

BANKRUPTCY CODE REFERENCES: §§ 702, 705 and 1104

## Rule 2007 Review of Appointment of Creditors' Committee Organized Before Commencement of the Case

(*a*) *Motion to Review Appointment.* If a committee appointed by the United States trustee pursuant to § 1102(a) of the Code consists of the members of a committee organized by creditors before the commencement of a chapter 9 or chapter 11 case, on motion of a party in interest and after a hearing on notice to the United States trustee and other entities as the court may direct, the court may determine whether the appointment of the committee satisfies the requirements of § 1102(b)(1) of the Code.

(*b*) *Selection of Members of Committee.* The court may find that a committee organized by unsecured creditors before the commencement of a chapter 9 or chapter 11 case was fairly chosen if:

(*1*) it was selected by a majority in number and amount of claims of unsecured creditors who may vote under § 702(a) of the Code and were present in person or represented at a meeting of which all creditors having unsecured claims of over $1,000 or the 100 unsecured creditors having the largest claims had at least seven days notice in writing, and of which meeting written minutes reporting the names of the creditors present or represented and voting and the amounts of their claims were kept and are available for inspection;

(*2*) all proxies voted at the meeting for the elected committee were solicited pursuant to Rule 2006 and the lists and statements required by subdivision (e) thereof have been transmitted to the United States trustee; and

(*3*) the organization of the committee was in all other respects fair and proper.

(*c*) *Failure to Comply with Requirements for Appointment.* After a hearing on notice pursuant to subdivision (a) of this rule, the court shall direct the United States trustee to vacate the appointment of the committee and may order other appropriate action if the court finds that such appointment failed to satisfy the requirements of § 1102(b)(1) of the Code.

BANKRUPTCY CODE REFERENCES: §§ 901 and 1102

## Rule 2007.1 Appointment of Trustee or Examiner in a Chapter 11 Reorganization Case

(*a*) *Order to Appoint Trustee or Examiner.* In a chapter 11 reorganization case, a motion for an order to appoint a trustee or an examiner under § 1104(a) or § 1104(c) of the Code shall be made in accordance with Rule 9014.

(*b*) *Election of Trustee.*

(*1*) *Request for an Election.* A request to convene a meeting of creditors for the purpose of electing a trustee in a chapter 11 reorganization case shall be filed and transmitted to the United States trustee in accordance with Rule 5005 within the time prescribed by § 1104(b) of the Code. Pending court approval of the person elected, any person appointed by the United States trustee under § 1104(d) and approved in accordance with subdivision (c) of this rule shall serve as trustee.

(2) *Manner of Election and Notice.* An election of a trustee under § 1104(b) of the Code shall be conducted in the manner provided in Rules 2003(b)(3) and 2006. Notice of the meeting of creditors convened under § 1104(b) shall be given as provided in Rule 2002. The United States trustee shall preside at the meeting. A proxy for the purpose of voting in the election may be solicited only by a committee of creditors appointed under § 1102 of the Code or by any other party entitled to solicit a proxy pursuant to Rule 2006.

(3) *Report of Election and Resolution of Disputes.*

(*A*) *Report of Undisputed Election.* If no dispute arises out of the election, the United States trustee shall promptly file a report certifying the election, including the name and address of the person elected and a statement that the election is undisputed. The report shall be accompanied by a verified statement of the person elected setting forth that person's connections with the debtor, creditors, any other party in interest, their respective attorneys and accountants, the United States trustee, or any person employed in the office of the United States trustee.

(*B*) *Dispute Arising Out of an Election.* If a dispute arises out of an election, the United States trustee shall promptly file a report stating that the election is disputed, informing the court of the nature of the dispute, and listing the name and address of any candidate elected under any alternative presented by the dispute. The report shall be accompanied by a verified statement by each candidate elected under each alternative presented by the dispute, setting forth the person's connections with the debtor, creditors, any other party in interest, their respective attorneys and accountants, the United States trustee, or any person employed in the office of the United States trustee. Not later than the date on which the report of the disputed election is filed, the United States trustee shall mail a copy of the report and each verified statement to any party in interest that has made a request to convene a meeting under § 1104(b) or to receive a copy of the report, and to any committee appointed under § 1102 of the Code.

(c) *Approval of Appointment.* An order approving the appointment of a trustee or an examiner under § 1104(d) of the Code shall be made on application of the United States trustee. The application shall state the name of the person appointed and, to the best of the applicant's knowledge, all the person's connections with the debtor, creditors, any other parties in interest, their respective attorneys and accountants, the United States trustee, or persons employed in the office of the United States trustee. The application shall state the names of the parties in interest with whom the United States trustee consulted regarding the appointment. The application shall be accompanied by a verified statement of the person appointed setting forth the person's connections with the debtor, creditors, any other party in interest, their respective attorneys and accountants, the United States trustee, or any person employed in the office of the United States trustee.

BANKRUPTCY CODE REFERENCES: §§ 321, 322, 702 and 1104

## Rule 2007.2 Appointment of Patient Care Ombudsman in a Health Care Business Case

(*a*) *Order to Appoint Patient Care Ombudsman.* In a chapter 7, chapter 9, or chapter 11 case in which the debtor is a health care business, the court shall order the appointment of a patient care ombudsman under § 333 of the Code, unless the court, on motion of the United States trustee or a party in interest filed no later than 21 days after the commencement of the case or within another time fixed by the court, finds that the appointment of a patient care ombudsman is not necessary under the specific circumstances of the case for the protection of patients.

(*b*) *Motion for Order to Appoint Ombudsman.* If the court has found that the appointment of an ombudsman is not necessary, or has terminated the appointment, the court, on motion of the United States trustee or a party in interest, may order the appointment at a later time if it finds that the appointment has become necessary to protect patients.

(*c*) *Notice of Appointment.* If a patient care ombudsman is appointed under § 333, the United States trustee shall promptly file a notice of the appointment, including the name and address of the person appointed. Unless the person appointed is a State Long-Term Care Ombudsman, the notice shall be accompanied by a verified statement of the person appointed setting forth the person's connections with the debtor, creditors, patients, any other party in interest, their respective attorneys and accountants, the United States trustee, and any person employed in the office of the United States trustee.

(*d*) *Termination of Appointment.* On motion of the United States trustee or a party in interest, the court may terminate the appointment of a patient care ombudsman if the court finds that the appointment is not necessary to protect patients.

(*e*) *Motion.* A motion under this rule shall be governed by Rule 9014. The motion shall be transmitted to the United States trustee and served on: the debtor; the trustee; any committee elected under § 705 or appointed under § 1102 of the Code or its authorized agent, or, if the case is a chapter 9 municipality case or a chapter 11 reorganization case and no committee of unsecured creditors has been appointed under § 1102, on the creditors included on the list filed under Rule 1007(d); and such other entities as the court may direct.

## Rule 2008 Notice to Trustee of Selection

The United States trustee shall immediately notify the person selected as trustee how to qualify and, if applicable, the amount of the trustee's bond. A trustee that has filed a blanket bond pursuant to Rule 2010 and has been selected as trustee in a chapter 7, chapter 12, or chapter 13 case that does not notify the court and the United States trustee in writing of rejection of the office within seven days after receipt of notice of selection shall be deemed to have accepted the office. Any other person selected as trustee shall notify the court and the United States trustee in writing of acceptance of the office within seven days after receipt of notice of selection or shall be deemed to have rejected the office.

Bankruptcy Code References: §§ 321 and 322

## Rule 2009 Trustees for Estates When Joint Administration Ordered

(*a*) *Election of Single Trustee for Estates Being Jointly Administered.* If the court orders a joint administration of two or more estates under Rule 1015(b), creditors may elect a single trustee for the estates being jointly administered, unless the case is under subchapter V of chapter 7 of the Code.

(*b*) *Right of Creditors to Elect Separate Trustee.* Notwithstanding entry of an order for joint administration under Rule 1015(b), the creditors of any debtor may elect a separate trustee for the estate of the debtor as provided in § 702 of the Code, unless the case is under subchapter V of chapter 7.

(*c*) *Appointment of Trustees for Estates Being Jointly Administered.*

(*1*) *Chapter 7 Liquidation Cases.* Except in a case governed by subchapter V of chapter 7, the United States trustee may appoint one or more interim trustees for estates being jointly administered in chapter 7 cases.

(*2*) *Chapter 11 Reorganization Cases.* If the appointment of a trustee is ordered, the United States trustee may appoint one or more trustees for estates being jointly administered in chapter 11 cases.

(*3*) *Chapter 12 Family Farmer's Debt Adjustment Cases.* The United States trustee may appoint one or more trustees for estates being jointly administered in chapter 12 cases.

(*4*) *Chapter 13 Individual's Debt Adjustment Cases.* The United States trustee may appoint one or more trustees for estates being jointly administered in chapter 13 cases.

(*d*) *Potential Conflicts of Interest.* On a showing that creditors or equity security holders of the different estates will be prejudiced by conflicts of interest of a common trustee who has been elected or appointed, the court shall order the selection of separate trustees for estates being jointly administered.

(*e*) *Separate Accounts.* The trustee or trustees of estates being jointly administered shall keep separate accounts of the property and distribution of each estate.

Bankruptcy Code References: §§ 302, 321, 322, 701, 702, 1104, 1202 and 1302

## Interim Rule 2009 Trustees for Estates When Joint Administration Ordered[5]

(*a*) *Election of Single Trustee for Estates Being Jointly Administered.* If the court orders a joint administration of two or more estates under Rule 1015(b), creditors may elect a single trustee for the estates being jointly administered, unless the case is under subchapter V of chapter 7 or subchapter V of chapter 11 of the Code.

(*b*) *Right of Creditors to Elect Separate Trustee.* Notwithstanding entry of an order for joint administration under Rule 1015(b), the creditors of any debtor may elect a separate trustee for the estate of the debtor as provided in § 702 of the Code, unless the case is under subchapter V of chapter 7 or subchapter V of chapter 11.

(*c*) *Appointment of Trustees for Estates Being Jointly Administered.*

* * * * *

(*2*) *Chapter 11 Reorganization Cases.* If the appointment of a trustee is ordered or is required by the Code, the United States trustee may appoint one or more trustees for estates being jointly administered in chapter 11 cases.

* * *

## Rule 2010 Qualification by Trustee; Proceeding on Bond

(*a*) *Blanket Bond.* The United States trustee may authorize a blanket bond in favor of the United States conditioned on the faithful performance of official duties by the trustee or trustees to cover (1) a person who qualifies as trustee in a number of cases, and (2) a number of trustees each of whom qualifies in a different case.

(*b*) *Proceeding on Bond.* A proceeding on the trustee's bond may be brought by any party in interest in the name of the United States for the use of the entity injured by the breach of the condition.

Bankruptcy Code Reference: § 322

## Rule 2011 Evidence of Debtor in Possession or Qualification of Trustee

(*a*) Whenever evidence is required that a debtor is a debtor in possession or that a trustee has qualified, the clerk may so certify and the certificate shall constitute conclusive evidence of that fact.

(*b*) If a person elected or appointed as trustee does not qualify within the time prescribed by § 322(a) of the Code, the clerk shall so notify the court and the United States trustee.

Bankruptcy Code References: §§ 322, 1101, 1107 and 1203

## Rule 2012 Substitution of Trustee or Successor Trustee; Accounting

(*a*) *Trustee.* If a trustee is appointed in a chapter 11 case or the debtor is removed

---

[5] Ed. Note: Interim Rule 2009 has been adopted by the bankruptcy courts to implement the Small Business Reorganization Act of 2019, Pub. L. No. 116-54 (2019). Additions to the existing rule are indicated with underscoring.

as debtor in possession in a chapter 12 case, the trustee is substituted automatically for the debtor in possession as a party in any pending action, proceeding, or matter.

(*b*) *Successor Trustee.* When a trustee dies, resigns, is removed, or otherwise ceases to hold office during the pendency of a case under the Code

(*1*) the successor is automatically substituted as a party in any pending action, proceeding, or matter; and

(*2*) the successor trustee shall prepare, file, and transmit to the United States trustee an accounting of the prior administration of the estate.

Bankruptcy Code References: §§ 321, 322, 323, 325, 701, 702, 703, 1104, 1202 and 1

### Interim Rule 2012 Substitution of Trustee or Successor Trustee; Accounting[6]

(*a*) *Trustee.* If a trustee is appointed in a chapter 11 case (other than under subchapter V), or the debtor is removed as debtor in possession in a chapter 12 case or in a case under subchapter V of chapter 11, the trustee is substituted automatically for the debtor in possession as a party in any pending action, proceeding, or matter.

* * * * *

### Rule 2013 Public Record of Compensation Awarded to Trustees, Examiners, and Professionals

(*a*) *Record to Be Kept.* The clerk shall maintain a public record listing fees awarded by the court (1) to trustees and attorneys, accountants, appraisers, auctioneers and other professionals employed by trustees; and (2) to examiners. The record shall include the name and docket number of the case, the name of the individual or firm receiving the fee and the amount of the fee awarded. The record shall be maintained chronologically and shall be kept current and open to examination by the public without charge. "Trustees," as used in this rule, does not include debtors in possession.

(*b*) *Summary of Record.* At the close of each annual period, the clerk shall prepare a summary of the public record by individual or firm name, to reflect total fees awarded during the preceding year. The summary shall be open to examination by the public without charge. The clerk shall transmit a copy of the summary to the United States trustee.

Bankruptcy Code References: §§ 326, 327, and 328

Bankruptcy Statutory Reference: 28 U.S.C. § 586

### Rule 2014 Employment of Professional Persons

(*a*) *Application for an Order of Employment.* An order approving the employment of attorneys, accountants, appraisers, auctioneers, agents, or other professionals

[6] Ed. note: Interim Rule 2012 has been adopted by the bankruptcy courts to implement the Small Business Reorganization Act of 2019, Pub. L. No. 116-54 (2019). Additions to the existing rule are indicated with underscoring.

BANKRUPTCY RULES

pursuant to § 327, § 1103, or § 1114 of the Code shall be made only on application of the trustee or committee. The application shall be filed and, unless the case is a chapter 9 municipality case, a copy of the application shall be transmitted by the applicant to the United States trustee. The application shall state the specific facts showing the necessity for the employment, the name of the person to be employed, the reasons for the selection, the professional services to be rendered, any proposed arrangement for compensation, and, to the best of the applicant's knowledge, all of the person's connections with the debtor, creditors, any other party in interest, their respective attorneys and accountants, the United States trustee, or any person employed in the office of the United States trustee. The application shall be accompanied by a verified statement of the person to be employed setting forth the person's connections with the debtor, creditors, any other party in interest, their respective attorneys and accountants, the United States trustee, or any person employed in the office of the United States trustee.

(*b*) *Services Rendered by Member or Associate of Firm of Attorneys or Accountants.* If, under the Code and this rule, a law partnership or corporation is employed as an attorney, or an accounting partnership or corporation is employed as an accountant, or if a named attorney or accountant is employed, any partner, member, or regular associate of the partnership, corporation or individual may act as attorney or accountant so employed, without further order of the court.

Bankruptcy Code References: §§ 101, 326, 327, 328, 1102, 1103 and 1114

Bankruptcy Statutory Reference: 28 U.S.C. § 586

## Rule 2015 Duty to Keep Records, Make Reports, and Give Notice of Case or Change of Status

(*a*) *Trustee or Debtor in Possession.* A trustee or debtor in possession shall:

(*1*) in a chapter 7 liquidation case and, if the court directs, in a chapter 11 reorganization case file and transmit to the United States trustee a complete inventory of the property of the debtor within 30 days after qualifying as a trustee or debtor in possession, unless such an inventory has already been filed;

(*2*) keep a record of receipts and the disposition of money and property received;

(*3*) file the reports and summaries required by § 704(a)(8) of the Code, which shall include a statement, if payments are made to employees, of the amounts of deductions for all taxes required to be withheld or paid for and in behalf of employees and the place where these amounts are deposited;

(*4*) as soon as possible after the commencement of the case, give notice of the case to every entity known to be holding money or property subject to withdrawal or order of the debtor, including every bank, savings or building and loan association, public utility company, and landlord with whom the debtor has a deposit, and to every insurance company which has issued a policy having a cash surrender value payable to the debtor, except that notice need not be given to any entity who has knowledge or has previously been notified of the case;

(5) in a chapter 11 reorganization case, on or before the last day of the month after each calendar quarter during which there is a duty to pay fees under 28 U.S.C. § 1930(a)(6), file and transmit to the United States trustee a statement of any disbursements made during that quarter and of any fees payable under 28 U.S.C. § 1930(a)(6) for that quarter; and

(6) in a chapter 11 small business case, unless the court, for cause, sets another reporting interval, file and transmit to the United States trustee for each calendar month after the order for relief, on the appropriate Official Form, the report required by § 308. If the order for relief is within the first 15 days of a calendar month, a report shall be filed for the portion of the month that follows the order for relief. If the order for relief is after the 15th day of a calendar month, the period for the remainder of the month shall be included in the report for the next calendar month. Each report shall be filed no later than 21 days after the last day of the calendar month following the month covered by the report. The obligation to file reports under this subparagraph terminates on the effective date of the plan, or conversion or dismissal of the case.

(b) *Chapter 12 Trustee and Debtor in Possession.* In a chapter 12 family farmer's debt adjustment case, the debtor in possession shall perform the duties prescribed in clauses (2)–(4) of subdivision (a) of this rule and, if the court directs, shall file and transmit to the United States trustee a complete inventory of the property of the debtor within the time fixed by the court. If the debtor is removed as debtor in possession, the trustee shall perform the duties of the debtor in possession prescribed in this paragraph.

(c) *Chapter 13 Trustee and Debtor.*

(1) *Business Cases.* In a chapter 13 individual's debt adjustment case, when the debtor is engaged in business, the debtor shall perform the duties prescribed by clauses (2)–(4) of subdivision (a) of this rule and, if the court directs, shall file and transmit to the United States trustee a complete inventory of the property of the debtor within the time fixed by the court.

(2) *Nonbusiness Cases.* In a chapter 13 individual's debt adjustment case, when the debtor is not engaged in business, the trustee shall perform the duties prescribed by clause (2) of subdivision (a) of this rule.

(d) *Foreign Representative.* In a case in which the court has granted recognition of a foreign proceeding under chapter 15, the foreign representative shall file any notice required under § 1518 of the Code within 14 days after the date when the representative becomes aware of the subsequent information.

(e) *Transmission of Reports.* In a chapter 11 case the court may direct that copies or summaries of annual reports and copies or summaries of other reports shall be mailed to the creditors, equity security holders, and indenture trustees. The court may also direct the publication of summaries of any such reports. A copy of every report or summary mailed or published pursuant to this subdivision shall be transmitted to the United States trustee.

BANKRUPTCY CODE REFERENCES: §§ 521, 704, 1106, 1107, 1116, 1202, 1302 and 1304

Bankruptcy Statutory Reference: 28 U.S.C. § 586

## Interim Rule 2015 Duty to Keep Records, Make Reports, and Give Notice of Case or Change of Status[7]

(*a*) *Trustee or Debtor in Possession.* A trustee or debtor in possession shall:

(*1*) in a chapter 7 liquidation case and, if the court directs, in a chapter 11 reorganization case (other than under subchapter V), file and transmit to the United States trustee a complete inventory of the property of the debtor within 30 days after qualifying as a trustee or debtor in possession, unless such an inventory has already been filed;

(*2*) keep a record of receipts and the disposition of money and property received;

(*3*) file the reports and summaries required by § 704(a)(8) of the Code, which shall include a statement, if payments are made to employees, of the amounts of deductions for all taxes required to be withheld or paid for and in behalf of employees and the place where these amounts are deposited;

(*4*) as soon as possible after the commencement of the case, give notice of the case to every entity known to be holding money or property subject to withdrawal or order of the debtor, including every bank, savings or building and loan association, public utility company, and landlord with whom the debtor has a deposit, and to every insurance company which has issued a policy having a cash surrender value payable to the debtor, except that notice need not be given to any entity who has knowledge or has previously been notified of the case;

(*5*) in a chapter 11 reorganization case (other than under subchapter V), on or before the last day of the month after each calendar quarter during which there is a duty to pay fees under 28 U.S.C. § 1930(a)(6), file and transmit to the United States trustee a statement of any disbursements made during that quarter and of any fees payable under 28 U.S.C. § 1930(a)(6) for that quarter; and

(*6*) in a chapter 11 small business case, unless the court, for cause, sets another reporting interval, file and transmit to the United States trustee for each calendar month after the order for relief, on the appropriate Official Form, the report required by § 308. If the order for relief is within the first 15 days of a calendar month, a report shall be filed for the portion of the month that follows the order for relief. If the order for relief is after the 15th day of a calendar month, the period for the remainder of the month shall be included in the report for the next calendar month. Each report shall be filed no later than 21 days after the last day of the calendar month following the month covered by the report. The obligation to file reports under this subparagraph

---

[7] Ed. note: Interim Rule 2015 has been adopted by the bankruptcy courts to implement the Small Business Reorganization Act of 2019, Pub. L. No. 116-54 (2019). Changes from the existing rule are indicated with strikeouts and underscoring.

terminates on the effective date of the plan, or conversion or dismissal of the case.

(*b*) *Trustee, Debtor in Possession, and Debtor in a Case under Subchapter V of Chapter 11.* In a case under subchapter V of chapter 11, the debtor in possession shall perform the duties prescribed in (a)(2)–(4) and, if the court directs, shall file and transmit to the United States trustee a complete inventory of the debtor's property within the time fixed by the court. If the debtor is removed as debtor in possession, the trustee shall perform the duties of the debtor in possession prescribed in this subdivision (b). The debtor shall perform the duties prescribed in (a)(6).

(*~~b~~c*) *Chapter 12 Trustee and Debtor in Possession.* In a chapter 12 family farmer's debt adjustment case, the debtor in possession shall perform the duties prescribed in clauses (2)–(4) of subdivision (a) of this rule and, if the court directs, shall file and transmit to the United States trustee a complete inventory of the property of the debtor within the time fixed by the court. If the debtor is removed as debtor in possession, the trustee shall perform the duties of the debtor in possession prescribed in this ~~paragraph.~~ subdivision (c).

(*~~c~~d*) *Chapter 13 Trustee and Debtor.*

(*1*) *Business Cases.* In a chapter 13 individual's debt adjustment case, when the debtor is engaged in business, the debtor shall perform the duties prescribed by clauses (2)–(4) of subdivision (a) of this rule and, if the court directs, shall file and transmit to the United States trustee a complete inventory of the property of the debtor within the time fixed by the court.

(*2*) *Nonbusiness Cases.* In a chapter 13 individual's debt adjustment case, when the debtor is not engaged in business, the trustee shall perform the duties prescribed by clause (2) of subdivision (a) of this rule.

(*~~d~~e*) *Foreign Representative.* In a case in which the court has granted recognition of a foreign proceeding under chapter 15, the foreign representative shall file any notice required under § 1518 of the Code within 14 days after the date when the representative becomes aware of the subsequent information.

(*~~e~~f*) *Transmission of Reports.* In a chapter 11 case the court may direct that copies or summaries of annual reports and copies or summaries of other reports shall be mailed to the creditors, equity security holders, and indenture trustees. The court may also direct the publication of summaries of any such reports. A copy of every report or summary mailed or published pursuant to this subdivision shall be transmitted to the United States trustee.

## Rule 2015.1 Patient Care Ombudsman

(*a*) *Reports.* A patient care ombudsman, at least 14 days before making a report under § 333(b)(2) of the Code, shall give notice that the report will be made to the court, unless the court orders otherwise. The notice shall be transmitted to the United States trustee, posted conspicuously at the health care facility that is the subject of the report, and served on: the debtor; the trustee; all patients; and any committee elected under § 705 or appointed under § 1102 of the Code or its authorized agent, or, if the case is a chapter 9 municipality case or a chapter 11 reorganization case and no committee of unsecured creditors has been appointed under § 1102, on the creditors included on the list filed under Rule 1007(d); and such other entities as the court may direct. The notice shall state the date and time when the report will be made, the manner in which the report will be made, and, if the report is in writing, the name, address, telephone number, email address, and website, if any, of the person from whom a copy of the report may be obtained at the debtor's expense.

(*b*) *Authorization to Review Confidential Patient Records.* A motion by a patient care ombudsman under § 333(c) to review confidential patient records shall be governed by Rule 9014, served on the patient and any family member or other contact person whose name and address have been given to the trustee or the debtor for the purpose of providing information regarding the patient's health care, and transmitted to the United States trustee subject to applicable nonbankruptcy law relating to patient privacy. Unless the court orders otherwise, a hearing on the motion may not be commenced earlier than 14 days after service of the motion.

## Rule 2015.2 Transfer of Patient in Health Care Business Case

Unless the court orders otherwise, if the debtor is a health care business, the trustee may not transfer a patient to another health care business under § 704(a)(12) of the Code unless the trustee gives at least 14 days' notice of the transfer to the patient care ombudsman, if any, the patient, and any family member or other contact person whose name and address have been given to the trustee or the debtor for the purpose of providing information regarding the patient's health care. The notice is subject to applicable nonbankruptcy law relating to patient privacy.

BANKRUPTCY CODE REFERENCES: §§ 303, 704(a)(12)

## Rule 2015.3 Reports of Financial Information on Entities in Which a Chapter 11 Estate Holds a Controlling or Substantial Interest

(*a*) *Reporting Requirement.* In a chapter 11 case, the trustee or debtor in possession shall file periodic financial reports of the value, operations, and profitability of each entity that is not a publicly traded corporation or a debtor in a case under title 11, and in which the estate holds a substantial or controlling interest. The reports shall be prepared as prescribed by the appropriate Official Form, and shall be based upon the most recent information reasonably available to the trustee or debtor in possession.

(*b*) *Time for Filing; Service.* The first report required by this rule shall be filed no later than seven days before the first date set for the meeting of creditors under § 341 of the Code. Subsequent reports shall be filed no less frequently than every six months thereafter, until the effective date of a plan or the case is dismissed or converted. Copies of the report shall be served on the United States trustee, any committee appointed under § 1102 of the Code, and any other party in interest that has filed a request therefor.

(*c*) *Presumption of Substantial or Controlling Interest; Judicial Determination.* For purposes of this rule, an entity of which the estate controls or owns at least a 20 percent interest, shall be presumed to be an entity in which the estate has a substantial or controlling interest. An entity in which the estate controls or owns less than a 20 percent interest shall be presumed not to be an entity in which the estate has a substantial or controlling interest. Upon motion, the entity, any holder of an interest therein, the United States trustee, or any other party in interest may seek to rebut either presumption, and the court shall, after notice and a hearing, determine whether the estate's interest in the entity is substantial or controlling.

(*d*) *Modification of Reporting Requirement.* The court may, after notice and a hearing, vary the reporting requirement established by subdivision (a) of this rule for cause, including that the trustee or debtor in possession is not able, after a good faith effort, to comply with those reporting requirements, or that the information required by subdivision (a) is publicly available.

(*e*) *Notice and Protective Orders.* No later than 14 days before filing the first report required by this rule, the trustee or debtor in possession shall send notice to the entity in which the estate has a substantial or controlling interest, and to all holders—known to the trustee or debtor in possession—of an interest in that entity, that the trustee or debtor in possession expects to file and serve financial information relating to the entity in accordance with this rule. The entity in which the estate has a substantial or controlling interest, or a person holding an interest in that entity, may request protection of the information under § 107 of the Code.

(*f*) *Effect of Request.* Unless the court orders otherwise, the pendency of a request under subdivisions (c), (d), or (e) of this rule shall not alter or stay the requirements of subdivision (a).

Bankruptcy Code Reference: § 107



## Rule 2016 Compensation for Services Rendered and Reimbursement of Expenses

(*a*) *Application for Compensation or Reimbursement.* An entity seeking interim or final compensation for services, or reimbursement of necessary expenses, from the estate shall file an application setting forth a detailed statement of (1) the services rendered, time expended and expenses incurred, and (2) the amounts requested. An application for compensation shall include a statement as to what payments have theretofore been made or promised to the applicant for services rendered or to be rendered in any capacity whatsoever in connection with the case, the source of the compensation so paid or promised, whether any compensation previously received has been shared and whether an agreement or understanding exists between the applicant and any other entity for the sharing of compensation received or to be received for services rendered in or in connection with the case, and the particulars of any sharing of compensation or agreement or understanding therefor, except that details of any agreement by the applicant for the sharing of compensation as a member or regular associate of a firm of lawyers or accountants shall not be required. The requirements of this subdivision shall apply to an application for compensation for services rendered by an attorney or accountant even though the application is filed by a creditor or other entity. Unless the case is a chapter 9 municipality case, the applicant shall transmit to the United States trustee a copy of the application.

(*b*) *Disclosure of Compensation Paid or Promised to Attorney for Debtor.* Every attorney for a debtor, whether or not the attorney applies for compensation, shall file and transmit to the United States trustee within 14 days after the order for relief, or at another time as the court may direct, the statement required by § 329 of the Code including whether the attorney has shared or agreed to share the compensation with any other entity. The statement shall include the particulars of any such sharing or agreement to share by the attorney, but the details of any agreement for the sharing of the compensation with a member or regular associate of the attorney's law firm shall not be required. A supplemental statement shall be filed and transmitted to the United States trustee within 14 days after any payment or agreement not previously disclosed.

(*c*) *Disclosure of Compensation Paid or Promised to Bankruptcy Petition Preparer.* Before a petition is filed, every bankruptcy petition preparer for a debtor shall deliver to the debtor, the declaration under penalty of perjury required by § 110(h)(2). The declaration shall disclose any fee, and the source of any fee, received from or on behalf of the debtor within 12 months of the filing of the case and all unpaid fees charged to the debtor. The declaration shall also describe the services performed and documents prepared or caused to be prepared by the bankruptcy petition preparer. The declaration shall be filed with the petition. The petition preparer shall file a supplemental statement within 14 days after any payment or agreement not previously disclosed.

Bankruptcy Code References: §§ 110, 326–331, 504, 1102, 1103, 1104 and 1114

Bankruptcy Statutory Reference: 28 U.S.C. § 586

## Rule 2017 Examination of Debtor's Transactions with Debtor's Attorney

(*a*) *Payment or Transfer to Attorney Before Order for Relief.* On motion by any party in interest or on the court's own initiative, the court after notice and a hearing may determine whether any payment of money or any transfer of property by the debtor, made directly or indirectly and in contemplation of the filing of a petition under the Code by or against the debtor or before entry of the order for relief in an involuntary case, to an attorney for services rendered or to be rendered is excessive.

(*b*) *Payment or Transfer to Attorney After Order for Relief.* On motion by the debtor, the United States trustee, or on the court's own initiative, the court after notice and a hearing may determine whether any payment of money or any transfer of property, or any agreement therefor, by the debtor to an attorney after entry of an order for relief in a case under the Code is excessive, whether the payment or transfer is made or is to be made directly or indirectly, if the payment, transfer, or agreement therefor is for services in any way related to the case.

Bankruptcy Code References: §§ 329, 330, 331 and 504

## Rule 2018 Intervention; Right to Be Heard

(*a*) *Permissive Intervention.* In a case under the Code, after hearing on such notice as the court directs and for cause shown, the court may permit any interested entity to intervene generally or with respect to any specified matter.

(*b*) *Intervention by Attorney General of a State.* In a chapter 7, 11, 12, or 13 case, the Attorney General of a State may appear and be heard on behalf of consumer creditors if the court determines the appearance is in the public interest, but the Attorney General may not appeal from any judgment, order, or decree in the case.

(*c*) *Chapter 9 Municipality Case.* The Secretary of the Treasury of the United States may, or if requested by the court shall, intervene in a chapter 9 case. Representatives of the state in which the debtor is located may intervene in a chapter 9 case with respect to matters specified by the court.

(*d*) *Labor Unions.* In a chapter 9, 11, or 12 case, a labor union or employees' association, representative of employees of the debtor, shall have the right to be heard on the economic soundness of a plan affecting the interests of the employees. A labor union or employees' association which exercises its right to be heard under this subdivision shall not be entitled to appeal any judgment, order, or decree relating to the plan, unless otherwise permitted by law.

(*e*) *Service on Entities Covered by This Rule.* The court may enter orders governing the service of notice and papers on entities permitted to intervene or be heard pursuant to this rule.

BANKRUPTCY CODE REFERENCES: §§ 901, 943, 1109 and 1164

## Rule 2019 Disclosure Regarding Creditors and Equity Security Holders in Chapter 9 and Chapter 11 Cases

(*a*) *Definitions.* In this rule the following terms have the meanings indicated:

(*1*) "Disclosable economic interest" means any claim, interest, pledge, lien, option, participation, derivative instrument, or any other right or derivative right granting the holder an economic interest that is affected by the value, acquisition, or disposition of a claim or interest.

(*2*) "Represent" or "represents" means to take a position before the court or to solicit votes regarding the confirmation of a plan on behalf of another.

(*b*) *Disclosure by Groups, Committees, and Entities.*

(*1*) In a chapter 9 or 11 case, a verified statement setting forth the information specified in subdivision (c) of this rule shall be filed by every group or committee that consists of or represents, and every entity that represents, multiple creditors or equity security holders that are

(*A*) acting in concert to advance their common interests, and

(*B*) not composed entirely of affiliates or insiders of one another.

(*2*) Unless the court orders otherwise, an entity is not required to file the verified statement described in paragraph (1) of this subdivision solely because of its status as:

(*A*) an indenture trustee;

BANKRUPTCY RULES

(*B*) an agent for one or more other entities under an agreement for the extension of credit;

(*C*) a class action representative; or

(*D*) a governmental unit that is not a person.

(c) *Information Required.* The verified statement shall include:

(*1*) the pertinent facts and circumstances concerning:

(*A*) with respect to a group or committee, other than a committee appointed under § 1102 or § 1114 of the Code, the formation of the group or committee, including the name of each entity at whose instance the group or committee was formed or for whom the group or committee has agreed to act; or

(*B*) with respect to an entity, the employment of the entity, including the name of each creditor or equity security holder at whose instance the employment was arranged;

(*2*) if not disclosed under subdivision (c)(1), with respect to an entity, and with respect to each member of a group or committee:

(*A*) name and address;

(*B*) the nature and amount of each disclosable economic interest held in relation to the debtor as of the date the entity was employed or the group or committee was formed; and

(*C*) with respect to each member of a group or committee that claims to represent any entity in addition to the members of the group or committee, other than a committee appointed under § 1102 or § 1114 of the Code, the date of acquisition by quarter and year of each disclosable economic interest, unless acquired more than one year before the petition was filed;

(*3*) if not disclosed under subdivision (c)(1) or (c)(2), with respect to each creditor or equity security holder represented by an entity, group, or committee, other than a committee appointed under § 1102 or § 1114 of the Code:

(*A*) name and address; and

(*B*) the nature and amount of each disclosable economic interest held in relation to the debtor as of the date of the statement; and

(*4*) a copy of the instrument, if any, authorizing the entity, group, or committee to act on behalf of creditors or equity security holders.

(d) *Supplemental Statements.* If any fact disclosed in its most recently filed statement has changed materially, an entity, group, or committee shall file a verified supplemental statement whenever it takes a position before the court or solicits votes on the confirmation of a plan. The supplemental statement shall set forth the material changes in the facts required by subdivision (c) to be disclosed.

(e) *Determination of Failure to Comply; Sanctions.*

(*1*) On motion of any party in interest, or on its own motion, the court may determine whether there has been a failure to comply with any provision of this rule.

(*2*) If the court finds such a failure to comply, it may:

(*A*) refuse to permit the entity, group, or committee to be heard or to intervene in the case;

(*B*) hold invalid any authority, acceptance, rejection, or objection given, procured, or received by the entity, group, or committee; or

(*C*) grant other appropriate relief.

BANKRUPTCY CODE REFERENCES: §§ 901, 1102, 1103 and 1114

## Rule 2020 Review of Acts by United States Trustee

A proceeding to contest any act or failure to act by the United States trustee is governed by Rule 9014.

BANKRUPTCY STATUTORY REFERENCE: 28 U.S.C. § 586

# PART III

# CLAIMS AND DISTRIBUTION TO CREDITORS AND EQUITY INTEREST HOLDERS; PLANS

## Rule 3001 Proof of Claim

(*a*) *Form and Content.* A proof of claim is a written statement setting forth a creditor's claim. A proof of claim shall conform substantially to the appropriate Official Form.

(*b*) *Who May Execute.* A proof of claim shall be executed by the creditor or the creditor's authorized agent except as provided in Rules 3004 and 3005.

(*c*) *Supporting Information.*

(*1*) *Claim Based on a Writing.* Except for a claim governed by paragraph (3) of this subdivision, when a claim, or an interest in property of the debtor securing the claim, is based on a writing, a copy of the writing shall be filed with the proof of claim. If the writing has been lost or destroyed, a statement of the circumstances of the loss or destruction shall be filed with the claim.

(*2*) *Additional Requirements in an Individual Debtor Case; Sanctions for Failure to Comply.* In a case in which the debtor is an individual:

(*A*) If, in addition to its principal amount, a claim includes interest, fees, expenses, or other charges incurred before the petition was filed, an itemized statement of the interest, fees, expenses, or charges shall be filed with the proof of claim.

(*B*) If a security interest is claimed in the debtor's property, a statement of the amount necessary to cure any default as of the date of the petition shall be filed with the proof of claim.

(*C*) If a security interest is claimed in property that is the debtor's principal residence, the attachment prescribed by the appropriate Official Form shall be filed with the proof of claim. If an escrow account has been established in connection with the claim, an escrow account statement prepared as of the date the petition was filed and in a form consistent with applicable nonbankruptcy law shall be filed with the attachment to the proof of claim.

(*D*) If the holder of a claim fails to provide any information required by this subdivision (c), the court may, after notice and hearing, take either or both of the following actions:

(*i*) preclude the holder from presenting the omitted information, in any form, as evidence in any contested matter or adversary proceeding in the case, unless the court determines that the failure was substantially justified or is harmless; or

(*ii*) award other appropriate relief, including reasonable expenses and attorney's fees caused by the failure.

(3) *Claim Based on an Open-End or Revolving Consumer Credit Agreement.*

(*A*) When a claim is based on an open-end or revolving consumer credit agreement—except one for which a security interest is claimed in the debtor's real property—a statement shall be filed with the proof of claim, including all of the following information that applies to the account:

(*i*) the name of the entity from whom the creditor purchased the account;

(*ii*) the name of the entity to whom the debt was owed at the time of an account holder's last transaction on the account;

(*iii*) the date of an account holder's last transaction;

(*iv*) the date of the last payment on the account; and

(*v*) the date on which the account was charged to profit and loss.

(*B*) On written request by a party in interest, the holder of a claim based on an open-end or revolving consumer credit agreement shall, within 30 days after the request is sent, provide the requesting party a copy of the writing specified in paragraph (1) of this subdivision.

(*d*) *Evidence of Perfection of Security Interest.* If a security interest in property of the debtor is claimed, the proof of claim shall be accompanied by evidence that the security interest has been perfected.

(*e*) *Transferred Claim.*

(1) *Transfer of Claim Other Than for Security Before Proof Filed.* If a claim has been transferred other than for security before proof of the claim has been filed, the proof of claim may be filed only by the transferee or an indenture trustee.

(2) *Transfer of Claim Other Than for Security After Proof Filed.* If a claim other than one based on a publicly traded note, bond, or debenture has been transferred other than for security after the proof of claim has been filed, evidence of the transfer shall be filed by the transferee. The clerk shall immediately notify the alleged transferor by mail of the filing of the evidence of transfer and that objection thereto, if any, must be filed within 21 days of the mailing of the notice or within any additional time allowed by the court. If the alleged transferor files a timely objection and the court finds, after notice and a hearing, that the claim has been transferred other than for security, it shall enter an order substituting the transferee for the transferor. If a timely objection is not filed by the alleged transferor, the transferee shall be substituted for the transferor.

(3) *Transfer of Claim for Security Before Proof Filed.* If a claim other than one based on a publicly traded note, bond, or debenture has been transferred for security before proof of the claim has been filed, the transferor or transferee or both may file a proof of claim for the full amount. The proof shall be supported by a statement setting forth the terms of the transfer. If either the transferor or

the transferee files a proof of claim, the clerk shall immediately notify the other by mail of the right to join in the filed claim. If both transferor and transferee file proofs of the same claim, the proofs shall be consolidated. If the transferor or transferee does not file an agreement regarding its relative rights respecting voting of the claim, payment of dividends thereon, or participation in the administration of the estate, on motion by a party in interest and after notice and a hearing, the court shall enter such orders respecting these matters as may be appropriate.

(4) *Transfer of Claim for Security After Proof Filed.* If a claim other than one based on a publicly traded note, bond, or debenture has been transferred for security after the proof of claim has been filed, evidence of the terms of the transfer shall be filed by the transferee. The clerk shall immediately notify the alleged transferor by mail of the filing of the evidence of transfer and that objection thereto, if any, must be filed within 21 days of the mailing of the notice or within any additional time allowed by the court. If a timely objection is filed by the alleged transferor, the court, after notice and a hearing, shall determine whether the claim has been transferred for security. If the transferor or transferee does not file an agreement regarding its relative rights respecting voting of the claim, payment of dividends thereon, or participation in the administration of the estate, on motion by a party in interest and after notice and a hearing, the court shall enter such orders respecting these matters as may be appropriate.

(5) *Service of Objection or Motion; Notice of Hearing.* A copy of an objection filed pursuant to paragraph (2) or (4) or a motion filed pursuant to paragraph (3) or (4) of this subdivision together with a notice of a hearing shall be mailed or otherwise delivered to the transferor or transferee, whichever is appropriate, at least 30 days prior to the hearing.

(*f*) *Evidentiary Effect.* A proof of claim executed and filed in accordance with these rules shall constitute prima facie evidence of the validity and amount of the claim.

(*g*) To the extent not inconsistent with the United States Warehouse Act or applicable State law, a warehouse receipt, scale ticket, or similar document of the type routinely issued as evidence of title by a grain storage facility, as defined in section 557 of title 11, shall constitute prima facie evidence of the validity and amount of a claim of ownership of a quantity of grain.

BANKRUPTCY CODE REFERENCES: §§ 501 and 502

## Rule 3002 Filing Proof of Claim or Interest

(*a*) *Necessity for Filing.* A secured creditor, unsecured creditor, or equity security holder must file a proof of claim or interest for the claim or interest to be allowed, except as provided in Rules 1019(3), 3003, 3004, and 3005. A lien that secures a claim against the debtor is not void due only to the failure of any entity to file a proof of claim.

(*b*) *Place of Filing.* A proof of claim or interest shall be filed in accordance with Rule 5005.

(*c*) *Time for Filing.* In a voluntary chapter 7 case, chapter 12 case, or chapter 13 case, a proof of claim is timely filed if it is filed not later than 70 days after the order for relief under that chapter or the date of the order of conversion to a case under chapter 12 or chapter 13. In an involuntary chapter 7 case, a proof of claim is timely filed if it is filed not later than 90 days after the order for relief under that chapter is entered. But in all these cases, the following exceptions apply:

(*1*) A proof of claim filed by a governmental unit, other than for a claim resulting from a tax return filed under § 1308, is timely filed if it is filed not later than 180 days after the date of the order for relief. A proof of claim filed by a governmental unit for a claim resulting from a tax return filed under § 1308 is timely filed if it is filed no later than 180 days after the date of the order for relief or 60 days after the date of the filing of the tax return. The court may, for cause, enlarge the time for a governmental unit to file a proof of claim only upon motion of the governmental unit made before expiration of the period for filing a timely proof of claim.

(*2*) In the interest of justice and if it will not unduly delay the administration of the case, the court may extend the time for filing a proof of claim by an infant or incompetent person or the representative of either.

(*3*) An unsecured claim which arises in favor of an entity or becomes allowable as a result of a judgment may be filed within 30 days after the judgment becomes final if the judgment is for the recovery of money or property from that entity or denies or avoids the entity's interest in property. If the judgment imposes a liability which is not satisfied, or a duty which is not performed within such period or such further time as the court may permit, the claim shall not be allowed.

(*4*) A claim arising from the rejection of an executory contract or unexpired lease of the debtor may be filed within such time as the court may direct.

(*5*) If notice of insufficient assets to pay a dividend was given to creditors under Rule 2002(e), and subsequently the trustee notifies the court that payment of a dividend appears possible, the clerk shall give at least 90 days' notice by mail to creditors of that fact and of the date by which proofs of claim must be filed.

(*6*) On motion filed by a creditor before or after the expiration of the time to file a proof of claim, the court may extend the time by not more than 60 days from the date of the order granting the motion. The motion may be granted if the court finds that:

(*A*) the notice was insufficient under the circumstances to give the creditor a reasonable time to file a proof of claim because the debtor failed to timely file the list of creditors' names and addresses required by Rule 1007(a); or

(*B*) the notice was insufficient under the circumstances to give the creditor a reasonable time to file a proof of claim, and the notice was mailed to the creditor at a foreign address.

(*7*) A proof of claim filed by the holder of a claim that is secured by a security interest in the debtor's principal residence is timely filed if:

(*A*) the proof of claim, together with the attachments required by Rule 3001(c)(2)(C), is filed not later than 70 days after the order for relief is entered; and

(*B*) any attachments required by Rule 3001(c)(1) and (d) are filed as a supplement to the holder's claim not later than 120 days after the order for relief is entered.

Bankruptcy Code References: §§ 501, 502, 503 and 726

## Rule 3002.1. Notice Relating to Claims Secured by Security Interest in the Debtor's Principal Residence

(*a*) *In General.* This rule applies in a chapter 13 case to claims (1) that are secured by a security interest in the debtor's principal residence, and (2) for which the plan provides that either the trustee or the debtor will make contractual installment payments. Unless the court orders otherwise, the notice requirements of this rule cease to apply when an order terminating or annulling the automatic stay becomes effective with respect to the residence that secures the claim.

(*b*) *Notice of Payment Changes; Objection.*

(*1*) *Notice.* The holder of the claim shall file and serve on the debtor, debtor's counsel, and the trustee a notice of any change in the payment amount, including any change that results from an interest-rate or escrow-account adjustment, no later than 21 days before a payment in the new amount is due. If the claim arises from a home-equity line of credit, this requirement may be modified by court order.

(*2*) *Objection.* A party in interest who objects to the payment change may file a motion to determine whether the change is required to maintain payments in accordance with § 1322(b)(5) of the Code. If no motion is filed by the day before the new amount is due, the change goes into effect, unless the court orders otherwise.

(*c*) *Notice of Fees, Expenses, and Charges.* The holder of the claim shall file and serve on the debtor, debtor's counsel, and the trustee a notice itemizing all fees, expenses, or charges (1) that were incurred in connection with the claim after the bankruptcy case was filed, and (2) that the holder asserts are recoverable against the debtor or against the debtor's principal residence. The notice shall be served within 180 days after the date on which the fees, expenses, or charges are incurred.

(*d*) *Form and Content.* A notice filed and served under subdivision (b) or (c) of this rule shall be prepared as prescribed by the appropriate Official Form, and filed as a supplement to the holder's proof of claim. The notice is not subject to Rule 3001(f).

(*e*) *Determination of Fees, Expenses, or Charges.* On motion of a party in interest filed within one year after service of a notice under subdivision (c) of this rule, the court shall, after notice and hearing, determine whether payment of any claimed fee, expense, or charge is required by the underlying agreement and applicable nonbankruptcy law to cure a default or maintain payments in accordance with § 1322(b)(5) of the Code.

(*f*) *Notice of Final Cure Payment.* Within 30 days after the debtor completes all payments under the plan, the trustee shall file and serve on the holder of the claim, the debtor, and debtor's counsel a notice stating that the debtor has paid in full the amount required to cure any default on the claim. The notice shall also inform the holder of its obligation to file and serve a response under subdivision (g). If the debtor contends that final cure payment has been made and all plan payments have been completed, and the trustee does not timely file and serve the notice required by this subdivision, the debtor may file and serve the notice.

(*g*) *Response to Notice of Final Cure Payment.* Within 21 days after service of the notice under subdivision (f) of this rule, the holder shall file and serve on the debtor, debtor's counsel, and the trustee a statement indicating (1) whether it agrees that the debtor has paid in full the amount required to cure the default on the claim, and (2) whether the debtor is otherwise current on all payments consistent with § 1322(b)(5) of the Code. The statement shall itemize the required cure or postpetition amounts, if any, that the holder contends remain unpaid as of the date of the statement. The statement shall be filed as a supplement to the holder's proof of claim and is not subject to Rule 3001(f).

(*h*) *Determination of Final Cure and Payment.* On motion of the debtor or trustee filed within 21 days after service of the statement under subdivision (g) of this rule, the court shall, after notice and hearing, determine whether the debtor has cured the default and paid all required postpetition amounts.

(*i*) *Failure to Notify.* If the holder of a claim fails to provide any information as required by subdivision (b), (c), or (g) of this rule, the court may, after notice and hearing, take either or both of the following actions:

(*1*) preclude the holder from presenting the omitted information, in any form, as evidence in any contested matter or adversary proceeding in the case, unless the court determines that the failure was substantially justified or is harmless; or

(2) award other appropriate relief, including reasonable expenses and attorney's fees caused by the failure.

## Rule 3003 Filing Proof of Claim or Equity Security Interest in Chapter 9 Municipality or Chapter 11 Reorganization Cases

(*a*) *Applicability of Rule.* This rule applies in chapter 9 and 11 cases.

(*b*) *Schedule of Liabilities and List of Equity Security Holders*

(*1*) *Schedule of Liabilities.* The schedule of liabilities filed pursuant to § 521(1) of the Code shall constitute prima facie evidence of the validity and amount of the claims of creditors, unless they are scheduled as disputed, contingent, or unliquidated. It shall not be necessary for a creditor or equity security holder to file a proof of claim or interest except as provided in subdivision (c)(2) of this rule.

BANKRUPTCY RULES

(2) *List of Equity Security Holders.* The list of equity security holders filed pursuant to Rule 1007(a)(3) shall constitute prima facie evidence of the validity and amount of the equity security interests and it shall not be necessary for the holders of such interests to file a proof of interest.

(c) *Filing Proof of Claim.*

(1) *Who May File.* Any creditor or indenture trustee may file a proof of claim within the time prescribed by subdivision (c)(3) of this rule.

(2) *Who Must File.* Any creditor or equity security holder whose claim or interest is not scheduled or scheduled as disputed, contingent, or unliquidated shall file a proof of claim or interest within the time prescribed by subdivision (c)(3) of this rule; any creditor who fails to do so shall not be treated as a creditor with respect to such claim for the purposes of voting and distribution.

(3) *Time for Filing.* The court shall fix and for cause shown may extend the time within which proofs of claim or interest may be filed. Notwithstanding the expiration of such time, a proof of claim may be filed to the extent and under the conditions stated in Rule 3002(c)(2), (c)(3), (c)(4), and (c)(6).

(4) *Effect of Filing Claim or Interest.* A proof of claim or interest executed and filed in accordance with this subdivision shall supersede any scheduling of that claim or interest pursuant to § 521(a)(1) of the Code.

(5) *Filing by Indenture Trustee.* An indenture trustee may file a claim on behalf of all known or unknown holders of securities issued pursuant to the trust instrument under which it is trustee.

(d) *Proof of Right to Record Status.* For the purposes of Rules 3017, 3018 and 3021 and for receiving notices, an entity who is not the record holder of a security may file a statement setting forth facts which entitle that entity to be treated as the record holder. An objection to the statement may be filed by any party in interest.

BANKRUPTCY CODE REFERENCES: §§ 501, 502, 503, 726 and 1111

### Rule 3004 Filing of Claims by Debtor or Trustee

If a creditor does not timely file a proof of claim under Rule 3002(c) or 3003(c), the debtor or trustee may file a proof of the claim within 30 days after the expiration of the time for filing claims prescribed by Rule 3002(c) or 3003(c), whichever is applicable. The clerk shall forthwith give notice of the filing to the creditor, the debtor and the trustee.

BANKRUPTCY CODE REFERENCES: §§ 501, 502, 503, 726 and 1111

### Rule 3005 Filing of Claim, Acceptance, or Rejection by Guarantor, Surety, Indorser, or Other Codebtor

(a) *Filing of Claim.* If a creditor does not timely file a proof of claim under Rule 3002(c) or 3003(c), any entity that is or may be liable with the debtor to that creditor, or who has secured that creditor, may file a proof of the claim within 30 days after the expiration of the time for filing claims prescribed by Rule 3002(c) or 3003(c) whichever is applicable. No distribution shall be made on the claim except on satisfactory proof that the original debt will be diminished by the amount of distribution.

(*b*) *Filing of Acceptance or Rejection; Substitution of Creditor.* An entity which has filed a claim pursuant to the first sentence of subdivision (a) of this rule may file an acceptance or rejection of a plan in the name of the creditor, if known, or if unknown, in the entity's own name but if the creditor files a proof of claim within the time permitted by Rule 3003(c) or files a notice prior to confirmation of a plan of the creditor's intention to act in the creditor's own behalf, the creditor shall be substituted for the obligor with respect to that claim.

Bankruptcy Code References: §§ 501, 502, 503, 726, 1111

## Rule 3006 Withdrawal of Claim; Effect on Acceptance or Rejection of Plan

A creditor may withdraw a claim as of right by filing a notice of withdrawal, except as provided in this rule. If after a creditor has filed a proof of claim an objection is filed thereto or a complaint is filed against that creditor in an adversary proceeding, or the creditor has accepted or rejected the plan or otherwise has participated significantly in the case, the creditor may not withdraw the claim except on order of the court after a hearing on notice to the trustee or debtor in possession, and any creditors' committee elected pursuant to § 705(a) or appointed pursuant to § 1102 of the Code. The order of the court shall contain such terms and conditions as the court deems proper. Unless the court orders otherwise, an authorized withdrawal of a claim shall constitute withdrawal of any related acceptance or rejection of a plan.

Bankruptcy Code References: §§ 501, 502, 503, 726 and 1111

## Rule 3007 Objections to Claims

(*a*) *Time and Manner of Service.*

(*1*) *Time of Service.* An objection to the allowance of a claim and a notice of objection that substantially conforms to the appropriate Official Form shall be filed and served at least 30 days before any scheduled hearing on the objection or any deadline for the claimant to request a hearing.

(*2*) *Manner of Service.*

(*A*) The objection and notice shall be served on a claimant by first-class mail to the person most recently designated on the claimant's original or amended proof of claim as the person to receive notices, at the address so indicated; and

(*i*) if the objection is to a claim of the United States, or any of its officers or agencies, in the manner provided for service of a summons and complaint by Rule 7004(b)(4) or (5); or

(*ii*) if the objection is to a claim of an insured depository institution as defined in section 3 of the Federal Deposit Insurance Act, in the manner provided in Rule 7004(h).

(*B*) Service of the objection and notice shall also be made by first-class mail or other permitted means on the debtor or debtor in possession, the trustee, and, if applicable, the entity filing the proof of claim under Rule 3005.

*(b) Demand for Relief Requiring an Adversary Proceeding.* A party in interest shall not include a demand for relief of a kind specified in Rule 7001 in an objection to the allowance of a claim, but may include the objection in an adversary proceeding.

*(c) Limitation on Joinder of Claims Objections.* Unless otherwise ordered by the court or permitted by subdivision (d), objections to more than one claim shall not be joined in a single objection.

*(d) Omnibus Objection.* Subject to subdivision (e), objections to more than one claim may be joined in an omnibus objection if all the claims were filed by the same entity, or the objections are based solely on the grounds that the claims should be disallowed, in whole or in part, because:

(*1*) they duplicate other claims;

(*2*) they have been filed in the wrong case;

(*3*) they have been amended by subsequently filed proofs of claim;

(*4*) they were not timely filed;

(*5*) they have been satisfied or released during the case in accordance with the Code, applicable rules, or a court order;

(*6*) they were presented in a form that does not comply with applicable rules, and the objection states that the objector is unable to determine the validity of the claim because of the noncompliance;

(*7*) they are interests, rather than claims; or

(*8*) they assert priority in an amount that exceeds the maximum amount under § 507 of the Code.

*(e) Requirements for Omnibus Objection.* An omnibus objection shall:

(*1*) state in a conspicuous place that claimants receiving the objection should locate their names and claims in the objection;

(*2*) list claimants alphabetically, provide a cross-reference to claim numbers, and, if appropriate, list claimants by category of claims;

(*3*) state the grounds of the objection to each claim and provide a cross-reference to the pages in the omnibus objection pertinent to the stated grounds;

(*4*) state in the title the identity of the objector and the grounds for the objections;

(*5*) be numbered consecutively with other omnibus objections filed by the same objector; and

(6) contain objections to no more than 100 claims.

(*f*) *Finality of Objection.* The finality of any order regarding a claim objection included in an omnibus objection shall be determined as though the claim had been subject to an individual objection.

Bankruptcy Code References: §§ 501, 502 and 1111

**Rule 3008 Reconsideration of Claims**

A party in interest may move for reconsideration of an order allowing or disallowing a claim against the estate. The court after a hearing on notice shall enter an appropriate order.

Bankruptcy Code References: §§ 102, 501, 502 and 1111

**Rule 3009 Declaration and Payment of Dividends in Chapter 7 Liquidation Cases**

In a chapter 7 case, dividends to creditors shall be paid as promptly as practicable. Dividend checks shall be made payable to and mailed to each creditor whose claim has been allowed, unless a power of attorney authorizing another entity to receive dividends has been executed and filed in accordance with Rule 9010. In that event, dividend checks shall be made payable to the creditor and to the other entity and shall be mailed to the other entity.

Bankruptcy Code References: §§ 704 and 726

**Rule 3010 Small Dividends and Payments in Chapter 7 Liquidation, Chapter 12 Family Farmer's Debt Adjustment, and Chapter 13 Individual's Debt Adjustment Cases**

(*a*) *Chapter 7 Cases.* In a chapter 7 case no dividend in an amount less than $5 shall be distributed by the trustee to any creditor unless authorized by local rule or order of the court. Any such dividend not distributed to a creditor shall be treated in the same manner as unclaimed funds as provided in § 347 of the Code.

(*b*) *Chapter 12 and Chapter 13 Cases.* In a chapter 12 or chapter 13 case no payment in an amount less than $15 shall be distributed by the trustee to any creditor unless authorized by local rule or order of the court. Funds not distributed because of this subdivision shall accumulate and shall be paid whenever the accumulation aggregates $15. Any funds remaining shall be distributed with the final payment.

Bankruptcy Code References: §§ 347, 704, 1202, 1226, 1302 and 1326

**Interim Rule 3010 Small Dividends and Payments in Cases Under Chapter 7 ~~Liquidation~~, Subchapter V of Chapter 11, Chapter 12 ~~Family Farmer's Debt Adjustment~~, and Chapter 13 ~~Individual's Debt Adjustment Cases~~[8]**

* * * * *

(*b*) *Cases Under Subchapter V of Chapter 11, Chapter 12, and Chapter 13 ~~Cases~~.* In

[8] Ed. Note: Interim Rule 3010 has been adopted by the bankruptcy courts to implement the Small Business Reorganization Act of 2019, Pub. L. No. 116-54 (2019). Changes from the existing rule are indicated with strikeouts and underscoring.

a case under subchapter V of chapter 11, chapter 12, or chapter 13, ~~case~~ no payment in an amount less than $15 shall be distributed by the trustee to any creditor unless authorized by local rule or order of the court. Funds not distributed because of this subdivision shall accumulate and shall be paid whenever the accumulation aggregates $15. Any funds remaining shall be distributed with the final payment.

### Rule 3011 Unclaimed Funds in Chapter 7 Liquidation, Chapter 12 Family Farmer's Debt Adjustment, and Chapter 13 Individual's Debt Adjustment Cases

The trustee shall file a list of all known names and addresses of the entities and the amounts which they are entitled to be paid from remaining property of the estate that is paid into court pursuant to § 347(a) of the Code.

BANKRUPTCY CODE REFERENCES: §§ 347, 704, 1202 and 1302

### Interim Rule 3011 Unclaimed Funds in Cases Under Chapter 7 ~~Liquidation~~, Subchapter V of Chapter 11, Chapter 12 ~~Family Farmer's Debt Adjustment~~, and Chapter 13 ~~Individual's Debt Adjustment Cases~~[9]

The trustee shall file a list of all known names and addresses of the entities and the amounts which they are entitled to be paid from remaining property of the estate that is paid into court pursuant to § 347(a) of the Code.

### Rule 3012 Determining the Amount of Secured and Priority Claims

(*a*) *Determination of Amount of Claim.* On request by a party in interest and after notice—to the holder of the claim and any other entity the court designates—and a hearing, the court may determine:

(*1*) the amount of a secured claim under § 506(a) of the Code; or

(*2*) the amount of a claim entitled to priority under § 507 of the Code.

(*b*) *Request for Determination; How Made.* Except as provided in subdivision (c), a request to determine the amount of a secured claim may be made by motion, in a claim objection, or in a plan filed in a chapter 12 or chapter 13 case. When the request is made in a chapter 12 or chapter 13 plan, the plan shall be served on the holder of the claim and any other entity the court designates in the manner provided for service of a summons and complaint by Rule 7004. A request to determine the amount of a claim entitled to priority may be made only by motion after a claim is filed or in a claim objection.

(*c*) *Claims of Governmental Units.* A request to determine the amount of a secured claim of a governmental unit may be made only by motion or in a claim objection after the governmental unit files a proof of claim or after the time for filing one under Rule 3002(c)(1) has expired.

BANKRUPTCY CODE REFERENCES: §§ 506 and 1325

---

[9] ED. NOTE: Interim Rule 3011 has been adopted by the bankruptcy courts to implement the Small Business Reorganization Act of 2019, Pub. L. No. 116-54 (2019). Changes from the existing rule are indicated with strikeouts and underscoring.

## Rule 3013 Classification of Claims and Interests

For the purposes of the plan and its acceptance, the court may, on motion after hearing on notice as the court may direct, determine classes of creditors and equity security holders pursuant to §§ 1122, 1222(b)(1), and 1322(b)(1) of the Code.

BANKRUPTCY CODE REFERENCES: §§ 501, 502, 901, 1122, 1222 and 1322

## Rule 3014 Election Under § 1111(b) by Secured Creditor in Chapter 9 Municipality or Chapter 11 Reorganization Case

An election of application of § 1111(b)(2) of the Code by a class of secured creditors in a chapter 9 or 11 case may be made at any time prior to the conclusion of the hearing on the disclosure statement or within such later time as the court may fix. If the disclosure statement is conditionally approved pursuant to Rule 3017.1, and a final hearing on the disclosure statement is not held, the election of application of § 1111(b)(2) may be made not later than the date fixed pursuant to Rule 3017.1(a)(2) or another date the court may fix. The election shall be in writing and signed unless made at the hearing on the disclosure statement. The election, if made by the majorities required by § 1111(b)(1)(A)(i), shall be binding on all members of the class with respect to the plan.

BANKRUPTCY CODE REFERENCES: §§ 901 and 1111

## Interim Rule 3014 Election Under § 1111(b) by Secured Creditor in Chapter 9 Municipality or Chapter 11 Reorganization Case[10]

An election of application of § 1111(b)(2) of the Code by a class of secured creditors in a chapter 9 or 11 case may be made at any time prior to the conclusion of the hearing on the disclosure statement or within such later time as the court may fix. If the disclosure statement is conditionally approved pursuant to Rule 3017.1, and a final hearing on the disclosure statement is not held, the election of application of § 1111(b)(2) may be made not later than the date fixed pursuant to Rule 3017.1(a)(2) or another date the court may fix. <u>In a case under subchapter V of chapter 11 in which § 1125 of the Code does not apply, the election may be made not later than a date the court may fix.</u> The election shall be in writing and signed unless made at the hearing on the disclosure statement. The election, if made by the majorities required by § 1111(b)(1)(A)(i), shall be binding on all members of the class with respect to the plan.

## Rule 3015 Filing, Objection to Confirmation, Effect of Confirmation, and Modification of a Plan in a Chapter 12 or a Chapter 13 Case

(*a*) *Filing a Chapter 12 Plan.* The debtor may file a chapter 12 plan with the petition. If a plan is not filed with the petition, it shall be filed within the time prescribed by § 1221 of the Code.

(*b*) *Filing a Chapter 13 Plan.* The debtor may file a chapter 13 plan with the petition. If a plan is not filed with the petition, it shall be filed within 14 days

---

10 ED. NOTE: Interim Rule 3014 has been adopted by the bankruptcy courts to implement the Small Business Reorganization Act of 2019, Pub. L. No. 116-54 (2019). Additions to the existing rule are indicated with underscoring.

BANKRUPTCY RULES

thereafter, and such time may not be further extended except for cause shown and on notice as the court may direct. If a case is converted to chapter 13, a plan shall be filed within 14 days thereafter, and such time may not be further extended except for cause shown and on notice as the court may direct.

(*c*) *Form of Chapter 13 Plan.* If there is an Official Form for a plan filed in a chapter 13 case, that form must be used unless a Local Form has been adopted in compliance with Rule 3015.1. With either the Official Form or a Local Form, a nonstandard provision is effective only if it is included in a section of the form designated for nonstandard provisions and is also identified in accordance with any other requirements of the form. As used in this rule and the Official Form or a Local Form, "nonstandard provision" means a provision not otherwise included in the Official or Local Form or deviating from it.

(*d*) *Notice.* If the plan is not included with the notice of the hearing on confirmation mailed under Rule 2002, the debtor shall serve the plan on the trustee and all creditors when it is filed with the court.

(*e*) *Transmission to United States Trustee.* The clerk shall forthwith transmit to the United States trustee a copy of the plan and any modification thereof filed under subdivision (a) or (b) of this rule.

(*f*) *Objection to Confirmation; Determination of Good Faith in the Absence of an Objection.* An objection to confirmation of a plan shall be filed and served on the debtor, the trustee, and any other entity designated by the court, and shall be transmitted to the United States trustee, at least seven days before the date set for the hearing on confirmation, unless the court orders otherwise. An objection to confirmation is governed by Rule 9014. If no objection is timely filed, the court may determine that the plan has been proposed in good faith and not by any means forbidden by law without receiving evidence on such issues.

(*g*) *Effect of Confirmation.* Upon the confirmation of a chapter 12 or chapter 13 plan:

(*1*) any determination in the plan made under Rule 3012 about the amount of a secured claim is binding on the holder of the claim, even if the holder files a contrary proof of claim or the debtor schedules that claim, and regardless of whether an objection to the claim has been filed; and

(*2*) any request in the plan to terminate the stay imposed by § 362(a), § 1201(a), or § 1301(a) is granted.

(*h*) *Modification of Plan after Confirmation.* A request to modify a plan under § 1229 or § 1329 of the Code shall identify the proponent and shall be filed together with the proposed modification. The clerk, or some other person as the court may direct, shall give the debtor, the trustee, and all creditors not less than 21 days' notice by mail of the time fixed for filing objections and, if an objection is filed, the hearing to consider the proposed modification, unless the court orders otherwise with respect to creditors who are not affected by the proposed modification. A copy of the notice shall be transmitted to the United States trustee. A copy of the proposed modification, or a summary thereof, shall be included with the notice. Any objection to the proposed modification shall be filed and served on the debtor, the trustee, and any other entity designated by the court, and shall be transmitted to the United States trustee. An objection to a proposed modification is governed by Rule 9014.

BANKRUPTCY CODE REFERENCES: §§ 1221, 1229, 1321 and 1329

### Rule 3015.1 Requirements for a Local Form for Plans Filed in a Chapter 13 Case

Notwithstanding Rule 9029(a)(1), a district may require that a Local Form for a plan filed in a chapter 13 case be used instead of an Official Form adopted for that purpose if the following conditions are satisfied:

(*a*) a single Local Form is adopted for the district after public notice and an opportunity for public comment;

(*b*) each paragraph is numbered and labeled in boldface type with a heading stating the general subject matter of the paragraph;

(*c*) the Local Form includes an initial paragraph for the debtor to indicate that the plan does or does not:

(*1*) contain any nonstandard provision;

(*2*) limit the amount of a secured claim based on a valuation of the collateral for the claim; or

(*3*) avoid a security interest or lien;

(*d*) the Local Form contains separate paragraphs for:

(*1*) curing any default and maintaining payments on a claim secured by the debtor's principal residence;

(*2*) paying a domestic-support obligation;

(*3*) paying a claim described in the final paragraph of § 1325(a) of the Bankruptcy Code; and

(*4*) surrendering property that secures a claim with a request that the stay under §§ 362(a) and 1301(a) be terminated as to the surrendered collateral; and

(*e*) the Local Form contains a final paragraph for:

(*1*) the placement of nonstandard provisions, as defined in Rule 3015(c), along with a statement that any nonstandard provision placed elsewhere in the plan is void; and

(*2*) certification by the debtor's attorney or by an unrepresented debtor that the plan contains no nonstandard provision other than those set out in the final paragraph.

BANKRUPTCY CODE REFERENCE: § 1321

## Rule 3016 Filing of Plan and Disclosure Statement in a Chapter 9 Municipality or Chapter 11 Reorganization Case

(*a*) *Identification of Plan.* Every proposed plan and any modification thereof shall be dated and, in a chapter 11 case, identified with the name of the entity or entities submitting or filing it.

(*b*) *Disclosure Statement.* In a chapter 9 or 11 case, a disclosure statement under § 1125 of the Code or evidence showing compliance with § 1126(b) shall be filed with the plan or within a time fixed by the court, unless the plan is intended to provide adequate information under § 1125(f)(1). If the plan is intended to provide adequate information under § 1125(f)(1), it shall be so designated and Rule 3017.1 shall apply as if the plan is a disclosure statement.

(*c*) *Injunction Under a Plan.* If a plan provides for an injunction against conduct not otherwise enjoined under the Code, the plan and disclosure statement shall describe in specific and conspicuous language (bold, italic, or underlined text) all acts to be enjoined and identify the entities that would be subject to the injunction.

(*d*) *Standard Form Small Business Disclosure Statement and Plan.* In a small business case, the court may approve a disclosure statement and may confirm a plan that conform substantially to the appropriate Official Forms or other standard forms approved by the court.

BANKRUPTCY CODE REFERENCES: §§ 941, 1121 and 1125

## Interim Rule 3016 Filing of Plan and Disclosure Statement in a Chapter 9 Municipality or Chapter 11 Reorganization Case[11]

(*a*) *Identification of Plan.* Every proposed plan and any modification thereof shall be dated and, in a chapter 11 case, identified with the name of the entity or entities submitting or filing it.

(*b*) *Disclosure Statement.* In a chapter 9 or 11 case, a disclosure statement, if required under § 1125 of the Code, or evidence showing compliance with § 1126(b) shall be filed with the plan or within a time fixed by the court, unless the plan is intended to provide adequate information under § 1125(f)(1). If the plan is intended to provide adequate information under § 1125(f)(1), it shall be so designated, and Rule 3017.1 shall apply as if the plan is a disclosure statement.

* * * * *

(*d*) *Standard Form Small Business Disclosure Statement and Plan.* In a small business case or a case under subchapter V of chapter 11, the court may approve a disclosure statement and may confirm a plan that conform substantially to the appropriate Official Forms or other standard forms approved by the court.

---

[11] ED. NOTE: Interim Rule 3016 has been adopted by the bankruptcy courts to implement the Small Business Reorganization Act of 2019, Pub. L. No. 116-54 (2019). Additions to the existing rule are indicated with underscoring.

## Rule 3017 Court Consideration of Disclosure Statement in a Chapter 9 Municipality or Chapter 11 Reorganization Case

(*a*) *Hearing on Disclosure Statement and Objections.* Except as provided in Rule 3017.1, after a disclosure statement is filed in accordance with Rule 3016(b), the court shall hold a hearing on at least 28 days' notice to the debtor, creditors, equity security holders and other parties in interest as provided in Rule 2002 to consider the disclosure statement and any objections or modifications thereto. The plan and the disclosure statement shall be mailed with the notice of the hearing only to the debtor, any trustee or committee appointed under the Code, the Securities and Exchange Commission, and any party in interest who requests in writing a copy of the statement or plan. Objections to the disclosure statement shall be filed and served on the debtor, the trustee, any committee appointed under the Code, and any other entity designated by the court, at any time before the disclosure statement is approved or by an earlier date as the court may fix. In a chapter 11 reorganization case, every notice, plan, disclosure statement, and objection required to be served or mailed pursuant to this subdivision shall be transmitted to the United States trustee within the time provided in this subdivision.

(*b*) *Determination on Disclosure Statement.* Following the hearing the court shall determine whether the disclosure statement should be approved.

(*c*) *Dates Fixed for Voting on Plan and Confirmation.* On or before approval of the disclosure statement, the court shall fix a time within which the holders of claims and interests may accept or reject the plan and may fix a date for the hearing on confirmation.

(*d*) *Transmission and Notice to United States Trustee, Creditors, and Equity Security Holders.* Upon approval of a disclosure statement,—except to the extent that the court orders otherwise with respect to one or more unimpaired classes of creditors or equity security holders—the debtor in possession, trustee, proponent of the plan, or clerk as the court orders shall mail to all creditors and equity security holders, and in a chapter 11 reorganization case shall transmit to the United States trustee,

(*1*) the plan or a court-approved summary of the plan;

(*2*) the disclosure statement approved by the court;

(*3*) notice of the time within which acceptances and rejections of the plan may be filed; and

(*4*) any other information as the court may direct, including any court opinion approving the disclosure statement or a court-approved summary of the opinion.

In addition, notice of the time fixed for filing objections and the hearing on confirmation shall be mailed to all creditors and equity security holders in accordance with Rule 2002(b), and a form of ballot conforming to the appropriate Official Form shall be mailed to creditors and equity security holders entitled to vote on the plan. If the court opinion is not transmitted or only a summary of the plan is transmitted, the court opinion or the plan shall be provided on request of a party in interest at the plan proponent's expense. If the court orders that the disclosure statement and the plan or a summary of the plan shall not be mailed to any unimpaired class, notice that the class is designated in the plan as unimpaired and notice of the name and address of the person from whom the plan or summary of the plan and disclosure statement may be obtained upon request and at the plan proponent's expense, shall be mailed to members of the unimpaired class together with the notice of the time fixed for filing objections to and the hearing on confirmation. For the purposes of this subdivision, creditors and equity security holders shall include holders of stock, bonds, debentures, notes, and other securities of record on the date the order approving the disclosure statement is entered or another date fixed by the court, for cause, after notice and a hearing.

(*e*) *Transmission to Beneficial Holders of Securities.* At the hearing held pursuant to subdivision (a) of this rule, the court shall consider the procedures for transmitting the documents and information required by subdivision (d) of this rule to beneficial holders of stock, bonds, debentures, notes, and other securities, determine the adequacy of the procedures, and enter any orders the court deems appropriate.

(*f*) *Notice and Transmission of Documents to Entities Subject to an Injunction Under a Plan.* If a plan provides for an injunction against conduct not otherwise enjoined under the Code and an entity that would be subject to the injunction is not a creditor or equity security holder, at the hearing held under Rule 3017(a), the court shall consider procedures for providing the entity with:

(*1*) at least 28 days' notice of the time fixed for filing objections and the hearing on confirmation of the plan containing the information described in Rule 2002(c)(3); and

(*2*) to the extent feasible, a copy of the plan and disclosure statement.

Bankruptcy Code References: §§ 1125 and 1126

## Rule 3017.1 Court Consideration of Disclosure Statement in a Small Business Case

(*a*) *Conditional Approval of Disclosure Statement.* In a small business case, the court may, on application of the plan proponent or on its own initiative, conditionally approve a disclosure statement filed in accordance with Rule 3016. On or before conditional approval of the disclosure statement, the court shall:

(*1*) fix a time within which the holders of claims and interests may accept or reject the plan;

(*2*) fix a time for filing objections to the disclosure statement;

(*3*) fix a date for the hearing on final approval of the disclosure statement to be held if a timely objection is filed; and

(*4*) fix a date for the hearing on confirmation.

(*b*) *Application of Rule 3017.* Rule 3017(a), (b), (c), and (e) do not apply to a conditionally approved disclosure statement. Rule 3017(d) applies to a conditionally approved disclosure statement, except that conditional approval is considered approval of the disclosure statement for the purpose of applying Rule 3017(d).

(c) *Final Approval.*

(1) *Notice.* Notice of the time fixed for filing objections and the hearing to consider final approval of the disclosure statement shall be given in accordance with Rule 2002 and may be combined with notice of the hearing on confirmation of the plan.

(2) *Objections.* Objections to the disclosure statement shall be filed, transmitted to the United States trustee, and served on the debtor, the trustee, any committee appointed under the Code and any other entity designated by the court at any time before final approval of the disclosure statement or by an earlier date as the court may fix.

(3) *Hearing.* If a timely objection to the disclosure statement is filed, the court shall hold a hearing to consider final approval before or combined with the hearing on confirmation of the plan.

BANKRUPTCY CODE REFERENCES: §§ 101, 1116, 1121 and 1125

## Interim Rule 3017.1 Court Consideration of Disclosure Statement in a Small Business Case or in a Case Under Subchapter V of Chapter 11[12]

(a) *Conditional Approval of Disclosure Statement.* In a small business case or in a case under subchapter V of chapter 11 in which the court has ordered that § 1125 applies, the court may, on application of the plan proponent or on its own initiative, Conditionally approve a disclosure statement filed in accordance with Rule 3016. On or before conditional approval of the disclosure statement, the court shall:

(1) fix a time within which the holders of claims and interests may accept or reject the plan;

(2) fix a time for filing objections to the disclosure statement;

(3) fix a date for the hearing on final approval of the disclosure statement to be held if a timely objection is filed; and

(4) fix a date for the hearing on confirmation.

* * * * *

## Interim Rule 3017.2 Fixing of Dates by the Court in Subchapter V Cases in Which There Is No Disclosure Statement[13]

In a case under subchapter V of chapter 11 in which § 1125 does not apply, the court shall:

[12] ED. NOTE: Interim Rule 3017.1 has been adopted by the bankruptcy courts to implement the Small Business Reorganization Act of 2019, Pub. L. No. 116-54 (2019). Additions to the existing rule are indicated with underscoring.

[13] ED. NOTE: Interim Rule 3017.2 has been adopted by the bankruptcy courts to implement the Small Business Reorganization Act of 2019, Pub. L. No. 116-54 (2019). The rule is new.

(*a*) fix a time within which the holders of claims and interests may accept or reject the plan;

(*b*) fix a date on which an equity security holder or creditor whose claim is based on a security must be the holder of record of the security in order to be eligible to accept or reject the plan;

(*c*) fix a date for the hearing on confirmation; and

(*d*) fix a date for transmission of the plan, notice of the time within which the holders of claims and interests may accept or reject the plan, and notice of the date for the hearing on confirmation.

### Rule 3018 Acceptance or Rejection of Plan in a Chapter 9 Municipality or a Chapter 11 Reorganization Case

(*a*) *Entities Entitled to Accept or Reject Plan; Time for Acceptance or Rejection.* A plan may be accepted or rejected in accordance with § 1126 of the Code within the time fixed by the court pursuant to Rule 3017. Subject to subdivision (b) of this rule, an equity security holder or creditor whose claim is based on a security of record shall not be entitled to accept or reject a plan unless the equity security holder or creditor is the holder of record of the security on the date the order approving the disclosure statement is entered or on another date fixed by the court, for cause, after notice and a hearing. For cause shown, the court after notice and hearing may permit a creditor or equity security holder to change or withdraw an acceptance or rejection. Notwithstanding objection to a claim or interest, the court after notice and hearing may temporarily allow the claim or interest in an amount which the court deems proper for the purpose of accepting or rejecting a plan.

(*b*) *Acceptances or Rejections Obtained Before Petition.* An equity security holder or creditor whose claim is based on a security of record who accepted or rejected the plan before the commencement of the case shall not be deemed to have accepted or rejected the plan pursuant to § 1126(b) of the Code unless the equity security holder or creditor was the holder of record of the security on the date specified in the solicitation of such acceptance or rejection for the purposes of such solicitation. A holder of a claim or interest who has accepted or rejected a plan before the commencement of the case under the Code shall not be deemed to have accepted or rejected the plan if the court finds after notice and hearing that the plan was not transmitted to substantially all creditors and equity security holders of the same class, that an unreasonably short time was prescribed for such creditors and equity security holders to accept or reject the plan, or that the solicitation was not in compliance with § 1126(b) of the Code.

(*c*) *Form of Acceptance or Rejection.* An acceptance or rejection shall be in writing, identify the plan or plans accepted or rejected, be signed by the creditor or equity security holder or an authorized agent, and conform to the appropriate Official Form. If more than one plan is transmitted pursuant to Rule 3017, an acceptance or rejection may be filed by each creditor or equity security holder for any number of plans transmitted and if acceptances are filed for more than one plan, the creditor or equity security holder may indicate a preference or preferences among the plans so accepted.

(*d*) *Acceptance or Rejection by Partially Secured Creditor.* A creditor whose claim has been allowed in part as a secured claim and in part as an unsecured claim shall be entitled to accept or reject a plan in both capacities.

Bankruptcy Code Reference: § 1126

**Interim Rule 3018 Acceptance or Rejection of Plan in a Chapter 9 Municipality or a Chapter 11 Reorganization Case**[14]

(*a*) *Entities Entitled to Accept or Reject Plan; Time for Acceptance or Rejection.* A plan may be accepted or rejected in accordance with § 1126 of the Code within the time fixed by the court pursuant to Rule 3017, 3017.1, or 3017.2. Subject to subdivision (b) of this rule, an equity security holder or creditor whose claim is based on a security of record shall not be entitled to accept or reject a plan unless the equity security holder or creditor is the holder of record of the security on the date the order approving the disclosure statement is entered or on another date fixed by the court under Rule 3017.2, or fixed for cause after notice and a hearing. For cause shown, the court after notice and hearing may permit a creditor or equity security holder to change or withdraw an acceptance or rejection. Notwithstanding objection to a claim or interest, the court after notice and hearing may temporarily allow the claim or interest in an amount which the court deems proper for the purpose of accepting or rejecting a plan.

* * * * *

**Rule 3019 Modification of Accepted Plan in a Chapter 9 Municipality or a Chapter 11 Reorganization Case**

(*a*) *Modification of Plan Before Confirmation.* In a chapter 9 or chapter 11 case, after a plan has been accepted and before its confirmation, the proponent may file a modification of the plan. If the court finds after hearing on notice to the trustee, any committee appointed under the Code, and any other entity designated by the court that the proposed modification does not adversely change the treatment of the claim of any creditor or the interest of any equity security holder who has not accepted in writing the modification, it shall be deemed accepted by all creditors and equity security holders who have previously accepted the plan.

(*b*) *Modification of Plan After Confirmation in Individual Debtor Case.* If the debtor is an individual, a request to modify the plan under § 1127(e) of the Code is governed by Rule 9014. The request shall identify the proponent and shall be filed together with the proposed modification. The clerk, or some other person as the court may direct, shall give the debtor, the trustee, and all creditors not less than 21 days' notice by mail of the time fixed to file objections and, if an objection is filed, the hearing to consider the proposed modification, unless the court orders otherwise with respect to creditors who are not affected by the proposed modification. A copy of the notice shall be transmitted to the United States trustee, together with a copy of the proposed modification. Any objection to the proposed modification shall be filed and served on the debtor, the proponent of

BANKRUPTCY RULES

[14] Ed. Note: Interim Rule 3018 has been adopted by the bankruptcy courts to implement the Small Business Reorganization Act of 2019, Pub. L. No. 116-54 (2019). Additions to the existing rule are indicated with underscoring.

the modification, the trustee, and any other entity designated by the court, and shall be transmitted to the United States trustee.

Bankruptcy Code References: §§ 942 and 1127

## Interim Rule 3019 Modification of Accepted Plan in a Chapter 9 Municipality or a Chapter 11 Reorganization Case[15]

* * * * *

(*b*) *Modification of Plan After Confirmation in Individual Debtor Case.* If the debtor is an individual, a request to modify the plan under § 1127(e) of the Code is governed by Rule 9014. The request shall identify the proponent and shall be filed together with the proposed modification. The clerk, or some other person as the court may direct, shall give the debtor, the trustee, and all creditors not less than 21 days' notice by mail of the time fixed to file objections and, if an objection is filed, the hearing to consider the proposed modification, unless the court orders otherwise with respect to creditors who are not affected by the proposed modification. A copy of the notice shall be transmitted to the United States trustee, together with a copy of the proposed modification. Any objection to the proposed modification shall be filed and served on the debtor, the proponent of the modification, the trustee, and any other entity designated by the court, and shall be transmitted to the United States trustee.

(*c*) *Modification of Plan After Confirmation in Subchapter V Case.* In a case under subchapter V of chapter 11, a request to modify the plan under § 1193(b) or (c) of the Code is governed by Rule 9014, and the provisions of this Rule 3019(b) apply.

## Rule 3020 Deposit; Confirmation of Plan in a Chapter 9 Municipality or Chapter 11 Reorganization Case

(*a*) *Deposit.* In a chapter 11 case, prior to entry of the order confirming the plan, the court may order the deposit with the trustee or debtor in possession of the consideration required by the plan to be distributed on confirmation. Any money deposited shall be kept in a special account established for the exclusive purpose of making the distribution.

(*b*) *Objection to and Hearing on Confirmation in a Chapter 9 or Chapter 11 Case.*

(*1*) *Objection.* An objection to confirmation of the plan shall be filed and served on the debtor, the trustee, the proponent of the plan, any committee appointed under the Code and any other entity designated by the court, within a time fixed by the court. Unless the case is a chapter 9 municipality case, a copy of every objection to confirmation shall be transmitted by the objecting party to the United States trustee within the time fixed for filing objections. An objection to confirmation is governed by Rule 9014.

(*2*) *Hearing.* The court shall rule on confirmation of the plan after notice and hearing as provided in Rule 2002. If no objection is timely filed, the court may

---

[15] Ed. note: Interim Rule 3019 has been adopted by the bankruptcy courts to implement the Small Business Reorganization Act of 2019, Pub. L. No. 116-54 (2019). Additions to the existing rule are indicated with underscoring.

determine that the plan has been proposed in good faith and not by any means forbidden by law without receiving evidence on such issues.

(c) *Order of Confirmation.*

(*1*) The order of confirmation shall conform to the appropriate Official Form. If the plan provides for an injunction against conduct not otherwise enjoined under the Code, the order of confirmation shall (1) describe in reasonable detail all acts enjoined; (2) be specific in its terms regarding the injunction; and (3) identify the entities subject to the injunction.

(*2*) Notice of entry of the order of confirmation shall be mailed promptly to the debtor, the trustee, creditors, equity security holders, other parties in interest, and, if known, to any identified entity subject to an injunction provided for in the plan against conduct not otherwise enjoined under the Code.

(*3*) Except in a chapter 9 municipality case, notice of entry of the order of confirmation shall be transmitted to the United States trustee as provided in Rule 2002(k).

(*d*) *Retained Power.* Notwithstanding the entry of the order of confirmation, the court may issue any other order necessary to administer the estate.

(*e*) *Stay of Confirmation Order.* An order confirming a plan is stayed until the expiration of 14 days after the entry of the order, unless the court orders otherwise.

Bankruptcy Code References: §§ 944, 1128 and 1129

## Rule 3021 Distribution Under Plan

Except as provided in Rule 3020(e), after a plan is confirmed, distribution shall be made to creditors whose claims have been allowed, to interest holders whose interests have not been disallowed, and to indenture trustees who have filed claims under Rule 3003(c)(5) that have been allowed. For purposes of this rule, creditors include holders of bonds, debentures, notes, and other debt securities, and interest holders include the holders of stock and other equity securities, of record at the time of commencement of distribution, unless a different time is fixed by the plan or the order confirming the plan.

Bankruptcy Code References: §§ 502, 1142, 1143, 1226 and 1326

## Rule 3022 Final Decree in Chapter 11 Reorganization Case

After an estate is fully administered in a chapter 11 reorganization case, the court, on its own motion or on motion of a party in interest, shall enter a final decree closing the case.

Bankruptcy Code Reference: § 350

# PART IV

# THE DEBTOR: DUTIES AND BENEFITS

## Rule 4001 Relief from Automatic Stay; Prohibiting or Conditioning the Use, Sale, or Lease of Property; Use of Cash Collateral; Obtaining Credit; Agreements

(*a*) *Relief from Stay; Prohibiting or Conditioning the Use, Sale, or Lease of Property.*

(*1*) *Motion.* A motion for relief from an automatic stay provided by the Code or a motion to prohibit or condition the use, sale, or lease of property pursuant to § 363(e) shall be made in accordance with Rule 9014 and shall be served on any committee elected pursuant to § 705 or appointed pursuant to § 1102 of the Code or its authorized agent, or, if the case is a chapter 9 municipality case or a chapter 11 reorganization case and no committee of unsecured creditors has been appointed pursuant to § 1102, on the creditors included on the list filed pursuant to Rule 1007(d), and on such other entities as the court may direct.

(*2*) *Ex Parte Relief.* Relief from a stay under § 362(a) or a request to prohibit or condition the use, sale, or lease of property pursuant to § 363(e) may be granted without prior notice only if (A) it clearly appears from specific facts shown by affidavit or by a verified motion that immediate and irreparable injury, loss, or damage will result to the movant before the adverse party or the attorney for the adverse party can be heard in opposition, and (B) the movant's attorney certifies to the court in writing the efforts, if any, which have been made to give notice and the reasons why notice should not be required. The party obtaining relief under this subdivision and § 362(f) or § 363(e) shall immediately give oral notice thereof to the trustee or debtor in possession and to the debtor and forthwith mail or otherwise transmit to such adverse party or parties a copy of the order granting relief. On two days notice to the party who obtained relief from the stay without notice or on shorter notice to that party as the court may prescribe, the adverse party may appear and move reinstatement of the stay or reconsideration of the order prohibiting or conditioning the use, sale, or lease of property. In that event, the court shall proceed expeditiously to hear and determine the motion.

(*3*) *Stay of Order.* An order granting a motion for relief from an automatic stay made in accordance with Rule 4001(a)(1) is stayed until the expiration of 14 days after the entry of the order, unless the court orders otherwise.

(*b*) *Use of Cash Collateral.*

(*1*) *Motion; Service.*

(*A*) *Motion.* A motion for authority to use cash collateral shall be made in accordance with Rule 9014 and shall be accompanied by a proposed form of order.

(*B*) *Contents.* The motion shall consist of or (if the motion is more than five pages in length) begin with a concise statement of the relief requested, not to exceed five pages, that lists or summarizes, and sets out the location within the relevant documents of, all material provisions, including:

(*i*) the name of each entity with an interest in the cash collateral;

(*ii*) the purposes for the use of the cash collateral;

(*iii*) the material terms, including duration, of the use of the cash collateral; and

(*iv*) any liens, cash payments, or other adequate protection that will be provided to each entity with an interest in the cash collateral or, if no additional adequate protection is proposed, an explanation of why each entity's interest is adequately protected.

(*C*) *Service.* The motion shall be served on: (1) any entity with an interest in the cash collateral; (2) any committee elected under § 705 or appointed under § 1102 of the Code, or its authorized agent, or, if the case is a chapter 9 municipality case or a chapter 11 reorganization case and no committee of unsecured creditors has been appointed under § 1102, the creditors included on the list filed under Rule 1007(d); and (3) any other entity that the court directs.

(2) *Hearing.* The court may commence a final hearing on a motion for authorization to use cash collateral no earlier than 14 days after service of the motion. If the motion so requests, the court may conduct a preliminary hearing before such 14 day period expires, but the court may authorize the use of only that amount of cash collateral as is necessary to avoid immediate and irreparable harm to the estate pending a final hearing.

(3) *Notice.* Notice of hearing pursuant to this subdivision shall be given to the parties on whom service of the motion is required by paragraph (1) of this subdivision and to such other entities as the court may direct.

(c) *Obtaining Credit.*

(1) *Motion; Service.*

(*A*) *Motion.* A motion for authority to obtain credit shall be made in accordance with Rule 9014 and shall be accompanied by a copy of the credit agreement and a proposed form of order.

(*B*) *Contents.* The motion shall consist of or (if the motion is more than five pages in length) begin with a concise statement of the relief requested, not to exceed five pages, that lists or summarizes, and sets out the location within the relevant documents of, all material provisions of the proposed credit agreement and form of order, including interest rate, maturity, events of default, liens, borrowing limits, and borrowing conditions. If the proposed credit agreement or form of order includes any of the provisions listed below, the concise statement shall also: briefly list or summarize each one; identify its specific location in the proposed agreement and form of order; and identify any such provision that is proposed to remain in effect if interim approval is granted, but final relief is denied, as provided under Rule

4001(c)(2). In addition, the motion shall describe the nature and extent of each provision listed below:

(*i*) a grant of priority or a lien on property of the estate under § 364(c) or (d);

(*ii*) the providing of adequate protection or priority for a claim that arose before the commencement of the case, including the granting of a lien on property of the estate to secure the claim, or the use of property of the estate or credit obtained under § 364 to make cash payments on account of the claim;

(*iii*) a determination of the validity, enforceability, priority, or amount of a claim that arose before the commencement of the case, or of any lien securing the claim;

(*iv*) a waiver or modification of Code provisions or applicable rules relating to the automatic stay;

(*v*) a waiver or modification of any entity's authority or right to file a plan, seek an extension of time in which the debtor has the exclusive right to file a plan, request the use of cash collateral under § 363(c), or request authority to obtain credit under § 364;

(*vi*) the establishment of deadlines for filing a plan of reorganization, for approval of a disclosure statement, for a hearing on confirmation, or for entry of a confirmation order;

(*vii*) a waiver or modification of the applicability of nonbankruptcy law relating to the perfection of a lien on property of the estate, or on the foreclosure or other enforcement of the lien;

(*viii*) a release, waiver, or limitation on any claim or other cause of action belonging to the estate or the trustee, including any modification of the statute of limitations or other deadline to commence an action;

(*ix*) the indemnification of any entity;

(*x*) a release, waiver, or limitation of any right under § 506(c); or

(*xi*) the granting of a lien on any claim or cause of action arising under §§ 544, 545, 547, 548, 549, 553(b), 723(a), or 724(a).

(C) *Service.* The motion shall be served on: (1) any committee elected under § 705 or appointed under § 1102 of the Code, or its authorized agent, or, if the case is a chapter 9 municipality case or a chapter 11 reorganization case and no committee of unsecured creditors has been appointed under § 1102, on the creditors included on the list filed under Rule 1007(d); and (2) on any other entity that the court directs.

(2) *Hearing.* The court may commence a final hearing on a motion for authority to obtain credit no earlier than 14 days after service of the motion. If the motion so requests, the court may conduct a hearing before such 14 day period expires, but the court may authorize the obtaining of credit only to the

extent necessary to avoid immediate and irreparable harm to the estate pending a final hearing.

(3) *Notice.* Notice of hearing pursuant to this subdivision shall be given to the parties on whom service of the motion is required by paragraph (1) of this subdivision and to such other entities as the court may direct.

(4) *Inapplicability in a Chapter 13 Case.* This subdivision (c) does not apply in a chapter 13 case.

(*d*) *Agreement Relating to Relief from the Automatic Stay, Prohibiting or Conditioning the Use, Sale, or Lease of Property, Providing Adequate Protection, Use of Cash Collateral, and Obtaining Credit.*

(*1*) *Motion; Service.*

(*A*) *Motion.* A motion for approval of any of the following shall be accompanied by a copy of the agreement and a proposed form of order:

(*i*) an agreement to provide adequate protection;

(*ii*) an agreement to prohibit or condition the use, sale, or lease of property;

(*iii*) an agreement to modify or terminate the stay provided for in § 362;

(*iv*) an agreement to use cash collateral; or

(*v*) an agreement between the debtor and an entity that has a lien or interest in property of the estate pursuant to which the entity consents to the creation of a lien senior or equal to the entity's lien or interest in such property.

(*B*) *Contents.* The motion shall consist of or (if the motion is more than five pages in length) begin with a concise statement of the relief requested, not to exceed five pages, that lists or summarizes, and sets out the location within the relevant documents of, all material provisions of the agreement. In addition, the concise statement shall briefly list or summarize, and identify the specific location of, each provision in the proposed form of order, agreement, or other document of the type listed in subdivision (c)(1)(B). The motion shall also describe the nature and extent of each such provision.

(*C*) *Service.* The motion shall be served on: (1) any committee elected under § 705 or appointed under § 1102 of the Code, or its authorized agent, or, if the case is a chapter 9 municipality case or a chapter 11 reorganization case and no committee of unsecured creditors has been appointed under § 1102, on the creditors included on the list filed under Rule 1007(d); and (2) on any other entity the court directs.

(2) *Objection.* Notice of the motion and the time within which objections may be filed and served on the debtor in possession or trustee shall be mailed to the parties on whom service is required by paragraph (1) of this subdivision and to

BANKRUPTCY RULES

such other entities as the court may direct. Unless the court fixes a different time, objections may be filed within 14 days of the mailing of notice.

(3) *Disposition; Hearing.* If no objection is filed, the court may enter an order approving or disapproving the agreement without conducting a hearing. If an objection is filed or if the court determines a hearing is appropriate, the court shall hold a hearing on no less than seven days' notice to the objector, the movant, the parties on whom service is required by paragraph (1) of this subdivision and such other entities as the court may direct.

(4) *Agreement in Settlement of Motion.* The court may direct that the procedures prescribed in paragraphs (1), (2), and (3) of this subdivision shall not apply and the agreement may be approved without further notice if the court determines that a motion made pursuant to subdivisions (a), (b), or (c) of this rule was sufficient to afford reasonable notice of the material provisions of the agreement and opportunity for a hearing.

Bankruptcy Code References: §§ 362, 363, 364, 1201 and 1301

## Rule 4002 Duties of Debtor

(*a*) *In General.* In addition to performing other duties prescribed by the Code and rules, the debtor shall

(*1*) attend and submit to an examination at the times ordered by the court;

(*2*) attend the hearing on a complaint objecting to discharge and testify, if called as a witness;

(*3*) inform the trustee immediately in writing as to the location of real property in which the debtor has an interest and the name and address of every person holding money or property subject to the debtor's withdrawal or order if a schedule of property has not yet been filed pursuant to Rule 1007;

(*4*) cooperate with the trustee in the preparation of an inventory, the examination of proofs of claim, and the administration of the estate, and

(*5*) file a statement of any change of the debtor's address.

(*b*) *Individual Debtor's Duty to Provide Documentation.*

(*1*) *Personal Identification.* Every individual debtor shall bring to the meeting of creditors under § 341:

(*A*) a picture identification issued by a governmental unit, or other personal identifying information that establishes the debtor's identity; and

(*B*) evidence of social-security number(s), or a written statement that such documentation does not exist.

(*2*) *Financial Information.* Every individual debtor shall bring to the meeting of creditors under § 341, and make available to the trustee, the following documents or copies of them, or provide a written statement that the documentation does not exist or is not in the debtor's possession:

(*A*) evidence of current income such as the most recent payment advice;

(*B*) unless the trustee or the United States trustee instructs otherwise, statements for each of the debtor's depository and investment accounts, including checking, savings, and money market accounts, mutual funds and brokerage accounts for the time period that includes the date of the filing of the petition; and

(*C*) documentation of monthly expenses claimed by the debtor if required by § 707(b)(2)(A) or (B).

(*3*) *Tax Return.* At least 7 days before the first date set for the meeting of creditors under § 341, the debtor shall provide to the trustee a copy of the debtor's federal income tax return for the most recent tax year ending immediately before the commencement of the case and for which a return was filed, including any attachments, or a transcript of the tax return, or provide a written statement that the documentation does not exist.

(*4*) *Tax Returns Provided to Creditors.* If a creditor, at least 14 days before the first date set for the meeting of creditors under § 341, requests a copy of the debtor's tax return that is to be provided to the trustee under subdivision (b)(3), the debtor, at least 7 days before the first date set for the meeting of creditors under § 341, shall provide to the requesting creditor a copy of the return, including any attachments, or a transcript of the tax return, or provide a written statement that the documentation does not exist.

(*5*) *Confidentiality of Tax Information.* The debtor's obligation to provide tax returns under Rule 4002(b)(3) and (b)(4) is subject to procedures for safeguarding the confidentiality of tax information established by the Director of the Administrative Office of the United States Courts.

Bankruptcy Code References: §§ 341, 343 and 521

## Rule 4003 Exemptions

(*a*) *Claim of Exemptions.* A debtor shall list the property claimed as exempt under § 522 of the Code on the schedule of assets required to be filed by Rule 1007. If the debtor fails to claim exemptions or file the schedule within the time specified in Rule 1007, a dependent of the debtor may file the list within 30 days thereafter.

(*b*) *Objecting to a Claim of Exemptions.*

(*1*) Except as provided in paragraphs (2) and (3), a party in interest may file an objection to the list of property claimed as exempt only within 30 days after the meeting of creditors held under § 341(a) is concluded or within 30 days after any amendment to the list or supplemental schedules is filed, whichever is later. The court may, for cause, extend the time for filing objections if, before the time to object expires, a party in interest files a request for an extension.

(*2*) The trustee may file an objection to a claim of exemption at any time prior to one year after the closing of the case if the debtor fraudulently asserted the claim of exemption. The trustee shall deliver or mail the objection to the debtor and the debtor's attorney, and to any person filing the list of exempt property and that person's attorney.

(*3*) An objection to a claim of exemption based on § 522(q) shall be filed before the closing of the case. If an exemption is first claimed after a case is reopened, an objection shall be filed before the reopened case is closed.

(*4*) A copy of any objection shall be delivered or mailed to the trustee, the debtor and the debtor's attorney, and the person filing the list and that person's attorney.

(*c*) *Burden of Proof.* In any hearing under this rule, the objecting party has the burden of proving that the exemptions are not properly claimed. After hearing on notice, the court shall determine the issues presented by the objections.

(*d*) *Avoidance by Debtor of Transfers of Exempt Property.* A proceeding under § 522(f) to avoid a lien or other transfer of property exempt under the Code shall be commenced by motion in the manner provided by Rule 9014, or by serving a chapter 12 or chapter 13 plan on the affected creditors in the manner provided by Rule 7004 for service of a summons and complaint. Notwithstanding the provisions of subdivision (b), a creditor may object to a request under § 522(f) by challenging the validity of the exemption asserted to be impaired by the lien.

BANKRUPTCY CODE REFERENCE: § 522

## Rule 4004 Grant or Denial of Discharge

(*a*) *Time for Objecting to Discharge; Notice of Time Fixed.* In a chapter 7 case, a complaint, or a motion under § 727(a)(8) or (a)(9) of the Code, objecting to the debtor's discharge shall be filed no later than 60 days after the first date set for the meeting of creditors under § 341(a). In a chapter 11 case, the complaint shall be filed no later than the first date set for the hearing on confirmation. In a chapter 13 case, a motion objecting to the debtor's discharge under § 1328(f) shall be filed no later than 60 days after the first date set for the meeting of creditors under § 341(a). At least 28 days' notice of the time so fixed shall be given to the United States trustee and all creditors as provided in Rule 2002(f) and (k) and to the trustee and the trustee's attorney.

(*b*) *Extension of Time.*

(*1*) On motion of any party in interest, after notice and hearing, the court may for cause extend the time to object to discharge. Except as provided in subdivision (b)(2), the motion shall be filed before the time has expired.

(*2*) A motion to extend the time to object to discharge may be filed after the time for objection has expired and before discharge is granted if (A) the objection is based on facts that, if learned after the discharge, would provide a basis for revocation under § 727(d) of the Code, and (B) the movant did not have knowledge of those facts in time to permit an objection. The motion shall be filed promptly after the movant discovers the facts on which the objection is based.

(*c*) *Grant of Discharge.*

(*1*) In a chapter 7 case, on expiration of the times fixed for objecting to discharge and for filing a motion to dismiss the case under Rule 1017(e), the court shall forthwith grant the discharge, except that the court shall not grant a discharge if:

(*A*) the debtor is not an individual;

(*B*) a complaint, or a motion under § 727(a)(8) or (a)(9), objecting to the discharge has been filed and not decided in the debtor's favor;

(*C*) the debtor has filed a waiver under § 727(a)(10);

(*D*) a motion to dismiss the case under § 707 is pending;

(*E*) a motion to extend the time for filing a complaint objecting to the discharge is pending;

(*F*) a motion to extend the time for filing a motion to dismiss the case under Rule 1017(e)(1) is pending;

(*G*) the debtor has not paid in full the filing fee prescribed by 28 U.S.C. § 1930(a) and any other fee prescribed by the Judicial Conference of the United States under 28 U.S.C. § 1930(b) that is payable to the clerk upon the commencement of a case under the Code, unless the court has waived the fees under 28 U.S.C. § 1930(f);

(*H*) the debtor has not filed with the court a statement of completion of a course concerning personal financial management if required by Rule 1007(b)(7);

(*I*) a motion to delay or postpone discharge under § 727(a)(12) is pending;

(*J*) a motion to enlarge the time to file a reaffirmation agreement under Rule 4008(a) is pending;

(*K*) a presumption is in effect under § 524(m) that a reaffirmation agreement is an undue hardship and the court has not concluded a hearing on the presumption; or

(*L*) a motion is pending to delay discharge, because the debtor has not filed with the court all tax documents required to be filed under § 521(f).

(*2*) Notwithstanding Rule 4004(c)(1), on motion of the debtor, the court may defer the entry of an order granting a discharge for 30 days and, on motion within that period, the court may defer entry of the order to a date certain.

(*3*) If the debtor is required to file a statement under Rule 1007(b)(8), the court shall not grant a discharge earlier than 30 days after the statement is filed.

(*4*) In a chapter 11 case in which the debtor is an individual, or a chapter 13 case, the court shall not grant a discharge if the debtor has not filed any statement required by Rule 1007(b)(7).

(*d*) *Applicability of Rules in Part VII and Rule 9014.* An objection to discharge is governed by Part VII of these rules, except that an objection to discharge under §§ 727(a)(8), (a)(9), or 1328(f) is commenced by motion and governed by Rule

9014.

(*e*) *Order of Discharge.* An order of discharge shall conform to the appropriate Official Form.

(*f*) *Registration in Other Districts.* An order of discharge that has become final may be registered in any other district by filing a certified copy of the order in the office of the clerk of that district. When so registered the order of discharge shall have the same effect as an order of the court of the district where registered.

(*g*) *Notice of Discharge.* The clerk shall promptly mail a copy of the final order of discharge to those specified in subdivision (a) of this rule.

BANKRUPTCY CODE REFERENCES: §§ 707, 727, 1141, 1228 and 1328

BANKRUPTCY STATUTORY REFERENCE: 28 U.S.C. § 1930

### Rule 4005 Burden of Proof in Objecting to Discharge

At the trial on a complaint objecting to a discharge, the plaintiff has the burden of proving the objection.

BANKRUPTCY CODE REFERENCES: §§ 727 and 1141

### Rule 4006 Notice of No Discharge

If an order is entered: denying a discharge; revoking a discharge; approving a waiver of discharge; or, in the case of an individual debtor, closing the case without the entry of a discharge, the clerk shall promptly notify all parties in interest in the manner provided by Rule 2002.

BANKRUPTCY CODE REFERENCES: §§ 108, 362, 727, 1141, 1228 and 1328

### Rule 4007 Determination of Dischargeability of a Debt

(*a*) *Persons Entitled to File Complaint.* A debtor or any creditor may file a complaint to obtain a determination of the dischargeability of any debt.

(*b*) *Time for Commencing Proceeding Other Than Under § 523(c) of the Code.* A complaint other than under § 523(c) may be filed at any time. A case may be reopened without payment of an additional filing fee for the purpose of filing a complaint to obtain a determination under this rule.

(*c*) *Time for Filing Complaint Under § 523(c) in a Chapter 7 Liquidation, Chapter 11 Reorganization, Chapter 12 Family Farmer's Debt Adjustment Case, or Chapter 13 Individual's Debt Adjustment Case; Notice of Time Fixed.* Except as otherwise provided in subdivision (d), a complaint to determine the dischargeability of a debt under § 523(c) shall be filed no later than 60 days after the first date set for the meeting of creditors under § 341(a). The court shall give all creditors no less than 30 days' notice of the time so fixed in the manner provided in Rule 2002. On motion of a party in interest, after hearing on notice, the court may for cause extend the time fixed under this subdivision. The motion shall be filed before the time has expired.

(*d*) *Time for Filing Complaint Under § 523(a)(6) in a Chapter 13 Individual's Debt Adjustment Case; Notice of Time Fixed.* On motion by a debtor for a discharge under § 1328(b), the court shall enter an order fixing the time to file a complaint to determine the dischargeability of any debt under § 523(a)(6) and shall give no less than 30 days' notice of the time fixed to all creditors in the manner provided in Rule 2002. On motion of any party in interest, after hearing on notice, the court may for cause extend the time fixed under this subdivision. The motion shall be filed before the time has expired.

(*e*) *Applicability of Rules in Part VII.* A proceeding commenced by a complaint filed under this rule is governed by Part VII of these rules.

BANKRUPTCY CODE REFERENCES: §§ 523, 707, 727, 1141, 1228 and 1328

## Rule 4008 Filing of Reaffirmation Agreement; Statement in Support of Reaffirmation Agreement

(*a*) *Filing of Reaffirmation Agreement.* A reaffirmation agreement shall be filed no later than 60 days after the first date set for the meeting of creditors under § 341(a) of the Code. The reaffirmation agreement shall be accompanied by a cover sheet, prepared as prescribed by the appropriate Official Form. The court may, at any time and in its discretion, enlarge the time to file a reaffirmation agreement.

(*b*) *Statement in Support of Reaffirmation Agreement.* The debtor's statement required under § 524(k)(6)(A) of the Code shall be accompanied by a statement of the total income and expenses stated on schedules I and J. If there is a difference between the total income and expenses stated on those schedules and the statement required under § 524(k)(6)(A), the statement required by this subdivision shall include an explanation of the difference.

BANKRUPTCY CODE REFERENCE: § 524

# PART V

# COURTS AND CLERKS

## Rule 5001 Courts and Clerks' Offices

(*a*) *Courts Always Open.* The courts shall be deemed always open for the purpose of filing any pleading or other proper paper, issuing and returning process, and filing, making, or entering motions, orders and rules.

(*b*) *Trials and Hearings; Orders in Chambers.* All trials and hearings shall be conducted in open court and so far as convenient in a regular court room. Except as otherwise provided in 28 U.S.C. § 152(c), all other acts or proceedings may be done or conducted by a judge in chambers and at any place either within or without the district; but no hearing, other than one ex parte, shall be conducted outside the district without the consent of all parties affected thereby.

(*c*) *Clerk's Office.* The clerk's office with the clerk or a deputy in attendance shall be open during business hours on all days except Saturdays, Sundays and the legal holidays listed in Rule 9006(a).

Bankruptcy Code Reference: § 107

## Rule 5002 Restrictions on Approval of Appointments

(*a*) *Approval of Appointment of Relatives Prohibited.* The appointment of an individual as a trustee or examiner pursuant to § 1104 of the Code shall not be approved by the court if the individual is a relative of the bankruptcy judge approving the appointment or the United States trustee in the region in which the case is pending. The employment of an individual as an attorney, accountant, appraiser, auctioneer, or other professional person pursuant to §§ 327, 1103, or 1114 shall not be approved by the court if the individual is a relative of the bankruptcy judge approving the employment. The employment of an individual as attorney, accountant, appraiser, auctioneer, or other professional person pursuant to §§ 327, 1103, or 1114 may be approved by the court if the individual is a relative of the United States trustee in the region in which the case is pending, unless the court finds that the relationship with the United States trustee renders the employment improper under the circumstances of the case. Whenever under this subdivision an individual may not be approved for appointment or employment, the individual's firm, partnership, corporation, or any other form of business association or relationship, and all members, associates and professional employees thereof also may not be approved for appointment or employment.

(*b*) *Judicial Determination that Approval of Appointment or Employment Is Improper.* A bankruptcy judge may not approve the appointment of a person as a trustee or examiner pursuant to § 1104 of the Code or approve the employment of a person as an attorney, accountant, appraiser, auctioneer, or other professional person pursuant to §§ 327, 1103, or 1114 of the Code if that person is or has been so connected with such judge or the United States trustee as to render the appointment or employment improper.

Bankruptcy Code References: §§ 101, 102, 327, 332, 333, 1102, 1103, 1104 and 1114

Bankruptcy Statutory Reference: 28 U.S.C. § 455

## Rule 5003 Records Kept by the Clerk

(*a*) *Bankruptcy Dockets.* The clerk shall keep a docket in each case under the Code and shall enter thereon each judgment, order, and activity in that case as prescribed by the Director of the Administrative Office of the United States Courts. The entry of a judgment or order in a docket shall show the date the entry is made.

(*b*) *Claims Register.* The clerk shall keep in a claims register a list of claims filed in a case when it appears that there will be a distribution to unsecured creditors.

(*c*) *Judgments and Orders.* The clerk shall keep, in the form and manner as the Director of the Administrative Office of the United States Courts may prescribe, a correct copy of every final judgment or order affecting title to or lien on real property or for the recovery of money or property, and any other order which the court may direct to be kept. On request of the prevailing party, a correct copy of every judgment or order affecting title to or lien upon real or personal property or for the recovery of money or property shall be kept and indexed with the civil judgments of the district court.

(*d*) *Index of Cases; Certificate of Search.* The clerk shall keep indices of all cases and adversary proceedings as prescribed by the Director of the Administrative Office of the United States Courts. On request, the clerk shall make a search of any index and papers in the clerk's custody and certify whether a case or proceeding has been filed in or transferred to the court or if a discharge has been entered in its records.

(*e*) *Register of Mailing Addresses of Federal and State Governmental Units and Certain Taxing Authorities.* The United States or the state or territory in which the court is located may file a statement designating its mailing address. The United States, state, territory, or local governmental unit responsible for collecting taxes within the district in which the case is pending may also file a statement designating an address for service of requests under § 505(b) of the Code, and the designation shall describe where further information concerning additional requirements for filing such requests may be found. The clerk shall keep, in the form and manner as the Director of the Administrative Office of the United States Courts may prescribe, a register that includes the mailing addresses designated under the first sentence of this subdivision, and a separate register of the addresses designated for the service of requests under § 505(b) of the Code. The clerk is not required to include in any single register more than one mailing address for each department, agency, or instrumentality of the United States or the state or territory. If more than one address for a department, agency, or instrumentality is included in the register, the clerk shall also include information that would enable a user of the register to determine the circumstances when each address is applicable, and mailing notice to only one applicable address is sufficient to provide effective notice. The clerk shall update the register annually, effective January 2 of each year. The mailing address in the register is conclusively presumed to be a proper address for the governmental unit, but the failure to use that mailing address does not invalidate any notice that is otherwise effective under applicable law.

(*f*) *Other Books and Records of the Clerk.* The clerk shall keep any other books and records required by the Director of the Administrative Office of the United States.

BANKRUPTCY CODE REFERENCES: §§ 107 and 505

## Rule 5004 Disqualification

(*a*) *Disqualification of Judge.* A bankruptcy judge shall be governed by 28 U.S.C. § 455, and disqualified from presiding over the proceeding or contested matter in which the disqualifying circumstances[16] arises or, if appropriate, shall be disqualified from presiding over the case.

(*b*) *Disqualification of Judge from Allowing Compensation.* A bankruptcy judge shall be disqualified from allowing compensation to a person who is a relative of the bankruptcy judge or with whom the judge is so connected as to render it improper for the judge to authorize such compensation.

BANKRUPTCY STATUTORY REFERENCE: 28 U.S.C. § 455

## Rule 5005 Filing and Transmittal of Papers

(*a*) *Filing.*

(*1*) *Place of Filing.* The lists, schedules, statements, proofs of claim or interest, complaints, motions, applications, objections and other papers required to be filed by these rules, except as provided in 28 U.S.C. § 1409, shall be filed with the clerk in the district where the case under the Code is pending. The judge of that court may permit the papers to be filed with the judge, in which event the filing date shall be noted thereon, and they shall be forthwith transmitted to the clerk. The clerk shall not refuse to accept for filing any petition or other paper presented for the purpose of filing solely because it is not presented in proper form as required by these rules or any local rules or practices.

(*2*) *Electronic Filing and Signing.*

(*A*) *By a Represented Entity—Generally Required; Exceptions.* An entity represented by an attorney shall file electronically, unless nonelectronic filing is allowed by the court for good cause or is allowed or required by local rule.

(*B*) *By an Unrepresented Individual—When Allowed or Required.* An individual not represented by an attorney:

(*i*) may file electronically only if allowed by court order or by local rule; and

(*ii*) may be required to file electronically only by court order, or by a local rule that includes reasonable exceptions.

(*C*) *Signing.* A filing made through a person's electronic-filing account and

---

[16] ED NOTE: So in original. The word should probably be "circumstance."

authorized by that person, together with that person's name on a signature block, constitutes the person's signature.

(*D*) *Same as a Written Paper.* A paper filed electronically is a written paper for purposes of these rules, the Federal Rules of Civil Procedure made applicable by these rules, and § 107 of the Code.

(*b*) *Transmittal to the United States Trustee.*

(*1*) The complaints, motions, applications, objections and other papers required to be transmitted to the United States trustee by these rules shall be mailed or delivered to an office of the United States trustee, or to another place designated by the United States trustee, in the district where the case under the Code is pending.

(*2*) The entity, other than the clerk, transmitting a paper to the United States trustee shall promptly file as proof of such transmittal a verified statement identifying the paper and stating the date on which it was transmitted to the United States trustee.

(*3*) Nothing in these rules shall require the clerk to transmit any paper to the United States trustee if the United States trustee requests in writing that the paper not be transmitted.

(*c*) *Error in Filing or Transmittal.* A paper intended to be filed with the clerk but erroneously delivered to the United States trustee, the trustee, the attorney for the trustee, a bankruptcy judge, a district judge, the clerk of the bankruptcy appellate panel, or the clerk of the district court shall, after the date of its receipt has been noted thereon, be transmitted forthwith to the clerk of the bankruptcy court. A paper intended to be transmitted to the United States trustee but erroneously delivered to the clerk, the trustee, the attorney for the trustee, a bankruptcy judge, a district judge, the clerk of the bankruptcy appellate panel, or the clerk of the district court shall, after the date of its receipt has been noted thereon, be transmitted forthwith to the United States trustee. In the interest of justice, the court may order that a paper erroneously delivered shall be deemed filed with the clerk or transmitted to the United States trustee as of the date of its original delivery.

**Rule 5006 Certification of Copies of Papers**

The clerk shall issue a certified copy of the record of any proceeding in a case under the Code or of any paper filed with the clerk on payment of any prescribed fee.

**Rule 5007 Record of Proceedings and Transcripts**

(*a*) *Filing of Record or Transcript.* The reporter or operator of a recording device shall certify the original notes of testimony, tape recording, or other original record of the proceeding and promptly file them with the clerk. The person preparing any transcript shall promptly file a certified copy.

(*b*) *Transcript Fees.* The fees for copies of transcripts shall be charged at rates prescribed by the Judicial Conference of the United States. No fee may be charged for the certified copy filed with the clerk.

(c) *Admissibility of Record in Evidence.* A certified sound recording or a transcript of a proceeding shall be admissible as prima facie evidence to establish the record.

## Rule 5008 Notice Regarding Presumption of Abuse in Chapter 7 Cases of Individual Debtors

If a presumption of abuse has arisen under § 707(b) in a chapter 7 case of an individual with primarily consumer debts, the clerk shall within 10 days after the date of the filing of the petition notify creditors of the presumption of abuse in accordance with Rule 2002. If the debtor has not filed a statement indicating whether a presumption of abuse has arisen, the clerk shall within 10 days after the date of the filing of the petition notify creditors that the debtor has not filed the statement and that further notice will be given if a later filed statement indicates that a presumption of abuse has arisen. If a debtor later files a statement indicating that a presumption of abuse has arisen, the clerk shall notify creditors of the presumption of abuse as promptly as practicable.

BANKRUPTCY CODE REFERENCES: §§ 342, 707(b)

## Rule 5009 Closing Chapter 7, Chapter 12, Chapter 13, and Chapter 15 Cases; Order Declaring Lien Satisfied

(a) *Closing of Cases Under Chapters 7, 12, and 13.* If in a chapter 7, chapter 12, or chapter 13 case the trustee has filed a final report and final account and has certified that the estate has been fully administered, and if within 30 days no objection has been filed by the United States trustee or a party in interest, there shall be a presumption that the estate has been fully administered.

(b) *Notice of Failure to File Rule 1007(b)(7) Statement.* If an individual debtor in a chapter 7 or 13 case is required to file a statement under Rule 1007(b)(7) and fails to do so within 45 days after the first date set for the meeting of creditors under § 341(a) of the Code, the clerk shall promptly notify the debtor that the case will be closed without entry of a discharge unless the required statement is filed within the applicable time limit under Rule 1007(c).

(c) *Cases Under Chapter 15.* A foreign representative in a proceeding recognized under § 1517 of the Code shall file a final report when the purpose of the representative's appearance in the court is completed. The report shall describe the nature and results of the representative's activities in the court. The foreign representative shall transmit the report to the United States trustee, and give notice of its filing to the debtor, all persons or bodies authorized to administer foreign proceedings of the debtor, all parties to litigation pending in the United States in which the debtor was a party at the time of the filing of the petition, and such other entities as the court may direct. The foreign representative shall file a certificate with the court that notice has been given. If no objection has been filed by the United States trustee or a party in interest within 30 days after the certificate is filed, there shall be a presumption that the case has been fully administered.

(d) *Order Declaring Lien Satisfied.* In a chapter 12 or chapter 13 case, if a claim that was secured by property of the estate is subject to a lien under applicable nonbankruptcy law, the debtor may request entry of an order declaring that the secured claim has been satisfied and the lien has been released under the terms of a confirmed plan. The request shall be made by motion and shall be served on the holder of the claim and any other entity the court designates in the manner provided by Rule 7004 for service of a summons and complaint.

BANKRUPTCY CODE REFERENCES: §§ 341, 350, 704, 1202 and 1302

BANKRUPTCY STATUTORY REFERENCE: 28 U.S.C. § 586

## Rule 5010 Reopening Cases

A case may be reopened on motion of the debtor or other party in interest pursuant to § 350(b) of the Code. In a chapter 7, 12, or 13 case a trustee shall not be appointed by the United States trustee unless the court determines that a trustee is necessary to protect the interests of creditors and the debtor or to insure efficient administration of the case.

BANKRUPTCY CODE REFERENCE: § 350

## Rule 5011 Withdrawal and Abstention from Hearing a Proceeding

(*a*) *Withdrawal.* A motion for withdrawal of a case or proceeding shall be heard by a district judge.

(*b*) *Abstention from Hearing a Proceeding.* A motion for abstention pursuant to 28 U.S.C. § 1334(c) shall be governed by Rule 9014 and shall be served on the parties to the proceeding.

(*c*) *Effect of Filing of Motion for Withdrawal or Abstention.* The filing of a motion for withdrawal of a case or proceeding or for abstention pursuant to 28 U.S.C. § 1334(c) shall not stay the administration of the case or any proceeding therein before the bankruptcy judge except that the bankruptcy judge may stay, on such terms and conditions as are proper, proceedings pending disposition of the motion. A motion for a stay ordinarily shall be presented first to the bankruptcy judge. A motion for a stay or relief from a stay filed in the district court shall state why it has not been presented to or obtained from the bankruptcy judge. Relief granted by the district judge shall be on such terms and conditions as the judge deems proper.

BANKRUPTCY CODE REFERENCE: § 305 (rule specifically *not* applicable to section 305 abstention motions)

BANKRUPTCY STATUTORY REFERENCES: 28 U.S.C. §§ 157 and 1334

## Rule 5012 Agreements Concerning Coordination of Proceedings in Chapter 15 Cases

Approval of an agreement under § 1527(4) of the Code shall be sought by motion. The movant shall attach to the motion a copy of the proposed agreement or protocol and, unless the court directs otherwise, give at least 30 days' notice of any hearing on the motion by transmitting the motion to the United States trustee, and serving it on the debtor, all persons or bodies authorized to administer foreign proceedings of the debtor, all entities against whom provisional relief is being sought under § 1519, all parties to litigation pending in the United States in which the debtor was a party at the time of the filing of the petition, and such other entities as the court may direct.

BANKRUPTCY CODE REFERENCES: §§ 1519 and 1527

# PART VI

# COLLECTION AND LIQUIDATION OF THE ESTATE

## Rule 6001 Burden of Proof as to Validity of Postpetition Transfer

Any entity asserting the validity of a transfer under § 549 of the Code shall have the burden of proof.

Bankruptcy Code References: §§ 522 and 549

## Rule 6002 Accounting by Prior Custodian of Property of the Estate

(*a*) *Accounting Required.* Any custodian required by the Code to deliver property in the custodian's possession or control to the trustee shall promptly file and transmit to the United States trustee a report and account with respect to the property of the estate and the administration thereof.

(*b*) *Examination of Administration.* On the filing and transmittal of the report and account required by subdivision (a) of this rule and after an examination has been made into the superseded administration, after notice and a hearing, the court shall determine the propriety of the administration, including the reasonableness of all disbursements.

Bankruptcy Code References: §§ 101 and 543

## Rule 6003 Interim and Final Relief Immediately Following the Commencement of the Case—Applications for Employment; Motions for Use, Sale, or Lease of Property; and Motions for Assumption or Assignment of Executory Contracts

Except to the extent that relief is necessary to avoid immediate and irreparable harm, the court shall not, within 21 days after the filing of the petition, issue an order granting the following:

(*a*) an application under Rule 2014;

(*b*) a motion to use, sell, lease, or otherwise incur an obligation regarding property of the estate, including a motion to pay all or part of a claim that arose before the filing of the petition, but not a motion under Rule 4001; or

(*c*) a motion to assume or assign an executory contract or unexpired lease in accordance with § 365.

## Rule 6004 Use, Sale, or Lease of Property

(*a*) *Notice of Proposed Use, Sale, or Lease of Property.* Notice of a proposed use, sale, or lease of property, other than cash collateral, not in the ordinary course of business shall be given pursuant to Rule 2002(a)(2), (c)(1), (i), and (k) and, if applicable, in accordance with § 363(b)(2) of the Code.

(*b*) *Objection to Proposal.* Except as provided in subdivisions (c) and (d) of this rule, an objection to a proposed use, sale, or lease of property shall be filed and served not less than seven days before the date set for the proposed action or within the time fixed by the court. An objection to the proposed use, sale, or lease of property is governed by Rule 9014.

(c) *Sale Free and Clear of Liens and Other Interests.* A motion for authority to sell property free and clear of liens or other interests shall be made in accordance with Rule 9014 and shall be served on the parties who have liens or other interests in the property to be sold. The notice required by subdivision (a) of this rule shall include the date of the hearing on the motion and the time within which objections may be filed and served on the debtor in possession or trustee.

(d) *Sale of Property Under $2,500.* Notwithstanding subdivision (a) of this rule, when all of the nonexempt property of the estate has an aggregate gross value less than $2,500, it shall be sufficient to give a general notice of intent to sell such property other than in the ordinary course of business to all creditors, indenture trustees, committees appointed or elected pursuant to the Code, the United States trustee and other persons as the court may direct. An objection to any such sale may be filed and served by a party in interest within 14 days of the mailing of the notice, or within the time fixed by the court. An objection is governed by Rule 9014.

(e) *Hearing.* If a timely objection is made pursuant to subdivision (b) or (d) of this rule, the date of the hearing thereon may be set in the notice given pursuant to subdivision (a) of this rule.

(f) *Conduct of Sale Not in the Ordinary Course of Business.*

(1) *Public or Private Sale.* All sales not in the ordinary course of business may be by private sale or by public auction. Unless it is impracticable, an itemized statement of the property sold, the name of each purchaser, and the price received for each item or lot or for the property as a whole if sold in bulk shall be filed on completion of a sale. If the property is sold by an auctioneer, the auctioneer shall file the statement, transmit a copy thereof to the United States trustee, and furnish a copy to the trustee, debtor in possession, or chapter 13 debtor. If the property is not sold by an auctioneer, the trustee, debtor in possession, or chapter 13 debtor shall file the statement and transmit a copy thereof to the United States trustee.

(2) *Execution of Instruments.* After a sale in accordance with this rule the debtor, the trustee, or debtor in possession, as the case may be, shall execute any instrument necessary or ordered by the court to effectuate the transfer to the purchaser.

(g) *Sale of Personally Identifiable Information.*

(1) *Motion.* A motion for authority to sell or lease personally identifiable information under § 363(b)(1)(B) shall include a request for an order directing the United States trustee to appoint a consumer privacy ombudsman under § 332. Rule 9014 governs the motion which shall be served on: any committee elected under § 705 or appointed under § 1102 of the Code, or if the case is a chapter 11 reorganization case and no committee of unsecured creditors has been appointed under § 1102, on the creditors included on the list of creditors filed under Rule 1007(d); and on such other entities as the court may direct. The motion shall be transmitted to the United States trustee.

(2) *Appointment.* If a consumer privacy ombudsman is appointed under § 332, no later than seven days before the hearing on the motion under § 363(b)(1)(B), the United States trustee shall file a notice of the appointment, including the name and address of the person appointed. The United States trustee's notice shall be accompanied by a verified statement of the person appointed setting forth the person's connections with the debtor, creditors, any other party in interest, their respective attorneys and accountants, the United States trustee, or any person employed in the office of the United States trustee.

(*h*) *Stay of Order Authorizing Use, Sale, or Lease of Property.* An order authorizing the use, sale, or lease of property other than cash collateral is stayed until the expiration of 14 days after entry of the order, unless the court orders otherwise.

Bankruptcy Code References: §§ 102, 332, 363 and 1109

## Rule 6005 Appraisers and Auctioneers

The order of the court approving the employment of an appraiser or auctioneer shall fix the amount or rate of compensation. No officer or employee of the Judicial Branch of the United States or the United States Department of Justice shall be eligible to act as appraiser or auctioneer. No residence or licensing requirement shall disqualify an appraiser or auctioneer from employment.

Bankruptcy Code References: §§ 327, 328, 330 and 331

## Rule 6006 Assumption, Rejection or Assignment of an Executory Contract or Unexpired Lease

(*a*) *Proceeding to Assume, Reject, or Assign.* A proceeding to assume, reject, or assign an executory contract or unexpired lease, other than as part of a plan, is governed by Rule 9014.

(*b*) *Proceeding to Require Trustee to Act.* A proceeding by a party to an executory contract or unexpired lease in a chapter 9 municipality case, chapter 11 reorganization case, chapter 12 family farmer's debt adjustment case, or chapter 13 individual's debt adjustment case, to require the trustee, debtor in possession, or debtor to determine whether to assume or reject the contract or lease is governed by Rule 9014.

(*c*) *Notice.* Notice of a motion made pursuant to subdivision (a) or (b) of this rule, shall be given to the other party to the contract or lease, to other parties in interest as the court may direct, and, except in a chapter 9 municipality case, to the United States trustee.

(*d*) *Stay of Order Authorizing Assignment.* An order authorizing the trustee to assign an executory contract or unexpired lease under § 365(f) is stayed until the expiration of 14 days after the entry of the order, unless the court orders otherwise.

(*e*) *Limitations.* The trustee shall not seek authority to assume or assign multiple executory contracts or unexpired leases in one motion unless: (1) all executory contracts or unexpired leases to be assumed or assigned are between the same parties or are to be assigned to the same assignee; (2) the trustee seeks to assume, but not assign to more than one assignee, unexpired leases of real property; or (3) the court otherwise authorizes the motion to be filed. Subject to subdivision (f), the trustee may join requests for authority to reject multiple executory contracts or unexpired leases in one motion.

*(f) Omnibus Motions.* A motion to reject or, if permitted under subdivision (e), a motion to assume or assign multiple executory contracts or unexpired leases that are not between the same parties shall:

(*1*) state in a conspicuous place that parties receiving the omnibus motion should locate their names and their contracts or leases listed in the motion;

(*2*) list parties alphabetically and identify the corresponding contract or lease;

(*3*) specify the terms, including the curing of defaults, for each requested assumption or assignment;

(*4*) specify the terms, including the identity of each assignee and the adequate assurance of future performance by each assignee, for each requested assignment;

(*5*) be numbered consecutively with other omnibus motions to assume, assign, or reject executory contracts or unexpired leases; and

(*6*) be limited to no more than 100 executory contracts or unexpired leases.

*(g) Finality of Determination.* The finality of any order respecting an executory contract or unexpired lease included in an omnibus motion shall be determined as though such contract or lease had been the subject of a separate motion.

BANKRUPTCY CODE REFERENCES: §§ 365 and 1113

## Rule 6007 Abandonment or Disposition of Property

(*a*) *Notice of Proposed Abandonment or Disposition; Objections, Hearing.* Unless otherwise directed by the court, the trustee or debtor in possession shall give notice of a proposed abandonment or disposition of property to the United States trustee, all creditors, indenture trustees, and committees elected pursuant to § 705 or appointed pursuant to § 1102 of the Code. A party in interest may file and serve an objection within 14 days of the mailing of the notice, or within the time fixed by the court. If a timely objection is made, the court shall set a hearing on notice to the United States trustee and to other entities as the court may direct.

(*b*) *Motion by Party in Interest.* A party in interest may file and serve a motion requiring the trustee or debtor in possession to abandon property of the estate. Unless otherwise directed by the court, the party filing the motion shall serve the motion and any notice of the motion on the trustee or debtor in possession, the United States trustee, all creditors, indenture trustees, and committees elected pursuant to § 705 or appointed pursuant to § 1102 of the Code. A party in interest may file and serve an objection within 14 days of service, or within the time fixed by the court. If a timely objection is made, the court shall set a hearing on notice to the United States trustee and to other entities as the court may direct. If the court grants the motion, the order effects the trustee's or debtor in possession's abandonment without further notice, unless otherwise directed by the court.

(*c*) [*Abrogated.*]

Bankruptcy Code References: §§ 102, 554, 705, 725 and 1102

Bankruptcy Statutory Reference: 28 U.S.C. § 586

## Rule 6008 Redemption of Property from Lien or Sale

On motion by the debtor, trustee, or debtor in possession and after hearing on notice as the court may direct, the court may authorize the redemption of property from a lien or from a sale to enforce a lien in accordance with applicable law.

Bankruptcy Code References: §§ 102, 524 and 722

## Rule 6009 Prosecution and Defense of Proceedings by Trustee or Debtor in Possession

With or without court approval, the trustee or debtor in possession may prosecute or may enter an appearance and defend any pending action or proceeding by or against the debtor, or commence and prosecute any action or proceeding in behalf of the estate before any tribunal.

Bankruptcy Code References: §§ 323, 325, 327, 1107 and 1203

## Rule 6010 Proceeding to Avoid Indemnifying Lien or Transfer to Surety

If a lien voidable under § 547 of the Code has been dissolved by the furnishing of a bond or other obligation and the surety thereon has been indemnified by the transfer of, or the creation of a lien upon, nonexempt property of the debtor, the surety shall be joined as a defendant in any proceeding to avoid the indemnifying transfer or lien. Such proceeding is governed by the rules in Part VII.

Bankruptcy Code References: §§ 547 and 550

## Rule 6011 Disposal of Patient Records in Health Care Business Case

(*a*) *Notice by Publication Under § 351(1)(A).* A notice regarding the claiming or disposing of patient records under § 351(1)(A) shall not identify any patient by name or other identifying information, but shall:

(*1*) identify with particularity the health care facility whose patient records the trustee proposes to destroy;

(*2*) state the name, address, telephone number, email address, and website, if any, of a person from whom information about the patient records may be obtained;

(*3*) state how to claim the patient records; and

(*4*) state the date by which patient records must be claimed, and that if they are not so claimed the records will be destroyed.

(*b*) *Notice by Mail Under § 351(1)(B).* Subject to applicable nonbankruptcy law relating to patient privacy, a notice regarding the claiming or disposing of patient records under § 351(1)(B) shall, in addition to including the information in subdivision (a), direct that a patient's family member or other representative who receives the notice inform the patient of the notice. Any notice under this subdivision shall be mailed to the patient and any family member or other contact person whose name and address have been given to the trustee or the debtor for the purpose of providing information regarding the patient's health care, to the Attorney General of the State where the health care facility is located, and to any insurance company known to have provided health care insurance to the patient.

(c) *Proof of Compliance with Notice Requirement.* Unless the court orders the trustee to file proof of compliance with § 351(1)(B) under seal, the trustee shall not file, but shall maintain, the proof of compliance for a reasonable time.

(d) *Report of Destruction of Records.* The trustee shall file, no later than 30 days after the destruction of patient records under § 351(3), a report certifying that the unclaimed records have been destroyed and explaining the method used to effect the destruction. The report shall not identify any patient by name or other identifying information.

Bankruptcy Code Reference: § 351

# PART VII

# ADVERSARY PROCEEDINGS

## Rule 7001 Scope of Rules of Part VII

An adversary proceeding is governed by the rules of this Part VII. The following are adversary proceedings:

(*1*) a proceeding to recover money or property, other than a proceeding to compel the debtor to deliver property to the trustee, or a proceeding under § 554(b) or § 725 of the Code, Rule 2017, or Rule 6002;

(*2*) a proceeding to determine the validity, priority, or extent of a lien or other interest in property, but not a proceeding under Rule 3012 or Rule 4003(d);

(*3*) a proceeding to obtain approval under § 363(h) for the sale of both the interest of the estate and of a co-owner in property;

(*4*) a proceeding to object to or revoke a discharge, other than an objection to discharge under §§ 727(a)(8), (a)(9), or 1328(f);

(*5*) a proceeding to revoke an order of confirmation of a chapter 11, chapter 12, or chapter 13 plan;

(*6*) a proceeding to determine the dischargeability of a debt;

(*7*) a proceeding to obtain an injunction or other equitable relief, except when a chapter 9, chapter 11, chapter 12, or chapter 13 plan provides for the relief;

(*8*) a proceeding to subordinate any allowed claim or interest, except when a chapter 9, chapter 11, chapter 12, or chapter 13 plan provides for subordination;

(*9*) a proceeding to obtain a declaratory judgment relating to any of the foregoing; or (10) a proceeding to determine a claim or cause of action removed under 28 U.S.C. § 1452.

Bankruptcy Code References: §§ 363, 510, 521, 523, 550, 554, 704, 725, 727, 1144, 1230 and 1330

Bankruptcy Statutory Reference: 28 U.S.C. § 1452

## Rule 7002 References to Federal Rules of Civil Procedure

Whenever a Federal Rule of Civil Procedure applicable to adversary proceedings makes reference to another Federal Rule of Civil Procedure, the reference shall be read as a reference to the Federal Rule of Civil Procedure as modified in this Part VII.

## Rule 7003 Commencement of Adversary Proceeding

Rule 3 F.R.Civ.P. applies in adversary proceedings.

### CIVIL RULE:

Federal Rule of Civil Procedure 3, which was last amended effective December 1, 2007, provides:

**Rule 3 Commencing an Action**

A civil action is commenced by filing a complaint with the court.

**Rule 7004 Process; Service of Summons, Complaint**

(*a*) *Summons; Service; Proof of Service.*

(*1*) Except as provided in Rule 7004(a)(2), Rule 4(a), (b), (c)(1), (d)(5), (e)–(j), (*l*), and (m) F.R.Civ.P. applies in adversary proceedings. Personal service under Rule 4(e)–(j) F.R.Civ.P. may be made by any person at least 18 years of age who is not a party, and the summons may be delivered by the clerk to any such person.

(*2*) The clerk may sign, seal, and issue a summons electronically by putting an "s/" before the clerk's name and including the court's seal on the summons.

(*b*) *Service by First Class Mail.* Except as provided in subdivision (h), in addition to the methods of service authorized by Rule 4(e)–(j) F.R.Civ.P., service may be made within the United States by first class mail postage prepaid as follows:

(*1*) Upon an individual other than an infant or incompetent, by mailing a copy of the summons and complaint to the individual's dwelling house or usual place of abode or to the place where the individual regularly conducts a business or profession.

(*2*) Upon an infant or an incompetent person, by mailing a copy of the summons and complaint to the person upon whom process is prescribed to be served by the law of the state in which service is made when an action is brought against such a defendant in the courts of general jurisdiction of that state. The summons and complaint in that case shall be addressed to the person required to be served at that person's dwelling house or usual place of abode or at the place where the person regularly conducts a business or profession.

(*3*) Upon a domestic or foreign corporation or upon a partnership or other unincorporated association, by mailing a copy of the summons and complaint to the attention of an officer, a managing or general agent, or to any other agent authorized by appointment or by law to receive service of process and, if the agent is one authorized by statute to receive service and the statute so requires, by also mailing a copy to the defendant.

(*4*) Upon the United States, by mailing a copy of the summons and complaint addressed to the civil process clerk at the office of the United States attorney for the district in which the action is brought and by mailing a copy of the summons and complaint to the Attorney General of the United States at Washington, District of Columbia, and in any action attacking the validity of an order of an officer or an agency of the United States not made a party, by also mailing a copy of the summons and complaint to that officer or agency. The court shall allow a reasonable time for service pursuant to this subdivision for the purpose of curing the failure to mail a copy of the summons and complaint to multiple officers, agencies, or corporations of the United States if the plaintiff has mailed a copy of the summons and complaint either to the civil process clerk at the office of the United States attorney or to the Attorney General of the United States.

(*5*) Upon any officer or agency of the United States, by mailing a copy of the summons and complaint to the United States as prescribed in paragraph (4) of this subdivision and also to the officer or agency. If the agency is a corporation, the mailing shall be as prescribed in paragraph (3) of this subdivision of this rule. The court shall allow a reasonable time for service pursuant to this subdivision for the purpose of curing the failure to mail a copy of the summons and complaint to multiple officers, agencies, or corporations of the United States if the plaintiff has mailed a copy of the summons and complaint either to the civil process clerk at the office of the United States attorney or to the Attorney General of the United States. If the United States trustee is the trustee in the case and service is made upon the United States trustee solely as trustee, service may be made as prescribed in paragraph (10) of this subdivision of this rule.

(*6*) Upon a state or municipal corporation or other governmental organization thereof subject to suit, by mailing a copy of the summons and complaint to the person or office upon whom process is prescribed to be served by the law of the state in which service is made when an action is brought against such a defendant in the courts of general jurisdiction of that state, or in the absence of the designation of any such person or office by state law, then to the chief executive officer thereof.

(*7*) Upon a defendant of any class referred to in paragraph (1) or (3) of this subdivision of this rule, it is also sufficient if a copy of the summons and complaint is mailed to the entity upon whom service is prescribed to be served by any statute of the United States or by the law of the state in which service is made when an action is brought against such a defendant in the court of general jurisdiction of that state.

(*8*) Upon any defendant, it is also sufficient if a copy of the summons and complaint is mailed to an agent of such defendant authorized by appointment or by law to receive service of process, at the agent's dwelling house or usual place of abode or at the place where the agent regularly carries on a business or profession and, if the authorization so requires, by mailing also a copy of the summons and complaint to the defendant as provided in this subdivision.

(*9*) Upon the debtor, after a petition has been filed by or served upon the debtor and until the case is dismissed or closed, by mailing a copy of the summons and complaint to the debtor at the address shown in the petition or to such other address as the debtor may designate in a filed writing.

(*10*) Upon the United States trustee, when the United States trustee is the trustee in the case and service is made upon the United States trustee solely as trustee, by mailing a copy of the summons and complaint to an office of the United States trustee or another place designated by the United States trustee in the district where the case under the Code is pending.

(c) *Service by Publication.* If a party to an adversary proceeding to determine or protect rights in property in the custody of the court cannot be served as provided in Rule 4(e)–(j) F.R.Civ.P. or subdivision (b) of this rule, the court may order the summons and complaint to be served by mailing copies thereof by first class mail, postage prepaid, to the party's last known address, and by at least one publication in such manner and form as the court may direct.

(*d*) *Nationwide Service of Process.* The summons and complaint and all other process except a subpoena may be served anywhere in the United States.

(*e*) *Summons: Time Limit for Service Within the United States.* Service made under Rule 4(e), (g), (h)(1), (i), or (j)(2) F.R.Civ.P. shall be by delivery of the summons and complaint within 7 days after the summons is issued. If service is by any authorized form of mail, the summons and complaint shall be deposited in the mail within 7 days after the summons is issued. If a summons is not timely delivered or mailed, another summons will be issued for service. This subdivision does not apply to service in a foreign country.

(*f*) *Personal Jurisdiction.* If the exercise of jurisdiction is consistent with the Constitution and laws of the United States, serving a summons or filing a waiver of service in accordance with this rule or the subdivisions of Rule 4 F.R.Civ.P. made applicable by these rules is effective to establish personal jurisdiction over the person of any defendant with respect to a case under the Code or a civil proceeding arising under the Code, or arising in or related to a case under the Code.

(*g*) *Service on Debtor's Attorney.* If the debtor is represented by an attorney, whenever service is made upon the debtor under this Rule, service shall also be made upon the debtor's attorney by any means authorized under Rule 5(b) F.R.Civ.P.

(*h*) *Service of Process on an Insured Depository Institution.* Service on an insured depository institution (as defined in section 3 of the Federal Deposit Insurance Act) in a contested matter or adversary proceeding shall be made by certified mail addressed to an officer of the institution unless—

(*1*) the institution has appeared by its attorney, in which case the attorney shall be served by first class mail;

(*2*) the court orders otherwise after service upon the institution by certified mail of notice of an application to permit service on the institution by first class mail sent to an officer of the institution designated by the institution; or

(*3*) the institution has waived in writing its entitlement to service by certified mail by designating an officer to receive service.

## CIVIL RULE:

Federal Rule of Civil Procedure 4, which was last amended effective December 1, 2017, provides:

**Rule 4 Summons**

(a) CONTENTS; AMENDMENTS.

(1) *Contents.* A summons must:

BANKRUPTCY RULES

(A) name the court and the parties;

(B) be directed to the defendant;

(C) state the name and address of the plaintiff's attorney or—if unrepresented—of the plaintiff;

(D) state the time within which the defendant must appear and defend;

(E) notify the defendant that a failure to appear and defend will result in a default judgment against the defendant for the relief demanded in the complaint;

(F) be signed by the clerk; and

(G) bear the court's seal.

(2) *Amendments.* The court may permit a summons to be amended.

(b) ISSUANCE. On or after filing the complaint, the plaintiff may present a summons to the clerk for signature and seal. If the summons is properly completed, the clerk must sign, seal, and issue it to the plaintiff for service on the defendant. A summons—or a copy of a summons that is addressed to multiple defendants—must be issued for each defendant to be served.

(c) SERVICE.

(1) *In General.* A summons must be served with a copy of the complaint. The plaintiff is responsible for having the summons and complaint served within the time allowed by Rule 4(m) and must furnish the necessary copies to the person who makes service.

(2) *By Whom.* Any person who is at least 18 years old and not a party may serve a summons and complaint.

(3) *By a Marshal or Someone Specially Appointed.* At the plaintiff's request, the court may order that service be made by a United States marshal or deputy marshal or by a person specially appointed by the court. The court must so order if the plaintiff is authorized to proceed in forma pauperis under 28 U.S.C. § 1915 or as a seaman under 28 U.S.C. § 1916.

(d) WAIVING SERVICE.

(1) *Requesting a Waiver.* An individual, corporation, or association that is subject to service under Rule 4(e), (f), or (h) has a duty to avoid unnecessary expenses of serving the summons. The plaintiff may notify such a defendant that an action has been commenced and request that the defendant waive service of a summons. The notice and request must:

(A) be in writing and be addressed:

(i) to the individual defendant; or

(ii) for a defendant subject to service under Rule 4(h), to an officer, a managing or general agent, or any other agent authorized by appointment or by law to receive service of process;

(B) name the court where the complaint was filed;

(C) be accompanied by a copy of the complaint, 2 copies of the waiver form appended to this Rule 4,[17] and a prepaid means for returning the form;

(D) inform the defendant, using the form appended to this Rule 4, of the consequences of waiving and not waiving service;

(E) state the date when the request is sent;

(F) give the defendant a reasonable time of at least 30 days after the request was sent—or at least 60 days if sent to the defendant outside any judicial district of the United States—to return the waiver; and

(G) be sent by first-class mail or other reliable means.

(2) *Failure to Waive.* If a defendant located within the United States fails, without good cause, to sign and return a waiver requested by a plaintiff located within the United States, the court must impose on the defendant:

(A) the expenses later incurred in making service; and

(B) the reasonable expenses, including attorney's fees, of any motion required to collect those service expenses.

(3) *Time to Answer After a Waiver.* A defendant who, before being served with process, timely returns a waiver need not serve an answer to the complaint until 60 days after the request was sent—or until 90 days after it was sent to the defendant outside any judicial district of the United States.

(4) *Results of Filing a Waiver.* When the plaintiff files a waiver, proof of service is not required and these rules apply as if a summons and complaint had been served at the time of filing the waiver.

(5) *Jurisdiction and Venue Not Waived.* Waiving service of a summons does not waive any objection to personal jurisdiction or to venue.

(e) SERVING AN INDIVIDUAL WITHIN A JUDICIAL DISTRICT OF THE UNITED STATES. Serving an Individual Within a Judicial District of the United States. Unless federal law provides otherwise, an individual—other than a minor, an incompetent person, or a person whose waiver has been filed—may be served in a judicial district of the United States by:

(1) following state law for serving a summons in an action brought in courts of general jurisdiction in the state where the district court is located or where service is made; or

(2) doing any of the following:

(A) delivering a copy of the summons and of the complaint to the individual personally;

(B) leaving a copy of each at the individual's dwelling or usual place of abode with someone of suitable age and discretion who resides there; or

(C) delivering a copy of each to an agent authorized by appoint-

[17] ED. NOTE: For the text of this form, *see* 1 Moore's Federal Practice, ch. 4 (Matthew Bender 3d ed.).

BANKRUPTCY RULES

ment or by law to receive service of process.

(f) SERVING AN INDIVIDUAL IN A FOREIGN COUNTRY. Unless federal law provides otherwise, an individual—other than a minor, an incompetent person, or a person whose waiver has been filed—may be served at a place not within any judicial district of the United States:

(1) by any internationally agreed means of service that is reasonably calculated to give notice, such as those authorized by the Hague Convention on the Service Abroad of Judicial and Extrajudicial Documents;

(2) if there is no internationally agreed means, or if an international agreement allows but does not specify other means, by a method that is reasonably calculated to give notice:

(A) as prescribed by the foreign country's law for service in that country in an action in its courts of general jurisdiction;

(B) as the foreign authority directs in response to a letter rogatory or letter of request; or

(C) unless prohibited by the foreign country's law, by:

(i) delivering a copy of the summons and of the complaint to the individual personally; or

(ii) using any form of mail that the clerk addresses and sends to the individual and that requires a signed receipt; or

(3) by other means not prohibited by international agreement, as the court orders.

(g) SERVING A MINOR OR AN INCOMPETENT PERSON. A minor or an incompetent person in a judicial district of the United States must be served by following state law for serving a summons or like process on such a defendant in an action brought in the courts of general jurisdiction of the state where service is made. A minor or an incompetent person who is not within any judicial district of the United States must be served in the manner prescribed by Rule 4(f)(2)(A), (f)(2)(B), or (f)(3).

(h) SERVING A CORPORATION, PARTNERSHIP, OR ASSOCIATION. Unless federal law provides otherwise or the defendant's waiver has been filed, a domestic or foreign corporation, or a partnership or other unincorporated association that is subject to suit under a common name, must be served:

(1) in a judicial district of the United States:

(A) in the manner prescribed by Rule 4(e)(1) for serving an individual; or

(B) by delivering a copy of the summons and of the complaint to an officer, a managing or general agent, or any other agent authorized by appointment or by law to receive service of process and—if the agent is one authorized by statute and the statute so requires—by also mailing a copy of each to the defendant; or

(2) at a place not within any judicial district of the United States, in any manner prescribed by Rule 4(f) for serving an individual, except personal delivery under (f)(2)(C)(i).

(i) Serving the United States and Its Agencies, Corporations, Officers, or Employees.

(1) *United States.* To serve the United States, a party must:

(A) (i) deliver a copy of the summons and of the complaint to the United States attorney for the district where the action is brought—or to an assistant United States attorney or clerical employee whom the United States attorney designates in a writing filed with the court clerk—or

(ii) send a copy of each by registered or certified mail to the civil-process clerk at the United States attorney's office;

(B) send a copy of each by registered or certified mail to the Attorney General of the United States at Washington, D.C.; and

(C) if the action challenges an order of a nonparty agency or officer of the United States, send a copy of each by registered or certified mail to the agency or officer.

(2) *Agency; Corporation; Officer or Employee Sued in an Official Capacity.* To serve a United States agency or corporation, or a United States officer or employee sued only in an official capacity, a party must serve the United States and also send a copy of the summons and of the complaint by registered or certified mail to the agency, corporation, officer, or employee.

(3) *Officer or Employee Sued Individually.* To serve a United States officer or employee sued in an individual capacity for an act or omission occurring in connection with duties performed on the United States' behalf (whether or not the officer or employee is also sued in an official capacity), a party must serve the United States and also serve the officer or employee under Rule 4(e), (f), or (g).

(4) *Extending Time.* The court must allow a party a reasonable time to cure its failure to:

(A) serve a person required to be served under Rule 4(i)(2), if the party has served either the United States attorney or the Attorney General of the United States; or

(B) serve the United States under Rule 4(i)(3), if the party has served the United States officer or employee.

(j) Serving a Foreign, State, or Local Government.

(1) *Foreign State.* A foreign state or its political subdivision, agency, or instrumentality must be served in accordance with 28 U.S.C. § 1608.

(2) *State or Local Government.* A state, a municipal corporation, or any other state-created governmental organization that is subject to suit must be served by:

(A) delivering a copy of the summons and of the complaint to its chief executive officer; or

(B) serving a copy of each in the manner prescribed by that state's law for serving a summons or like process on such a defendant.

* * *

(*l*) PROVING SERVICE.

(1) *Affidavit Required.* Unless service is waived, proof of service must be made to the court. Except for service by a United States marshal or deputy marshal, proof must be by the server's affidavit.

(2) *Service Outside the United States.* Service not within any judicial district of the United States must be proved as follows:

(A) if made under Rule 4(f)(1), as provided in the applicable treaty or convention; or

(B) if made under Rule 4(f)(2) or (f)(3), by a receipt signed by the addressee, or by other evidence satisfying the court that the summons and complaint were delivered to the addressee.

(3) *Validity of Service; Amending Proof.* Failure to prove service does not affect the validity of service. The court may permit proof of service to be amended.

(m) TIME LIMIT FOR SERVICE. If a defendant is not served within 90 days after the complaint is filed, the court—on motion or on its own after notice to the plaintiff—must dismiss the action without prejudice against that defendant or order that service be made within a specified time. But if the plaintiff shows good cause for the failure, the court must extend the time for service for an appropriate period. This subdivision (m) does not apply to service in a foreign country under Rule 4(f), 4(h)(2), or 4(j)(1), or to service of a notice under Rule 71.1(d)(3)(A).

* * *

BANKRUPTCY CODE REFERENCES: §§ 101 and 342

## Rule 7005 Service and Filing of Pleadings and Other Papers

Rule 5 F.R.Civ.P. applies in adversary proceedings.

## CIVIL RULE:

Federal Rule of Civil Procedure 5, which was last amended effective December 1, 2018, provides:

### Rule 5 Serving and Filing Pleadings and Other Papers

(a) SERVICE: WHEN REQUIRED.

(1) *In General.* Unless these rules provide otherwise, each of the following papers must be served on every party:

(A) an order stating that service is required;

(B) a pleading filed after the original complaint, unless the court orders otherwise under Rule 5(c) because there are numerous defendants;

(C) a discovery paper required to be served on a party, unless the court orders otherwise;

(D) a written motion, except one that may be heard ex parte; and

(E) a written notice, appearance, demand, or offer of judgment, or any similar paper.

(2) *If a Party Fails to Appear.* No service is required on a party who is in default for failing to appear. But a pleading that asserts a new claim for relief against such a party must be served on that party under Rule 4.

(3) *Seizing Property.* If an action is begun by seizing property and no person is or need be named as a defendant, any service required before the filing of an appearance, answer, or claim must be made on the person who had custody or possession of the property when it was seized.

(b) SERVICE: HOW MADE.

(1) *Serving an Attorney.* If a party is represented by an attorney, service under this rule must be made on the attorney unless the court orders service on the party.

(2) *Service in General.* A paper is served under this rule by:

(A) handing it to the person;

(B) leaving it:

(i) at the person's office with a clerk or other person in charge or, if no one is in charge, in a conspicuous place in the office; or

(ii) if the person has no office or the office is closed, at the person's dwelling or usual place of abode with someone of suitable age and discretion who resides there;

(C) mailing it to the person's last known address—in which event service is complete upon mailing;

(D) leaving it with the court clerk if the person has no known address;

(E) sending it to a registered user by filing it with the court's electronic-filing system or sending it by other electronic means that the person consented to in writing—in either of which events service is complete upon filing or sending, but is not effective if the filer or sender learns that it did not reach the person to be served; or

(F) delivering it by any other means that the person consented to in writing—in which event service is complete when the person making service delivers it to the agency designated to make delivery.

(3) *Using Court Facilities.* [Abrogated effective December 1, 2018.]

(c) SERVING NUMEROUS DEFENDANTS.

(1) *In General.* If an action involves an unusually large number of defendants, the court may, on motion or on its own, order that:

(A) defendants' pleadings and replies to them need not be served on other defendants;

(B) any crossclaim, counterclaim, avoidance, or affirmative defense in those pleadings and replies to them will be treated as denied or avoided by all other parties; and

BANKRUPTCY RULES

(C) filing any such pleading and serving it on the plaintiff constitutes notice of the pleading to all parties.

(2) *Notifying Parties.* A copy of every such order must be served on the parties as the court directs.

(d) FILING.

(1) *Required Filings; Certificate of Service.*

(A) *Papers after the Complaint.* Any paper after the complaint that is required to be served must be filed no later than a reasonable time after service. But disclosures under Rule 26(a)(1) or (2) and the following discovery requests and responses must not be filed until they are used in the proceeding or the court orders filing: depositions, interrogatories, requests for documents or tangible things or to permit entry onto land, and requests for admission.

(B) *Certificate of Service.* No certificate of service is required when a paper is served by filing it with the court's electronic-filing system. When a paper that is required to be served is served by other means:

(i) if the paper is filed, a certificate of service must be filed with it or within a reasonable time after service; and

(ii) if the paper is not filed, a certificate of service need not be filed unless filing is required by court order or by local rule.

(2) *Nonelectronic Filing.* A paper not filed electronically is filed by delivering it:

(A) to the clerk; or

(B) to a judge who agrees to accept it for filing, and who must then note the filing date on the paper and promptly send it to the clerk.

(3) *Electronic Filing and Signing.*

(A) *By a Represented Person—Generally Required; Exceptions.* A person represented by an attorney must file electronically, unless nonelectronic filing is allowed by the court for good cause or is allowed or required by local rule.

(B) *By an Unrepresented Person—When Allowed or Required.* A person not represented by an attorney:

(i) may file electronically only if allowed by court order or by local rule; and

(ii) may be required to file electronically only by court order, or by a local rule that includes reasonable exceptions.

(C) *Signing.* A filing made through a person's electronic-filing account and authorized by that person, together with that person's name on a signature block, constitutes the person's signature.

(D) *Same as a Written Paper.* A paper filed electronically is a written paper for purposes of these rules.

(4) *Acceptance by the Clerk.* The clerk must not refuse to file a paper

solely because it is not in the form prescribed by these rules or by a local rule or practice.

**Rule 7007 Pleadings Allowed**

Rule 7 F. R. Civ.P. applies in adversary proceedings.

## CIVIL RULE:

Federal Rule of Civil Procedure 7, which was last amended effective December 1, 2007, provides:

**Rule 7 Pleadings Allowed; Form of Motion and Other Papers**

(a) Pleadings. Only these pleadings are allowed:

(1) a complaint;

(2) an answer to a complaint;

(3) an answer to a counterclaim designated as a counterclaim;

(4) an answer to a crossclaim;

(5) a third-party complaint;

(6) an answer to a third-party complaint; and

(7) if the court orders one, a reply to an answer.

(b) Motions and other Papers.

(1) *In General.* A request for a court order must be made by motion. The motion must:

(A) be in writing unless made during a hearing or trial;

(B) state with particularity the grounds for seeking the order; and

(C) state the relief sought.

(2) *Form.* The rules governing captions and other matters of form in pleadings apply to motions and other papers.

**Rule 7007.1 Corporate Ownership Statement**

(*a*) *Required Disclosure.* Any nongovernmental corporation that is a party to an adversary proceeding, other than the debtor, shall file a statement that identifies any parent corporation and any publicly held corporation that owns 10% or more of its stock or states that there is no such corporation. The same requirement applies to a nongovernmental corporation that seeks to intervene.

(*b*) *Time for Filing; Supplemental Filing.* The corporate ownership statement shall:

(*1*) be filed with the corporation's first appearance, pleading, motion, response, or other request addressed to the court; and

(*2*) be supplemented whenever the information required by this rule changes.

**Rule 7008 General Rules of Pleading**

Rule 8 F.R.Civ.P. applies in adversary proceedings. The allegation of jurisdiction required by Rule 8(a) shall also contain a reference to the name, number, and

BANKRUPTCY RULES

chapter of the case under the Code to which the adversary proceeding relates and to the district and division where the case under the Code is pending. In an adversary proceeding before a bankruptcy court, the complaint, counterclaim, cross-claim, or third-party complaint shall contain a statement that the pleader does or does not consent to entry of final orders or judgment by the bankruptcy court.

## CIVIL RULE:

Federal Rule of Civil Procedure 8, which was last amended effective December 1, 2010, provides:

### Rule 8. General Rules of Pleading

(a) CLAIM FOR RELIEF. A pleading that states a claim for relief must contain:

(1) a short and plain statement of the grounds for the court's jurisdiction, unless the court already has jurisdiction and the claim needs no new jurisdictional support;

(2) a short and plain statement of the claim showing that the pleader is entitled to relief; and

(3) a demand for the relief sought, which may include relief in the alternative or different types of relief.

(b) DEFENSES; ADMISSIONS AND DENIALS.

(1) *In General.* In responding to a pleading, a party must:

(A) state in short and plain terms its defenses to each claim asserted against it; and

(B) admit or deny the allegations asserted against it by an opposing party.

(2) *Denials—Responding to the Substance.* A denial must fairly respond to the substance of the allegation.

(3) *General and Specific Denials.* A party that intends in good faith to deny all the allegations of a pleading—including the jurisdictional grounds—may do so by a general denial. A party that does not intend to deny all the allegations must either specifically deny designated allegations or generally deny all except those specifically admitted.

(4) *Denying Part of an Allegation.* A party that intends in good faith to deny only part of an allegation must admit the part that is true and deny the rest.

(5) *Lacking Knowledge or Information.* A party that lacks knowledge or information sufficient to form a belief about the truth of an allegation must so state, and the statement has the effect of a denial.

(6) *Effect of Failing to Deny.* An allegation—other than one relating to the amount of damages—is admitted if a responsive pleading is required and the allegation is not denied. If a responsive pleading is not required, an allegation is considered denied or avoided.

(c) AFFIRMATIVE DEFENSES.

(1) *In General.* In responding to a pleading, a party must affirmatively state any avoidance or affirmative defense, including:

- accord and satisfaction;
- arbitration and award;
- assumption of risk;
- contributory negligence;
- duress;
- estoppel;
- failure of consideration;
- fraud;
- illegality;
- injury by fellow servant;
- laches;
- license;
- payment;
- release;
- res judicata;
- statute of frauds;
- statute of limitations; and
- waiver.

(2) *Mistaken Designation.* If a party mistakenly designates a defense as a counterclaim, or a counterclaim as a defense, the court must, if justice requires, treat the pleading as though it were correctly designated, and may impose terms for doing so.

(d) PLEADING TO BE CONCISE AND DIRECT; ALTERNATIVE STATEMENTS; INCONSISTENCY.

(1) *In General.* Each allegation must be simple, concise, and direct. No technical form is required.

(2) *Alternative Statements of a Claim or Defense.* A party may set out 2 or more statements of a claim or defense alternatively or hypothetically, either in a single count or defense or in separate ones. If a party makes alternative statements, the pleading is sufficient if any one of them is sufficient.

(3) *Inconsistent Claims or Defenses.* A party may state as many separate claims or defenses as it has, regardless of consistency.

(e) CONSTRUING PLEADINGS. Pleadings must be construed so as to do justice.

## Rule 7009 Pleading Special Matters

Rule 9 F.R.Civ.P. applies in adversary proceedings.

## CIVIL RULE:

Federal Rule of Civil Procedure 9, which was last amended effective December 1, 2007, provides:

**Rule 9 Pleading Special Matters**

(a) CAPACITY OR AUTHORITY TO SUE; LEGAL EXISTENCE.

(1) *In General.* Except when required to show that the court has jurisdiction, a pleading need not allege:

(A) a party's capacity to sue or be sued;

(B) a party's authority to sue or be sued in a representative capacity; or

(C) the legal existence of an organized association of persons that is made a party.

(2) *Raising Those Issues.* To raise any of those issues, a party must do so by a specific denial, which must state any supporting facts that are peculiarly within the party's knowledge.

(b) FRAUD OR MISTAKE; CONDITIONS OF MIND. In alleging fraud or mistake, a party must state with particularity the circumstances constituting fraud or mistake. Malice, intent, knowledge, and other conditions of a person's mind may be alleged generally.

(c) CONDITIONS PRECEDENT. In pleading conditions precedent, it suffices to allege generally that all conditions precedent have occurred or been performed. But when denying that a condition precedent has occurred or been performed, a party must do so with particularity.

(d) OFFICIAL DOCUMENT OR ACT. In pleading an official document or official act, it suffices to allege that the document was legally issued or the act legally done.

(e) JUDGMENT. In pleading a judgment or decision of a domestic or foreign court, a judicial or quasi-judicial tribunal, or a board or officer, it suffices to plead the judgment or decision without showing jurisdiction to render it.

(f) TIME AND PLACE. An allegation of time or place is material when testing the sufficiency of a pleading.

(g) SPECIAL DAMAGES. If an item of special damage is claimed, it must be specifically stated.

(h) ADMIRALTY OR MARITIME CLAIM.

(1) *How Designated.* If a claim for relief is within the admiralty or maritime jurisdiction and also within the court's subject-matter jurisdiction on some other ground, the pleading may designate the claim as an admiralty or maritime claim for purposes of Rules 14(c), 38(e), and 82 and the Supplemental Rules for Admiralty or Maritime Claims and Asset Forfeiture Actions. A claim cognizable only in the admiralty or maritime jurisdiction is an admiralty or maritime claim for those purposes, whether or not so designated.

(2) *Designation for Appeal.* A case that includes an admiralty or maritime claim within this subdivision (h) is an admiralty case within 28 U.S.C. § 1292(a)(3).

**Rule 7010 Form of Pleadings**

Rule 10 F.R.Civ.P. applies in adversary proceedings, except that the caption of each pleading in such a proceeding shall conform substantially to the appropriate Official Form.

## CIVIL RULE:

Federal Rule of Civil Procedure 10, which was last amended effective December 1, 2007, provides:

**Rule 10 Form of Pleadings**

(a) CAPTION; NAMES OF PARTIES. Every pleading must have a caption with the court's name, a title, a file number, and a Rule 7(a) designation. The title of the complaint must name all the parties; the title of other pleadings, after naming the first party on each side, may refer generally to other parties.

(b) PARAGRAPHS; SEPARATE STATEMENTS. A party must state its claims or defenses in numbered paragraphs, each limited as far as practicable to a single set of circumstances. A later pleading may refer by number to a paragraph in an earlier pleading. If doing so would promote clarity, each claim founded on a separate transaction or occurrence—and each defense other than a denial—must be stated in a separate count or defense.

(c) ADOPTION BY REFERENCE; EXHIBITS. A statement in a pleading may be adopted by reference elsewhere in the same pleading or in any other pleading or motion. A copy of a written instrument that is an exhibit to a pleading is a part of the pleading for all purposes.

## Rule 7012 Defenses and Objections—When and How Presented—By Pleading or Motion—Motion for Judgment on the Pleadings

(*a*) *When Presented.* If a complaint is duly served, the defendant shall serve an answer within 30 days after the issuance of the summons, except when a different time is prescribed by the court. The court shall prescribe the time for service of the answer when service of a complaint is made by publication or upon a party in a foreign country. A party served with a pleading stating a cross-claim shall serve an answer thereto within 21 days after service. The plaintiff shall serve a reply to a counterclaim in the answer within 21 days after service of the answer or, if a reply is ordered by the court, within 21 days after service of the order, unless the order otherwise directs. The United States or an officer or agency thereof shall serve an answer to a complaint within 35 days after the issuance of the summons, and shall serve an answer to a cross-claim, or a reply to a counterclaim, within 35 days after service upon the United States attorney of the pleading in which the claim is asserted. The service of a motion permitted under this rule alters these periods of time as follows, unless a different time is fixed by order of the court: (1) if the court denies the motion or postpones its disposition until the trial on the merits, the responsive pleading shall be served within 14 days after notice of the court's action; (2) if the court grants a motion for a more definite statement, the responsive pleading shall be served within 14 days after the service of a more definite statement.

(*b*) *Applicability of Rule 12(b)–(i) F.R.Civ.P.* Rule 12(b)–(i) F.R.Civ.P. applies in adversary proceedings. A responsive pleading shall include a statement that the party does or does not consent to entry of final orders or judgment by the bankruptcy court.

## CIVIL RULE:

Federal Rule of Civil Procedure 12, which was last amended effective December 1, 2009, provides:

### Rule 12 Defenses and Objections: When and How Presented; Motion for Judgment on the Pleadings; Consolidating Motions; Waiving Defenses; Pretrial Hearing

(a) TIME TO SERVE A RESPONSIVE PLEADING.

(1) *In General.* Unless another time is specified by this rule or a federal statute, the time for serving a responsive pleading is as follows:

(A) A defendant must serve an answer:

(i) within 21 days after being served with the summons and complaint; or

(ii) if it has timely waived service under Rule 4(d), within 60 days after the request for a waiver was sent, or within 90 days after it was sent to the defendant outside any judicial district of the United States.

(B) A party must serve an answer to a counterclaim or crossclaim within 21 days after being served with the pleading that states the counterclaim or crossclaim.

(C) A party must serve a reply to an answer within 21 days after being served with an order to reply, unless the order specifies a different time.

(2) *United States and Its Agencies, Officers, or Employees Sued in an Official Capacity.* The United States, a United States agency, or a United States officer or employee sued only in an official capacity must serve an answer to a complaint, counterclaim, or crossclaim within 60 days after service on the United States attorney.

(3) *United States Officers or Employees Sued in an Individual Capacity.* A United States officer or employee sued in an individual capacity for an act or omission occurring in connection with duties performed on the United States' behalf must serve an answer to a complaint, counterclaim, or crossclaim within 60 days after service on the officer or employee or service on the United States attorney, whichever is later.

(4) *Effect of a Motion.* Unless the court sets a different time, serving a motion under this rule alters these periods as follows:

(A) if the court denies the motion or postpones its disposition until trial, the responsive pleading must be served within 14 days after notice of the court's action; or

(B) if the court grants a motion for a more definite statement, the responsive pleading must be served within 14 days after the more definite statement is served.

(b) How to Present Defenses. Every defense to a claim for relief in any pleading must be asserted in the responsive pleading if one is required. But a party may assert the following defenses by motion:

(1) lack of subject-matter jurisdiction;

(2) lack of personal jurisdiction;

(3) improper venue;

(4) insufficient process;

(5) insufficient service of process;

(6) failure to state a claim upon which relief can be granted; and

(7) failure to join a party under Rule 19.

A motion asserting any of these defenses must be made before pleading if a responsive pleading is allowed. If a pleading sets out a claim for relief that does not require a responsive pleading, an opposing party may assert at trial any defense to that claim. No defense or objection is waived by joining it with one or more other defenses or objections in a responsive pleading or in a motion.

(c) Motion for Judgment on the Pleadings. After the pleadings are closed—but early enough not to delay trial—a party may move for judgment on the pleadings.

(d) Result of Presenting Matters Outside the Pleadings. If, on a motion under Rule 12(b)(6) or 12(c), matters outside the pleadings are presented to and not excluded by the court, the motion must be treated as one for summary judgment under Rule 56. All parties must be given a reasonable opportunity to present all the material that is pertinent to the motion.

(e) Motion for a More Definite Statement. A party may move for a more definite statement of a pleading to which a responsive pleading is allowed but which is so vague or ambiguous that the party cannot reasonably prepare a response. The motion must be made before filing a responsive pleading and must point out the defects complained of and the details desired. If the court orders a more definite statement and the order is not obeyed within 14 days after notice of the order or within the time the court sets, the court may strike the pleading or issue any other appropriate order.

(f) Motion to Strike. The court may strike from a pleading an insufficient defense or any redundant, immaterial, impertinent, or scandalous matter. The court may act:

(1) on its own; or

(2) on motion made by a party either before responding to the pleading or, if a response is not allowed, within 21 days after being served with the pleading.

(g) Joining Motions.

(1) *Right to Join.* A motion under this rule may be joined with any other motion allowed by this rule.

(2) *Limitation on Further Motions.* Except as provided in Rule

12(h)(2) or (3), a party that makes a motion under this rule must not make another motion under this rule raising a defense or objection that was available to the party but omitted from its earlier motion.

(h) WAIVING AND PRESERVING CERTAIN DEFENSES.

(1) *When Some Are Waived.* A party waives any defense listed in Rule 12(b)(2)–(5) by:

(A) omitting it from a motion in the circumstances described in Rule 12(g)(2); or

(B) failing to either:

(i) make it by motion under this rule; or

(ii) include it in a responsive pleading or in an amendment allowed by Rule 15(a)(1) as a matter of course.

(2) *When to Raise Others.* Failure to state a claim upon which relief can be granted, to join a person required by Rule 19(b), or to state a legal defense to a claim may be raised:

(A) in any pleading allowed or ordered under Rule 7(a);

(B) by a motion under Rule 12(c); or

(C) at trial.

(3) *Lack of Subject-Matter Jurisdiction.* If the court determines at any time that it lacks subject-matter jurisdiction, the court must dismiss the action.

(i) HEARING BEFORE TRIAL. If a party so moves, any defense listed in Rule 12(b)(1)–(7)—whether made in a pleading or by motion—and a motion under Rule 12(c) must be heard and decided before trial unless the court orders a deferral until trial.

## Rule 7013 Counterclaim and Cross-Claim

Rule 13 F.R.Civ.P. applies in adversary proceedings, except that a party sued by a trustee or debtor in possession need not state as a counterclaim any claim that the party has against the debtor, the debtor's property, or the estate, unless the claim arose after the entry of an order for relief. A trustee or debtor in possession who fails to plead a counterclaim through oversight, inadvertence, or excusable neglect, or when justice so requires, may by leave of court amend the pleading, or commence a new adversary proceeding or separate action.

## CIVIL RULE:

Federal Rule of Civil Procedure 13, which was last amended effective December 1, 2009, provides:

### Rule 13 Counterclaim and Crossclaim

(a) COMPULSORY COUNTERCLAIM.

(1) *In General.* A pleading must state as a counterclaim any claim that—at the time of its service—the pleader has against an opposing party if the claim:

(A) arises out of the transaction or occurrence that is the subject matter of the opposing party's claim; and

(B) does not require adding another party over whom the court cannot acquire jurisdiction.

(2) *Exceptions.* The pleader need not state the claim if:

(A) when the action was commenced, the claim was the subject of another pending action; or

(B) the opposing party sued on its claim by attachment or other process that did not establish personal jurisdiction over the pleader on that claim, and the pleader does not assert any counterclaim under this rule.

(b) PERMISSIVE COUNTERCLAIM. A pleading may state as a counterclaim against an opposing party any claim that is not compulsory.

(c) RELIEF SOUGHT IN A COUNTERCLAIM. A counterclaim need not diminish or defeat the recovery sought by the opposing party. It may request relief that exceeds in amount or differs in kind from the relief sought by the opposing party.

(d) COUNTERCLAIM AGAINST THE UNITED STATES. These rules do not expand the right to assert a counterclaim—or to claim a credit—against the United States or a United States officer or agency.

(e) COUNTERCLAIM MATURING OR ACQUIRED AFTER PLEADING. The court may permit a party to file a supplemental pleading asserting a counterclaim that matured or was acquired by the party after serving an earlier pleading.

(f) [ABROGATED.]

(g) CROSSCLAIM AGAINST A COPARTY. A pleading may state as a crossclaim any claim by one party against a coparty if the claim arises out of the transaction or occurrence that is the subject matter of the original action or of a counterclaim, or if the claim relates to any property that is the subject matter of the original action. The crossclaim may include a claim that the coparty is or may be liable to the crossclaimant for all or part of a claim asserted in the action against the crossclaimant.

(h) JOINING ADDITIONAL PARTIES. Rules 19 and 20 govern the addition of a person as a party to a counterclaim or crossclaim.

(i) SEPARATE TRIALS; SEPARATE JUDGMENTS. If the court orders separate trials under Rule 42(b), it may enter judgment on a counterclaim or crossclaim under Rule 54(b) when it has jurisdiction to do so, even if the opposing party's claims have been dismissed or otherwise resolved.

## Rule 7014 Third-Party Practice

Rule 14 F.R.Civ.P. applies in adversary proceedings.

## CIVIL RULE:

Federal Rule of Civil Procedure 14, which was last amended effective December 1, 2009, provides:

### Rule 14 Third-Party Practice

(a) WHEN A DEFENDING PARTY MAY BRING IN A THIRD PARTY.

(1) *Timing of the Summons and Complaint.* A defending party may, as

third-party plaintiff, serve a summons and complaint on a nonparty who is or may be liable to it for all or part of the claim against it. But the third-party plaintiff must, by motion, obtain the court's leave if it files the third-party complaint more than 14 days after serving its original answer.

(2) *Third-Party Defendant's Claims and Defenses.* The person served with the summons and third-party complaint—the "third-party defendant":

(A) must assert any defense against the third-party plaintiff's claim under Rule 12;

(B) must assert any counterclaim against the third-party plaintiff under Rule 13(a), and may assert any counterclaim against the third-party plaintiff under Rule 13(b) or any crossclaim against another third-party defendant under Rule 13(g);

(C) may assert against the plaintiff any defense that the third-party plaintiff has to the plaintiff's claim; and

(D) may also assert against the plaintiff any claim arising out of the transaction or occurrence that is the subject matter of the plaintiff's claim against the third-party plaintiff.

(3) *Plaintiff's Claims Against a Third-Party Defendant.* The plaintiff may assert against the third-party defendant any claim arising out of the transaction or occurrence that is the subject matter of the plaintiff's claim against the third-party plaintiff. The third-party defendant must then assert any defense under Rule 12 and any counterclaim under Rule 13(a), and may assert any counterclaim under Rule 13(b) or any crossclaim under Rule 13(g).

(4) *Motion to Strike, Sever, or Try Separately.* Any party may move to strike the third-party claim, to sever it, or to try it separately.

(5) *Third-Party Defendant's Claim Against a Nonparty.* A third-party defendant may proceed under this rule against a nonparty who is or may be liable to the third-party defendant for all or part of any claim against it.

(6) *Third-Party Complaint In Rem.* If it is within the admiralty or maritime jurisdiction, a third-party complaint may be in rem. In that event, a reference in this rule to the "summons" includes the warrant of arrest, and a reference to the defendant or third-party plaintiff includes, when appropriate, a person who asserts a right under Supplemental Rule C(6)(a)(i) in the property arrested.

(b) When a Plaintiff May Bring in a Third Party. When a claim is asserted against a plaintiff, the plaintiff may bring in a third party if this rule would allow a defendant to do so.

(c) Admiralty or Maritime Claim.

(1) *Scope of Impleader.* If a plaintiff asserts an admiralty or maritime claim under Rule 9(h), the defendant or a person who asserts a right under Supplemental Rule C(6)(a)(i) may, as a third-party plaintiff, bring in a third-party defendant who may be wholly or partly

liable—either to the plaintiff or to the third-party plaintiff—for remedy over, contribution, or otherwise on account of the same transaction, occurrence, or series of transactions or occurrences.

(2) *Defending Against a Demand for Judgment for the Plaintiff.* The third-party plaintiff may demand judgment in the plaintiff's favor against the third-party defendant. In that event, the third-party defendant must defend under Rule 12 against the plaintiff's claim as well as the third-party plaintiff's claim; and the action proceeds as if the plaintiff had sued both the third-party defendant and the third-party plaintiff.

**Rule 7015 Amended and Supplemental Pleadings**

Rule 15 F.R.Civ.P. applies in adversary proceedings.

## CIVIL RULE:

Federal Rule of Civil Procedure 15, which was last amended effective December 1, 2009, provides:

**Rule 15 Amended and Supplemental Pleadings**

(a) AMENDMENTS BEFORE TRIAL.

(1) *Amending as a Matter of Course.* A party may amend its pleading once as a matter of course within:

(A) 21 days after serving it, or

(B) if the pleading is one to which a responsive pleading is required, 21 days after service of a responsive pleading or 21 days after service of a motion under Rule 12(b), (e), or (f), whichever is earlier.

(2) *Other Amendments.* In all other cases, a party may amend its pleading only with the opposing party's written consent or the court's leave. The court should freely give leave when justice so requires.

(3) *Time to Respond.* Unless the court orders otherwise, any required response to an amended pleading must be made within the time remaining to respond to the original pleading or within 14 days after service of the amended pleading, whichever is later.

(b) AMENDMENTS DURING AND AFTER TRIAL.

(1) *Based on an Objection at Trial.* If, at trial, a party objects that evidence is not within the issues raised in the pleadings, the court may permit the pleadings to be amended. The court should freely permit an amendment when doing so will aid in presenting the merits and the objecting party fails to satisfy the court that the evidence would prejudice that party's action or defense on the merits. The court may grant a continuance to enable the objecting party to meet the evidence.

(2) *For Issues Tried by Consent.* When an issue not raised by the pleadings is tried by the parties' express or implied consent, it must be treated in all respects as if raised in the pleadings. A party may move—at any time, even after judgment—to amend the pleadings to

conform them to the evidence and to raise an unpleaded issue. But failure to amend does not affect the result of the trial of that issue.

(c) Relation Back of Amendments.

(1) *When an Amendment Relates Back.* An amendment to a pleading relates back to the date of the original pleading when:

(A) the law that provides the applicable statute of limitations allows relation back;

(B) the amendment asserts a claim or defense that arose out of the conduct, transaction, or occurrence set out—or attempted to be set out—in the original pleading; or

(C) the amendment changes the party or the naming of the party against whom a claim is asserted, if Rule 15(c)(1)(B) is satisfied and if, within the period provided by Rule 4(m) for serving the summons and complaint, the party to be brought in by amendment:

(i) received such notice of the action that it will not be prejudiced in defending on the merits; and

(ii) knew or should have known that the action would have been brought against it, but for a mistake concerning the proper party's identity.

(2) *Notice to the United States.* When the United States or a United States officer or agency is added as a defendant by amendment, the notice requirements of Rule 15(c)(1)(C)(i) and (ii) are satisfied if, during the stated period, process was delivered or mailed to the United States attorney or the United States attorney's designee, to the Attorney General of the United States, or to the officer or agency.

(d) Supplemental Pleadings. On motion and reasonable notice, the court may, on just terms, permit a party to serve a supplemental pleading setting out any transaction, occurrence, or event that happened after the date of the pleading to be supplemented. The court may permit supplementation even though the original pleading is defective in stating a claim or defense. The court may order that the opposing party plead to the supplemental pleading within a specified time.

Bankruptcy Code Reference: § 105

## Rule 7016 Pretrial Procedures

(*a*) *Pretrial Conferences; Scheduling; Management.* Rule 16 F.R.Civ.P. applies in adversary proceedings.

(*b*) *Determining Procedure.* The bankruptcy court shall decide, on its own motion or a party's timely motion, whether:

(*1*) to hear and determine the proceeding;

(*2*) to hear the proceeding and issue proposed findings of fact and conclusions of law; or

(3) to take some other action.

## CIVIL RULE:

Federal Rule of Civil Procedure 16, which was last amended effective December 1, 2015, provides:

**Rule 16 Pretrial Conferences; Scheduling; Management**

(a) PURPOSES OF A PRETRIAL CONFERENCE. In any action, the court may order the attorneys and any unrepresented parties to appear for one or more pretrial conferences for such purposes as:

(1) expediting disposition of the action;

(2) establishing early and continuing control so that the case will not be protracted because of lack of management;

(3) discouraging wasteful pretrial activities;

(4) improving the quality of the trial through more thorough preparation; and

(5) facilitating settlement.

(b) SCHEDULING.

(1) *Scheduling Order.* Except in categories of actions exempted by local rule, the district judge—or a magistrate judge when authorized by local rule—must issue a scheduling order:

(A) after receiving the parties' report under Rule 26(f); or

(B) after consulting with the parties' attorneys and any unrepresented parties at a scheduling conference.

(2) *Time to Issue.* The judge must issue the scheduling order as soon as practicable, but unless the judge finds good cause for delay, the judge must issue it within the earlier of 90 days after any defendant has been served with the complaint or 60 days after any defendant has appeared.

(3) *Contents of the Order.*

(A) *Required Contents.* The scheduling order must limit the time to join other parties, amend the pleadings, complete discovery, and file motions.

(B) *Permitted Contents.* The scheduling order may:

(i) modify the timing of disclosures under Rules 26(a) and 26(e)(1);

(ii) modify the extent of discovery;

(iii) provide for disclosure, discovery, or preservation of electronically stored information;

(iv) include any agreements the parties reach for asserting claims of privilege or of protection as trial-preparation material after information is produced, including agreements reached under Federal Rule of Evidence 502;

(v) direct that before moving for an order relating to discovery, the movant must request a conference with the court;

(vi) set dates for pretrial conferences and for trial; and

(vii) include other appropriate matters.

(4) *Modifying a Schedule.* A schedule may be modified only for good cause and with the judge's consent.

(c) ATTENDANCE AND MATTERS FOR CONSIDERATION AT A PRETRIAL CONFERENCE.

(1) *Attendance.* A represented party must authorize at least one of its attorneys to make stipulations and admissions about all matters that can reasonably be anticipated for discussion at a pretrial conference. If appropriate, the court may require that a party or its representative be present or reasonably available by other means to consider possible settlement.

(2) *Matters for Consideration.* At any pretrial conference, the court may consider and take appropriate action on the following matters:

(A) formulating and simplifying the issues, and eliminating frivolous claims or defenses;

(B) amending the pleadings if necessary or desirable;

(C) obtaining admissions and stipulations about facts and documents to avoid unnecessary proof, and ruling in advance on the admissibility of evidence;

(D) avoiding unnecessary proof and cumulative evidence, and limiting the use of testimony under Federal Rule of Evidence 702;

(E) determining the appropriateness and timing of summary adjudication under Rule 56;

(F) controlling and scheduling discovery, including orders affecting disclosures and discovery under Rule 26 and Rules 29 through 37;

(G) identifying witnesses and documents, scheduling the filing and exchange of any pretrial briefs, and setting dates for further conferences and for trial;

(H) referring matters to a magistrate judge or a master;

(I) settling the case and using special procedures to assist in resolving the dispute when authorized by statute or local rule;

(J) determining the form and content of the pretrial order;

(K) disposing of pending motions;

(L) adopting special procedures for managing potentially difficult or protracted actions that may involve complex issues, multiple parties, difficult legal questions, or unusual proof problems;

(M) ordering a separate trial under Rule 42(b) of a claim, counterclaim, crossclaim, third-party claim, or particular issue;

(N) ordering the presentation of evidence early in the trial on a manageable issue that might, on the evidence, be the basis for a judgment as a matter of law under Rule 50(a) or a judgment on partial findings under Rule 52(c);

(O) establishing a reasonable limit on the time allowed to

present evidence; and

(P) facilitating in other ways the just, speedy, and inexpensive disposition of the action.

(d) PRETRIAL ORDERS. After any conference under this rule, the court should issue an order reciting the action taken. This order controls the course of the action unless the court modifies it.

(e) FINAL PRETRIAL CONFERENCE AND ORDERS. The court may hold a final pretrial conference to formulate a trial plan, including a plan to facilitate the admission of evidence. The conference must be held as close to the start of trial as is reasonable, and must be attended by at least one attorney who will conduct the trial for each party and by any unrepresented party. The court may modify the order issued after a final pretrial conference only to prevent manifest injustice.

(f) SANCTIONS.

(1) *In General.* On motion or on its own, the court may issue any just orders, including those authorized by Rule 37(b)(2)(A)(ii)–(vii), if a party or its attorney:

(A) fails to appear at a scheduling or other pretrial conference;

(B) is substantially unprepared to participate—or does not participate in good faith—in the conference; or

(C) fails to obey a scheduling or other pretrial order.

(2) *Imposing Fees and Costs.* Instead of or in addition to any other sanction, the court must order the party, its attorney, or both to pay the reasonable expenses—including attorney's fees—incurred because of any noncompliance with this rule, unless the noncompliance was substantially justified or other circumstances make an award of expenses unjust.

BANKRUPTCY CODE REFERENCE: § 105

## Rule 7017 Parties Plaintiff and Defendant; Capacity

Rule 17 F.R.Civ.P. applies in adversary proceedings, except as provided in Rule 2010(b).

## CIVIL RULE:

Federal Rule of Civil Procedure 17, which was last amended effective December 1, 2007, provides:

### Rule 17 Plaintiff and Defendant; Capacity; Public Officers

(a) REAL PARTY IN INTEREST.

(1) *Designation in General.* An action must be prosecuted in the name of the real party in interest. The following may sue in their own names without joining the person for whose benefit the action is brought:

(A) an executor;

(B) an administrator;

(C) a guardian;

(D) a bailee;

(E) a trustee of an express trust;

(F) a party with whom or in whose name a contract has been made for another's benefit; and

(G) a party authorized by statute.

(2) *Action in the Name of the United States for Another's Use or Benefit.* When a federal statute so provides, an action for another's use or benefit must be brought in the name of the United States.

(3) *Joinder of the Real Party in Interest.* The court may not dismiss an action for failure to prosecute in the name of the real party in interest until, after an objection, a reasonable time has been allowed for the real party in interest to ratify, join, or be substituted into the action. After ratification, joinder, or substitution, the action proceeds as if it had been originally commenced by the real party in interest.

(b) Capacity to Sue or be Sued. Capacity to sue or be sued is determined as follows:

(1) for an individual who is not acting in a representative capacity, by the law of the individual's domicile;

(2) for a corporation, by the law under which it was organized; and

(3) for all other parties, by the law of the state where the court is located, except that:

(A) a partnership or other unincorporated association with no such capacity under that state's law may sue or be sued in its common name to enforce a substantive right existing under the United States Constitution or laws; and

(B) 28 U.S.C. §§ 754 and 959(a) govern the capacity of a receiver appointed by a United States court to sue or be sued in a United States court.

(c) Minor or Incompetent Person.

(1) *With a Representative.* The following representatives may sue or defend on behalf of a minor or an incompetent person:

(A) a general guardian;

(B) a committee;

(C) a conservator; or

(D) a like fiduciary.

(2) *Without a Representative.* A minor or an incompetent person who does not have a duly appointed representative may sue by a next friend or by a guardian ad litem. The court must appoint a guardian ad litem—or issue another appropriate order—to protect a minor or incompetent person who is unrepresented in an action.

(d) Public Officer's Title and Name. A public officer who sues or is sued in an official capacity may be designated by official title rather than by name, but the court may order that the officer's name be added.

## Rule 7018 Joinder of Claims and Remedies

Rule 18 F.R.Civ.P. applies in adversary proceedings.

### CIVIL RULE:

Federal Rule of Civil Procedure 18, which was last amended effective December 1, 2007, provides:

**Rule 18 Joinder of Claims**

(a) IN GENERAL. A party asserting a claim, counterclaim, crossclaim, or third-party claim may join, as independent or alternative claims, as many claims as it has against an opposing party.

(b) JOINDER OF CONTINGENT CLAIMS. A party may join two claims even though one of them is contingent on the disposition of the other; but the court may grant relief only in accordance with the parties' relative substantive rights. In particular, a plaintiff may state a claim for money and a claim to set aside a conveyance that is fraudulent as to that plaintiff, without first obtaining a judgment for the money.

BANKRUPTCY CODE REFERENCE: § 544

## Rule 7019 Joinder of Persons Needed for Just Determination

Rule 19 F.R.Civ.P. applies in adversary proceedings, except that (1) if an entity joined as a party raises the defense that the court lacks jurisdiction over the subject matter and the defense is sustained, the court shall dismiss such entity from the adversary proceedings and (2) if an entity joined as a party properly and timely raises the defense of improper venue, the court shall determine, as provided in 28 U.S.C. § 1412, whether that part of the proceeding involving the joined party shall be transferred to another district, or whether the entire adversary proceeding shall be transferred to another district.



### CIVIL RULE:

Federal Rule of Civil Procedure 19, which was last amended effective December 1, 2007, provides:

**Rule 19 Required Joinder of Parties**

(a) PERSONS REQUIRED TO BE JOINED IF FEASIBLE.

(1) *Required Party.* A person who is subject to service of process and whose joinder will not deprive the court of subject-matter jurisdiction must be joined as a party if:

(A) in that person's absence, the court cannot accord complete relief among existing parties; or

(B) that person claims an interest relating to the subject of the action and is so situated that disposing of the action in the person's absence may:

(i) as a practical matter impair or impede the person's ability to protect the interest; or

(ii) leave an existing party subject to a substantial risk of incurring double, multiple, or otherwise inconsistent obligations because of the interest.

(2) *Joinder by Court Order.* If a person has not been joined as required, the court must order that the person be made a party. A person who refuses to join as a plaintiff may be made either a defendant or, in a proper case, an involuntary plaintiff.

(3) *Venue.* If a joined party objects to venue and the joinder would make venue improper, the court must dismiss that party.

(b) WHEN JOINDER IS NOT FEASIBLE. If a person who is required to be joined if feasible cannot be joined, the court must determine whether, in equity and good conscience, the action should proceed among the existing parties or should be dismissed. The factors for the court to consider include:

(1) the extent to which a judgment rendered in the person's absence might prejudice that person or the existing parties;

(2) the extent to which any prejudice could be lessened or avoided by:

(A) protective provisions in the judgment;

(B) shaping the relief; or

(C) other measures;

(3) whether a judgment rendered in the person's absence would be adequate; and

(4) whether the plaintiff would have an adequate remedy if the action were dismissed for nonjoinder.

(c) PLEADING THE REASONS FOR NONJOINDER. When asserting a claim for relief, a party must state:

(1) the name, if known, of any person who is required to be joined if feasible but is not joined; and

(2) the reasons for not joining that person.

(d) EXCEPTION FOR CLASS ACTIONS. This rule is subject to Rule 23.

BANKRUPTCY STATUTORY REFERENCE: 28 U.S.C. § 1412

## Rule 7020 Permissive Joinder of Parties

Rule 20 F.R.Civ.P. applies in adversary proceedings.

## CIVIL RULE:

Federal Rule of Civil Procedure 20, which was last amended effective December 1, 2007, provides:

### Rule 20 Permissive Joinder of Parties

(a) PERSONS WHO MAY JOIN OR BE JOINED.

(1) *Plaintiffs.* Persons may join in one action as plaintiffs if:

(A) they assert any right to relief jointly, severally, or in the alternative with respect to or arising out of the same transaction, occurrence, or series of transactions or occurrences; and

(B) any question of law or fact common to all plaintiffs will arise in the action.

(2) *Defendants.* Persons—as well as a vessel, cargo, or other property subject to admiralty process in rem—may be joined in one action as defendants if:

(A) any right to relief is asserted against them jointly, severally, or in the alternative with respect to or arising out of the same transaction, occurrence, or series of transactions or occurrences; and

(B) any question of law or fact common to all defendants will arise in the action.

(3) *Extent of Relief.* Neither a plaintiff nor a defendant need be interested in obtaining or defending against all the relief demanded. The court may grant judgment to one or more plaintiffs according to their rights, and against one or more defendants according to their liabilities.

(b) Protective Measures. The court may issue orders—including an order for separate trials—to protect a party against embarrassment, delay, expense, or other prejudice that arises from including a person against whom the party asserts no claim and who asserts no claim against the party.

### Rule 7021 Misjoinder and Non-Joinder of Parties

Rule 21 F.R.Civ.P. applies in adversary proceedings.

## CIVIL RULE:

Federal Rule of Civil Procedure 21, which was last amended effective December 1, 2007, provides:

#### Rule 21 Misjoinder and Nonjoinder of Parties

Misjoinder of parties is not a ground for dismissing an action. On motion or on its own, the court may at any time, on just terms, add or drop a party. The court may also sever any claim against a party.

Bankruptcy Code Reference: § 302

### Rule 7022 Interpleader

Rule 22(a) F.R.Civ.P. applies in adversary proceedings. This rule supplements—and does not limit—the joinder of parties allowed by Rule 7020.

## CIVIL RULE:

Federal Rule of Civil Procedure 22, which was last amended effective December 1, 2007, provides:

#### Rule 22 Interpleader

(a) Grounds.

(1) *By a Plaintiff.* Persons with claims that may expose a plaintiff to double or multiple liability may be joined as defendants and required to interplead. Joinder for interpleader is proper even though:

(A) the claims of the several claimants, or the titles on which their claims depend, lack a common origin or are adverse and independent rather than identical; or

(B) the plaintiff denies liability in whole or in part to any or all of the claimants.

(2) *By a Defendant.* A defendant exposed to similar liability may seek interpleader through a crossclaim or counterclaim.

(b) Relation to Other Rules and Statutes. This rule supplements—and does not limit—the joinder of parties allowed by Rule 20. The remedy this rule provides is in addition to—and does not supersede or limit—the remedy provided by 28 U.S.C. §§ 1335, 1397, and 2361. An action under those statutes must be conducted under these rules.

**Rule 7023 Class Proceedings**

Rule 23 F.R.Civ.P. applies in adversary proceedings.

## CIVIL RULE:

Federal Rule of Civil Procedure 23, which was last amended effective December 1, 2018, provides:

**Rule 23 Class Actions**

(a) Prerequisites. One or more members of a class may sue or be sued as representative parties on behalf of all members only if:

(1) the class is so numerous that joinder of all members is impracticable;

(2) there are questions of law or fact common to the class;

(3) the claims or defenses of the representative parties are typical of the claims or defenses of the class; and

(4) the representative parties will fairly and adequately protect the interests of the class.

(b) Types of Class Actions. A class action may be maintained if Rule 23(a) is satisfied and if:

(1) prosecuting separate actions by or against individual class members would create a risk of:

(A) inconsistent or varying adjudications with respect to individual class members that would establish incompatible standards of conduct for the party opposing the class; or

(B) adjudications with respect to individual class members that, as a practical matter, would be dispositive of the interests of the other members not parties to the individual adjudications or would substantially impair or impede their ability to protect their interests;

(2) the party opposing the class has acted or refused to act on grounds that apply generally to the class, so that final injunctive relief or corresponding declaratory relief is appropriate respecting the class as a whole; or

(3) the court finds that the questions of law or fact common to class members predominate over any questions affecting only individual members, and that a class action is superior to other available methods for fairly and efficiently adjudicating the controversy. The matters pertinent to these findings include:

(A) the class members' interests in individually controlling the prosecution or defense of separate actions;

(B) the extent and nature of any litigation concerning the controversy already begun by or against class members;

(C) the desirability or undesirability of concentrating the litigation of the claims in the particular forum; and

(D) the likely difficulties in managing a class action.

(c) CERTIFICATION ORDER; NOTICE TO CLASS MEMBERS; JUDGMENT; ISSUES CLASSES; SUBCLASSES.

(1) *Certification Order.*

(A) *Time to Issue.* At an early practicable time after a person sues or is sued as a class representative, the court must determine by order whether to certify the action as a class action.

(B) *Defining the Class; Appointing Class Counsel.* An order that certifies a class action must define the class and the class claims, issues, or defenses, and must appoint class counsel under Rule 23(g).

(C) *Altering or Amending the Order.* An order that grants or denies class certification may be altered or amended before final judgment.

(2) *Notice.*

(A) *For (b)(1) or (b)(2) Classes.* For any class certified under Rule 23(b)(1) or (b)(2), the court may direct appropriate notice to the class.

(B) *For (b)(3) Classes.* For any class certified under Rule 23(b)(3)—or upon ordering notice under Rule 23(e)(1) to a class proposed to be certified for purposes of settlement under Rule 23(b)(3)—the court must direct to class members the best notice that is practicable under the circumstances, including individual notice to all members who can be identified through reasonable effort. The notice may be by one or more of the following: United States mail, electronic means, or other appropriate means. The notice must clearly and concisely state in plain, easily understood language:

(i) the nature of the action;

(ii) the definition of the class certified;

(iii) the class claims, issues, or defenses;

(iv) that a class member may enter an appearance through an attorney if the member so desires;

(v) that the court will exclude from the class any member who requests exclusion;

(vi) the time and manner for requesting exclusion; and

(vii) the binding effect of a class judgment on members under Rule 23(c)(3).

(3) *Judgment.* Whether or not favorable to the class, the judgment in a class action must:

(A) for any class certified under Rule 23(b)(1) or (b)(2), include and describe those whom the court finds to be class members; and

(B) for any class certified under Rule 23(b)(3), include and specify or describe those to whom the Rule 23(c)(2) notice was directed, who have not requested exclusion, and whom the court finds to be class members.

(4) *Particular Issues.* When appropriate, an action may be brought or maintained as a class action with respect to particular issues.

(5) *Subclasses.* When appropriate, a class may be divided into subclasses that are each treated as a class under this rule.

(d) CONDUCTING THE ACTION.

(1) *In General.* In conducting an action under this rule, the court may issue orders that:

(A) determine the course of proceedings or prescribe measures to prevent undue repetition or complication in presenting evidence or argument;

(B) require—to protect class members and fairly conduct the action—giving appropriate notice to some or all class members of:

(i) any step in the action;

(ii) the proposed extent of the judgment; or

(iii) the members' opportunity to signify whether they consider the representation fair and adequate, to intervene and present claims or defenses, or to otherwise come into the action;

(C) impose conditions on the representative parties or on intervenors;

(D) require that the pleadings be amended to eliminate allegations about representation of absent persons and that the action proceed accordingly; or

(E) deal with similar procedural matters.

(2) *Combining and Amending Orders.* An order under Rule 23(d)(1) may be altered or amended from time to time and may be combined with an order under Rule 16.

(e) SETTLEMENT, VOLUNTARY DISMISSAL, OR COMPROMISE. The claims, issues, or defenses of a certified class—or a class proposed to be certified for purposes of settlement—may be settled, voluntarily dismissed, or compromised only with the court's approval. The following procedures apply to a proposed settlement, voluntary dismissal, or compromise:

(1) *Notice to the Class.*

(A) *Information That Parties Must Provide to the Court.* The parties must provide the court with information sufficient to enable it to determine whether to give notice of the proposal to the class.

(B) *Grounds for a Decision to Give Notice.* The court must direct notice in a reasonable manner to all class members who would be bound by the proposal if giving notice is justified by the parties' showing that the court will likely be able to:

(i) approve the proposal under Rule 23(e)(2); and

(ii) certify the class for purposes of judgment on the proposal.

(2) *Approval of the Proposal.* If the proposal would bind class members, the court may approve it only after a hearing and only on finding that it is fair, reasonable, and adequate after considering whether:

(A) the class representatives and class counsel have adequately represented the class;

(B) the proposal was negotiated at arm's length;

(C) the relief provided for the class is adequate, taking into account:

(i) the costs, risks, and delay of trial and appeal;

(ii) the effectiveness of any proposed method of distributing relief to the class, including the method of processing class-member claims;

(iii) the terms of any proposed award of attorney's fees, including timing of payment; and

(iv) any agreement required to be identified under Rule 23(e)(3); and

(D) the proposal treats class members equitably relative to each other.

(3) *Identifying Agreements.* The parties seeking approval must file a statement identifying any agreement made in connection with the proposal.

(4) *New Opportunity to Be Excluded.* If the class action was previously certified under Rule 23(b)(3), the court may refuse to approve a settlement unless it affords a new opportunity to request exclusion to individual class members who had an earlier opportunity to request exclusion but did not do so.

(5) *Class-Member Objections.*

(A) *In General.* Any class member may object to the proposal if it requires court approval under this subdivision (e). The objection must state whether it applies only to the objector, to a specific subset of the class, or to the entire class, and also state with specificity the grounds for the objection.

(B) *Court Approval Required for Payment in Connection with an Objection.* Unless approved by the court after a hearing, no payment or other consideration may be provided in connection with:

(i) forgoing or withdrawing an objection, or

(ii) forgoing, dismissing, or abandoning an appeal from a judgment approving the proposal.

(C) *Procedure for Approval After an Appeal.* If approval under Rule 23(e)(5)(B) has not been obtained before an appeal is docketed in the court of appeals, the procedure of Rule 62.1 applies while the appeal remains pending.

(f) APPEALS. A court of appeals may permit an appeal from an order granting or denying class-action certification under this rule, but not from an order under Rule 23(e)(1). A party must file a petition for permission to appeal with the circuit clerk within 14 days after the order is entered, or within 45 days after the order is entered if any party is the United States, a United States agency, or a United States officer or employee sued for an act or omission occurring in connection with duties performed on the United States' behalf. An appeal does not stay proceedings in the district court unless the district judge or the court of appeals so orders.

(g) CLASS COUNSEL.

(1) *Appointing Class Counsel.* Unless a statute provides otherwise, a court that certifies a class must appoint class counsel. In appointing class counsel, the court:

(A) must consider:

(i) the work counsel has done in identifying or investigating potential claims in the action;

(ii) counsel's experience in handling class actions, other complex litigation, and the types of claims asserted in the action;

(iii) counsel's knowledge of the applicable law; and

(iv) the resources that counsel will commit to representing the class;

(B) may consider any other matter pertinent to counsel's ability to fairly and adequately represent the interests of the class;

(C) may order potential class counsel to provide information on any subject pertinent to the appointment and to propose terms for attorney's fees and nontaxable costs;

(D) may include in the appointing order provisions about the award of attorney's fees or nontaxable costs under Rule 23(h); and

(E) may make further orders in connection with the appointment.

(2) *Standard for Appointing Class Counsel.* When one applicant seeks appointment as class counsel, the court may appoint that applicant only if the applicant is adequate under Rule 23(g)(1) and (4). If more than one adequate applicant seeks appointment, the court must appoint the applicant best able to represent the interests of the class.

(3) *Interim Counsel.* The court may designate interim counsel to act on behalf of a putative class before determining whether to certify the action as a class action.

(4) *Duty of Class Counsel.* Class counsel must fairly and adequately represent the interests of the class.

(h) ATTORNEY'S FEES AND NONTAXABLE COSTS. In a certified class action, the court may award reasonable attorney's fees and nontaxable costs that are authorized by law or by the parties' agreement. The following procedures apply:

(1) A claim for an award must be made by motion under Rule 54(d)(2), subject to the provisions of this subdivision (h), at a time the court sets. Notice of the motion must be served on all parties and, for motions by class counsel, directed to class members in a reasonable manner.

(2) A class member, or a party from whom payment is sought, may object to the motion.

(3) The court may hold a hearing and must find the facts and state its legal conclusions under Rule 52(a).

(4) The court may refer issues related to the amount of the award to a special master or a magistrate judge, as provided in Rule 54(d)(2)(D).

## Rule 7023.1 Derivative Actions

Rule 23.1 F.R.Civ.P. applies in adversary proceedings.

## CIVIL RULE:

Federal Rule of Civil Procedure 23.1, which was last amended effective December 1, 2007, provides:

### Rule 23.1 Derivative Actions

(a) Prerequisites. This rule applies when one or more shareholders or members of a corporation or an unincorporated association bring a derivative action to enforce a right that the corporation or association may properly assert but has failed to enforce. The derivative action may not be maintained if it appears that the plaintiff does not fairly and adequately represent the interests of shareholders or members who are similarly situated in enforcing the right of the corporation or association.

(b) Pleading Requirements. The complaint must be verified and must:

(1) allege that the plaintiff was a shareholder or member at the time of the transaction complained of, or that the plaintiff's share or membership later devolved on it by operation of law;

(2) allege that the action is not a collusive one to confer jurisdiction that the court would otherwise lack; and

(3) state with particularity:

(A) any effort by the plaintiff to obtain the desired action from the directors or comparable authority and, if necessary, from the shareholders or members; and

(B) the reasons for not obtaining the action or not making the effort.

(c) Settlement, Dismissal, and Compromise. A derivative action may be settled, voluntarily dismissed, or compromised only with the court's approval. Notice of a proposed settlement, voluntary dismissal, or compromise must be given to shareholders or members in the manner that the court orders.

**Rule 7023.2 Adversary Proceedings Relating to Unincorporated Associations**

Rule 23.2 F.R.Civ.P. applies in adversary proceedings.

## CIVIL RULE:

Federal Rule of Civil Procedure 23.2, which was last amended effective December 1, 2007, provides:

**Rule 23.2 Actions Relating to Unincorporated Associations**

This rule applies to an action brought by or against the members of an unincorporated association as a class by naming certain members as representative parties. The action may be maintained only if it appears that those parties will fairly and adequately protect the interests of the association and its members. In conducting the action, the court may issue any appropriate orders corresponding with those in Rule 23(d), and the procedure for settlement, voluntary dismissal, or compromise must correspond with the procedure in Rule 23(e).

**Rule 7024 Intervention**

Rule 24 F.R.Civ.P. applies in adversary proceedings.

## CIVIL RULE:

Federal Rule of Civil Procedure 24, which was last amended effective December 1, 2007, provides:

**Rule 24 Intervention**

(a) Intervention of Right. On timely motion, the court must permit anyone to intervene who:

(1) is given an unconditional right to intervene by a federal statute; or

(2) claims an interest relating to the property or transaction that is the subject of the action, and is so situated that disposing of the action may as a practical matter impair or impede the movant's ability to protect its interest, unless existing parties adequately represent that interest.

(b) Permissive Intervention.

(1) *In General.* On timely motion, the court may permit anyone to intervene who:

(A) is given a conditional right to intervene by a federal statute; or

(B) has a claim or defense that shares with the main action a common question of law or fact.

(2) *By a Government Officer or Agency.* On timely motion, the court may permit a federal or state governmental officer or agency to intervene if a party's claim or defense is based on:

(A) a statute or executive order administered by the officer or agency; or

(B) any regulation, order, requirement, or agreement issued or made under the statute or executive order.

(3) *Delay or Prejudice.* In exercising its discretion, the court must consider whether the intervention will unduly delay or prejudice the adjudication of the original parties' rights.

(c) NOTICE AND PLEADING REQUIRED. A motion to intervene must be served on the parties as provided in Rule 5. The motion must state the grounds for intervention and be accompanied by a pleading that sets out the claim or defense for which intervention is sought.

BANKRUPTCY CODE REFERENCE: § 1109

## Rule 7025 Substitution of Parties

Subject to the provisions of Rule 2012, Rule 25 F.R.Civ.P. applies in adversary proceedings.

### CIVIL RULE:

Federal Rule of Civil Procedure 25, which was last amended effective December 1, 2007, provides:

**Rule 25 Substitution of Parties**

(a) DEATH.

(1) *Substitution if the Claim Is Not Extinguished.* If a party dies and the claim is not extinguished, the court may order substitution of the proper party. A motion for substitution may be made by any party or by the decedent's successor or representative. If the motion is not made within 90 days after service of a statement noting the death, the action by or against the decedent must be dismissed.

(2) *Continuation Among the Remaining Parties.* After a party's death, if the right sought to be enforced survives only to or against the remaining parties, the action does not abate, but proceeds in favor of or against the remaining parties. The death should be noted on the record.

(3) *Service.* A motion to substitute, together with a notice of hearing, must be served on the parties as provided in Rule 5 and on nonparties as provided in Rule 4. A statement noting death must be served in the same manner. Service may be made in any judicial district.

(b) INCOMPETENCY. If a party becomes incompetent, the court may, on motion, permit the action to be continued by or against the party's representative. The motion must be served as provided in Rule 25(a)(3).

(c) TRANSFER OF INTEREST. If an interest is transferred, the action may be continued by or against the original party unless the court, on motion, orders the transferee to be substituted in the action or joined with the original party. The motion must be served as provided in Rule 25(a)(3).

(d) PUBLIC OFFICERS; DEATH OR SEPARATION FROM OFFICE. An action does not abate when a public officer who is a party in an official capacity dies, resigns, or otherwise ceases to hold office while the action is pending. The officer's successor is automatically substituted as a party. Later proceedings should be in the substituted party's name, but any misnomer not affecting the parties' substantial rights must be disregarded. The court may order substitution at any time, but the absence of such an order does not affect the substitution.

Bankruptcy Code Reference: § 325

## Rule 7026 General Provisions Governing Discovery

Rule 26 F.R.Civ.P. applies in adversary proceedings.

### CIVIL RULE:

Federal Rule of Civil Procedure 26, which was last amended effective December 1, 2015, provides:

#### Rule 26 Duty to Disclose; General Provisions Governing Discovery

(a) Required Disclosures.

(1) *Initial Disclosure.*

(A) *In General.* Except as exempted by Rule 26(a)(1)(B) or as otherwise stipulated or ordered by the court, a party must, without awaiting a discovery request, provide to the other parties:

(i) the name and, if known, the address and telephone number of each individual likely to have discoverable information—along with the subjects of that information—that the disclosing party may use to support its claims or defenses, unless the use would be solely for impeachment;

(ii) a copy—or a description by category and location—of all documents, electronically stored information, and tangible things that the disclosing party has in its possession, custody, or control and may use to support its claims or defenses, unless the use would be solely for impeachment;

(iii) a computation of each category of damages claimed by the disclosing party—who must also make available for inspection and copying as under Rule 34 the documents or other evidentiary material, unless privileged or protected from disclosure, on which each computation is based, including materials bearing on the nature and extent of injuries suffered; and

(iv) for inspection and copying as under Rule 34, any insurance agreement under which an insurance business may be liable to satisfy all or part of a possible judgment in the action or to indemnify or reimburse for payments made to satisfy the judgment.

(B) *Proceedings Exempt from Initial Disclosure.* The following proceedings are exempt from initial disclosure:

(i) an action for review on an administrative record;

(ii) a forfeiture action in rem arising from a federal statute;

(iii) a petition for habeas corpus or any other proceeding to challenge a criminal conviction or sentence;

(iv) an action brought without an attorney by a person in the custody of the United States, a state, or a state subdivision;

(v) an action to enforce or quash an administrative summons or subpoena;

(vi) an action by the United States to recover benefit payments;

(vii) an action by the United States to collect on a student loan guaranteed by the United States;

(viii) a proceeding ancillary to a proceeding in another court; and

(ix) an action to enforce an arbitration award.

(C) *Time for Initial Disclosures—In General.* A party must make the initial disclosures at or within 14 days after the parties' Rule 26(f) conference unless a different time is set by stipulation or court order, or unless a party objects during the conference that initial disclosures are not appropriate in this action and states the objection in the proposed discovery plan. In ruling on the objection, the court must determine what disclosures, if any, are to be made and must set the time for disclosure.

(D) *Time for Initial Disclosures—For Parties Served or Joined Later.* A party that is first served or otherwise joined after the Rule 26(f) conference must make the initial disclosures within 30 days after being served or joined, unless a different time is set by stipulation or court order.

(E) *Basis for Initial Disclosure; Unacceptable Excuses.* A party must make its initial disclosures based on the information then reasonably available to it. A party is not excused from making its disclosures because it has not fully investigated the case or because it challenges the sufficiency of another party's disclosures or because another party has not made its disclosures.

(2) *Disclosure of Expert Testimony.*

(A) *In General.* In addition to the disclosures required by Rule 26(a)(1), a party must disclose to the other parties the identity of any witness it may use at trial to present evidence under Federal Rule of Evidence 702, 703, or 705.

(B) *Witnesses Who Must Provide a Written Report.* Unless otherwise stipulated or ordered by the court, this disclosure must be accompanied by a written report—prepared and signed by the witness—if the witness is one retained or specially employed to provide expert testimony in the case or one whose duties as the party's employee regularly involve giving expert testimony. The report must contain:

(i) a complete statement of all opinions the witness will express and the basis and reasons for them;

(ii) the facts or data considered by the witness in forming them;

(iii) any exhibits that will be used to summarize or support them;

(iv) the witness's qualifications, including a list of all publications authored in the previous 10 years;

(v) a list of all other cases in which, during the previous 4 years, the witness testified as an expert at trial or by deposition; and

(vi) a statement of the compensation to be paid for the study and testimony in the case.

(C) *Witnesses Who Do Not Provide a Written Report.* Unless otherwise stipulated or ordered by the court, if the witness is not required to provide a written report, this disclosure must state:

(i) the subject matter on which the witness is expected to present evidence under Federal Rule of Evidence 702, 703, or 705; and

(ii) a summary of the facts and opinions to which the witness is expected to testify.

(D) *Time to Disclose Expert Testimony.* A party must make these disclosures at the times and in the sequence that the court orders. Absent a stipulation or a court order, the disclosures must be made:

(i) at least 90 days before the date set for trial or for the case to be ready for trial; or

(ii) if the evidence is intended solely to contradict or rebut evidence on the same subject matter identified by another party under Rule 26(a)(2)(B) or (C), within 30 days after the other party's disclosure.

(E) *Supplementing the Disclosure.* The parties must supplement these disclosures when required under Rule 26(e).

(3) *Pretrial Disclosures.*

(A) *In General.* In addition to the disclosures required by Rule 26(a)(1) and (2), a party must provide to the other parties and promptly file the following information about the evidence that it may present at trial other than solely for impeachment:

(i) the name and, if not previously provided, the address and telephone number of each witness—separately identifying those the party expects to present and those it may call if the need arises;

(ii) the designation of those witnesses whose testimony the party expects to present by deposition and, if not taken stenographically, a transcript of the pertinent parts of the deposition; and

(iii) an identification of each document or other exhibit, including summaries of other evidence—separately identifying those items the party expects to offer and those it may offer if the need arises.

(B) *Time for Pretrial Disclosures; Objections.* Unless the court orders otherwise, these disclosures must be made at least 30 days before trial. Within 14 days after they are made, unless the court sets a different time, a party may serve and promptly file a list of the following objections: any objections to the use under Rule 32(a) of a deposition designated by another party under Rule 26(a)(3)(A)(ii); and any objection, together with the grounds for it, that may be made to the admissibility of materials identified under Rule 26(a)(3)(A)(iii). An objection not so made—except for one under Federal Rule of Evidence 402 or 403—is waived unless excused by the court for good cause.

(4) *Form of Disclosures.* Unless the court orders otherwise, all disclosures under Rule 26(a) must be in writing, signed, and served.

(b) DISCOVERY SCOPE AND LIMITS.

(1) *Scope in General.* Unless otherwise limited by court order, the scope of discovery is as follows: Parties may obtain discovery regarding any nonprivileged matter that is relevant to any party's claim or defense and proportional to the needs of the case, considering the importance of the issues at stake in the action, the amount in controversy, the parties' relative access to relevant information, the parties' resources, the importance of the discovery in resolving the issues, and whether the burden or expense of the proposed discovery outweighs its likely benefit. Information within this scope of discovery need not be admissible in evidence to be discoverable.

(2) *Limitations on Frequency and Extent.*

(A) *When Permitted.* By order, the court may alter the limits in these rules on the number of depositions and interrogatories or on the length of depositions under Rule 30. By order or local rule, the court may also limit the number of requests under Rule 36.

(B) *Specific Limitations on Electronically Stored Information.* A party need not provide discovery of electronically stored information from sources that the party identifies as not reasonably accessible because of undue burden or cost. On motion to compel discovery or for a protective order, the party from whom discovery is sought must show that the information is not reasonably accessible because of undue burden or cost. If that showing is made, the court may nonetheless order discovery from such sources if the requesting party shows good cause, considering the limitations of Rule 26(b)(2)(C). The court may specify conditions for the discovery.

(C) *When Required.* On motion or on its own, the court must limit the frequency or extent of discovery otherwise allowed by these rules or by local rule if it determines that:

(i) the discovery sought is unreasonably cumulative or duplicative, or can be obtained from some other source that is more convenient, less burdensome, or less expensive;

(ii) the party seeking discovery has had ample opportunity to obtain the information by discovery in the action; or

(iii) the proposed discovery is outside the scope permitted by Rule 26(b)(1).

(3) *Trial Preparation: Materials.*

(A) *Documents and Tangible Things.* Ordinarily, a party may not discover documents and tangible things that are prepared in anticipation of litigation or for trial by or for another party or its representative (including the other party's attorney, consultant, surety, indemnitor, insurer, or agent). But, subject to Rule 26(b)(4), those materials may be discovered if:

(i) they are otherwise discoverable under Rule 26(b)(1); and

(ii) the party shows that it has substantial need for the materials to prepare its case and cannot, without undue hardship, obtain their substantial equivalent by other means.

(B) *Protection Against Disclosure.* If the court orders discovery of those materials, it must protect against disclosure of the mental impressions, conclusions, opinions, or legal theories of a party's attorney or other representative concerning the litigation.

(C) *Previous Statement.* Any party or other person may, on request and without the required showing, obtain the person's own previous statement about the action or its subject matter. If the request is refused, the person may move for a court order, and Rule 37(a)(5) applies to the award of expenses. A previous statement is either:

(i) a written statement that the person has signed or otherwise adopted or approved; or

(ii) a contemporaneous stenographic, mechanical, electrical, or other recording—or a transcription of it—that recites substantially verbatim the person's oral statement.

(4) *Trial Preparation: Experts.*

(A) *Deposition of an Expert Who May Testify.* A party may depose any person who has been identified as an expert whose opinions may be presented at trial. If Rule 26(a)(2)(B) requires a report from the expert, the deposition may be conducted only after the report is provided.

(B) *Trial-Preparation Protection for Draft Reports or Disclosures.* Rules 26(b)(3)(A) and (B) protect drafts of any report or disclosure required under Rule 26(a)(2), regardless of the form in which the draft is recorded.

(C) *Trial-Preparation Protection for Communications Between a Party's Attorney and Expert Witnesses.* Rules 26(b)(3)(A) and (B) protect communications between the party's attorney and any witness required to provide a report under Rule 26(a)(2)(B), regardless of the form of the communications, except to the extent that the communications:

(i) relate to compensation for the expert's study or testimony;

(ii) identify facts or data that the party's attorney provided and that the expert considered in forming the opinions to be expressed; or

(iii) identify assumptions that the party's attorney provided and that the expert relied on in forming the opinions to be expressed.

(D) *Expert Employed Only for Trial Preparation.* Ordinarily, a party may not, by interrogatories or deposition, discover facts known or opinions held by an expert who has been retained or specially employed by another party in anticipation of litigation or to prepare for trial and who is not expected to be called as a witness at trial. But a party may do so only:

(i) as provided in Rule 35(b); or

(ii) on showing exceptional circumstances under which it is impracticable for the party to obtain facts or opinions on the same subject by other means.

(E) *Payment.* Unless manifest injustice would result, the court must require that the party seeking discovery:

(i) pay the expert a reasonable fee for time spent in responding to discovery under Rule 26(b)(4)(A) or (D); and

(ii) for discovery under (D), also pay the other party a fair portion of the fees and expenses it reasonably incurred in obtaining the expert's facts and opinions.

(5) *Claiming Privilege or Protecting Trial-Preparation Materials.*

(A) *Information Withheld.* When a party withholds information otherwise discoverable by claiming that the information is privileged or subject to protection as trial-preparation material, the party must:

(i) expressly make the claim; and

(ii) describe the nature of the documents, communications, or tangible things not produced or disclosed—and do so in a manner that, without revealing information itself privileged or protected, will enable other parties to assess the claim.

(B) *Information Produced.* If information produced in discovery is subject to a claim of privilege or of protection as trial-preparation material, the party making the claim may notify any party that received the information of the claim and the basis for it. After being notified, a party must promptly return, sequester, or destroy the specified information and any copies it has; must not use or disclose the information until the claim is resolved; must take reasonable steps to retrieve the information if the party disclosed it before being notified; and may promptly present the information to the court under seal for a determination of the claim. The producing party must preserve the information until the claim is resolved.

(c) PROTECTIVE ORDERS.

(1) *In General.* A party or any person from whom discovery is sought may move for a protective order in the court where the action is pending—or as an alternative on matters relating to a deposition, in the court for the district where the deposition will be taken. The motion must include a certification that the movant has in good faith conferred or attempted to confer with other affected parties in an effort to resolve the dispute without court action. The court may, for good cause, issue an order to protect a party or person from annoyance, embarrassment, oppression, or undue burden or expense, including one or more of the following:

(A) forbidding the disclosure or discovery;

(B) specifying terms, including time and place or the allocation of expenses, for the disclosure or discovery;

(C) prescribing a discovery method other than the one selected by the party seeking discovery;

(D) forbidding inquiry into certain matters, or limiting the scope of disclosure or discovery to certain matters;

(E) designating the persons who may be present while the discovery is conducted;

(F) requiring that a deposition be sealed and opened only on court order;

(G) requiring that a trade secret or other confidential research, development, or commercial information not be revealed or be revealed only in a specified way; and

(H) requiring that the parties simultaneously file specified documents or information in sealed envelopes, to be opened as the court directs.

(2) *Ordering Discovery.* If a motion for a protective order is wholly or partly denied, the court may, on just terms, order that any party or person provide or permit discovery.

(3) *Awarding Expenses.* Rule 37(a)(5) applies to the award of expenses.

(d) TIMING AND SEQUENCE OF DISCOVERY.

(1) *Timing.* A party may not seek discovery from any source before the parties have conferred as required by Rule 26(f), except in a proceeding exempted from initial disclosure under Rule 26(a)(1)(B), or when authorized by these rules, by stipulation, or by court order.

(2) *Early Rule 34 Requests.*

(A) *Time to Deliver.* More than 21 days after the summons and complaint are served on a party, a request under Rule 34 may be delivered:

(i) to that party by any other party, and

(ii) by that party to any plaintiff or to any other party that has been served.

(B) *When Considered Served.* The request is considered to have been served at the first Rule 26(f) conference.

(3) *Sequence.* Unless the parties stipulate or the court orders otherwise for the parties' and witnesses' convenience and in the interests of justice:

(A) methods of discovery may be used in any sequence; and

(B) discovery by one party does not require any other party to delay its discovery.

(e) Supplementing Disclosures and Responses.

(1) *In General.* A party who has made a disclosure under Rule 26(a)—or who has responded to an interrogatory, request for production, or request for admission—must supplement or correct its disclosure or response:

(A) in a timely manner if the party learns that in some material respect the disclosure or response is incomplete or incorrect, and if the additional or corrective information has not otherwise been made known to the other parties during the discovery process or in writing; or

(B) as ordered by the court.

(2) *Expert Witness.* For an expert whose report must be disclosed under Rule 26(a)(2)(B), the party's duty to supplement extends both to information included in the report and to information given during the expert's deposition. Any additions or changes to this information must be disclosed by the time the party's pretrial disclosures under Rule 26(a)(3) are due.

(f) Conference of the Parties; Planning for Discovery.

(1) *Conference Timing.* Except in a proceeding exempted from initial disclosure under Rule 26(a)(1)(B) or when the court orders otherwise, the parties must confer as soon as practicable—and in any event at least 21 days before a scheduling conference is to be held or a scheduling order is due under Rule 16(b).

(2) *Conference Content; Parties' Responsibilities.* In conferring, the parties must consider the nature and basis of their claims and defenses and the possibilities for promptly settling or resolving the case; make or arrange for the disclosures required by Rule 26(a)(1); discuss any issues about preserving discoverable information; and develop a proposed discovery plan. The attorneys of record and all unrepresented parties that have appeared in the case are jointly responsible for arranging the conference, for attempting in good faith to agree on the proposed discovery plan, and for submitting to the court within 14 days after the conference a written report outlining the plan. The court may order the parties or attorneys to attend the conference in person.

(3) *Discovery Plan.* A discovery plan must state the parties' views and proposals on:

(A) what changes should be made in the timing, form, or requirement for disclosures under Rule 26(a), including a statement of when initial disclosures were made or will be made;

(B) the subjects on which discovery may be needed, when discovery should be completed, and whether discovery should be conducted in phases or be limited to or focused on particular issues;

(C) any issues about disclosure, discovery, or preservation of electronically stored information, including the form or forms in which it should be produced;

(D) any issues about claims of privilege or of protection as trial-preparation materials, including—if the parties agree on a procedure to assert these claims after production—whether to ask the court to include their agreement in an order under Federal Rule of Evidence 502;

(E) what changes should be made in the limitations on discovery imposed under these rules or by local rule, and what other limitations should be imposed; and

(F) any other orders that the court should issue under Rule 26(c) or under Rule 16(b) and (c).

(4) *Expedited Schedule.* If necessary to comply with its expedited schedule for Rule 16(b) conferences, a court may by local rule:

(A) require the parties' conference to occur less than 21 days before the scheduling conference is held or a scheduling order is due under Rule 16(b); and

(B) require the written report outlining the discovery plan to be filed less than 14 days after the parties' conference, or excuse the parties from submitting a written report and permit them to report orally on their discovery plan at the Rule 16(b) conference.

(g) SIGNING DISCLOSURES AND DISCOVERY REQUESTS, RESPONSES, AND OBJECTIONS.

(1) *Signature Required; Effect of Signature.* Every disclosure under Rule 26(a)(1) or (a)(3) and every discovery request, response, or objection must be signed by at least one attorney of record in the attorney's own name—or by the party personally, if unrepresented—and must state the signer's address, e-mail address, and telephone number. By signing, an attorney or party certifies that to the best of the person's knowledge, information, and belief formed after a reasonable inquiry:

(A) with respect to a disclosure, it is complete and correct as of the time it is made; and

(B) with respect to a discovery request, response, or objection, it is:

(i) consistent with these rules and warranted by existing law or by a nonfrivolous argument for extending, modifying, or reversing existing law, or for establishing new law;

(ii) not interposed for any improper purpose, such as to harass, cause unnecessary delay, or needlessly increase the cost of litigation; and

(iii) neither unreasonable nor unduly burdensome or expensive, considering the needs of the case, prior discovery in the case, the amount in controversy, and the importance of the issues at stake in the action.

(2) *Failure to Sign.* Other parties have no duty to act on an unsigned disclosure, request, response, or objection until it is signed, and the court must strike it unless a signature is promptly supplied after the omission is called to the attorney's or party's attention.

(3) *Sanction for Improper Certification.* If a certification violates this rule without substantial justification, the court, on motion or on its own, must impose an appropriate sanction on the signer, the party on whose behalf the signer was acting, or both. The sanction may include an order to pay the reasonable expenses, including attorney's fees, caused by the violation.

## Rule 7027 Depositions Before Adversary Proceeding or Pending Appeal

Rule 27 F.R.Civ.P. applies in adversary proceedings.

## CIVIL RULE:

Federal Rule of Civil Procedure 27, which was last amended effective December 1, 2009, provides:

### Rule 27 Depositions to Perpetuate Testimony

(a) Before an Action Is Filed.

(1) *Petition.* A person who wants to perpetuate testimony about any matter cognizable in a United States court may file a verified petition in the district court for the district where any expected adverse party resides. The petition must ask for an order authorizing the petitioner to depose the named persons in order to perpetuate their testimony. The petition must be titled in the petitioner's name and must show:

(A) that the petitioner expects to be a party to an action cognizable in a United States court but cannot presently bring it or cause it to be brought;

(B) the subject matter of the expected action and the petitioner's interest;

(C) the facts that the petitioner wants to establish by the proposed testimony and the reasons to perpetuate it;

(D) the names or a description of the persons whom the petitioner expects to be adverse parties and their addresses, so far as known; and

(E) the name, address, and expected substance of the testimony of each deponent.

(2) *Notice and Service.* At least 21 days before the hearing date, the

petitioner must serve each expected adverse party with a copy of the petition and a notice stating the time and place of the hearing. The notice may be served either inside or outside the district or state in the manner provided in Rule 4. If that service cannot be made with reasonable diligence on an expected adverse party, the court may order service by publication or otherwise. The court must appoint an attorney to represent persons not served in the manner provided in Rule 4 and to cross-examine the deponent if an unserved person is not otherwise represented. If any expected adverse party is a minor or is incompetent, Rule 17(c) applies.

(3) *Order and Examination.* If satisfied that perpetuating the testimony may prevent a failure or delay of justice, the court must issue an order that designates or describes the persons whose depositions may be taken, specifies the subject matter of the examinations, and states whether the depositions will be taken orally or by written interrogatories. The depositions may then be taken under these rules, and the court may issue orders like those authorized by Rules 34 and 35. A reference in these rules to the court where an action is pending means, for purposes of this rule, the court where the petition for the deposition was filed.

(4) *Using the Deposition.* A deposition to perpetuate testimony may be used under Rule 32(a) in any later-filed district-court action involving the same subject matter if the deposition either was taken under these rules or, although not so taken, would be admissible in evidence in the courts of the state where it was taken.

(b) PENDING APPEAL.

(1) *In General.* The court where a judgment has been rendered may, if an appeal has been taken or may still be taken, permit a party to depose witnesses to perpetuate their testimony for use in the event of further proceedings in that court.

(2) *Motion.* The party who wants to perpetuate testimony may move for leave to take the depositions, on the same notice and service as if the action were pending in the district court. The motion must show:

(A) the name, address, and expected substance of the testimony of each deponent; and

(B) the reasons for perpetuating the testimony.

(3) *Court Order.* If the court finds that perpetuating the testimony may prevent a failure or delay of justice, the court may permit the depositions to be taken and may issue orders like those authorized by Rules 34 and 35. The depositions may be taken and used as any other deposition taken in a pending district-court action.

(c) PERPETUATION BY AN ACTION. This rule does not limit a court's power to entertain an action to perpetuate testimony.

## Rule 7028 Persons Before Whom Depositions May Be Taken

Rule 28 F.R.Civ.P. applies in adversary proceedings.

### CIVIL RULE:

Federal Rule of Civil Procedure 28, which was last amended effective December 1, 2007, provides:

**Rule 28 Persons Before Whom Depositions May Be Taken**

(a) WITHIN THE UNITED STATES.

(1) *In General.* Within the United States or a territory or insular possession subject to United States jurisdiction, a deposition must be taken before:

(A) an officer authorized to administer oaths either by federal law or by the law in the place of examination; or

(B) a person appointed by the court where the action is pending to administer oaths and take testimony.

(2) *Definition of "Officer."* The term "officer" in Rules 30, 31, and 32 includes a person appointed by the court under this rule or designated by the parties under Rule 29(a).

(b) IN A FOREIGN COUNTRY.

(1) *In General.* A deposition may be taken in a foreign country:

(A) under an applicable treaty or convention;

(B) under a letter of request, whether or not captioned a "letter rogatory";

(C) on notice, before a person authorized to administer oaths either by federal law or by the law in the place of examination; or

(D) before a person commissioned by the court to administer any necessary oath and take testimony.

(2) *Issuing a Letter of Request or a Commission.* A letter of request, a commission, or both may be issued:

(A) on appropriate terms after an application and notice of it; and

(B) without a showing that taking the deposition in another manner is impracticable or inconvenient.

(3) *Form of a Request, Notice, or Commission.* When a letter of request or any other device is used according to a treaty or convention, it must be captioned in the form prescribed by that treaty or convention. A letter of request may be addressed "To the Appropriate Authority in [name of country]." A deposition notice or a commission must designate by name or descriptive title the person before whom the deposition is to be taken.

(4) *Letter of Request—Admitting Evidence.* Evidence obtained in response to a letter of request need not be excluded merely because it is not a verbatim transcript, because the testimony was not taken under oath, or because of any similar departure from the requirements

for depositions taken within the United States.

(c) DISQUALIFICATION. A deposition must not be taken before a person who is any party's relative, employee, or attorney; who is related to or employed by any party's attorney; or who is financially interested in the action.

## Rule 7029 Stipulations Regarding Discovery Procedure

Rule 29 F.R.Civ.P. applies in adversary proceedings.

### CIVIL RULE:

Federal Rule of Civil Procedure 29, which was last amended effective December 1, 2007, provides:

**Rule 29 Stipulations About Discovery Procedure**

Unless the court orders otherwise, the parties may stipulate that:

(a) a deposition may be taken before any person, at any time or place, on any notice, and in the manner specified—in which event it may be used in the same way as any other deposition; and

(b) other procedures governing or limiting discovery be modified—but a stipulation extending the time for any form of discovery must have court approval if it would interfere with the time set for completing discovery, for hearing a motion, or for trial.

## Rule 7030 Depositions upon Oral Examination

Rule 30 F.R.Civ.P. applies in adversary proceedings.

### CIVIL RULE:

Federal Rule of Civil Procedure 30, which was last amended effective December 1, 2020, provides:

**Rule 30 Depositions by Oral Examination**

(a) WHEN A DEPOSITION MAY BE TAKEN.

(1) *Without Leave.* A party may, by oral questions, depose any person, including a party, without leave of court except as provided in Rule 30(a)(2). The deponent's attendance may be compelled by subpoena under Rule 45.

(2) *With Leave.* A party must obtain leave of court, and the court must grant leave to the extent consistent with Rule 26(b)(1) and (2):

(A) if the parties have not stipulated to the deposition and:

(i) the deposition would result in more than 10 depositions being taken under this rule or Rule 31 by the plaintiffs, or by the defendants, or by the third-party defendants;

(ii) the deponent has already been deposed in the case; or

(iii) the party seeks to take the deposition before the time specified in Rule 26(d), unless the party certifies in the notice, with supporting facts, that the deponent is expected to leave the United States and be unavailable for examination in this country after that time; or

(B) if the deponent is confined in prison.

(b) Notice of the Deposition; Other Formal Requirements.

(1) *Notice in General.* A party who wants to depose a person by oral questions must give reasonable written notice to every other party. The notice must state the time and place of the deposition and, if known, the deponent's name and address. If the name is unknown, the notice must provide a general description sufficient to identify the person or the particular class or group to which the person belongs.

(2) *Producing Documents.* If a subpoena duces tecum is to be served on the deponent, the materials designated for production, as set out in the subpoena, must be listed in the notice or in an attachment. The notice to a party deponent may be accompanied by a request under Rule 34 to produce documents and tangible things at the deposition.

(3) *Method of Recording.*

(A) *Method Stated in the Notice.* The party who notices the deposition must state in the notice the method for recording the testimony. Unless the court orders otherwise, testimony may be recorded by audio, audiovisual, or stenographic means. The noticing party bears the recording costs. Any party may arrange to transcribe a deposition.

(B) *Additional Method.* With prior notice to the deponent and other parties, any party may designate another method for recording the testimony in addition to that specified in the original notice. That party bears the expense of the additional record or transcript unless the court orders otherwise.

(4) *By Remote Means.* The parties may stipulate—or the court may on motion order—that a deposition be taken by telephone or other remote means. For the purpose of this rule and Rules 28(a), 37(a)(2), and 37(b)(1), the deposition takes place where the deponent answers the questions.

(5) *Officer's Duties.*

(A) *Before the Deposition.* Unless the parties stipulate otherwise, a deposition must be conducted before an officer appointed or designated under Rule 28. The officer must begin the deposition with an on-the-record statement that includes:

(i) the officer's name and business address;

(ii) the date, time, and place of the deposition;

(iii) the deponent's name;

(iv) the officer's administration of the oath or affirmation to the deponent; and

(v) the identity of all persons present.

(B) *Conducting the Deposition; Avoiding Distortion.* If the deposition is recorded nonstenographically, the officer must repeat the items in Rule 30(b)(5)(A)(i)–(iii) at the beginning of each unit of the recording medium. The deponent's and attorneys' appearance or demeanor must not be distorted through recording techniques.

(C) *After the Deposition.* At the end of a deposition, the officer must state on the record that the deposition is complete and must set out any stipulations made by the attorneys about custody of the transcript or recording and of the exhibits, or about any other pertinent matters.

(6) *Notice or Subpoena Directed to an Organization.* In its notice or subpoena, a party may name as the deponent a public or private corporation, a partnership, an association, a governmental agency, or other entity and must describe with reasonable particularity the matters for examination. The named organization must designate one or more officers, directors, or managing agents, or designate other persons who consent to testify on its behalf; and it may set out the matters on which each person designated will testify. Before or promptly after the notice or subpoena is served, the serving party and the organization must confer in good faith about the matters for examination. A subpoena must advise a nonparty organization of its duty to confer with the serving party and to designate each person who will testify. The persons designated must testify about information known or reasonably available to the organization. This paragraph (6) does not preclude a deposition by any other procedure allowed by these rules.

(c) EXAMINATION AND CROSS-EXAMINATION; RECORD OF THE EXAMINATION; OBJECTIONS; WRITTEN QUESTIONS.

(1) *Examination and Cross-Examination.* The examination and cross-examination of a deponent proceed as they would at trial under the Federal Rules of Evidence, except Rules 103 and 615. After putting the deponent under oath or affirmation, the officer must record the testimony by the method designated under Rule 30(b)(3)(A). The testimony must be recorded by the officer personally or by a person acting in the presence and under the direction of the officer.

(2) *Objections.* An objection at the time of the examination—whether to evidence, to a party's conduct, to the officer's qualifications, to the manner of taking the deposition, or to any other aspect of the deposition—must be noted on the record, but the examination still proceeds; the testimony is taken subject to any objection. An objection must be stated concisely in a nonargumentative and nonsuggestive manner. A person may instruct a deponent not to answer only when necessary to preserve a privilege, to enforce a limitation ordered by the court, or to present a motion under Rule 30(d)(3).

(3) *Participating Through Written Questions.* Instead of participating in the oral examination, a party may serve written questions in a sealed envelope on the party noticing the deposition, who must deliver them to the officer. The officer must ask the deponent those questions and record the answers verbatim.

(d) DURATION; SANCTION; MOTION TO TERMINATE OR LIMIT.

(1) *Duration.* Unless otherwise stipulated or ordered by the court, a deposition is limited to one day of 7 hours. The court must allow additional time consistent with Rule 26(b)(1) and (2) if needed to fairly examine the deponent or if the deponent, another person, or any other circumstance impedes or delays the examination.

(2) *Sanction.* The court may impose an appropriate sanction—including the reasonable expenses and attorney's fees incurred by any party—on a person who impedes, delays, or frustrates the fair examination of the deponent.

(3) *Motion to Terminate or Limit.*

(A) *Grounds.* At any time during a deposition, the deponent or a party may move to terminate or limit it on the ground that it is being conducted in bad faith or in a manner that unreasonably annoys, embarrasses, or oppresses the deponent or party. The motion may be filed in the court where the action is pending or the deposition is being taken. If the objecting deponent or party so demands, the deposition must be suspended for the time necessary to obtain an order.

(B) *Order.* The court may order that the deposition be terminated or may limit its scope and manner as provided in Rule 26(c). If terminated, the deposition may be resumed only by order of the court where the action is pending.

(C) *Award of Expenses.* Rule 37(a)(5) applies to the award of expenses.

(e) Review by the Witness; Changes.

(1) *Review; Statement of Changes.* On request by the deponent or a party before the deposition is completed, the deponent must be allowed 30 days after being notified by the officer that the transcript or recording is available in which:

(A) to review the transcript or recording; and

(B) if there are changes in form or substance, to sign a statement listing the changes and the reasons for making them.

(2) *Changes Indicated in the Officer's Certificate.* The officer must note in the certificate prescribed by Rule 30(f)(1) whether a review was requested and, if so, must attach any changes the deponent makes during the 30-day period.

(f) Certification and Delivery; Exhibits; Copies of the Transcript or Recording; Filing.

(1) *Certification and Delivery.* The officer must certify in writing that the witness was duly sworn and that the deposition accurately records the witness's testimony. The certificate must accompany the record of the deposition. Unless the court orders otherwise, the officer must seal the deposition in an envelope or package bearing the title of the action and marked "Deposition of [witness's name]" and must promptly send it to the attorney who arranged for the transcript or recording. The attorney must store it under conditions that will protect it against loss,

destruction, tampering, or deterioration.

(2) *Documents and Tangible Things.*

(A) *Originals and Copies.* Documents and tangible things produced for inspection during a deposition must, on a party's request, be marked for identification and attached to the deposition. Any party may inspect and copy them. But if the person who produced them wants to keep the originals, the person may:

(i) offer copies to be marked, attached to the deposition, and then used as originals—after giving all parties a fair opportunity to verify the copies by comparing them with the originals; or

(ii) give all parties a fair opportunity to inspect and copy the originals after they are marked—in which event the originals may be used as if attached to the deposition.

(B) *Order Regarding the Originals.* Any party may move for an order that the originals be attached to the deposition pending final disposition of the case.

(3) *Copies of the Transcript or Recording.* Unless otherwise stipulated or ordered by the court, the officer must retain the stenographic notes of a deposition taken stenographically or a copy of the recording of a deposition taken by another method. When paid reasonable charges, the officer must furnish a copy of the transcript or recording to any party or the deponent.

(4) *Notice of Filing.* A party who files the deposition must promptly notify all other parties of the filing.

(g) FAILURE TO ATTEND A DEPOSITION OR SERVE A SUBPOENA; EXPENSES. A party who, expecting a deposition to be taken, attends in person or by an attorney may recover reasonable expenses for attending, including attorney's fees, if the noticing party failed to:

(1) attend and proceed with the deposition; or

(2) serve a subpoena on a nonparty deponent, who consequently did not attend.

## Rule 7031 Deposition upon Written Questions

Rule 31 F.R.Civ.P. applies in adversary proceedings.

## CIVIL RULE:

Federal Rule of Civil Procedure 31, which was last amended effective December 1, 2015, provides:

### Rule 31 Depositions by Written Questions

(a) WHEN A DEPOSITION MAY BE TAKEN.

(1) *Without Leave.* A party may, by written questions, depose any person, including a party, without leave of court except as provided in Rule 31(a)(2). The deponent's attendance may be compelled by subpoena under Rule 45.

(2) *With Leave.* A party must obtain leave of court, and the court

must grant leave to the extent consistent with Rule 26(b)(1) and (2):

(A) if the parties have not stipulated to the deposition and:

(i) the deposition would result in more than 10 depositions being taken under this rule or Rule 30 by the plaintiffs, or by the defendants, or by the third-party defendants;

(ii) the deponent has already been deposed in the case; or

(iii) the party seeks to take a deposition before the time specified in Rule 26(d); or

(B) if the deponent is confined in prison.

(3) *Service; Required Notice.* A party who wants to depose a person by written questions must serve them on every other party, with a notice stating, if known, the deponent's name and address. If the name is unknown, the notice must provide a general description sufficient to identify the person or the particular class or group to which the person belongs. The notice must also state the name or descriptive title and the address of the officer before whom the deposition will be taken.

(4) *Questions Directed to an Organization.* A public or private corporation, a partnership, an association, or a governmental agency may be deposed by written questions in accordance with Rule 30(b)(6).

(5) *Questions from Other Parties.* Any questions to the deponent from other parties must be served on all parties as follows: cross-questions, within 14 days after being served with the notice and direct questions; redirect questions, within 7 days after being served with cross-questions; and recross-questions, within 7 days after being served with redirect questions. The court may, for good cause, extend or shorten these times.

(b) Delivery to the Officer; Officer's Duties. The party who noticed the deposition must deliver to the officer a copy of all the questions served and of the notice. The officer must promptly proceed in the manner provided in Rule 30(c), (e), and (f) to:

(1) take the deponent's testimony in response to the questions;

(2) prepare and certify the deposition; and

(3) send it to the party, attaching a copy of the questions and of the notice.

(c) Notice of Completion or Filing. When the deposition is filed the party taking it shall promptly give notice thereof to all other parties.

(1) *Completion.* The party who noticed the deposition must notify all other parties when it is completed.

(2) *Filing.* A party who files the deposition must promptly notify all other parties of the filing.

**Rule 7032 Use of Depositions in Adversary Proceedings**

Rule 32 F.R.Civ.P. applies in adversary proceedings.

## CIVIL RULE:

Federal Rule of Civil Procedure 32, which was last amended effective December 1, 2009, provides:

**Rule 32 Using Depositions in Court Proceedings**

(a) Using Depositions.

(1) *In General.* At a hearing or trial, all or part of a deposition may be used against a party on these conditions:

(A) the party was present or represented at the taking of the deposition or had reasonable notice of it;

(B) it is used to the extent it would be admissible under the Federal Rules of Evidence if the deponent were present and testifying; and

(C) the use is allowed by Rule 32(a)(2) through (8).

(2) *Impeachment and Other Uses.* Any party may use a deposition to contradict or impeach the testimony given by the deponent as a witness, or for any other purpose allowed by the Federal Rules of Evidence.

(3) *Deposition of Party, Agent, or Designee.* An adverse party may use for any purpose the deposition of a party or anyone who, when deposed, was the party's officer, director, managing agent, or designee under Rule 30(b)(6) or 31(a)(4).

(4) *Unavailable Witness.* A party may use for any purpose the deposition of a witness, whether or not a party, if the court finds:

(A) that the witness is dead;

(B) that the witness is more than 100 miles from the place of hearing or trial or is outside the United States, unless it appears that the witness's absence was procured by the party offering the deposition;

(C) that the witness cannot attend or testify because of age, illness, infirmity, or imprisonment;

(D) that the party offering the deposition could not procure the witness's attendance by subpoena; or

(E) on motion and notice, that exceptional circumstances make it desirable—in the interest of justice and with due regard to the importance of live testimony in open court—to permit the deposition to be used.

(5) *Limitations on Use.*

(A) *Deposition Taken on Short Notice.* A deposition must not be used against a party who, having received less than 14 days' notice of the deposition, promptly moved for a protective order under Rule 26(c)(1)(B) requesting that it not be taken or be taken at a different time or place—and this motion was still pending when the deposition was taken.

(B) *Unavailable Deponent; Party Could Not Obtain an Attorney.* A deposition taken without leave of court under the unavailability provision of Rule 30(a)(2)(A)(iii) must not be used against a party who shows that, when served with the notice, it could not, despite diligent efforts, obtain an attorney to represent it at the deposition.

(6) *Using Part of a Deposition.* If a party offers in evidence only part of a deposition, an adverse party may require the offeror to introduce other parts that in fairness should be considered with the part introduced, and any party may itself introduce any other parts.

(7) *Substituting a Party.* Substituting a party under Rule 25 does not affect the right to use a deposition previously taken.

(8) *Deposition Taken in an Earlier Action.* A deposition lawfully taken and, if required, filed in any federal-or state-court action may be used in a later action involving the same subject matter between the same parties, or their representatives or successors in interest, to the same extent as if taken in the later action. A deposition previously taken may also be used as allowed by the Federal Rules of Evidence.

(b) Objections to Admissibility. Subject to Rules 28(b) and 32(d)(3), an objection may be made at a hearing or trial to the admission of any deposition testimony that would be inadmissible if the witness were present and testifying.

(c) Form of Presentation. Unless the court orders otherwise, a party must provide a transcript of any deposition testimony the party offers, but may provide the court with the testimony in nontranscript form as well. On any party's request, deposition testimony offered in a jury trial for any purpose other than impeachment must be presented in nontranscript form, if available, unless the court for good cause orders otherwise.

(d) Waiver of Objections.

(1) *To the Notice.* An objection to an error or irregularity in a deposition notice is waived unless promptly served in writing on the party giving the notice.

(2) *To the Officer's Qualification.* An objection based on disqualification of the officer before whom a deposition is to be taken is waived if not made:

(A) before the deposition begins; or

(B) promptly after the basis for disqualification becomes known or, with reasonable diligence, could have been known.

(3) *To the Taking of the Deposition.*

(A) *Objection to Competence, Relevance, or Materiality.* An objection to a deponent's competence—or to the competence, relevance, or materiality of testimony—is not waived by a failure to make the objection before or during the deposition, unless the ground for it might have been corrected at that time.

(B) *Objection to an Error or Irregularity.* An objection to an error or irregularity at an oral examination is waived if:

(i) it relates to the manner of taking the deposition, the form of a question or answer, the oath or affirmation, a party's conduct, or other matters that might have been corrected at that time; and

(ii) it is not timely made during the deposition.

(C) *Objection to a Written Question.* An objection to the form of a written question under Rule 31 is waived if not served in writing on the party submitting the question within the time for serving responsive questions or, if the question is a recross-question, within 7 days after being served with it.

(4) *To Completing and Returning the Deposition.* An objection to how the officer transcribed the testimony—or prepared, signed, certified, sealed, endorsed, sent, or otherwise dealt with the deposition—is waived unless a motion to suppress is made promptly after the error or irregularity becomes known or, with reasonable diligence, could have been known.

## Rule 7033 Interrogatories to Parties

Rule 33 F.R.Civ.P. applies in adversary proceedings.

## CIVIL RULE:

Federal Rule of Civil Procedure 33, which was last amended effective December 1, 2015, provides:

### Rule 33 Interrogatories to Parties

(a) IN GENERAL.

(1) *Number.* Unless otherwise stipulated or ordered by the court, a party may serve on any other party no more than 25 written interrogatories, including all discrete subparts. Leave to serve additional interrogatories may be granted to the extent consistent with Rule 26(b)(1) and (2).

(2) *Scope.* An interrogatory may relate to any matter that may be inquired into under Rule 26(b). An interrogatory is not objectionable merely because it asks for an opinion or contention that relates to fact or the application of law to fact, but the court may order that the interrogatory need not be answered until designated discovery is complete, or until a pretrial conference or some other time.

(b) ANSWERS AND OBJECTIONS.

(1) *Responding Party.* The interrogatories must be answered:

(A) by the party to whom they are directed; or

(B) if that party is a public or private corporation, a partnership, an association, or a governmental agency, by any officer or agent, who must furnish the information available to the party.

(2) *Time to Respond.* The responding party must serve its answers and any objections within 30 days after being served with the interrogatories. A shorter or longer time may be stipulated to under

Rule 29 or be ordered by the court.

(3) *Answering Each Interrogatory.* Each interrogatory must, to the extent it is not objected to, be answered separately and fully in writing under oath.

(4) *Objections.* The grounds for objecting to an interrogatory must be stated with specificity. Any ground not stated in a timely objection is waived unless the court, for good cause, excuses the failure.

(5) *Signature.* The person who makes the answers must sign them, and the attorney who objects must sign any objections.

(c) Use. An answer to an interrogatory may be used to the extent allowed by the Federal Rules of Evidence.

(d) Option to Produce Business Records. If the answer to an interrogatory may be determined by examining, auditing, compiling, abstracting, or summarizing a party's business records (including electronically stored information), and if the burden of deriving or ascertaining the answer will be substantially the same for either party, the responding party may answer by:

(1) specifying the records that must be reviewed, in sufficient detail to enable the interrogating party to locate and identify them as readily as the responding party could; and

(2) giving the interrogating party a reasonable opportunity to examine and audit the records and to make copies, compilations, abstracts, or summaries.

## Rule 7034 Production of Documents and Things and Entry upon Land for Inspection and Other Purposes

Rule 34 F.R.Civ.P. applies in adversary proceedings.

BANKRUPTCY RULES

## CIVIL RULE:

Federal Rule of Civil Procedure 34, which was last amended effective December 1, 2015, provides:

### Rule 34 Producing Documents, Electronically Stored Information, and Tangible Things, or Entering onto Land, for Inspection and Other Purposes

(a) In General. A party may serve on any other party a request within the scope of Rule 26(b):

(1) to produce and permit the requesting party or its representative to inspect, copy, test, or sample the following items in the responding party's possession, custody, or control:

(A) any designated documents or electronically stored information—including writings, drawings, graphs, charts, photographs, sound recordings, images, and other data or data compilations—stored in any medium from which information can be obtained either directly or, if necessary, after translation by the responding party into a reasonably usable form; or

(B) any designated tangible things; or

(2) to permit entry onto designated land or other property possessed or controlled by the responding party, so that the requesting party may inspect, measure, survey, photograph, test, or sample the property or any designated object or operation on it.

(b) PROCEDURE.

(1) *Contents of the Request.* The request:

(A) must describe with reasonable particularity each item or category of items to be inspected;

(B) must specify a reasonable time, place, and manner for the inspection and for performing the related acts; and

(C) may specify the form or forms in which electronically stored information is to be produced.

(2) *Responses and Objections.*

(A) *Time to Respond.* The party to whom the request is directed must respond in writing within 30 days after being served or—if the request was delivered under Rule 26(d)(2)—within 30 days after the parties' first Rule 26(f) conference. A shorter or longer time may be stipulated to under Rule 29 or be ordered by the court.

(B) *Responding to Each Item.* For each item or category, the response must either state that inspection and related activities will be permitted as requested or state with specificity the grounds for objecting to the request, including the reasons. The responding party may state that it will produce copies of documents or of electronically stored information instead of permitting inspection. The production must then be completed no later than the time for inspection specified in the request or another reasonable time specified in the response.

(C) *Objections.* An objection must state whether any responsive materials are being withheld on the basis of that objection. An objection to part of a request must specify the part and permit inspection of the rest.

(D) *Responding to a Request for Production of Electronically Stored Information.* The response may state an objection to a requested form for producing electronically stored information. If the responding party objects to a requested form—or if no form was specified in the request—the party must state the form or forms it intends to use.

(E) *Producing the Documents or Electronically Stored Information.* Unless otherwise stipulated or ordered by the court, these procedures apply to producing documents or electronically stored information:

(i) A party must produce documents as they are kept in the usual course of business or must organize and label them to correspond to the categories in the request;

(ii) If a request does not specify a form for producing electronically stored information, a party must produce it in a form or forms in which it is ordinarily maintained or in a reasonably usable form or forms; and

(iii) A party need not produce the same electronically stored information in more than one form.

(c) Nonparties. As provided in Rule 45, a nonparty may be compelled to produce documents and tangible things or to permit an inspection.

## Rule 7035 Physical and Mental Examination of Persons

Rule 35 F.R.Civ.P. applies in adversary proceedings.

## CIVIL RULE:

Federal Rule of Civil Procedure 35, which was last amended effective December 1, 2007, provides:

### Rule 35 Physical and Mental Examinations

(a) Order for an Examination.

(1) *In General.* The court where the action is pending may order a party whose mental or physical condition—including blood group—is in controversy to submit to a physical or mental examination by a suitably licensed or certified examiner. The court has the same authority to order a party to produce for examination a person who is in its custody or under its legal control.

(2) *Motion and Notice; Contents of the Order.* The order:

(A) may be made only on motion for good cause and on notice to all parties and the person to be examined; and

(B) must specify the time, place, manner, conditions, and scope of the examination, as well as the person or persons who will perform it.

(b) Examiner's Report.

(1) *Request by the Party or Person Examined.* The party who moved for the examination must, on request, deliver to the requester a copy of the examiner's report, together with like reports of all earlier examinations of the same condition. The request may be made by the party against whom the examination order was issued or by the person examined.

(2) *Contents.* The examiner's report must be in writing and must set out in detail the examiner's findings, including diagnoses, conclusions, and the results of any tests.

(3) *Request by the Moving Party.* After delivering the reports, the party who moved for the examination may request—and is entitled to receive—from the party against whom the examination order was issued like reports of all earlier or later examinations of the same condition. But those reports need not be delivered by the party with custody or control of the person examined if the party shows that it could not obtain them.

(4) *Waiver of Privilege.* By requesting and obtaining the examiner's report, or by deposing the examiner, the party examined waives any

privilege it may have—in that action or any other action involving the same controversy—concerning testimony about all examinations of the same condition.

(5) *Failure to Deliver a Report.* The court on motion may order—on just terms—that a party deliver the report of an examination. If the report is not provided, the court may exclude the examiner's testimony at trial.

(6) *Scope.* This subdivision (b) applies also to an examination made by the parties' agreement, unless the agreement states otherwise. This subdivision does not preclude obtaining an examiner's report or deposing an examiner under other rules.

## Rule 7036 Requests for Admission

Rule 36 F.R.Civ.P. applies in adversary proceedings.

## CIVIL RULE:

Federal Rule of Civil Procedure 36, which was last amended effective December 1, 2007, provides:

### Rule 36 Requests for Admission

(a) Scope and Procedure.

(1) *Scope.* A party may serve on any other party a written request to admit, for purposes of the pending action only, the truth of any matters within the scope of Rule 26(b)(1) relating to:

(A) facts, the application of law to fact, or opinions about either; and

(B) the genuineness of any described documents.

(2) *Form; Copy of a Document.* Each matter must be separately stated. A request to admit the genuineness of a document must be accompanied by a copy of the document unless it is, or has been, otherwise furnished or made available for inspection and copying.

(3) *Time to Respond; Effect of Not Responding.* A matter is admitted unless, within 30 days after being served, the party to whom the request is directed serves on the requesting party a written answer or objection addressed to the matter and signed by the party or its attorney. A shorter or longer time for responding may be stipulated to under Rule 29 or be ordered by the court.

(4) *Answer.* If a matter is not admitted, the answer must specifically deny it or state in detail why the answering party cannot truthfully admit or deny it. A denial must fairly respond to the substance of the matter; and when good faith requires that a party qualify an answer or deny only a part of a matter, the answer must specify the part admitted and qualify or deny the rest. The answering party may assert lack of knowledge or information as a reason for failing to admit or deny only if the party states that it has made reasonable inquiry and that the information it knows or can readily obtain is insufficient to enable it to admit or deny.

(5) *Objections.* The grounds for objecting to a request must be stated. A party must not object solely on the ground that the request presents a genuine issue for trial.

(6) *Motion Regarding the Sufficiency of an Answer or Objection.* The requesting party may move to determine the sufficiency of an answer or objection. Unless the court finds an objection justified, it must order that an answer be served. On finding that an answer does not comply with this rule, the court may order either that the matter is admitted or that an amended answer be served. The court may defer its final decision until a pretrial conference or a specified time before trial. Rule 37(a)(5) applies to an award of expenses.

(b) EFFECT OF AN ADMISSION; WITHDRAWING OR AMENDING IT. A matter admitted under this rule is conclusively established unless the court, on motion, permits the admission to be withdrawn or amended. Subject to Rule 16(e), the court may permit withdrawal or amendment if it would promote the presentation of the merits of the action and if the court is not persuaded that it would prejudice the requesting party in maintaining or defending the action on the merits. An admission under this rule is not an admission for any other purpose and cannot be used against the party in any other proceeding.

## Rule 7037 Failure to Make Discovery: Sanctions

Rule 37 F.R.Civ.P. applies in adversary proceedings.

## CIVIL RULE:

Federal Rule of Civil Procedure 37, which was last amended effective December 1, 2015, provides:

### Rule 37 Failure to Make Disclosures or to Cooperate in Discovery; Sanctions

(a) MOTION FOR AN ORDER COMPELLING DISCLOSURE OR DISCOVERY.

(1) *In General.* On notice to other parties and all affected persons, a party may move for an order compelling disclosure or discovery. The motion must include a certification that the movant has in good faith conferred or attempted to confer with the person or party failing to make disclosure or discovery in an effort to obtain it without court action.

(2) *Appropriate Court.* A motion for an order to a party must be made in the court where the action is pending. A motion for an order to a nonparty must be made in the court where the discovery is or will be taken.

(3) *Specific Motions.*

(A) *To Compel Disclosure.* If a party fails to make a disclosure required by Rule 26(a), any other party may move to compel disclosure and for appropriate sanctions.

(B) *To Compel a Discovery Response.* A party seeking discovery may move for an order compelling an answer, designation, production, or inspection. This motion may be made if:

(i) a deponent fails to answer a question asked under Rule 30 or 31;

(ii) a corporation or other entity fails to make a designation under Rule 30(b)(6) or 31(a)(4);

(iii) a party fails to answer an interrogatory submitted under Rule 33; or

(iv) a party fails to produce documents or fails to respond that inspection will be permitted—or fails to permit inspection—as requested under Rule 34.

(C) *Related to a Deposition.* When taking an oral deposition, the party asking a question may complete or adjourn the examination before moving for an order.

(4) *Evasive or Incomplete Disclosure, Answer, or Response.* For purposes of this subdivision (a), an evasive or incomplete disclosure, answer, or response must be treated as a failure to disclose, answer, or respond.

(5) *Payment of Expenses; Protective Orders.*

(A) *If the Motion Is Granted (or Disclosure or Discovery Is Provided After Filing).* If the motion is granted—or if the disclosure or requested discovery is provided after the motion was filed—the court must, after giving an opportunity to be heard, require the party or deponent whose conduct necessitated the motion, the party or attorney advising that conduct, or both to pay the movant's reasonable expenses incurred in making the motion, including attorney's fees. But the court must not order this payment if:

(i) the movant filed the motion before attempting in good faith to obtain the disclosure or discovery without court action;

(ii) the opposing party's nondisclosure, response, or objection was substantially justified; or

(iii) other circumstances make an award of expenses unjust.

(B) *If the Motion Is Denied.* If the motion is denied, the court may issue any protective order authorized under Rule 26(c) and must, after giving an opportunity to be heard, require the movant, the attorney filing the motion, or both to pay the party or deponent who opposed the motion its reasonable expenses incurred in opposing the motion, including attorney's fees. But the court must not order this payment if the motion was substantially justified or other circumstances make an award of expenses unjust.

(C) *If the Motion Is Granted in Part and Denied in Part.* If the motion is granted in part and denied in part, the court may issue any protective order authorized under Rule 26(c) and may, after giving an opportunity to be heard, apportion the reasonable expenses for the motion.

(b) FAILURE TO COMPLY WITH A COURT ORDER.

(1) *Sanctions Sought in the District Where the Deposition Is Taken.* If

the court where the discovery is taken orders a deponent to be sworn or to answer a question and the deponent fails to obey, the failure may be treated as contempt of court. If a deposition-related motion is transferred to the court where the action is pending, and that court orders a deponent to be sworn or to answer a question and the deponent fails to obey, the failure may be treated as contempt of either the court where the discovery is taken or the court where the action is pending.

(2) *Sanctions Sought in the District Where the Action Is Pending.*

(A) *For Not Obeying a Discovery Order.* If a party or a party's officer, director, or managing agent—or a witness designated under Rule 30(b)(6) or 31(a)(4)—fails to obey an order to provide or permit discovery, including an order under Rule 26(f), 35, or 37(a), the court where the action is pending may issue further just orders. They may include the following:

(i) directing that the matters embraced in the order or other designated facts be taken as established for purposes of the action, as the prevailing party claims;

(ii) prohibiting the disobedient party from supporting or opposing designated claims or defenses, or from introducing designated matters in evidence;

(iii) striking pleadings in whole or in part;

(iv) staying further proceedings until the order is obeyed;

(v) dismissing the action or proceeding in whole or in part;

(vi) rendering a default judgment against the disobedient party; or

(vii) treating as contempt of court the failure to obey any order except an order to submit to a physical or mental examination.

(B) *For Not Producing a Person for Examination.* If a party fails to comply with an order under Rule 35(a) requiring it to produce another person for examination, the court may issue any of the orders listed in Rule 37(b)(2)(A)(i)–(vi), unless the disobedient party shows that it cannot produce the other person.

(C) *Payment of Expenses.* Instead of or in addition to the orders above, the court must order the disobedient party, the attorney advising that party, or both to pay the reasonable expenses, including attorney's fees, caused by the failure, unless the failure was substantially justified or other circumstances make an award of expenses unjust.

(c) Failure to Disclose, to Supplement an Earlier Response, or to Admit.

(1) *Failure to Disclose or Supplement.* If a party fails to provide information or identify a witness as required by Rule 26(a) or (e), the party is not allowed to use that information or witness to supply evidence on a motion, at a hearing, or at a trial, unless the failure was substantially justified or is harmless. In addition to or instead of this sanction, the court, on motion and after giving an opportunity to be

heard:

(A) may order payment of the reasonable expenses, including attorney's fees, caused by the failure;

(B) may inform the jury of the party's failure; and

(C) may impose other appropriate sanctions, including any of the orders listed in Rule 37(b)(2)(A)(i)–(vi).

(2) *Failure to Admit.* If a party fails to admit what is requested under Rule 36 and if the requesting party later proves a document to be genuine or the matter true, the requesting party may move that the party who failed to admit pay the reasonable expenses, including attorney's fees, incurred in making that proof. The court must so order unless:

(A) the request was held objectionable under Rule 36(a);

(B) the admission sought was of no substantial importance;

(C) the party failing to admit had a reasonable ground to believe that it might prevail on the matter; or

(D) there was other good reason for the failure to admit.

(d) PARTY'S FAILURE TO ATTEND ITS OWN DEPOSITION, SERVE ANSWERS TO INTERROGATORIES, OR RESPOND TO A REQUEST FOR INSPECTION.

(1) *In General.*

(A) *Motion; Grounds for Sanctions.* The court where the action is pending may, on motion, order sanctions if:

(i) a party or a party's officer, director, or managing agent—or a person designated under Rule 30(b)(6) or 31(a)(4)—fails, after being served with proper notice, to appear for that person's deposition; or

(ii) a party, after being properly served with interrogatories under Rule 33 or a request for inspection under Rule 34, fails to serve its answers, objections, or written response.

(B) *Certification.* A motion for sanctions for failing to answer or respond must include a certification that the movant has in good faith conferred or attempted to confer with the party failing to act in an effort to obtain the answer or response without court action.

(2) *Unacceptable Excuse for Failing to Act.* A failure described in Rule 37(d)(1)(A) is not excused on the ground that the discovery sought was objectionable, unless the party failing to act has a pending motion for a protective order under Rule 26(c).

(3) *Types of Sanctions.* Sanctions may include any of the orders listed in Rule 37(b)(2)(A)(i)–(vi). Instead of or in addition to these sanctions, the court must require the party failing to act, the attorney advising that party, or both to pay the reasonable expenses, including attorney's fees, caused by the failure, unless the failure was substantially justified or other circumstances make an award of expenses unjust.

(e) FAILURE TO PRESERVE ELECTRONICALLY STORED INFORMATION. If electronically stored information that should have been preserved in the anticipation or conduct of litigation is lost because a party failed to take reasonable steps to preserve it, and it cannot be restored or replaced through additional discovery, the court:

(1) upon finding prejudice to another party from loss of the information, may order measures no greater than necessary to cure the prejudice; or

(2) only upon finding that the party acted with the intent to deprive another party of the information's use in the litigation may:

(A) presume that the lost information was unfavorable to the party;

(B) instruct the jury that it may or must presume the information was unfavorable to the party; or

(C) dismiss the action or enter a default judgment.

(f) FAILURE TO PARTICIPATE IN FRAMING A DISCOVERY PLAN. If a party or its attorney fails to participate in good faith in developing and submitting a proposed discovery plan as required by Rule 26(f), the court may, after giving an opportunity to be heard, require that party or attorney to pay to any other party the reasonable expenses, including attorney's fees, caused by the failure.

## Rule 7040 Assignment of Cases for Trial

Rule 40 F.R.Civ.P. applies in adversary proceedings.

### CIVIL RULE:

Federal Rule of Civil Procedure 40, which was last amended effective December 1, 2007, provides:

**Rule 40 Scheduling Cases for Trial**

Each court must provide by rule for scheduling trials. The court must give priority to actions entitled to priority by a federal statute.

BANKRUPTCY CODE REFERENCE: § 362

## Rule 7041 Dismissal of Adversary Proceedings

Rule 41 F.R.Civ.P. applies in adversary proceedings, except that a complaint objecting to the debtor's discharge shall not be dismissed at the plaintiff's instance without notice to the trustee, the United States trustee, and such other persons as the court may direct, and only on order of the court containing terms and conditions which the court deems proper.

### CIVIL RULE:

Federal Rule of Civil Procedure 41, which was last amended effective December 1, 2007, provides:

**Rule 41 Dismissal of Actions**

(a) VOLUNTARY DISMISSAL.

(1) *By the Plaintiff.*

(A) *Without a Court Order.* Subject to Rules 23(e), 23.1(c), 23.2,

BANKRUPTCY RULES

and 66 and any applicable federal statute, the plaintiff may dismiss an action without a court order by filing:

(i) a notice of dismissal before the opposing party serves either an answer or a motion for summary judgment; or

(ii) a stipulation of dismissal signed by all parties who have appeared.

(B) *Effect.* Unless the notice or stipulation states otherwise, the dismissal is without prejudice. But if the plaintiff previously dismissed any federal-or state-court action based on or including the same claim, a notice of dismissal operates as an adjudication on the merits.

(2) *By Court Order; Effect.* Except as provided in Rule 41(a)(1), an action may be dismissed at the plaintiff's request only by court order, on terms that the court considers proper. If a defendant has pleaded a counterclaim before being served with the plaintiff's motion to dismiss, the action may be dismissed over the defendant's objection only if the counterclaim can remain pending for independent adjudication. Unless the order states otherwise, a dismissal under this paragraph (2) is without prejudice.

(b) Involuntary Dismissal; Effect. If the plaintiff fails to prosecute or to comply with these rules or a court order, a defendant may move to dismiss the action or any claim against it. Unless the dismissal order states otherwise, a dismissal under this subdivision (b) and any dismissal not under this rule—except one for lack of jurisdiction, improper venue, or failure to join a party under Rule 19—operates as an adjudication on the merits.

(c) Dismissing a Counterclaim, Crossclaim, or Third-Party Claim. This rule applies to a dismissal of any counterclaim, crossclaim, or third-party claim. A claimant's voluntary dismissal under Rule 41(a)(1)(A)(i) must be made:

(1) before a responsive pleading is served; or

(2) if there is no responsive pleading, before evidence is introduced at a hearing or trial.

(d) Costs of a Previously Dismissed Action. If a plaintiff who previously dismissed an action in any court files an action based on or including the same claim against the same defendant, the court:

(1) may order the plaintiff to pay all or part of the costs of that previous action; and

(2) may stay the proceedings until the plaintiff has complied.

Bankruptcy Code Reference: § 727

## Rule 7042 Consolidation of Adversary Proceedings; Separate Trials

Rule 42 F.R.Civ.P. applies in adversary proceedings.

### CIVIL RULE:

Federal Rule of Civil Procedure 42, which was last amended effective

December 1, 2007, provides:

**Rule 42 Consolidation; Separate Trials**

(a) CONSOLIDATION. If actions before the court involve a common question of law or fact, the court may:

(1) join for hearing or trial any or all matters at issue in the actions;

(2) consolidate the actions; or

(3) issue any other orders to avoid unnecessary cost or delay.

(b) SEPARATE TRIALS. For convenience, to avoid prejudice, or to expedite and economize, the court may order a separate trial of one or more separate issues, claims, crossclaims, counterclaims, or third-party claims. When ordering a separate trial, the court must preserve any federal right to a jury trial.

## Rule 7052 Findings by the Court

Rule 52 F.R.Civ.P. applies in adversary proceedings, except that any motion under subdivision (b) of that rule for amended or additional findings shall be filed no later than 14 days after entry of judgment. In these proceedings, the reference in Rule 52 F.R.Civ.P. to the entry of judgment under Rule 58 F.R.Civ.P. shall be read as a reference to the entry of a judgment or order under Rule 5003(a).

## CIVIL RULE:

Federal Rule of Civil Procedure 52, which was last amended effective December 1, 2009, provides:

**Rule 52 Findings and Conclusions by the Court; Judgment on Partial Findings**

(a) FINDINGS AND CONCLUSIONS.

(1) *In General.* In an action tried on the facts without a jury or with an advisory jury, the court must find the facts specially and state its conclusions of law separately. The findings and conclusions may be stated on the record after the close of the evidence or may appear in an opinion or a memorandum of decision filed by the court. Judgment must be entered under Rule 58.

(2) *For an Interlocutory Injunction.* In granting or refusing an interlocutory injunction, the court must similarly state the findings and conclusions that support its action.

(3) *For a Motion.* The court is not required to state findings or conclusions when ruling on a motion under Rule 12 or 56 or, unless these rules provide otherwise, on any other motion.

(4) *Effect of a Master's Findings.* A master's findings, to the extent adopted by the court, must be considered the court's findings.

(5) *Questioning the Evidentiary Support.* A party may later question the sufficiency of the evidence supporting the findings, whether or not the party requested findings, objected to them, moved to amend them, or moved for partial findings.

(6) *Setting Aside the Findings.* Findings of fact, whether based on oral

or other evidence, must not be set aside unless clearly erroneous, and the reviewing court must give due regard to the trial court's opportunity to judge the witnesses' credibility.

(b) Amended or Additional Findings. On a party's motion filed no later than 28 days after the entry of judgment, the court may amend its findings—or make additional findings—and may amend the judgment accordingly. The motion may accompany a motion for a new trial under Rule 59.

(c) Judgment on Partial Findings. If a party has been fully heard on an issue during a nonjury trial and the court finds against the party on that issue, the court may enter judgment against the party on a claim or defense that, under the controlling law, can be maintained or defeated only with a favorable finding on that issue. The court may, however, decline to render any judgment until the close of the evidence. A judgment on partial findings must be supported by findings of fact and conclusions of law as required by Rule 52(a).

### Rule 7054 Judgments; Costs

(*a*) *Judgments.* Rule 54(a)–(c) F.R.Civ.P. applies in adversary proceedings.

(*b*) *Costs; Attorney's Fees.*

(*1*) *Costs Other Than Attorney's Fees.* The court may allow costs to the prevailing party except when a statute of the United States or these rules otherwise provides. Costs against the United States, its officers and agencies shall be imposed only to the extent permitted by law. Costs may be taxed by the clerk on 14 days' notice; on motion served within seven days thereafter, the action of the clerk may be reviewed by the court.

(*2*) *Attorney's Fees.*

(*A*) Rule 54(d)(2)(A)–(C) and (E) F.R.Civ.P. applies in adversary proceedings except for the reference in Rule 54(d)(2)(C) to Rule 78.

(*B*) By local rule, the court may establish special procedures to resolve fee-related issues without extensive evidentiary hearings

## CIVIL RULE:

Federal Rule of Civil Procedure 54(a)–(c), which was last amended effective December 1, 2009, provides:

**Rule 54 Judgments; Costs**

(a) Definition; Form. "Judgment" as used in these rules includes a decree and any order from which an appeal lies. A judgment should not include recitals of pleadings, a master's report, or a record of prior proceedings.

(b) Judgment on Multiple Claims or Involving Multiple Parties. When an action presents more than one claim for relief—whether as a claim, counterclaim, crossclaim, or third-party claim—or when multiple parties are involved, the court may direct entry of a final judgment as to one or more, but fewer than all, claims or parties only if the court expressly determines that there is no just reason for delay. Otherwise, any order or other decision, however designated, that adjudicates fewer than all the claims or the rights and liabilities of fewer than all the parties does not end the action as to any of the claims or parties and may be revised at any time before the entry of a judgment adjudicating all the claims and all the parties' rights and liabilities.

(c) DEMAND FOR JUDGMENT; RELIEF TO BE GRANTED. A default judgment must not differ in kind from, or exceed in amount, what is demanded in the pleadings. Every other final judgment should grant the relief to which each party is entitled, even if the party has not demanded that relief in its pleadings.

* * *

(d) COSTS; ATTORNEY'S FEES.

(1) *Costs Other Than Attorney's Fees.* Unless a federal statute, these rules, or a court order provides otherwise, costs—other than attorney's fees—should be allowed to the prevailing party. But costs against the United States, its officers, and its agencies may be imposed only to the extent allowed by law. The clerk may tax costs on 14 days' notice. On motion served within the next 7 days, the court may review the clerk's action.

(2) *Attorney's Fees.*

(A) *Claim to Be by Motion.* A claim for attorney's fees and related nontaxable expenses must be made by motion unless the substantive law requires those fees to be proved at trial as an element of damages.

(B) *Timing and Contents of the Motion.* Unless a statute or a court order provides otherwise, the motion must:

(i) be filed no later than 14 days after the entry of judgment;

(ii) specify the judgment and the statute, rule, or other grounds entitling the movant to the award;

(iii) state the amount sought or provide a fair estimate of it; and

(iv) disclose, if the court so orders, the terms of any agreement about fees for the services for which the claim is made.

(C) *Proceedings.* Subject to Rule 23(h), the court must, on a party's request, give an opportunity for adversary submissions on the motion in accordance with Rule 43(c) or 78. The court may decide issues of liability for fees before receiving submissions on the value of services. The court must find the facts and state its conclusions of law as provided in Rule 52(a).

(D) *Special Procedures by Local Rule; Reference to a Master or a Magistrate Judge.* By local rule, the court may establish special procedures to resolve fee-related issues without extensive evidentiary hearings. Also, the court may refer issues concerning the value of services to a special master under Rule 53 without regard to the limitations of Rule 53(a)(1), and may refer a motion for attorney's fees to a magistrate judge under Rule 72(b) as if it were a dispositive pretrial matter.

(E) *Exceptions.* Subparagraphs (A)–(D) do not apply to claims for fees and expenses as sanctions for violating these rules or as sanctions under 28 U.S.C. § 1927.

**Rule 7055 Default**

Rule 55 F.R.Civ.P. applies in adversary proceedings.

## CIVIL RULE:

Federal Rule of Civil Procedure 55, which was last amended effective December 1, 2015, provides:

**Rule 55 Default; Default Judgment**

(a) ENTERING A DEFAULT. When a party against whom a judgment for affirmative relief is sought has failed to plead or otherwise defend, and that failure is shown by affidavit or otherwise, the clerk must enter the party's default.

(b) ENTERING A DEFAULT JUDGMENT.

(1) *By the Clerk.* If the plaintiff's claim is for a sum certain or a sum that can be made certain by computation, the clerk—on the plaintiff's request, with an affidavit showing the amount due—must enter judgment for that amount and costs against a defendant who has been defaulted for not appearing and who is neither a minor nor an incompetent person.

(2) *By the Court.* In all other cases, the party must apply to the court for a default judgment. A default judgment may be entered against a minor or incompetent person only if represented by a general guardian, conservator, or other like fiduciary who has appeared. If the party against whom a default judgment is sought has appeared personally or by a representative, that party or its representative must be served with written notice of the application at least 7 days before the hearing. The court may conduct hearings or make referrals—preserving any federal statutory right to a jury trial—when, to enter or effectuate judgment, it needs to:

(A) conduct an accounting;

(B) determine the amount of damages;

(C) establish the truth of any allegation by evidence; or

(D) investigate any other matter.

(c) SETTING ASIDE A DEFAULT OR A DEFAULT JUDGMENT. The court may set aside an entry of default for good cause, and it may set aside a final default judgment under Rule 60(b).

(d) JUDGMENT AGAINST THE UNITED STATES. A default judgment may be entered against the United States, its officers, or its agencies only if the claimant establishes a claim or right to relief by evidence that satisfies the court.

## Rule 7056 Summary Judgment

Rule 56 F.R.Civ.P. applies in adversary proceedings, except that any motion for summary judgment must be made at least 30 days before the initial date set for an evidentiary hearing on any issue for which summary judgment is sought, unless a different time is set by local rule or the court orders otherwise.

### CIVIL RULE:

Federal Rule of Civil Procedure 56, which was last amended effective December 1, 2010, provides:

**Rule 56 Summary Judgment**

(a) Motion for Summary Judgment or Partial Summary Judgment. A party may move for summary judgment, identifying each claim or defense—or the part of each claim or defense—on which summary judgment is sought. The court shall grant summary judgment if the movant shows that there is no genuine dispute as to any material fact and the movant is entitled to judgment as a matter of law. The court should state on the record the reasons for granting or denying the motion.

(b) Time to File a Motion. Unless a different time is set by local rule or the court orders otherwise, a party may file a motion for summary judgment at any time until 30 days after the close of all discovery.

(c) Procedures.

(1) *Supporting Factual Positions.* A party asserting that a fact cannot be or is genuinely disputed must support the assertion by:

(A) citing to particular parts of materials in the record, including depositions, documents, electronically stored information, affidavits or declarations, stipulations (including those made for purposes of the motion only), admissions, interrogatory answers, or other materials; or

(B) showing that the materials cited do not establish the absence or presence of a genuine dispute, or that an adverse party cannot produce admissible evidence to support the fact.

(2) *Objection That a Fact Is Not Supported by Admissible Evidence.* A party may object that the material cited to support or dispute a fact cannot be presented in a form that would be admissible in evidence.

(3) *Materials Not Cited.* The court need consider only the cited materials, but it may consider other materials in the record.

(4) *Affidavits or Declarations.* An affidavit or declaration used to support or oppose a motion must be made on personal knowledge, set out facts that would be admissible in evidence, and show that the affiant or declarant is competent to testify on the matters stated.

(d) When Facts are Unavailable to the Nonmovant. If a nonmovant shows by affidavit or declaration that, for specified reasons, it cannot present facts essential to justify its opposition, the court may:

(1) defer considering the motion or deny it;

(2) allow time to obtain affidavits or declarations or to take

discovery; or

(3) issue any other appropriate order.

(e) Failing to Properly Support or Address a Fact. If a party fails to properly support an assertion of fact or fails to properly address another party's assertion of fact as required by Rule 56(c), the court may:

(1) give an opportunity to properly support or address the fact;

(2) consider the fact undisputed for purposes of the motion;

(3) grant summary judgment if the motion and supporting materials—including the facts considered undisputed—show that the movant is entitled to it; or

(4) issue any other appropriate order.

(f) Judgment Independent of the Motion. After giving notice and a reasonable time to respond, the court may:

(1) grant summary judgment for a nonmovant;

(2) grant the motion on grounds not raised by a party; or

(3) consider summary judgment on its own after identifying for the parties material facts that may not be genuinely in dispute.

(g) Failing to Grant All the Requested Relief. If the court does not grant all the relief requested by the motion, it may enter an order stating any material fact—including an item of damages or other relief—that is not genuinely in dispute and treating the fact as established in the case.

(h) Affidavit or Declaration Submitted in Bad Faith. If satisfied that an affidavit or declaration under this rule is submitted in bad faith or solely for delay, the court—after notice and a reasonable time to respond—may order the submitting party to pay the other party the reasonable expenses, including attorney's fees, it incurred as a result. An offending party or attorney may also be held in contempt or subjected to other appropriate sanctions.

## Rule 7058 Entering Judgment in Adversary Proceeding

Rule 58 F.R. Civ. P. applies in adversary proceedings. In these proceedings, the reference in Rule 58 F.R. Civ. P. to the civil docket shall be read as a reference to the docket maintained by the clerk under Rule 5003(a).

### CIVIL RULE:

Federal Rule of Civil Procedure 58, which was last amended effective December 1, 2007, provides:

#### Rule 58 Entering Judgment

(a) Separate Document. Every judgment and amended judgment must be set out in a separate document, but a separate document is not required for an order disposing of a motion:

(1) for judgment under Rule 50(b);

(2) to amend or make additional findings of fact under Rule 52(b);

(3) for attorney's fees under Rule 54;

(4) for a new trial, or to alter or amend the judgment, under Rule

59; or

(5) for relief under Rule 60.

(b) ENTERING JUDGMENT.

(1) *Without the Court's Direction.* Subject to Rule 54(b) and unless the court orders otherwise, the clerk must, without awaiting the court's direction, promptly prepare, sign, and enter the judgment when:

(A) the jury returns a general verdict;

(B) the court awards only costs or a sum certain; or

(C) the court denies all relief.

(2) *Court's Approval Required.* Subject to Rule 54(b), the court must promptly approve the form of the judgment, which the clerk must promptly enter, when:

(A) the jury returns a special verdict or a general verdict with answers to written questions; or

(B) the court grants other relief not described in this subdivision (b).

(c) TIME OF ENTRY. For purposes of these rules, judgment is entered at the following times:

(1) if a separate document is not required, when the judgment is entered in the civil docket under Rule 79(a); or

(2) if a separate document is required, when the judgment is entered in the civil docket under Rule 79(a) and the earlier of these events occurs:

(A) it is set out in a separate document; or

(B) 150 days have run from the entry in the civil docket.

(d) REQUEST FOR ENTRY. A party may request that judgment be set out in a separate document as required by Rule 58(a).

(e) COST OR FEE AWARDS. Ordinarily, the entry of judgment may not be delayed, nor the time for appeal extended, in order to tax costs or award fees. But if a timely motion for attorney's fees is made under Rule 54(d)(2), the court may act before a notice of appeal has been filed and become effective to order that the motion have the same effect under Federal Rule of Appellate Procedure 4(a)(4) as a timely motion under Rule 59.

## Rule 7062 Stay of Proceedings to Enforce a Judgment

Rule 62 F.R.Civ.P. applies in adversary proceedings, except that proceedings to enforce a judgment are stayed for 14 days after its entry.

### CIVIL RULE:

Federal Rule of Civil Procedure 62, which was last amended effective December 1, 2018, provides:

**Rule 62 Stay of Proceedings to Enforce a Judgment**

(a) AUTOMATIC STAY. Except as provided in Rule 62(c) and (d), execution on a judgment and proceedings to enforce it are stayed for 30 days after its entry, unless the court orders otherwise.

(b) Stay by Bond or Other Security. At any time after judgment is entered, a party may obtain a stay by providing a bond or other security. The stay takes effect when the court approves the bond or other security and remains in effect for the time specified in the bond or other security.

(c) Stay of an Injunction, Receivership, or Patent Accounting Order. Unless the court orders otherwise, the following are not stayed after being entered, even if an appeal is taken:

(1) an interlocutory or final judgment in an action for an injunction or receivership; or

(2) a judgment or order that directs an accounting in an action for patent infringement.

(d) Injunction Pending an Appeal. While an appeal is pending from an interlocutory order or final judgment that grants, continues, modifies, refuses, dissolves, or refuses to dissolve or modify an injunction, the court may suspend, modify, restore, or grant an injunction on terms for bond or other terms that secure the opposing party's rights. If the judgment appealed from is rendered by a statutory three-judge district court, the order must be made either:

(1) by that court sitting in open session; or

(2) by the assent of all its judges, as evidenced by their signatures.

(e) Stay Without Bond on an Appeal by the United States, Its Officers, or Its Agencies. The court must not require a bond, obligation, or other security from the appellant when granting a stay on an appeal by the United States, its officers, or its agencies or on an appeal directed by a department of the federal government.

(f) Stay in Favor of a Judgment Debtor Under State Law. If a judgment is a lien on the judgment debtor's property under the law of the state where the court is located, the judgment debtor is entitled to the same stay of execution the state court would give.

(g) Appellate Court's Power Not Limited. This rule does not limit the power of the appellate court or one of its judges or justices:

(1) to stay proceedings—or suspend, modify, restore, or grant an injunction—while an appeal is pending; or

(2) to issue an order to preserve the status quo or the effectiveness of the judgment to be entered.

(h) Stay with Multiple Claims or Parties. A court may stay the enforcement of a final judgment entered under Rule 54(b) until it enters a later judgment or judgments, and may prescribe terms necessary to secure the benefit of the stayed judgment for the party in whose favor it was entered.

## Rule 7064 Seizure of Person or Property

Rule 64 F.R.Civ.P. applies in adversary proceedings.

### CIVIL RULE:

Federal Rule of Civil Procedure 64, which was last amended effective December 1, 2007, provides:

**Rule 64 Seizing a Person or Property**

(a) Remedies Under State Law—In General. At the commencement of and throughout an action, every remedy is available that, under the law of the state where the court is located, provides for seizing a person or property to secure satisfaction of the potential judgment. But a federal statute governs to the extent it applies.

(b) Specific Kinds of Remedies. The remedies available under this rule include the following—however designated and regardless of whether state procedure requires an independent action:

- arrest;
- attachment;
- garnishment;
- replevin;
- sequestration; and
- other corresponding or equivalent remedies.

## Rule 7065 Injunctions

Rule 65 F.R.Civ.P. applies in adversary proceedings, except that a temporary restraining order or preliminary injunction may be issued on application of a debtor, trustee, or debtor in possession without compliance with Rule 65(c).

### CIVIL RULE:

Federal Rule of Civil Procedure 65, which was last amended effective December 1, 2009, provides:

**Rule 65 Injunctions and Restraining Orders**

(a) Preliminary Injunction.

(1) *Notice.* The court may issue a preliminary injunction only on notice to the adverse party.

(2) *Consolidating the Hearing with the Trial on the Merits.* Before or after beginning the hearing on a motion for a preliminary injunction, the court may advance the trial on the merits and consolidate it with the hearing. Even when consolidation is not ordered, evidence that is received on the motion and that would be admissible at trial becomes part of the trial record and need not be repeated at trial. But the court must preserve any party's right to a jury trial.

(b) Temporary Restraining Order.

(1) *Issuing Without Notice.* The court may issue a temporary restraining order without written or oral notice to the adverse party or its attorney only if:

(A) specific facts in an affidavit or a verified complaint clearly show that immediate and irreparable injury, loss, or damage will result to the movant before the adverse party can be heard in opposition; and

(B) the movant's attorney certifies in writing any efforts made to give notice and the reasons why it should not be required.

(2) *Contents; Expiration.* Every temporary restraining order issued without notice must state the date and hour it was issued; describe the injury and state why it is irreparable; state why the order was issued without notice; and be promptly filed in the clerk's office and entered in the record. The order expires at the time after entry—not to exceed 14 days—that the court sets, unless before that time the court, for good cause, extends it for a like period or the adverse party consents to a longer extension. The reasons for an extension must be entered in the record.

(3) *Expediting the Preliminary-Injunction Hearing.* If the order is issued without notice, the motion for a preliminary injunction must be set for hearing at the earliest possible time, taking precedence over all other matters except hearings on older matters of the same character. At the hearing, the party who obtained the order must proceed with the motion; if the party does not, the court must dissolve the order.

(4) *Motion to Dissolve.* On 2 days' notice to the party who obtained the order without notice—or on shorter notice set by the court—the adverse party may appear and move to dissolve or modify the order. The court must then hear and decide the motion as promptly as justice requires.

(c) SECURITY. The court may issue a preliminary injunction or a temporary restraining order only if the movant gives security in an amount that the court considers proper to pay the costs and damages sustained by any party found to have been wrongfully enjoined or restrained. The United States, its officers, and its agencies are not required to give security.

(d) CONTENTS AND SCOPE OF EVERY INJUNCTION AND RESTRAINING ORDER.

(1) *Contents.* Every order granting an injunction and every restraining order must:

(A) state the reasons why it issued;

(B) state its terms specifically; and

(C) describe in reasonable detail—and not by referring to the complaint or other document—the act or acts restrained or required.

(2) *Persons Bound.* The order binds only the following who receive actual notice of it by personal service or otherwise:

(A) the parties;

(B) the parties' officers, agents, servants, employees, and attorneys; and

(C) other persons who are in active concert or participation with anyone described in Rule 65(d)(2)(A) or (B).

(e) OTHER LAWS NOT MODIFIED. These rules do not modify the following:

(1) any federal statute relating to temporary restraining orders or preliminary injunctions in actions affecting employer and employee;

(2) 28 U.S.C. § 2361, which relates to preliminary injunctions in actions of interpleader or in the nature of interpleader; or

(3) 28 U.S.C. § 2284, which relates to actions that must be heard and decided by a three-judge district court.

(f) COPYRIGHT IMPOUNDMENT. This rule applies to copyright-impoundment proceedings.

BANKRUPTCY CODE REFERENCE: §§ 105, 362 and 524

## Rule 7067 Deposit in Court

Rule 67 F.R.Civ.P. applies in adversary proceedings.

### CIVIL RULE:

Federal Rule of Civil Procedure 67, which was last amended effective December 1, 2007, provides:

**Rule 67 Deposit into Court**

(a) DEPOSITING PROPERTY. If any part of the relief sought is a money judgment or the disposition of a sum of money or some other deliverable thing, a party—on notice to every other party and by leave of court—may deposit with the court all or part of the money or thing, whether or not that party claims any of it. The depositing party must deliver to the clerk a copy of the order permitting deposit.

(b) INVESTING AND WITHDRAWING FUNDS. Money paid into court under this rule must be deposited and withdrawn in accordance with 28 U.S.C. §§ 2041 and 2042 and any like statute. The money must be deposited in an interest-bearing account or invested in a court-approved, interest-bearing instrument.

BANKRUPTCY CODE REFERENCES: §§ 345, 347 and 541

## Rule 7068 Offer of Judgment

Rule 68 F.R.Civ.P. applies in adversary proceedings.

### CIVIL RULE:

Federal Rule of Civil Procedure 68, which was last amended effective December 1, 2009, provides:

**Rule 68 Offer of Judgment**

(a) MAKING AN OFFER; JUDGMENT ON AN ACCEPTED OFFER. At least 14 days before the date set for trial, a party defending against a claim may serve on an opposing party an offer to allow judgment on specified terms, with the costs then accrued. If, within 14 days after being served, the opposing party serves written notice accepting the offer, either party may then file the offer and notice of acceptance, plus proof of service. The clerk must then enter judgment.

(b) UNACCEPTED OFFER. An unaccepted offer is considered withdrawn, but it does not preclude a later offer. Evidence of an unaccepted offer is not admissible except in a proceeding to determine costs.

(c) OFFER AFTER LIABILITY IS DETERMINED. When one party's liability to another has been determined but the extent of liability remains to be determined by further proceedings, the party held liable may make an offer of judgment. It must be served within a reasonable time—but at least 14 days—before the date set for a hearing to determine the extent of liability.

(d) PAYING COSTS AFTER AN UNACCEPTED OFFER. If the judgment that the offeree finally obtains is not more favorable than the unaccepted offer, the offeree must pay the costs incurred after the offer was made.

## Rule 7069 Execution

Rule 69 F. R. Civ. P applies in adversary proceedings.

### CIVIL RULE:

Federal Rule of Civil Procedure 69, which was last amended effective December 1, 2007, provides:

**Rule 69 Execution**

(a) IN GENERAL.

(1) *Money Judgment; Applicable Procedure.* A money judgment is enforced by a writ of execution, unless the court directs otherwise. The procedure on execution—and in proceedings supplementary to and in aid of judgment or execution—must accord with the procedure of the state where the court is located, but a federal statute governs to the extent it applies.

(2) *Obtaining Discovery.* In aid of the judgment or execution, the judgment creditor or a successor in interest whose interest appears of record may obtain discovery from any person—including the judgment debtor—as provided in these rules or by the procedure of the state where the court is located.

(b) AGAINST CERTAIN PUBLIC OFFICERS. When a judgment has been entered against a revenue officer in the circumstances stated in 28 U.S.C. § 2006, or against an officer of Congress in the circumstances stated in 2 U.S.C. § 118, the judgment must be satisfied as those statutes provide.

## Rule 7070 Judgment for Specific Acts; Vesting Title

Rule 70 F.R.Civ.P. applies in adversary proceedings and the court may enter a judgment divesting the title of any party and vesting title in others whenever the real or personal property involved is within the jurisdiction of the court.

### CIVIL RULE:

Federal Rule of Civil Procedure 70, which was last amended effective December 1, 2007, provides:

**Rule 70 Enforcing a Judgment for a Specific Act**

(a) Party's Failure to Act; Ordering Another to Act. If a judgment requires a party to convey land, to deliver a deed or other document, or to perform any other specific act and the party fails to comply within the time specified, the court may order the act to be done—at the disobedient party's expense—by another person appointed by the court. When done, the act has the same effect as if done by the party.

(b) Vesting Title. If the real or personal property is within the district, the court—instead of ordering a conveyance—may enter a judgment divesting any party's title and vesting it in others. That judgment has the effect of a legally executed conveyance.

(c) Obtaining a Writ of Attachment or Sequestration. On application by a party entitled to performance of an act, the clerk must issue a writ of attachment or sequestration against the disobedient party's property to compel obedience.

(d) Obtaining a Writ of Execution or Assistance. On application by a party who obtains a judgment or order for possession, the clerk must issue a writ of execution or assistance.

(e) Holding in Contempt. The court may also hold the disobedient party in contempt.

## Rule 7071 Process in Behalf of and Against Persons Not Parties

Rule 71 F.R.Civ.P. applies in adversary proceedings.

### CIVIL RULE:

Federal Rule of Civil Procedure 71, which was last amended effective December 1, 2007, provides:

**Rule 71 Enforcing Relief for or Against a Nonparty**

When an order grants relief for a nonparty or may be enforced against a nonparty, the procedure for enforcing the order is the same as for a party.

## Rule 7087 Transfer of Adversary Proceeding

On motion and after a hearing, the court may transfer an adversary proceeding or any part thereof to another district pursuant to 28 U.S.C. § 1412, except as provided in Rule 7019(2).

Bankruptcy Statutory Reference: 28 U.S.C. § 1412

# PART VIII

# APPEALS TO DISTRICT COURT OR BANKRUPTCY APPELLATE PANEL

## Rule 8001 Scope of Part VIII Rules; Definition of "BAP"; Method of Transmission

*(a) General Scope.* These Part VIII rules govern the procedure in a United States district court and a bankruptcy appellate panel on appeal from a judgment, order, or decree of a bankruptcy court. They also govern certain procedures on appeal to a United States court of appeals under 28 U.S.C. § 158(d).

*(b) Definition of "BAP."* "BAP" means a bankruptcy appellate panel established by a circuit's judicial council and authorized to hear appeals from a bankruptcy court under 28 U.S.C. § 158.

*(c) Method of Transmitting Documents.* A document must be sent electronically under these Part VIII rules, unless it is being sent by or to an individual who is not represented by counsel or the court's governing rules permit or require mailing or other means of delivery.

## Rule 8002 Time for Filing Notice of Appeal

*(a) In General.*

*(1) Fourteen-Day Period.* Except as provided in subdivisions (b) and (c), a notice of appeal must be filed with the bankruptcy clerk within 14 days after entry of the judgment, order, or decree being appealed.

*(2) Filing Before the Entry of Judgment.* A notice of appeal filed after the bankruptcy court announces a decision or order-but before entry of the judgment, order, or decree-is treated as filed on the date of and after the entry.

*(3) Multiple Appeals.* If one party files a timely notice of appeal, any other party may file a notice of appeal within 14 days after the date when the first notice was filed, or within the time otherwise allowed by this rule, whichever period ends later.

*(4) Mistaken Filing in Another Court.* If a notice of appeal is mistakenly filed in a district court, BAP, or court of appeals, the clerk of that court must state on the notice the date on which it was received and transmit it to the bankruptcy clerk. The notice of appeal is then considered filed in the bankruptcy court on the date so stated.

*(5) Entry Defined.*

*(A)* A judgment, order, or decree is entered for purposes of this Rule 8002(a):

*(i)* when it is entered in the docket under Rule 5003(a), or

*(ii)* if Rule 7058 applies and Rule 58(a) F.R.Civ.P. requires a separate document, when the judgment, order, or decree is entered in the docket

under Rule 5003(a) and when the earlier of these events occurs:

- the judgment, order, or decree is set out in a separate document; or
- 150 days have run from entry of the judgment, order, or decree in the docket under Rule 5003(a).

*(B)* A failure to set out a judgment, order, or decree in a separate document when required by Rule 58(a) F.R.Civ.P. does not affect the validity of an appeal from that judgment, order, or decree.

*(b) Effect of a Motion on the Time to Appeal.*

*(1) In General.* If a party files in the bankruptcy court any of the following motions and does so within the time allowed by these rules, the time to file an appeal runs for all parties from the entry of the order disposing of the last such remaining motion:

*(A)* to amend or make additional findings under Rule 7052, whether or not granting the motion would alter the judgment;

*(B)* to alter or amend the judgment under Rule 9023;

*(C)* for a new trial under Rule 9023; or

*(D)* for relief under Rule 9024 if the motion is filed within 14 days after the judgment is entered.

*(2) Filing an Appeal Before the Motion is Decided.* If a party files a notice of appeal after the court announces or enters a judgment, order, or decree-but before it disposes of any motion listed in subdivision (b)(1)-the notice becomes effective when the order disposing of the last such remaining motion is entered.

*(3) Appealing the Ruling on the Motion.* If a party intends to challenge an order disposing of any motion listed in subdivision (b)(1)-or the alteration or amendment of a judgment, order, or decree upon the motion-the party must file a notice of appeal or an amended notice of appeal. The notice or amended notice must comply with Rule 8003 or 8004 and be filed within the time prescribed by this rule, measured from the entry of the order disposing of the last such remaining motion.

*(4) No Additional Fee.* No additional fee is required to file an amended notice of appeal.

*(c) Appeal by an Inmate Confined in an Institution.*

*(1) In General.* If an institution has a system designed for legal mail, an inmate confined there must use that system to receive the benefit of this Rule 8002(c)(1). If an inmate files a notice of appeal from a judgment, order, or decree of a bankruptcy court, the notice is timely if it is deposited in the institution's internal mail system on or before the last day for filing and:

*(A)* it is accompanied by:

*(i)* a declaration in compliance with 28 U.S.C. § 1746—or a notarized statement—setting out the date of deposit and stating that first-class postage is being prepaid; or

*(ii)* evidence (such as a postmark or date stamp) showing that the notice was so deposited and that postage was prepaid; or

*(B)* the appellate court exercises its discretion to permit the later filing of a declaration or notarized statement that satisfies Rule 8002(c)(1)(A)(i).

*(2) Multiple Appeals.* If an inmate files under this subdivision the first notice of appeal, the 14-day period provided in subdivision (a)(3) for another party to file a notice of appeal runs from the date when the bankruptcy clerk dockets the first notice.

*(d) Extending the Time to Appeal.*

*(1) When the Time May Be Extended.* Except as provided in subdivision (d)(2), the bankruptcy court may extend the time to file a notice of appeal upon a party's motion that is filed:

*(A)* within the time prescribed by this rule; or

*(B)* within 21 days after that time, if the party shows excusable neglect.

*(2) When the Time May Not Be Extended.* The bankruptcy court may not extend the time to file a notice of appeal if the judgment, order, or decree appealed from:

*(A)* grants relief from an automatic stay under § 362, 922, 1201, or 1301 of the Code;

*(B)* authorizes the sale or lease of property or the use of cash collateral under § 363 of the Code;

*(C)* authorizes the obtaining of credit under § 364 of the Code;

*(D)* authorizes the assumption or assignment of an executory contract or unexpired lease under § 365 of the Code;

*(E)* approves a disclosure statement under § 1125 of the Code; or

*(F)* confirms a plan under § 943, 1129, 1225, or 1325 of the Code.

*(3) Time Limits on an Extension.* No extension of time may exceed 21 days after the time prescribed by this rule, or 14 days after the order granting the motion to extend time is entered, whichever is later.

## Rule 8003 Appeal as of Right—How Taken; Docketing the Appeal

*(a) Filing the Notice of Appeal.*

*(1) In General.* An appeal from a judgment, order, or decree of a bankruptcy court to a district court or BAP under 28 U.S.C. § 158(a)(1) or (a)(2) may be taken only by filing a notice of appeal with the bankruptcy clerk within the time allowed by Rule 8002.

*(2) Effect of Not Taking Other Steps.* An appellant's failure to take any step other than the timely filing of a notice of appeal does not affect the validity of the appeal, but is ground only for the district court or BAP to act as it considers appropriate, including dismissing the appeal.

*(3) Contents.* The notice of appeal must:

*(A)* conform substantially to the appropriate Official Form;

*(B)* be accompanied by the judgment, order, or decree, or the part of it, being appealed; and

*(C)* be accompanied by the prescribed fee.

*(4) Additional Copies.* If requested to do so, the appellant must furnish the bankruptcy clerk with enough copies of the notice to enable the clerk to comply with subdivision (c).

*(b) Joint or Consolidated Appeals.*

*(1) Joint Notice of Appeal.* When two or more parties are entitled to appeal from a judgment, order, or decree of a bankruptcy court and their interests make joinder practicable, they may file a joint notice of appeal. They may then proceed on appeal as a single appellant.

*(2) Consolidating Appeals.* When parties have separately filed timely notices of appeal, the district court or BAP may join or consolidate the appeals.

*(c) Serving the Notice of Appeal.*

*(1) Serving Parties and Transmitting to the United States Trustee.* The bankruptcy clerk must serve the notice of appeal on counsel of record for each party to the appeal, excluding the appellant, and transmit it to the United States trustee. If a party is proceeding pro se, the clerk must send the notice of appeal to the party's last known address. The clerk must note, on each copy, the date when the notice of appeal was filed.

*(2) Effect of Failing to Serve or Transmit Notice.* The bankruptcy clerk's failure to serve notice on a party or transmit notice to the United States trustee does not affect the validity of the appeal.

*(3) Noting Service on the Docket.* The clerk must note on the docket the names of the parties served and the date and method of the service.

*(d) Transmitting the Notice of Appeal to the District Court or BAP; Docketing the Appeal.*

*(1) Transmitting the Notice.* The bankruptcy clerk must promptly transmit the notice of appeal to the BAP clerk if a BAP has been established for appeals from that district and the appellant has not elected to have the district court hear the appeal. Otherwise, the bankruptcy clerk must promptly transmit the notice to the district clerk.

*(2) Docketing in the District Court or BAP.* Upon receiving the notice of appeal, the district or BAP clerk must docket the appeal under the title of the

bankruptcy case and the title of any adversary proceeding, and must identify the appellant, adding the appellant's name if necessary.

**Rule 8004 Appeal by Leave—How Taken; Docketing the Appeal**

*(a) Notice of Appeal and Motion for Leave to Appeal.* To appeal from an interlocutory order or decree of a bankruptcy court under 28 U.S.C. § 158(a)(3), a party must file with the bankruptcy clerk a notice of appeal as prescribed by Rule 8003(a). The notice must:

*(1)* be filed within the time allowed by Rule 8002;

*(2)* be accompanied by a motion for leave to appeal prepared in accordance with subdivision (b); and

*(3)* unless served electronically using the court's transmission equipment, include proof of service in accordance with Rule 8011(d).

*(b) Contents of the Motion; Response.*

*(1) Contents.* A motion for leave to appeal under 28 U.S.C. § 158(a)(3) must include the following:

*(A)* the facts necessary to understand the question presented;

*(B)* the question itself;

*(C)* the relief sought;

*(D)* the reasons why leave to appeal should be granted; and

*(E)* a copy of the interlocutory order or decree and any related opinion or memorandum.

*(2) Response.* A party may file with the district or BAP clerk a response in opposition or a cross-motion within 14 days after the motion is served.

*(c) Transmitting the Notice of Appeal and the Motion; Docketing the Appeal; Determining the Motion.*

*(1) Transmitting to the District Court or BAP.* The bankruptcy clerk must promptly transmit the notice of appeal and the motion for leave to the BAP clerk if a BAP has been established for appeals from that district and the appellant has not elected to have the district court hear the appeal. Otherwise, the bankruptcy clerk must promptly transmit the notice and motion to the district clerk.

*(2) Docketing in the District Court or BAP.* Upon receiving the notice and motion, the district or BAP clerk must docket the appeal under the title of the bankruptcy case and the title of any adversary proceeding, and must identify the appellant, adding the appellant's name if necessary.

*(3) Oral Argument Not Required.* The motion and any response or cross-motion are submitted without oral argument unless the district court or BAP orders otherwise.

*(d) Failure to File a Motion with a Notice of Appeal.* If an appellant timely files a notice of appeal under this rule but does not include a motion for leave, the district court or BAP may order the appellant to file a motion for leave, or treat the notice of appeal as a motion for leave and either grant or deny it. If the court orders that a motion for leave be filed, the appellant must do so within 14 days after the order is entered, unless the order provides otherwise.

*(e) Direct Appeal to a Court of Appeals.* If leave to appeal an interlocutory order or decree is required under 28 U.S.C. § 158(a)(3), an authorization of a direct appeal by the court of appeals under 28 U.S.C. § 158(d)(2) satisfies the requirement.

## Rule 8005 Election to Have an Appeal Heard by the District Court Instead of the BAP

*(a) Filing of a Statement of Election.* To elect to have an appeal heard by the district court, a party must:

*(1)* file a statement of election that conforms substantially to the appropriate Official Form; and

*(2)* do so within the time prescribed by 28 U.S.C. § 158(c)(1).

*(b) Transmitting the Documents Related to the Appeal.* Upon receiving an appellant's timely statement of election, the bankruptcy clerk must transmit to the district clerk all documents related to the appeal. Upon receiving a timely statement of election by a party other than the appellant, the BAP clerk must transmit to the district clerk all documents related to the appeal and notify the bankruptcy clerk of the transmission.

*(c) Determining the Validity of an Election.* A party seeking a determination of the validity of an election must file a motion in the court where the appeal is then pending. The motion must be filed within 14 days after the statement of election is filed.

*(d) Motion for Leave Without a Notice of Appeal—Effect on the Timing of an Election.* If an appellant moves for leave to appeal under Rule 8004 but fails to file a separate notice of appeal with the motion, the motion must be treated as a notice of appeal for purposes of determining the timeliness of a statement of election.

## Rule 8006 Certifying a Direct Appeal to the Court of Appeals

*(a) Effective Date of a Certification.* A certification of a judgment, order, or decree of a bankruptcy court for direct review in a court of appeals under 28 U.S.C. § 158(d)(2) is effective when:

*(1)* the certification has been filed;

*(2)* a timely appeal has been taken under Rule 8003 or 8004; and

*(3)* the notice of appeal has become effective under Rule 8002.

*(b) Filing the Certification.* The certification must be filed with the clerk of the court where the matter is pending. For purposes of this rule, a matter remains pending in the bankruptcy court for 30 days after the effective date under Rule

8002 of the first notice of appeal from the judgment, order, or decree for which direct review is sought. A matter is pending in the district court or BAP thereafter.

*(c) Joint Certification by All Appellants and Appellees.*

*(1) How Accomplished.* A joint certification by all the appellants and appellees under 28 U.S.C. § 158(d)(2)(A) must be made by using the appropriate Official Form. The parties may supplement the certification with a short statement of the basis for the certification, which may include the information listed in subdivision (f)(2).

*(2) Supplemental Statement by the Court.* Within 14 days after the parties' certification, the bankruptcy court or the court in which the matter is then pending may file a short supplemental statement about the merits of the certification.

*(d) The Court That May Make the Certification.* Only the court where the matter is pending, as provided in subdivision (b), may certify a direct review on request of parties or on its own motion.

*(e) Certification on the Court's Own Motion.*

*(1) How Accomplished.* A certification on the court's own motion must be set forth in a separate document. The clerk of the certifying court must serve it on the parties to the appeal in the manner required for service of a notice of appeal under Rule 8003(c)(1). The certification must be accompanied by an opinion or memorandum that contains the information required by subdivision (f)(2)(A)–(D).

*(2) Supplemental Statement by a Party.* Within 14 days after the court's certification, a party may file with the clerk of the certifying court a short supplemental statement regarding the merits of certification.

*(f) Certification by the Court on Request.*

*(1) How Requested.* A request by a party for certification that a circumstance specified in 28 U.S.C. § 158(d)(2)(A)(i)–(iii) applies—or a request by a majority of the appellants and a majority of the appellees—must be filed with the clerk of the court where the matter is pending within 60 days after the entry of the judgment, order, or decree.

*(2) Service and Contents.* The request must be served on all parties to the appeal in the manner required for service of a notice of appeal under Rule 8003(c)(1), and it must include the following:

*(A)* the facts necessary to understand the question presented;

*(B)* the question itself;

*(C)* the relief sought;

*(D)* the reasons why the direct appeal should be allowed, including which circumstance specified in 28 U.S.C. § 158(d)(2)(A)(i)–(iii) applies; and

*(E)* a copy of the judgment, order, or decree and any related opinion or

memorandum.

*(3) Time to File a Response or a Cross-Request.* A party may file a response to the request within 14 days after the request is served, or such other time as the court where the matter is pending allows. A party may file a cross-request for certification within 14 days after the request is served, or within 60 days after the entry of the judgment, order, or decree, whichever occurs first.

*(4) Oral Argument Not Required.* The request, cross-request, and any response are submitted without oral argument unless the court where the matter is pending orders otherwise.

*(5) Form and Service of the Certification.* If the court certifies a direct appeal in response to the request, it must do so in a separate document. The certification must be served on the parties to the appeal in the manner required for service of a notice of appeal under Rule 8003(c)(1).

*(g) Proceeding in the Court of Appeals Following a Certification.* Within 30 days after the date the certification becomes effective under subdivision (a), a request for permission to take a direct appeal to the court of appeals must be filed with the circuit clerk in accordance with F.R.App.P. 6(c).

## Rule 8007 Stay Pending Appeal; Bonds; Suspension of Proceedings

*(a) Initial Motion in the Bankruptcy Court.*

*(1) In General.* Ordinarily, a party must move first in the bankruptcy court for the following relief:

*(A)* a stay of a judgment, order, or decree of the bankruptcy court pending appeal;

*(B)* the approval of a bond or other security provided to obtain a stay of judgment;

*(C)* an order suspending, modifying, restoring, or granting an injunction while an appeal is pending; or

*(D)* the suspension or continuation of proceedings in a case or other relief permitted by subdivision (e).

*(2) Time to File.* The motion may be made either before or after the notice of appeal is filed.

*(b) Motion in the District Court, the BAP, or the Court of Appeals on Direct Appeal.*

*(1) Request for Relief.* A motion for the relief specified in subdivision (a)(1)—or to vacate or modify a bankruptcy court's order granting such relief—may be made in the court where the appeal is pending.

*(2) Showing or Statement Required.* The motion must:

*(A)* show that moving first in the bankruptcy court would be impracticable; or

*(B)* if a motion was made in the bankruptcy court, either state that the

BANKRUPTCY RULES

court has not yet ruled on the motion, or state that the court has ruled and set out any reasons given for the ruling.

*(3) Additional Content.* The motion must also include:

*(A)* the reasons for granting the relief requested and the facts relied upon;

*(B)* affidavits or other sworn statements supporting facts subject to dispute; and

*(C)* relevant parts of the record.

*(4) Serving Notice.* The movant must give reasonable notice of the motion to all parties.

*(c) Filing a Bond or Other Security.* The district court, BAP, or court of appeals may condition relief on filing a bond or other security with the bankruptcy court.

*(d) Bond or Other Security for a Trustee or the United States.* The court may require a trustee to file a bond or other security when the trustee appeals. A bond or other security is not required when an appeal is taken by the United States, its officer, or its agency or by direction of any department of the federal government.

*(e) Continuation of Proceedings in the Bankruptcy Court.* Despite Rule 7062 and subject to the authority of the district court, BAP, or court of appeals, the bankruptcy court may:

*(1)* suspend or order the continuation of other proceedings in the case; or

*(2)* issue any other appropriate orders during the pendency of an appeal to protect the rights of all parties in interest.

**Rule 8008 Indicative Rulings**

*(a) Relief Pending Appeal.* If a party files a timely motion in the bankruptcy court for relief that the court lacks authority to grant because of an appeal that has been docketed and is pending, the bankruptcy court may:

*(1)* defer considering the motion;

*(2)* deny the motion; or

*(3)* state that the court would grant the motion if the court where the appeal is pending remands for that purpose, or state that the motion raises a substantial issue.

*(b) Notice to the Court Where the Appeal Is Pending.* The movant must promptly notify the clerk of the court where the appeal is pending if the bankruptcy court states that it would grant the motion or that the motion raises a substantial issue.

*(c) Remand After an Indicative Ruling.* If the bankruptcy court states that it would grant the motion or that the motion raises a substantial issue, the district court or BAP may remand for further proceedings, but it retains jurisdiction unless it expressly dismisses the appeal. If the district court or BAP remands but retains jurisdiction, the parties must promptly notify the clerk of that court when the bankruptcy court has decided the motion on remand.

## Rule 8009 Record on Appeal; Sealed Documents

*(a) Designating the Record on Appeal; Statement of the Issues.*

*(1) Appellant.*

*(A)* The appellant must file with the bankruptcy clerk and serve on the appellee a designation of the items to be included in the record on appeal and a statement of the issues to be presented.

*(B)* The appellant must file and serve the designation and statement within 14 days after:

*(i)* the appellant's notice of appeal as of right becomes effective under Rule 8002; or

*(ii)* an order granting leave to appeal is entered.

A designation and statement served prematurely must be treated as served on the first day on which filing is timely.

*(2) Appellee and Cross-Appellant.*Within 14 days after being served, the appellee may file with the bankruptcy clerk and serve on the appellant a designation of additional items to be included in the record. An appellee who files a cross-appeal must file and serve a designation of additional items to be included in the record and a statement of the issues to be presented on the cross-appeal.

*(3) Cross-Appellee.* Within 14 days after service of the cross-appellant's designation and statement, a cross-appellee may file with the bankruptcy clerk and serve on the cross-appellant a designation of additional items to be included in the record.

*(4) Record on Appeal.* The record on appeal must include the following:

- docket entries kept by the bankruptcy clerk;
- items designated by the parties;
- the notice of appeal;
- the judgment, order, or decree being appealed;
- any order granting leave to appeal;
- any certification required for a direct appeal to the court of appeals;
- any opinion, findings of fact, and conclusions of law relating to the issues on appeal, including transcripts of all oral rulings;
- any transcript ordered under subdivision (b);
- any statement required by subdivision (c); and
- any additional items from the record that the court where the appeal is pending orders.

*(5) Copies for the Bankruptcy Clerk.* If paper copies are needed, a party filing a designation of items must provide a copy of any of those items that the bankruptcy clerk requests. If the party fails to do so, the bankruptcy clerk must

prepare the copy at the party's expense.

*(b) Transcript of Proceedings.*

*(1) Appellant's Duty to Order.* Within the time period prescribed by subdivision (a)(1), the appellant must:

*(A)* order in writing from the reporter, as defined in Rule 8010(a)(1), a transcript of such parts of the proceedings not already on file as the appellant considers necessary for the appeal, and file a copy of the order with the bankruptcy clerk; or

*(B)* file with the bankruptcy clerk a certificate stating that the appellant is not ordering a transcript.

*(2) Cross-Appellant's Duty to Order.* Within 14 days after the appellant files a copy of the transcript order or a certificate of not ordering a transcript, the appellee as cross-appellant must:

*(A)* order in writing from the reporter, as defined in Rule 8010(a)(1), a transcript of such additional parts of the proceedings as the cross-appellant considers necessary for the appeal, and file a copy of the order with the bankruptcy clerk; or

*(B)* file with the bankruptcy clerk a certificate stating that the cross-appellant is not ordering a transcript.

*(3) Appellee's or Cross-Appellee's Right to Order.* Within 14 days after the appellant or cross-appellant files a copy of a transcript order or certificate of not ordering a transcript, the appellee or cross-appellee may order in writing from the reporter a transcript of such additional parts of the proceedings as the appellee or cross-appellee considers necessary for the appeal. A copy of the order must be filed with the bankruptcy clerk.

*(4) Payment.* At the time of ordering, a party must make satisfactory arrangements with the reporter for paying the cost of the transcript.

*(5) Unsupported Finding or Conclusion.* If the appellant intends to argue on appeal that a finding or conclusion is unsupported by the evidence or is contrary to the evidence, the appellant must include in the record a transcript of all relevant testimony and copies of all relevant exhibits.

*(c) Statement of the Evidence When a Transcript Is Unavailable.* If a transcript of a hearing or trial is unavailable, the appellant may prepare a statement of the evidence or proceedings from the best available means, including the appellant's recollection. The statement must be filed within the time prescribed by subdivision (a)(1) and served on the appellee, who may serve objections or proposed amendments within 14 days after being served. The statement and any objections or proposed amendments must then be submitted to the bankruptcy court for settlement and approval. As settled and approved, the statement must be included by the bankruptcy clerk in the record on appeal.

*(d) Agreed Statement as the Record on Appeal.* Instead of the record on appeal as

defined in subdivision (a), the parties may prepare, sign, and submit to the bankruptcy court a statement of the case showing how the issues presented by the appeal arose and were decided in the bankruptcy court. The statement must set forth only those facts alleged and proved or sought to be proved that are essential to the court's resolution of the issues. If the statement is accurate, it—together with any additions that the bankruptcy court may consider necessary to a full presentation of the issues on appeal—must be approved by the bankruptcy court and must then be certified to the court where the appeal is pending as the record on appeal. The bankruptcy clerk must then transmit it to the clerk of that court within the time provided by Rule 8010. A copy of the agreed statement may be filed in place of the appendix required by Rule 8018(b) or, in the case of a direct appeal to the court of appeals, by F.R.App.P. 30.

*(e) Correcting or Modifying the Record.*

*(1) Submitting to the Bankruptcy Court.* If any difference arises about whether the record accurately discloses what occurred in the bankruptcy court, the difference must be submitted to and settled by the bankruptcy court and the record conformed accordingly. If an item has been improperly designated as part of the record on appeal, a party may move to strike that item.

*(2) Correcting in Other Ways.* If anything material to either party is omitted from or misstated in the record by error or accident, the omission or misstatement may be corrected, and a supplemental record may be certified and transmitted:

*(A)* on stipulation of the parties;

*(B)* by the bankruptcy court before or after the record has been forwarded; or

*(C)* by the court where the appeal is pending.

*(3) Remaining Questions.* All other questions as to the form and content of the record must be presented to the court where the appeal is pending.

*(f) Sealed Documents.* A document placed under seal by the bankruptcy court may be designated as part of the record on appeal. In doing so, a party must identify it without revealing confidential or secret information, but the bankruptcy clerk must not transmit it to the clerk of the court where the appeal is pending as part of the record. Instead, a party must file a motion with the court where the appeal is pending to accept the document under seal. If the motion is granted, the movant must notify the bankruptcy court of the ruling, and the bankruptcy clerk must promptly transmit the sealed document to the clerk of the court where the appeal is pending.

*(g) Other Necessary Actions.* All parties to an appeal must take any other action necessary to enable the bankruptcy clerk to assemble and transmit the record.

### Rule 8010 Completing and Transmitting the Record

*(a) Reporter's Duties.*

*(1) Proceedings Recorded Without a Reporter Present.* If proceedings were

recorded without a reporter being present, the person or service selected under bankruptcy court procedures to transcribe the recording is the reporter for purposes of this rule.

*(2) Preparing and Filing the Transcript.* The reporter must prepare and file a transcript as follows:

*(A)* Upon receiving an order for a transcript in accordance with Rule 8009(b), the reporter must file in the bankruptcy court an acknowledgment of the request that shows when it was received, and when the reporter expects to have the transcript completed.

*(B)* After completing the transcript, the reporter must file it with the bankruptcy clerk, who will notify the district, BAP, or circuit clerk of its filing.

*(C)* If the transcript cannot be completed within 30 days after receiving the order, the reporter must request an extension of time from the bankruptcy clerk. The clerk must enter on the docket and notify the parties whether the extension is granted.

*(D)* If the reporter does not file the transcript on time, the bankruptcy clerk must notify the bankruptcy judge.

*(b) Clerk's Duties.*

*(1) Transmitting the Record—In General.* Subject to Rule 8009(f) and subdivision (b)(5) of this rule, when the record is complete, the bankruptcy clerk must transmit to the clerk of the court where the appeal is pending either the record or a notice that the record is available electronically.

*(2) Multiple Appeals.* If there are multiple appeals from a judgment, order, or decree, the bankruptcy clerk must transmit a single record.

*(3) Receiving the Record.* Upon receiving the record or notice that it is available electronically, the district, BAP, or circuit clerk must enter that information on the docket and promptly notify all parties to the appeal.

*(4) If Paper Copies Are Ordered.* If the court where the appeal is pending directs that paper copies of the record be provided, the clerk of that court must so notify the appellant. If the appellant fails to provide them, the bankruptcy clerk must prepare them at the appellant's expense.

*(5) When Leave to Appeal is Requested.* Subject to subdivision (c), if a motion for leave to appeal has been filed under Rule 8004, the bankruptcy clerk must prepare and transmit the record only after the district court, BAP, or court of appeals grants leave.

*(c) Record for a Preliminary Motion in the District Court, BAP, or Court of Appeals.* This subdivision (c) applies if, before the record is transmitted, a party moves in the district court, BAP, or court of appeals for any of the following relief:

- leave to appeal;
- dismissal;
- a stay pending appeal;

- approval of a bond or other security provided to obtain a stay of judgment; or
- any other intermediate order.

The bankruptcy clerk must then transmit to the clerk of the court where the relief is sought any parts of the record designated by a party to the appeal or a notice that those parts are available electronically.

**Rule 8011 Filing and Service; Signature**

*(a) Filing.*

*(1) With the Clerk.* A document required or permitted to be filed in a district court or BAP must be filed with the clerk of that court.

*(2) Method and Timeliness.*

*(A) Nonelectronic Filing.*

*(i) In General.* For a document not filed electronically, filing may be accomplished by mail addressed to the clerk of the district court or BAP. Except as provided in subdivision (a)(2)(A)(ii) and (iii), filing is timely only if the clerk receives the document within the time fixed for filing.

*(ii) Brief or Appendix.* A brief or appendix not filed electronically is also timely filed if, on or before the last day for filing, it is:

- mailed to the clerk by first-class mail—or other class of mail that is at least as expeditious—postage prepaid; or
- dispatched to a third-party commercial carrier for delivery within 3 days to the clerk.

*(iii) Inmate Filing.* If an institution has a system designed for legal mail, an inmate confined there must use that system to receive the benefit of this Rule 8011(a)(2)(A)(iii). A document not filed electronically by an inmate confined in an institution is timely if it is deposited in the institution's internal mailing system on or before the last day for filing and:

- it is accompanied by a declaration in compliance with 28 U.S.C. § 1746—or a notarized statement—setting out the date of deposit and stating that first-class postage is being prepaid; or evidence (such as a postmark or date stamp) showing that the notice was so deposited and that postage was prepaid; or
- the appellate court exercises its discretion to permit the later filing of a declaration or notarized statement that satisfies this Rule 8011(a)(2)(A)(iii).

*(B) Electronic Filing.*

*(i) By a Represented Person—Generally Required; Exceptions.* An entity represented by an attorney must file electronically, unless nonelectronic filing is allowed by the court for good cause or is allowed or required by local rule.

*(ii) By an Unrepresented Individual—When Allowed or Required.* An individual not represented by an attorney:

- may file electronically only if allowed by court order or by local rule; and
- may be required to file electronically only by court order, or by a local rule that includes reasonable exceptions.

*(iii) Same as a Written Paper.* A document filed electronically is a written paper for purposes of these rules.

*(C) Copies.* If a document is filed electronically, no paper copy is required. If a document is filed by mail or delivery to the district court or BAP, no additional copies are required. But the district court or BAP may require by local rule or by order in a particular case the filing or furnishing of a specified number of paper copies.

*(3) Clerk's Refusal of Documents.* The court's clerk must not refuse to accept for filing any document transmitted for that purpose solely because it is not presented in proper form as required by these rules or by any local rule or practice.

*(b) Service of All Documents Required.* Unless a rule requires service by the clerk, a party must, at or before the time of the filing of a document, serve it on the other parties to the appeal. Service on a party represented by counsel must be made on the party's counsel.

*(c) Manner of Service.*

*(1) Nonelectronic Service.* Nonelectronic service may be by any of the following:

*(A)* personal delivery;

*(B)* mail; or

*(C)* third-party commercial carrier for delivery within 3 days.

*(2) Electronic Service.* Electronic service may be made by sending a document to a registered user by filing it with the court's electronic-filing system or by using other electronic means that the person served consented to in writing.

*(3) When Service Is Complete.* Service by electronic means is complete on filing or sending, unless the person making service receives notice that the document was not received by the person served. Service by mail or by commercial carrier is complete on mailing or delivery to the carrier.

*(d) Proof of Service.*

*(1) What Is Required.* A document presented for filing must contain either of the following if it was served other than through the court's electronic-filing system:

*(A)* an acknowledgment of service by the person served; or

*(B)* proof of service consisting of a statement by the person who made service certifying:

*(i)* the date and manner of service;

*(ii)* the names of the persons served; and

*(iii)* the mail or electronic address, the fax number, or the address of the place of delivery, as appropriate for the manner of service, for each person served.

*(2) Delayed Proof.* The district or BAP clerk may permit documents to be filed without acknowledgment or proof of service, but must require the acknowledgment or proof to be filed promptly thereafter.

*(3) Brief or Appendix.* When a brief or appendix is filed, the proof of service must also state the date and manner by which it was filed.

*(e) Signature.* Every document filed electronically must include the electronic signature of the person filing it or, if the person is represented, the electronic signature of counsel. A filing made through a person's electronic-filing account and authorized by that person, together with that person's name on a signature block, constitutes the person's signature. Every document filed in paper form must be signed by the person filing the document or, if the person is represented, by counsel.

**Rule 8012 Disclosure Statement**

*(a) Nongovernmental Corporations.* Any nongovernmental corporation that is a party to a proceeding in the district court or BAP must file a statement that identifies any parent corporation and any publicly held corporation that owns 10% or more of its stock or states that there is no such corporation. The same requirement applies to a nongovernmental corporation that seeks to intervene.

*(b) Disclosure About the Debtor.* The debtor, the trustee, or, if neither is a party, the appellant must file a statement that:

*(1)* identifies each debtor not named in the caption; and

*(2)* for each debtor that is a corporation, discloses the information required by Rule 8012(a).

*(c) Time to File; Supplemental Filing.* A Rule 8012 statement must:

*(1)* be filed with the principal brief or upon filing a motion, response, petition, or answer in the district court or BAP, whichever occurs first, unless a local rule requires earlier filing;

*(2)* be included before the table of contents in the principal brief; and

*(3)* be supplemented whenever the information required by Rule 8012 changes.

**Rule 8013 Motions; Intervention**

*(a) Contents of a Motion; Response; Reply.*

*(1) Request for Relief.* A request for an order or other relief is made by filing a motion with the district or BAP clerk.

*(2) Contents of a Motion.*

*(A) Grounds and the Relief Sought.* A motion must state with particularity the grounds for the motion, the relief sought, and the legal argument necessary to support it.

*(B) Motion to Expedite an Appeal.* A motion to expedite an appeal must explain what justifies considering the appeal ahead of other matters. If the district court or BAP grants the motion, it may accelerate the time to transmit the record, the deadline for filing briefs and other documents, oral argument, and the resolution of the appeal. A motion to expedite an appeal may be filed as an emergency motion under subdivision (d).

*(C) Accompanying Documents.*

*(i)* Any affidavit or other document necessary to support a motion must be served and filed with the motion.

*(ii)* An affidavit must contain only factual information, not legal argument.

*(iii)* A motion seeking substantive relief must include a copy of the bankruptcy court's judgment, order, or decree, and any accompanying opinion as a separate exhibit.

*(D) Documents Barred or Not Required.*

*(i)* A separate brief supporting or responding to a motion must not be filed.

*(ii)* Unless the court orders otherwise, a notice of motion or a proposed order is not required.

*(3) Response and Reply; Time to File.* Unless the district court or BAP orders otherwise,

*(A)* any party to the appeal may file a response to the motion within 7 days after service of the motion; and

*(B)* the movant may file a reply to a response within 7 days after service of the response, but may only address matters raised in the response.

*(b) Disposition of a Motion for a Procedural Order.* The district court or BAP may rule on a motion for a procedural order—including a motion under Rule 9006(b) or (c)—at any time without awaiting a response. A party adversely affected by the ruling may move to reconsider, vacate, or modify it within 7 days after the procedural order is served.

*(c) Oral Argument.* A motion will be decided without oral argument unless the district court or BAP orders otherwise.

*(d) Emergency Motion.*

*(1) Noting the Emergency.* When a movant requests expedited action on a motion because irreparable harm would occur during the time needed to consider a response, the movant must insert the word "Emergency" before the title of the motion.

*(2) Contents of the Motion.* The emergency motion must

*(A)* be accompanied by an affidavit setting out the nature of the emergency;

*(B)* state whether all grounds for it were submitted to the bankruptcy court and, if not, why the motion should not be remanded for the bankruptcy court to consider;

*(C)* include the e-mail addresses, office addresses, and telephone numbers of moving counsel and, when known, of opposing counsel and any unrepresented parties to the appeal; and

*(D)* be served as prescribed by Rule 8011.

*(3) Notifying Opposing Parties.* Before filing an emergency motion, the movant must make every practicable effort to notify opposing counsel and any unrepresented parties in time for them to respond. The affidavit accompanying the emergency motion must state when and how notice was given or state why giving it was impracticable.

*(e) Power of a Single BAP Judge to Entertain a Motion.*

*(1) Single Judge's Authority.* A BAP judge may act alone on any motion, but may not dismiss or otherwise determine an appeal, deny a motion for leave to appeal, or deny a motion for a stay pending appeal if denial would make the appeal moot.

*(2) Reviewing a Single Judge's Action.* The BAP may review a single judge's action, either on its own motion or on a party's motion.

*(f) Form of Documents; Length Limits; Number of Copies.*

*(1)* Format of a paper document. Rule 27(d)(1) F.R.App.P. applies in the district court or BAP to a paper version of a motion, response, or reply.

*(2) Format of an Electronically Filed Document.* A motion, response, or reply filed electronically must comply with the requirements for a paper version regarding covers, line spacing, margins, typeface, and type style. It must also comply with the length limits under paragraph (3).

*(3) Length Limits.* Except by the district court's or BAP's permission, and excluding the accompanying documents authorized by subdivision (a)(2)(C):

*(A)* a motion or a response to a motion produced using a computer must include a certificate under Rule 8015(h) and not exceed 5,200 words;

*(B)* a handwritten or typewritten motion or a response to a motion must not exceed 20 pages;

*(C)* a reply produced using a computer must include a certificate under Rule 8015(h) and not exceed 2,600 words; and

*(D)* a handwritten or typewritten reply must not exceed 10 pages.

*(4) Paper Copies.* Paper copies must be provided only if required by local rule or by an order in a particular case.

*(g) Intervening in an Appeal.* Unless a statute provides otherwise, an entity that seeks to intervene in an appeal pending in the district court or BAP must move for leave to intervene and serve a copy of the motion on the parties to the appeal. The motion or other notice of intervention authorized by statute must be filed within 30 days after the appeal is docketed. It must concisely state the movant's interest, the grounds for intervention, whether intervention was sought in the bankruptcy court, why intervention is being sought at this stage of the proceeding, and why participating as an amicus curiae would not be adequate.

**Rule 8014 Briefs**

*(a) Appellant's Brief.* The appellant's brief must contain the following under appropriate headings and in the order indicated:

*(1)* a corporate disclosure statement, if required by Rule 8012;

*(2)* a table of contents, with page references;

*(3)* a table of authorities—cases (alphabetically arranged), statutes, and other authorities—with references to the pages of the brief where they are cited;

*(4)* a jurisdictional statement, including:

*(A)* the basis for the bankruptcy court's subject-matter jurisdiction, with citations to applicable statutory provisions and stating relevant facts establishing jurisdiction;

*(B)* the basis for the district court's or BAP's jurisdiction, with citations to applicable statutory provisions and stating relevant facts establishing jurisdiction;

*(C)* the filing dates establishing the timeliness of the appeal; and

*(D)* an assertion that the appeal is from a final judgment, order, or decree, or information establishing the district court's or BAP's jurisdiction on another basis;

*(5)* a statement of the issues presented and, for each one, a concise statement of the applicable standard of appellate review;

*(6)* a concise statement of the case setting out the facts relevant to the issues submitted for review, describing the relevant procedural history, and identifying the rulings presented for review, with appropriate references to the record;

*(7)* a summary of the argument, which must contain a succinct, clear, and accurate statement of the arguments made in the body of the brief, and which

must not merely repeat the argument headings;

*(8)* the argument, which must contain the appellant's contentions and the reasons for them, with citations to the authorities and parts of the record on which the appellant relies;

*(9)* a short conclusion stating the precise relief sought; and

*(10)* the certificate of compliance, if required by Rule 8015(a)(7) or (b).

*(b) Appellee's Brief.* The appellee's brief must conform to the requirements of subdivision (a)(1)–(8) and (10), except that none of the following need appear unless the appellee is dissatisfied with the appellant's statement:

*(1)* the jurisdictional statement;

*(2)* the statement of the issues and the applicable standard of appellate review; and

*(3)* the statement of the case.

*(c) Reply Brief.* The appellant may file a brief in reply to the appellee's brief. A reply brief must comply with the requirements of subdivision (a)(2)–(3).

*(d) Statutes, Rules, Regulations, or Similar Authority.* If the court's determination of the issues presented requires the study of the Code or other statutes, rules, regulations, or similar authority, the relevant parts must be set out in the brief or in an addendum.

*(e) Briefs in a Case Involving Multiple Appellants or Appellees.* In a case involving more than one appellant or appellee, including consolidated cases, any number of appellants or appellees may join in a brief, and any party may adopt by reference a part of another's brief. Parties may also join in reply briefs.

*(f) Citation of Supplemental Authorities.* If pertinent and significant authorities come to a party's attention after the party's brief has been filed—or after oral argument but before a decision—a party may promptly advise the district or BAP clerk by a signed submission setting forth the citations. The submission, which must be served on the other parties to the appeal, must state the reasons for the supplemental citations, referring either to the pertinent page of a brief or to a point argued orally. The body of the submission must not exceed 350 words. Any response must be made within 7 days after the party is served, unless the court orders otherwise, and must be similarly limited.

## Rule 8015 Form and Length of Briefs; Form of Appendices and Other Papers

*(a) Paper Copies of a Brief.* If a paper copy of a brief may or must be filed, the following provisions apply:

*(1) Reproduction.*

*(A)* A brief may be reproduced by any process that yields a clear black image on light paper. The paper must be opaque and unglazed. Only one side of the paper may be used.

*(B)* Text must be reproduced with a clarity that equals or exceeds the output of a laser printer.

*(C)* Photographs, illustrations, and tables may be reproduced by any method that results in a good copy of the original. A glossy finish is acceptable if the original is glossy.

*(2) Cover.* The front cover of a brief must contain:

*(A)* the number of the case centered at the top;

*(B)* the name of the court;

*(C)* the title of the case as prescribed by Rule 8003(d)(2) or 8004(c)(2);

*(D)* the nature of the proceeding and the name of the court below;

*(E)* the title of the brief, identifying the party or parties for whom the brief is filed; and

*(F)* the name, office address, telephone number, and e-mail address of counsel representing the party for whom the brief is filed.

*(3) Binding.* The brief must be bound in any manner that is secure, does not obscure the text, and permits the brief to lie reasonably flat when open.

*(4) Paper Size, Line Spacing, and Margins.* The brief must be on 8½-by-11 inch paper. The text must be double-spaced, but quotations more than two lines long may be indented and single-spaced. Headings and footnotes may be single-spaced. Margins must be at least one inch on all four sides. Page numbers may be placed in the margins, but no text may appear there.

*(5) Typeface.* Either a proportionally spaced or monospaced face may be used.

*(A)* A proportionally spaced face must include serifs, but sans-serif type may be used in headings and captions. A proportionally spaced face must be 14-point or larger.

*(B)* A monospaced face may not contain more than 10½ characters per inch.

*(6) Type Styles.* A brief must be set in plain, roman style, although italics or boldface may be used for emphasis. Case names must be italicized or underlined.

*(7) Length.*

*(A) Page Limitation.* A principal brief must not exceed 30 pages, or a reply brief 15 pages, unless it complies with subparagraph (B).

*(B) Type-Volume Limitation.*

*(i)* A principal brief is acceptable if it contains a certificate under Rule 8015(h) and:

- contains no more than 13,000 words; or
- uses a monospaced face and contains no more than 1,300 lines

of text.

*(ii)* A reply brief is acceptable if it includes a certificate under Rule 8015(h) and contains no more than half of the type volume specified in item (i).

*(b) Electronically Filed Briefs.* A brief filed electronically must comply with subdivision (a), except for (a)(1), (a)(3), and the paper requirement of (a)(4).

*(c) Paper Copies of Appendices.* A paper copy of an appendix must comply with subdivision (a)(1), (2), (3), and (4), with the following exceptions:

*(1)* An appendix may include a legible photocopy of any document found in the record or of a printed decision.

*(2)* When necessary to facilitate inclusion of odd-sized documents such as technical drawings, an appendix may be a size other than 8½-by-11 inches, and need not lie reasonably flat when opened.

*(d) Electronically Filed Appendices.* An appendix filed electronically must comply with subdivision (a)(2) and (4), except for the paper requirement of (a)(4).

*(e) Other Documents.*

*(1) Motion.* Rule 8013(f) governs the form of a motion, response, or reply.

*(2) Paper Copies of Other Documents.* A paper copy of any other document, other than a submission under Rule 8014(f), must comply with subdivision (a), with the following exceptions:

*(A)* A cover is not necessary if the caption and signature page together contain the information required by subdivision (a)(2).

*(B)* Subdivision (a)(7) does not apply.

*(3) Other Documents Filed Electronically.* Any other document filed electronically, other than a submission under Rule 8014(f), must comply with the appearance requirements of paragraph (2).

*(f) Local Variation.* A district court or BAP must accept documents that comply with the form requirements of this rule and the length limits set by Part VIII of these rules. By local rule or order in a particular case, a district court or BAP may accept documents that do not meet all the form requirements of this rule or the length limits set by Part VIII of these rules.

*(g) Items Excluded from Length.* In computing any length limit, headings, footnotes, and quotations count toward the limit, but the following items do not:

- cover page;
- disclosure statement under Rule 8012;
- table of contents;
- table of citations;
- statement regarding oral argument;
- addendum containing statutes, rules, or regulations;

BANKRUPTCY RULES

- certificates of counsel;
- signature block;
- proof of service; and
- any item specifically excluded by these rules or by local rule.

*(h) Certificate of Compliance.*

*(1) Briefs and Documents That Require a Certificate.* A brief submitted under Rule 8015(a)(7)(B), 8016(d)(2), or 8017(b)(4)—and a document submitted under Rule 8013(f)(3)(A), 8013(f)(3)(C), or 8022(b)(1)—must include a certificate by the attorney, or an unrepresented party, that the document complies with the type-volume limitation. The individual preparing the certificate may rely on the word or line count of the word-processing system used to prepare the document. The certificate must state the number of words—or the number of lines of monospaced type—in the document.

*(2) Acceptable Form.* The certificate requirement is satisfied by a certificate of compliance that conforms substantially to the appropriate Official Form.

**Rule 8016 Cross-Appeals**

*(a) Applicability.* This rule applies to a case in which a cross-appeal is filed. Rules 8014(a)-(c), 8015(a)(7)(A)-(B), and 8018(a)(1)-(3) do not apply to such a case, except as otherwise provided in this rule.

*(b) Designation of Appellant.* The party who files a notice of appeal first is the appellant for purposes of this rule and Rule 8018(a)(4) and (b) and Rule 8019. If notices are filed on the same day, the plaintiff, petitioner, applicant, or movant in the proceeding below is the appellant. These designations may be modified by the parties' agreement or by court order.

*(c) Briefs.* In a case involving a cross-appeal:

*(1) Appellant's Principal Brief.* The appellant must file a principal brief in the appeal. That brief must comply with Rule 8014(a).

*(2) Appellee's Principal and Response Brief.* The appellee must file a principal brief in the cross-appeal and must, in the same brief, respond to the principal brief in the appeal. That brief must comply with Rule 8014(a), except that the brief need not include a statement of the case unless the appellee is dissatisfied with the appellant's statement.

*(3) Appellant's Response and Reply Brief.* The appellant must file a brief that responds to the principal brief in the cross-appeal and may, in the same brief, reply to the response in the appeal. That brief must comply with Rule 8014(a)(2)-(8) and (10), except that none of the following need appear unless the appellant is dissatisfied with the appellee's statement in the cross-appeal:

*(A)* the jurisdictional statement;

*(B)* the statement of the issues and the applicable standard of appellate review; and

(C) the statement of the case.

(4) *Appellee's Reply Brief.* The appellee may file a brief in reply to the response in the cross-appeal. That brief must comply with Rule 8014(a)(2)–(3) and (10) and must be limited to the issues presented by the cross-appeal.

(d) *Length.*

(1) *Page Limitation.* Unless it complies with paragraph (2), the appellant's principal brief must not exceed 30 pages; the appellee's principal and response brief, 35 pages; the appellant's response and reply brief, 30 pages; and the appellee's reply brief, 15 pages.

(2) *Type-Volume Limitation.*

(A) The appellant's principal brief or the appellant's response and reply brief is acceptable if it includes a certificate under Rule 8015(h) and:

(i) contains no more than 13,000 words; or

(ii) uses a monospaced face and contains no more than 1,300 lines of text.

(B) The appellee's principal and response brief is acceptable if it includes a certificate under Rule 8015(h) and:

(i) contains no more than 15,300 words; or

(ii) uses a monospaced face and contains no more than 1,500 lines of text.

(C) The appellee's reply brief is acceptable if it includes a certificate under Rule 8015(h) and contains no more than half of the type volume specified in subparagraph (A).

(e) *Time to Serve and File a Brief.* Briefs must be served and filed as follows, unless the district court or BAP by order in a particular case excuses the filing of briefs or specifies different time limits:

(1) the appellant's principal brief, within 30 days after the docketing of notice that the record has been transmitted or is available electronically;

(2) the appellee's principal and response brief, within 30 days after the appellant's principal brief is served;

(3) the appellant's response and reply brief, within 30 days after the appellee's principal and response brief is served; and

(4) the appellee's reply brief, within 14 days after the appellant's response and reply brief is served, but at least 7 days before scheduled argument unless the district court or BAP, for good cause, allows a later filing.

## Rule 8017 Brief of an Amicus Curiae

(a) *During Initial Consideration of Case on the Merits.*

(1) *Applicability.* This Rule 8017(a) governs amicus filings during a court's

initial consideration of a case on the merits.

*(2) When Permitted.* The United States or its officer or agency or a state may file an amicus brief without the consent of the parties or leave of court. Any other amicus curiae may file a brief only by leave of court or if the brief states that all parties have consented to its filing, but a district court or BAP may prohibit the filing of or may strike an amicus brief that would result in a judge's disqualification. On its own motion, and with notice to all parties to an appeal, the district court or BAP may request a brief by an amicus curiae.

*(3) Motion for Leave to File.* The motion must be accompanied by the proposed brief and state:

*(A)* the movant's interest; and

*(B)* the reason why an amicus brief is desirable and why the matters asserted are relevant to the disposition of the appeal.

*(4) Contents and Form.* An amicus brief must comply with Rule 8015. In addition to the requirements of Rule 8015, the cover must identify the party or parties supported and indicate whether the brief supports affirmance or reversal. If an amicus curiae is a corporation, the brief must include a disclosure statement like that required of parties by Rule 8012. An amicus brief need not comply with Rule 8014, but must include the following:

*(A)* a table of contents, with page references;

*(B)* a table of authorities—cases (alphabetically arranged), statutes, and other authorities—with references to the pages of the brief where they are cited;

*(C)* a concise statement of the identity of the amicus curiae, its interest in the case, and the source of its authority to file;

*(D)* unless the amicus curiae is one listed in the first sentence of subdivision (a)(2), a statement that indicates whether:

*(i)* a party's counsel authored the brief in whole or in part;

*(ii)* a party or a party's counsel contributed money that was intended to fund preparing or submitting the brief; and

*(iii)* a person—other than the amicus curiae, its members, or its counsel—contributed money that was intended to fund preparing or submitting the brief and, if so, identifies each such person;

*(E)* an argument, which may be preceded by a summary and need not include a statement of the applicable standard of review; and

*(F)* a certificate of compliance, if required by Rule 8015(h).

*(5) Length.* Except by the district court's or BAP's permission, an amicus brief must be no more than one-half the maximum length authorized by these rules for a party's principal brief. If the court grants a party permission to file a longer brief, that extension does not affect the length of an amicus brief.

(6) *Time for Filing.* An amicus curiae must file its brief, accompanied by a motion for filing when necessary, no later than 7 days after the principal brief of the party being supported is filed. An amicus curiae that does not support either party must file its brief no later than 7 days after the appellant's principal brief is filed. The district court or BAP may grant leave for later filing, specifying the time within which an opposing party may answer.

(7) *Reply Brief.* Except by the district court's or BAP's permission, an amicus curiae may not file a reply brief.

(8) *Oral Argument.* An amicus curiae may participate in oral argument only with the district court's or BAP's permission.

(b) *During Consideration of Whether to Grant Rehearing.*

(1) *Applicability.* This Rule 8017(b) governs amicus filings during a district court's or BAP's consideration of whether to grant rehearing, unless a local rule or order in a case provides otherwise.

(2) *When Permitted.* The United States or its officer or agency or a state may file an amicus brief without the consent of the parties or leave of court. Any other amicus curiae may file a brief only by leave of court.

(3) *Motion for Leave to File.* Rule 8017(a)(3) applies to a motion for leave.

(4) *Contents, Form, and Length.* Rule 8017(a)(4) applies to the amicus brief. The brief must include a certificate under Rule 8015(h) and not exceed 2,600 words.

(5) *Time for Filing.* An amicus curiae supporting the motion for rehearing or supporting neither party must file its brief, accompanied by a motion for filing when necessary, no later than 7 days after the motion is filed. An amicus curiae opposing the motion for rehearing must file its brief, accompanied by a motion for filing when necessary, no later than the date set by the court for the response.

**Rule 8018 Serving and Filing Briefs; Appendices**

(a) *Time to Serve and File a Brief.* The following rules apply unless the district court or BAP by order in a particular case excuses the filing of briefs or specifies different time limits:

(1) The appellant must serve and file a brief within 30 days after the docketing of notice that the record has been transmitted or is available electronically.

(2) The appellee must serve and file a brief within 30 days after service of the appellant's brief.

(3) The appellant may serve and file a reply brief within 14 days after service of the appellee's brief, but a reply brief must be filed at least 7 days before scheduled argument unless the district court or BAP, for good cause, allows a later filing.

(4) If an appellant fails to file a brief on time or within an extended time

authorized by the district court or BAP, an appellee may move to dismiss the appeal—or the district court or BAP, after notice, may dismiss the appeal on its own motion. An appellee who fails to file a brief will not be heard at oral argument unless the district court or BAP grants permission.

*(b) Duty to Serve and File an Appendix to the Brief.*

*(1) Appellant.* Subject to subdivision (e) and Rule 8009(d), the appellant must serve and file with its principal brief excerpts of the record as an appendix. It must contain the following:

*(A)* the relevant entries in the bankruptcy docket;

*(B)* the complaint and answer, or other equivalent filings;

*(C)* the judgment, order, or decree from which the appeal is taken;

*(D)* any other orders, pleadings, jury instructions, findings, conclusions, or opinions relevant to the appeal;

*(E)* the notice of appeal; and

*(F)* any relevant transcript or portion of it.

*(2) Appellee.* The appellee may also serve and file with its brief an appendix that contains material required to be included by the appellant or relevant to the appeal or cross-appeal, but omitted by the appellant.

*(3) Cross-Appellee.* The appellant as cross-appellee may also serve and file with its response an appendix that contains material relevant to matters raised initially by the principal brief in the cross-appeal, but omitted by the cross-appellant.

*(c) Format of the Appendix.* The appendix must begin with a table of contents identifying the page at which each part begins. The relevant docket entries must follow the table of contents. Other parts of the record must follow chronologically. When pages from the transcript of proceedings are placed in the appendix, the transcript page numbers must be shown in brackets immediately before the included pages. Omissions in the text of documents or of the transcript must be indicated by asterisks. Immaterial formal matters (captions, subscriptions, acknowledgments, and the like) should be omitted.

*(d) Exhibits.* Exhibits designated for inclusion in the appendix may be reproduced in a separate volume or volumes, suitably indexed.

*(e) Appeal on the Original Record Without an Appendix.* The district court or BAP may, either by rule for all cases or classes of cases or by order in a particular case, dispense with the appendix and permit an appeal to proceed on the original record, with the submission of any relevant parts of the record that the district court or BAP orders the parties to file.

**Rule 8018.1 District-Court Review of a Judgment that the Bankruptcy Court Lacked the Constitutional Authority to Enter**

If, on appeal, a district court determines that the bankruptcy court did not have the power under Article III of the Constitution to enter the judgment, order, or decree appealed from, the district court may treat it as proposed findings of fact and conclusions of law.

**Rule 8019 Oral Argument**

*(a) Party's Statement.* Any party may file, or a district court or BAP may require, a statement explaining why oral argument should, or need not, be permitted.

*(b) Presumption of Oral Argument and Exceptions.* Oral argument must be allowed in every case unless the district judge—or all the BAP judges assigned to hear the appeal—examine the briefs and record and determine that oral argument is unnecessary because

*(1)* the appeal is frivolous;

*(2)* the dispositive issue or issues have been authoritatively decided; or

*(3)* the facts and legal arguments are adequately presented in the briefs and record, and the decisional process would not be significantly aided by oral argument.

*(c) Notice of Argument; Postponement.* The district court or BAP must advise all parties of the date, time, and place for oral argument, and the time allowed for each side. A motion to postpone the argument or to allow longer argument must be filed reasonably in advance of the hearing date.

*(d) Order and Contents of Argument.* The appellant opens and concludes the argument. Counsel must not read at length from briefs, the record, or authorities.

*(e) Cross-Appeals and Separate Appeals.* If there is a cross-appeal, Rule 8016(b) determines which party is the appellant and which is the appellee for the purposes of oral argument. Unless the district court or BAP directs otherwise, a cross-appeal or separate appeal must be argued when the initial appeal is argued. Separate parties should avoid duplicative argument.

*(f) Nonappearance of a Party.* If the appellee fails to appear for argument, the district court or BAP may hear the appellant's argument. If the appellant fails to appear for argument, the district court or BAP may hear the appellee's argument. If neither party appears, the case will be decided on the briefs unless the district court or BAP orders otherwise.

*(g) Submission on Briefs.* The parties may agree to submit a case for decision on the briefs, but the district court or BAP may direct that the case be argued.

*(h) Use of Physical Exhibits at Argument; Removal.* Counsel intending to use physical exhibits other than documents at the argument must arrange to place them in the courtroom on the day of the argument before the court convenes. After the argument, counsel must remove the exhibits from the courtroom unless the district court or BAP directs otherwise. The clerk may destroy or dispose of the exhibits if counsel does not reclaim them within a reasonable time after the clerk gives notice to remove them.

**Rule 8020 Frivolous Appeal and Other Misconduct**

*(a) Frivolous Appeal—Damages and Costs.* If the district court or BAP determines that an appeal is frivolous, it may, after a separately filed motion or notice from the court and reasonable opportunity to respond, award just damages and single or double costs to the appellee.

*(b) Other Misconduct.* The district court or BAP may discipline or sanction an attorney or party appearing before it for other misconduct, including failure to comply with any court order. First, however, the court must afford the attorney or party reasonable notice, an opportunity to show cause to the contrary, and, if requested, a hearing.

**Rule 8021 Costs**

*(a) Against Whom Assessed.* The following rules apply unless the law provides or the district court or BAP orders otherwise:

*(1)* if an appeal is dismissed, costs are taxed against the appellant, unless the parties agree otherwise;

*(2)* if a judgment, order, or decree is affirmed, costs are taxed against the appellant;

*(3)* if a judgment, order, or decree is reversed, costs are taxed against the appellee;

*(4)* if a judgment, order, or decree is affirmed or reversed in part, modified, or vacated, costs are taxed only as the district court or BAP orders.

*(b) Costs for and Against the United States.* Costs for or against the United States, its agency, or its officer may be assessed under subdivision (a) only if authorized by law.

*(c) Costs on Appeal Taxable in the Bankruptcy Court.* The following costs on appeal are taxable in the bankruptcy court for the benefit of the party entitled to costs under this rule:

*(1)* the production of any required copies of a brief, appendix, exhibit, or the record;

*(2)* the preparation and transmission of the record;

*(3)* the reporter's transcript, if needed to determine the appeal;

*(4)* premiums paid for a bond or other security to preserve rights pending appeal; and

*(5)* the fee for filing the notice of appeal.

*(d) Bill of Costs; Objections.* A party who wants costs taxed must, within 14 days after entry of judgment on appeal, file with the bankruptcy clerk and serve an itemized and verified bill of costs. Objections must be filed within 14 days after service of the bill of costs, unless the bankruptcy court extends the time.

## Rule 8022 Motion for Rehearing

*(a) Time to File; Contents; Response; Action by the District Court or BAP If Granted.*

*(1) Time.* Unless the time is shortened or extended by order or local rule, any motion for rehearing by the district court or BAP must be filed within 14 days after entry of judgment on appeal.

*(2) Contents.* The motion must state with particularity each point of law or fact that the movant believes the district court or BAP has overlooked or misapprehended and must argue in support of the motion. Oral argument is not permitted.

*(3) Response.* Unless the district court or BAP requests, no response to a motion for rehearing is permitted. But ordinarily, rehearing will not be granted in the absence of such a request.

*(4) Action by the District Court or BAP.* If a motion for rehearing is granted, the district court or BAP may do any of the following:

*(A)* make a final disposition of the appeal without reargument;

*(B)* restore the case to the calendar for reargument or resubmission; or

*(C)* issue any other appropriate order.

*(b) Form of the Motion; Length.* The motion must comply in form with Rule 8013(f)(1) and (2). Copies must be served and filed as provided by Rule 8011. Except by the district court's or BAP's permission:

*(1)* a motion for rehearing produced using a computer must include a certificate under Rule 8015(h) and not exceed 3,900 words; and

*(2)* a handwritten or typewritten motion must not exceed 15 pages.

## Rule 8023 Voluntary Dismissal

The clerk of the district court or BAP must dismiss an appeal if the parties file a signed dismissal agreement specifying how costs are to be paid and pay any fees that are due. An appeal may be dismissed on the appellant's motion on terms agreed to by the parties or fixed by the district court or BAP.

## Rule 8024 Clerk's Duties on Disposition of the Appeal

*(a) Judgment on Appeal.* The district or BAP clerk must prepare, sign, and enter the judgment after receiving the court's opinion or, if there is no opinion, as the court instructs. Noting the judgment on the docket constitutes entry of judgment.

*(b) Notice of a Judgment.* Immediately upon the entry of a judgment, the district or BAP clerk must:

*(1)* transmit a notice of the entry to each party to the appeal, to the United States trustee, and to the bankruptcy clerk, together with a copy of any opinion; and

*(2)* note the date of the transmission on the docket.

*(c) Returning Physical Items.* If any physical items were transmitted as the record on appeal, they must be returned to the bankruptcy clerk on disposition of the appeal.

**Rule 8025 Stay of a District Court or BAP Judgment**

*(a) Automatic Stay of Judgment on Appeal.* Unless the district court or BAP orders otherwise, its judgment is stayed for 14 days after entry.

*(b) Stay Pending Appeal to the Court of Appeals.*

*(1) In General.* On a party's motion and notice to all other parties to the appeal, the district court or BAP may stay its judgment pending an appeal to the court of appeals.

*(2) Time Limit.* The stay must not exceed 30 days after the judgment is entered, except for cause shown.

*(3) Stay Continued.* If, before a stay expires, the party who obtained the stay appeals to the court of appeals, the stay continues until final disposition by the court of appeals.

*(4) Bond or Other Security.* A bond or other security may be required as a condition for granting or continuing a stay of the judgment. A bond or other security may be required if a trustee obtains a stay, but not if a stay is obtained by the United States or its officer or agency or at the direction of any department of the United States government.

*(c) Automatic Stay of an Order, Judgment, or Decree of a Bankruptcy Court.* If the district court or BAP enters a judgment affirming an order, judgment, or decree of the bankruptcy court, a stay of the district court's or BAP's judgment automatically stays the bankruptcy court's order, judgment, or decree for the duration of the appellate stay.

*(d) Power of a Court of Appeals Not Limited.* This rule does not limit the power of a court of appeals or any of its judges to do the following:

*(1)* stay a judgment pending appeal;

*(2)* stay proceedings while an appeal is pending;

*(3)* suspend, modify, restore, vacate, or grant a stay or an injunction while an appeal is pending; or

*(4)* issue any order appropriate to preserve the status quo or the effectiveness of any judgment to be entered.

**Rule 8026 Rules by Circuit Councils and District Courts; Procedure When There Is No Controlling Law**

*(a) Local Rules by Circuit Councils and District Courts.*

*(1) Adopting Local Rules.* A circuit council that has authorized a BAP under 28 U.S.C. § 158(b) may make and amend rules governing the practice and procedure on appeal from a judgment, order, or decree of a bankruptcy court to the BAP. A district court may make and amend rules governing the practice

and procedure on appeal from a judgment, order, or decree of a bankruptcy court to the district court. Local rules must be consistent with, but not duplicative of, Acts of Congress and these Part VIII rules. Rule 83 F.R.Civ.P. governs the procedure for making and amending rules to govern appeals.

*(2) Numbering.* Local rules must conform to any uniform numbering system prescribed by the Judicial Conference of the United States.

*(3) Limitation on Imposing Requirements of Form.* A local rule imposing a requirement of form must not be enforced in a way that causes a party to lose any right because of a nonwillful failure to comply.

*(b) Procedure When There Is No Controlling Law.*

*(1) In General.* A district court or BAP may regulate practice in any manner consistent with federal law, applicable federal rules, the Official Forms, and local rules.

*(2) Limitation on Sanctions.* No sanction or other disadvantage may be imposed for noncompliance with any requirement not in federal law, applicable federal rules, the Official Forms, or local rules unless the alleged violator has been furnished in the particular case with actual notice of the requirement.

## Rule 8027 Notice of a Mediation Procedure

If the district court or BAP has a mediation procedure applicable to bankruptcy appeals, the clerk must notify the parties promptly after docketing the appeal of:

*(a)* the requirements of the mediation procedure; and

*(b)* any effect the mediation procedure has on the time to file briefs.

## Rule 8028 Suspension of Rules in Part VIII

In the interest of expediting decision or for other cause in a particular case, the district court or BAP, or where appropriate the court of appeals, may suspend the requirements or provisions of the rules in Part VIII, except Rules 8001, 8002, 8003, 8004, 8005, 8006, 8007, 8012, 8020, 8024, 8025, 8026, and 8028.

# Appendix

## Length Limits Stated in Part VIII of the Federal Rules of Bankruptcy Procedure

This chart shows the length limits stated in Part VIII of the Federal Rules of Bankruptcy Procedure. Please bear in mind the following:

- In computing these limits, you can exclude the items listed in Rule 8015(g).
- If you are using a word limit or line limit (other than the word limit in Rule 8014(f)), you must include the certificate required by Rule 8015(h).
- If you are using a line limit, your document must be in monospaced typeface. A typeface is monospaced when each character occupies the same amount of horizontal space.
- For the limits in Rules 8013 and 8022:
  - You must use the word limit if you produce your document on a computer; and
  - You must use the page limit if you handwrite your document or type it on a typewriter.

| | **Rule** | **Document Type** | **Word Limit** | **Page Limit** | **Line Limit** |
|---|---|---|---|---|---|
| **Motions** | 8013(f)(3) | • Motion | 5,200 | 20 | Not applicable |
| | | • Response to a motion | | | |
| | 8013(f)(3) | • Reply to a response to a motion | 2,600 | 10 | Not applicable |
| **Parties' brief (where no cross-appeal)** | 8015(a)(7) | • Principal brief | 13,000 | 30 | 1,300 |
| | 8015(a)(7) | • Reply brief | 6,500 | 15 | 650 |
| **Parties' briefs (where cross-appeal)** | 8016(d) | • Appellant's principal brief | 13,000 | 30 | 1,300 |
| | | • Appellant's response and reply brief | | | |
| | 8016(d) | • Appellee's principal and response brief | 15,300 | 35 | 1,500 |
| | 8016(d) | • Appellee's reply brief | 6,500 | 15 | 650 |
| **Party's supplemental letter** | 8014(f) | • Letter citing supplemental authorities | 350 | Not applicable | Not applicable |

| **Amicus briefs** | 8017(a)(5) | • Amicus brief during initial consideration of case on merits | One-half the length set by the Part VIII Rules for a party's principal brief | One-half the length set by the Part VIII Rules for a party's principal brief | One-half the length set by the Part VIII Rules for a party's principal brief |
|---|---|---|---|---|---|
| | 8017(b)(4) | • Amicus brief during consideration of whether to grant rehearing | 2,600 | Not applicable | Not applicable |
| **Motion for rehearing** | 8022(b) | • Motion for rehearing | 3,900 | 15 | Not applicable |

# PART IX
# GENERAL PROVISIONS

## Rule 9001 General Definitions

The definitions of words and phrases in §§ 101, 902, 1101, and 1502 of the Code, and the rules of construction in § 102, govern their use in these rules. In addition, the following words and phrases used in these rules have the meanings indicated:

(*1*) "Bankruptcy clerk" means a clerk appointed pursuant to 28 U.S.C. § 156(b).

(*2*) "Bankruptcy Code" or "Code" means title 11 of the United States Code.

(*3*) "Clerk" means bankruptcy clerk, if one has been appointed, otherwise clerk of the district court.

(*4*) "Court" or "judge" means the judicial officer before whom a case or proceeding is pending.

(*5*) "Debtor." When any act is required by these rules to be performed by a debtor or when it is necessary to compel attendance of a debtor for examination and the debtor is not a natural person: (A) if the debtor is a corporation, "debtor" includes, if designated by the court, any or all of its officers, members of its board of directors or trustees or of a similar controlling body, a controlling stockholder or member, or any other person in control; (B) if the debtor is a partnership, "debtor" includes any or all of its general partners or, if designated by the court, any other person in control.

(*6*) "Firm" includes a partnership or professional corporation of attorneys or accountants.

(*7*) "Judgment" means any appealable order.

(*8*) "Mail" means first class, postage prepaid.

(*9*) "Notice provider" means any entity approved by the Administrative Office of the United States Courts to give notice to creditors under Rule 2002(g)(4).

(*10*) "Regular associate" means any attorney regularly employed by, associated with, or counsel to an individual or firm.

(*11*) "Trustee" includes a debtor in possession in a chapter 11 case.

(*12*) "United States trustee" includes an assistant United States trustee and any designee of the United States trustee.

BANKRUPTCY CODE REFERENCES: §§ 101, 102, 902 and 1101

## Rule 9002 Meanings of Words in the Federal Rules of Civil Procedure When Applicable to Cases Under the Code

The following words and phrases used in the Federal Rules of Civil Procedure made applicable to cases under the Code by these rules have the meanings indicated unless they are inconsistent with the context:

(*1*) "Action" or "civil action" means an adversary proceeding or, when appropriate, a contested petition, or proceedings to vacate an order for relief or to determine any other contested matter.

(*2*) "Appeal" means an appeal as provided by 28 U.S.C. § 158.

(*3*) "Clerk" or "clerk of the district court" means the court officer responsible for the bankruptcy records in the district.

(*4*) "District court," "trial court," "court," "district judges," or "judge" means bankruptcy judge if the case or proceeding is pending before a bankruptcy judge.

(*5*) "Judgment" includes any order appealable to an appellate court.

Bankruptcy Code References: §§ 101, 102, 902 and 1101

Bankruptcy Statutory Reference: 28 U.S.C. § 586

## Rule 9003 Prohibition of Ex Parte Contacts

(*a*) *General Prohibition.* Except as otherwise permitted by applicable law, any examiner, any party in interest, and any attorney, accountant, or employee of a party in interest shall refrain from ex parte meetings and communications with the court concerning matters affecting a particular case or proceeding.

(*b*) *United States Trustee.* Except as otherwise permitted by applicable law, the United States trustee and assistants to and employees or agents of the United States trustee shall refrain from ex parte meetings and communications with the court concerning matters affecting a particular case or proceeding. This rule does not preclude communications with the court to discuss general problems of administration and improvement of bankruptcy administration, including the operation of the United States trustee system.

## Rule 9004 General Requirements of Form

(*a*) *Legibility; Abbreviations.* All petitions, pleadings, schedules and other papers shall be clearly legible. Abbreviations in common use in the English language may be used.

(*b*) *Caption.* Each paper filed shall contain a caption setting forth the name of the court, the title of the case, the bankruptcy docket number, and a brief designation of the character of the paper.

## Rule 9005 Harmless Error

Rule 61 F.R.Civ.P. applies in cases under the Code. When appropriate, the court may order the correction of any error or defect or the cure of any omission which does not affect substantial rights.

### CIVIL RULE:

Federal Rule of Civil Procedure 61, which was last amended effective December 1, 2007, provides:

**Rule 61 Harmless Error**

Unless justice requires otherwise, no error in admitting or excluding

BANKRUPTCY RULES

evidence—or any other error by the court or a party—is ground for granting a new trial, for setting aside a verdict, or for vacating, modifying, or otherwise disturbing a judgment or order. At every stage of the proceeding, the court must disregard all errors and defects that do not affect any party's substantial rights.

## Rule 9005.1 Constitutional Challenge to a Statute—Notice, Certification, and Intervention

Rule 5.1 F.R.Civ.P. applies in cases under the Code.

## CIVIL RULE:

Federal Rule of Civil Procedure 5.1, which was last amended effective December 1, 2007, provides:

**Rule 5.1 Constitutional Challenge to a Statute—Notice, Certification, and Intervention**

(a) Notice by a Party. A party that files a pleading, written motion, or other paper drawing into question the constitutionality of a federal or state statute must promptly:

(1) file a notice of constitutional question stating the question and identifying the paper that raises it, if:

(A) a federal statute is questioned and the parties do not include the United States, one of its agencies, or one of its officers or employees in an official capacity; or

(B) a state statute is questioned and the parties do not include the state, one of its agencies, or one of its officers or employees in an official capacity; and

(2) serve the notice and paper on the Attorney General of the United States if a federal statute is questioned—or on the state attorney general if a state statute is questioned—either by certified or registered mail or by sending it to an electronic address designated by the attorney general for this purpose.

(b) Certification by the Court. The court must, under 28 U.S.C. § 2403, certify to the appropriate attorney general that a statute has been questioned.

(c) Intervention; Final Decision on the Merits. Unless the court sets a later time, the attorney general may intervene within 60 days after the notice is filed or after the court certifies the challenge, whichever is earlier. Before the time to intervene expires, the court may reject the constitutional challenge, but may not enter a final judgment holding the statute unconstitutional.

(d) No Forfeiture. A party's failure to file and serve the notice, or the court's failure to certify, does not forfeit a constitutional claim or defense that is otherwise timely asserted.

## Rule 9006 Computing and Extending Time; Time for Motion Papers

(a) *Computing Time.* The following rules apply in computing any time period specified in these rules, in the Federal Rules of Civil Procedure, in any local rule or court order, or in any statute that does not specify a method of computing time.

(*1*) *Period Stated in Days or a Longer Unit.* When the period is stated in days or a longer unit of time:

(*A*) exclude the day of the event that triggers the period;

(*B*) count every day, including intermediate Saturdays, Sundays, and legal holidays; and

(*C*) include the last day of the period, but if the last day is a Saturday, Sunday, or legal holiday, the period continues to run until the end of the next day that is not a Saturday, Sunday, or legal holiday.

(*2*) *Period Stated in Hours.* When the period is stated in hours:

(*A*) begin counting immediately on the occurrence of the event that triggers the period;

(*B*) count every hour, including hours during intermediate Saturdays, Sundays, and legal holidays; and

(*C*) if the period would end on a Saturday, Sunday, or legal holiday, then continue the period until the same time on the next day that is not a Saturday, Sunday, or legal holiday.

(*3*) *Inaccessibility of Clerk's Office.* Unless the court orders otherwise, if the clerk's office is inaccessible:

(*A*) on the last day for filing under Rule 9006(a)(1), then the time for filing is extended to the first accessible day that is not a Saturday, Sunday, or legal holiday; or

(*B*) during the last hour for filing under Rule 9006(a)(2), then the time for filing is extended to the same time on the first accessible day that is not a Saturday, Sunday, or legal holiday.

(*4*) *"Last Day" Defined.* Unless a different time is set by a statute, local rule, or order in the case, the last day ends:

(*A*) for electronic filing, at midnight in the court's time zone; and

(*B*) for filing by other means, when the clerk's office is scheduled to close.

(*5*) *"Next Day" Defined.* The "next day" is determined by continuing to count forward when the period is measured after an event and backward when measured before an event.

(*6*) *"Legal Holiday" Defined.* "Legal holiday" means:

(*A*) the day set aside by statute for observing New Year's Day, Martin Luther King Jr.'s Birthday, Washington's Birthday, Memorial Day, Independence Day, Labor Day, Columbus Day, Veterans' Day, Thanksgiving Day, or Christmas Day;

(*B*) any day declared a holiday by the President or Congress; and

(*C*) for periods that are measured after an event, any other day declared a holiday by the state where the district court is located. (In this rule, "state" includes the District of Columbia and any United States commonwealth or territory.)

(*b*) *Enlargement.*

(*1*) *In General.* Except as provided in paragraphs (2) and (3) of this subdivision, when an act is required or allowed to be done at or within a specified period by these rules or by a notice given thereunder or by order of court, the court for cause shown may at any time in its discretion (1) with or without motion or notice order the period enlarged if the request therefor is made before the expiration of the period originally prescribed or as extended by a previous order or (2) on motion made after the expiration of the specified period permit the act to be done where the failure to act was the result of excusable neglect.

(*2*) *Enlargement Not Permitted.* The court may not enlarge the time for taking action under Rules 1007(d), 2003(a) and (d), 7052, 9023, and 9024.

(*3*) *Enlargement Governed by Other Rules.* The court may enlarge the time for taking action under Rules 1006(b)(2), 1017(e), 3002(c), 4003(b), 4004(a), 4007(c), 4008(a), 8002, and 9033, only to the extent and under the conditions stated in those rules. In addition, the court may enlarge the time to file the statement required under Rule 1007(b)(7), and to file schedules and statements in a small business case under § 1116(3) of the Code, only to the extent and under the conditions stated in Rule 1007(c).

(*c*) *Reduction.*

(*1*) *In General.* Except as provided in paragraph (2) of this subdivision, when an act is required or allowed to be done at or within a specified time by these rules or by a notice given thereunder or by order of court, the court for cause shown may in its discretion with or without motion or notice order the period reduced.

(*2*) *Reduction Not Permitted.* The court may not reduce the time for taking action under Rules 2002(a)(7), 2003(a), 3002(c), 3014, 3015, 4001(b)(2), (c)(2), 4003(a), 4004(a), 4007(c), 4008(a), 8002, and 9033(b). In addition, the court may not reduce the time under Rule 1007(c) to file the statement required by Rule 1007(b)(7).

(*d*) *Motion Papers.* A written motion, other than one which may be heard ex parte, and notice of any hearing shall be served not later than seven days before the time specified for such hearing, unless a different period is fixed by these rules or by order of the court. Such an order may for cause shown be made on ex parte application. When a motion is supported by affidavit, the affidavit shall be served with the motion. Except as otherwise provided in Rule 9023, any written response shall be served not later than one day before the hearing, unless the court permits otherwise.

(*e*) *Time of Service.* Service of process and service of any paper other than process or of notice by mail is complete on mailing.

(*f*) *Additional Time After Service by Mail or Under Rule 5(b)(2)(D) or (F) F.R.Civ.P.* When there is a right or requirement to act or undertake some proceedings within a prescribed period after being served and that service is by mail or under Rule 5(b)(2)(D) (leaving with the clerk) or (F) (other means consented to) F.R.Civ.P.,[18] three days are added after the prescribed period would otherwise expire under Rule 9006(a).

(*g*) *Grain Storage Facility Cases.* This rule shall not limit the court's authority under § 557 of the Code to enter orders governing procedures in cases in which the debtor is an owner or operator of a grain storage facility.

BANKRUPTCY CODE REFERENCES: §§ 108, 363, 364, 502, 522, 523, and 727

## Rule 9007 General Authority to Regulate Notices

When notice is to be given under these rules, the court shall designate, if not otherwise specified herein, the time within which, the entities to whom, and the form and manner in which the notice shall be given. When feasible, the court may order any notices under these rules to be combined.

## Rule 9008 Service or Notice by Publication

Whenever these rules require or authorize service or notice by publication, the court shall, to the extent not otherwise specified in these rules, determine the form and manner thereof, including the newspaper or other medium to be used and the number of publications.

BANKRUPTCY CODE REFERENCE: § 923

## Rule 9009 Forms

(*a*) *Official Forms.* The Official Forms prescribed by the Judicial Conference of the United States shall be used without alteration, except as otherwise provided in these rules, in a particular Official Form, or in the national instructions for a particular Official Form. Official Forms may be modified to permit minor changes not affecting wording or the order of presenting information, including changes that:

(*1*) expand the prescribed areas for responses in order to permit complete responses;

(*2*) delete space not needed for responses; or

(*3*) delete items requiring detail in a question or category if the filer indicates—either by checking "no" or "none" or by stating in words—that there is nothing to report on that question or category.

(*b*) *Director's Forms.* The Director of the Administrative Office of the United States Courts may issue additional forms for use under the Code.

(*c*) *Construction.* The forms shall be construed to be consistent with these rules and the Code.

[18] ED. NOTE: For the text of Fed. R. Civ. P. 5, *see* Fed. R. Bankr. P. 7005 *supra.*

## Rule 9010 Representation and Appearances; Powers of Attorney

(*a*) *Authority to Act Personally or by Attorney.* A debtor, creditor, equity security holder, indenture trustee, committee or other party may (1) appear in a case under the Code and act either in the entity's own behalf or by an attorney authorized to practice in the court, and (2) perform any act not constituting the practice of law, by an authorized agent, attorney in fact, or proxy.

(*b*) *Notice of Appearance.* An attorney appearing for a party in a case under the Code shall file a notice of appearance with the attorney's name, office address and telephone number, unless the attorney's appearance is otherwise noted in the record.

(*c*) *Power of Attorney.* The authority of any agent, attorney in fact, or proxy to represent a creditor for any purpose other than the execution and filing of a proof of claim or the acceptance or rejection of a plan shall be evidenced by a power of attorney conforming substantially to the appropriate Official Form. The execution of any such power of attorney shall be acknowledged before one of the officers enumerated in 28 U.S.C. § 459, § 953, Rule 9012, or a person authorized to administer oaths under the laws of the state where the oath is administered.

Bankruptcy Code Reference: § 110

## Rule 9011 Signing of Papers; Representations to the Court; Sanctions; Verification and Copies of Papers

(*a*) *Signature.* Every petition, pleading, written motion, and other paper, except a list, schedule, or statement, or amendments thereto, shall be signed by at least one attorney of record in the attorney's individual name. A party who is not represented by an attorney shall sign all papers. Each paper shall state the signer's address and telephone number, if any. An unsigned paper shall be stricken unless omission of the signature is corrected promptly after being called to the attention of the attorney or party.

(*b*) *Representations to the Court.* By presenting to the court (whether by signing, filing, submitting, or later advocating) a petition, pleading, written motion, or other paper, an attorney or unrepresented party is certifying that to the best of the person's knowledge, information, and belief, formed after an inquiry reasonable under the circumstances,—

(*1*) it is not being presented for any improper purpose, such as to harass or to cause unnecessary delay or needless increase in the cost of litigation;

(2) the claims, defenses, and other legal contentions therein are warranted by existing law or by a nonfrivolous argument for the extension, modification, or reversal of existing law or the establishment of new law;

(3) the allegations and other factual contentions have evidentiary support or, if specifically so identified, are likely to have evidentiary support after a reasonable opportunity for further investigation or discovery; and

(4) the denials of factual contentions are warranted on the evidence or, if specifically so identified, are reasonably based on a lack of information or belief.

(*c*) *Sanctions.* If, after notice and a reasonable opportunity to respond, the court determines that subdivision (b) has been violated, the court may, subject to the conditions stated below, impose an appropriate sanction upon the attorneys, law firms, or parties that have violated subdivision (b) or are responsible for the violation.

(*1*) *How Initiated.*

(*A*) *By Motion.* A motion for sanctions under this rule shall be made separately from other motions or requests and shall describe the specific conduct alleged to violate subdivision (b). It shall be served as provided in Rule 7004. The motion for sanctions may not be filed with or presented to the court unless, within 21 days after service of the motion (or such other period as the court may prescribe), the challenged paper, claim, defense, contention, allegation, or denial is not withdrawn or appropriately corrected, except that this limitation shall not apply if the conduct alleged is the filing of a petition in violation of subdivision (b). If warranted, the court may award to the party prevailing on the motion the reasonable expenses and attorney's fees incurred in presenting or opposing the motion. Absent exceptional circumstances, a law firm shall be held jointly responsible for violations committed by its partners, associates, and employees.

(*B*) *On Court's Initiative.* On its own initiative, the court may enter an order describing the specific conduct that appears to violate subdivision (b) and directing an attorney, law firm, or party to show cause why it has not violated subdivision (b) with respect thereto.

(*2*) *Nature of Sanction; Limitations.* A sanction imposed for violation of this rule shall be limited to what is sufficient to deter repetition of such conduct or comparable conduct by others similarly situated. Subject to the limitations in subparagraphs (A) and (B), the sanction may consist of, or include, directives of a nonmonetary nature, an order to pay a penalty into court, or, if imposed on motion and warranted for effective deterrence, an order directing payment to the movant of some or all of the reasonable attorneys' fees and other expenses incurred as a direct result of the violation.

(*A*) Monetary sanctions may not be awarded against a represented party for a violation of subdivision (b)(2).

(*B*) Monetary sanctions may not be awarded on the court's initiative unless the court issues its order to show cause before a voluntary dismissal or settlement of the claims made by or against the party which is, or whose attorneys are, to be sanctioned.

(*3*) *Order.* When imposing sanctions, the court shall describe the conduct determined to constitute a violation of this rule and explain the basis for the sanction imposed.

(*d*) *Inapplicability to Discovery.* Subdivisions (a) through (c) of this rule do not apply to disclosures and discovery requests, responses, objections, and motions that are subject to the provisions of Rules 7026 through 7037.

(*e*) *Verification.* Except as otherwise specifically provided by these rules, papers filed in a case under the Code need not be verified. Whenever verification is required by these rules, an unsworn declaration as provided in 28 U.S.C. § 1746 satisfies the requirement of verification.

(*f*) *Copies of Signed or Verified Papers.* When these rules require copies of a signed or verified paper, it shall suffice if the original is signed or verified and the copies are conformed to the original.

BANKRUPTCY CODE REFERENCES: §§ 105 and 707

## Rule 9012 Oaths and Affirmations

(*a*) *Persons Authorized to Administer Oaths.* The following persons may administer oaths and affirmations and take acknowledgments: a bankruptcy judge, clerk, deputy clerk, United States trustee, officer authorized to administer oaths in proceedings before the courts of the United States or under the laws of the state where the oath is to be taken, or a diplomatic or consular officer of the United States in any foreign country.

(*b*) *Affirmation in Lieu of Oath.* When in a case under the Code an oath is required to be taken, a solemn affirmation may be accepted in lieu thereof.

BANKRUPTCY CODE REFERENCES: §§ 341 and 343

## Rule 9013 Motions: Form and Service

A request for an order, except when an application is authorized by the rules, shall be by written motion, unless made during a hearing. The motion shall state with particularity the grounds therefor, and shall set forth the relief or order sought. Every written motion, other than one which may be considered ex parte, shall be served by the moving party within the time determined under Rule 9006(d). The moving party shall serve the motion on:

(a) the trustee or debtor in possession and on those entities specified by these rules; or

(b) the entities the court directs if these rules do not require service or specify the entities to be served.

## Rule 9014 Contested Matters

(*a*) *Motion.* In a contested matter not otherwise governed by these rules, relief shall be requested by motion, and reasonable notice and opportunity for hearing shall be afforded the party against whom relief is sought. No response is required under this rule unless the court directs otherwise.

(*b*) *Service.* The motion shall be served in the manner provided for service of a summons and complaint by Rule 7004 and within the time determined under Rule 9006(d). Any written response to the motion shall be served within the time determined under Rule 9006(d). Any paper served after the motion shall be served in the manner provided by Rule 5(b) F.R. Civ. P.[19]

---

[19] ED. NOTE: For the text of Fed. R. Civ. P. 5, *see* Fed. R. Bankr. P. 7005 *supra.*

(c) *Application of Part VII rules.* Except as otherwise provided in this rule, and unless the court directs otherwise, the following rules shall apply: 7009, 7017, 7021, 7025, 7026, 7028–7037, 7041, 7042, 7052, 7054–7056, 7064, 7069, and 7071. The following subdivisions of Fed. R. Civ. P. 26, as incorporated by Rule 7026, shall not apply in a contested matter unless the court directs otherwise: 26(a)(1) (mandatory disclosure), 26(a)(2) (disclosures regarding expert testimony) and 26(a)(3) (additional pre-trial disclosure), and 26(f) (mandatory meeting before scheduling conference/discovery plan). An entity that desires to perpetuate testimony may proceed in the same manner as provided in Rule 7027 for the taking of a deposition before an adversary proceeding. The court may at any stage in a particular matter direct that one or more of the other rules in Part VII shall apply. The court shall give the parties notice of any order issued under this paragraph to afford them a reasonable opportunity to comply with the procedures prescribed by the order.

(d) *Testimony of witnesses.* Testimony of witnesses with respect to disputed material factual issues shall be taken in the same manner as testimony in an adversary proceeding.

(e) *Attendance of witnesses.* The court shall provide procedures that enable parties to ascertain at a reasonable time before any scheduled hearing whether the hearing will be an evidentiary hearing at which witnesses may testify.

Bankruptcy Code Reference: § 102

**Rule 9015 Jury Trials**

(a) *Applicability of Certain Federal Rules of Civil Procedure.* Rules 38, 39, 47–49, and 51, F.R.Civ.P., and Rule 81(c) F.R.Civ.P. insofar as it applies to jury trials, apply in cases and proceedings, except that a demand made under Rule 38(b) F.R.Civ.P. shall be filed in accordance with Rule 5005.

(b) *Consent to Have Trial Conducted by Bankruptcy Judge.* If the right to a jury trial applies, a timely demand has been filed pursuant to Rule 38(b) F.R.Civ.P., and the bankruptcy judge has been specially designated to conduct the jury trial, the parties may consent to have a jury trial conducted by a bankruptcy judge under 28 U.S.C. § 157(e) by jointly or separately filing a statement of consent within any applicable time limits specified by local rule.

(c) *Applicability of Rule 50 F.R.Civ.P.* Rule 50 F.R.Civ.P. applies in cases and proceedings, except that any renewed motion for judgment or request for a new trial shall be filed no later than 14 days after the entry of judgment.

CIVIL RULE:

Federal Rule of Civil Procedure 38, which was last amended effective December 1, 2009, provides:

**Rule 38 Right to a Jury Trial; Demand**

(a) Right Preserved. The right of trial by jury as declared by the Seventh Amendment to the Constitution—or as provided by a federal statute—is preserved to the parties inviolate.

(b) Demand. On any issue triable of right by a jury, a party may demand a jury trial by:

(1) serving the other parties with a written demand—which may be included in a pleading—no later than 14 days after the last pleading directed to the issue is served; and

(2) filing the demand in accordance with Rule 5(d).

(c) SPECIFYING ISSUES. In its demand, a party may specify the issues that it wishes to have tried by a jury; otherwise, it is considered to have demanded a jury trial on all the issues so triable. If the party has demanded a jury trial on only some issues, any other party may—within 14 days after being served with the demand or within a shorter time ordered by the court—serve a demand for a jury trial on any other or all factual issues triable by jury.

(d) WAIVER; WITHDRAWAL. A party waives a jury trial unless its demand is properly served and filed. A proper demand may be withdrawn only if the parties consent.

(e) ADMIRALTY AND MARITIME CLAIMS. These rules do not create a right to a jury trial on issues in a claim that is an admiralty or maritime claim under Rule 9(h).

## CIVIL RULE:

Federal Rule of Civil Procedure 39, which was last amended effective December 1, 2007, provides:

**Rule 39 Trial by Jury or by the Court**

(a) WHEN A DEMAND IS MADE. When a jury trial has been demanded under Rule 38, the action must be designated on the docket as a jury action. The trial on all issues so demanded must be by jury unless:

(1) the parties or their attorneys file a stipulation to a nonjury trial or so stipulate on the record; or

(2) the court, on motion or on its own, finds that on some or all of those issues there is no federal right to a jury trial.

(b) WHEN NO DEMAND IS MADE. Issues on which a jury trial is not properly demanded are to be tried by the court. But the court may, on motion, order a jury trial on any issue for which a jury might have been demanded.

(c) ADVISORY JURY; JURY TRIAL BY CONSENT. In an action not triable of right by a jury, the court, on motion or on its own:

(1) may try any issue with an advisory jury; or

(2) may, with the parties' consent, try any issue by a jury whose verdict has the same effect as if a jury trial had been a matter of right, unless the action is against the United States and a federal statute provides for a nonjury trial.

## CIVIL RULE:

Federal Rule of Civil Procedure 47, which was last amended effective December 1, 2007, provides:

**Rule 47 Selecting of Jurors**

(a) EXAMINING JURORS. The court may permit the parties or their attorneys to examine prospective jurors or may itself do so. If the court examines the jurors, it must permit the parties or their attorneys to make any further inquiry it considers proper, or must itself ask any of their additional questions it considers proper.

(b) PEREMPTORY CHALLENGES. The court must allow the number of peremptory challenges provided by 28 U.S.C. § 1870.

(c) EXCUSING A JUROR. During trial or deliberation, the court may excuse a juror for good cause.

## CIVIL RULE:

Federal Rule of Civil Procedure 48, which was last amended effective December 1, 2009, provides:

**Rule 48 Number of Jurors; Verdict; Polling**

(a) NUMBER OF JURORS. A jury must begin with at least 6 and no more than 12 members, and each juror must participate in the verdict unless excused under Rule 47(c).

(b) VERDICT. Unless the parties stipulate otherwise, the verdict must be unanimous and must be returned by a jury of at least 6 members.

(c) POLLING. After a verdict is returned but before the jury is discharged, the court must on a party's request, or may on its own, poll the jurors individually. If the poll reveals a lack of unanimity or lack of assent by the number of jurors that the parties stipulated to, the court may direct the jury to deliberate further or may order a new trial.



## CIVIL RULE:

Federal Rule of Civil Procedure 49, which was last amended effective December 1, 2007, provides:

**Rule 49 Special Verdict; General Verdict and Questions**

(a) SPECIAL VERDICT.

(1) *In General.* The court may require a jury to return only a special verdict in the form of a special written finding on each issue of fact. The court may do so by:

(A) submitting written questions susceptible of a categorical or other brief answer;

(B) submitting written forms of the special findings that might properly be made under the pleadings and evidence; or

(C) using any other method that the court considers appropriate.

(2) *Instructions.* The court must give the instructions and explanations necessary to enable the jury to make its findings on each submitted issue.

(3) *Issues Not Submitted.* A party waives the right to a jury trial on any issue of fact raised by the pleadings or evidence but not submitted to the jury unless, before the jury retires, the party demands its

submission to the jury. If the party does not demand submission, the court may make a finding on the issue. If the court makes no finding, it is considered to have made a finding consistent with its judgment on the special verdict.

(b) General Verdict With Answers to Written Questions.

(1) *In General.* The court may submit to the jury forms for a general verdict, together with written questions on one or more issues of fact that the jury must decide. The court must give the instructions and explanations necessary to enable the jury to render a general verdict and answer the questions in writing, and must direct the jury to do both.

(2) *Verdict and Answers Consistent.* When the general verdict and the answers are consistent, the court must approve, for entry under Rule 58, an appropriate judgment on the verdict and answers.

(3) *Answers Inconsistent with the Verdict.* When the answers are consistent with each other but one or more is inconsistent with the general verdict, the court may:

(A) approve, for entry under Rule 58, an appropriate judgment according to the answers, notwithstanding the general verdict;

(B) direct the jury to further consider its answers and verdict; or

(C) order a new trial.

(4) *Answers Inconsistent with Each Other and the Verdict.* When the answers are inconsistent with each other and one or more is also inconsistent with the general verdict, judgment must not be entered; instead, the court must direct the jury to further consider its answers and verdict, or must order a new trial.

## CIVIL RULE:

Federal Rule of Civil Procedure 50, which was last amended effective December 1, 2009, provides:

**Rule 50 Judgment as a Matter of Law in a Jury Trial; Related Motion for a New Trial; Conditional Ruling**

(a) Judgment as a Matter of Law.

(1) *In General.* If a party has been fully heard on an issue during a jury trial and the court finds that a reasonable jury would not have a legally sufficient evidentiary basis to find for the party on that issue, the court may:

(A) resolve the issue against the party; and

(B) grant a motion for judgment as a matter of law against the party on a claim or defense that, under the controlling law, can be maintained or defeated only with a favorable finding on that issue.

(2) *Motion.* A motion for judgment as a matter of law may be made at any time before the case is submitted to the jury. The motion must specify the judgment sought and the law and facts that entitle the movant to the judgment.

(b) Renewing the Motion After Trial; Alternative Motion for a New Trial. If the court does not grant a motion for judgment as a matter of law made under Rule 50(a), the court is considered to have submitted the action to the jury subject to the court's later deciding the legal questions raised by the motion. No later than 28 days after the entry of judgment—or if the motion addresses a jury issue not decided by a verdict, no later than 28 days after the jury was discharged—the movant may file a renewed motion for judgment as a matter of law and may include an alternative or joint request for a new trial under Rule 59. In ruling on the renewed motion, the court may:

(1) allow judgment on the verdict, if the jury returned a verdict;

(2) order a new trial; or

(3) direct the entry of judgment as a matter of law.

(c) Granting the Renewed Motion; Conditional Ruling on a Motion for a New Trial.

(1) *In General.* If the court grants a renewed motion for judgment as a matter of law, it must also conditionally rule on any motion for a new trial by determining whether a new trial should be granted if the judgment is later vacated or reversed. The court must state the grounds for conditionally granting or denying the motion for a new trial.

(2) *Effect of a Conditional Ruling.* Conditionally granting the motion for a new trial does not affect the judgment's finality; if the judgment is reversed, the new trial must proceed unless the appellate court orders otherwise. If the motion for a new trial is conditionally denied, the appellee may assert error in that denial; if the judgment is reversed, the case must proceed as the appellate court orders.

(d) Time for a Losing Party's New-Trial Motion. Any motion for a new trial under Rule 59 by a party against whom judgment as a matter of law is rendered must be filed no later than 28 days after the entry of the judgment.

(e) Denying the Motion for Judgment as a Matter of Law; Reversal on Appeal. If the court denies the motion for judgment as a matter of law, the prevailing party may, as appellee, assert grounds entitling it to a new trial should the appellate court conclude that the trial court erred in denying the motion. If the appellate court reverses the judgment, it may order a new trial, direct the trial court to determine whether a new trial should be granted, or direct the entry of judgment.

## CIVIL RULE:

Federal Rule of Civil Procedure 51, which was last amended effective December 1, 2007, provides:

### Rule 51 Instructions to Jury; Objections; Preserving a Claim of Error

(a) Requests.

(1) *Before or at the Close of the Evidence.* At the close of the evidence or at any earlier reasonable time that the court orders, a party may file

and furnish to every other party written requests for the jury instructions it wants the court to give.

(2) *After the Close of the Evidence.* After the close of the evidence, a party may:

(A) file requests for instructions on issues that could not reasonably have been anticipated at an earlier time that the court set for requests; and

(B) with the court's permission file untimely requests for instructions on any issue.

(b) INSTRUCTIONS. The court:

(1) must inform the parties of its proposed instructions and proposed action on the requests before instructing the jury and before final jury arguments;

(2) must give the parties an opportunity to object on the record and out of the jury's hearing before the instructions and arguments are delivered; and

(3) may instruct the jury at any time after trial begins and before the jury is discharged.

(c) OBJECTIONS.

(1) *How to Make.* A party who objects to an instruction or the failure to give an instruction must do so on the record, stating distinctly the matter objected to and the grounds of the objection.

(2) *When to Make.* An objection is timely if:

(A) a party objects at the opportunity provided under Rule 51(b)(2); or

(B) a party was not informed of an instruction or action on a request before that opportunity to object, and the party objects promptly after learning that the instruction or request will be, or has been, given or refused.

(d) ASSIGNING ERROR; PLAIN ERROR.

(1) *Assigning Error.* A party may assign as error:

(A) an error in an instruction actually given, if that party properly objected; or

(B) a failure to give an instruction, if that party properly requested it and—unless the court rejected the request in a definitive ruling on the record—also properly objected.

(2) *Plain Error.* A court may consider a plain error in the instructions that has not been preserved as required by Rule 51(d)(1) if the error affects substantial rights.

## CIVIL RULE:

Federal Rule of Civil Procedure 81(c), which was last amended effective December 1, 2009, provides:

**Rule 81 Applicability of the Rules in General; Removed Actions**

* * *

(c) REMOVED ACTIONS.

(1) *Applicability.* These rules apply to a civil action after it is removed from a state court.

(2) *Further Pleading.* After removal, repleading is unnecessary unless the court orders it. A defendant who did not answer before removal must answer or present other defenses or objections under these rules within the longest of these periods:

(A) 21 days after receiving—through service or otherwise—a copy of the initial pleading stating the claim for relief;

(B) 21 days after being served with the summons for an initial pleading on file at the time of service; or

(C) 7 days after the notice of removal is filed.

(3) *Demand for a Jury Trial.*

(A) *As Affected by State Law.* A party who, before removal, expressly demanded a jury trial in accordance with state law need not renew the demand after removal. If the state law did not require an express demand for a jury trial, a party need not make one after removal unless the court orders the parties to do so within a specified time. The court must so order at a party's request and may so order on its own. A party who fails to make a demand when so ordered waives a jury trial.

(B) *Under Rule 38.* If all necessary pleadings have been served at the time of removal, a party entitled to a jury trial under Rule 38 must be given one if the party serves a demand within 14 days after:

(i) it files a notice of removal; or

(ii) it is served with a notice of removal filed by another party.

BANKRUPTCY RULES

BANKRUPTCY STATUTORY REFERENCES: 28 U.S.C. §§ 157 and 1411

## Rule 9016 Subpoena

Rule 45 F.R.Civ.P. applies in cases under the Code.

## CIVIL RULE:

Federal Rule of Civil Procedure 45, which was last amended effective December 1, 2013, provides:

**Rule 45 Subpoena**

(a) IN GENERAL.

(1) *Form and Contents.*

(A) *Requirements-In General.* Every subpoena must:

(i) state the court from which it issued;

(ii) state the title of the action and its civil-action number;

(iii) command each person to whom it is directed to do the following at a specified time and place: attend and testify; produce designated documents, electronically stored information, or tangible things in that person's possession, custody, or control; or permit the inspection of premises; and

(iv) set out the text of Rule 45(d) and (e).

(B) *Command to Attend a Deposition-Notice of the Recording Method.* A subpoena commanding attendance at a deposition must state the method for recording the testimony.

(C) *Combining or Separating a Command to Produce or to Permit Inspection; Specifying the Form for Electronically Stored Information.* A command to produce documents, electronically stored information, or tangible things or to permit the inspection of premises may be included in a subpoena commanding attendance at a deposition, hearing, or trial, or may be set out in a separate subpoena. A subpoena may specify the form or forms in which electronically stored information is to be produced.

(D) *Command to Produce; Included Obligations.* A command in a subpoena to produce documents, electronically stored information, or tangible things requires the responding person to permit inspection, copying, testing, or sampling of the materials.

(2) *Issuing Court.* A subpoena must issue from the court where the action is pending.

(3) *Issued by Whom.* The clerk must issue a subpoena, signed but otherwise in blank, to a party who requests it. That party must complete it before service. An attorney also may issue and sign a subpoena if the attorney is authorized to practice in the issuing court.

(4) *Notice to Other Parties Before Service.* If the subpoena commands the production of documents, electronically stored information, or tangible things or the inspection of premises before trial, then before it is served on the person to whom it is directed, a notice and a copy of the subpoena must be served on each party.

(b) SERVICE.

(1) *By Whom and How; Tendering Fees.* Any person who is at least 18 years old and not a party may serve a subpoena. Serving a subpoena requires delivering a copy to the named person and, if the subpoena requires that person's attendance, tendering the fees for 1 day's attendance and the mileage allowed by law. Fees and mileage need not be tendered when the subpoena issues on behalf of the United States or any of its officers or agencies.

(2) *Service in the United States.* A subpoena may be served at any place within the United States.

(3) *Service in a Foreign Country.* 28 U.S.C. § 1783 governs issuing and serving a subpoena directed to a United States national or resident who is in a foreign country.

(4) *Proof of Service.* Proving service, when necessary, requires filing

with the issuing court a statement showing the date and manner of service and the names of the persons served. The statement must be certified by the server.

(c) Place of Compliance.

(1) *For a Trial, Hearing, or Deposition.* A subpoena may command a person to attend a trial, hearing, or deposition only as follows:

(A) within 100 miles of where the person resides, is employed, or regularly transacts business in person; or

(B) within the state where the person resides, is employed, or regularly transacts business in person, if the person

(i) is a party or a party's officer; or

(ii) is commanded to attend a trial and would not incur substantial expense.

(2) *For Other Discovery.* A subpoena may command:

(A) production of documents, electronically stored information, or tangible things at a place within 100 miles of where the person resides, is employed, or regularly transacts business in person; and

(B) inspection of premises at the premises to be inspected.

(d) Protecting a Person Subject to a Subpoena; Enforcement.

(1) *Avoiding Undue Burden or Expense; Sanctions.* A party or attorney responsible for issuing and serving a subpoena must take reasonable steps to avoid imposing undue burden or expense on a person subject to the subpoena. The court for the district where compliance is required must enforce this duty and impose an appropriate sanction—which may include lost earnings and reasonable attorney's fees—on a party or attorney who fails to comply.

(2) *Command to Produce Materials or Permit Inspection.*

(A) *Appearance Not Required.* A person commanded to produce documents, electronically stored information, or tangible things, or to permit the inspection of premises, need not appear in person at the place of production or inspection unless also commanded to appear for a deposition, hearing, or trial.

(B) *Objections.* A person commanded to produce documents or tangible things or to permit inspection may serve on the party or attorney designated in the subpoena a written objection to inspecting, copying, testing, or sampling any or all of the materials or to inspecting the premises—or to producing electronically stored information in the form or forms requested. The objection must be served before the earlier of the time specified for compliance or 14 days after the subpoena is served. If an objection is made, the following rules apply:

(i) At any time, on notice to the commanded person, the serving party may move the court for the district where compliance is required for an order compelling production or inspection.

(ii) These acts may be required only as directed in the order, and the order must protect a person who is neither a party nor a party's officer from significant expense resulting from compliance.

(3) *Quashing or Modifying a Subpoena.*

(A) *When Required.* On timely motion, the court for the district where compliance is required must quash or modify a subpoena that:

(i) fails to allow a reasonable time to comply;

(ii) requires a person to comply beyond the geographical limits specified in Rule 45(c);

(iii) requires disclosure of privileged or other protected matter, if no exception or waiver applies; or

(iv) subjects a person to undue burden.

(B) *When Permitted.* To protect a person subject to or affected by a subpoena, the court for the district where compliance is required may, on motion, quash or modify the subpoena if it requires:

(i) disclosing a trade secret or other confidential research, development, or commercial information; or

(ii) disclosing an unretained expert's opinion or information that does not describe specific occurrences in dispute and results from the expert's study that was not requested by a party.

(C) *Specifying Conditions as an Alternative.* In the circumstances described in Rule 45(d)(3)(B), the court may, instead of quashing or modifying a subpoena, order appearance or production under specified conditions if the serving party:

(i) shows a substantial need for the testimony or material that cannot be otherwise met without undue hardship; and

(ii) ensures that the subpoenaed person will be reasonably compensated.

(e) DUTIES IN RESPONDING TO A SUBPOENA.

(1) *Producing Documents or Electronically Stored Information.* These procedures apply to producing documents or electronically stored information:

(A) *Documents.* A person responding to a subpoena to produce documents must produce them as they are kept in the ordinary course of business or must organize and label them to correspond to the categories in the demand.

(B) *Form for Producing Electronically Stored Information Not Specified.* If a subpoena does not specify a form for producing electronically stored information, the person responding must produce it in a form or forms in which it is ordinarily maintained or in a reasonably usable form or forms.

(C) *Electronically Stored Information Produced in Only One Form.* The person responding need not produce the same electronically stored information in more than one form.

(D) *Inaccessible Electronically Stored Information.* The person responding need not provide discovery of electronically stored information from sources that the person identifies as not reasonably accessible because of undue burden or cost. On motion to compel discovery or for a protective order, the person responding must show that the information is not reasonably accessible because of undue burden or cost. If that showing is made, the court may nonetheless order discovery from such sources if the requesting party shows good cause, considering the limitations of Rule 26(b)(2)(C). The court may specify conditions for the discovery.

(2) *Claiming Privilege or Protection.*

(A) *Information Withheld.* A person withholding subpoenaed information under a claim that it is privileged or subject to protection as trial-preparation material must:

(i) expressly make the claim; and

(ii) describe the nature of the withheld documents, communications, or tangible things in a manner that, without revealing information itself privileged or protected, will enable the parties to assess the claim.

(B) *Information Produced.* If information produced in response to a subpoena is subject to a claim of privilege or of protection as trial-preparation material, the person making the claim may notify any party that received the information of the claim and the basis for it. After being notified, a party must promptly return, sequester, or destroy the specified information and any copies it has; must not use or disclose the information until the claim is resolved; must take reasonable steps to retrieve the information if the party disclosed it before being notified; and may promptly present the information under seal to the court for the district where compliance is required for a determination of the claim. The person who produced the information must preserve the information until the claim is resolved.

(f) Transferring a Subpoena-Related Motion. When the court where compliance is required did not issue the subpoena, it may transfer a motion under this rule to the issuing court if the person subject to the subpoena consents or if the court finds exceptional circumstances. Then, if the attorney for a person subject to a subpoena is authorized to practice in the court where the motion was made, the attorney may file papers and appear on the motion as an officer of the issuing court. To enforce its order, the issuing court may transfer the order to the court where the motion was made.

(g) Contempt. The court for the district where compliance is required—and also, after a motion is transferred, the issuing court—may hold in contempt a person who, having been served, fails without adequate excuse to obey the subpoena or an order related to it.

**Rule 9017 Evidence**

The Federal Rules of Evidence and Rules 43, 44 and 44.1 F.R.Civ.P. apply in cases under the Code.

## CIVIL RULES:

Federal Rule of Civil Procedure 43, which was last amended effective December 1, 2007, provides:

**Rule 43 Taking of Testimony**

(a) In Open Court. At trial, the witnesses' testimony must be taken in open court unless a federal statute, the Federal Rules of Evidence, these rules, or other rules adopted by the Supreme Court provide otherwise. For good cause in compelling circumstances and with appropriate safeguards, the court may permit testimony in open court by contemporaneous transmission from a different location.

(b) Affirmation Instead of an Oath. When these rules require an oath, a solemn affirmation suffices.

(c) Evidence on a Motion. When a motion relies on facts outside the record, the court may hear the matter on affidavits or may hear it wholly or partly on oral testimony or on depositions.

(d) Interpreter. The court may appoint an interpreter of its choosing; fix reasonable compensation to be paid from funds provided by law or by one or more parties; and tax the compensation as costs.

Federal Rule of Civil Procedure 44, which was last amended effective December 1, 2007, provides:

**Rule 44 Proving an Official Record**

(a) Means of Proving.

(1) *Domestic Record.* Each of the following evidences an official record—or an entry in it—that is otherwise admissible and is kept within the United States, any state, district, or commonwealth, or any territory subject to the administrative or judicial jurisdiction of the United States:

(A) an official publication of the record; or

(B) a copy attested by the officer with legal custody of the record—or by the officer's deputy—and accompanied by a certificate that the officer has custody. The certificate must be made under seal:

(i) by a judge of a court of record in the district or political subdivision where the record is kept; or

(ii) by any public officer with a seal of office and with official duties in the district or political subdivision where the record is kept.

(2) *Foreign Record.*

(A) In General. Each of the following evidences a foreign official record—or an entry in it—that is otherwise admissible:

(i) an official publication of the record; or

(ii) the record—or a copy—that is attested by an authorized person and is accompanied either by a final certification of genuineness or by a certification under a treaty or convention to which the United States and the country where the record is located are parties.

(B) *Final Certification of Genuineness.* A final certification must certify the genuineness of the signature and official position of the attester or of any foreign official whose certificate of genuineness relates to the attestation or is in a chain of certificates of genuineness relating to the attestation. A final certification may be made by a secretary of a United States embassy or legation; by a consul general, vice consul, or consular agent of the United States; or by a diplomatic or consular official of the foreign country assigned or accredited to the United States.

(C) *Other Means of Proof.* If all parties have had a reasonable opportunity to investigate a foreign record's authenticity and accuracy, the court may, for good cause, either:

(i) admit an attested copy without final certification; or

(ii) permit the record to be evidenced by an attested summary with or without a final certification.

(b) Lack of a Record. A written statement that a diligent search of designated records revealed no record or entry of a specified tenor is admissible as evidence that the records contain no such record or entry. For domestic records, the statement must be authenticated under Rule 44(a)(1). For foreign records, the statement must comply with (a)(2)(C)(ii).

(c) Other Proof. A party may prove an official record—or an entry or lack of an entry in it—by any other method authorized by law.

Federal Rule of Civil Procedure 44.1, which was last amended effective December 1, 2007, provides:

**Rule 44.1 Determining Foreign Law**

A party who intends to raise an issue about a foreign country's law must give notice by a pleading or other writing. In determining foreign law, the court may consider any relevant material or source, including testimony, whether or not submitted by a party or admissible under the Federal Rules of Evidence. The court's determination must be treated as a ruling on a question of law.

## Rule 9018 Secret, Confidential, Scandalous, or Defamatory Matter

On motion or on its own initiative, with or without notice, the court may make any order which justice requires (1) to protect the estate or any entity in respect of a trade secret or other confidential research, development, or commercial information, (2) to protect any entity against scandalous or defamatory matter contained in any paper filed in a case under the Code, or (3) to protect governmental matters that are made confidential by statute or regulation. If an order is entered under this rule without notice, any entity affected thereby may move to vacate or modify the order, and after a hearing on notice the court shall determine the motion.

BANKRUPTCY CODE REFERENCES: §§ 101 and 107

## Rule 9019 Compromise and Arbitration

(*a*) *Compromise.* On motion by the trustee and after notice and a hearing, the court may approve a compromise or settlement. Notice shall be given to creditors, the United States trustee, the debtor, and indenture trustees as provided in Rule 2002 and to any other entity as the court may direct.

(*b*) *Authority to Compromise or Settle Controversies Within Classes.* After a hearing on such notice as the court may direct, the court may fix a class or classes of controversies and authorize the trustee to compromise or settle controversies within such class or classes without further hearing or notice.

(*c*) *Arbitration.* On stipulation of the parties to any controversy affecting the estate the court may authorize the matter to be submitted to final and binding arbitration.

BANKRUPTCY CODE REFERENCES: §§ 102 and 1107

## Rule 9020 Contempt Proceedings

Rule 9014 governs a motion for an order of contempt made by the United States trustee or a party in interest.

## Rule 9021 Entry of Judgment

A judgment or order is effective when entered under Rule 5003.

## Rule 9022 Notice of Judgment or Order

(*a*) *Judgment or Order of Bankruptcy Judge.* Immediately on the entry of a judgment or order the clerk shall serve a notice of entry in the manner provided in Rule 5(b) F. R.Civ.P.[20] on the contesting parties and on other entities as the court directs. Unless the case is a chapter 9 municipality case, the clerk shall forthwith transmit to the United States trustee a copy of the judgment or order. Service of the notice shall be noted in the docket. Lack of notice of the entry does not affect the time to appeal or relieve or authorize the court to relieve a party for failure to appeal within the time allowed, except as permitted in Rule 8002.

(*b*) *Judgment or Order of District Judge.* Notice of a judgment or order entered by a district judge is governed by Rule 77(d) F.R.Civ.P. Unless the case is a chapter 9 municipality case, the clerk shall forthwith transmit to the United States trustee a copy of a judgment or order entered by a district judge.

### CIVIL RULE:

Federal Rule of Civil Procedure 77(d), which was last amended effective December 1, 2007, provides:

**Rule 77 Conducting Business; Clerk's Authority; Notice of an Order or Judgment**

---

[20] ED. NOTE: For the text of Fed. R. Civ. P. 5, *see* Fed. R. Bankr. P. 7005 *supra*.

* * *

(d) Serving Notice of an Order or Judgment.

(1) *Service.* Immediately after entering an order or judgment, the clerk must serve notice of the entry, as provided in Rule 5(b), on each party who is not in default for failing to appear. The clerk must record the service on the docket. A party also may serve notice of the entry as provided in Rule 5(b).

(2) *Time to Appeal Not Affected by Lack of Notice.* Lack of notice of the entry does not affect the time for appeal or relieve—or authorize the court to relieve—a party for failing to appeal within the time allowed, except as allowed by Federal Rule of Appellate Procedure (4)(a).

**Rule 9023 New Trials; Amendment of Judgments**

Except as provided in this rule and Rule 3008, Rule 59 F.R. Civ. P. applies in cases under the Code. A motion for a new trial or to alter or amend a judgment shall be filed, and a court may on its own order a new trial, no later than 14 days after entry of judgment. In some circumstances, Rule 8008 governs post-judgment motion practice after an appeal has been docketed and is pending.

## CIVIL RULE:

Federal Rule of Civil Procedure 59, which was last amended effective December 1, 2009, provides:

**Rule 59 New Trial; Altering or Amending a Judgment**

(a) In General.

(1) *Grounds for New Trial.* The court may, on motion, grant a new trial on all or some of the issues—and to any party—as follows:

(A) after a jury trial, for any reason for which a new trial has heretofore been granted in an action at law in federal court; or

(B) after a nonjury trial, for any reason for which a rehearing has heretofore been granted in a suit in equity in federal court.

(2) *Further Action After a Nonjury Trial.* After a nonjury trial, the court may, on motion for a new trial, open the judgment if one has been entered, take additional testimony, amend findings of fact and conclusions of law or make new ones, and direct the entry of a new judgment.

(b) Time to File a Motion for a New Trial. A motion for a new trial must be filed no later than 28 days after the entry of judgment.

(c) Time to Serve Affidavits. When a motion for a new trial is based on affidavits, they must be filed with the motion. The opposing party has 14 days after being served to file opposing affidavits. The court may permit reply affidavits.

(d) New Trial on the Court's Initiative or for Reasons Not in the Motion. No later than 28 days after the entry of judgment, the court, on its own, may order a new trial for any reason that would justify granting one on a party's motion. After giving the parties notice and an opportunity to be heard, the court may grant a timely motion for a new trial for a reason not stated in the motion. In either event, the court must specify the reasons in its order.

(e) MOTION TO ALTER OR AMEND A JUDGMENT. A motion to alter or amend a judgment must be filed no later than 28 days after the entry of the judgment.

## Rule 9024 Relief from Judgment or Order

Rule 60 F.R.Civ.P. applies in cases under the Code except that (1) a motion to reopen a case under the Code or for the reconsideration of an order allowing or disallowing a claim against the estate entered without a contest is not subject to the one year limitation prescribed in Rule 60(c), (2) a complaint to revoke a discharge in a chapter 7 liquidation case may be filed only within the time allowed by § 727(e) of the Code, and (3) a complaint to revoke an order confirming a plan may be filed only within the time allowed by § 1144, § 1230, or § 1330. In some circumstances, Rule 8008 governs post-judgment motion practice after an appeal has been docketed and is pending.

### CIVIL RULE:

Federal Rule of Civil Procedure 60, which was last amended effective December 1, 2007, provides:

#### Rule 60 Relief from a Judgment or Order

(a) CORRECTIONS BASED ON CLERICAL MISTAKES; OVERSIGHTS AND OMISSIONS. The court may correct a clerical mistake or a mistake arising from oversight or omission whenever one is found in a judgment, order, or other part of the record. The court may do so on motion or on its own, with or without notice. But after an appeal has been docketed in the appellate court and while it is pending, such a mistake may be corrected only with the appellate court's leave.

(b) GROUNDS FOR RELIEF FROM A FINAL JUDGMENT, ORDER, OR PROCEEDING. On motion and just terms, the court may relieve a party or its legal representative from a final judgment, order, or proceeding for the following reasons:

(1) mistake, inadvertence, surprise, or excusable neglect;

(2) newly discovered evidence that, with reasonable diligence, could not have been discovered in time to move for a new trial under Rule 59(b);

(3) fraud (whether previously called intrinsic or extrinsic), misrepresentation, or misconduct by an opposing party;

(4) the judgment is void;

(5) the judgment has been satisfied, released, or discharged; it is based on an earlier judgment that has been reversed or vacated; or applying it prospectively is no longer equitable; or

(6) any other reason that justifies relief.

(c) TIMING AND EFFECT OF THE MOTION.

(1) *Timing.* A motion under Rule 60(b) must be made within a reasonable time—and for reasons (1), (2), and (3) no more than a year

after the entry of the judgment or order or the date of the proceeding.

(2) *Effect on Finality.* The motion does not affect the judgment's finality or suspend its operation.

(d) OTHER POWERS TO GRANT RELIEF. This rule does not limit a court's power to:

(1) entertain an independent action to relieve a party from a judgment, order, or proceeding;

(2) grant relief under 28 U.S.C. § 1655 to a defendant who was not personally notified of the action; or

(3) set aside a judgment for fraud on the court.

(e) BILLS AND WRITS ABOLISHED. The following are abolished: bills of review, bills in the nature of bills of review, and writs of coram nobis, coram vobis, and audita querela.

BANKRUPTCY CODE REFERENCES: §§ 350, 727, 1144, 1230 and 1330

## Rule 9025 Security: Proceedings Against Security Providers

Whenever the Code or these rules require or permit a party to give security, and security is given with one or more security providers, each provider submits to the jurisdiction of the court, and liability may be determined in an adversary proceeding governed by the rules in Part VII.

BANKRUPTCY CODE REFERENCES: §§ 303 and 322

## Rule 9026 Exceptions Unnecessary

Rule 46 F.R.Civ.P. applies in cases under the Code.

### CIVIL RULE:

Federal Rule of Civil Procedure 46, which was last amended effective December 1, 2007, provides:

**Rule 46 Objecting to a Ruling or Order**

A formal exception to a ruling or order is unnecessary. When the ruling or order is requested or made, a party need only state the action that it wants the court to take or objects to, along with the grounds for the request or objection. Failing to object does not prejudice a party who had no opportunity to do so when the ruling or order was made.

## Rule 9027 Removal

(a) *Notice of Removal.*

(1) *Where Filed; Form and Content.* A notice of removal shall be filed with the clerk for the district and division within which is located the state or federal court where the civil action is pending. The notice shall be signed pursuant to Rule 9011 and contain a short and plain statement of the facts which entitle the party filing the notice to remove, contain a statement that upon removal of the claim or cause of action, the party filing the notice does or does not consent to entry of final orders or judgment by the bankruptcy court, and be accompanied by a copy of all process and pleadings.

(2) *Time for Filing; Civil Action Initiated Before Commencement of the Case Under the Code.* If the claim or cause of action in a civil action is pending when a case under the Code is commenced, a notice of removal may be filed only within the longest of (A) 90 days after the order for relief in the case under the Code, (B) 30 days after entry of an order terminating a stay, if the claim or cause of action in a civil action has been stayed under § 362 of the Code, or (C) 30 days after a trustee qualifies in a chapter 11 reorganization case but not later than 180 days after the order for relief.

(3) *Time for Filing; Civil Action Initiated After Commencement of the Case Under the Code.* If a claim or cause of action is asserted in another court after the commencement of a case under the Code, a notice of removal may be filed with the clerk only within the shorter of (A) 30 days after receipt, through service or otherwise, of a copy of the initial pleading setting forth the claim or cause of action sought to be removed, or (B) 30 days after receipt of the summons if the initial pleading has been filed with the court but not served with the summons.

(*b*) *Notice.* Promptly after filing the notice of removal, the party filing the notice shall serve a copy of it on all parties to the removed claim or cause of action.

(*c*) *Filing in Non-Bankruptcy Court.* Promptly after filing the notice of removal, the party filing the notice shall file a copy of it with the clerk of the court from which the claim or cause of action is removed. Removal of the claim or cause of action is effected on such filing of a copy of the notice of removal. The parties shall proceed no further in that court unless and until the claim or cause of action is remanded.

(*d*) *Remand.* A motion for remand of the removed claim or cause of action shall be governed by Rule 9014 and served on the parties to the removed claim or cause of action.

(*e*) *Procedure After Removal.*

(*1*) After removal of a claim or cause of action to a district court the district court or, if the case under the Code has been referred to a bankruptcy judge of the district, the bankruptcy judge, may issue all necessary orders and process to bring before it all proper parties whether served by process issued by the court from which the claim or cause of action was removed or otherwise.

(*2*) The district court or, if the case under the Code has been referred to a bankruptcy judge of the district, the bankruptcy judge, may require the party filing the notice of removal to file with the clerk copies of all records and proceedings relating to the claim or cause of action in the court from which the claim or cause of action was removed.

(*3*) Any party who has filed a pleading in connection with the removed claim or cause of action, other than the party filing the notice of removal, shall file a statement that the party does or does not consent to entry of final orders or judgment by the bankruptcy court. A statement required by this paragraph shall be signed pursuant to Rule 9011 and shall be filed not later than 14 days after the filing of the notice of removal. Any party who files a statement pursuant to this paragraph shall mail a copy to every other party to the removed claim or cause of action.

(*f*) *Process After Removal.* If one or more of the defendants has not been served with process, the service has not been perfected prior to removal, or the process served proves to be defective, such process or service may be completed or new process issued pursuant to Part VII of these rules. This subdivision shall not deprive any defendant on whom process is served after removal of the defendant's right to move to remand the case.

(*g*) *Applicability of Part VII.* The rules of Part VII apply to a claim or cause of action removed to a district court from a federal or state court and govern procedure after removal. Repleading is not necessary unless the court so orders. In a removed action in which the defendant has not answered, the defendant shall answer or present the other defenses or objections available under the rules of Part VII within 21 days following the receipt through service or otherwise of a copy of the initial pleading setting forth the claim for relief on which the action or proceeding is based, or within 21 days following the service of summons on such initial pleading, or within seven days following the filing of the notice of removal, whichever period is longest.

(*h*) *Record Supplied.* When a party is entitled to copies of the records and proceedings in any civil action or proceeding in a federal or a state court, to be used in the removed civil action or proceeding, and the clerk of the federal or state court, on demand accompanied by payment or tender of the lawful fees, fails to deliver certified copies, the court may, on affidavit reciting the facts, direct such record to be supplied by affidavit or otherwise. Thereupon the proceedings, trial and judgment may be had in the court, and all process awarded, as if certified copies had been filed.

(*i*) *Attachment or Sequestration; Securities.* When a claim or cause of action is removed to a district court, any attachment or sequestration of property in the court from which the claim or cause of action was removed shall hold the property to answer the final judgment or decree in the same manner as the property would have been held to answer final judgment or decree had it been rendered by the court from which the claim or cause of action was removed. All bonds, undertakings, or security given by either party to the claim or cause of action prior to its removal shall remain valid and effectual notwithstanding such removal. All injunctions issued, orders entered and other proceedings had prior to removal shall remain in full force and effect until dissolved or modified by the court.



Bankruptcy Statutory Reference: 28 U.S.C. § 1452

**Rule 9028 Disability of a Judge**

Rule 63 F.R.Civ.P. applies in cases under the Code.

## CIVIL RULE:

Federal Rule of Civil Procedure 63, which was last amended effective December 1, 2007, provides:

**Rule 63 Judge's Inability to Proceed**

If a judge conducting a hearing or trial is unable to proceed, any other judge may proceed upon certifying familiarity with the record and determining that the case may be completed without prejudice to the parties. In a hearing or a nonjury trial, the successor judge must, at a party's request, recall any witness whose testimony is material and disputed and who is available to testify again without undue burden. The successor judge may also recall any other witness.

## Rule 9029 Local Bankruptcy Rules; Procedure When There Is No Controlling Law

(*a*) *Local Bankruptcy Rules.*

(*1*) Each district court acting by a majority of its district judges may make and amend rules governing practice and procedure in all cases and proceedings within the district court's bankruptcy jurisdiction which are consistent with—but not duplicative of—Acts of Congress and these rules and which do not prohibit or limit the use of the Official Forms. Rule 83 F.R.Civ.P. governs the procedure for making local rules. A district court may authorize the bankruptcy judges of the district, subject to any limitation or condition it may prescribe and the requirements of Rule 83 F.R.Civ.P., to make and amend rules of practice and procedure which are consistent with—but not duplicative of—Acts of Congress and these rules and which do not prohibit or limit the use of the Official Forms. Local rules shall conform to any uniform numbering system prescribed by the Judicial Conference of the United States.

(*2*) A local rule imposing a requirement of form shall not be enforced in a manner that causes a party to lose rights because of a nonwillful failure to comply with the requirement.

(*b*) *Procedure When There is No Controlling Law.* A judge may regulate practice in any manner consistent with federal law, these rules, Official Forms, and local rules of the district. No sanction or other disadvantage may be imposed for noncompliance with any requirement not in federal law, federal rules, Official Forms, or the local rules of the district unless the alleged violator has been furnished in the particular case with actual notice of the requirement.

## CIVIL RULE:

Federal Rule of Civil Procedure 83, which was last amended effective December 1, 2007, provides:

**Rule 83 Rules by District Courts; Judge's Directives**

(a) LOCAL RULES.

(1) *In General.* After giving public notice and an opportunity for comment, a district court, acting by a majority of its district judges, may adopt and amend rules governing its practice. A local rule must be consistent with—but not duplicate—federal statutes and rules adopted under 28 U.S.C. §§ 2072 and 2075, and must conform to any uniform numbering system prescribed by the Judicial Conference of the United States. A local rule takes effect on the date specified by the

district court and remains in effect unless amended by the court or abrogated by the judicial council of the circuit. Copies of rules and amendments must, on their adoption, be furnished to the judicial council and the Administrative Office of the United States Courts and be made available to the public.

(2) *Requirement of Form.* A local rule imposing a requirement of form must not be enforced in a way that causes a party to lose any right because of a nonwillful failure to comply.

(b) PROCEDURE WHEN THERE IS NO CONTROLLING LAW. A judge may regulate practice in any manner consistent with federal law, rules adopted under 28 U.S.C. §§ 2072 and 2075, and the district's local rules. No sanction or other disadvantage may be imposed for noncompliance with any requirement not in federal law, federal rules, or the local rules unless the alleged violator has been furnished in the particular case with actual notice of the requirement.

BANKRUPTCY STATUTORY REFERENCE: 28 U.S.C. § 2075

## Rule 9030 Jurisdiction and Venue Unaffected

These rules shall not be construed to extend or limit the jurisdiction of the courts or the venue of any matters therein.

## Rule 9031 Masters Not Authorized

Rule 53 F.R.Civ.P. does not apply in cases under the Code.

## Rule 9032 Effect of Amendment of Federal Rules of Civil Procedure

The Federal Rules of Civil Procedure which are incorporated by reference and made applicable by these rules shall be the Federal Rules of Civil Procedure in effect on the effective date of these rules and as thereafter amended, unless otherwise provided by such amendment or by these rules.

## Rule 9033 Findings of Fact and Conclusions of Law

(*a*) *Service.* In a proceeding in which the bankruptcy court has issued proposed findings of fact and conclusions of law, the clerk shall serve forthwith copies on all parties by mail and note the date of mailing on the docket.

(*b*) *Objections: Time for Filing.* Within 14 days after being served with a copy of the proposed findings of fact and conclusions of law a party may serve and file with the clerk written objections which identify the specific proposed findings or conclusions objected to and state the grounds for such objection. A party may respond to another party's objections within 14 days after being served with a copy thereof. A party objecting to the bankruptcy judge's proposed findings or conclusions shall arrange promptly for the transcription of the record, or such portions of it as all parties may agree upon or the bankruptcy judge deems sufficient, unless the district judge otherwise directs.

(*c*) *Extension of Time.* The bankruptcy judge may for cause extend the time for filing objections by any party for a period not to exceed 21 days from the expiration of the time otherwise prescribed by this rule. A request to extend the time for filing objections must be made before the time for filing objections has expired, except that a request made no more than 21 days after the expiration of the time for filing objections may be granted upon a showing of excusable neglect.

(*d*) *Standard of Review.* The district judge shall make a de novo review upon the record or, after additional evidence, of any portion of the bankruptcy judge's findings of fact or conclusions of law to which specific written objection has been made in accordance with this rule. The district judge may accept, reject, or modify the proposed findings of fact or conclusions of law, receive further evidence, or recommit the matter to the bankruptcy judge with instructions.

Bankruptcy Statutory Reference: 28 U.S.C. § 157

## Rule 9034 Transmittal of Pleadings, Motion Papers, Objections, and Other Papers to the United States Trustee

Unless the United States trustee requests otherwise or the case is a chapter 9 municipality case, any entity that files a pleading, motion, objection, or similar paper relating to any of the following matters shall transmit a copy thereof to the United States trustee within the time required by these rules for service of the paper:

(*a*) a proposed use, sale, or lease of property of the estate other than in the ordinary course of business;

(*b*) the approval of a compromise or settlement of a controversy;

(*c*) the dismissal or conversion of a case to another chapter;

(*d*) the employment of professional persons;

(*e*) an application for compensation or reimbursement of expenses;

(*f*) a motion for, or approval of an agreement relating to, the use of cash collateral or authority to obtain credit;

(*g*) the appointment of a trustee or examiner in a chapter 11 reorganization case;

(*h*) the approval of a disclosure statement;

(*i*) the confirmation of a plan;

(*j*) an objection to, or waiver or revocation of, the debtor's discharge;

(*k*) any other matter in which the United States trustee requests copies of filed papers or the court orders copies transmitted to the United States trustee.

Bankruptcy Code Reference: § 307

Bankruptcy Statutory Reference: 28 U.S.C. § 586

## Rule 9035 Applicability of Rules in Judicial Districts in Alabama and North Carolina

In any case under the Code that is filed in or transferred to a district in the State of Alabama or the State of North Carolina and in which a United States trustee is not authorized to act, these rules apply to the extent that they are not inconsistent with any federal statute effective in the case.

**Rule 9036 Notice and Service by Electronic Transmission**

(*a*) *In General.* This rule applies whenever these rules require or permit sending a notice or serving a paper by mail or other means.

(*b*) *Notices from and Service by the Court.*

(*1*) *Registered Users.* The clerk may send notice to or serve a registered user by filing the notice or paper with the court's electronic-filing system.

(*2*) *All Recipients.* For any recipient, the clerk may send notice or serve a paper by electronic means that the recipient consented to in writing, including by designating an electronic address for receipt of notices. But these exceptions apply:

(*A*) if the recipient has registered an electronic address with the Administrative Office of the United States Courts' bankruptcy-noticing program, the clerk shall send the notice to or serve the paper at that address; and

(*B*) if an entity has been designated by the Director of the Administrative Office of the United States Courts as a high-volume paper-notice recipient, the clerk may send the notice to or serve the paper electronically at an address designated by the Director, unless the entity has designated an address under § 342(e) or (f) of the Code.

(*c*) *Notices from and Service by an Entity.* An entity may send notice or serve a paper in the same manner that the clerk does under (b), excluding (b)(2)(A) and (B).

(*d*) *Completing Notice or Service.* Electronic notice or service is complete upon filing or sending but is not effective if the filer or sender receives notice that it did not reach the person to be served. It is the recipient's responsibility to keep its electronic address current with the clerk.

(*e*) *Inapplicability.* This rule does not apply to any paper required to be served in accordance with Rule 7004.

**Rule 9037 Privacy Protection for Filings Made with the Court**

(*a*) *Redacted Filings.* Unless the court orders otherwise, in an electronic or paper filing made with the court that contains an individual's social-security number, taxpayer-identification number, or birth date, the name of an individual, other than the debtor, known to be and identified as a minor, or a financial-account number, a party or nonparty making the filing may include only:

(*1*) the last four digits of the social-security number and taxpayer-identification number;

(*2*) the year of the individual's birth;

(*3*) the minor's initials; and

(*4*) the last four digits of the financial-account number.

(*b*) *Exemptions from the Redaction Requirement.* The redaction requirement does not apply to the following:

(*1*) a financial-account number that identifies the property allegedly subject to forfeiture in a forfeiture proceeding;

(*2*) the record of an administrative or agency proceeding unless filed with a proof of claim;

(*3*) the official record of a state-court proceeding;

(*4*) the record of a court or tribunal, if that record was not subject to the redaction requirement when originally filed;

(*5*) a filing covered by subdivision (c) of this rule; and

(*6*) a filing that is subject to § 110 of the Code.

(*c*) *Filings Made Under Seal.* The court may order that a filing be made under seal without redaction. The court may later unseal the filing or order the entity that made the filing to file a redacted version for the public record.

(*d*) *Protective Orders.* For cause, the court may by order in a case under the Code:

(*1*) require redaction of additional information; or

(*2*) limit or prohibit a nonparty's remote electronic access to a document filed with the court.

(*e*) *Option for Additional Unredacted Filing Under Seal.* An entity making a redacted filing may also file an unredacted copy under seal. The court must retain the unredacted copy as part of the record.

(*f*) *Option for Filing a Reference List.* A filing that contains redacted information may be filed together with a reference list that identifies each item of redacted information and specifies an appropriate identifier that uniquely corresponds to each item listed. The list must be filed under seal and may be amended as of right. Any reference in the case to a listed identifier will be construed to refer to the corresponding item of information.

(*g*) *Waiver of Protection of Identifiers.* An entity waives the protection of subdivision (a) as to the entity's own information by filing it without redaction and not under seal.

(*h*) *Motion to Redact a Previously Filed Document.*

(*1*) *Content of the Motion; Service.* Unless the court orders otherwise, if an entity seeks to redact from a previously filed document information that is protected under subdivision (a), the entity must:

(*A*) file a motion to redact identifying the proposed redactions;

(*B*) attach to the motion the proposed redacted document;

(*C*) include in the motion the docket or proof-of-claim number of the previously filed document; and

(*D*) serve the motion and attachment on the debtor, debtor's attorney, trustee (if any), United States trustee, filer of the unredacted document, and any individual whose personal identifying information is to be redacted.

(2) *Restricting Public Access to the Unredacted Document; Docketing the Redacted Document.* The court must promptly restrict public access to the motion and the unredacted document pending its ruling on the motion. If the court grants it, the court must docket the redacted document. The restrictions on public access to the motion and unredacted document remain in effect until a further court order. If the court denies it, the restrictions must be lifted, unless the court orders otherwise.

# Time Periods Prescribed by the Bankruptcy Rules

The following timetables set forth the various time periods prescribed by the Federal Rules of Bankruptcy Procedure. The timetables are arranged in the following groupings, which follow to the degree possible the usual sequence of events in bankruptcy cases:

- Deadlines in Connection with Commencement of the Case
- Time Periods Related to Plans
- Deadlines Throughout the Case
- Time Periods in Connection with Claims
- Time Periods in Connection with Dismissal or Discharge
- Time Periods in Connection with Adversary Proceedings
- Time Periods in Connection with Discovery
- Time Periods in Connection with Appeals

In each table, the column on the left indicates the entity responsible for taking action. The next column indicates the deadline for that action. The third column describes the act that is required of the responsible entity. The final column cites the applicable Federal Rule of Bankruptcy Procedure.

Practitioners should consult the cited rule for whether "for cause shown" or if "unless the court orders otherwise" applies to enlarge or reduce a time period, and Federal Rule of Bankruptcy Procedure 9006(b), (c) for when enlargement or reduction is not permitted. In addition, Federal Rule of Bankruptcy Procedure 9006(a) explains how to count time periods; Rule 9006(e) sets forth what constitutes the time for service by mail; and Rule 9006(f) sets forth when three additional days are added to prescribed time periods. Note also that some deadlines instead are found in the Bankruptcy Code.

Finally, practitioners should consult their court's local rules for additional or altered time periods "consistent with" the federal rules. Fed. R. Bankr. P. 9029(a)(1).

## Deadlines in Connection with Commencement of the Case

| DEADLINES IN CONNECTION WITH COMMENCEMENT OF THE CASE | | | |
|---|---|---|---|
| **Entity** | **Deadline** | **Act to Be Performed** | **Rule** |
| Involuntary debtor | 7 days after entry of the order for relief | File a list containing the name and address of each entity included or to be included on Schedules D, E/F, G, and H | 1007(a)(2)[1] |
| Chapter 11 debtor | 14 days after entry of the order for relief | File a list of the debtor's equity security holders, with the number and kind of interests, and the last known address or place of business of each holder | 1007(a)(3) |
| Voluntary debtor | 14 days after filing the petition | File the schedules, statements and other documents required by Rule 1007(b)(1) | 1007(c) |
| Chapter 7 individual debtor | 14 days after filing the petition | File a statement of current monthly income and, if above median, the information and calculations required by § 707(b)[2] | 1007(c) |
| Individual chapter 11 debtor | 14 days after filing the petition | File a statement of current monthly income | 1007(c) |
| Chapter 13 debtor | 14 days after filing the petition | File a statement of current monthly income and, if above median, the information and calculations required by § 1325(b)(3) | 1007(c) |
| Voluntary debtor | 14 days after entry of the order for relief | File a certificate of credit counseling if debtor filed a statement that debtor received the counseling but did not have the certificate on the filing date | 1007(c) |

[1] All references are to the Federal Rules of Bankruptcy Procedure unless otherwise specified.

[2] All statutory references are to title 11 of the United States Code unless otherwise specified.

| DEADLINES IN CONNECTION WITH COMMENCEMENT OF THE CASE | | | |
|---|---|---|---|
| **Entity** | **Deadline** | **Act to Be Performed** | **Rule** |
| Clerk, or some other person as the court may direct | 21 days after the order for relief | Provide notice by mail of the order for relief in a voluntary case commenced by an individual debtor whose debts are primarily consumer debts | 2002(o) |
| Petitioning creditor(s) in an involuntary case | 7 days after issuance | Serve summons | 1010(a), 7004(e) |
| Involuntary debtor | 14 days after entry of the order for relief | File the schedules, statements and other documents required by Rule 1007(b)(1) | 1007(c) |
| Involuntary chapter 11 reorganization debtor | 2 days after entry of the order for relief | File a list of the creditors holding the 20 largest unsecured claims | 1007(d) |
| Individual involuntary debtor | 14 days after entry of the order for relief | File a verified statement that sets out the debtor's Social Security number, or states that the debtor does not have a Social Security number | 1007(f) |
| Involuntary debtor | 21 days after service of the summons, unless made by publication on a party not residing or found within the state in which the court sits | File and serve defenses and objections to an involuntary petition | 1011(b) |
| Involuntary chapter 11 debtor | 14 days after entry of the order for relief | File statement as to whether the debtor is a small business debtor | 1020(a) |
| Objectors to election of chapter 7 trustee | 14 days after the United States trustee files the report of the disputed election | File motion for the resolution of disputed chapter 7 trustee election | 2003(d)(2) |
| United States trustee in a chapter 7, 9, or 11 health care business case | 21 days after the commencement of the case | File motion to not appoint a patient care ombudsman | 2007.2(a) |
| Chapter 7, 12, or 13 panel trustee | 7 days after receipt of notice of selection as trustee | Notify court and United State trustee of rejection of the office | 2008 |
| Person selected as trustee who is not a panel trustee | 7 days after receipt of notice of selection as trustee | Notify court and United States trustee of acceptance of the office | 2008 |

| DEADLINES IN CONNECTION WITH COMMENCEMENT OF THE CASE | | | |
|---|---|---|---|
| **Entity** | **Deadline** | **Act to Be Performed** | **Rule** |
| Debtor's attorney | 14 days after the order for relief | File statement whether the attorney has shared or agreed to share the compensation with any other entity | 2016(b) |
| United States trustee or party in interest | 7 days before the date set for the hearing on the petition | File motion in a chapter 15 case for determination that the debtor's center of main interests is other than as stated in the petition | 1004.2(b) |
| Chapter 15 debtor or any party in interest | 7 days before the date set for the hearing on the petition | File objections and other responses to a chapter 15 petition | 1012(b) |
| Chapter 15 corporate entity | With first pleading, motion, response or other request addressed to the court | File corporate ownership statement | 1012(c) |
| Clerk, or some other person as the court may direct | 21 days | Provide notice by mail of hearing on provisional relief being sought under § 1519 | 2002(q) |
| Voluntary individual debtor | 120 days after filing the petition | Pay filing fee in installments | 1006(b)(2) |
| Clerk of court | 10 days after the filing of the petition | Provide notice of presumption of abuse in a chapter 7 case | 5008 |

## Time Periods Related to Plans[3]

| TIME PERIODS RELATED TO PLANS | | | |
|---|---|---|---|
| **Entity** | **Deadline** | **Act to Be Performed** | **Rule** |
| Chapter 12 debtor | 90 days after the order for relief | File a chapter 12 plan | 3015(a) |
| Chapter 13 debtor | 14 days after filing the petition | File a chapter 13 plan | 3015(b) |
| Chapter 13 debtor | 14 days after conversion | File a chapter 13 plan in a case converted to chapter 13 | 3015(b) |
| Chapter 9 or 11 plan proponent | With the plan or within a time fixed by the court | File a disclosure statement or evidence of prepetition acceptance of a plan | 3016(b) |
| Clerk, or some other person as the court may direct | 21 days | Provide notice by mail of time fixed for filing objection to modification of chapter 12 or 13 plan and, if objection is filed, the hearing on the proposed modification | 2002(a)(5), 3015(h) |
| Clerk, or some other person as the court may direct | 21 days | Provide notice by mail of time fixed for filing objections and the hearing to consider chapter 12 plan confirmation | 2002(a)(8) |
| Clerk, or some other person as the court may direct | 21 days | Provide notice by mail of time fixed for filing objections to chapter 13 plan confirmation | 2002(a)(9) |
| Clerk, or some other person as the court may direct | 28 days | Provide notice by mail of time for filing objections and the hearing to consider confirmation of a chapter 9 or 11 plan | 2002(b) |
| Clerk, or some other person as the court may direct | 28 days | Provide notice by mail of time fixed for filing objections and the hearing to consider approval of a disclosure statement | 2002(b) |

[3] *See* 11 U.S.C. § 941 for the time for filing a chapter 9 plan, and 11 U.S.C. § 1121 for deadlines in connection with the filing of plans under chapter 11. *See* 11 U.S.C. § 1224 for the time for holding a chapter 12 confirmation hearing, and 11 U.S.C. § 1324(b) for the time for holding a chapter 13 confirmation hearing.

| TIME PERIODS RELATED TO PLANS | | | |
|---|---|---|---|
| **Entity** | **Deadline** | **Act to Be Performed** | **Rule** |
| Clerk, or some other person as the court may direct | 28 days | Provide notice by mail of the time fixed in a chapter 11 small business case to make a final determination whether the plan provides adequate information so that a separate disclosure statement is not necessary | 2002(b) |
| Clerk, or some other person as the court may direct | 28 days | Provide notice by mail of the time for the hearing to consider confirmation of a chapter 13 plan | 2002(b) |
| Objectors to chapter 12 or 13 plan | 7 days before the date set for hearing on confirmation | File objection to confirmation of chapter 12 or 13 plan[4] | 3015(f) |
| Clerk, or some other person as the court may direct | 28 days | Provide notice of time for filing objections to an injunction provided in a chapter 9 or 11 plan | 3017(f)(1) |
| Clerk, or some other person as the court may direct | 28 days | Provide notice of hearing on disclosure statement and objections in a chapter 9 or 11 case | 3017(a) |
| Clerk, or some other person as the court may direct | 21 days | Provide notice by mail of time for filing objections to chapter 11 individual's plan and of hearing on objections | 3019(b) |
| Chapter 9 or 11 parties in interest | 14 days after entry of the order | Stay of order confirming a chapter 9 or 11 plan | 3020(e) |

[4] The time for filing a complaint to revoke a chapter 12 or 13 confirmation order as procured by fraud may be filed any time within 180 days after the date of the entry of the order of confirmation. 11 U.S.C. §§ 1230, 1330.

# Deadlines Throughout the Case

| DEADLINES THROUGHOUT THE CASE | | | |
|---|---|---|---|
| **Entity** | **Deadline** | **Act to Be Performed** | **Rule** |
| Debtor | 14 days after the information comes to the debtor's knowledge | File supplemental schedule disclosing acquisition of property by bequest, devise, inheritance, property settlement agreement, or as a beneficiary of a life insurance policy or death benefit plan | 1007(h) |
| Debtor | At any time before the case is closed | File an amendment of any voluntary petition, list, schedule, or statement | 1009(a) |
| Chapter 7 debtor | 30 days after the date of the filing of the petition, or on or before the date of the meeting of creditors, whichever is earlier | File an amendment to the statement of intention | 1009(b)[5] |
| Chapter 7 debtor | 30 days after the entry of the order of conversion or before the first date set for the meeting of creditors, whichever is earlier | File of a statement of intention after conversion to chapter 7 | 1019(1)(B) |
| Chapter 11 or 12 debtor in possession ("DIP") or trustee in case converted from chapter 7 | 14 days after conversion of the case | File a schedule of unpaid debts incurred after the filing of the petition and before conversion of the case, including the name and address of each holder of a claim | 1019(5)(A)(i) |
| Chapter 11 or 12 DIP or trustee in case converted to chapter 7 | 30 days after conversion of the case | File and transmit to the United States trustee a final report and account | 1019(5)(A)(ii) |
| Chapter 7 debtor in case converted from chapter 13 | 14 days after conversion of the case | File a schedule of unpaid debts incurred after the filing of the petition and before conversion of the case, including the name and address of each holder of a claim | 1019(5)(B)(i) |

[5] *See* 11 U.S.C. § 521(a).

| DEADLINES THROUGHOUT THE CASE | | | |
|---|---|---|---|
| **Entity** | **Deadline** | **Act to Be Performed** | **Rule** |
| Chapter 13 trustee in case converted to chapter 7 | 30 days after conversion of the case | File and transmit to the United States trustee a final report and account | 1019(5)(B)(ii) |
| Chapter 11 parties in interest | 30 days after the conclusion of the § 341(a) meeting or 30 days after any amendment to the statement, whichever is later | File objection to the chapter 11 debtor's designation as a small business debtor | 1020(b) |
| Clerk, or some other person as the court may direct | 21 days | Provide notice by mail of meeting of creditors under § 341 or § 1104(b) | 2002(a)(1) |
| Clerk, or some other person as the court may direct | 21 days | Provide notice by mail of proposed use, sale, or lease of property of the estate other than in the ordinary course of business | 2002(a)(2) |
| Clerk, or some other person as the court may direct | 21 days | Provide notice by mail of hearing on approval of a compromise or settlement of a controversy other than pursuant to Rule 4001(d) | 2002(a)(3) |
| Clerk, or some other person as the court may direct | 21 days | Provide notice by mail of hearing on any entity's request for compensation or reimbursement of expenses in excess of $1,000 | 2002(a)(6) |
| Court in a voluntary chapter 7, 12, or 13 case | After 70 days following the order for relief under that chapter or of the order converting the case to chapter 12 or 13 | Direction by court that all notices required by Rule 2002(a) be mailed only to certain entities | 2002(h)(1) |
| Court in an involuntary chapter 7 case | After 90 days following the order for relief | Direction by court that all notices required by Rule 2002(a) be mailed only to certain entities | 2002(h)(2) |
| Court in a chapter 7 case originally noticed as a no asset case | After 90 days following the mailing of a notice of the time for filing claims | Direction by court that notices be mailed only to specified entities | 2002(h)(3) |

| DEADLINES THROUGHOUT THE CASE | | | |
|---|---|---|---|
| **Entity** | **Deadline** | **Act to Be Performed** | **Rule** |
| United States trustee in a chapter 7 liquidation or chapter 11 reorganization case | Between 21 and 40 days after the order for relief | Call a meeting of creditors, except where a prepetition plan has been accepted | 2003(a) |
| United States trustee in a chapter 12 case | Between 21 and 35 days after the order for relief | Call a meeting of creditors | 2003(a) |
| United States trustee in a chapter 13 case | Between 21 and 50 days after the order for relief | Call a meeting of creditors | 2003(a) |
| United States trustee | 2 years after the conclusion of the meeting of creditors | Period of time to preserve recording of § 341 meeting available for public access | 2003(c) |
| Chapter 7 or 11 trustee or DIP | 30 days after qualifying as a trustee or DIP | File and transmit to the United States trustee a complete inventory of the property of the debtor | 2015(a)(1) |
| Chapter 11 reorganization case trustee or DIP | The last day of the month after each calendar quarter during which there is a duty to pay fees under 28 U.S.C. § 1930(a)(6) | File and transmit to the United States trustee a statement of any disbursements made during that quarter and of any fees payable under 28 U.S.C. § 1930(a)(6) for that quarter | 2015(a)(5) |
| Chapter 11 small business case trustee or DIP | 21 days after the last day of the calendar month fol lowing the month covered by the report | File reports required by § 308 | 2015(a)(6) |
| Chapter 15 foreign representative | 14 days after becoming aware of new information | File notice of a change in status as required under § 1518 | 2015(d) |
| Patient care ombudsman | 14 days prior to making a report under § 333(b)(2) | Notice of a report regarding quality of patient care | 2015.1(a) |
| Patient care ombudsman | No earlier than 14 days after service of the motion | Time of hearing on motion to review confidential patient records | 2015.1(b) |
| Trustee in a health care business case | 14 days | Provide notice to the patient care ombudsman and any family member or contact person of transfer by trustee of a patient to another health care business | 2015.2 |

| DEADLINES THROUGHOUT THE CASE | | | |
|---|---|---|---|
| **Entity** | **Deadline** | **Act to Be Performed** | **Rule** |
| Chapter 11 trustee or DIP | 7 days before the first date set for the § 341 meeting of creditors | File first periodic report of the value, operations, and profitability of each entity that is not a publicly traded corporation or a chapter 11 debtor and in which the estate holds a substantial or controlling interest | 2015.3(b) |
| Chapter 11 trustee or DIP | No less frequently than every six months thereafter, until the effective date of a plan or the case is dismissed or converted | File subsequent periodic reports of the value, operations, and profitability of each entity that is not a publicly traded corporation or a chapter 11 debtor and in which the estate holds a substantial or controlling interest | 2015.3(b) |
| Chapter 11 trustee or DIP | 14 days before filing the first periodic financial report required by this rule | Send notice to the entity in which the estate has a substantial or controlling interest, and to all holders of an interest in that entity, that it expects to file and serve financial information relating to that entity | 2015.3(e) |
| Debtor's attorney | 14 days after any payment or agreement not previously disclosed | File and transmit a supplemental statement of any payment or agreement not previously disclosed | 2016(b) |
| Petition preparer | 14 days after any payment or agreement not previously disclosed | File a supplemental statement of any payment or agreement not previously disclosed | 2016(c) |
| Debtor or trustee | 2 days | Provide notice to party who obtained ex parte stay or § 363(e) relief that adverse party is moving for reinstatement of the stay or reconsideration of the order prohibiting or conditioning the use, sale, or lease of property | 4001(a)(2) |

| DEADLINES THROUGHOUT THE CASE | | | |
|---|---|---|---|
| **Entity** | **Deadline** | **Act to Be Performed** | **Rule** |
| Debtor or creditor | 14 days after entry of the order | Stay of order granting a motion for relief from the automatic stay | 4001(a)(3) |
| Debtor | 14 days after service of the motion | Time of holding final hearing on a motion for authorization to use cash collateral | 4001(b)(2) |
| Debtor | 14 days after service of the motion | Time of holding final hearing on a motion for authority to obtain credit | 4001(c)(2) |
| Parties in interest | 14 days of the mailing of notice of the motion | File objection to agreement to provide relief from the automatic stay; prohibit or condition the use, sale, or lease of property; provide adequate protection; use cash collateral; or obtain credit | 4001(d)(2) |
| Parties in interest | 7 days' notice to required parties | Time of holding hearing on objection to agreement relating to relief from the automatic stay; prohibiting or conditioning the use, sale, or lease of property; adequate protection; use of cash collateral; or for obtaining credit | 4001(d)(3) |
| Individual debtor | 7 days before the first date set for the § 341 meeting of creditors | Provide to the trustee, and to a creditor if requested 14 days before the first date set for the § 341 meeting, a copy of the debtor's federal income tax return for the most recent tax year ending immediately before the commencement of the case and for which a return was filed, or a statement that it does not exist | 4002(b)(3), (4) |
| Dependent of debtor | 30 days after expiration of the Rule 1007 deadline (with the petition or within 14 days thereafter) | File list of property exempt under § 522 when the debtor fails to do so | 4003(a) |

| DEADLINES THROUGHOUT THE CASE | | | |
|---|---|---|---|
| **Entity** | **Deadline** | **Act to Be Performed** | **Rule** |
| Party in interest | 30 days after the meeting of creditors held under § 341(a) is concluded or within 30 days after any amendment to the list or supplemental schedules is filed, whichever is later | File objection to claim of exemption | 4003(b)(1) |
| Trustee | Any time prior to one year after the closing of the case | File objection to claim of exemption on the basis that the debtor fraudulently asserted the claim of exemption | 4003(b)(2) |
| Party in interest | Any time prior to the closing of the case | File objection to a claim of exemption based on § 522(q) | 4003(b)(3) |
| Chapter 7 debtor, creditor | 60 days after the first date set for the § 341(a) meeting of creditors | File reaffirmation agreement | 4008(a) |
| Chapter 15 movant | At least 30 days | Provide notice of any hearing on a motion for approval of an agreement of coordination in chapter 15 | 5012 |
| Court | For the first 21 days of the case, unless granting relief is necessary to avoid immediate and irreparable harm | Time within which court is prohibited from granting relief on applications for the employment of professional persons, motions for the use, sale, or lease of property of the estate other than such a motion under Rule 4001, and motions to assume or assign executory contracts and unexpired leases | 6003(a)–(c) |
| Debtor, trustee | 21 days | Provide notice by mail of proposed use, sale, or lease of property not in the ordinary course of business | 6004(a), incorporating 2002(a)(2) |

| DEADLINES THROUGHOUT THE CASE | | | |
|---|---|---|---|
| **Entity** | **Deadline** | **Act to Be Performed** | **Rule** |
| Party in interest | 7 days before the date set for the proposed action | File and serve objection to a proposed use, sale, or lease of property, except as provided in 6004(c) and (d) | 6004(b) |
| Clerk, or some other person as the court may direct | 21 days | Provide notice of filing and service of a motion for authority to sell property free and clear of liens or other interests not in the ordinary course | 6004(c), incorporating 2002(a)(2) |
| Party in interest | 14 days of the mailing of the notice of intent to sell | File objection to notice of intent to sell property of the estate with an aggregate gross value less than $2,500 | 6004(d) |
| United States trustee | 7 days before the hearing on the motion to sell personally identifiable information | Provide notice of appointment of consumer privacy ombudsman | 6004(g)(2) |
| Creditor | 14 days after entry of the order | Stay of order authorizing the use, sale, or lease of property other than cash collateral | 6004(h) |
| Trustee | 14 days after entry of the order | Stay of order authorizing the trustee to assign an executory contract or unexpired lease under § 365(f) | 6006(d) |
| Party in interest | 14 days of the mailing of the notice | File objection to notice of a proposed abandonment or disposition of property | 6007(a) |
| Trustee | 30 days after the destruction | File report of destruction of patient records under § 351(3) | 6011(d) |
| Movant | 7 days before the time specified for such hearing, unless a different period is fixed by the rules or by order of the court | Serve written motion other than ex parte | 9006(d), 9014(b) |
| Respondent | 1 day before the hearing | File written response to written motion | 9006(d), 9014(b) |

| DEADLINES THROUGHOUT THE CASE | | | |
|---|---|---|---|
| **Entity** | **Deadline** | **Act to Be Performed** | **Rule** |
| Clerk, or some other person as the court may direct | 21 days | Provide notice by mail of hearing on motion by the trustee for approval of compromise or settlement | 9019(a), incorporating 2002(a)(3) |

## Time Periods in Connection with Claims

| TIME PERIODS IN CONNECTION WITH CLAIMS | | | |
|---|---|---|---|
| **Entity** | **Deadline** | **Act to Be Performed** | **Rule** |
| Creditor in a chapter 7, 12, or 13 case | 70 days after the order for relief or order of conversion to chapter 12 or 13 | File proof of claim | 3002(c) |
| Creditor in a chapter 9 or 11 case | As fixed by the court, or under the conditions stated in Rule 3002(c)(2), (c)(3), (c)(4), and (c)(6). | File proof of claim or equity security interest | 3003(c)(3) |
| Creditor in an involuntary chapter 7 case | 90 days after the order for relief | File proof of claim | 3002(c) |
| Governmental unit in a chapter 13 case | 180 days after the date of the order for relief | File proof of claim, other than for a claim resulting from a tax return filed under § 1308 | 3002(c)(1) |
| Governmental unit in a chapter 7, 12, or 13 case | 180 days after the date of the order for relief, or 60 days after the filing of the tax return | File proof of claim resulting from a tax return filed under § 1308 | 3002(c)(1) |
| Unsecured creditor in a chapter 7, 11, 12, or 13 case | 30 days after the judgment becomes final | File proof of claim that arises in favor of an entity or becomes allowable as a result of a judgment, if the judgment is for the recovery of money or property from that entity or denies or avoids the entity's interest in property | 3002(c)(3) |
| Creditor in a chapter 7, 11, 12, or 13 case | Within such time as the court may direct | File proof of claim arising from the rejection of an executory contract or unexpired lease of the debtor | 3002(c)(4) |
| Creditor in a formerly no asset chapter 7 case | Such time as the clerk provides on 90 days' notice by mail | File proof of claim | 3002(c)(5) |
| Holder of a claim secured by the debtor's principal residence in a chapter 7, 12, or 13 case | 70 days after the order for relief | File proof of claim if filed with attachments required by Rule 3001(c)(2)(C) | 3002(c)(7)(A) |

| TIME PERIODS IN CONNECTION WITH CLAIMS | | | |
|---|---|---|---|
| **Entity** | **Deadline** | **Act to Be Performed** | **Rule** |
| Governmental unit | Before expiration of the period for timely filing a proof of claim | File motion to enlarge the time to file proof of claim | 3002(c)(1) |
| Foreign creditor | Before or after the expiration of the time to file proof of claim | File motion to extend the time by not more than 60 days to file proof of claim, where notice of the deadline was insufficient | 3002(c)(6) |
| Creditor in a chapter 7, 12, or 13 case | 30 days after the request is sent | Provide a copy of the writing on which a proof of claim concerning an open-end or revolving consumer credit agreement is based | 3001(c)(3)(B) |
| Holder of a claim secured by the debtor's principal residence | 120 days after the order for relief is entered | File any attachments required by Rule 3001(c)(1), (d) as a supplement to the claim | 3002(c)(7)(B) |
| Debtor or trustee | 30 days after the expiration of the time for filing claims prescribed by Rule 3002(c) or 3003(c), whichever is applicable | File proof of claim when creditor does not timely file proof of claim | 3004 |
| Any entity liable with the debtor to a creditor or that has secured that creditor | 30 days after the expiration of the time for filing claims prescribed by Rule 3002(c) or 3003(c), whichever is applicable | File proof of claim | 3005(a) |
| Administrative claimant | Before conversion or a time fixed by the court if filed by a governmental unit, or within 180 days after the date of conversion or the time fixed by the court, whichever is later | File request for payment incurred before conversion of the case | 1019(6) |
| Party in interest | 30 days before any scheduled hearing on the objection or any deadline for the claimant to request a hearing | File and serve an objection to the allowance of a claim and a notice of objection | 3007(a)(1) |

| TIME PERIODS IN CONNECTION WITH CLAIMS | | | |
|---|---|---|---|
| **Entity** | **Deadline** | **Act to Be Performed** | **Rule** |
| Clerk, or some other person as the court may direct | 21 days | Provide notice of time fixed for filing proofs of claims pursuant to Rule 3003(c) | 2002(a)(7) |
| Clerk, or some other person as the court may direct | 30 days | Provide notice to a creditor with a foreign address of time fixed for filing a proof of claim | 2002(p)(2) |
| Transferor of claim | 21 days after the mailing of the notice of the transfer by the clerk | File objection to the transfer of a claim after the proof of claim was filed | 3001(e)(2), (4) |
| Transferor or transferee | 30 days prior to the hearing | Serve objection and notice of hearing on transferee or transferor of a claim | 3001(e)(5) |
| Holder of a claim secured by security interest in chapter 13 debtor's principal residence | 21 days before a payment in the new amount is due | File notice of any change in payment amount | 3002.1(b) |
| Party in interest | Day before the new amount is due | Object to payment amount change going into effect | 3002.1(b)(2) |
| Holder of a claim secured by security interest in chapter 13 debtor's principal residence | 180 days after the date on which the fees, expenses, or charges are incurred | File and serve notice itemizing all fees, expenses, or charges (1) that were incurred in connection with the claim after the bankruptcy case was filed, and (2) that the holder asserts are recoverable against the debtor or against the debtor's principal residence | 3002.1(c) |
| Party in interest | One year after service of a notice under 3002.1(c) | File motion to determine whether payment of any claimed fee, expense, or charge is required by the underlying agreement and applicable nonbankruptcy law to cure a default or maintain payments in accordance with § 1322(b)(5) | 3002.1(e) |

| TIME PERIODS IN CONNECTION WITH CLAIMS | | | |
|---|---|---|---|
| **Entity** | **Deadline** | **Act to Be Performed** | **Rule** |
| Chapter 13 trustee | 30 days after the debtor completes all payments under the plan | File and serve notice stating that the debtor has paid in full the amount required to cure any default on the claim | 3002.1(f) |
| Holder of a claim secured by security interest in chapter 13 debtor's principal residence | 21 days after service of the notice under Rule 3002.1(f) | File and serve statement indicating (1) whether the holder agrees that the debtor has paid in full the amount required to cure the default on the claim, and (2) whether the debtor is otherwise current on all payments consistent with § 1322(b)(5) | 3002.1(g) |
| Chapter 13 debtor or trustee | 21 days after service of the Rule 3002.1(g) statement | File motion to determine whether the debtor has cured the default and paid all required postpetition amounts to holder of a claim secured by security interest in chapter 13 debtor's principal residence and for which the plan provides for contractual installment payments | 3002.1(h) |

| TIME PERIODS IN CONNECTION WITH ADVERSARY PROCEEDINGS | | | |
|---|---|---|---|
| **Entity** | **Deadline** | **Act to Be Performed** | **Rule** |
| Cross-claim defendant | 21 days after service, unless a motion is filed and denied or postponed, or motion for a more definite statement granted, then 14 days after notice of the court's action | Serve answer to cross-claim | 7012(a) |
| Counterclaim defendant | 21 days after service of the answer, or if a reply is ordered by the court, within 21 days after service of the order, unless a motion is filed and denied or postponed, or motion for a more definite statement granted, then 14 days after notice of the court's action | Serve reply to counterclaim in the answer | 7012(a) |
| United States or an officer or agency as defendant | 35 days after the issuance of the summons of service of the pleading in which the claim is asserted, unless a motion is filed and denied or postponed, or motion for a more definite statement granted, then 14 days after notice of the court's action | Serve answer to complaint, cross-claim, or reply to counterclaim | 7012(a) |
| Plaintiff or defendant | 14 days after the last pleading directed to the issue is served | File and serve written demand for a jury trial | 9015(a), incorporating FRCP 38(b) |
| Plaintiff or defendant | 14 days after being served with the original demand | File and serve demand for a jury trial when one party demanded on only some issues | 9015(a), (b), incorporating FRCP 38(c) |
| Defendant | Before pleading if a responsive pleading is allowed | Serve a motion to dismiss under FRCP 12(b) | 7012, incorporating FRCP 12(b) |
| Plaintiff or defendant | Before filing a responsive pleading | File motion for a more definite statement of a pleading to which responsive pleading allowed | 7012(b), incorporating FRCP 12(e) |

| TIME PERIODS IN CONNECTION WITH ADVERSARY PROCEEDINGS | | | |
|---|---|---|---|
| **Entity** | **Deadline** | **Act to Be Performed** | **Rule** |
| Plaintiff or defendant | 14 days after notice of the order | File more definite statement of a pleading | 7012(b), incorporating FRCP 12(e) |
| Plaintiff or defendant | Before responding to the pleading, or if a response is not allowed, 21 days after being served with the pleading | File motion to strike insufficient defense or any redundant, immaterial, impertinent, or scandalous matter | 7012(b), incorporating FRCP 12(f)(2) |
| Plaintiff or defendant | After the pleadings are closed, but early enough not to delay trial | File motion for judgment on the pleadings | 7012, incorporating FRCP 12(c) |
| Third-party plaintiff | 14 days after serving the original answer, else by leave of court on motion | File third-party summons and complaint on a nonparty | 7014, incorporating FRCP 14(a)(1) |
| Plaintiff or defendant or decedent's successor or representative | 90 days after service of a statement noting the death | File motion for substitution of a party following the death of the party | 7025, incorporating FRCP 25(a)(1) |
| Plaintiff or defendant | 21 days after service of it on the offending party and that party does not withdraw or appropriately correct the challenged paper, claim, defense, contention, allegation, or denial, except if the challenged conduct is the filing of a petition | File motion for Rule 9011 sanctions | 9011(c)(1)(A) |
| Plaintiff or defendant | The longer of 90 days after the order for relief in the case under the Code, 30 days after entry of an order terminating a stay, if the claim or cause of action in a civil action has been stayed under § 362, or 30 days after a trustee qualifies in a chapter 11 reorganization case but not later than 180 days after the order for relief | File notice of removal of a civil action filed prepetition | 9027(a)(2) |

| TIME PERIODS IN CONNECTION WITH ADVERSARY PROCEEDINGS | | | |
|---|---|---|---|
| **Entity** | **Deadline** | **Act to Be Performed** | **Rule** |
| Plaintiff or defendant | The shorter of 30 days after receipt of a copy of the initial pleading setting forth the claim or cause of action sought to be removed, or 30 days after receipt of the summons if the initial pleading has been filed with the court but not served with the summons | Remove a civil action that was filed postpetition | 9027(a)(3) |
| Party who has filed a pleading in connection with the removed claim or cause of action, other than the party filing the notice of removal | 14 days after the filing of the notice of removal | File statement regarding consent to entry of final orders or judgment by the bankruptcy court | 9027(e)(3) |
| Defendant | The longer of 21 days after receiving a copy of the initial pleading stating the claim for relief, 21 days after being served with the summons for an initial pleading on file at the time of service, or 7 days after the notice of removal is filed | Time to answer or present defenses or objections in removed action in which the defendant has not yet answered | 9027(g); 9015(a), incorporating FRCP 81(c)(2) |
| Plaintiff or defendant where all necessary pleadings had been served at the time of removal | 14 days after filing a notice of removal or after being served with a notice of removal filed by another party | Serve demand for jury trial in removed action | 9015(a), incorporating FRCP 81(c)(3)(B) |
| Plaintiff or defendant or deponent | 30 days after availability | Review transcript and submit changes in form or substance | 7030, incorporating FRCP 30(e)(1) |
| Plaintiff | 7 days before the hearing | Serve written notice of application for entry of default judgment by the court when party against whom plaintiff is seeking default judgment has appeared | 7055, incorporating FRCP 55(b)(2) |

| TIME PERIODS IN CONNECTION WITH ADVERSARY PROCEEDINGS | | | |
|---|---|---|---|
| **Entity** | **Deadline** | **Act to Be Performed** | **Rule** |
| Plaintiff or defendant | 30 days before the initial date set for an evidentiary hearing on any issue for which summary judgment is sought | File motion for summary judgment | 7056 |
| Plaintiff or defendant | 14 days from service of the proposed findings of facts or conclusions of law | File and serve written objections to proposed findings of fact and conclusions of law of another party when court not authorized to enter final judgment | 9033(b) |
| Plaintiff or defendant | Before the time for filing objections has expired, except that a request made no more than 21 days after the expiration of the time for filing objections may be granted upon a showing of excusable neglect | File request to extend time, not to exceed 21 days, for filing objections to proposed findings of fact and conclusions of law | 9033(c) |
| Plaintiff or defendant | On 14 days' notice to the clerk; review on motion served within 7 days thereafter | Request for taxing of costs other than attorney's fees | 7054 |
| Plaintiff or defendant | 14 days after its entry | Stay of execution on a judgment and proceedings to enforce it | 7062, incorporating FRCP 62(a) |
| Plaintiff | Not to exceed 14 days after time of entry | Expiration of temporary restraining order issued without notice | 7065, incorporating FRCP 65(b)(2) |
| Enjoined party | On 2 days' notice or on shorter notice set by the court | Appear and move to dissolve TRO by adverse party against whom ex parte TRO was granted | 7065, incorporating FRCP 65(b)(4) |
| Defendant | 14 days before the date set for trial | Make an offer of judgment | 7068, incorporating FRCP 68(a) |
| Plaintiff | 14 days after being served with offer | Serve written notice of acceptance of offer of judgment | 7068, incorporating FRCP 68(a) |
| Defendant | 14 days before the date set for a hearing to determine the extent of liability | Serve offer of judgment after liability determined | 7068, incorporating FRCP 68(c) |

| TIME PERIODS IN CONNECTION WITH ADVERSARY PROCEEDINGS | | | |
|---|---|---|---|
| **Entity** | **Deadline** | **Act to Be Performed** | **Rule** |
| Party against whom judgment as a matter of law is rendered | 28 days after the entry of the judgment | File motion for a new trial under FRCP 59 | 9015(c), incorporating FRCP 50(d) |
| Plaintiff or defendant | 14 days after the entry of the judgment | File renewed motion for judgment or request for a new trial | 9015(c) |
| Plaintiff or defendant or court | 14 days after entry of judgment | File motion for a new trial or to alter or amend a judgment or for a court to order on its own a new trial | 9023, 7052 |
| Plaintiff or defendant | 14 days after being served with the affidavits | Serve affidavits opposing those included in a motion for a new trial | 9023, incorporating FRCP 59(c) |
| Plaintiff or defendant | Within a reasonable time and no more than 1 year after the entry of the judgment or order or the date of the proceeding | File motion for relief from a judgment or order ("reconsideration") under FRCP 60(b)(1)–(3), except for motion to reopen or for reconsideration of an order allowing or disallowing a claim entered without a contest, complaint to revoke discharge in chapter 7, or complaint to revoke order confirming chapter 11, 12, or 13 plan[11] | 9024, incorporating FRCP 60(c) |
| Plaintiff or defendant | Within a reasonable time | File motion for relief from a judgment or order ("reconsideration") under FRCP 60(b)(4)–(6) | 9024, incorporating FRCP 60(c) |

11 *See* 11 U.S.C. §§ 727(e), 1144, 1230, 1330.

# Time Periods in Connection with Discovery

| TIME PERIODS IN CONNECTION WITH DISCOVERY | | | |
|---|---|---|---|
| **Entity** | **Deadline** | **Act to Be Performed** | **Rule** |
| Court | 90 days after any defendant has been served with the complaint or 60 days after any defendant has appeared | Issue scheduling order | 7016, incorporating FRCP 16(b)(2) |
| Defendant | 30 days after being served or joined | Make initial disclosures if first served or joined after the Rule 26(f) conference | 7026, incorporating FRCP 26(a)(1)(D) |
| Plaintiff and defendant | 90 days before the date set for trial or for the case to be ready for trial, or, if the evidence is intended solely to contradict or rebut evidence on the same subject matter identified by another party under Rule 26(a)(2)(B) or (C), within 30 days after the other party's disclosure | Disclose expert testimony | 7026, incorporating FRCP 26(a)(2)(D) |
| Plaintiff and defendant | 30 days before trial | Make pretrial disclosures | 7026, incorporating FRCP 26(a)(3)(B) |
| Plaintiff and defendant | 14 days after pretrial disclosures made | Object to pretrial disclosures | 7026, incorporating FRCP 26(a)(3)(B) |
| Plaintiff and defendant | More than 21 days after the summons and complaint are served on a party | Deliver Rule 34 request (production of documents and things and entry upon land for inspection and other purposes) | 7026, incorporating FRCP 26(d)(2) |
| Plaintiff and defendant | 21 days before a scheduling conference is to be held or a scheduling order is due under Rule 16(b) | Hold initial conference of the parties | 7026, incorporating FRCP 26(f)(1) |
| Plaintiff and defendant | 14 days after the Rule 26(f)(1) conference | Submit report on proposed discovery plan | 7026, incorporating FRCP 26(f)(2) |
| Plaintiff or defendant | 21 days before the hearing date | Provide notice and serve verified petition for deposition to perpetrate testimony | 7027, incorporating FRCP 27(a)(2) |

| TIME PERIODS IN CONNECTION WITH DISCOVERY | | | |
|---|---|---|---|
| **Entity** | **Deadline** | **Act to Be Performed** | **Rule** |
| Plaintiff or defendant | 14 days after being served with the notice and direct questions | Serve written questions to deponent from other parties | 7031, incorporating FRCP 31(a)(5) |
| Plaintiff or defendant | 7 days after being served cross-questions | Serve written re-direct questions to deponent from other parties | 7031, incorporating FRCP 31(a)(5) |
| Plaintiff or defendant | Within 7 days after being served redirect questions | Serve written cross-questions to deponent from other parties | 7031, incorporating FRCP 31(a)(5) |
| Deponent | Within time for serving responsive questions or, if objection to a re-cross question, within 7 days of service | Serve written objections to written questions under Rule 31 | 7032, incorporating FRCP 32(d)(3)(C) |
| Plaintiff or defendant | 30 days after being served | Respond to interrogatories | 7033, incorporating FRCP 33(b)(2) |
| Plaintiff or defendant | 30 days after being served, or if request is delivered under Rule 26(d)(2), within 30 days after the parties' first Rule 26(f) conference | Respond in writing to request for production of documents, electronically stored information, and tangible things, or entering onto land for inspection and other purposes | 7034, incorporating FRCP 34(b)(2)(A) |
| Plaintiff or defendant | 30 days after being served | Serve written answer or objection to request for admissions; otherwise, matter is admitted | 7036, incorporating FRCP 36(a)(3) |
| Target of subpoena | Before the earlier of the time specified for compliance or 14 days after the subpoena is served | Serve written objection to subpoena to produce documents or tangible things or to permit inspection | 9016, incorporating FRCP 45(d)(2)(B) |

# Time Periods in Connection with Appeals[12]

| TIME PERIODS IN CONNECTION WITH APPEALS | | | |
|---|---|---|---|
| **Entity** | **Deadline** | **Act to Be Performed** | **Rule** |
| Plaintiff and defendant | The earlier of the setting out of the judgment in a separate document or 150 days from the entry in the civil docket | Time that judgment is considered entered if a separate document is required | 7058, incorporating FRCP 58(c)(2)(B) |
| Appellant | 14 days after entry, or, if separate document is required, after entry of the judgment, order, or decree set out in a separate document or 150 days after entry of the judgment, order, or decree | File notice of appeal of judgment, order, or decree being appealed, or after disposition of motion to amend, to make additional findings, for a new trial, or for relief under Rule 9024 | 8002(a)(1), (b)(1) |
| Another appellant | 14 days after the date the first notice of appeal was filed, or from the date the first notice is docketed if filed by an inmate confined in an institution | Filing by another party of notice of appeal after one party has filed a timely notice of appeal | 8002(a)(3), (c)(2) |
| Appellant | Within the time to file a notice of appeal, or 21 days after that time if party shows excusable neglect | File motion requesting an extension of time to file a notice of appeal | 8002(d)(1)(B) |
| Appellant | The later of 21 days after the time to file a notice of appeal or 14 days after the order granting the motion to extend time is entered | Limit on time of extension to file notice of appeal | 8002(d)(3) |
| Appellant | 14 days after entry of the order or decree | File notice of leave to appeal from an interlocutory order or decree | 8004(a)(1) |

[12] *See* Fed. R. Bankr. P. 8011(a) for timeliness of filing of documents.

| TIME PERIODS IN CONNECTION WITH APPEALS | | | |
|---|---|---|---|
| **Entity** | **Deadline** | **Act to Be Performed** | **Rule** |
| Appellee | 14 days after the motion is served | File response or opposition to, or cross-motion to, motion for leave to appeal from an interlocutory order or decree | 8004(b)(2) |
| Appellant | 14 days after entry of order requiring that a motion for leave be filed | File leave to appeal from an interlocutory order if appellant filed a notice of appeal without filing a motion for leave | 8004(d) |
| Appellant | 14 days after the order is entered | File petition with circuit clerk for permission to appeal to court of appeals from an order granting or denying class-action certification | 7023, incorporating FRCP 23(f) |
| Appellant or appellee | 30 days after service of notice of the appeal | Elect to have appeal heard by the district court instead of the bankruptcy appellate panel ("BAP") | 8005(a)(2) |
| Appellant or appellee | 14 days after the statement of election is filed | File motion seeking determination of the validity of an election to have appeal heard by the district court instead of the BAP | 8005(c) |
| Appellant, appellee, or the court | 30 days after the effective date under Rule 8002(b) of the first notice of appeal from the judgment, order, or decree for which direct review is sought | File certification in the bankruptcy court for direct appeal to the court of appeals | 8006(b) |
| Appellant, appellee, or the court | 30 days after the effective date under Rule 8002(b) of the first notice of appeal from the judgment, order, or decree for which direct review is sought | File certification in the district court or BAP for direct appeal to the court of appeals | 8006(b) |
| Court | 14 days after the parties' certification | File short supplemental statement about the merits of a certification | 8006(c)(2) |

| TIME PERIODS IN CONNECTION WITH APPEALS | | | |
|---|---|---|---|
| **Entity** | **Deadline** | **Act to Be Performed** | **Rule** |
| Appellant or appellee | 14 days after the court's certification | File supplemental statement in the certifying court regarding the merits of certification of direct review in a court of appeals when request for certification was by the court's own motion | 8006(e)(2) |
| Appellant, appellee, or majority of appellants and appellees | 60 days after the entry of the judgment, order, or decree | File request for certification that the judgment, order, or decree involves a question of law as to which there is no controlling decision of the court of appeals for the circuit or of the Supreme Court of the United States, is a matter of public importance, or is a question of law requiring resolution of conflicting decisions; or that an immediate appeal may materially advance the progress of the case or proceeding in which the appeal is taken | 8006(f)(1) |
| Appellant or appellee | 14 days after the request is served | File response to a Rule 8006(f)(1) request (certification to court of appeals) | 8006(f)(3) |
| Appellant or appellee | 14 days after the request is served or within 60 days after the entry of the judgment, order, or decree, whichever occurs first | File cross-request to a Rule 8006(f)(1) request (certification to court of appeals) | 8006(f)(3) |
| Appellant or appellee | Within 30 days after the date the certification becomes effective under Rule 8006(a) | File with the circuit clerk a request for permission to take a direct appeal to the court of appeals | 8006(g) |
| Appellant | 14 days after notice of appeal becomes effective under Rule 8002 or an order granting leave to appeal is entered | File and serve designation of items to be included in the record on appeal and a statement of issues to be presented | 8009(a)(1)(B) |

| TIME PERIODS IN CONNECTION WITH APPEALS | | | |
|---|---|---|---|
| **Entity** | **Deadline** | **Act to Be Performed** | **Rule** |
| Appellee and cross-appellant | 14 days after being served the record on appeal | File and serve designation of additional items to be included in the record | 8009(a)(2) |
| Cross-appellee | 14 days after service of cross-appellant's designation and statement | File and serve additional items to be included in the record | 8009(a)(3) |
| Appellant | 14 days after the appellant's notice of appeal becomes effective under Rule 8002 or an order granting leave to appeal is entered | Order transcript of parts of the proceedings not already on file and necessary for the appeal, or certificate stating that the party is not ordering a transcript | 8009(b)(1)(A) |
| Cross-appellant | 14 days after the appellant files a copy of the transcript or a certification that the party is not ordering a transcript | Order transcript of such additional parts of the proceedings not already on file and considered necessary for the appeal, or certificate stating that the party is not ordering a transcript | 8009(b)(2) |
| Appellee or cross-appellee | 14 days after the appellant or cross-appellant files a copy of the transcript or a certification that the party is not ordering a transcript | Order transcript of such additional parts of the proceedings not already on file and considered necessary for the appeal | 8009(b)(3) |
| Appellant | 14 days after the appellant's notice of appeal becomes effective under Rule 8002 or an order granting leave to appeal is entered | File statement of evidence when a transcript is unavailable | 8009(c) |
| Appellee | 14 days after being served with the statement | File objections to statement of the evidence by the appellant when a transcript is unavailable | 8009(c) |
| Transcriber | 30 days after receiving the order for a transcript | Complete transcript | 8010(a)(2)(C) |
| Any party | 7 days after service of the motion | File response to a motion for an order or other relief made to the district court or BAP | 8013(a)(3)(A) |

| TIME PERIODS IN CONNECTION WITH APPEALS | | | |
|---|---|---|---|
| **Entity** | **Deadline** | **Act to Be Performed** | **Rule** |
| Movant | 7 days after service of the response | File reply to response to a motion made to the district court or BAP | 8013(a)(3)(B) |
| Party adversely affected by ruling | 7 days after the procedural order is served | File motion to reconsider, vacate, or modify procedural ruling by the district court or BAP | 8013(b) |
| Intervenor | 30 days after the appeal is docketed | File motion to intervene in appeal pending in a district court or BAP | 8013(g) |
| Any party | 7 days after the party is served with the supplement | File response to filing by other party of citation to supplemental authorities | 8014(f) |
| Appellant | 30 days after the docketing of notice that the record has been transmitted or is available electronically | File and serve brief | 8018(a)(1) |
| Appellee | 30 days after service of the appellant's brief | File and serve brief | 8018(a)(2) |
| Appellant | 14 days after service of the appellee's brief and at least 7 days before scheduled argument | File and serve reply brief | 8018(a)(3) |
| Appellant | Within 30 days after the docketing of notice that the record has been transmitted or is available electronically | File and serve principal brief in case in which a cross-appeal is filed | 8016(e)(1) |
| Appellee | 30 days after the appellant's principal brief is served | File and serve principal and response brief in case in which a cross-appeal is filed | 8016(e)(2) |
| Appellant | 30 days after the appellee's principal and response brief is served | File and serve response and reply brief to appellee's principal and response brief in case in which a cross-appeal is filed | 8016(e)(3) |

| TIME PERIODS IN CONNECTION WITH APPEALS | | | |
|---|---|---|---|
| **Entity** | **Deadline** | **Act to Be Performed** | **Rule** |
| Appellee | 14 days after the appellant's response and reply brief is served, but at least 7 days before scheduled argument | File and serve reply brief to appellant's response and reply brief in case in which a cross-appeal is filed | 8016(e)(4) |
| Amici | 7 days after the principal brief of the party being supported is filed, or, if does not support either party, 7 days after the appellant's principal brief is filed | File amicus curiae brief | 8017(a)(6) |
| Amici | 7 days after the motion for rehearing is filed | File amicus curiae brief supporting a motion for rehearing or supporting neither party | 8017(b)(5) |
| Prevailing party | 14 days after entry of judgment on appeal | File itemized and verified bill of appeal costs with the bankruptcy court | 8021(d) |
| Losing party | 14 days after service of the bill of costs | File objection to itemized and verified bill of costs of appeal | 8021(d) |
| Losing party | 14 days after entry of judgment on appeal | File motion for rehearing of appeal by the district court or BAP | 8022(a)(1) |
| Prevailing party | 14 days after entry of judgment | Stay of judgment on appeal | 8025(a) |
| Prevailing party | No more than 30 days after the judgment is entered | Limit on stay of judgment pending appeal to the court of appeals | 8025(b)(2) |

# Federal Rules of Evidence[1]

## ARTICLE I GENERAL PROVISIONS

### Fed. R. Evid. 101. Scope; Definitions.

(a) Scope. These rules apply to proceedings in United States courts. The specific courts and proceedings to which the rules apply, along with exceptions, are set out in Rule 1101.

(b) Definitions. In these rules:

(1) "civil case" means a civil action or proceeding;

(2) "criminal case" includes a criminal proceeding;

(3) "public office" includes a public agency;

(4) "record" includes a memorandum, report, or data compilation;

(5) a "rule prescribed by the Supreme Court" means a rule adopted by the Supreme Court under statutory authority; and

(6) a reference to any kind of written material or any other medium includes electronically stored information.

### Fed. R. Evid. 102. Purpose.

These rules should be construed so as to administer every proceeding fairly, eliminate unjustifiable expense and delay, and promote the development of evidence law, to the end of ascertaining the truth and securing a just determination.

### Fed. R. Evid. 103. Rulings on Evidence.

(a) Preserving a Claim of Error. A party may claim error in a ruling to admit or exclude evidence only if the error affects a substantial right of the party and:

(1) if the ruling admits evidence, a party, on the record:

(A) timely objects or moves to strike; and

(B) states the specific ground, unless it was apparent from the context; or

(2) if the ruling excludes evidence, a party informs the court of its substance by an offer of proof, unless the substance was apparent from the context.

(b) Not Needing to Renew an Objection or Offer of Proof. Once the court rules definitively on the record—either before or at trial—a party need not renew an objection or offer of proof to preserve a claim of error for appeal.

(c) Court's Statement About the Ruling; Directing an Offer of Proof. The court may make any statement about the character or form of the evidence, the objection made, and the ruling. The court may direct that an offer of proof be made in question-and-answer form.

---

[1] As last amended effective December 1, 2020.

(d) Preventing the Jury from Hearing Inadmissible Evidence. To the extent practicable, the court must conduct a jury trial so that inadmissible evidence is not suggested to the jury by any means.

(e) Taking Notice of Plain Error. A court may take notice of a plain error affecting a substantial right, even if the claim of error was not properly preserved.

### Fed. R. Evid. 104. Preliminary Questions.

(a) In General. The court must decide any preliminary question about whether a witness is qualified, a privilege exists, or evidence is admissible. In so deciding, the court is not bound by evidence rules, except those on privilege.

(b) Relevance That Depends on a Fact. When the relevance of evidence depends on whether a fact exists, proof must be introduced sufficient to support a finding that the fact does exist. The court may admit the proposed evidence on the condition that the proof be introduced later.

(c) Conducting a Hearing So That the Jury Cannot Hear It. The court must conduct any hearing on a preliminary question so that the jury cannot hear it if:

(1) the hearing involves the admissibility of a confession;

(2) a defendant in a criminal case is a witness and so requests; or

(3) justice so requires.

(d) Cross-Examining a Defendant in a Criminal Case. By testifying on a preliminary question, a defendant in a criminal case does not become subject to cross-examination on other issues in the case.

(e) Evidence Relevant to Weight and Credibility. This rule does not limit a party's right to introduce before the jury evidence that is relevant to the weight or credibility of other evidence.

### Fed. R. Evid. 105. Limiting Evidence That Is Not Admissible Against Other Parties or for Other Purposes.

If the court admits evidence that is admissible against a party or for a purpose—but not against another party or for another purpose—the court, on timely request, must restrict the evidence to its proper scope and instruct the jury accordingly.

### Fed. R. Evid. 106. Remainder of or Related Writings or Recorded Statements.

If a party introduces all or part of a writing or recorded statement, an adverse party may require the introduction, at that time, of any other part—or any other writing or recorded statement—that in fairness ought to be considered at the same time.

## ARTICLE II JUDICIAL NOTICE

### Fed. R. Evid. 201. Judicial Notice of Adjudicative Facts.

(a) Scope. This rule governs judicial notice of an adjudicative fact only, not a legislative fact.

(b) KINDS OF FACTS THAT MAY BE JUDICIALLY NOTICED. The court may judicially notice a fact that is not subject to reasonable dispute because it:

(1) is generally known within the trial court's territorial jurisdiction; or

(2) can be accurately and readily determined from sources whose accuracy cannot reasonably be questioned.

(c) TAKING NOTICE. The court:

(1) may take judicial notice on its own; or

(2) must take judicial notice if a party requests it and the court is supplied with the necessary information.

(d) TIMING. The court may take judicial notice at any stage of the proceeding.

(e) OPPORTUNITY TO BE HEARD. On timely request, a party is entitled to be heard on the propriety of taking judicial notice and the nature of the fact to be noticed. If the court takes judicial notice before notifying a party, the party, on request, is still entitled to be heard.

(f) INSTRUCTING THE JURY. In a civil case, the court must instruct the jury to accept the noticed fact as conclusive. In a criminal case, the court must instruct the jury that it may or may not accept the noticed fact as conclusive.

## ARTICLE III PRESUMPTIONS IN CIVIL CASES

### Fed. R. Evid. 301. Presumptions in Civil Cases Generally.

In a civil case, unless a federal statute or these rules provide otherwise, the party against whom a presumption is directed has the burden of producing evidence to rebut the presumption. But this rule does not shift the burden of persuasion, which remains on the party who had it originally.

### Fed. R. Evid. 302. Applying State Law to Presumptions in Civil Cases.

In a civil case, state law governs the effect of a presumption regarding a claim or defense for which state law supplies the rule of decision.

## ARTICLE IV RELEVANCE AND ITS LIMITS

### Fed. R. Evid. 401. Test for Relevant Evidence.

Evidence is relevant if:

(a) it has any tendency to make a fact more or less probable than it would be without the evidence; and

(b) the fact is of consequence in determining the action.

### Fed. R. Evid. 402. General Admissibility of Relevant Evidence.

Relevant evidence is admissible unless any of the following provides otherwise:

- the United States Constitution;

- a federal statute;
- these rules; or
- other rules prescribed by the Supreme Court.

Irrelevant evidence is not admissible.

### Fed. R. Evid. 403. Excluding Relevant Evidence for Prejudice, Confusion, Waste of Time, or Other Reasons.

The court may exclude relevant evidence if its probative value is substantially outweighed by a danger of one or more of the following: unfair prejudice, confusing the issues, misleading the jury, undue delay, wasting time, or needlessly presenting cumulative evidence.

### Fed. R. Evid. 404. Character Evidence; Other Crimes, Wrongs or Acts.

(a) CHARACTER EVIDENCE.

(1) *Prohibited Uses.* Evidence of a person's character or character trait is not admissible to prove that on a particular occasion the person acted in accordance with the character or trait.

(2) *Exceptions for a Defendant or Victim in a Criminal Case.* The following exceptions apply in a criminal case:

(A) a defendant may offer evidence of the defendant's pertinent trait, and if the evidence is admitted, the prosecutor may offer evidence to rebut it;

(B) subject to the limitations in Rule 412, a defendant may offer evidence of an alleged victim's pertinent trait, and if the evidence is admitted, the prosecutor may:

(i) offer evidence to rebut it; and

(ii) offer evidence of the defendant's same trait; and

(C) in a homicide case, the prosecutor may offer evidence of the alleged victim's trait of peacefulness to rebut evidence that the victim was the first aggressor.

(3) *Exceptions for a Witness.* Evidence of a witness's character may be admitted under Rules 607, 608, and 609.

(b) OTHER CRIMES, WRONGS, OR ACTS.

(1) *Prohibited Uses.* Evidence of any other crime, wrong, or act is not admissible to prove a person's character in order to show that on a particular occasion the person acted in accordance with the character.

(2) *Permitted Uses.* This evidence may be admissible for another purpose, such as proving motive, opportunity, intent, preparation, plan, knowledge, identity, absence of mistake, or lack of accident.

(3) *Notice in a Criminal Case.* In a criminal case, the prosecutor must:

(A) provide reasonable notice of any such evidence that the prosecutor intends to offer at trial, so that the defendant has a fair opportunity to meet it;

(B) articulate in the notice the permitted purpose for which the prosecutor intends to offer the evidence and the reasoning that supports the purpose; and

(C) do so in writing before trial—or in any form during trial if the court, for good cause, excuses lack of pretrial notice.

**Fed. R. Evid. 405. Methods of Proving Character.**

(a) BY REPUTATION OR OPINION. When evidence of a person's character or character trait is admissible, it may be proved by testimony about the person's reputation or by testimony in the form of an opinion. On cross-examination of the character witness, the court may allow an inquiry into relevant specific instances of the person's conduct.

(b) BY SPECIFIC INSTANCES OF CONDUCT. When a person's character or character trait is an essential element of a charge, claim, or defense, the character or trait may also be proved by relevant specific instances of the person's conduct.

**Fed. R. Evid. 406. Habit; Routine Practice.**

Evidence of a person's habit or an organization's routine practice may be admitted to prove that on a particular occasion the person or organization acted in accordance with the habit or routine practice. The court may admit this evidence regardless of whether it is corroborated or whether there was an eyewitness.

**Fed. R. Evid. 407. Subsequent Remedial Measures.**

When measures are taken that would have made an earlier injury or harm less likely to occur, evidence of the subsequent measures is not admissible to prove:

- negligence;
- culpable conduct;
- a defect in a product or its design; or
- a need for a warning or instruction.

But the court may admit this evidence for another purpose, such as impeachment or—if disputed—proving ownership, control, or the feasibility of precautionary measures.

**Fed. R. Evid. 408. Compromise Offers and Negotiations.**

(a) PROHIBITED USES. Evidence of the following is not admissible—on behalf of any party—either to prove or disprove the validity or amount of a disputed claim or to impeach by a prior inconsistent statement or a contradiction:

(1) furnishing, promising, or offering—or accepting, promising to accept, or offering to accept—a valuable consideration in compromising or attempting to compromise the claim; and

(2) conduct or a statement made during compromise negotiations about the claim—except when offered in a criminal case and when the negotiations related to a claim by a public office in the exercise of its regulatory, investigative, or enforcement authority.

(b) EXCEPTIONS. The court may admit this evidence for another purpose, such as proving a witness's bias or prejudice, negating a contention of undue delay, or proving an effort to obstruct a criminal investigation or prosecution.

**Fed. R. Evid. 409. Offers to Pay Medical and Similar Expenses.** Evidence of furnishing, promising to pay, or offering to pay medical, hospital, or similar expenses resulting from an injury is not admissible to prove liability for the injury.

**Fed. R. Evid. 410. Pleas, Plea Discussions, and Related Statements.**

(a) Prohibited Uses. In a civil or criminal case, evidence of the following is not admissible against the defendant who made the plea or participated in the plea discussions:

(1) a guilty plea that was later withdrawn;

(2) a nolo contendere plea;

(3) a statement made during a proceeding on either of those pleas under Federal Rule of Criminal Procedure 11 or a comparable state procedure; or

(4) a statement made during plea discussions with an attorney for the prosecuting authority if the discussions did not result in a guilty plea or they resulted in a later-withdrawn guilty plea.

(b) Exceptions. The court may admit a statement described in Rule 410(a)(3) or (4):

(1) in any proceeding in which another statement made during the same plea or plea discussions has been introduced, if in fairness the statements ought to be considered together; or

(2) in a criminal proceeding for perjury or false statement, if the defendant made the statement under oath, on the record, and with counsel present.

**Fed. R. Evid. 411. Liability Insurance.**

Evidence that a person was or was not insured against liability is not admissible to prove whether the person acted negligently or otherwise wrongfully. But the court may admit this evidence for another purpose, such as proving a witness's bias or prejudice or proving agency, ownership, or control.

**Fed. R. Evid. 412. Sex-Offense Cases: The Victim's Sexual Behavior or Predisposition.**

(a) Prohibited Uses. The following evidence is not admissible in a civil or criminal proceeding involving alleged sexual misconduct:

(1) evidence offered to prove that a victim engaged in other sexual behavior; or

(2) evidence offered to prove a victim's sexual predisposition.

(b) Exceptions.

(1) *Criminal Cases.* The court may admit the following evidence in a criminal case:

(A) evidence of specific instances of a victim's sexual behavior, if offered to prove that someone other than the defendant was the source of semen, injury, or other physical evidence;

(B) evidence of specific instances of a victim's sexual behavior with respect to the person accused of the sexual misconduct, if offered by the defendant to prove consent or if offered by the prosecutor; and

(C) evidence whose exclusion would violate the defendant's constitutional rights.

(2) *Civil Cases.* In a civil case, the court may admit evidence offered to prove a victim's sexual behavior or sexual predisposition if its probative value substantially outweighs the danger of harm to any victim and of unfair prejudice to any party. The court may admit evidence of a victim's reputation only if the victim has placed it in controversy.

(c) PROCEDURE TO DETERMINE ADMISSIBILITY.

(1) *Motion.* If a party intends to offer evidence under Rule 412(b), the party must:

(A) file a motion that specifically describes the evidence and states the purpose for which it is to be offered;

(B) do so at least 14 days before trial unless the court, for good cause, sets a different time;

(C) serve the motion on all parties; and

(D) notify the victim or, when appropriate, the victim's guardian or representative.

(2) *Hearing.* Before admitting evidence under this rule, the court must conduct an in camera hearing and give the victim and parties a right to attend and be heard. Unless the court orders otherwise, the motion, related materials, and the record of the hearing must be and remain sealed.

(d) DEFINITION OF "VICTIM." In this rule, "victim" includes an alleged victim.

**Fed. R. Evid. 413. Similar Crimes in Sexual-Assault Cases.**

(a) PERMITTED USES. In a criminal case in which a defendant is accused of a sexual assault, the court may admit evidence that the defendant committed any other sexual assault. The evidence may be considered on any matter to which it is relevant.

(b) DISCLOSURE TO THE DEFENDANT. If the prosecutor intends to offer this evidence, the prosecutor must disclose it to the defendant, including witnesses' statements or a summary of the expected testimony. The prosecutor must do so at least 15 days before trial or at a later time that the court allows for good cause.

(c) EFFECT ON OTHER RULES. This rule does not limit the admission or consideration of evidence under any other rule.

(d) DEFINITION OF "SEXUAL ASSAULT." In this rule and Rule 415, "sexual assault" means a crime under federal law or under state law (as "state" is defined in 18 U.S.C. § 513) involving:

(1) any conduct prohibited by 18 U.S.C. chapter 109A;

(2) contact, without consent, between any part of the defendant's body—or an object—and another person's genitals or anus;

(3) contact, without consent, between the defendant's genitals or anus and any part of another person's body;

(4) deriving sexual pleasure or gratification from inflicting death, bodily injury, or physical pain on another person; or

(5) an attempt or conspiracy to engage in conduct described in subparagraphs (1)–(4).

**Fed. R. Evid. 414. Similar Crimes in Child-Molestation Cases.**

(a) Permitted Uses. In a criminal case in which a defendant is accused of child molestation, the court may admit evidence that the defendant committed any other child molestation. The evidence may be considered on any matter to which it is relevant.

(b) Disclosure to the Defendant. If the prosecutor intends to offer this evidence, the prosecutor must disclose it to the defendant, including witnesses' statements or a summary of the expected testimony. The prosecutor must do so at least 15 days before trial or at a later time that the court allows for good cause.

(c) Effect on Other Rules. This rule does not limit the admission or consideration of evidence under any other rule.

(d) Definition of "Child" and "Child Molestation." In this rule and Rule 415:

(1) "child" means a person below the age of 14; and

(2) "child molestation" means a crime under federal law or under state law (as "state" is defined in 18 U.S.C. § 513) involving:

(A) any conduct prohibited by 18 U.S.C. chapter 109A and committed with a child;

(B) any conduct prohibited by 18 U.S.C. chapter 110;

(C) contact between any part of the defendant's body—or an object—and a child's genitals or anus;

(D) contact between the defendant's genitals or anus and any part of a child's body;

(E) deriving sexual pleasure or gratification from inflicting death, bodily injury, or physical pain on a child; or

(F) an attempt or conspiracy to engage in conduct described in subparagraphs (A)–(E).

**Fed. R. Evid. 415. Similar Acts in Civil Cases Involving Sexual Assault or Child Molestation.**

(a) Permitted Uses. In a civil case involving a claim for relief based on a party's alleged sexual assault or child molestation, the court may admit evidence that the party committed any other sexual assault or child molestation. The evidence may be considered as provided in Rules 413 and 414.

(b) Disclosure to the Opponent. If a party intends to offer this evidence, the party must disclose it to the party against whom it will be offered, including witnesses' statements or a summary of the expected testimony. The party must do so at least 15 days before trial or at a later time that the court allows for good cause.

(c) Effect on Other Rules. This rule does not limit the admission or consideration of evidence under any other rule.

## ARTICLE V PRIVILEGES

### Fed. R. Evid. 501. Privilege in General.

The common law—as interpreted by United States courts in the light of reason and experience—governs a claim of privilege unless any of the following provides otherwise:

- the United States Constitution;
- a federal statute; or
- rules prescribed by the Supreme Court.

But in a civil case, state law governs privilege regarding a claim or defense for which state law supplies the rule of decision.

### Fed. R. Evid. 502. Attorney-Client Privilege and Work Product; Limitations on Waiver.

The following provisions apply, in the circumstances set out, to disclosure of a communication or information covered by the attorney-client privilege or work-product protection.

(a) Disclosure Made in a Federal Proceeding or to a Federal Office or Agency; Scope of a Waiver. When the disclosure is made in a federal proceeding or to a federal office or agency and waives the attorney-client privilege or work-product protection, the waiver extends to an undisclosed communication or information in a federal or state proceeding only if:

(1) the waiver is intentional;

(2) the disclosed and undisclosed communications or information concern the same subject matter; and

(3) they ought in fairness to be considered together.

(b) Inadvertent Disclosure. When made in a federal proceeding or to a federal office or agency, the disclosure does not operate as a waiver in a federal or state proceeding if:

(1) the disclosure is inadvertent;

(2) the holder of the privilege or protection took reasonable steps to prevent disclosure; and

(3) the holder promptly took reasonable steps to rectify the error, including (if applicable) following Federal Rule of Civil Procedure 26(b)(5)(B).

(c) Disclosure Made in a State Proceeding. When the disclosure is made in a state proceeding and is not the subject of a state-court order concerning waiver, the disclosure does not operate as a waiver in a federal proceeding if the disclosure:

(1) would not be a waiver under this rule if it had been made in

a federal proceeding; or

(2) is not a waiver under the law of the state where the disclosure occurred.

(d) Controlling Effect of a Court Order. A federal court may order that the privilege or protection is not waived by disclosure connected with the litigation pending before the court—in which event the disclosure is also not a waiver in any other federal or state proceeding.

(e) Controlling Effect of a Party Agreement. An agreement on the effect of disclosure in a federal proceeding is binding only on the parties to the agreement, unless it is incorporated into a court order.

(f) Controlling Effect of This Rule. Notwithstanding Rules 101 and 1101, this rule applies to state proceedings and to federal court-annexed and federal court-mandated arbitration proceedings, in the circumstances set out in the rule. And notwithstanding Rule 501, this rule applies even if state law provides the rule of decision.

(g) Definitions. In this rule:

(1) "attorney-client privilege" means the protection that applicable law provides for confidential attorney-client communications; and

(2) "work-product protection" means the protection that applicable law provides for tangible material (or its intangible equivalent) prepared in anticipation of litigation or for trial.

## ARTICLE VI WITNESSES

### Fed. R. Evid. 601. Competency to Testify in General.

Every person is competent to be a witness unless these rules provide otherwise. But in a civil case, state law governs the witness's competency regarding a claim or defense for which state law supplies the rule of decision.

### Fed. R. Evid. 602. Need for Personal Knowledge.

A witness may testify to a matter only if evidence is introduced sufficient to support a finding that the witness has personal knowledge of the matter. Evidence to prove personal knowledge may consist of the witness's own testimony. This rule does not apply to a witness's expert testimony under Rule 703.

### Fed. R. Evid. 603. Oath or Affirmation to Testify Truthfully.

Before testifying, a witness must give an oath or affirmation to testify truthfully. It must be in a form designed to impress that duty on the witness's conscience.

### Fed. R. Evid. 604. Interpreter.

An interpreter must be qualified and must give an oath or affirmation to make a true translation.

**Fed. R. Evid. 605. Judge's Competency as a Witness.**

The presiding judge may not testify as a witness at the trial. A party need not object to preserve the issue.

**Fed. R. Evid. 606. Juror's Competency as a Witness.**

(a) At the Trial. A juror may not testify as a witness before the other jurors at the trial. If a juror is called to testify, the court must give a party an opportunity to object outside the jury's presence.

(b) During an Inquiry Into the Validity of a Verdict or Indictment.

(1) *Prohibited Testimony or Other Evidence.* During an inquiry into the validity of a verdict or indictment, a juror may not testify about any statement made or incident that occurred during the jury's deliberations; the effect of anything on that juror's or another juror's vote; or any juror's mental processes concerning the verdict or indictment. The court may not receive a juror's affidavit or evidence of a juror's statement on these matters.

(2) *Exceptions.* A juror may testify about whether:

(A) extraneous prejudicial information was improperly brought to the jury's attention;

(B) an outside influence was improperly brought to bear on any juror; or

(C) a mistake was made in entering the verdict on the verdict form.

**Fed. R. Evid. 607. Who May Impeach a Witness.**

Any party, including the party that called the witness, may attack the witness's credibility.

**Fed. R. Evid. 608. A Witness's Character for Truthfulness or Untruthfulness.**

(a) Reputation or Opinion Evidence. A witness's credibility may be attacked or supported by testimony about the witness's reputation for having a character for truthfulness or untruthfulness, or by testimony in the form of an opinion about that character. But evidence of truthful character is admissible only after the witness's character for truthfulness has been attacked.

(b) Specific Instances of Conduct. Except for a criminal conviction under Rule 609, extrinsic evidence is not admissible to prove specific instances of a witness's conduct in order to attack or support the witness's character for truthfulness. But the court may, on cross-examination, allow them to be inquired into if they are probative of the character for truthfulness or untruthfulness of:

(1) the witness; or

(2) another witness whose character the witness being cross-examined has testified about.

By testifying on another matter, a witness does not waive any privilege against self-incrimination for testimony that relates only to the witness's character for truthfulness.

## Fed. R. Evid. 609. Impeachment by Evidence of a Criminal Conviction.

(a) In General. The following rules apply to attacking a witness's character for truthfulness by evidence of a criminal conviction:

(1) for a crime that, in the convicting jurisdiction, was punishable by death or by imprisonment for more than one year, the evidence:

(A) must be admitted, subject to Rule 403, in a civil case or in a criminal case in which the witness is not a defendant; and

(B) must be admitted in a criminal case in which the witness is a defendant, if the probative value of the evidence outweighs its prejudicial effect to that defendant; and

(2) for any crime regardless of the punishment, the evidence must be admitted if the court can readily determine that establishing the elements of the crime required proving—or the witness's admitting—a dishonest act or false statement.

(b) Limit on Using the Evidence After 10 Years. This subdivision (b) applies if more than 10 years have passed since the witness's conviction or release from confinement for it, whichever is later. Evidence of the conviction is admissible only if:

(1) its probative value, supported by specific facts and circumstances, substantially outweighs its prejudicial effect; and

(2) the proponent gives an adverse party reasonable written notice of the intent to use it so that the party has a fair opportunity to contest its use.

(c) Effect of a Pardon, Annulment, or Certificate of Rehabilitation. Evidence of a conviction is not admissible if:

(1) the conviction has been the subject of a pardon, annulment, certificate of rehabilitation, or other equivalent procedure based on a finding that the person has been rehabilitated, and the person has not been convicted of a later crime punishable by death or by imprisonment for more than one year; or

(2) the conviction has been the subject of a pardon, annulment, or other equivalent procedure based on a finding of innocence.

(d) Juvenile Adjudications. Evidence of a juvenile adjudication is admissible under this rule only if:

(1) it is offered in a criminal case;

(2) the adjudication was of a witness other than the defendant;

(3) an adult's conviction for that offense would be admissible to attack the adult's credibility; and

(4) admitting the evidence is necessary to fairly determine guilt or innocence.

(e) Pendency of an Appeal. A conviction that satisfies this rule is admissible even if an appeal is pending. Evidence of the pendency is also admissible.

### Fed. R. Evid. 610. Religious Beliefs or Opinions.

Evidence of a witness's religious beliefs or opinions is not admissible to attack or support the witness's credibility.

### Fed. R. Evid. 611. Mode and Order of Examining Witnesses and Presenting Evidence.

(a) CONTROL BY THE COURT; PURPOSES. The court should exercise reasonable control over the mode and order of examining witnesses and presenting evidence so as to:

(1) make those procedures effective for determining the truth;

(2) avoid wasting time; and

(3) protect witnesses from harassment or undue embarrassment.

(b) SCOPE OF CROSS-EXAMINATION. Cross-examination should not go beyond the subject matter of the direct examination and matters affecting the witness's credibility. The court may allow inquiry into additional matters as if on direct examination.

(c) LEADING QUESTIONS. Leading questions should not be used on direct examination except as necessary to develop the witness's testimony. Ordinarily, the court should allow leading questions:

(1) on cross-examination; and

(2) when a party calls a hostile witness, an adverse party, or a witness identified with an adverse party.

### Fed. R. Evid. 612. Writing Used to Refresh a Witness's Memory.

(a) SCOPE. This rule gives an adverse party certain options when a witness uses a writing to refresh memory:

(1) while testifying; or

(2) before testifying, if the court decides that justice requires the party to have those options.

(b) ADVERSE PARTY'S OPTIONS; DELETING UNRELATED MATTER. Unless 18 U.S.C. § 3500 provides otherwise in a criminal case, an adverse party is entitled to have the writing produced at the hearing, to inspect it, to cross-examine the witness about it, and to introduce in evidence any portion that relates to the witness's testimony. If the producing party claims that the writing includes unrelated matter, the court must examine the writing in camera, delete any unrelated portion, and order that the rest be delivered to the adverse party. Any portion deleted over objection must be preserved for the record.

(c) FAILURE TO PRODUCE OR DELIVER THE WRITING. If a writing is not produced or is not delivered as ordered, the court may issue any appropriate order. But if the prosecution does not comply in a criminal case, the court must strike the witness's testimony or—if justice so requires—declare a mistrial.

### Fed. R. Evid. 613. Witness's Prior Statement.

(a) SHOWING OR DISCLOSING THE STATEMENT DURING EXAMINATION. When examining a witness about the witness's prior statement, a party need not show it or disclose its contents to the witness. But the party must, on request, show it or disclose its contents to an adverse party's attorney.

(b) Extrinsic Evidence of a Prior Inconsistent Statement. Extrinsic evidence of a witness's prior inconsistent statement is admissible only if the witness is given an opportunity to explain or deny the statement and an adverse party is given an opportunity to examine the witness about it, or if justice so requires. This subdivision (b) does not apply to an opposing party's statement under Rule 801(d)(2).

**Fed. R. Evid. 614. Court's Calling or Examining a Witness.**

(a) Calling. The court may call a witness on its own or at a party's request. Each party is entitled to cross-examine the witness.

(b) Examining. The court may examine a witness regardless of who calls the witness.

(c) Objections. A party may object to the court's calling or examining a witness either at that time or at the next opportunity when the jury is not present.

**Fed. R. Evid. 615. Excluding Witnesses.**

At a party's request, the court must order witnesses excluded so that they cannot hear other witnesses' testimony. Or the court may do so on its own. But this rule does not authorize excluding:

(a) a party who is a natural person;

(b) an officer or employee of a party that is not a natural person, after being designated as the party's representative by its attorney;

(c) a person whose presence a party shows to be essential to presenting the party's claim or defense; or

(d) a person authorized by statute to be present.

## ARTICLE VII OPINIONS AND EXPERT TESTIMONY

**Fed. R. Evid. 701. Opinion Testimony by Lay Witnesses.**

If a witness is not testifying as an expert, testimony in the form of an opinion is limited to one that is:

(a) rationally based on the witness's perception;

(b) helpful to clearly understanding the witness's testimony or to determining a fact in issue; and

(c) not based on scientific, technical, or other specialized knowledge within the scope of Rule 702.

**Fed. R. Evid. 702. Testimony by Expert Witnesses.**

A witness who is qualified as an expert by knowledge, skill, experience, training, or education may testify in the form of an opinion or otherwise if:

(a) the expert's scientific, technical, or other specialized knowledge will help the trier of fact to understand the evidence or to determine a fact in issue;

(b) the testimony is based on sufficient facts or data;

(c) the testimony is the product of reliable principles and methods;

and

(d) the expert has reliably applied the principles and methods to the facts of the case.

**Fed. R. Evid. 703. Bases of an Expert's Opinion Testimony.**

An expert may base an opinion on facts or data in the case that the expert has been made aware of or personally observed. If experts in the particular field would reasonably rely on those kinds of facts or data in forming an opinion on the subject, they need not be admissible for the opinion to be admitted. But if the facts or data would otherwise be inadmissible, the proponent of the opinion may disclose them to the jury only if their probative value in helping the jury evaluate the opinion substantially outweighs their prejudicial effect.

**Fed. R. Evid. 704. Opinion on an Ultimate Issue.**

(a) In General—Not Automatically Objectionable. An opinion is not objectionable just because it embraces an ultimate issue.

(b) Exception. In a criminal case, an expert witness must not state an opinion about whether the defendant did or did not have a mental state or condition that constitutes an element of the crime charged or of a defense. Those matters are for the trier of fact alone.

**Fed. R. Evid. 705. Disclosing the Facts or Data Underlying an Expert's Opinion.**

Unless the court orders otherwise, an expert may state an opinion—and give the reasons for it—without first testifying to the underlying facts or data. But the expert may be required to disclose those facts or data on cross-examination.

**Fed. R. Evid. 706. Court-Appointed Expert Witnesses.**

(a) Appointment Process. On a party's motion or on its own, the court may order the parties to show cause why expert witnesses should not be appointed and may ask the parties to submit nominations. The court may appoint any expert that the parties agree on and any of its own choosing. But the court may only appoint someone who consents to act.

(b) Expert's Role. The court must inform the expert of the expert's duties. The court may do so in writing and have a copy filed with the clerk or may do so orally at a conference in which the parties have an opportunity to participate. The expert:

(1) must advise the parties of any findings the expert makes;

(2) may be deposed by any party;

(3) may be called to testify by the court or any party; and

(4) may be cross-examined by any party, including the party that called the expert.

(c) Compensation. The expert is entitled to a reasonable compensation, as set by the court. The compensation is payable as follows:

(1) in a criminal case or in a civil case involving just compensation under the Fifth Amendment, from any funds that are provided by law;

and

(2) in any other civil case, by the parties in the proportion and at the time that the court directs—and the compensation is then charged like other costs.

(d) Disclosing The Appointment to the Jury. The court may authorize disclosure to the jury that the court appointed the expert.

(e) Parties' Choice of Their Own Experts. This rule does not limit a party in calling its own experts.

## ARTICLE VIII HEARSAY

### Fed. R. Evid. 801. Definitions That Apply to This Article; Exclusions from Hearsay.

(a) Statement. "Statement" means a person's oral assertion, written assertion, or nonverbal conduct, if the person intended it as an assertion.

(b) Declarant. "Declarant" means the person who made the statement.

(c) Hearsay. "Hearsay" means a statement that:

(1) the declarant does not make while testifying at the current trial or hearing; and

(2) a party offers in evidence to prove the truth of the matter asserted in the statement.

(d) Statements That Are Not Hearsay. A statement that meets the following conditions is not hearsay:

(1) *A Declarant-Witness's Prior Statement.* The declarant testifies and is subject to cross-examination about a prior statement, and the statement:

(A) is inconsistent with the declarant's testimony and was given under penalty of perjury at a trial, hearing, or other proceeding or in a deposition;

(B) is consistent with the declarant's testimony and is offered:

(i) to rebut an express or implied charge that the declarant recently fabricated it or acted from a recent improper influence or motive in so testifying; or

(ii) to rehabilitate the declarant's credibility as a witness when attacked on another ground; or

(C) identifies a person as someone the declarant perceived earlier.

(2) *An Opposing Party's Statement.* The statement is offered against an opposing party and:

(A) was made by the party in an individual or representative capacity;

(B) is one the party manifested that it adopted or believed to be true;

(C) was made by a person whom the party authorized to make a statement on the subject;

(D) was made by the party's agent or employee on a matter within the scope of that relationship and while it existed; or

(E) was made by the party's coconspirator during and in furtherance of the conspiracy.

The statement must be considered but does not by itself establish the declarant's authority under (C); the existence or scope of the relationship under (D); or the existence of the conspiracy or participation in it under (E).

### Fed. R. Evid. 802. The Rule Against Hearsay.

Hearsay is not admissible unless any of the following provides otherwise:

- a federal statute;
- these rules; or
- other rules prescribed by the Supreme Court.

### Fed. R. Evid. 803. Exceptions to the Rule Against Hearsay—Regardless of Whether the Declarant Is Available as a Witness.

The following are not excluded by the rule against hearsay, regardless of whether the declarant is available as a witness:

(1) *Present Sense Impression.* A statement describing or explaining an event or condition, made while or immediately after the declarant perceived it.

(2) *Excited Utterance.* A statement relating to a startling event or condition, made while the declarant was under the stress of excitement that it caused.

(3) *Then-Existing Mental, Emotional, or Physical Condition.* A statement of the declarant's then-existing state of mind (such as motive, intent, or plan) or emotional, sensory, or physical condition (such as mental feeling, pain, or bodily health), but not including a statement of memory or belief to prove the fact remembered or believed unless it relates to the validity or terms of the declarant's will.

(4) *Statement Made for Medical Diagnosis or Treatment.* A statement that:

(A) is made for—and is reasonably pertinent to—medical diagnosis or treatment; and

(B) describes medical history; past or present symptoms or sensations; their inception; or their general cause.

(5) *Recorded Recollection.* A record that:

(A) is on a matter the witness once knew about but now cannot recall well enough to testify fully and accurately;

(B) was made or adopted by the witness when the matter was fresh in the witness's memory; and

(C) accurately reflects the witness's knowledge.

If admitted, the record may be read into evidence but may be received as an exhibit only if offered by an adverse party.

(6) *Records of a Regularly Conducted Activity*. A record of an act, event, condition, opinion, or diagnosis if:

(A) the record was made at or near the time by—or from information transmitted by—someone with knowledge;

(B) the record was kept in the course of a regularly conducted activity of a business, organization, occupation, or calling, whether or not for profit;

(C) making the record was a regular practice of that activity;

(D) all these conditions are shown by the testimony of the custodian or another qualified witness, or by a certification that complies with Rule 902(11) or (12) or with a statute permitting certification; and

(E) the opponent does not show that the source of information or the method or circumstances of preparation indicate a lack of trustworthiness.

(7) *Absence of a Record of a Regularly Conducted Activity*. Evidence that a matter is not included in a record described in paragraph (6) if:

(A) the evidence is admitted to prove that the matter did not occur or exist;

(B) a record was regularly kept for a matter of that kind; and

(C) the opponent does not show that the possible source of the information or other circumstances indicate a lack of trustworthiness.

(8) *Public Records*. A record or statement of a public office if:

(A) it sets out:

(i) the office's activities;

(ii) a matter observed while under a legal duty to report, but not including, in a criminal case, a matter observed by law-enforcement personnel; or

(iii) in a civil case or against the government in a criminal case, factual findings from a legally authorized investigation; and

(B) the opponent does not show that the source of information or other circumstances indicate a lack of trustworthiness.

(9) *Public Records of Vital Statistics*. A record of a birth, death, or marriage, if reported to a public office in accordance with a legal duty.

(10) *Absence of a Public Record.*[2] Testimony—or a certification under Rule 902—that a diligent search failed to disclose a public record or

---

[2] The 2013 Committee Note states:

Rule 803(10) has been amended in response to Melendez-Diaz v. Massachusetts, 557 U.S. 305 (2009). The *Melendez-Diaz* Court declared that a testimonial certificate could be admitted if the accused is given advance notice and does not timely demand the presence of the official who prepared the certificate. The amendment incorporates, with minor variations, a "notice-and-demand" procedure that was approved by the *Melendez-Diaz* Court. *See* Tex. Code Crim. P. Ann., art. 38.41.

statement if:

(A) the testimony or certification is admitted to prove that

(i) the record or statement does not exist; or

(ii) a matter did not occur or exist, if a public office regularly kept a record or statement for a matter of that kind; and

(B) in a criminal case, a prosecutor who intends to offer a certification provides written notice of that intent at least 14 days before trial, and the defendant does not object in writing within 7 days of receiving the notice—unless the court sets a different time for the notice or the objection.

(11) *Records of Religious Organizations Concerning Personal or Family History*. A statement of birth, legitimacy, ancestry, marriage, divorce, death, relationship by blood or marriage, or similar facts of personal or family history, contained in a regularly kept record of a religious organization.

(12) *Certificates of Marriage, Baptism, and Similar Ceremonies*. A statement of fact contained in a certificate:

(A) made by a person who is authorized by a religious organization or by law to perform the act certified;

(B) attesting that the person performed a marriage or similar ceremony or administered a sacrament; and

(C) purporting to have been issued at the time of the act or within a reasonable time after it.

(13) *Family Records*. A statement of fact about personal or family history contained in a family record, such as a Bible, genealogy, chart, engraving on a ring, inscription on a portrait, or engraving on an urn or burial marker.

(14) *Records of Documents That Affect an Interest in Property*. The record of a document that purports to establish or affect an interest in property if:

(A) the record is admitted to prove the content of the original recorded document, along with its signing and its delivery by each person who purports to have signed it;

(B) the record is kept in a public office; and

(C) a statute authorizes recording documents of that kind in that office.

(15) *Statements in Documents That Affect an Interest in Property*. A statement contained in a document that purports to establish or affect an interest in property if the matter stated was relevant to the document's purpose—unless later dealings with the property are inconsistent with the truth of the statement or the purport of the document.

(16) *Statements in Ancient Documents*. A statement in a document that was prepared before January 1, 1998, and whose authenticity is established.

(17) *Market Reports and Similar Commercial Publications.* Market quotations, lists, directories, or other compilations that are generally relied on by the public or by persons in particular occupations.

(18) *Statements in Learned Treatises, Periodicals, or Pamphlets.* A statement contained in a treatise, periodical, or pamphlet if:

(A) the statement is called to the attention of an expert witness on cross-examination or relied on by the expert on direct examination; and

(B) the publication is established as a reliable authority by the expert's admission or testimony, by another expert's testimony, or by judicial notice.

If admitted, the statement may be read into evidence but not received as an exhibit.

(19) *Reputation Concerning Personal or Family History.* A reputation among a person's family by blood, adoption, or marriage—or among a person's associates or in the community—concerning the person's birth, adoption, legitimacy, ancestry, marriage, divorce, death, relationship by blood, adoption, or marriage, or similar facts of personal or family history.

(20) *Reputation Concerning Boundaries or General History.* A reputation in a community—arising before the controversy—concerning boundaries of land in the community or customs that affect the land, or concerning general historical events important to that community, state, or nation.

(21) *Reputation Concerning Character.* A reputation among a person's associates or in the community concerning the person's character.

(22) *Judgment of a Previous Conviction.* Evidence of a final judgment of conviction if:

(A) the judgment was entered after a trial or guilty plea, but not a nolo contendere plea;

(B) the conviction was for a crime punishable by death or by imprisonment for more than a year;

(C) the evidence is admitted to prove any fact essential to the judgment; and

(D) when offered by the prosecutor in a criminal case for a purpose other than impeachment, the judgment was against the defendant.

The pendency of an appeal may be shown but does not affect admissibility.

(23) *Judgments Involving Personal, Family, or General History, or a Boundary.* A judgment that is admitted to prove a matter of personal, family, or general history, or boundaries, if the matter:

(A) was essential to the judgment; and

(B) could be proved by evidence of reputation.

(24) [*Other Exceptions.*] [Transferred to Rule 807.]

## Fed. R. Evid. 804. Exceptions to the Rule Against Hearsay—When the Declarant Is Unavailable as a Witness.

(a) Criteria for Being Unavailable. A declarant is considered to be unavailable as a witness if the declarant:

(1) is exempted from testifying about the subject matter of the declarant's statement because the court rules that a privilege applies;

(2) refuses to testify about the subject matter despite a court order to do so;

(3) testifies to not remembering the subject matter;

(4) cannot be present or testify at the trial or hearing because of death or a then-existing infirmity, physical illness, or mental illness; or

(5) is absent from the trial or hearing and the statement's proponent has not been able, by process or other reasonable means, to procure:

(A) the declarant's attendance, in the case of a hearsay exception under Rule 804(b)(1) or (6); or

(B) the declarant's attendance or testimony, in the case of a hearsay exception under Rule 804(b)(2), (3), or (4).

But this subdivision (a) does not apply if the statement's proponent procured or wrongfully caused the declarant's unavailability as a witness in order to prevent the declarant from attending or testifying.

(b) The Exceptions. The following are not excluded by the rule against hearsay if the declarant is unavailable as a witness:

(1) *Former Testimony.* Testimony that:

(A) was given as a witness at a trial, hearing, or lawful deposition, whether given during the current proceeding or a different one; and

(B) is now offered against a party who had—or, in a civil case, whose predecessor in interest had—an opportunity and similar motive to develop it by direct, cross-, or redirect examination.

(2) *Statement Under the Belief of Imminent Death.* In a prosecution for homicide or in a civil case, a statement that the declarant, while believing the declarant's death to be imminent, made about its cause or circumstances.

(3) *Statement Against Interest.* A statement that:

(A) a reasonable person in the declarant's position would have made only if the person believed it to be true because, when made, it was so contrary to the declarant's proprietary or pecuniary interest or had so great a tendency to invalidate the declarant's claim against someone else or to expose the declarant to civil or criminal liability; and

(B) is supported by corroborating circumstances that clearly indicate its trustworthiness, if it is offered in a criminal case as one that tends to expose the declarant to criminal liability.

(4) *Statement of Personal or Family History.* A statement about:

(A) the declarant's own birth, adoption, legitimacy, ancestry, marriage, divorce, relationship by blood, adoption, or marriage, or similar facts of personal or family history, even though the declarant had no way of acquiring personal knowledge about that fact; or

(B) another person concerning any of these facts, as well as death, if the declarant was related to the person by blood, adoption, or marriage or was so intimately associated with the person's family that the declarant's information is likely to be accurate.

(5) [*Other Exceptions.*] [Transferred to Rule 807.]

(6) *Statement Offered Against a Party That Wrongfully Caused the Declarant's Unavailability.* A statement offered against a party that wrongfully caused—or acquiesced in wrongfully causing—the declarant's unavailability as a witness, and did so intending that result.

### Fed. R. Evid. 805. Hearsay Within Hearsay.

Hearsay within hearsay is not excluded by the rule against hearsay if each part of the combined statements conforms with an exception to the rule.

### Fed. R. Evid. 806. Attacking and Supporting the Declarant's Credibility.

When a hearsay statement—or a statement described in Rule 801(d)(2)(C), (D), or (E)—has been admitted in evidence, the declarant's credibility may be attacked, and then supported, by any evidence that would be admissible for those purposes if the declarant had testified as a witness. The court may admit evidence of the declarant's inconsistent statement or conduct, regardless of when it occurred or whether the declarant had an opportunity to explain or deny it. If the party against whom the statement was admitted calls the declarant as a witness, the party may examine the declarant on the statement as if on cross-examination.

### Fed. R. Evid. 807. Residual Exception.

(a) In General. Under the following conditions, a hearsay statement is not excluded by the rule against hearsay even if the statement is not admissible under a hearsay exception in Rule 803 or 804:

(1) the statement is supported by sufficient guarantees of trustworthiness—after considering the totality of circumstances under which it was made and evidence, if any, corroborating the statement; and

(2) it is more probative on the point for which it is offered than any other evidence that the proponent can obtain through reasonable efforts.

(b) Notice. The statement is admissible only if the proponent gives an adverse party reasonable notice of the intent to offer the statement—including its substance and the declarant's name—so that the party has a fair opportunity to meet it. The notice must be provided in writing before the trial or hearing—or in any form during the trial or hearing if the court, for good cause, excuses a lack of earlier notice.

## ARTICLE IX AUTHENTICATION AND IDENTIFICATION

### Fed. R. Evid. 901. Authenticating or Identifying Evidence.

(a) IN GENERAL. To satisfy the requirement of authenticating or identifying an item of evidence, the proponent must produce evidence sufficient to support a finding that the item is what the proponent claims it is.

(b) EXAMPLES. The following are examples only—not a complete list—of evidence that satisfies the requirement:

(1) *Testimony of a Witness with Knowledge.* Testimony that an item is what it is claimed to be.

(2) *Nonexpert Opinion About Handwriting.* A nonexpert's opinion that handwriting is genuine, based on a familiarity with it that was not acquired for the current litigation.

(3) *Comparison by an Expert Witness or the Trier of Fact.* A comparison with an authenticated specimen by an expert witness or the trier of fact.

(4) *Distinctive Characteristics and the Like.* The appearance, contents, substance, internal patterns, or other distinctive characteristics of the item, taken together with all the circumstances.

(5) *Opinion About a Voice.* An opinion identifying a person's voice—whether heard firsthand or through mechanical or electronic transmission or recording—based on hearing the voice at any time under circumstances that connect it with the alleged speaker.

(6) *Evidence About a Telephone Conversation.* For a telephone conversation, evidence that a call was made to the number assigned at the time to:

(A) a particular person, if circumstances, including self-identification, show that the person answering was the one called; or

(B) a particular business, if the call was made to a business and the call related to business reasonably transacted over the telephone.

(7) *Evidence About Public Records.* Evidence that:

(A) a document was recorded or filed in a public office as authorized by law; or

(B) a purported public record or statement is from the office where items of this kind are kept.

(8) *Evidence About Ancient Documents or Data Compilations.* For a document or data compilation, evidence that it:

(A) is in a condition that creates no suspicion about its authenticity;

(B) was in a place where, if authentic, it would likely be; and

(C) is at least 20 years old when offered.

(9) *Evidence About a Process or System.* Evidence describing a process or system and showing that it produces an accurate result.

(10) *Methods Provided by a Statute or Rule.* Any method of authentication or identification allowed by a federal statute or a rule prescribed by the Supreme Court.

**Fed. R. Evid. 902. Evidence That Is Self-Authenticating.** The following items of evidence are self-authenticating; they require no extrinsic evidence of authenticity in order to be admitted:

(1) *Domestic Public Documents That Are Sealed and Signed.* A document that bears:

(A) a seal purporting to be that of the United States; any state, district, commonwealth, territory, or insular possession of the United States; the former Panama Canal Zone; the Trust Territory of the Pacific Islands; a political subdivision of any of these entities; or a department, agency, or officer of any entity named above; and

(B) a signature purporting to be an execution or attestation.

(2) *Domestic Public Documents That Are Not Sealed but Are Signed and Certified.* A document that bears no seal if:

(A) it bears the signature of an officer or employee of an entity named in Rule 902(1)(A); and

(B) another public officer who has a seal and official duties within that same entity certifies under seal—or its equivalent—that the signer has the official capacity and that the signature is genuine.

(3) *Foreign Public Documents.* A document that purports to be signed or attested by a person who is authorized by a foreign country's law to do so. The document must be accompanied by a final certification that certifies the genuineness of the signature and official position of the signer or attester—or of any foreign official whose certificate of genuineness relates to the signature or attestation or is in a chain of certificates of genuineness relating to the signature or attestation. The certification may be made by a secretary of a United States embassy or legation; by a consul general, vice consul, or consular agent of the United States; or by a diplomatic or consular official of the foreign country assigned or accredited to the United States. If all parties have been given a reasonable opportunity to investigate the document's authenticity and accuracy, the court may, for good cause, either:

(A) order that it be treated as presumptively authentic without final certification; or

(B) allow it to be evidenced by an attested summary with or without final certification.

(4) *Certified Copies of Public Records.* A copy of an official record—or a copy of a document that was recorded or filed in a public office as authorized by law—if the copy is certified as correct by:

(A) the custodian or another person authorized to make the certification; or

(B) a certificate that complies with Rule 902(1), (2), or (3), a federal statute, or a rule prescribed by the Supreme Court.

(5) *Official Publications.* A book, pamphlet, or other publication purporting to be issued by a public authority.

(6) *Newspapers and Periodicals.* Printed material purporting to be a newspaper or periodical.

(7) *Trade Inscriptions and the Like.* An inscription, sign, tag, or label purporting to have been affixed in the course of business and indicating origin, ownership, or control.

(8) *Acknowledged Documents.* A document accompanied by a certificate of acknowledgment that is lawfully executed by a notary public or another officer who is authorized to take acknowledgments.

(9) *Commercial Paper and Related Documents.* Commercial paper, a signature on it, and related documents, to the extent allowed by general commercial law.

(10) *Presumptions Under a Federal Statute.* A signature, document, or anything else that a federal statute declares to be presumptively or prima facie genuine or authentic.

(11) *Certified Domestic Records of a Regularly Conducted Activity.* The original or a copy of a domestic record that meets the requirements of Rule 803(6)(A)–(C), as shown by a certification of the custodian or another qualified person that complies with a federal statute or a rule prescribed by the Supreme Court. Before the trial or hearing, the proponent must give an adverse party reasonable written notice of the intent to offer the record—and must make the record and certification available for inspection—so that the party has a fair opportunity to challenge them.

(12) *Certified Foreign Records of a Regularly Conducted Activity.* In a civil case, the original or a copy of a foreign record that meets the requirements of Rule 902(11), modified as follows: the certification, rather than complying with a federal statute or Supreme Court rule, must be signed in a manner that, if falsely made, would subject the maker to a criminal penalty in the country where the certification is signed. The proponent must also meet the notice requirements of Rule 902(11).

(13) *Certified Records Generated by an Electronic Process or System.* A record generated by an electronic process or system that produces an accurate result, as shown by a certification of a qualified person that complies with the certification requirements of Rule 902(11) or (12). The proponent must also meet the notice requirements of Rule 902(11).

(14) *Certified Data Copied from an Electronic Device, Storage Medium, or File.* Data copied from an electronic device, storage medium, or file, if authenticated by a process of digital identification, as shown by a certification of a qualified person that complies with the certification requirements of Rule 902(11) or (12). The proponent must meet the notice requirements of Rule 902(11).

**Fed. R. Evid. 903. Subscribing Witness's Testimony.**

A subscribing witness's testimony is necessary to authenticate a writing only if required by the law of the jurisdiction that governs its validity.

## ARTICLE X CONTENTS OF WRITINGS, RECORDINGS, AND PHOTOGRAPHS

**Fed. R. Evid. 1001. Definitions That Apply to This Article.**

In this article:

(a) A "writing" consists of letters, words, numbers, or their equivalent set down in any form.

(b) A "recording" consists of letters, words, numbers, or their equivalent recorded in any manner.

(c) A "photograph" means a photographic image or its equivalent stored in any form.

(d) An "original" of a writing or recording means the writing or recording itself or any counterpart intended to have the same effect by the person who executed or issued it. For electronically stored information, "original" means any printout—or other output readable by sight—if it accurately reflects the information. An "original" of a photograph includes the negative or a print from it.

(e) A "duplicate" means a counterpart produced by a mechanical, photographic, chemical, electronic, or other equivalent process or technique that accurately reproduces the original.

**Fed. R. Evid. 1002. Requirement of the Original.**

An original writing, recording, or photograph is required in order to prove its content unless these rules or a federal statute provides otherwise.

**Fed. R. Evid. 1003. Admissibility of Duplicates.**

A duplicate is admissible to the same extent as the original unless a genuine question is raised about the original's authenticity or the circumstances make it unfair to admit the duplicate.

**Fed. R. Evid. 1004. Admissibility of Other Evidence of Content.**

An original is not required and other evidence of the content of a writing, recording, or photograph is admissible if:

(a) all the originals are lost or destroyed, and not by the proponent acting in bad faith;

(b) an original cannot be obtained by any available judicial process;

(c) the party against whom the original would be offered had control of the original; was at that time put on notice, by pleadings or otherwise, that the original would be a subject of proof at the trial or hearing; and fails to produce it at the trial or hearing; or

(d) the writing, recording, or photograph is not closely related to a controlling issue.

**Fed. R. Evid. 1005. Copies of Public Records to Prove Content.**
The proponent may use a copy to prove the content of an official record—or of a document that was recorded or filed in a public office as authorized by law—if these conditions are met: the record or document is otherwise admissible; and the copy is certified as correct in accordance with Rule 902(4) or is testified to be correct by a witness who has compared it with the original. If no such copy can be obtained by reasonable diligence, then the proponent may use other evidence to prove the content.

**Fed. R. Evid. 1006. Summaries to Prove Content.**
The proponent may use a summary, chart, or calculation to prove the content of voluminous writings, recordings, or photographs that cannot be conveniently examined in court. The proponent must make the originals or duplicates available for examination or copying, or both, by other parties at a reasonable time and place. And the court may order the proponent to produce them in court.

**Fed. R. Evid. 1007. Testimony or Statement of a Party to Prove Content.**
The proponent may prove the content of a writing, recording, or photograph by the testimony, deposition, or written statement of the party against whom the evidence is offered. The proponent need not account for the original.

**Fed. R. Evid. 1008. Functions of the Court and Jury.**
Ordinarily, the court determines whether the proponent has fulfilled the factual conditions for admitting other evidence of the content of a writing, recording, or photograph under Rule 1004 or 1005. But in a jury trial, the jury determines—in accordance with Rule 104(b)—any issue about whether:

(a) an asserted writing, recording, or photograph ever existed;

(b) another one produced at the trial or hearing is the original; or

(c) other evidence of content accurately reflects the content.

## ARTICLE XI MISCELLANEOUS RULES

**Fed. R. Evid. 1101. Applicability of the Rules.**

(a) To Courts and Judges. These rules apply to proceedings before:

- United States district courts;
- United States bankruptcy and magistrate judges;
- United States courts of appeals;
- the United States Court of Federal Claims; and
- the district courts of Guam, the Virgin Islands, and the Northern Mariana Islands.

(b) To Cases and Proceedings. These rules apply in:

- civil cases and proceedings, including bankruptcy, admiralty, and maritime cases;

- criminal cases and proceedings; and
- contempt proceedings, except those in which the court may act summarily.

(c) Rules on Privilege. The rules on privilege apply to all stages of a case or proceeding.

(d) Exceptions. These rules—except for those on privilege—do not apply to the following:

(1) the court's determination, under Rule 104(a), on a preliminary question of fact governing admissibility;

(2) grand-jury proceedings; and

(3) miscellaneous proceedings such as:

- extradition or rendition;
- issuing an arrest warrant, criminal summons, or search warrant;
- a preliminary examination in a criminal case;
- sentencing;
- granting or revoking probation or supervised release; and
- considering whether to release on bail or otherwise.

(e) Other Statutes and Rules. A federal statute or a rule prescribed by the Supreme Court may provide for admitting or excluding evidence independently from these rules.

**Fed. R. Evid. 1102. Amendments.**

These rules may be amended as provided in 28 U.S.C. § 2072.

**Fed. R. Evid. 1103. Title.**

These rules may be cited as the Federal Rules of Evidence.

# INDEX

[References are to Code Sections of U.S.C. Title 11 and Bankruptcy Rules (Ex. R7030). References to other U.S.C. titles are cited, for example, as 28 U.S.C. 1334, and references to Public Laws are cited, for example, as 106-518 §501. Title 28 materials are located in the Judicial section.]

## A

[References are to Code Sections of U.S.C. Title 11 and Bankruptcy Rules (Ex. R7030). References to other U.S.C. titles are cited, for example, as 28 U.S.C. 1334, and references to Public Laws are cited, for example, as 106-518 §501. Title 28 materials are located in the Judicial section.]

[References are to Code Sections of U.S.C. Title 11 and Bankruptcy Rules (Ex. R7030). References to other U.S.C. titles are cited, for example, as 28 U.S.C. 1334, and references to Public Laws are cited, for example, as 106-518 §501. Title 28 materials are located in the Judicial section.]

[References are to Code Sections of U.S.C. Title 11 and Bankruptcy Rules (Ex. R7030). References to other U.S.C. titles are cited, for example, as 28 U.S.C. 1334, and references to Public Laws are cited, for example, as 106-518 §501. Title 28 materials are located in the Judicial section.]

[References are to Code Sections of U.S.C. Title 11 and Bankruptcy Rules (Ex. R7030). References to other U.S.C. titles are cited, for example, as 28 U.S.C. 1334, and references to Public Laws are cited, for example, as 106-518 §501. Title 28 materials are located in the Judicial section.]

[References are to Code Sections of U.S.C. Title 11 and Bankruptcy Rules (Ex. R7030). References to other U.S.C. titles are cited, for example, as 28 U.S.C. 1334, and references to Public Laws are cited, for example, as 106-518 §501. Title 28 materials are located in the Judicial section.]

[References are to Code Sections of U.S.C. Title 11 and Bankruptcy Rules (Ex. R7030). References to other U.S.C. titles are cited, for example, as 28 U.S.C. 1334, and references to Public Laws are cited, for example, as 106-518 §501. Title 28 materials are located in the Judicial section.]

[References are to Code Sections of U.S.C. Title 11 and Bankruptcy Rules (Ex. R7030). References to other U.S.C. titles are cited, for example, as 28 U.S.C. 1334, and references to Public Laws are cited, for example, as 106-518 §501. Title 28 materials are located in the Judicial section.]

[References are to Code Sections of U.S.C. Title 11 and Bankruptcy Rules (Ex. R7030). References to other U.S.C. titles are cited, for example, as 28 U.S.C. 1334, and references to Public Laws are cited, for example, as 106-518 §501. Title 28 materials are located in the Judicial section.]

[References are to Code Sections of U.S.C. Title 11 and Bankruptcy Rules (Ex. R7030). References to other U.S.C. titles are cited, for example, as 28 U.S.C. 1334, and references to Public Laws are cited, for example, as 106-518 §501. Title 28 materials are located in the Judicial section.]

[References are to Code Sections of U.S.C. Title 11 and Bankruptcy Rules (Ex. R7030). References to other U.S.C. titles are cited, for example, as 28 U.S.C. 1334, and references to Public Laws are cited, for example, as 106-518 §501. Title 28 materials are located in the Judicial section.]

[References are to Code Sections of U.S.C. Title 11 and Bankruptcy Rules (Ex. R7030). References to other U.S.C. titles are cited, for example, as 28 U.S.C. 1334, and references to Public Laws are cited, for example, as 106-518 §501. Title 28 materials are located in the Judicial section.]

[References are to Code Sections of U.S.C. Title 11 and Bankruptcy Rules (Ex. R7030). References to other U.S.C. titles are cited, for example, as 28 U.S.C. 1334, and references to Public Laws are cited, for example, as 106-518 §501. Title 28 materials are located in the Judicial section.]



# C

[References are to Code Sections of U.S.C. Title 11 and Bankruptcy Rules (Ex. R7030). References to other U.S.C. titles are cited, for example, as 28 U.S.C. 1334, and references to Public Laws are cited, for example, as 106-518 §501. Title 28 materials are located in the Judicial section.]

[References are to Code Sections of U.S.C. Title 11 and Bankruptcy Rules (Ex. R7030). References to other U.S.C. titles are cited, for example, as 28 U.S.C. 1334, and references to Public Laws are cited, for example, as 106-518 §501. Title 28 materials are located in the Judicial section.]

[References are to Code Sections of U.S.C. Title 11 and Bankruptcy Rules (Ex. R7030). References to other U.S.C. titles are cited, for example, as 28 U.S.C. 1334, and references to Public Laws are cited, for example, as 106-518 §501. Title 28 materials are located in the Judicial section.]

[References are to Code Sections of U.S.C. Title 11 and Bankruptcy Rules (Ex. R7030). References to other U.S.C. titles are cited, for example, as 28 U.S.C. 1334, and references to Public Laws are cited, for example, as 106-518 §501. Title 28 materials are located in the Judicial section.]

[References are to Code Sections of U.S.C. Title 11 and Bankruptcy Rules (Ex. R7030). References to other U.S.C. titles are cited, for example, as 28 U.S.C. 1334, and references to Public Laws are cited, for example, as 106-518 §501. Title 28 materials are located in the Judicial section.]

[References are to Code Sections of U.S.C. Title 11 and Bankruptcy Rules (Ex. R7030). References to other U.S.C. titles are cited, for example, as 28 U.S.C. 1334, and references to Public Laws are cited, for example, as 106-518 §501. Title 28 materials are located in the Judicial section.]

[References are to Code Sections of U.S.C. Title 11 and Bankruptcy Rules (Ex. R7030). References to other U.S.C. titles are cited, for example, as 28 U.S.C. 1334, and references to Public Laws are cited, for example, as 106-518 §501. Title 28 materials are located in the Judicial section.]

[References are to Code Sections of U.S.C. Title 11 and Bankruptcy Rules (Ex. R7030). References to other U.S.C. titles are cited, for example, as 28 U.S.C. 1334, and references to Public Laws are cited, for example, as 106-518 §501. Title 28 materials are located in the Judicial section.]

[References are to Code Sections of U.S.C. Title 11 and Bankruptcy Rules (Ex. R7030). References to other U.S.C. titles are cited, for example, as 28 U.S.C. 1334, and references to Public Laws are cited, for example, as 106-518 §501. Title 28 materials are located in the Judicial section.]

[References are to Code Sections of U.S.C. Title 11 and Bankruptcy Rules (Ex. R7030). References to other U.S.C. titles are cited, for example, as 28 U.S.C. 1334, and references to Public Laws are cited, for example, as 106-518 §501. Title 28 materials are located in the Judicial section.]

[References are to Code Sections of U.S.C. Title 11 and Bankruptcy Rules (Ex. R7030). References to other U.S.C. titles are cited, for example, as 28 U.S.C. 1334, and references to Public Laws are cited, for example, as 106-518 §501. Title 28 materials are located in the Judicial section.]

[References are to Code Sections of U.S.C. Title 11 and Bankruptcy Rules (Ex. R7030). References to other U.S.C. titles are cited, for example, as 28 U.S.C. 1334, and references to Public Laws are cited, for example, as 106-518 §501. Title 28 materials are located in the Judicial section.]

[References are to Code Sections of U.S.C. Title 11 and Bankruptcy Rules (Ex. R7030). References to other U.S.C. titles are cited, for example, as 28 U.S.C. 1334, and references to Public Laws are cited, for example, as 106-518 §501. Title 28 materials are located in the Judicial section.]

[References are to Code Sections of U.S.C. Title 11 and Bankruptcy Rules (Ex. R7030). References to other U.S.C. titles are cited, for example, as 28 U.S.C. 1334, and references to Public Laws are cited, for example, as 106-518 §501. Title 28 materials are located in the Judicial section.]

[References are to Code Sections of U.S.C. Title 11 and Bankruptcy Rules (Ex. R7030). References to other U.S.C. titles are cited, for example, as 28 U.S.C. 1334, and references to Public Laws are cited, for example, as 106-518 §501. Title 28 materials are located in the Judicial section.]

[References are to Code Sections of U.S.C. Title 11 and Bankruptcy Rules (Ex. R7030). References to other U.S.C. titles are cited, for example, as 28 U.S.C. 1334, and references to Public Laws are cited, for example, as 106-518 §501. Title 28 materials are located in the Judicial section.]

[References are to Code Sections of U.S.C. Title 11 and Bankruptcy Rules (Ex. R7030). References to other U.S.C. titles are cited, for example, as 28 U.S.C. 1334, and references to Public Laws are cited, for example, as 106-518 §501. Title 28 materials are located in the Judicial section.]

[References are to Code Sections of U.S.C. Title 11 and Bankruptcy Rules (Ex. R7030). References to other U.S.C. titles are cited, for example, as 28 U.S.C. 1334, and references to Public Laws are cited, for example, as 106-518 §501. Title 28 materials are located in the Judicial section.]

[References are to Code Sections of U.S.C. Title 11 and Bankruptcy Rules (Ex. R7030). References to other U.S.C. titles are cited, for example, as 28 U.S.C. 1334, and references to Public Laws are cited, for example, as 106-518 §501. Title 28 materials are located in the Judicial section.]



## F

[References are to Code Sections of U.S.C. Title 11 and Bankruptcy Rules (Ex. R7030). References to other U.S.C. titles are cited, for example, as 28 U.S.C. 1334, and references to Public Laws are cited, for example, as 106-518 §501. Title 28 materials are located in the Judicial section.]

[References are to Code Sections of U.S.C. Title 11 and Bankruptcy Rules (Ex. R7030). References to other U.S.C. titles are cited, for example, as 28 U.S.C. 1334, and references to Public Laws are cited, for example, as 106-518 §501. Title 28 materials are located in the Judicial section.]

[References are to Code Sections of U.S.C. Title 11 and Bankruptcy Rules (Ex. R7030). References to other U.S.C. titles are cited, for example, as 28 U.S.C. 1334, and references to Public Laws are cited, for example, as 106-518 §501. Title 28 materials are located in the Judicial section.]

[References are to Code Sections of U.S.C. Title 11 and Bankruptcy Rules (Ex. R7030). References to other U.S.C. titles are cited, for example, as 28 U.S.C. 1334, and references to Public Laws are cited, for example, as 106-518 §501. Title 28 materials are located in the Judicial section.]

[References are to Code Sections of U.S.C. Title 11 and Bankruptcy Rules (Ex. R7030). References to other U.S.C. titles are cited, for example, as 28 U.S.C. 1334, and references to Public Laws are cited, for example, as 106-518 §501. Title 28 materials are located in the Judicial section.]

[References are to Code Sections of U.S.C. Title 11 and Bankruptcy Rules (Ex. R7030). References to other U.S.C. titles are cited, for example, as 28 U.S.C. 1334, and references to Public Laws are cited, for example, as 106-518 §501. Title 28 materials are located in the Judicial section.]

[References are to Code Sections of U.S.C. Title 11 and Bankruptcy Rules (Ex. R7030). References to other U.S.C. titles are cited, for example, as 28 U.S.C. 1334, and references to Public Laws are cited, for example, as 106-518 §501. Title 28 materials are located in the Judicial section.]

[References are to Code Sections of U.S.C. Title 11 and Bankruptcy Rules (Ex. R7030). References to other U.S.C. titles are cited, for example, as 28 U.S.C. 1334, and references to Public Laws are cited, for example, as 106-518 §501. Title 28 materials are located in the Judicial section.]

[References are to Code Sections of U.S.C. Title 11 and Bankruptcy Rules (Ex. R7030). References to other U.S.C. titles are cited, for example, as 28 U.S.C. 1334, and references to Public Laws are cited, for example, as 106-518 §501. Title 28 materials are located in the Judicial section.]

[References are to Code Sections of U.S.C. Title 11 and Bankruptcy Rules (Ex. R7030). References to other U.S.C. titles are cited, for example, as 28 U.S.C. 1334, and references to Public Laws are cited, for example, as 106-518 §501. Title 28 materials are located in the Judicial section.]

[References are to Code Sections of U.S.C. Title 11 and Bankruptcy Rules (Ex. R7030). References to other U.S.C. titles are cited, for example, as 28 U.S.C. 1334, and references to Public Laws are cited, for example, as 106-518 §501. Title 28 materials are located in the Judicial section.]

[References are to Code Sections of U.S.C. Title 11 and Bankruptcy Rules (Ex. R7030). References to other U.S.C. titles are cited, for example, as 28 U.S.C. 1334, and references to Public Laws are cited, for example, as 106-518 §501. Title 28 materials are located in the Judicial section.]

[References are to Code Sections of U.S.C. Title 11 and Bankruptcy Rules (Ex. R7030). References to other U.S.C. titles are cited, for example, as 28 U.S.C. 1334, and references to Public Laws are cited, for example, as 106-518 §501. Title 28 materials are located in the Judicial section.]





## J

[References are to Code Sections of U.S.C. Title 11 and Bankruptcy Rules (Ex. R7030). References to other U.S.C. titles are cited, for example, as 28 U.S.C. 1334, and references to Public Laws are cited, for example, as 106-518 §501. Title 28 materials are located in the Judicial section.]

[References are to Code Sections of U.S.C. Title 11 and Bankruptcy Rules (Ex. R7030). References to other U.S.C. titles are cited, for example, as 28 U.S.C. 1334, and references to Public Laws are cited, for example, as 106-518 §501. Title 28 materials are located in the Judicial section.]

[References are to Code Sections of U.S.C. Title 11 and Bankruptcy Rules (Ex. R7030). References to other U.S.C. titles are cited, for example, as 28 U.S.C. 1334, and references to Public Laws are cited, for example, as 106-518 §501. Title 28 materials are located in the Judicial section.]

[References are to Code Sections of U.S.C. Title 11 and Bankruptcy Rules (Ex. R7030). References to other U.S.C. titles are cited, for example, as 28 U.S.C. 1334, and references to Public Laws are cited, for example, as 106-518 §501. Title 28 materials are located in the Judicial section.]

[References are to Code Sections of U.S.C. Title 11 and Bankruptcy Rules (Ex. R7030). References to other U.S.C. titles are cited, for example, as 28 U.S.C. 1334, and references to Public Laws are cited, for example, as 106-518 §501. Title 28 materials are located in the Judicial section.]

[References are to Code Sections of U.S.C. Title 11 and Bankruptcy Rules (Ex. R7030). References to other U.S.C. titles are cited, for example, as 28 U.S.C. 1334, and references to Public Laws are cited, for example, as 106-518 §501. Title 28 materials are located in the Judicial section.]

[References are to Code Sections of U.S.C. Title 11 and Bankruptcy Rules (Ex. R7030). References to other U.S.C. titles are cited, for example, as 28 U.S.C. 1334, and references to Public Laws are cited, for example, as 106-518 §501. Title 28 materials are located in the Judicial section.]

[References are to Code Sections of U.S.C. Title 11 and Bankruptcy Rules (Ex. R7030). References to other U.S.C. titles are cited, for example, as 28 U.S.C. 1334, and references to Public Laws are cited, for example, as 106-518 §501. Title 28 materials are located in the Judicial section.]



## N

[References are to Code Sections of U.S.C. Title 11 and Bankruptcy Rules (Ex. R7030). References to other U.S.C. titles are cited, for example, as 28 U.S.C. 1334, and references to Public Laws are cited, for example, as 106-518 §501. Title 28 materials are located in the Judicial section.]

[References are to Code Sections of U.S.C. Title 11 and Bankruptcy Rules (Ex. R7030). References to other U.S.C. titles are cited, for example, as 28 U.S.C. 1334, and references to Public Laws are cited, for example, as 106-518 §501. Title 28 materials are located in the Judicial section.]



## O

[References are to Code Sections of U.S.C. Title 11 and Bankruptcy Rules (Ex. R7030). References to other U.S.C. titles are cited, for example, as 28 U.S.C. 1334, and references to Public Laws are cited, for example, as 106-518 §501. Title 28 materials are located in the Judicial section.]

[References are to Code Sections of U.S.C. Title 11 and Bankruptcy Rules (Ex. R7030). References to other U.S.C. titles are cited, for example, as 28 U.S.C. 1334, and references to Public Laws are cited, for example, as 106-518 §501. Title 28 materials are located in the Judicial section.]



## P

[References are to Code Sections of U.S.C. Title 11 and Bankruptcy Rules (Ex. R7030). References to other U.S.C. titles are cited, for example, as 28 U.S.C. 1334, and references to Public Laws are cited, for example, as 106-518 §501. Title 28 materials are located in the Judicial section.]

[References are to Code Sections of U.S.C. Title 11 and Bankruptcy Rules (Ex. R7030). References to other U.S.C. titles are cited, for example, as 28 U.S.C. 1334, and references to Public Laws are cited, for example, as 106-518 §501. Title 28 materials are located in the Judicial section.]

[References are to Code Sections of U.S.C. Title 11 and Bankruptcy Rules (Ex. R7030). References to other U.S.C. titles are cited, for example, as 28 U.S.C. 1334, and references to Public Laws are cited, for example, as 106-518 §501. Title 28 materials are located in the Judicial section.]

[References are to Code Sections of U.S.C. Title 11 and Bankruptcy Rules (Ex. R7030). References to other U.S.C. titles are cited, for example, as 28 U.S.C. 1334, and references to Public Laws are cited, for example, as 106-518 §501. Title 28 materials are located in the Judicial section.]

[References are to Code Sections of U.S.C. Title 11 and Bankruptcy Rules (Ex. R7030). References to other U.S.C. titles are cited, for example, as 28 U.S.C. 1334, and references to Public Laws are cited, for example, as 106-518 §501. Title 28 materials are located in the Judicial section.]

[References are to Code Sections of U.S.C. Title 11 and Bankruptcy Rules (Ex. R7030). References to other U.S.C. titles are cited, for example, as 28 U.S.C. 1334, and references to Public Laws are cited, for example, as 106-518 §501. Title 28 materials are located in the Judicial section.]

[References are to Code Sections of U.S.C. Title 11 and Bankruptcy Rules (Ex. R7030). References to other U.S.C. titles are cited, for example, as 28 U.S.C. 1334, and references to Public Laws are cited, for example, as 106-518 §501. Title 28 materials are located in the Judicial section.]

[References are to Code Sections of U.S.C. Title 11 and Bankruptcy Rules (Ex. R7030). References to other U.S.C. titles are cited, for example, as 28 U.S.C. 1334, and references to Public Laws are cited, for example, as 106-518 §501. Title 28 materials are located in the Judicial section.]

[References are to Code Sections of U.S.C. Title 11 and Bankruptcy Rules (Ex. R7030). References to other U.S.C. titles are cited, for example, as 28 U.S.C. 1334, and references to Public Laws are cited, for example, as 106-518 §501. Title 28 materials are located in the Judicial section.]

[References are to Code Sections of U.S.C. Title 11 and Bankruptcy Rules (Ex. R7030). References to other U.S.C. titles are cited, for example, as 28 U.S.C. 1334, and references to Public Laws are cited, for example, as 106-518 §501. Title 28 materials are located in the Judicial section.]

[References are to Code Sections of U.S.C. Title 11 and Bankruptcy Rules (Ex. R7030). References to other U.S.C. titles are cited, for example, as 28 U.S.C. 1334, and references to Public Laws are cited, for example, as 106-518 §501. Title 28 materials are located in the Judicial section.]

[References are to Code Sections of U.S.C. Title 11 and Bankruptcy Rules (Ex. R7030). References to other U.S.C. titles are cited, for example, as 28 U.S.C. 1334, and references to Public Laws are cited, for example, as 106-518 §501. Title 28 materials are located in the Judicial section.]

[References are to Code Sections of U.S.C. Title 11 and Bankruptcy Rules (Ex. R7030). References to other U.S.C. titles are cited, for example, as 28 U.S.C. 1334, and references to Public Laws are cited, for example, as 106-518 §501. Title 28 materials are located in the Judicial section.]

[References are to Code Sections of U.S.C. Title 11 and Bankruptcy Rules (Ex. R7030). References to other U.S.C. titles are cited, for example, as 28 U.S.C. 1334, and references to Public Laws are cited, for example, as 106-518 §501. Title 28 materials are located in the Judicial section.]

[References are to Code Sections of U.S.C. Title 11 and Bankruptcy Rules (Ex. R7030). References to other U.S.C. titles are cited, for example, as 28 U.S.C. 1334, and references to Public Laws are cited, for example, as 106-518 §501. Title 28 materials are located in the Judicial section.]

[References are to Code Sections of U.S.C. Title 11 and Bankruptcy Rules (Ex. R7030). References to other U.S.C. titles are cited, for example, as 28 U.S.C. 1334, and references to Public Laws are cited, for example, as 106-518 §501. Title 28 materials are located in the Judicial section.]

[References are to Code Sections of U.S.C. Title 11 and Bankruptcy Rules (Ex. R7030). References to other U.S.C. titles are cited, for example, as 28 U.S.C. 1334, and references to Public Laws are cited, for example, as 106-518 §501. Title 28 materials are located in the Judicial section.]

[References are to Code Sections of U.S.C. Title 11 and Bankruptcy Rules (Ex. R7030). References to other U.S.C. titles are cited, for example, as 28 U.S.C. 1334, and references to Public Laws are cited, for example, as 106-518 §501. Title 28 materials are located in the Judicial section.]

[References are to Code Sections of U.S.C. Title 11 and Bankruptcy Rules (Ex. R7030). References to other U.S.C. titles are cited, for example, as 28 U.S.C. 1334, and references to Public Laws are cited, for example, as 106-518 §501. Title 28 materials are located in the Judicial section.]

[References are to Code Sections of U.S.C. Title 11 and Bankruptcy Rules (Ex. R7030). References to other U.S.C. titles are cited, for example, as 28 U.S.C. 1334, and references to Public Laws are cited, for example, as 106-518 §501. Title 28 materials are located in the Judicial section.]

[References are to Code Sections of U.S.C. Title 11 and Bankruptcy Rules (Ex. R7030). References to other U.S.C. titles are cited, for example, as 28 U.S.C. 1334, and references to Public Laws are cited, for example, as 106-518 §501. Title 28 materials are located in the Judicial section.]

[References are to Code Sections of U.S.C. Title 11 and Bankruptcy Rules (Ex. R7030). References to other U.S.C. titles are cited, for example, as 28 U.S.C. 1334, and references to Public Laws are cited, for example, as 106-518 §501. Title 28 materials are located in the Judicial section.]

[References are to Code Sections of U.S.C. Title 11 and Bankruptcy Rules (Ex. R7030). References to other U.S.C. titles are cited, for example, as 28 U.S.C. 1334, and references to Public Laws are cited, for example, as 106-518 §501. Title 28 materials are located in the Judicial section.]

[References are to Code Sections of U.S.C. Title 11 and Bankruptcy Rules (Ex. R7030). References to other U.S.C. titles are cited, for example, as 28 U.S.C. 1334, and references to Public Laws are cited, for example, as 106-518 §501. Title 28 materials are located in the Judicial section.]

[References are to Code Sections of U.S.C. Title 11 and Bankruptcy Rules (Ex. R7030). References to other U.S.C. titles are cited, for example, as 28 U.S.C. 1334, and references to Public Laws are cited, for example, as 106-518 §501. Title 28 materials are located in the Judicial section.]

[References are to Code Sections of U.S.C. Title 11 and Bankruptcy Rules (Ex. R7030). References to other U.S.C. titles are cited, for example, as 28 U.S.C. 1334, and references to Public Laws are cited, for example, as 106-518 §501. Title 28 materials are located in the Judicial section.]

[References are to Code Sections of U.S.C. Title 11 and Bankruptcy Rules (Ex. R7030). References to other U.S.C. titles are cited, for example, as 28 U.S.C. 1334, and references to Public Laws are cited, for example, as 106-518 §501. Title 28 materials are located in the Judicial section.]

[References are to Code Sections of U.S.C. Title 11 and Bankruptcy Rules (Ex. R7030). References to other U.S.C. titles are cited, for example, as 28 U.S.C. 1334, and references to Public Laws are cited, for example, as 106-518 §501. Title 28 materials are located in the Judicial section.]

[References are to Code Sections of U.S.C. Title 11 and Bankruptcy Rules (Ex. R7030). References to other U.S.C. titles are cited, for example, as 28 U.S.C. 1334, and references to Public Laws are cited, for example, as 106-518 §501. Title 28 materials are located in the Judicial section.]



## V

[References are to Code Sections of U.S.C. Title 11 and Bankruptcy Rules (Ex. R7030). References to other U.S.C. titles are cited, for example, as 28 U.S.C. 1334, and references to Public Laws are cited, for example, as 106-518 §501. Title 28 materials are located in the Judicial section.]